Other Books By Bill Welch

The Tenth Man
*How A Major League Team
Can Gain A 2 To 3 Run Advantage
Every Game*

**The Baseball Analysis And Reporting System
American League Report**

The Baseball Analysis And Reporting System
National League Report
Ballpark Edition

By Bill Welch

With Jeff Moses

A Baseball Analysis And Reporting System Publication

A BARS System Book
Published by Baseball Analysis And Reporting System, Inc.
Box 50
Chillicothe, Missouri 64601
The BARS System is a registered trademark of
Baseball Analysis And Reporting System. Inc.
Manufactured in the United States of America
Library of Congress Catalogue Number Applied For

The Baseball Analysis And Reporting System
National League Report
Ballpark Edition

"A BARS book."
Includes index.

ISBN 0-929633-02-4

Contents

The New Age Of Baseball Statistics

When a Don Mattingly or a Dale Murphy — or any of the great hitters active in baseball today — comes to the plate with runners in scoring position during the late innings of a close game, everyone in the ballpark knows he is capable of driving in the runners. The opposing pitcher knows it. The opposing fielders know it. And every fan watching the game knows it.

Everyone knows that certain hitters usually have good batting averages, get a lot of hits and drive in a lot of runs. But when a hitter is at the plate, the opposing team needs specific information about how to get him out. The opposing team needs to know what strengths and weaknesses the hitter has, what types and locations of pitches the hitter is most vulnerable to on specific ball-and-strike counts, and where fielders should be positioned to be most effective on every pitch. In other words, the team in the field needs specific, practicable information that will help on the spot and at the moment.

The Baseball Analysis And Reporting System

Such statistics are exactly what the Baseball Analysis And Reporting System attempts to provide.

The Baseball Analysis and Reporting System (The BARS System) is a privately owned organization using a nationwide scouting system and a powerful computer to generate practical baseball statistics that can be used in actual game situations by any major league team.

The key word here is "practical." "Practical statistics" are defined as statistics that can be of use in actual play — during key moments in an actual game. The BARS System generates statistics that are meant to be used. In this book many of these statistics will be presented for the fans' enjoyment (and perhaps a deeper understanding of the game), but overall the statistics are designed for actual use.

The BARS System has scouted over 800 major league games each of the last five seasons and has collected an enormous amount of data on every player in both leagues. This data is coordinated by a powerful computer to generate scouting and reporting charts that could revolutionize the game if used regularly by any team.

When put into play by major league teams, the BARS System can increase the effectiveness of pitchers and hitters, set up defensive strategy that is much more effective than the strategy now being used in the majors, and — when used in conjunction with other BARS strategies — prevent an average of two to three runs that each team is now allowing every game. Over the course of a 162-game schedule, this would make a tremendous difference in a team's final standing.

This book will show how this can be done, and will give detailed team-by-team BARS records for hitters in the National League.

The BARS System Super Summary Report

The BARS System calculates batting averages for nine locations in the strike zone for every player in the majors. Nine-location batting grids are calculated for four types of pitches: fastballs, curves, sliders and change-ups. In addition, batting grids are calculated for each of these four types of pitches in several different situations that can affect a hitter's performance: when he is ahead, behind, and even in the count, and when facing right- and left-handed pitchers. These batting charts are called Super Summary Reports in the BARS System, because they are a summary of several other BARS Reports.

The chart shown below illustrates how the BARS Super Summary batting grid is set up. The chart below is for a right-handed hitter. It shows the strike zone as the hitter would see it from the batter's box looking out at the pitcher. Inside and outside would be reversed for a left-handed hitter.

	Inside	Middle	Outside
High	High Inside	High Over The Middle	High Outside
Medium	Medium-High Inside	Medium Over The Middle	Medium-High Outside
Low	Low Inside	Low Over The Middle	Low Outside

The BARS System calculates a separate batting percentage in each of the nine locations. The sample chart on the next page shows how the batting average and other statistics are displayed.

(Please see the chart on the following page.)

BARS System Batting Chart
Sample Nine-Location Grid

	Inside	Middle	Outside
High	185 / 50 — **270**	222 / 75 — **338**	136 / 35 — **257**
Medium	310 / 98 — **316**	108 / 45 — **417**	268 / 75 — **280**
Low	140 / 31 — **221**	191 / 59 — **309**	155 / 28 — **181**

Batting average for the specific location. (the bold number in each cell)

Total at-bats. (the number above and to the left of the slash)

Total base hits resulting from pitches to the location. (the number below and to the right of the slash)

The sample chart above shows how information is displayed. Notice that a separate batting percentage is shown in bold for each of the nine locations. For greater clarity, the decimal point is not included.

The number above and to the left of the slash is the total number of at-bats ended by pitches to that particular location. This includes all strike outs, fly-ball outs, ground-ball outs, base hits (singles, doubles, triples and home runs), hit balls resulting in fielders' errors or fielders' choices, and pop-outs into foul or fair territory. It does not include walks and sacrifices.

The number below and to the right of the slash is the number of base hits resulting from pitches to the location (singles, doubles, triples and home runs). Dividing the number below the slash by the number above the slash results in the batting average for the location.

This exactness gives a new dimension to baseball scouting and analysis. It's no longer adequate to speak in generalities, saying that a certain hitter has difficulties with inside fastballs, or problems with curves against right-handers. When pitchers can know with great precision what a hitter's strong and weak locations are, great accuracy can be achieved. In key moments of games, use of the BARS System can give managers and pitchers the practical information they need to plan the best strategy.

The BARS System Fielding Strategy

In each Super Summary Report there are areas of strength and weakness. By focussing on a hitter's weak batting locations, a pitcher will have a greater chance of getting the hitter out. But there is another aspect to getting a hitter out: positioning fielders properly.

Much of the success of any pitcher, or of the pitchers on a team as a whole, is based on the quality of the team's defense. Low ERAs can mean that the pitching is good, but often a pitcher who has a low ERA with one team will have a higher ERA when transferred to a team with a weaker defense.

It is often said that a pitcher can make hitters hit ground balls but can't make them hit the grounders to fielders. But is that really the case? Is there no way for fielders to know where to position themselves to be most effective? The BARS System has developed such a way.

The BARS System has determined that trends can be found in a hitter's performance when large numbers of instances are taken into consideration. Each hitter has his own characteristic trends. For instance, a player may hit a medium-high inside fastball a different distance and direction than he would hit a medium-high outside fastball. BARS research shows that many hitters tend to hit even the same type and location of pitch different distances and directions when ahead and behind in the count. Direction and distance of hit balls will vary with the type of pitch, location of pitch, when the batter faces right- and left-handed pitchers, and when he is ahead and behind in the count.

Generally, hitters tend to pull the ball more when they are ahead in the count than when they are behind. This is probably because when they are ahead they look for fastballs and time their swing accordingly. It's not unusual to see a batter hit medium-high outside fastballs, for example, completely differently when ahead and when behind in the count. This could be true for any of the pitch types and locations.

Since the distance and direction of each hit ball is recorded by the BARS scouts along with the type of each pitch and location of each pitch, it is not difficult for the BARS computer to calculate the best position for the fielders on a pitch-by-pitch basis.

For example, say that 310 instances have been recorded for a hitter in a certain location. This means that 310 at-bats for the hitter have ended with pitches to that particular location. Other than strikeouts, all instances would have resulted in the ball being hit. (Remember that walks and sacrifices are not included in the total.) Some of the hit balls would have been pop flies, some line drives and some ground balls. Some of these would have been base hits (singles, doubles, triples and home runs) and some would have been outs.

Based on this information, the BARS computer calculates the best possible fielding position for each of the fielders — for that type of pitch and location of pitch on that particular count. Thus if a hitter had 310 at-bats ended by pitches to a certain location, the BARS computer would calculate where each fielder should be positioned when the hitter is thrown pitches to that location.

How The Fielding Strategy Works

In the BARS System fielding strategy, the baseball field is divided into designated areas. Optimal fielding positions are calculated for the three outfielders, the shortstop and the second baseman. Each of the outfielders has nine suggested positions. The left fielder's positions are shown below. The center and right fielders have similar designated positions:

Deep and shifted toward the left field line
Deep in straightaway left field
Deep and shifted toward center field
Medium-deep and shifted toward the left field line
Medium-deep in straightaway left field
Medium-deep and shifted toward center field
Short and shifted toward the left field line
Short in straightaway left field
Short and shifted toward center field.

The positions for the shortstop are:

Shifted toward third base
Normal position
Up middle (shifted toward second base).

The positions for the second baseman are:

Up middle (shifted toward second base)
Normal position
Shifted toward first base.

Fielding strategy is not calculated for the first and third basemen. The first baseman is often forced to hold runners close to the base, and BARS strategy would not affect him as much as the other fielders. Although strategy is not presently calculated for the third baseman, BARS research has shown that the third baseman is out of position much more often than was originally thought. Because of this, the BARS System will soon begin calculating the third baseman's best position on a pitch-by-pitch basis.

There has long been a debate in baseball about whether in certain situations it is better to place the third baseman close to the bag so he can cut off potential extra-base hits down the line, or to place him in his normal position so he can field ground balls hit into the hole between third and short. When the BARS analysis is completed, this decision can be based on the comprehensive study of each hitter's past performance, rather than on theory or conjecture. The two designated fielding positions for the third baseman will be *Shifted toward the line* and *Normal position*.

The BARS System positions fielders for each of the nine locations in each batting grid. Taking the batting chart on the opposite page as an example, the .181 average in the low-outside location is the lowest. As will be seen throughout this book, the suggested positions for each fielder vary greatly with the pitching locations, the types of pitches, when the batter is ahead or behind in the count, and when he is facing a right- or left-handed pitcher. Assuming that the fielding strategy would require each fielder to be in the straightaway position, the BARS fielding information for the location would look like this:

LOW-OUTSIDE

BATTING AVERAGE .181
Play
Left Deep in straightaway left field
Center Deep in straightaway center field
Right Deep in straightaway right field
Short Normal position
Second Normal position

The next-lowest average is .221 in the low-inside location. The fielding strategy for that location would be similarly designated, depending on where the BARS strategy has found it best for each fielder to be positioned. Each of the nine locations would have designations for each of the fielders.

The next two chapters go into greater detail about the BARS Super Summary batting charts and fielding strategy, using the records of Dale Murphy and Andres Dawson as examples.

The chart on the following page shows how the field is divided for the purpose of positioning fielders.

The field chart is a graphic representation of a baseball field, divided into fielding positions.

Field Chart

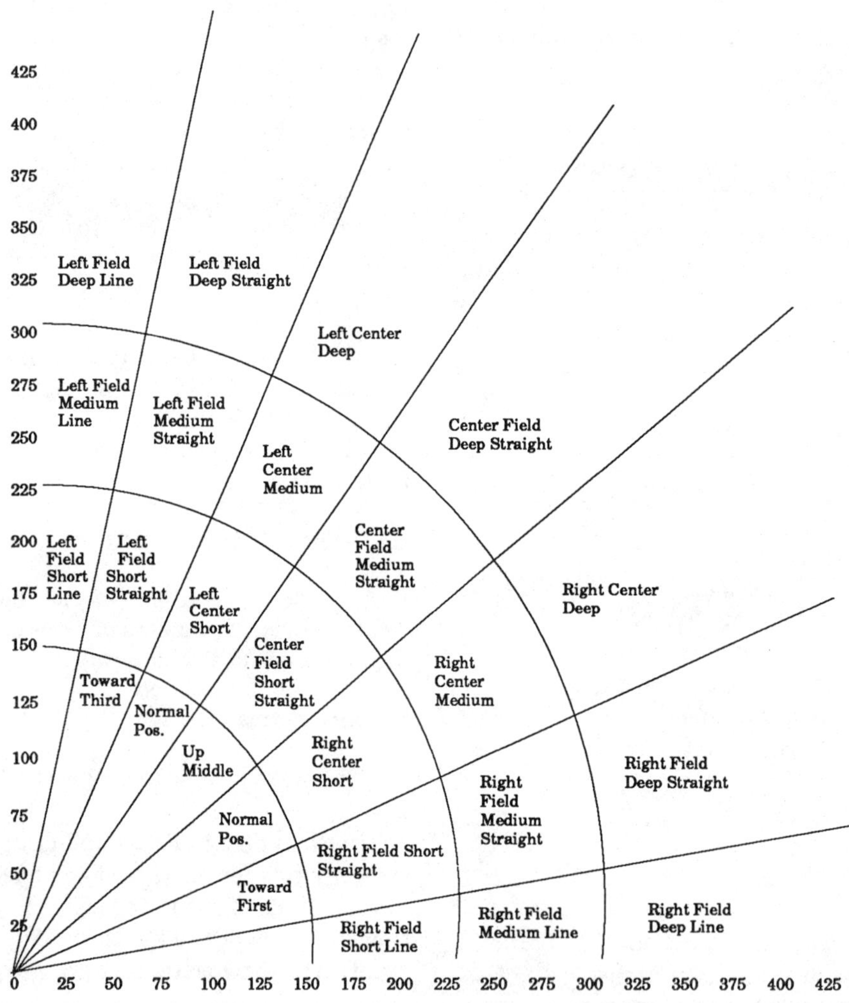

The BARS System records all balls hit to these field positions. Coordinating this information with the type and location of pitch (and with the ball-and-strike count when the pitch was made) allows the BARS computer to calculate the best possible position for each fielder when pitches are made to each location.

Such a high number of instances are recorded by the BARS System that when all the balls hit by a batter are recorded graphically on the Field Chart, the human eye can't differentiate one hit from another. Fortunately, the computer can make sense out the information. Without use of a computer, the computations necessary to position fielders would be extremely complicated and time consuming.

The BARS System is unique in that it gathers an enormous amount of information — more than can be calculated by human beings — and analyzes it with a powerful computer to generate simple, easily understood charts that can be practically implemented by any major league team.

The BARS Super Summary fielding strategy positions fielders for every pitch, based on the Field Chart shown on the opposite page. The positions for the shortstop and the second baseman are shown below. The positions for the outfielders are shown on the following page. These diagrams are for descriptive purposes only. The size of the players and their positions on the field are not meant to be exact.

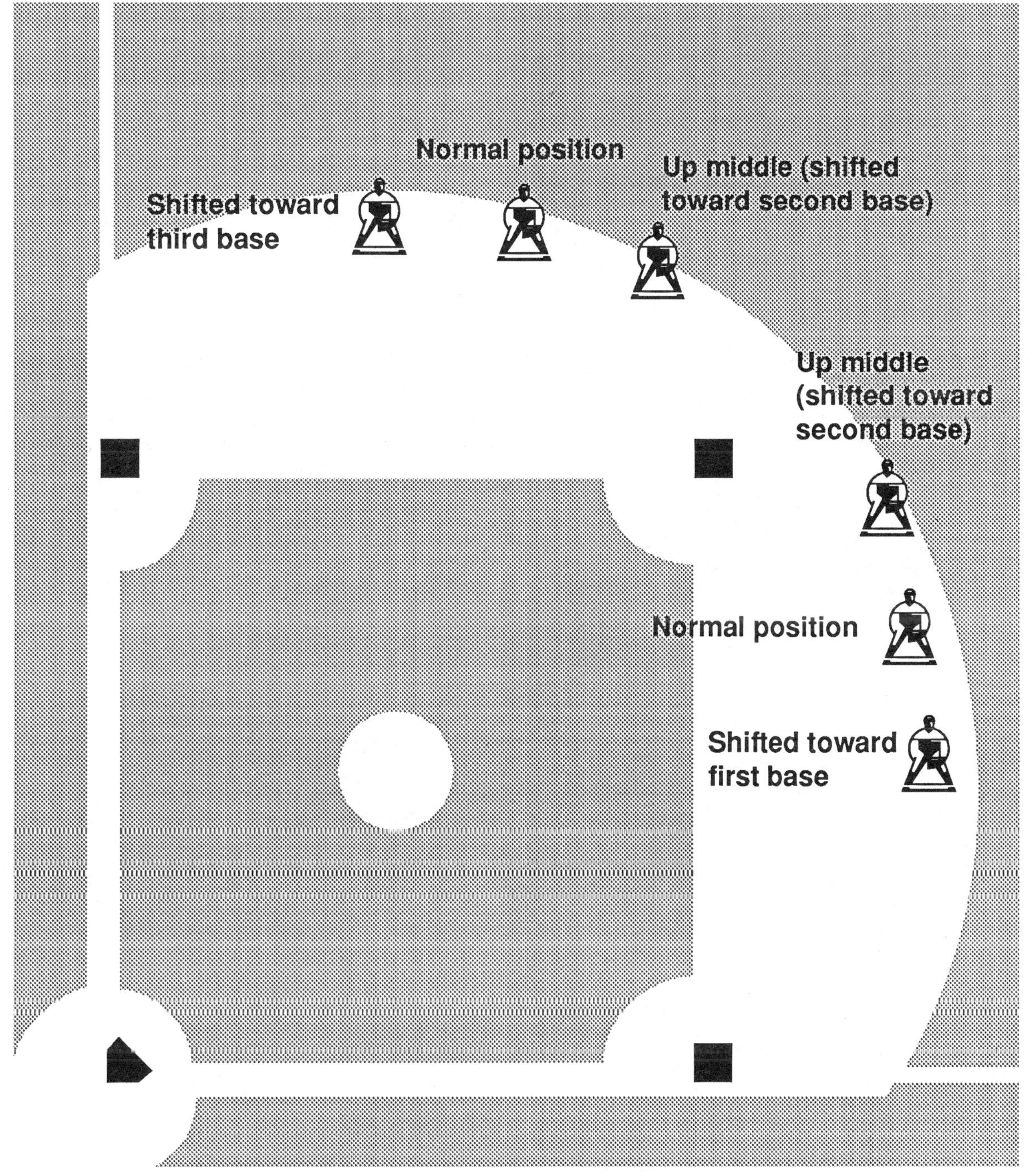

The left fielder's nine designated fielding locations are shown in the diagram below. The center fielder and right fielder are positioned similarly in their respective fields but for the sake of clearness in the diagram they are not shown.

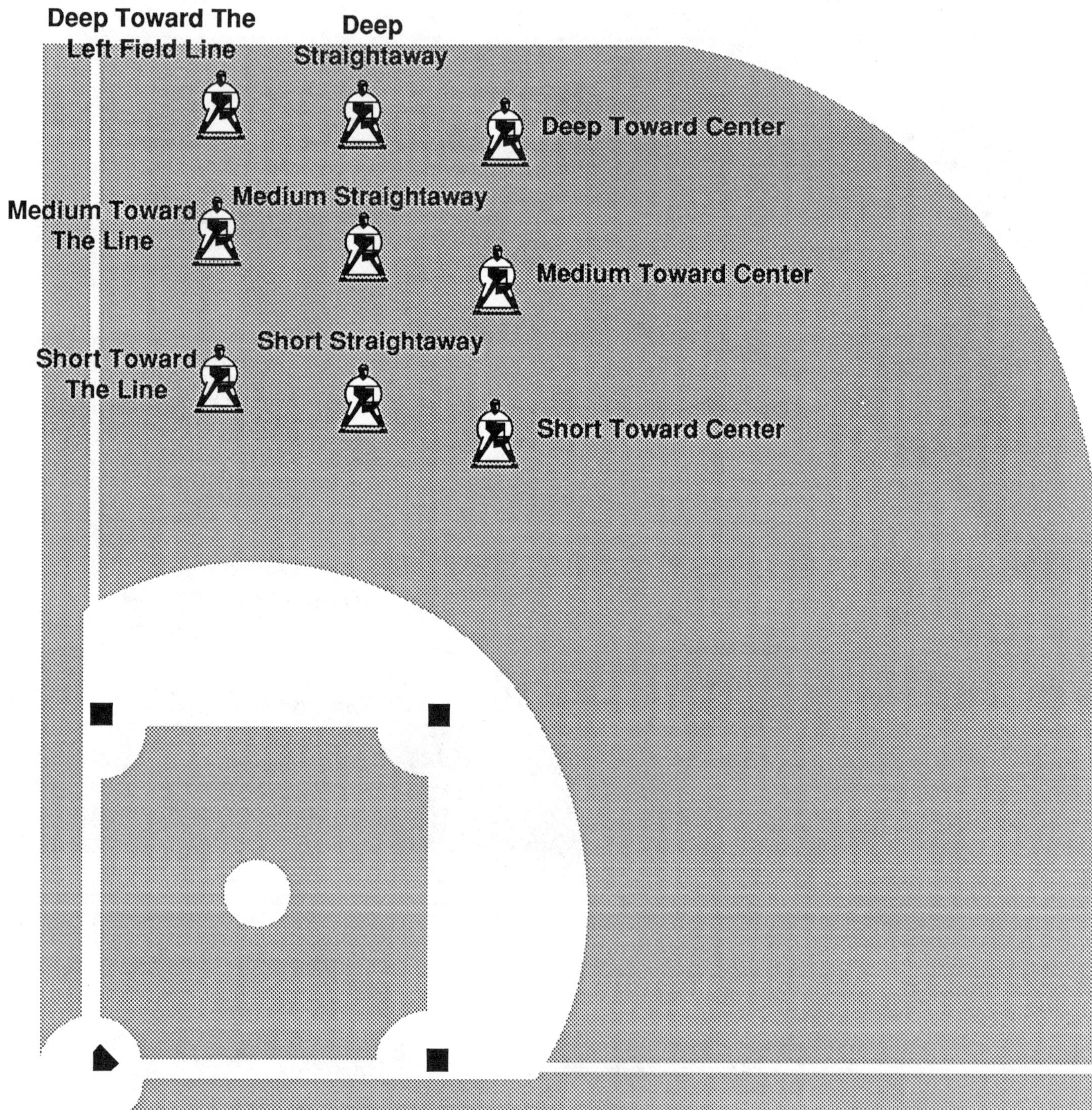

BARS Fielding Strategy Correct Over 90 Percent Of The Time

Sometimes during crucial moments in a game you'll see a coach come out of the dugout and wave to his fielders to take certain positions against a hitter. Maybe the coach will wave the outfielders more toward the right, or toward the left, or to come in, or to play deeper. These efforts are well-intended, but when the ensuing pattern of pitches to the hitter is, for example, a high-inside fastball followed by a low-outside curve, a low-inside slider and a low-outside fastball, the batter is being thrown pitches that he will tend to hit varying directions and distances. It's almost a waste of time for fielders to take set positions and hold them through all the pitches. They can be right only in the most general sense.

BARS analysis has shown that traditional fielding strategy is right about 75 percent of the time. This means that fielders are out of position about 25 percent of the time when balls are hit in their direction. When a "seeing eye" ground ball slips past an infielder or a line drive single falls just in front of a charging outfielder who was playing deep, that 25 percent factor is coming into effect.

The BARS System fielding strategy is accurate more than 90 percent of the time. This means that by following the BARS strategy, fielders would be in the right position nine times out of ten to field balls hit in their direction. The difference between 90 percent and 75 percent means that about two to three base hits that could have been prevented by using the BARS fielding strategy are being allowed by each team in every game.

This 15 percent differential — two to three hits per game — could make a tremendous difference in a team's final standing. It could turn any team into a highly organized defensive unit. If a team is made up of good defensive players, the team would become even better. If the team has weak defensive players, it would become more than adequate. Almost any fielder can field the ball when he is in the right position to start with.

I know that some teams have tried to make charts on where to put their fielders against certain hitters. These teams have kept records of the distance and direction hitters have hit against them. But these records are based only on how hitters have performed against that team, or against specific pitchers on that team. At best, this can give inconclusive information.

The BARS System consistently has gained 90 percent accuracy by breaking its batting and fielding strategy into specific charts for hitters against right- and left-handed pitchers, and for when ahead and behind in the count.

The previously-published BARS book, *The Tenth Man: How A Major League Team Can Gain A Two To Three Run Advantage Every Game*, goes into great detail about the BARS fielding strategy. *The Tenth Man* gives dozens of examples of games won and lost because of hits that could have been prevented by using the BARS fielding strategy.

The Number of Games Scouted

Over the last five years, the BARS System has scouted over one-third of all major league games on a pitch-by-pitch basis. Many teams have had over half of their games scouted during the past few seasons. The Chicago Cubs had 137 games scouted in 1988, the Kansas City Royals had 118, the Baltimore Orioles 95, the Boston Red Sox 93, the New York Yankees 89, and the Atlanta Braves 88. Many teams had 50, 60 or 70 games scouted. (Team-by-team scouting records for 1983-1987 are available in *The Tenth Man*.) Overall, more than 800 games have been scouted during each of the last five seasons. This has resulted in a large amount of information that the BARS computer uses with great accuracy.

The BARS System records:

1. The exact location of every pitch in and around the strike zone.

2. The type of pitch: fastball, curve, slider, knuckleball, screwball, sinkerball, split-fingered fastball and change-up.

3. Exact details of the results of every hit: distance and direction of hit ball (fair or foul), fielder fielding the ball, accuracy of throws made, result of hit, runners advanced, runs scored, RBIs, errors, etc.

4. Called strikes and swing strikes, balls, fouls, bunts and bunt attempts, passed balls, balks, stolen bases, sacrifices, etc. — all events are recorded so that complete accuracy can be attained.

The computer is a powerful tool that has not yet come into its own in baseball. Many other sports utilize the computer's great potential, both in scouting and in game situations. Baseball today is such big business, on both the major and minor league levels, that it is only a matter of time until computers are used. The BARS System fielding strategy combined with other BARS strategies can give any team a two to three run advantage every game. Once a team implements the BARS System, it will have an edge for three or four years, until other teams have the chance to catch up.

The Best Way To Get A Batter Out

The BARS System calculates exact batting percentages by dividing the strike zone and the area immediately around the strike zone into nine locations. The BARS System batting report, which is called the Super Summary Report because it is a composite of several BARS System reports, calculates a separate nine-location batting-average grid for fastballs, curves and sliders. The BARS System can calculate batting averages for any type of pitch (change-ups, knuckleballs, sinkers and split-fingered fastballs, etc.), but this book shows only the charts for fastballs, curves and sliders because these are the three most common types of pitches.

Overall, six separate Super Summary Reports are printed for each batter:

Against Right-Handed Pitchers

1. When ahead in the count
2. When behind in the count
3. Overall for all counts

Against Left-Handed Pitchers

4. When ahead in the count
5. When behind in the count
6. Overall for all counts

The breakdown into these different categories is important because, as will be seen, a batter may hit very differently not only against left- and right-handed pitchers and against different types of pitches, but when ahead and behind in the count.

The BARS System batting average may not correspond exactly with a player's official batting average, because the BARS batting charts are composites of a player's records over many seasons.

Batting Reports For Dale Murphy

The BARS batting charts for Dale Murphy, Atlanta Braves' right-handed hitter, will be used as examples.

Dale Murphy Against Right-Handed Pitchers
Overall BARS Batting Average .269

Fastball Average .319

	Inside	Middle	Outside
High	37 / 81 / 3	68 / 367 / 25	58 / 275 / 16
Med	94 / 329 / 31	70 / 385 / 27	188 / 361 / 68
Low	44 / 250 / 11	142 / 359 / 51	91 / 230 / 21

Curve Average .224

	Inside	Middle	Outside
High	0 / 0 / 0	15 / 533 / 8	12 / 416 / 5
Med	7 / 428 / 3	19 / 421 / 8	54 / 203 / 11
Low	11 / 181 / 2	42 / 142 / 6	98 / 153 / 15

Slider Average .278

	Inside	Middle	Outside
High	1 / 0 / 0	11 / 454 / 5	5 / 400 / 2
Med	9 / 111 / 1	7 / 571 / 4	43 / 325 / 14
Low	7 / 142 / 1	29 / 448 / 13	71 / 154 / 11

Dale Murphy Against Left-Handed Pitchers
Overall BARS Batting Average .277

Fastball Average .311

	Inside	Middle	Outside
High	7 / 142 / 1	23 / 347 / 8	38 / 289 / 11
Med	24 / 208 / 5	19 / 421 / 8	77 / 467 / 36
Low	16 / 187 / 3	43 / 255 / 11	58 / 206 / 12

Curve Average .228

	Inside	Middle	Outside
High	1 / 1000 / 1	4 / 500 / 2	3 / 0 / 0
Med	11 / 90 / 1	2 / 0 / 0	14 / 428 / 6
Low	12 / 83 / 1	12 / 250 / 3	11 / 181 / 2

Slider Average .333

	Inside	Middle	Outside
High	1 / 0 / 0	2 / 0 / 0	1 / 0 / 0
Med	10 / 400 / 4	0 / 0 / 0	7 / 714 / 5
Low	10 / 100 / 1	10 / 300 / 3	10 / 400 / 4

Murphy's Super Summary Report shows that he hits slightly better against left-handed than against right-handed pitchers. His overall BARS Super Summary average against left-handers is .277. Against right-handers it is .269.

Notice the strengths and weaknesses in Murphy's charts. Against right-handed pitchers he hits well against medium-over-the-middle fastballs (.385), high-over-the-middle fastballs (.367), medium-high outside fastballs (.361), low-over-the-middle fastballs (.359) and medium-high inside fastballs (.329). He hits well in a few of his curve and slider locations as well.

But Murphy has distinct weaknesses in his charts. Against right-handed pitchers he hits only .081 against high-inside fastballs, .230 against low-outside fastballs, and .250 against low-inside fastballs. He hits poorly in all low curve locations against right-handed pitchers (.181, .142 and .153), the medium-outside curve location (.203) and in several slider locations.

Against left-handed pitchers, Murphy is weak in all inside and low fastball locations. Notice, however, his strength against medium-high outside fastballs.

Against curves thrown by left-handed pitchers, he is strong in the medium-high outside location (.428). But he is weak in the other highly pitched curve locations, most notably low-inside (.083), medium-high inside (.090) and low-outside (.181).

When thrown sliders by left-handed pitchers, he seems to have difficulty only in the low-inside location (.100). The BARS System has recorded only a few high sliders thrown to him, but his hitlessness in those locations indicates a possible weakness.

Murphy Ahead And Behind In The Count

Murphy's BARS reports show that he hits better when he is ahead in the count against right-handed pitchers (.354 when ahead, .316 when behind). In the charts below, notice the strength of his fastball averages when he is ahead in the count. With the exception of the high-inside fastball location (0-for-10) and the low-inside location (.250), all of Murphy's fastball averages are solid. Notice how few curves he is thrown when he's ahead in the count. Murphy obviously is aware of this. He expects fastballs when ahead and feasts on them.

In the ongoing battle between pitcher and batter, the batter is considered to be ahead in the count when the count is 1-0 (one ball and no strikes), 3-0, 3-1, 2-0 and 2-1. The batter is considered behind when the count is 0-1, 0-2, 1-2 and 2-2. The other ball and strike counts — 0-0, 1-1 and 3-2 — are considered even counts.

Behind Against Right-Handed Pitchers .316

Fastball Average .333

	Inside	Middle	Outside
High	4/250 /1	15/266 /4	13/153 /2
Med	24/291 /7	18/444 /8	28/357 /10
Low	4/0 /0	19/526 /10	13/307 /4

Curve Average .305

	Inside	Middle	Outside
High	0/0 /0	4/250 /1	3/333 /1
Med	0/0 /0	7/571 /4	17/294 /5
Low	2/0 /0	8/375 /3	18/222 /4

Ahead Against Right-Handed Pitchers .354

Fastball Average .414

	Inside	Middle	Outside
High	10/0 /0	28/607 /17	22/409 /9
Med	38/473 /18	30/400 /12	89/471 /42
Low	20/250 /5	69/376 /26	29/344 /10

Curve Average .349

	Inside	Middle	Outside
High	0/0 /0	7/571 /4	5/400 /2
Med	2/1000 /2	7/428 /3	14/285 /4
Low	2/500 /1	5/0 /0	21/285 /6

Murphy Ahead And Behind Against Left-Handed Pitchers

Murphy has a slightly higher overall average against left-handed pitchers when he is behind in the count.

Behind Against Left-Handed Pitchers .373

Fastball Average .400

	Inside	Middle	Outside
High	0 / 0 / 0	7 / 285 / 2	8 / 500 / 4
Med	1 / 0 / 0	2 / 1000 / 2	8 / 500 / 4
Low	2 / 500 / 1	4 / 500 / 2	8 / 125 / 1

Curve Average .357

	Inside	Middle	Outside
High	1 / 1000 / 1	0 / 0 / 0	2 / 0 / 0
Med	2 / 0 / 0	0 / 0 / 0	3 / 666 / 2
Low	2 / 500 / 1	1 / 0 / 0	3 / 333 / 1

Ahead Against Left-Handed Pitchers .355

Fastball Average .391

	Inside	Middle	Outside
High	1 / 0 / 0	10 / 500 / 5	9 / 333 / 3
Med	10 / 300 / 3	7 / 571 / 4	35 / 457 / 16
Low	1 / 1000 / 1	25 / 280 / 7	22 / 363 / 8

Curve Average .315

	Inside	Middle	Outside
High	0 / 0 / 0	2 / 500 / 1	0 / 0 / 0
Med	5 / 200 / 1	0 / 0 / 0	4 / 500 / 2
Low	1 / 0 / 0	6 / 333 / 2	1 / 0 / 0

Examples Of The Fielding Strategy

The Super Summary shows fielding strategy for each of the nine locations for fastballs, curves and sliders. The chart below shows the fastball fielding strategy from Murphy's Super Summary. Below the nine-location batting grid for fastballs are the best fielding positions for each of the nine locations.

Fastball Average .319

	Inside	Middle	Outside
High	37 / 81 / 3	68 / 367 / 25	58 / 275 / 16
Med	94 / 329 / 31	70 / 385 / 27	188 / 361 / 68
Low	44 / 250 / 11	142 / 359 / 51	91 / 230 / 21

(Taken from Murphy's overall BARS Super Summary against right-handed pitchers.)

Notice that there are nine fielding categories listed below, one for each of the nine locations in the strike zone for that particular type of pitch. These positions are calculated by the BARS computer, based on the way Murphy has hit balls thrown to each pitch location during the past seasons.

1. HIGH-INSIDE FASTBALLS

BATTING AVERAGE .081

Play

Left	Deep and shifted toward the left field line
Center	Medium-deep in straightaway center field
Right	Short in straightaway right field
Short	Shifted toward third base
Second	Shifted toward first base

2. LOW-OUTSIDE FASTBALLS

BATTING AVERAGE .230

Play

Left	Medium-deep and shifted toward center field
Center	Deep and shifted toward right field
Right	Deep and shifted toward the right field line
Short	Up middle (shifted toward second base)
Second	Normal position

3. LOW-INSIDE FASTBALLS

BATTING AVERAGE .250
Play

Left	Deep and shifted toward the left field line
Center	Medium-deep in straightaway center field
Right	Deep and shifted toward center field
Short	Normal position
Second	Shifted toward first base

4. HIGH-OUTSIDE FASTBALLS

BATTING AVERAGE .275
Play

Left	Deep and shifted toward the left field line
Center	Medium-deep in straightaway center field
Right	Deep and shifted toward center field
Short	Up middle (shifted toward second base)
Second	Normal position

5. MEDIUM-HIGH INSIDE FASTBALLS

BATTING AVERAGE .329
Play

Left	Deep and shifted toward the left field line
Center	Medium-deep and shifted toward left field
Right	Medium-deep in straightaway right field
Short	Normal position
Second	Shifted toward first base

6. LOW-OVER-THE-MIDDLE FASTBALLS

BATTING AVERAGE .359
Play

Left	Deep and shifted toward the left field line
Center	Medium-deep and shifted toward left field
Right	Medium-deep in straightaway right field
Short	Normal position
Second	Normal position

7. MEDIUM-HIGH OUTSIDE FASTBALLS

BATTING AVERAGE .361
Play

Left	Deep and shifted toward center field
Center	Deep and shifted toward right field
Right	Deep in straightaway right field
Short	Up middle (shifted toward second base)
Second	Shifted toward first base

8. HIGH-OVER-THE-MIDDLE FASTBALLS

BATTING AVERAGE .367
Play

Left	Deep in straightaway left field
Center	Deep and shifted toward left field
Right	Deep and shifted toward center field
Short	Shifted toward third base
Second	Normal position

9. MEDIUM-OVER-THE-MIDDLE FASTBALLS

BATTING AVERAGE .385
Play

Left	Deep in straightaway left field
Center	Deep in straightaway center field
Right	Deep and shifted toward center field
Short	Shifted toward third base
Second	Normal position

It has been found that when each fielder plays in the suggested position for the specific type and location of pitch, the overall BARS fielding strategy will be correct slightly over 90 percent of the time.

An Overall Defensive Strategy

In general, the best way for a right-handed pitcher to get Murphy out with a fastball would be to throw to the location in which he has the lowest average (.081 in his high-inside fastball location). But positioning fielders according to the BARS fielding strategy for a particular location of fastball will increase the chances of getting Murphy out. (This of course assumes that the pitch is not hit for a home run. The BARS System will soon include the number of home runs hit in each location of the batting grid.)

Since the fielding strategy is accurate more than 90 percent of the time, positioning fielders according to the suggested strategy for any particular pitch location will tend to lower the hitter's average in that location.

Murphy hits .361 against medium-high outside fastballs, but if all fielders were properly positioned, his average in that location would decline. The same is true for all locations in Murphy's and any other hitter's Super Summary.

Thus, it is just as important — if not more important — to position fielders correctly for particular types and locations of pitches as it is to pitch to a hitter's weak locations. It doesn't matter whether the batter has been hitting .300 or even .400 in a location, if the fielders position themselves correctly, he will hit only about .100 in the location.

As in any system that works with probability, the larger the number of instances that a computer has to work with, the greater the accuracy will be. In the BARS System, the larger the number of instances that have been recorded in any particular location, the greater the accuracy of the BARS fielding strategy will be for that location.

In some cases it may be better to pitch to a location with a high average than to pitch to a location with a low average — if the location with a high average has a large number of recorded instances.

Exactness Of The BARS System

The BARS System produces such accurate batting averages and fielding strategy that fielders are required to shift even for pitches that are in adjacent locations of the strike zone. Pitchers and fielders should be in coordination so that the fielding strategy can be the most effective.

The following example in Murphy's Super Summary shows how critical even a few inches in the strike zone can be.

4. HIGH-OUTSIDE FASTBALLS

BATTING AVERAGE .275

Play

Left	Deep and shifted toward the left field line
Center	Medium-deep in straightaway center field
Right	Deep and shifted toward center field
Short	Up middle (shifted toward second base)
Second	Normal position

Notice how differently the fielders would have to be positioned when a fastball is thrown to the medium-high outside location, which is only inches away in the strike zone. The diagram on the opposite page shows how each fielder would be required to shift.

7. MEDIUM-HIGH OUTSIDE FASTBALLS

BATTING AVERAGE .361

Play

Left	Deep and shifted toward center field
Center	Deep and shifted toward right field
Right	Deep in straightaway right field
Short	Up middle (shifted toward second base)
Second	Shifted toward first base

Every fielder except the shortstop would be required to shift in order to be correctly positioned for a high-outside fastball as compared to a medium-high outside fastball. If they did not shift, they would be completely out of position for one of the pitches, and probably would have difficulty fielding a hit ball.

BARS Fielding Strategy
High-Outside Fastballs
Overall Against Right-Handed Pitchers

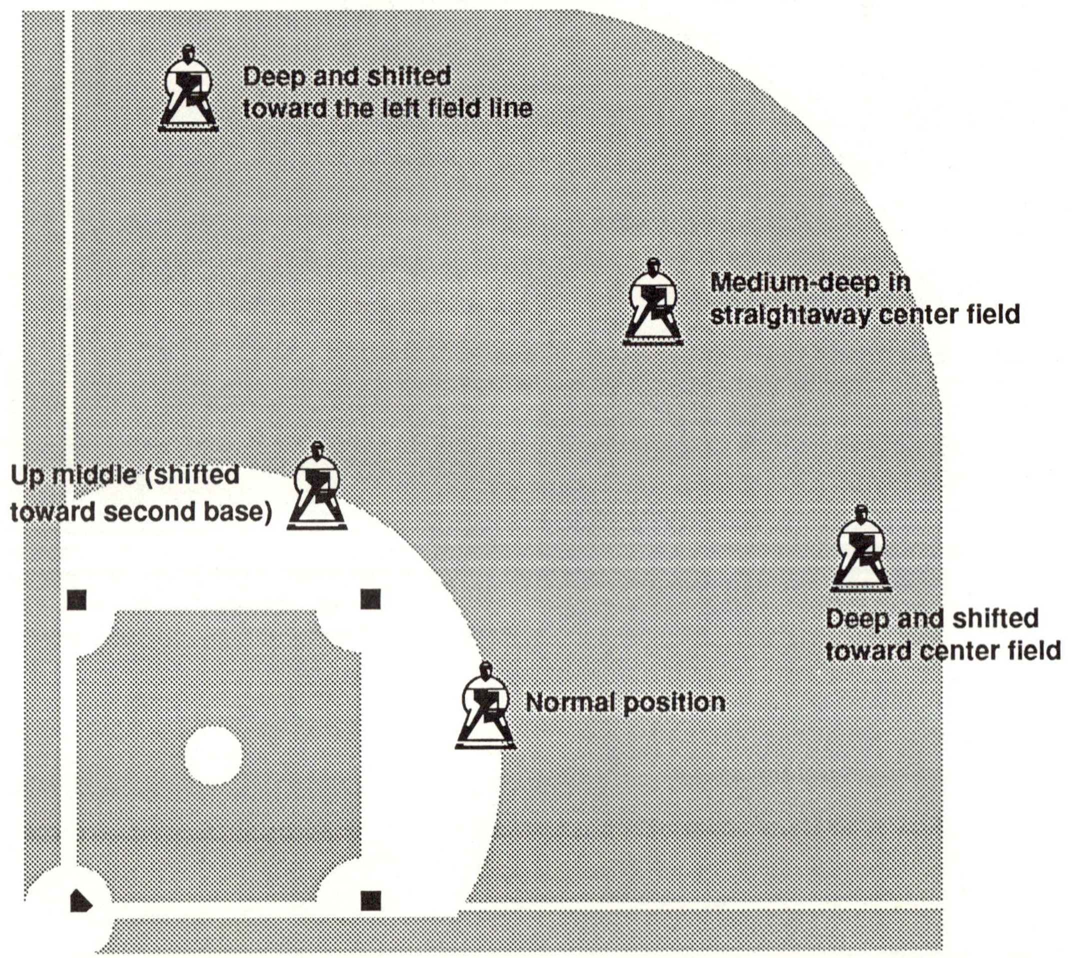

The same is true for many of the pitch types and locations to Murphy, as it is with all hitters. It is not enough for fielders to play a hitter to hit straightaway, or to play him to pull the ball or to go to the opposite field. If each fielder takes a position when a batter comes to the plate and holds that position through all the pitches to the batter, he will be out of position for some of the pitches.

The Tenth Man: How A Major League Team Can Gain A 2 To 3 Run Advantage Every Game goes into great detail about the BARS fielding strategy. *The Tenth Man* gives numerous examples of games won and lost because of hits that could have been prevented by using the BARS fielding strategy.

BARS Fielding Strategy
Medium-High Outside Fastballs
(As Compared To High-Outside)
Overall Against Right-Handed Pitchers

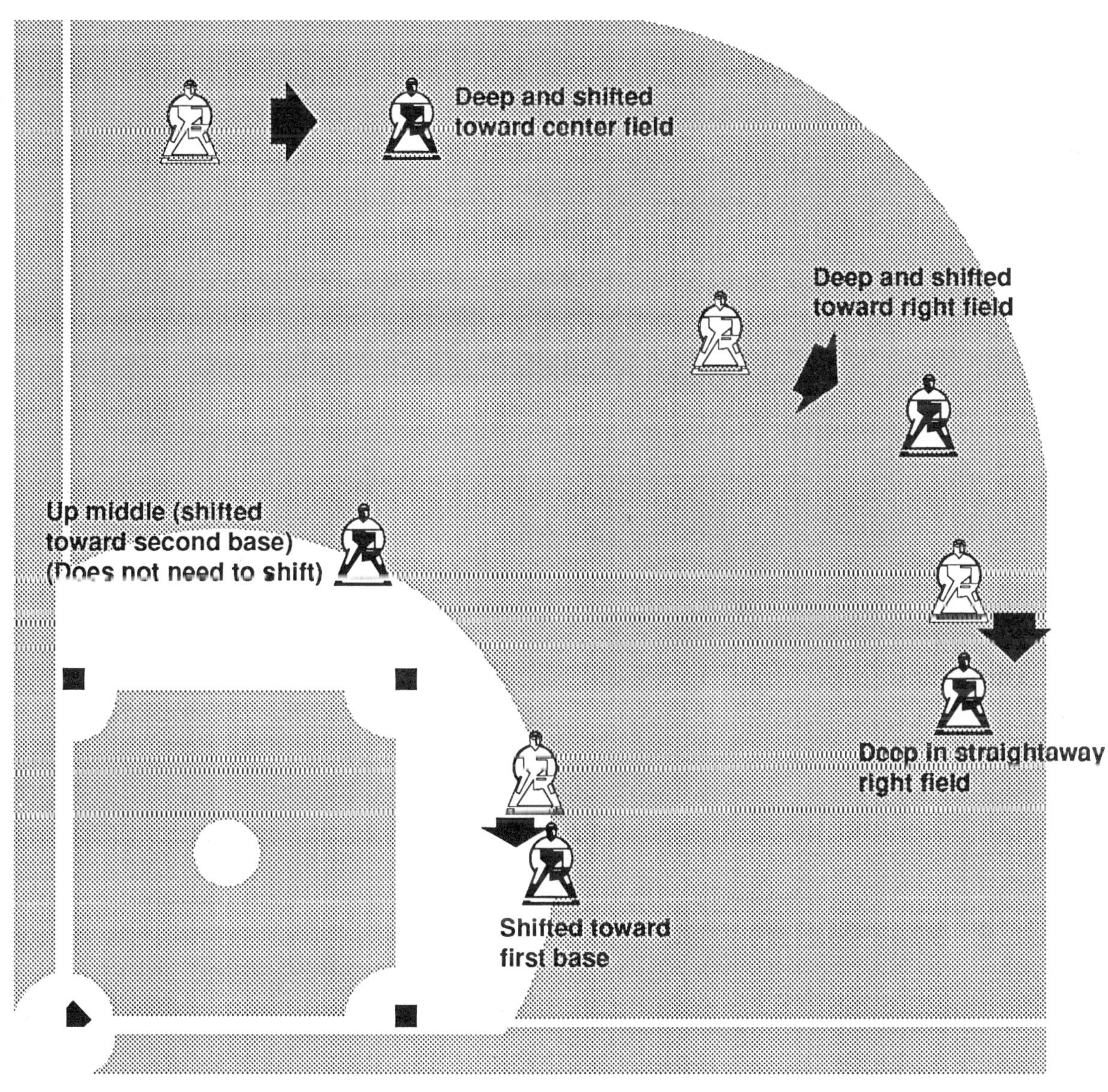

How To Get Andre Dawson Out, or The Anatomy Of A Hitter, BARS Style

In sports, as in life generally, the difference between a champion and an also-ran can be exceedingly small. In a horse race, the difference between the winning horse and a horse finishing out of the money is often measured in fractions of a second. Olympic running events and ski races are just as close. Hundredths of a second separate gold medalists from also-rans. It's not unusual for golf tournaments to be determined by a single stroke after 72 holes, and more and more it seems that golf tournaments end in ties and have to be settled in playoffs. And the difference between a .300 hitter and a .250 hitter in major league baseball is only 25 hits during the season, assuming that a hitter has 500 official at-bats. That averages out to about one hit per week during the season.

That extra hit per week can be a fluke, a bloop hit that falls in for a single, or a ground ball that takes a lucky hop over a fielder's glove.

But for the most part the same players hit .300 or better year after year. They keep finding ways to get that extra bloop single or lucky bounce every week. Somehow they find a way to succeed. Those who hit .300 year in and year out are among the best, but only the great hitters consistently move into the .330-.350 range

Andre Dawson is an excellent hitter. He hits for average, he hits home runs and, year in year out, he has high RBI totals. In '87 he was National League MVP, leading the league in both homers and RBIs. Then in '88 he followed up with a fine .303 average with 179 hits in 591 at-bats, including 24 homers and 79 RBIs. He had a slugging average of .504 and an on-base average of .344. There are other great hitters in the game today, and this book will talk about them. But let's focus on Andre Dawson in this chapter.

The Best Way To Get Andre Dawson Out

When it comes to the best way to get a batter out, there are two things to consider:

(1) pitching to the batter's weaknesses
(2) positioning the fielders correctly on a pitch-by-pitch basis.

Of these, the more important is positioning the fielders correctly. It's true that when a batter's BARS charts show that he has very low batting percentages in certain locations, in general it may be better to pitch to those locations. But even if a batter is hitting .400 in a certain location, when the fielders are positioned correctly, the batter's average in that location will drop. Since the BARS fielding strategy is correct 90 percent of the time, a player would hit no more than .100 in any location if the fielders followed the BARS strategy for that location.

The charts in this chapter will show that the right-handed hitting Dawson hits much better against left-handed pitchers. Overall, Dawson is a good fastball and curve hitter. He hits sliders fairly well against left-handers, but poorly against right-handers.

First let's look at his performance against right-handed pitchers:

Andre Dawson Against Right-Handed Pitchers
Overall BARS Batting Average .265

Fastball Average .295

	Inside	Middle	Outside
High	38 / 157 / 6	63 / 349 / 22	45 / 222 / 10
Med	49 / 346 / 17	11 / 454 / 5	100 / 300 / 30
Low	47 / 276 / 13	61 / 459 / 28	74 / 175 / 13

Curve Average .296

	Inside	Middle	Outside
High	6 / 0 / 0	16 / 375 / 6	12 / 333 / 4
Med	4 / 750 / 3	8 / 375 / 3	44 / 454 / 20
Low	4 / 250 / 1	16 / 250 / 4	62 / 161 / 10

Slider Average .228

	Inside	Middle	Outside
High	3 / 333 / 1	10 / 300 / 3	14 / 214 / 3
Med	1 / 1000 / 1	3 / 333 / 1	61 / 311 / 19
Low	2 / 0 / 0	15 / 400 / 6	92 / 130 / 12

Even though Dawson hits fastballs and curves well (.295 overall against fastballs and .296 overall against curves), he has a few weak locations. No hitter can hit well against all types and locations of pitches. Notice in the charts that Dawson hits several fastball locations very well. He hits low-over-the-middle fastballs at a .459 clip. He hits .349 against high-over-the-middle fastballs, .346 against medium-high inside fastballs, and .300 against medium-high outside fastballs.

But he has weaknesses in the high-inside location (.157), the low-outside location (.175), and the high-outside location (.222).

Notice in Dawson's curve chart that he hits medium-high outside curves extremely well (.454), but hits low-outside curves very poorly (.161). He is strong against medium-high outside sliders (.311), but weak against low-outside sliders (.130).

There is one great similarity in Dawson's three charts: he has a much higher average against medium-high outside pitches than against low-outside pitches.

These charts show that many pitchers have been pitching Dawson outside. In fact, the medium-high outside fastball location is almost always the most highly pitched location for a batter. The BARS fielding strategy shows that Dawson pulls medium-high outside fastballs deep to left and center fields, while hitting to the right side of the infield when he hits grounders.

MEDIUM-HIGH OUTSIDE FASTBALLS

BATTING AVERAGE .300

Play

Left	Deep and shifted toward the left field line
Center	Deep and shifted toward left field
Right	Medium-deep in straightaway right field
Short	Up middle (shifted toward second base)
Second	Shifted toward first base

(Please see diagram below)

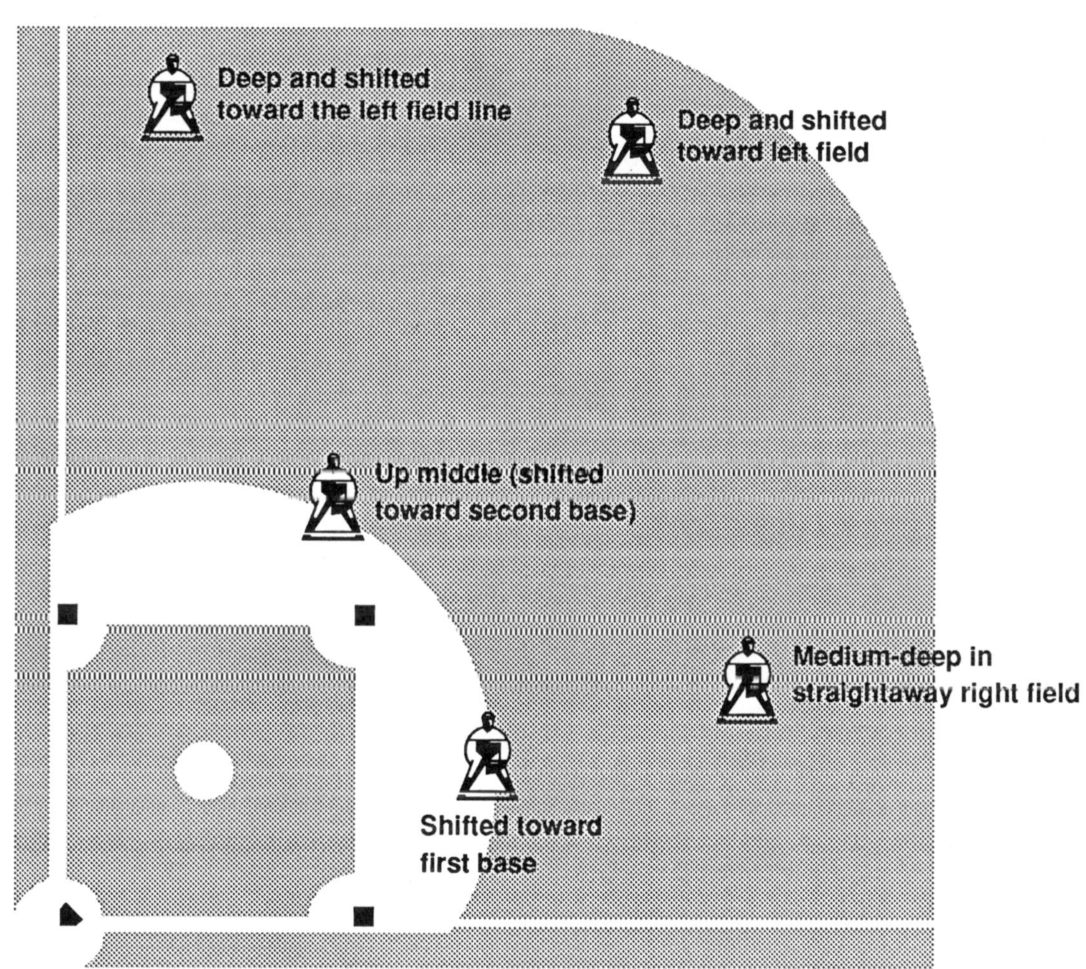

Dawson also pulls medium-high inside fastballs deep to left and center fields, but notice in the chart below that for pitches to this location the right fielder would have to play short in straightaway right and the shortstop would have to shift toward third base.

MEDIUM-HIGH INSIDE FASTBALLS

BATTING AVERAGE .346
Play

Left	Deep and shifted toward the left field line
Center	Deep and shifted toward left field
Right	Short in straightaway right field
Short	Shifted toward third base
Second	Shifted toward first base

The charts below show that fielders would have to be positioned much differently for low-outside fastballs compared to low-over-the-middle fastballs. Every fielder except the shortstop would be required to shift for the two pitches.

LOW-OUTSIDE FASTBALLS

BATTING AVERAGE .175
Play

Left	Deep and shifted toward the left field line
Center	Deep and shifted toward right field
Right	Deep in straightaway right field
Short	Shifted toward third base
Second	Normal position

LOW-OVER-THE-MIDDLE FASTBALLS

BATTING AVERAGE .459
Play

Left	Deep in straightaway left field
Center	Deep in straightaway center field
Right	Deep and shifted toward center field
Short	Shifted toward third base
Second	Shifted toward first base

Each of the outfielders and the shortstop would be required to shift for a low-outside curve as compared to a medium-high outside curve.

MEDIUM-HIGH OUTSIDE CURVEBALLS

BATTING AVERAGE .454
Play

Left	Deep and shifted toward the left field line
Center	Deep and shifted toward left field

Right	Deep in straightaway right field
Short	Up middle (shifted toward second base)
Second	Normal position

LOW-OUTSIDE CURVEBALLS

BATTING AVERAGE .161
Play

Left	Deep in straightaway left field
Center	Deep and shifted toward right field
Right	Short in straightaway right field
Short	Shifted toward third base
Second	Normal position

When thrown sliders, Dawson hits the ball deep to all fields from most pitch locations.

MEDIUM-HIGH OUTSIDE SLIDERS

BATTING AVERAGE .311
Play

Left	Deep in straightaway left field
Center	Deep and shifted toward left field
Right	Deep and shifted toward center field
Short	Up middle (shifted toward second base)
Second	*No instances recorded*

LOW-OUTSIDE SLIDERS

BATTING AVERAGE .130
Play

Left	Deep and shifted toward the left field line
Center	Deep in straightaway center field
Right	Deep and shifted toward center field
Short	Normal position
Second	Normal position

It is apparent that Dawson hits some types and locations of pitches much differently than other types and locations of pitches. By positioning themselves specifically on a pitch-by-pitch basis, outfielders and infielders could reach many of the balls that now get past them.

These examples from the performance of Andre Dawson are not isolated instances: every hitter hits different types and locations of pitches in a wide variety of distances and directions. The BARS fielding strategy calculates the positions for fielders with 90 percent accuracy. When operating together as a highly coordinated unit, a team could prevent about one-third of all base hits that are now being allowed.

Ahead Against Right-Handed Pitchers

Fastball Average .351

	Inside	Middle	Outside
High	11 / 363 / 4	19 / 473 / 9	14 / 214 / 3
Med	21 / 285 / 6	7 / 571 / 4	43 / 418 / 18
Low	19 / 157 / 3	26 / 576 / 15	25 / 120 / 3

Curve Average .413

	Inside	Middle	Outside
High	0 / 0 / 0	9 / 222 / 2	5 / 400 / 2
Med	3 / 666 / 2	5 / 400 / 2	22 / 454 / 10
Low	0 / 0 / 0	4 / 500 / 2	10 / 400 / 4

Behind Against Right-Handed Pitchers

Fastball Average .321

	Inside	Middle	Outside
High	8 / 0 / 0	19 / 368 / 7	16 / 312 / 5
Med	11 / 636 / 7	1 / 0 / 0	21 / 285 / 6
Low	12 / 333 / 4	11 / 272 / 3	16 / 312 / 5

Curve Average .333

	Inside	Middle	Outside
High	3 / 0 / 0	4 / 500 / 2	4 / 250 / 1
Med	1 / 1000 / 1	2 / 500 / 1	7 / 428 / 3
Low	0 / 0 / 0	4 / 500 / 2	17 / 235 / 4

Although Dawson hits fastballs better overall when he is ahead in the count (.351 when ahead, .321 when behind), he hits medium-high inside fastballs extremely well when behind (.636). He pulls these pitches deep down the line to left but also punches them into short right field. If fielders would position themselves correctly for these pitches, they would probably be able to take away some of his base hits.

**MEDIUM-HIGH INSIDE FASTBALLS
(THROWN WHEN DAWSON IS
BEHIND IN THE COUNT)**

BATTING AVERAGE .636
Play

Left	Deep and shifted toward the left field line
Center	Medium-deep and shifted toward left field
Right	Short in straightaway right field
Short	Shifted toward third base
Second	Shifted toward first base

When ahead, Dawson hits medium-high outside fastballs and low-over-the-middle fastballs very well (.418 and .576 respectively).

**MEDIUM-HIGH OUTSIDE FASTBALLS
(THROWN WHEN DAWSON IS AHEAD IN THE COUNT)**

BATTING AVERAGE .418
Play

Left	Deep and shifted toward the left field line
Center	Deep and shifted toward left field
Right	Deep and shifted toward center field
Short	Normal position
Second	Shifted toward first base

**LOW-OVER-THE-MIDDLE FASTBALLS
(THROWN WHEN DAWSON IS AHEAD IN THE COUNT)**

BATTING AVERAGE .576
Play

Left	Deep in straightaway left field
Center	Deep in straightaway center field
Right	Deep and shifted toward center field
Short	Normal position
Second	Normal position

Notice in the two preceding fielding-strategy charts that only the right fielder and the shortstop would be properly positioned for both pitches. This emphasizes the importance of adjusting fielders for all types and locations of pitches.

Andre Dawson Against Left-Handed Pitchers
Overall BARS Batting Average .302

Fastball Average .371				Curve Average .285				Slider Average .275		
	Inside	Middle	Outside		Inside	Middle	Outside		Inside	Middle	Outside
High	10/300 /3	12/333 /4	24/458 /11		0/0 /0	1/0 /0	2/1000 /2		1/1000 /1	1/0 /0	2/500 /1
Med	11/363 /4	2/500 /1	33/454 /15		4/250 /1	1/1000 /1	12/333 /4		2/0 /0	1/1000 /1	2/500 /1
Low	8/250 /2	20/350 /7	44/318 /14		5/0 /0	12/250 /3	5/200 /1		9/0 /0	6/500 /3	5/200 /1

Dawson has a considerably higher overall BARS batting average against left-handed pitchers than against right-handed pitchers (.302 overall against left-handers, .265 overall against right-handers).

Notice in the above fastball chart how well Dawson hits outside fastballs thrown by lefties. He is especially strong against medium-high outside and high-outside fastballs. Left-handed pitchers should avoid throwing these pitches to Dawson. The charts below show that fielders need to be positioned differently for pitches to these locations.

MEDIUM-HIGH OUTSIDE FASTBALLS
(THROWN TO DAWSON BY
LEFT-HANDED PITCHERS)

BATTING AVERAGE .454
Play
Left	Deep and shifted toward the left field line
Center	Medium-deep in straightaway center field
Right	Deep and shifted toward center field
Short	Normal position
Second	Normal position

HIGH-OUTSIDE FASTBALLS
(THROWN TO DAWSON BY
LEFT-HANDED PITCHERS)

BATTING AVERAGE .458
Play
Left	Deep and shifted toward the left field line
Center	Deep in straightaway center field
Right	Deep in straightaway right field
Short	Shifted toward third base
Second	Shifted toward first base

Dawson has weaknesses against both low-inside curves and low-inside sliders. He does not have a recorded hit ball against low-inside curves. He hits low-inside sliders very weakly.

LOW-INSIDE SLIDERS
(THROWN TO DAWSON BY
LEFT-HANDED PITCHERS)

BATTING AVERAGE .000 (0 for 9)
Play
Left	*No instances recorded*
Center	*No instances recorded*
Right	Short in straightaway right field
Short	Shifted toward third base
Second	*No instances recorded*

Looking back at Dawson's fastball chart, it is interesting to note that he hits high-outside fastballs much differently against left-handers when he is ahead and when he is behind in the count. His ahead and behind charts against left-handers are not shown here, but the fielding strategy shown below emphasizes the point that fielders may need to shift when the count changes on a batter. The diagram on the opposite page illustrates how fielders need to shift for high-outside fastballs when Dawson is ahead and behind.

HIGH-OUTSIDE FASTBALLS
(THROWN BY LEFT-HANDED PITCHERS
WHEN DAWSON IS BEHIND IN THE COUNT)

BATTING AVERAGE .375
Play
Left	Deep and shifted toward center field
Center	Deep in straightaway center field
Right	Deep and shifted toward center field
Short	Normal position
Second	Shifted toward first base

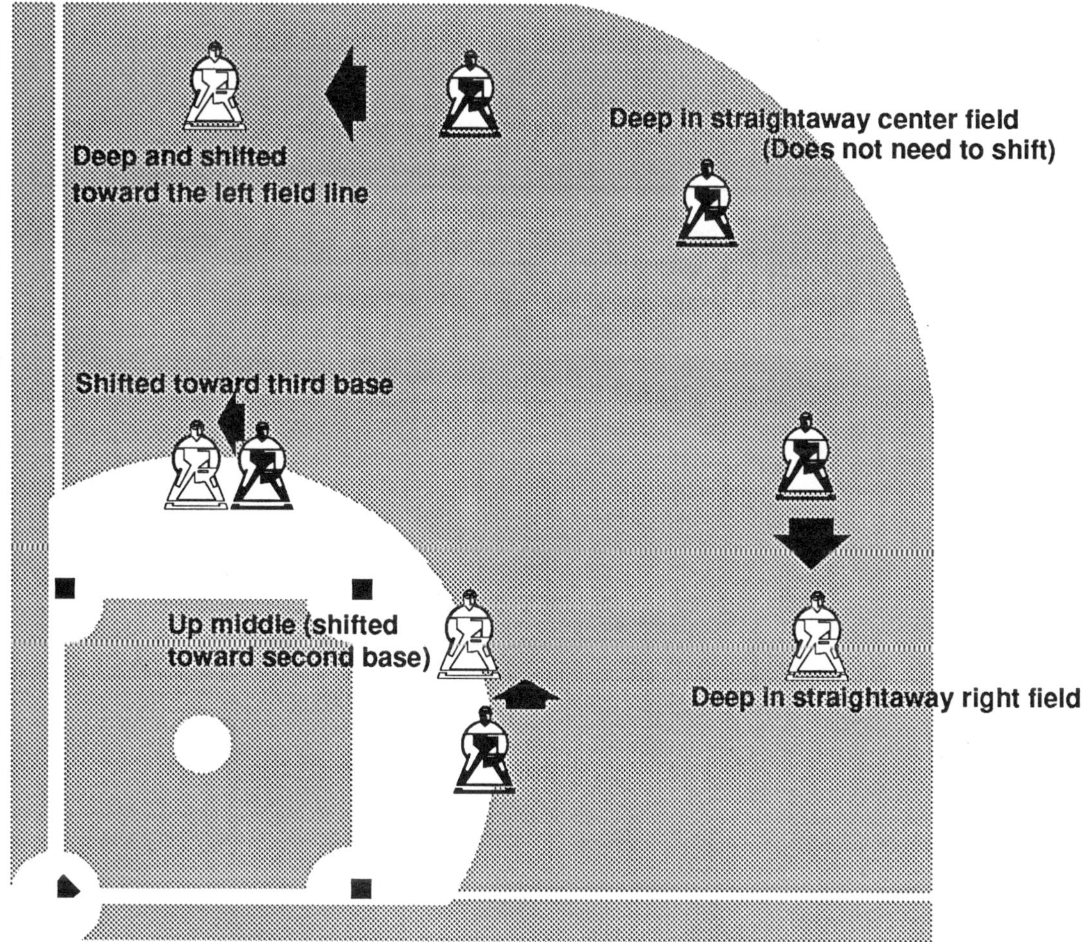

Darker men represent behind-in-the-count positions
Lighter men represent ahead-in-the-count positions

HIGH-OUTSIDE FASTBALLS
(THROWN BY LEFT-HANDED PITCHERS
WHEN DAWSON IS AHEAD IN THE COUNT)

BATTING AVERAGE .545

Play

Left	Deep and shifted toward the left field line
Center	Deep in straightaway center field
Right	Deep in straightaway right field
Short	Shifted toward third base
Second	Up middle (shifted toward second base)

It is not uncommon for batters to hit the same type and location of pitch much differently when ahead and when behind in the count. Therefore it is just as important for fielders to coordinate their positions according to the count as it is with the type and location of pitch.

A Comprehensive BARS Analysis

This analysis of Andre Dawson's BARS batting records is by no means comprehensive. The fielding strategy for a few key locations have been shown in this chapter but, for the greatest possible accuracy, fielders should position themselves on a pitch-by-pitch basis for Dawson, as they should for any hitter. That would mean examining the fielding strategy for every type and location of pitch when ahead and behind in the count against both right- and left-handed pitchers.

The easiest way for a team to start using BARS fielding strategy would be to position fielders only for fastballs. Communication could be worked out between the fielders and the bench. Shifting only for fastballs would make the transition to BARS fielding strategy easier and, since most pitches are fastballs, most pitches would be covered.

A lot of people think that it would be too complicated for the fielders to shift before each pitch, but there are always at least twenty to thirty seconds between pitches. This is more than enough time to transfer information around the field.

If someone twenty years ago had suggested that professional football teams analyze opposing teams and shift on every play, based on computer read-outs of strengths, weaknesses and probable patterns of plays, he probably would have been told that it's too complicated and would take too much time.

Now every professional and major-college football team does just that. Before a game, a staff of coaches analyzes the opposing team, and their accuracy of analysis has a strong bearing on winning or losing.

During a game, each team has scouts and analysts in the pressbox, calling game plans and changes in strategy to the coaches on the sidelines. This procedure is familiar to all football fans, and the complexity of the modern game has made it much more enjoyable for fans both at the stadium and on television.

The same will happen in baseball. The time will come when a strategic scouting system like the BARS System will be used by a team. When a team starts with the BARS System, it will have a three- or four-year advantage on the rest of the league, because it will take time for other teams to gather as much information as the BARS System has gathered. Once a team does start, others will follow. They will have to just to maintain the accelerating pace of fielding excellence that will result.

Fielding Strategy In Action

Few game-winning RBIs have had greater potential for lasting significance than Gary Carter's game-winning double in game one of the 1988 National League playoffs.

The event was dramatic enough to have been written by a Hollywood scriptwriter. The Mets came to bat in the top of the ninth trailing 2-0. Dodger pitcher Orel Hershiser, who had finished the regular season with a major-league record 59 scoreless innings, had handcuffed the Mets to that point. But when Gregg Jefferies singled to lead off the inning, moved to second on Keith Hernandez's ground out and scored on Darryl Strawberry's double to right center, the Dodgers lead was cut to 2-1 and Hershiser was taken out.

Right-handed reliever Jay Howell came in to face Kevin McReynolds. McReynolds drew a walk, but Howell then fanned Howard Johnson for the second out. That brought up Mets catcher Gary Carter.

With Strawberry on second and McReynolds on first, Howell threw Carter two straight low-outside curves. Carter reached for the next pitch, another curve low and away, and hit a soft line drive into shallow center field. Dodger centerfielder John Shelby, who had been playing very deep in center, made a mad dash and dived for the ball. He got it in his glove but it popped out as he hit the ground. Strawberry and McReynolds scored, giving the Mets a dramatic come-from-behind 3-2 victory.

The Much-Publicized Fielding Strategy

Only moments before Carter's hit, T.V. announcer Tim McCarver had mentioned that he thought the Dodger outfielders were playing Carter extremely deep — too deep for the way Carter hits the ball today as opposed to five years ago. The camera scanned the field, showing each of the outfielders playing straightaway and backed up nearly to the wall.

One pitch later, Carter's bloop hit made a prophet out of McCarver, and left millions of baseball fans with the impression that the Dodgers blew the game by playing Carter incorrectly. Next morning the papers called McCarver's observation one of the best in television history. Perhaps more than any other hit in recent years, this base hit brought national attention to the vital importance of fielding strategy.

Pitch-By-Pitch Fielding Strategy

The important fact to note is that the Dodger outfielders were not necessarily out of position simply because they were playing Carter deep. The BARS fielding strategy shows that it is often correct for the outfielders to play Carter deep — but only for specific types and locations of pitches. The Dodger fielding strategy broke down because the outfielders played Carter deep for all pitches to him, even though the pitches thrown to him did not call for them to be playing deep.

If some of the pitches to Carter had been medium-high outside fastballs, high-over-the-middle fastballs or even medium-high outside curves (among many other types and locations of pitches), it would have been correct for the outfielders to be positioned deep — *for those particular types and locations of pitches.* But by positioning themselves deep and staying deep for each of the three low-outside curves thrown to Carter, the Dodger outfielders found themselves out of position for Carter's hit.

The BARS System fielding strategy shows that for a low-outside curve thrown to Carter by a right-handed pitcher, the center fielder should play short in straight-away center field.

The BARS batting charts below show Carter's overall performance against right-handed pitchers. In particular, note his average against low-outside curves.

Gary Carter Against Right-Handed Pitchers
Overall BARS Batting Average .257

Fastball Average .291

	Inside	Middle	Outside
High	29/ 137 / 4	41/ 292 / 12	28/ 285 / 8
Med	37/ 486 / 18	17/ 235 / 4	101/ 237 / 24
Low	22/ 227 / 5	51/ 392 / 20	52/ 288 / 15

Curve Average .266

	Inside	Middle	Outside
High	5/ 200 / 1	8/ 375 / 3	6/ 166 / 1
Med	4/ 500 / 2	3/ 333 / 1	43/ 302 / 13
Low	0/ 0 / 0	8/ 375 / 3	28/ 142 / 4

Slider Average .237

	Inside	Middle	Outside
High	3/ 333 / 1	7/ 571 / 4	4/ 500 / 2
Med	5/ 0 / 0	5/ 400 / 2	30/ 133 / 4
Low	5/ 0 / 0	12/ 333 / 4	30/ 233 / 7

There was nothing wrong with the pitch itself. In fact, Carter's .142 against low-outside curves is his lowest curve average. But when the fielders are not positioned correctly, it really doesn't matter how good the pitch is, unless of course it results in a strikeout.

The opposite is also true: a pitcher can safely throw to the locations in which a hitter has a high average, if the fielders are correctly positioned for how the hitter tends to hit those pitches. Since the BARS System fielding strategy is correct over 90 percent of the time, a hitter will not have an average of over .100 in any location — if the fielders play him correctly for that location.

The BARS fielding chart shows where each of the fielders should have been playing for the low-outside curve thrown to Carter. These fielding positions are based on the computer analysis of Carter's past performance against this type of pitch.

LOW-OUTSIDE CURVEBALLS

BATTING AVERAGE .142
Play

Left	*No instances recorded*
Center	Short in straightaway center field
Right	Medium-deep and shifted toward center field
Short	Normal position
Second	Normal position

The ball was hit so softly that if the center fielder had been playing as suggested by the BARS System, he could have caught the ball. Even though the center fielder was playing very deep, he nearly made the catch. He had it in his glove but lost it in his fall. The following diagram shows Carter's hit and the fielding position of John Shelby, the Dodger's center fielder, in the actual game.

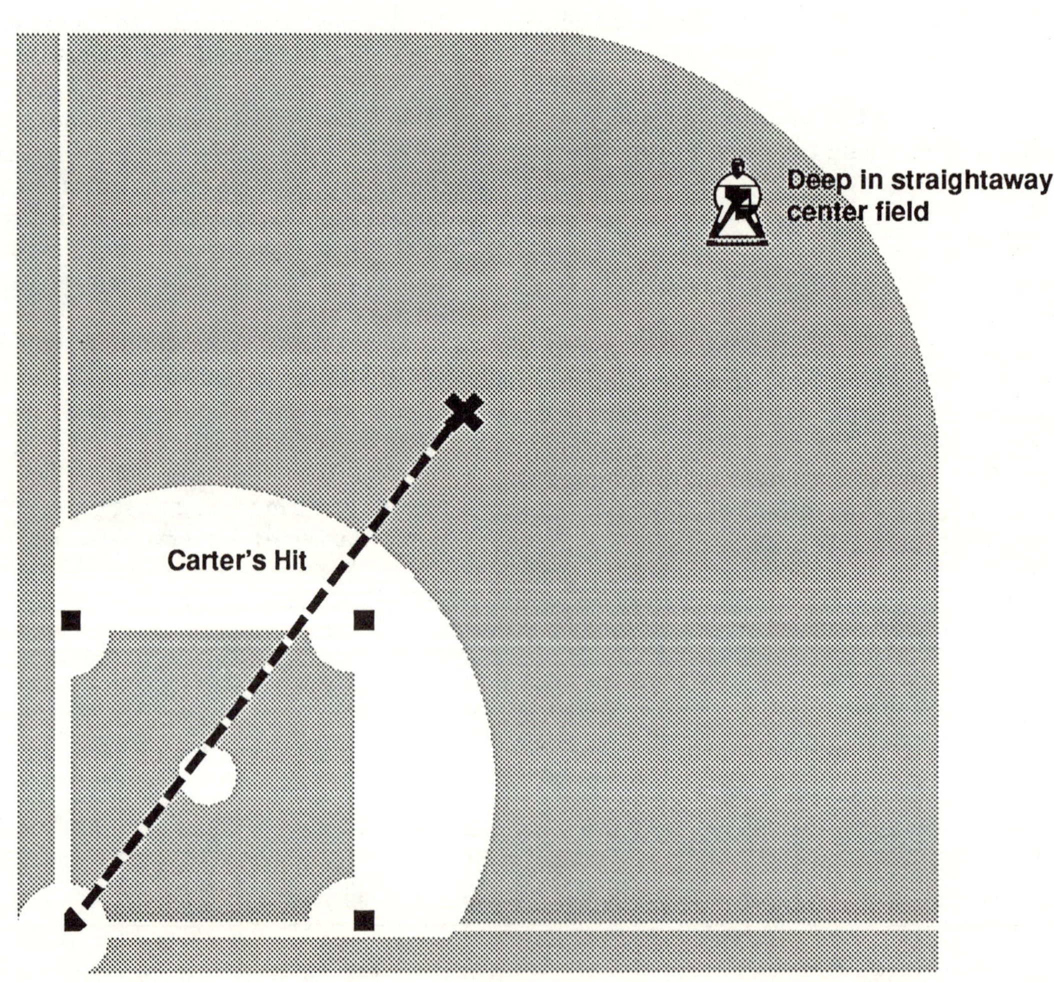

Dodger Center Fielder John Shelby's Position For Carter's Hit In Actual Game

If Shelby had been playing short in center, the ball would have been hit almost directly to him. Even if he had not wanted to play Carter short, Shelby could have played medium-deep (to guard against long hits), while realizing that the BARS fielding strategy indicates that Carter tends to hit low-outside curves short to straight-away center field.

The following diagram shows how Shelby would have been positioned had he followed the BARS fielding strategy.

BARS Fielding Strategy
Low-Outside Curveballs
Against Right-Handed Pitchers

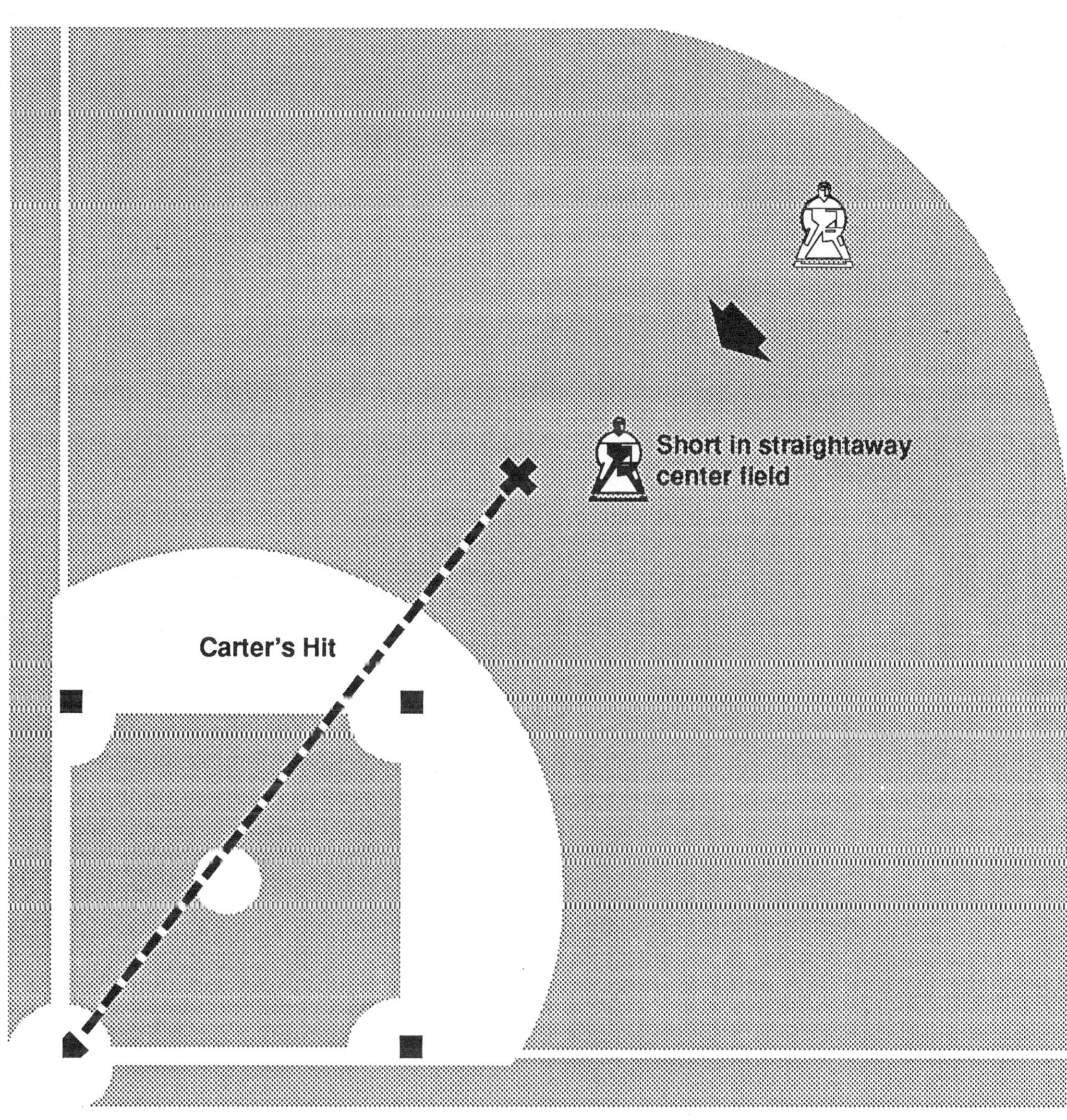

Thus, if Shelby had been playing short (or even medium-deep) in straightaway center field on this particular pitch, he would have been correctly positioned to catch the ball. As it was, he couldn't reach the ball and two runners scored, giving the Mets a 3-2 ninth-inning victory.

Fielding Strategy Varies For Different Types And Locations Of Pitches

It is typical to hear managers, announcers and players comment that teams should position fielders a specific way when a certain hitter comes up. They say that fielders should play the hitter deep, or play him to pull the ball or to hit it to the opposite field. But the fact is that the same hitter will hit various types and locations of pitches differently, and if fielders do not adjust for each pitch, they run the risk of being out of position when the ball is hit.

Taking right-handed hitting Gary Carter as an example, when right-handed pitchers throw him a high-outside fastball, each of the outfielders should play deep.

HIGH-OUTSIDE FASTBALLS

BATTING AVERAGE .285
Play

Left	Deep and shifted toward the left field line
Center	Deep in straightaway center field
Right	Deep in straightaway right field
Short	Normal position
Second	Shifted toward first base

But when pitchers throw him a high-inside fastball, the center and right fielders need to play short. Only the left fielder should play deep for this particular type and location of pitch.

HIGH-INSIDE FASTBALLS

BATTING AVERAGE .137
Play

Left	Deep in straightaway left field
Center	Short in straightaway center field
Right	Short and shifted toward center field
Short	Shifted toward third base
Second	Normal position

When pitchers throw Carter a medium-high outside curve, the left and right fielders need to play deep and the center fielder needs to be medium-deep.

MEDIUM-HIGH OUTSIDE CURVEBALLS

BATTING AVERAGE .302
Play

Left	Deep in straightaway left field
Center	Medium-deep and shifted toward left field
Right	Deep and shifted toward the right field line
Short	Shifted toward third base
Second	Normal position

When pitchers throw Carter a low-outside slider, the left fielder needs to play short and the center and right fielders need to play medium-deep.

LOW-OUTSIDE SLIDERS

BATTING AVERAGE .233
Play

Left	Short and shifted toward the left field line
Center	Medium-deep in straightaway center field
Right	Medium-deep and shifted toward the right
Short	Up middle (shifted toward second base)
Second	Normal position

You may notice in each of these fielding strategies that the shortstop and second baseman are also required to shift for different types and locations of pitches. Notice too that the outfielders often are required to shift significantly to the left or to the right, in addition to adjusting by moving deep, medium-deep or short.

A Coordinated Defensive Unit

The bottom line is that fielders cannot take one position and hold that position through all the pitches to a hitter, unless all the pitches are going to the same location.

In game one of the NL playoffs, the Dodgers threw Carter three straight low-outside curves but they were not positioned correctly for how Carter tends to hit that pitch. It cost them the game.

This chapter is certainly not meant to single out the Dodger's fine organization for making a strategic error. The fact is that nearly every team does the same thing time and time again — in every game. BARS research has shown that if a team aligned itself on a pitch-by-pitch basis using the BARS fielding strategy, it would prevent an average of two to three base hits that it is now allowing in every game. Since teams allow an average of about nine hits per game, preventing two to three of those hits would make a tremendous improvement in a team's performance. Over the course of an entire season, the effect on a team's final standing would be dramatic.

A Game Of Yards

It's been said that baseball is a game of inches. A ball hit down the line can be fair or foul by a matter of inches — or even less. Throws to first base often beat runners by surprisingly small margins; even instant replays in slow motion leave viewers undecided about whether the runner was safe or out. An attempted pick-off, a pitch just missing the corner of the plate, a ball hitting a pebble and bouncing over an infielder's glove — time and again inches make the difference in a baseball game.

Outfielders and infielders are instructed from their earliest years in baseball that it is vital to get a jump on the ball when it's hit. Again, the rule is that even inches can make the difference, and we see that this is true. Almost every game has a base hit (or extra-base hit) that falls just out of a fielder's reach. These hits often make the difference in the game.

But positioning fielders according to the BARS strategy can make a difference of not mere inches — it can position fielders *yards* closer to where the ball will be hit. Getting a good jump on the ball is and always will be important, but when a player can be positioned yards closer to where he ultimately needs to be, the

difference in fielding effectiveness will be immense.

For example, if the center fielder were playing deep in center field and the ball were lined to medium-deep or short center, he most likely would not be able to reach it in time to prevent the base hit. If, however, the BARS fielding strategy called for him to be playing medium-deep or short (see Example A below), by following the BARS strategy he would be a dozen or more yards closer to where he ultimately needs to be. Fast reaction time and a jump on the ball are certainly important, but when a fielder can be yards closer to where the ball is going to fall — and be there before the pitch is made — he is going to have a tremendously increased chance of making the play.

Another example, even more dramatic but no less likely, would be when a center fielder is playing deep and shifted toward left field. A ball hit short or medium-deep into *right center* would almost certainly fall in for a base hit, or slip through for an extra-base hit. But if the center fielder were positioned medium-deep or short and shifted toward right field, he would be 20 or 25 yards closer to where the ball will land. This is illustrated in Example B on the following page.

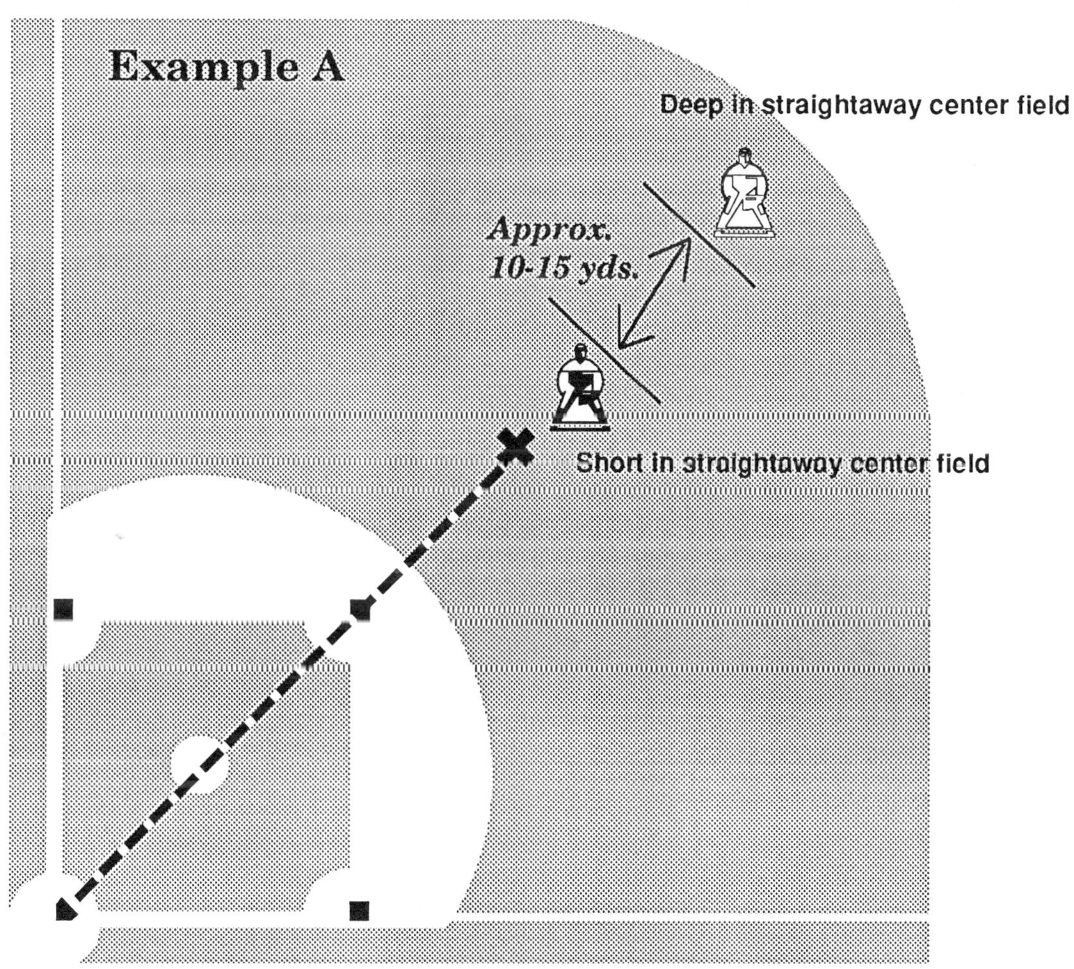

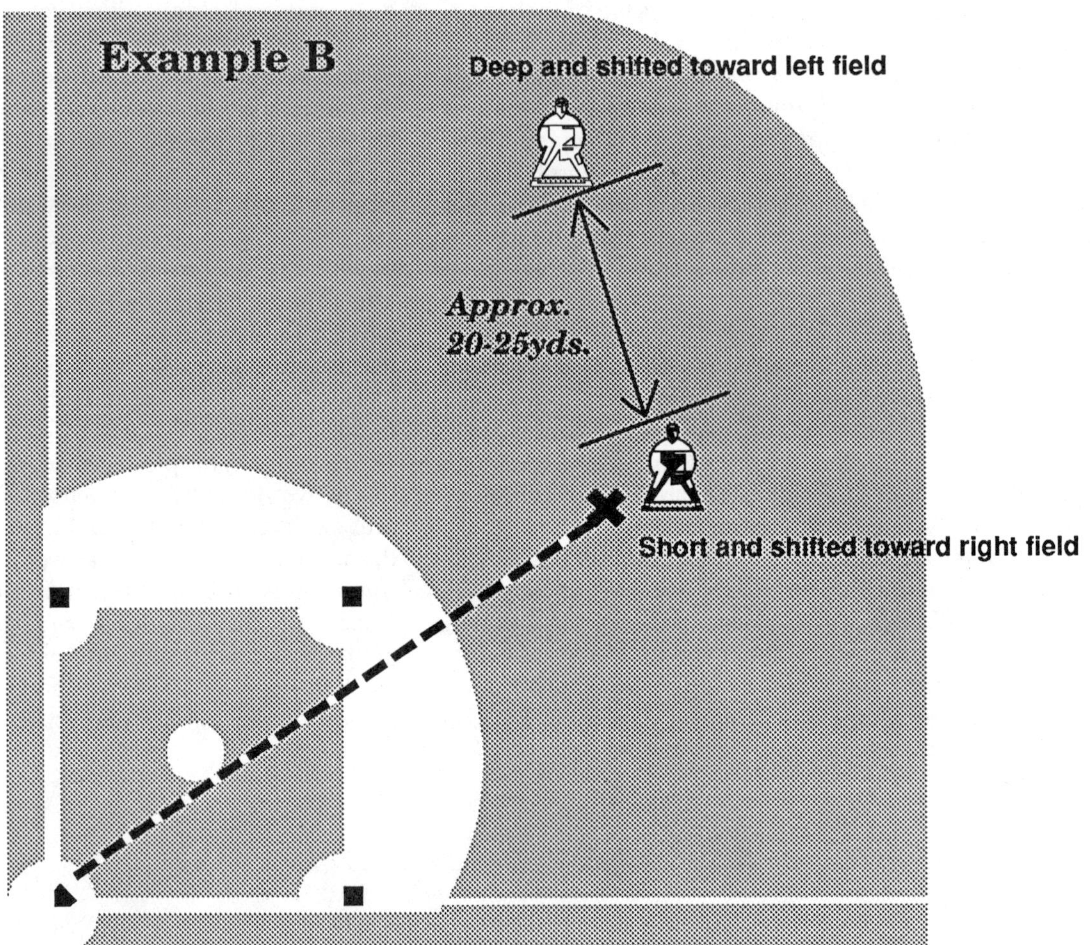

Hard-Hit Balls

Some hit balls are easy to field. A pop-up to the infield often results in two or three infielders deciding among them who will take it. A lazy fly ball to the outfield is easy to catch no matter where the outfielder is playing. But hard-hit line drives require fielders to be in just the right positions. If they're not, the ball is past them in a second or less.

If a shortstop, for example, plays shifted toward second base and the ball is hit like a shot into the hole between short and third, the ball will be into left field before he even has time to take a step or two. (See Example C on following page.) If a right fielder plays deep and shifted toward center field and the ball is hit hard down the right-field line, the ball will go to the wall. (See Example D on following page.)

Example C

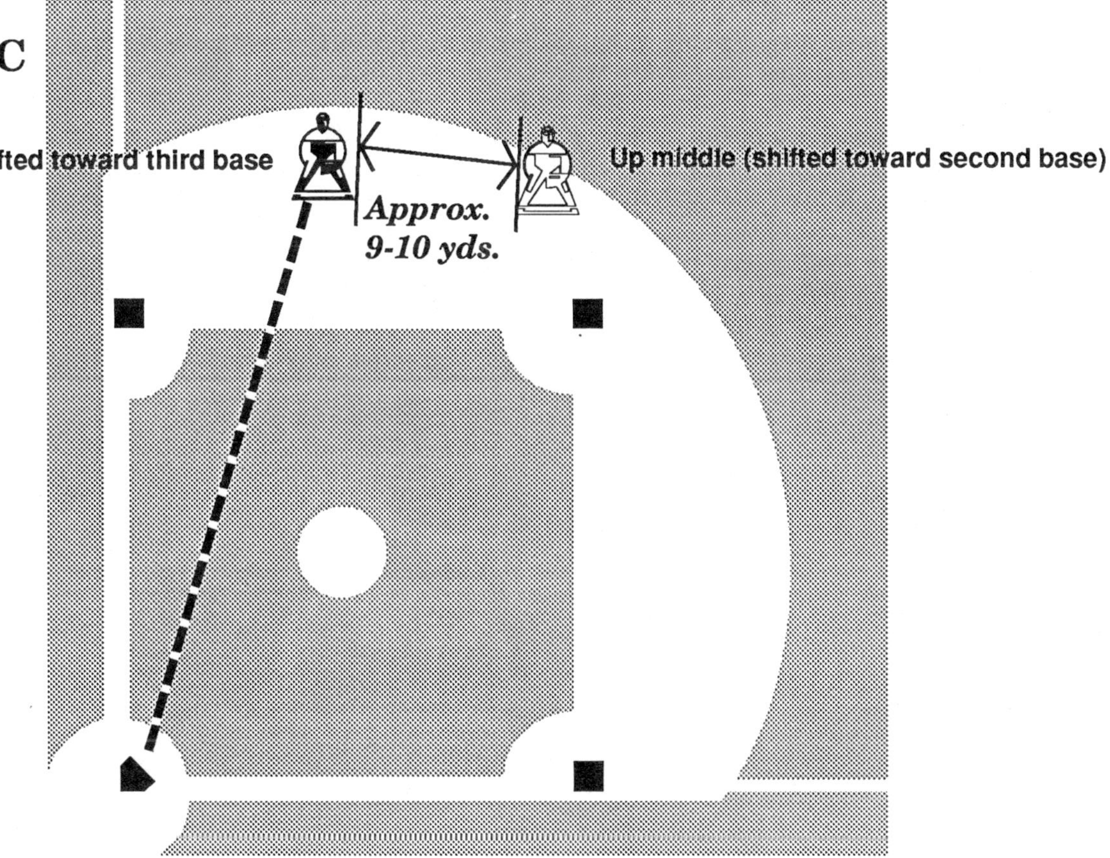

Example D

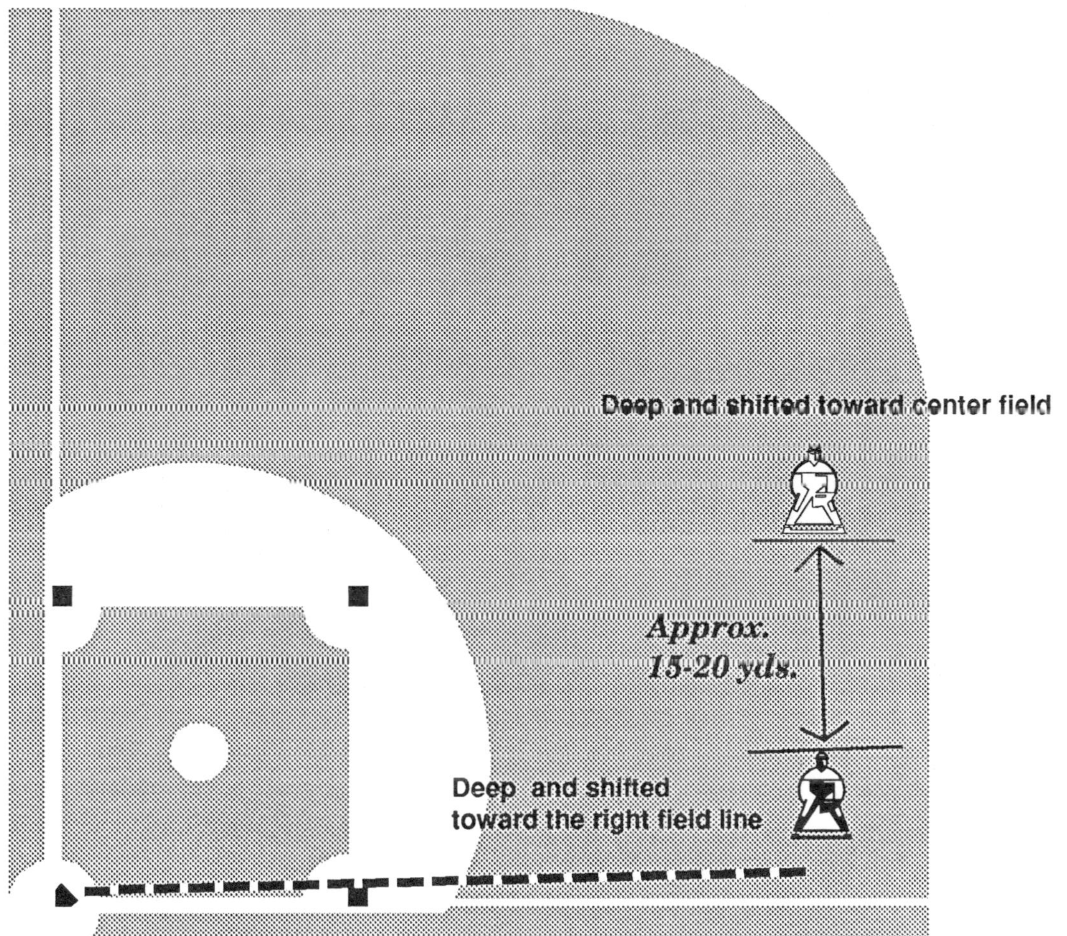

Soft fly balls or easy grounders usually don't demand perfect fielding strategy. It's only when the ball is hit hard or to an unusual spot that accurate fielding strategy is essential. In these key moments, which often determine the course of a game, the action takes place so quickly that fielders are either in the right spot or not. There's little time after the pitch for adjusting or reacting.

Fielders need to be positioned correctly before the pitch is made. Positioning fielders in the best possible way for every pitch is exactly what the BARS System fielding strategy attempts to do. It's been found that by positioning fielders according to the type and location of pitch, and according to whether the hitter is ahead and behind in the count, the BARS fielding strategy is right over 90 percent of the time. Since traditional fielding strategy is right about 75 percent of the time, using the BARS strategy will prevent an average of two to three base hits that are now being allowed very game.

As a rule it's best to position fielders for every pitch according to the BARS fielding strategy. Key hits can happen at any time. They can change the complexion of a game in a matter of seconds. By placing fielders in the best possible positions *before the pitch is made*, the greatest number of hits can be prevented.

The Overall Evaluation

Each player discussed in this book is given an Overall Evaluation. To make this more catchy to the eye and quicker to read, the Overall Evaluation is set up in chart form, with performance in each category designated as follows:

Excellent ⚾ ⚾ ⚾ ⚾
Good ⚾ ⚾ ⚾
Fair ⚾ ⚾
Poor ⚾

Since most players hit fastballs better than they hit curves and sliders, the excellent, good, fair and poor criteria are slightly higher for fastballs than for curves and sliders.

Fastballs

Excellent	.325 and above
Good	.300-.324
Fair	.275-.299
Poor	Below .275

Curves and Sliders

Excellent	.300 and above
Good	.275-.299
Fair	.250-.274
Poor	Below .250

When looking through the BARS records it can be seen that the above designations are appropriate for most hitters. Many players hit over .300 against fastballs, while few hit over .300 against curves and sliders.

The BARS Overall Batting Averages

In addition to batting averages for fastballs, curves and sliders, the BARS System gives an overall average against right-handed pitchers and against left-handed pitchers. In some instances these overall averages may be higher or lower than the collective fastball, curve and slider averages would seem to indicate. This discrepancy can occur because the overall averages take into consideration types of pitches other than fastballs, curves and sliders. Among these other pitches are knuckleballs, sinkerballs, screwballs and change-ups. In particular, many pitchers have added split-fingered fastballs to their collection of pitches. Certain hitters may have a very high — or, in many cases, — a very low average against split-fingered fastballs. This can cause the overall averages against right- or left-handed pitchers to be higher or lower than the fastball, curve and slider averages would suggest.

Realizing this, the BARS System will soon redesign its charts to account for the increasing number of split-fingered fastballs that are being thrown. Next year the BARS System will either replace the slider chart with a split-fingered fastball chart or simply add a split-fingered fastball chart to the analysis.

The BARS overall batting averages for a player against right- and left-handed pitchers may differ from his official averages against right- and left-handers because the BARS System scouts only about one-third of all major league games played. A player's BARS records and his official records are usually similar, but some variance is inevitable.

The Overall Evaluation shown for each player discussed in this book contains six overall categories:

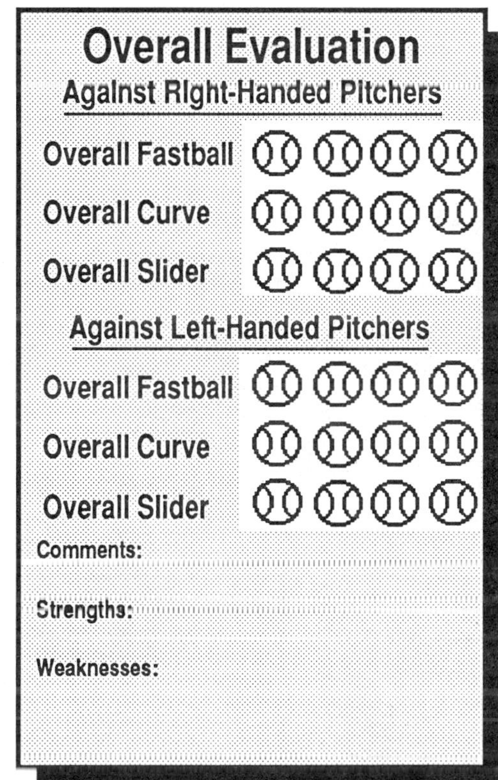

The number of baseballs shown for each category corresponds with the player's overall BARS average in that category. The Overall Evaluation includes a brief comment about each player's batting performance and a brief description of his most significant batting strengths and weaknesses.

The BARS System currently does not show home runs in the Super Summary. Starting next year it will. This will give a more complete indication of strength and weakness in each location of the batting grids.

Chicago Cubs

31

Dawson, Andre
Dunston, Shawon
Grace, Mark
Law, Vance
Sandberg, Ryne
Webster, Mitch
Wilkerson, Curtis

Chicago Cubs
BARS System
Hitting Analysis

Andre Dawson Against Right-Handed Pitchers
Overall BARS Batting Average .269

Fastball Average .306

	Inside	Middle	Outside
High	44/ 181/8	64/ 359/23	53/ 283/15
Med	55/ 327/18	11/ 454/5	105/ 304/32
Low	51/ 313/16	68/ 470/32	78/ 166/13

Curve Average .288

	Inside	Middle	Outside
High	7/ 0/0	16/ 375/6	13/ 307/4
Med	4/ 750/3	8/ 375/3	48/ 416/20
Low	5/ 400/2	16/ 250/4	67/ 164/11

Slider Average .225

	Inside	Middle	Outside
High	3/ 333/1	10/ 300/3	15/ 200/3
Med	1/ 1000/1	3/ 333/1	63/ 301/19
Low	3/ 0/0	15/ 400/6	95/ 136/13

Andre Dawson Against Left-Handed Pitchers
Overall BARS Batting Average .302

Fastball Average .357

	Inside	Middle	Outside
High	13/ 230/3	12/ 333/4	27/ 407/11
Med	11/ 363/4	2/ 500/1	35/ 457/16
Low	9/ 333/3	24/ 291/7	49/ 326/16

Curve Average .285

	Inside	Middle	Outside
High	0/ 0/0	2/ 500/1	2/ 1000/2
Med	5/ 200/1	1/ 1000/1	13/ 307/4
Low	6/ 0/0	12/ 250/3	8/ 250/2

Slider Average .290

	Inside	Middle	Outside
High	1/ 1000/1	1/ 0/0	2/ 500/1
Med	2/ 0/0	1/ 1000/1	2/ 500/1
Low	9/ 0/0	6/ 500/3	7/ 285/2

Andre Dawson, right-handed hitter, has a good fastball average against right-handed pitchers (.306 overall) and an excellent .357 overall fastball average against left-handed pitchers. You may notice that these statistics are slightly different from Dawson's statistics in the third chapter. The BARS System continually updates its records; these are the latest available at the time of publication.

Starting first with right-handers, notice that Dawson is strong against waist-high fastballs (.327, .454 and .304, inside to outside). He is even stronger down the middle top to bottom (.359, .454 and .470). If right-handers are going to give Dawson fastballs, it would be best to keep them up and in or down and away. His .313 against low-inside fastballs shows he is dangerous in that location.

Dawson hits .304 against medium-high outside fastballs thrown by right-handers. He hits this pitch deep down both lines. By positioning themselves as indicated by the BARS System, fielders could prevent most of his base hits resulting from this location. Note that the shortstop needs to play him shifted toward second and the first baseman shifted toward first for this pitch.

MEDIUM-HIGH OUTSIDE FASTBALLS

BATTING AVERAGE .304

Play

Left	Deep and shifted toward the left field line
Center	Deep and shifted toward left field
Right	Deep and shifted toward the right field line
Short	Up middle (shifted toward second base)
Second	Shifted toward first base

Dawson's .470 in the low-over-the-middle location is outstanding. He hits this pitch deep to all fields.

LOW-OVER-THE-MIDDLE FASTBALLS

BATTING AVERAGE .470

Play

Left	Deep in straightaway left field
Center	Deep in straightaway center field
Right	Deep and shifted toward center field
Short	Up middle (shifted toward second base)
Second	Shifted toward first base

Dawson hits high-over-the-middle fastballs at a brisk .359 clip.

HIGH-OVER-THE-MIDDLE FASTBALLS

BATTING AVERAGE .359

Play

Left	Deep in straightaway left field
Center	Medium-deep in straightaway center field
Right	Deep and shifted toward center field
Short	Up middle (shifted toward second base)
Second	Shifted toward first base

He hits only .166 against low-outside fastballs. This weakness against low-outside pitches is also seen in his curve and slider charts.

Dawson Against Curves And Sliders

Dawson hits only .164 against low-outside curves thrown by right-handed pitchers but he hits .416 against medium-high outside curves. He pulls this pitch deep down the left line and into the deep right-center gap. Even so, the shortstop needs to play shifted toward second.

MEDIUM-HIGH OUTSIDE CURVEBALLS

BATTING AVERAGE .416
Play

Left	Deep and shifted toward the left field line
Center	Deep and shifted toward left field
Right	Deep in straightaway right field
Short	Up middle (shifted toward second base)
Second	Normal position

He also hits weakly against low-outside sliders (.136). His medium-high outside slider average is excellent, however (.301).

Dawson Against Left-Handed Pitchers

Notice that left-handed pitchers throw Dawson many more outside than inside fastballs. This is a mistake because Dawson is outstanding against outside fastballs thrown by left-handers.

His .457 against medium-high outside fastballs serves as a warning for lefties to steer away from the outside locations. He pulls this pitch deep down the left line and into the right-center gap, but the shortstop again needs to play shifted toward second.

**MEDIUM-HIGH OUTSIDE FASTBALLS
(THROWN BY LEFT-HANDED PITCHERS)**

BATTING AVERAGE .457
Play

Left	Deep and shifted toward the left field line
Center	Medium-deep in straightaway center field
Right	Deep and shifted toward center field
Short	Up middle (shifted toward second base)
Second	Normal position

His .326 against low-outside fastballs is excellent. He goes deep to all fields with this pitch.

**LOW-OUTSIDE FASTBALLS
(THROWN BY LEFT-HANDED PITCHERS)**

BATTING AVERAGE .326
Play

Left	Deep in straightaway left field
Center	Deep and shifted toward left field
Right	Deep and shifted toward the right field line
Short	Up middle (shifted toward second base)
Second	Shifted toward first base

Dawson hits all fastballs well, so left-handers should throw to locations from which he does not hit the ball deep. This is the best way to keep the ball in the park.

Ahead And Behind In The Count Vs. RH

Ahead

Fastball Average .348

	Inside	Middle	Outside
High	14/357 /5	19/473 /9	16/250 /4
Med	25/240 /6	7/571 /4	45/422 /19
Low	21/190 /4	31/548 /17	26/115 /3

Curve Average .396

	Inside	Middle	Outside
High	0/0 /0	9/222 /2	5/400 /2
Med	3/666 /2	5/400 /2	25/400 /10
Low	1/1000 /1	4/500 /2	11/363 /4

Behind

Fastball Average .338

	Inside	Middle	Outside
High	10/100 /1	19/368 /7	18/388 /7
Med	12/666 /8	1/0 /0	23/304 /7
Low	12/333 /4	11/272 /3	18/277 /5

Curve Average .333

	Inside	Middle	Outside
High	4/0 /0	4/500 /2	4/250 /1
Med	1/1000 /1	2/500 /1	8/375 /3
Low	0/0 /0	4/500 /2	18/277 /5

Overall Evaluation

Against Right-Handed Pitchers

Overall Fastball	⚾ ⚾ ⚾
Overall Curve	⚾ ⚾ ⚾
Overall Slider	⚾

Against Left-Handed Pitchers

Overall Fastball	⚾ ⚾ ⚾ ⚾
Overall Curve	⚾ ⚾ ⚾
Overall Slider	⚾ ⚾ ⚾

Comments: An excellent fastball hitter vs. LH.
Strengths: All waist-high and over-the-middle fastballs and sliders, waist-high curves, high-middle and high-outside curves vs. RH; all fastballs (except high-inside), medium-outside curves vs. LH.
Weaknesses: High-inside and low-outside fastballs, low-outside curves and sliders vs. RH; high-inside fastballs, inside curves and low curves, inside sliders vs. LH.

Shawon Dunston (Right Handed) — *Chicago Cubs*

Shawon Dunston Against Right-Handed Pitchers
Overall BARS Batting Average .259

Fastball Average .289

	Inside	Middle	Outside
High	58/ 172 /10	38/ 315 /12	49/ 102 /5
Med	55/ 309 /17	2/ 0 /0	79/ 354 /28
Low	52/ 365 /19	79/ 392 /31	72/ 250 /18

Curve Average .237

	Inside	Middle	Outside
High	11/ 90 /1	12/ 250 /3	10/ 100 /1
Med	11/ 363 /4	0/ 0 /0	37/ 378 /14
Low	3/ 333 /1	23/ 434 /10	87/ 137 /12

Slider Average .320

	Inside	Middle	Outside
High	1/ 1000 /1	4/ 500 /2	11/ 272 /3
Med	4/ 750 /3	2/ 500 /1	53/ 358 /19
Low	7/ 571 /4	13/ 769 /10	92/ 184 /17

Shawon Dunston Against Left-Handed Pitchers
Overall BARS Batting Average .196

Fastball Average .183

	Inside	Middle	Outside
High	13/ 230 /3	12/ 166 /2	21/ 95 /2
Med	17/ 176 /3	2/ 500 /1	43/ 232 /10
Low	10/ 100 /1	35/ 200 /7	32/ 156 /5

Curve Average .214

	Inside	Middle	Outside
High	1/ 0 /0	2/ 0 /0	7/ 428 /3
Med	5/ 200 /1	1/ 0 /0	7/ 571 /4
Low	10/ 200 /2	9/ 222 /2	14/ 0 /0

Slider Average .470

	Inside	Middle	Outside
High	0/ 0 /0	1/ 1000 /1	1/ 1000 /1
Med	3/ 666 /2	0/ 0 /0	1/ 0 /0
Low	5/ 400 /2	4/ 500 /2	2/ 0 /0

Right-handed hitter Shawon Dunston hits .289 overall against fastballs thrown by right-handed pitchers. This is over 100 points higher than his .183 overall fastball average against left-handed pitchers.

Dunston's .354 against medium-high outside fastballs thrown by right-handers is excellent. He hits this ball deep to all fields. Notice that the shortstop needs to play shifted toward third base, the second baseman shifted toward first.

MEDIUM-HIGH OUTSIDE FASTBALLS

BATTING AVERAGE .354
Play

Left	Deep in straightaway left field
Center	Deep and shifted toward right field
Right	Deep in straightaway right field
Short	Shifted toward third base
Second	Shifted toward first base

Dunston's .392 in his low-over-the-middle fastball location is outstanding. He pulls this pitch deep down the left line and into the right-center gap. Even so, the shortstop needs to play shifted toward second and the second baseman shifted toward first.

LOW-OVER-THE-MIDDLE FASTBALLS

BATTING AVERAGE .392

Play

Left	Deep and shifted toward the left field line
Center	Medium-deep in straightaway center field
Right	Medium-deep and shifted toward center field
Short	Up middle (shifted toward second base)
Second	Shifted toward first base

Dunston is weak against low-outside fastballs (.250) but he is very strong against low-inside fastballs (.365). Both the center and right fielders need to shift to be positioned properly for each of these pitches. This shows how necessary it is for fielders to shift for many inside and outside pitches.

LOW-INSIDE FASTBALLS

BATTING AVERAGE .365
Play

Left	Deep in straightaway left field
Center	Medium-deep and shifted toward left field
Right	Medium-deep and shifted toward the right line
Short	Up middle (shifted toward second base)
Second	Normal position

LOW-OUTSIDE FASTBALLS

BATTING AVERAGE .250
Play

Left	Deep in straightaway left field
Center	Deep and shifted toward left field

Right	Deep in straightaway right field
Short	Up middle (shifted toward second base)
Second	Normal position

Dunston Against Curves And Sliders

Dunston has trouble with low-outside curves and sliders, but he hits these pitches well in the medium-high outside locations.

He hits medium-high outside curves for a .378 average.

MEDIUM-HIGH OUTSIDE CURVEBALLS

BATTING AVERAGE .378
Play

Left	Deep and shifted toward the left field line
Center	Medium-deep in straightaway center field
Right	Deep and shifted toward center field
Short	Shifted toward third base
Second	Shifted toward first base

Notice also how well he hits low-over-the-middle curves and sliders (.434 and .769, respectively). Pitchers should be aware of this when throwing him low curves.

LOW-OVER-THE-MIDDLE SLIDERS

BATTING AVERAGE .769
Play

Left	Deep and shifted toward the left field line
Center	Deep and shifted toward left field
Right	Deep and shifted toward the right field line

His .358 against medium-high outside sliders is also very strong. He hits this pitch deep down the left line and straightaway to the other fields.

Dunston Against Left-Handed Pitchers

Dunston, though a right-handed hitter, has low BARS averages against fastballs and curves thrown by left-handed pitchers. He is weak in all fastball locations except medium-over-the-middle. He hits medium-outside fastballs thrown by lefties deep down the left line and into the left-center gap, but his low average in this location indicates that most of his hit balls are probably easy outs.

MEDIUM-HIGH OUTSIDE FASTBALLS
(THROWN BY LEFT-HANDED PITCHERS)

BATTING AVERAGE .232
Play

Left	Deep and shifted toward the left field line
Center	Medium-deep and shifted toward left field
Right	Deep in straightaway right field
Short	Normal position
Second	Shifted toward first base

He is ineffective against low curves thrown by left-handers. His 0-for-14 against low-outside curves is a weakness left-handers can concentrate on.

Ahead And Behind In The Count Vs. RH

Ahead

Fastball Average .361

	Inside	Middle	Outside
High	24/208 /5	14/285 /4	7/0 /0
Med	27/407 /11	0/0 /0	32/500 /16
Low	16/437 /7	41/439 /18	27/259 /7

Curve Average .305

	Inside	Middle	Outside
High	2/0 /0	2/500 /1	2/0 /0
Med	3/333 /1	0/0 /0	12/500 /6
Low	0/0 /0	5/400 /2	10/100 /1

Behind

Fastball Average .329

	Inside	Middle	Outside
High	17/235 /4	5/200 /1	7/428 /3
Med	12/250 /3	0/0 /0	15/400 /6
Low	15/400 /6	14/357 /5	9/333 /3

Curve Average .363

	Inside	Middle	Outside
High	2/0 /0	6/333 /2	2/0 /0
Med	1/1000 /1	0/0 /0	11/545 /6
Low	1/1000 /1	9/555 /5	23/217 /5

Overall Evaluation
Against Right-Handed Pitchers

Overall Fastball ⚾⚾ ⚾⚾

Overall Curve ⚾⚾

Overall Slider ⚾⚾ ⚾⚾ ⚾⚾

Against Left-Handed Pitchers

Overall Fastball ⚾⚾

Overall Curve ⚾⚾

Overall Slider ⚾⚾ ⚾⚾ ⚾⚾

Comments: Has very few recorded hit balls through the heart of the plate. He should be more patient.
Strengths: Medium-outside, low-middle and low-inside fastballs, medium-outside curves and sliders, low-middle curves and sliders vs. RH; medium-outside and high outside curves vs. LH.
Weaknesses: High-inside, high-inside and low-outside fastballs, high curves and low-outside curves, low-outside sliders vs. RH; all fastballs, low curves vs. LH.

Mark Grace (Left Handed) — *Chicago Cubs*

Mark Grace Against Right-Handed Pitchers
Overall BARS Batting Average .324

Fastball Average .325

	Outside	Middle	Inside
High	8/ 125/1	11/ 454/5	24/ 166/4
Med	17/ 411/7	0/ 0/0	25/ 400/10
Low	9/ 111/1	10/ 400/4	25/ 400/10

Curve Average .440

	Outside	Middle	Inside
High	1/ 1000/1	2/ 500/1	2/ 500/1
Med	6/ 500/3	0/ 0/0	4/ 500/2
Low	1/ 0/0	5/ 400/2	4/ 250/1

Slider Average .454

	Outside	Middle	Inside
High	0/ 0/0	0/ 0/0	1/ 1000/1
Med	1/ 1000/1	0/ 0/0	6/ 333/2
Low	2/ 0/0	0/ 0/0	1/ 1000/1

Mark Grace Against Left-Handed Pitchers
Overall BARS Batting Average .223

Fastball Average .200

	Outside	Middle	Inside
High	1/ 0/0	7/ 142/1	11/ 272/3
Med	6/ 333/2	0/ 0/0	12/ 250/3
Low	3/ 0/0	1/ 0/0	9/ 111/1

Curve Average .300

	Outside	Middle	Inside
High	0/ 0/0	2/ 500/1	2/ 500/1
Med	2/ 0/0	0/ 0/0	2/ 500/1
Low	8/ 250/2	3/ 333/1	1/ 0/0

Slider Average .250

	Outside	Middle	Inside
High	0/ 0/0	0/ 0/0	0/ 0/0
Med	1/ 1000/1	0/ 0/0	0/ 0/0
Low	3/ 0/0	0/ 0/0	0/ 0/0

Left-handed hitter Mark Grace has an excellent .325 overall BARS fastball average against right-handed pitchers. He has scattered weak fastball locations (.166 high-inside, .111 low-outside and .125 high-outside) but he has five fastball locations in the .400s.

His .400 against medium-high inside fastballs is very strong. He goes down the left line (his opposite field) with this inside pitch. The following strategy and the field diagram on the opposite page show how fielders should be positioned for fastballs to this location.

MEDIUM-HIGH INSIDE FASTBALLS

BATTING AVERAGE .400

Play

Left	Medium-deep and shifted toward the left field line
Center	Deep in straightaway center field
Right	Medium-deep in straightaway right field
Short	Shifted toward third base
Second	Shifted toward first base

He also hits .400 against low-inside and low-over-the-middle fastballs. Right-handers should avoid throwing to the low-over-the-middle/low-inside/medium-high inside fastball sector.

He goes to the opposite field with low-inside fastballs. Note, however, that the shortstop needs to play shifted toward second base.

LOW-INSIDE FASTBALLS

BATTING AVERAGE .400

Play

Left	Medium-deep and shifted toward the left field line
Center	Deep and shifted toward left field
Right	Deep in straightaway right field
Short	Up middle (shifted toward second base)
Second	Normal position

Grace's .411 against medium-high outside fastballs is also very strong.

MEDIUM-HIGH OUTSIDE FASTBALLS

BATTING AVERAGE .411

Play

Left	Deep and shifted toward the left field line
Center	*No instances recorded*
Right	Medium-deep in straightaway right field
Short	Up middle (shifted toward second base)
Second	Normal position

The BARS System has fewer instances recorded for Grace against left-handed pitchers. He does seem to have potential weaknesses against all high fastballs and all inside fastballs. His .272 against high inside fastballs and his .250 against medium-high inside fastballs are both weak.

Medium-High Inside Fastballs

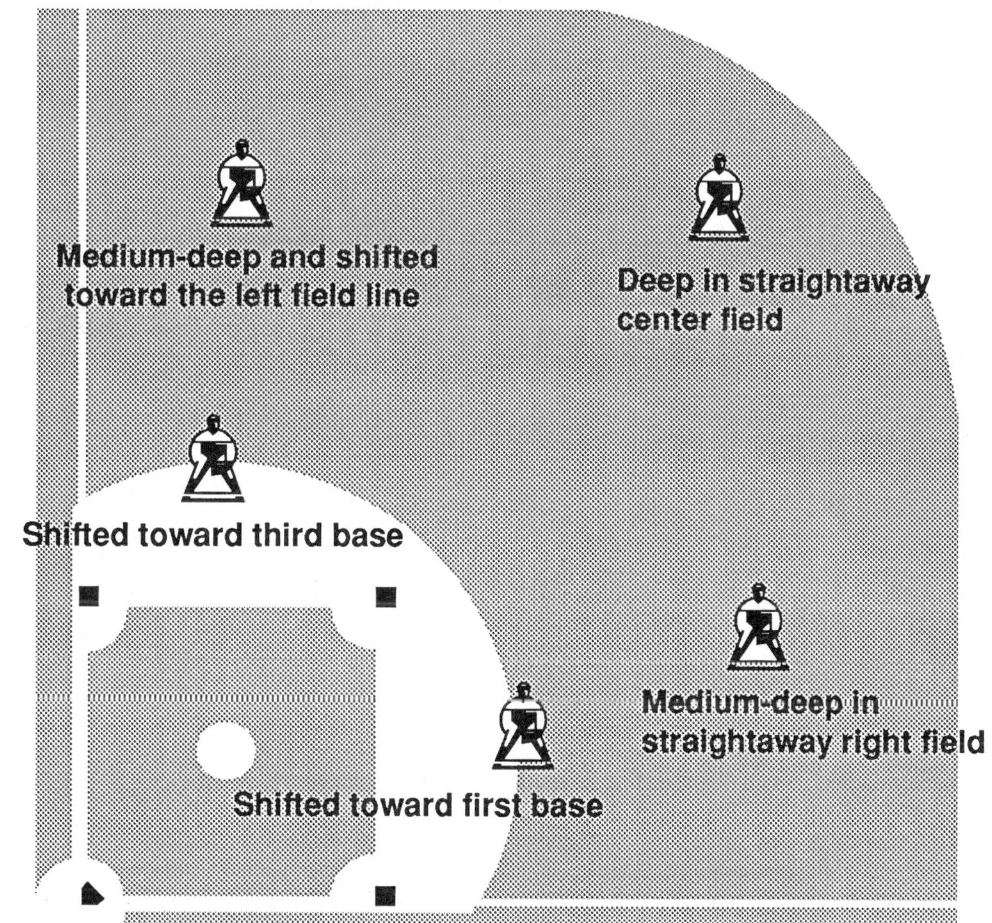

Ahead And Behind In The Count Vs. RH

Ahead

Fastball Average .367

	Outside	Middle	Inside
High	5/ 200 /1	7/ 571 /4	11/ 272 /3
Med	9/ 333 /3	0/ 0 /0	17/ 470 /8
Low	7/ 0 /0	8/ 375 /3	15/ 466 /7

Curve Average .250

	Outside	Middle	Inside
High	0/ 0 /0	0/ 0 /0	0/ 0 /0
Med	0/ 0 /0	0/ 0 /0	2/ 0 /0
Low	1/ 0 /0	1/ 1000 /1	0/ 0 /0

Behind

Fastball Average .250

	Outside	Middle	Inside
High	2/ 0 /0	2/ 0 /0	6/ 0 /0
Med	6/ 500 /3	0/ 0 /0	2/ 500 /1
Low	1/ 1000 /1	0/ 0 /0	5/ 200 /1

Curve Average .538

	Outside	Middle	Inside
High	1/ 1000 /1	1/ 0 /0	2/ 500 /1
Med	4/ 750 /3	0/ 0 /0	2/ 1000/2
Low	0/ 0 /0	1/ 0 /0	2/ 0 /0

Overall Evaluation

Against Right-Handed Pitchers

Overall Fastball	⚾⚾ ⚾⚾ ⚾⚾ ⚾⚾
Overall Curve	⚾⚾ ⚾⚾ ⚾⚾ ⚾⚾
Overall Slider	⚾⚾ ⚾⚾ ⚾⚾ ⚾⚾

Against Left-Handed Pitchers

Overall Fastball	⚾⚾
Overall Curve	⚾⚾ ⚾⚾ ⚾⚾ ⚾⚾
Overall Slider	Not enough information

Comments: Has adjacent strong and weak fastball locations against RH.

Strengths: High-middle, medium-outside, medium-inside, low-middle and low-inside fastballs vs. RH.

Weaknesses: High-outside, high-inside, low-outside fastballs vs. RH; high fastballs, low-inside fastballs vs. LH.

Vance Law Against Right-Handed Pitchers
Overall BARS Batting Average .244

Fastball Average .265

	Inside	Middle	Outside
High	27/148 /4	27/222 /6	20/100 /2
Med	55/327 /18	16/375 /6	62/290 /18
Low	46/260 /12	74/283 /21	54/259 /14

Curve Average .200

	Inside	Middle	Outside
High	3/333 /1	6/166 /1	8/250 /2
Med	10/200 /2	7/428 /3	31/258 /8
Low	6/333 /2	14/214 /3	50/100 /5

Slider Average .328

	Inside	Middle	Outside
High	2/0 /0	2/500 /1	5/200 /1
Med	6/666 /4	3/333 /1	16/500 /8
Low	3/0 /0	5/400 /2	28/214 /6

Vance Law Against Left-Handed Pitchers
Overall BARS Batting Average .283

Fastball Average .322

	Inside	Middle	Outside
High	10/500 /5	8/250 /2	12/166 /2
Med	22/363 /8	12/250 /3	47/340 /16
Low	12/250 /3	22/500 /11	32/218 /7

Curve Average .195

	Inside	Middle	Outside
High	0/0 /0	1/0 /0	1/0 /0
Med	5/600 /3	3/666 /2	12/166 /2
Low	2/0 /0	7/142 /1	10/0 /0

Slider Average .307

	Inside	Middle	Outside
High	1/0 /0	1/1000 /1	0/0 /0
Med	2/500 /1	2/500 /1	2/0 /0
Low	2/0 /0	1/1000 /1	2/0 /0

Vance Law, right-handed hitter, is strong against waist-high fastballs thrown by right-handed pitchers. He is weak against high fastballs thrown by right-handers (.148, .222 and .100, inside to outside).

He hits .290 against medium-high outside fastballs. He hits this pitch deep into the left-center gap and deep down the right line.

MEDIUM-HIGH OUTSIDE FASTBALLS

BATTING AVERAGE .290
Play
Left	Deep in straightaway left field
Center	Deep and shifted toward left field
Right	Deep and shifted toward the right field line
Short	Up middle (shifted toward second base)
Second	Normal position

His .327 against medium-high inside fastballs is excellent. The strategy below and the field diagram on the opposite page show how fielders need to be positioned for this pitch.

MEDIUM-HIGH INSIDE FASTBALLS

BATTING AVERAGE .327
Play
Left	Deep and shifted toward the left field line
Center	Medium-deep in straightaway center field
Right	Deep and shifted toward the right field line
Short	Up middle (shifted toward second base)
Second	Normal position

Law hits medium-high outside curves fairly well, but he has a lot of trouble with low-outside curves (.100 on 5-for-50). Right-handers are attacking this location. He needs to hold off on this pitch until he has two strikes.

He also has trouble with low-outside sliders (.214). But he hits medium-high outside sliders for .500. He lines this pitch medium-deep to all fields.

Law Against Left-Handed Pitchers

Law hits an excellent .340 against medium-high outside fastballs thrown by left-handed pitchers.

**MEDIUM-HIGH OUTSIDE FASTBALLS
(THROWN BY LEFT-HANDED PITCHERS)**

BATTING AVERAGE .340
Play
Left	Deep in straightaway left field
Center	Medium-deep in straightaway center field
Right	Medium-deep in straightaway right field
Short	Normal position
Second	Shifted toward first base

Medium-High Inside Fastballs

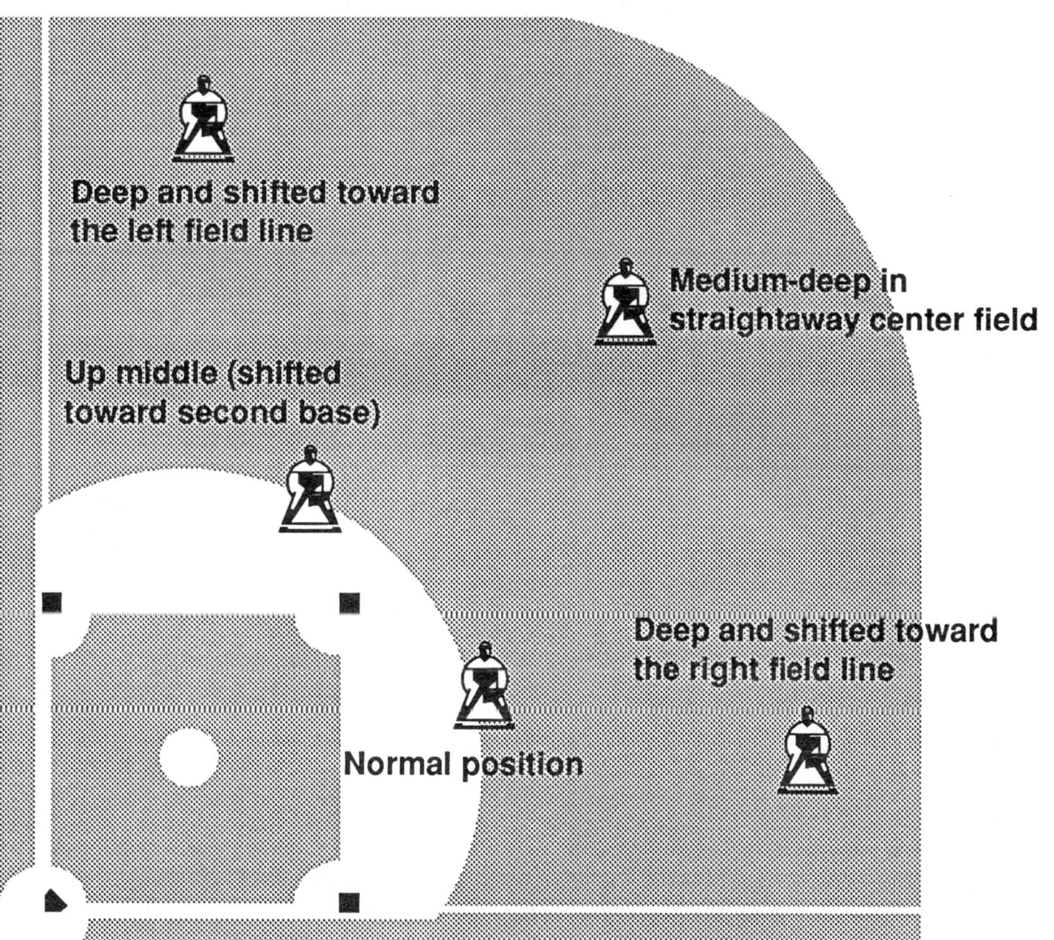

Ahead And Behind In The Count Vs. RH

Ahead

	Fastball Average .313			Curve Average .384		
	Inside	Middle	Outside	Inside	Middle	Outside
High	12/ 83 /1	14/ 214 /3	7/ 142 /1	0/ 0 /0	0/ 0 /0	1/ 1000 /1
Mod	25/ 360 /9	5/ 400 /2	28/ 357 /10	4/ 250 /1	2/ 1000 /2	6/ 500 /3
Low	15/ 333 /5	42/ 333 /14	24/ 375 /9	0/ 0 /0	3/ 666 /2	10/ 100 /1

Behind

	Fastball Average .302			Curve Average .250		
	Inside	Middle	Outside	Inside	Middle	Outside
High	6/ 500 /3	3/ 333 /1	3/ 0 /0	2/ 500 /1	3/ 0 /0	4/ 250 /1
Med	11/ 363 /4	5/ 200 /1	14/ 285 /4	1/ 0 /0	1/ 0 /0	9/ 333 /3
Low	11/ 363 /4	14/ 285 /4	9/ 222 /2	1/ 1000 /1	5/ 200 /1	14/ 214 /3

Overall Evaluation

Against Right-Handed Pitchers

Overall Fastball ⚾

Overall Curve ⚾

Overall Slider ⚾ ⚾ ⚾ ⚾

Against Left-Handed Pitchers

Overall Fastball ⚾ ⚾ ⚾

Overall Curve ⚾

Overall Slider ⚾ ⚾ ⚾ ⚾

Comments: Weak vs. high fastballs, low-outside curves and low-outside sliders vs. RH.

Strengths: Waist-high fastballs, medium-outside sliders vs. RH; high-inside, medium-inside, low-middle and medium-outside fastballs vs. LH.

Weaknesses: High fastballs, low-inside and low-outside fastballs, low-outside curves and sliders vs. RH; low-inside, low-outside and high-outside fastballs, low and outside curves vs. LH.

Ryne Sandberg (Right Handed) — *Chicago Cubs*

Ryne Sandberg Against Right-Handed Pitchers
Overall BARS Batting Average .291

Fastball Average .347

High/Med/Low	Inside	Middle	Outside
High	60 / 383 / 23	122 / 393 / 48	79 / 303 / 24
Med	114 / 377 / 43	55 / 563 / 31	249 / 373 / 93
Low	54 / 259 / 14	225 / 351 / 79	213 / 244 / 52

Curve Average .230

High/Med/Low	Inside	Middle	Outside
High	7 / 285 / 2	12 / 333 / 4	22 / 90 / 2
Med	14 / 214 / 3	5 / 600 / 3	72 / 291 / 21
Low	12 / 166 / 2	27 / 333 / 9	120 / 175 / 21

Slider Average .258

High/Med/Low	Inside	Middle	Outside
High	3 / 0 / 0	7 / 285 / 2	12 / 83 / 1
Med	11 / 363 / 4	6 / 500 / 3	105 / 361 / 38
Low	6 / 0 / 0	19 / 263 / 5	125 / 184 / 23

Ryne Sandberg Against Left-Handed Pitchers
Overall BARS Batting Average .276

Fastball Average .314

High/Med/Low	Inside	Middle	Outside
High	14 / 285 / 4	22 / 227 / 5	31 / 161 / 5
Med	34 / 264 / 9	10 / 300 / 3	83 / 337 / 28
Low	17 / 176 / 3	63 / 476 / 30	76 / 302 / 23

Curve Average .276

High/Med/Low	Inside	Middle	Outside
High	2 / 500 / 1	4 / 250 / 1	5 / 200 / 1
Med	7 / 714 / 5	1 / 0 / 0	21 / 285 / 6
Low	17 / 117 / 2	25 / 280 / 7	30 / 266 / 8

Slider Average .190

High/Med/Low	Inside	Middle	Outside
High	3 / 0 / 0	0 / 0 / 0	1 / 0 / 0
Med	5 / 0 / 0	0 / 0 / 0	7 / 285 / 2
Low	11 / 0 / 0	9 / 444 / 4	6 / 333 / 2

Right-handed hitter Ryne Sandberg has two weak locations in his fastball chart against right-handed pitchers (.259 low-inside and .244 low-outside). His other fastball locations are very strong.

Sandberg hits an outstanding .373 in the medium-high outside fastball location. He hits this pitch straightaway to all fields. But notice that the shortstop and second baseman need to shift.

MEDIUM-HIGH OUTSIDE FASTBALLS

BATTING AVERAGE .373

Play

Left	Deep in straightaway left field
Center	Medium-deep in straightaway center field
Right	Deep in straightaway right field
Short	Up middle (shifted toward second base)
Second	Shifted toward first base

Sandberg's Ahead and Behind charts on the opposite page show that he hits medium-high outside fastballs for a higher average when ahead in the count. In general, Sandberg hits for a higher average when ahead.

In part, this higher average could be because in certain locations he tends to pull the ball more when ahead. This is the case with his low-over-the-middle fastball location. Notice that the left and right fielder and the shortstop need to play Sandberg differently for this pitch when he is ahead and behind in the count.

LOW-OVER-THE-MIDDLE FASTBALLS (WHEN AHEAD IN THE COUNT)

BATTING AVERAGE .414

Play

Left	Medium-deep and shifted toward the left field line
Center	Medium-deep in straightaway center field
Right	Deep in straightaway right field
Short	Shifted toward third base
Second	Normal position

LOW-OVER-THE-MIDDLE FASTBALLS (WHEN BEHIND IN THE COUNT)

BATTING AVERAGE .325

Play

Left	Deep and shifted toward center field
Center	Medium-deep in straightaway center field
Right	Deep and shifted toward the right field line
Short	Up middle (shifted toward second base)
Second	Normal position

His .393 against high-over-the-middle fastballs is exceptional.

HIGH-OVER-THE-MIDDLE FASTBALLS

BATTING AVERAGE .393

Play

Left	Deep and shifted toward the left field line
Center	Medium-deep in straightaway center field
Right	Medium-deep in straightaway right field

Short   Up middle (shifted toward second base)
Second   Shifted toward first base

His .377 medium-high inside fastball average is also excellent.

MEDIUM-HIGH INSIDE FASTBALLS

BATTING AVERAGE .377
Play
Left   Medium-deep and shifted toward the left field line
Center   Deep and shifted toward left field
Right   Medium-deep and shifted toward the right line
Short   Up middle (shifted toward second base)
Second   Normal position

Sandberg Against Curves And Sliders

Sandberg has trouble with curves thrown by right-handed pitchers. He has several strong locations, such as high-over-the-middle (.333) and medium-high outside (.291), but his weak .175 in the highly pitched low-outside curve location brings down his curve average.

He has trouble with low sliders against right-handers, but his .361 against medium-high outside sliders is excellent.

MEDIUM-HIGH OUTSIDE SLIDERS

BATTING AVERAGE .361
Play
Left   Deep in straightaway left field
Center   Medium-deep in straightaway center field
Right   Medium-deep in straightaway right field
Short   Shifted toward third base
Second   Shifted toward first base

Sandberg Against Left-Handed Pitchers

Sandberg's overall fastball average is lower against left-handed pitchers (.314), but he has some excellent locations. He hits a brilliant .476 against low-over-the-middle fastballs.

LOW-OVER-THE-MIDDLE FASTBALLS (THROWN BY LEFT-HANDED PITCHERS)

BATTING AVERAGE .476
Play
Left   Deep and shifted toward the left field line
Center   Deep in straightaway center field
Right   Deep in straightaway right field
Short   Normal position
Second   Shifted toward first base

His .337 against medium-high outside fastballs is also very strong.

MEDIUM-HIGH OUTSIDE FASTBALLS (THROWN BY LEFT-HANDED PITCHERS)

BATTING AVERAGE .337
Play
Left   Deep and shifted toward the left field line
Center   Deep and shifted toward left field
Right   Deep in straightaway right field
Short   Shifted toward third base
Second   Normal position

He has trouble with high fastballs and inside fastballs against lefties. He also has trouble with inside sliders thrown by lefties.

Ahead And Behind In The Count Vs. RH

Ahead

Fastball Average .409

	Inside	Middle	Outside
High	26/ 538 /14	50/ 460 /23	29/ 344 /10
Med	46/ 413 /19	22/ 590 /13	112/ 446 /50
Low	11/ 181 /2	111/ 414 /46	101/ 306 /31

Curve Average .263

	Inside	Middle	Outside
High	0/ 0 /0	1/ 1000 /1	3/ 0 /0
Med	0/ 0 /0	0/ 0 /0	11/ 272 /3
Low	2/ 500 /1	5/ 200 /1	16/ 250 /4

Behind

Fastball Average .354

	Inside	Middle	Outside
High	9/ 444 /4	20/ 450 /9	14/ 428 /6
Med	26/ 384 /10	8/ 500 /4	41/ 292 /12
Low	15/ 400 /6	43/ 325 /14	30/ 266 /8

Curve Average .264

	Inside	Middle	Outside
High	1/ 1000 /1	3/ 666 /2	7/ 0 /0
Med	3/ 0 /0	3/ 333 /1	35/ 314 /11
Low	2/ 0 /0	13/ 461 /6	39/ 179 /7

Overall Evaluation

Against Right-Handed Pitchers

Overall Fastball (4 balls)
Overall Curve (1 ball)
Overall Slider (2 balls)

Against Left-Handed Pitchers

Overall Fastball (3 balls)
Overall Curve (3 balls)
Overall Slider (1 ball)

Comments: An excellent fastball hitter vs. RH. Strengths: All fastballs except low-inside and low-outside, over-the-middle curves, waist-high sliders vs. RH; medium-outside and low-middle fastballs vs. LH. Weaknesses: Low-inside and low-outside fastballs, low- and medium-inside, high- and low-outside curves, low sliders and high-outside sliders vs. RH; low-inside, medium-inside, high-middle and high-outside fastballs, low-inside curves and inside sliders vs. LH.

Mitch Webster Against Right-Handed Pitchers
Overall BARS Batting Average .251

Fastball Average .299

	Outside	Middle	Inside
High	16 / 250 / 4	25 / 360 / 9	15 / 266 / 4
Med	57 / 280 / 16	9 / 222 / 2	31 / 290 / 9
Low	31 / 193 / 6	42 / 333 / 14	28 / 428 / 12

Curve Average .181

	Outside	Middle	Inside
High	1 / 0 / 0	1 / 1000 / 1	1 / 0 / 0
Med	4 / 0 / 0	4 / 500 / 2	10 / 100 / 1
Low	7 / 142 / 1	8 / 250 / 2	8 / 125 / 1

Slider Average .333

	Outside	Middle	Inside
High	0 / 0 / 0	1 / 1000 / 1	1 / 0 / 0
Med	1 / 0 / 0	0 / 0 / 0	4 / 750 / 3
Low	1 / 0 / 0	4 / 250 / 1	3 / 0 / 0

Mitch Webster Against Left-Handed Pitchers
Overall BARS Batting Average .301

Fastball Average .344

	Inside	Middle	Outside
High	14 / 428 / 6	9 / 555 / 5	12 / 250 / 3
Med	14 / 214 / 3	2 / 500 / 1	25 / 520 / 13
Low	7 / 285 / 2	22 / 318 / 7	17 / 117 / 2

Curve Average .342

	Inside	Middle	Outside
High	0 / 0 / 0	2 / 500 / 1	1 / 1000 / 1
Med	4 / 500 / 2	2 / 1000 / 2	6 / 500 / 3
Low	6 / 0 / 0	7 / 428 / 3	7 / 0 / 0

Slider Average .500

	Inside	Middle	Outside
High	1 / 0 / 0	0 / 0 / 0	0 / 0 / 0
Med	1 / 1000 / 1	0 / 0 / 0	2 / 500 / 1
Low	3 / 333 / 1	3 / 666 / 2	0 / 0 / 0

Switch-hitting Mitch Webster hits .280 against medium-high outside fastballs thrown by right-handed pitchers. Batting left-handed, he hits this pitch medium-deep down the left line and into the left-center gap. The shortstop needs to play toward second base.

MEDIUM-HIGH OUTSIDE FASTBALLS

BATTING AVERAGE .280
Play
Left Medium-deep and shifted toward the left field line
Center Medium-deep and shifted toward left field
Right Deep in straightaway right field
Short Up middle (shifted toward second base)
Second Normal position

He is weak against low-outside fastballs (.193) but he hits low-over-the-middle and low-inside fastballs excellently.

LOW-OVER-THE-MIDDLE FASTBALLS

BATTING AVERAGE .333
Play
Left Deep in straightaway left field
Center Medium-deep in straightaway center field
Right Medium-deep and shifted toward the right line
Short Normal position
Second Shifted toward first base

LOW-INSIDE FASTBALLS

BATTING AVERAGE .428
Play
Left Medium-deep and shifted toward the left field line
Center Medium-deep in straightaway center field
Right Deep in straightaway right field
Short *No instances recorded*
Second Shifted toward first base

Webster has trouble with curves against right-handers. By mixing in more curves, right-handers could get an advantage.

Webster has some excellent fastball locations against left-handed pitchers. His .520 against medium-high outside fastballs is exceptional. Batting right-handed, he pulls this pitch down the left line.

MEDIUM-HIGH OUTSIDE FASTBALLS
(THROWN BY LEFT-HANDED PITCHERS)

BATTING AVERAGE .520
Play
Left Deep and shifted toward the left field line
Center Medium-deep in straightaway center field
Right Medium-deep in straightaway right field
Short Up middle (shifted toward second base)
Second Normal position

Medium-High Outside Fastballs

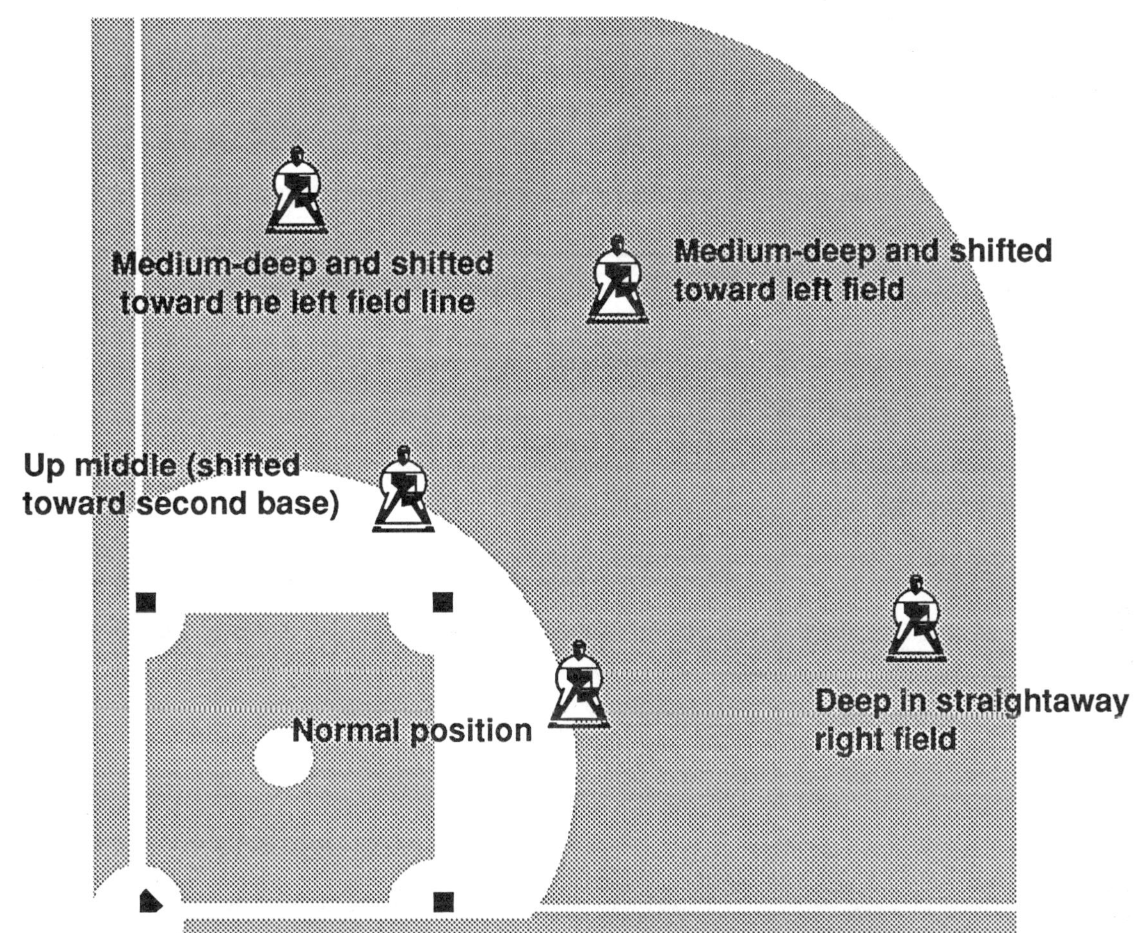

Ahead And Behind In The Count Vs. RH

Ahead

	Fastball Average .368			Curve Average .153		
	Outside	Middle	Inside	Outside	Middle	Inside
High	6/ 333 /2	12/ 333 /4	9/ 222 /2	0/ 0 /0	0/ 0 /0	1/ 0 /0
Med	27/ 333 /9	3/ 333 /1	16/ 375 /6	1/ 0 /0	1/ 0 /0	4/ 0 /0
Low	12/ 166 /2	21/ 523 /11	16/ 500 /8	1/ 0 /0	3/ 333 /1	2/ 500 /1

Behind

	Fastball Average .307			Curve Average .571		
	Outside	Middle	Inside	Outside	Middle	Inside
High	1/ 1000 /1	5/ 400 /2	3/ 333 /1	1/ 0 /0	1/ 1000 /1	0/ 0 /0
Med	7/ 428 /3	2/ 0 /0	6/ 166 /1	0/ 0 /0	1/ 1000 /1	3/ 333 /1
Low	6/ 333 /2	5/ 200 /1	4/ 250 /1	0/ 0 /0	1/ 1000 /1	0/ 0 /0

Overall Evaluation

Against Right-Handed Pitchers

Overall Fastball 
Overall Curve
Overall Slider

Against Left-Handed Pitchers

Overall Fastball
Overall Curve
Overall Slider — Not enough information

Comments: Very strong overall vs. LH.
Strengths: High-middle, low middle and low-inside fastballs vs. RH; high-inside fastballs, all over-the-middle fastballs, medium-high outside fastballs, low-middle and medium-high outside curves vs. LH.
Weaknesses: High-outside, high-inside and low-outside fastballs, curves in general, low sliders vs. RH; medium-inside, high-outside and low-outside fastballs, low-outside and low-inside curves vs. LH.

Curtis Wilkerson Against Right-Handed Pitchers
Overall BARS Batting Average .266

Fastball Average .299

	Outside	Middle	Inside
High	15/ 66 /1	42/ 261 /11	13/ 384 /5
Med	114/ 333 /38	30/ 533 /16	47/ 170 /8
Low	22/ 181 /4	40/ 250 /10	38/ 394 /15

Curve Average .212

	Outside	Middle	Inside
High	2/ 0 /0	6/ 0 /0	1/ 1000 /1
Med	11/ 181 /2	4/ 250 /1	8/ 375 /3
Low	1/ 0 /0	8/ 250 /2	6/ 166 /1

Slider Average .241

	Outside	Middle	Inside
High	1/ 0 /0	1/ 1000 /1	1/ 1000 /1
Med	2/ 0 /0	1/ 0 /0	7/ 142 /1
Low	2/ 0 /0	2/ 500 /1	12/ 250 /3

Curtis Wilkerson Against Left-Handed Pitchers
Overall BARS Batting Average .232

Fastball Average .243

	Inside	Middle	Outside
High	2/ 1000 /2	9/ 222 /2	2/ 0 /0
Med	11/ 363 /4	11/ 181 /2	17/ 117 /2
Low	4/ 250 /1	12/ 83 /1	10/ 500 /5

Curve Average .210

	Inside	Middle	Outside
High	2/ 0 /0	1/ 1000 /1	0/ 0 /0
Med	2/ 0 /0	1/ 1000 /1	2/ 0 /0
Low	6/ 0 /0	2/ 0 /0	3/ 666 /2

Slider Average .000

	Inside	Middle	Outside
High	1/ 0 /0	2/ 0 /0	0/ 0 /0
Med	0/ 0 /0	0/ 0 /0	0/ 0 /0
Low	3/ 0 /0	2/ 0 /0	0/ 0 /0

Switch-hitting Curtis Wilkerson hits fastballs very well when batting left-handed against right-handed pitchers (.299 overall). But he hits fastballs very poorly batting right-handed against left-handed pitchers (.243 overall).

Looking through his fastball, curve and slider charts shown above, notice how few curves and sliders are thrown in comparison to fastballs. Considering that he hits outside curves so poorly, pitchers should try mixing in more curves.

Against right-handed pitchers, Wilkerson hits medium-high outside fastballs for an excellent average (.333). Batting left-handed against right-handers, he hits this pitch deep into left center and deep down the right line.

MEDIUM-HIGH OUTSIDE FASTBALLS

BATTING AVERAGE .333
Play

Left	Medium-deep in straightaway left field
Center	Deep and shifted toward left field
Right	Deep and shifted toward the right field line
Short	Up middle (shifted toward second base)
Second	Normal position

In contrast, he hits medium-high inside fastballs more to the opposite field (left field).

MEDIUM-HIGH INSIDE FASTBALLS

BATTING AVERAGE .170
Play

Left	Medium-deep and shifted toward the left field line
Center	Medium-deep in straightaway center field
Right	Deep and shifted toward center field
Short	Normal position
Second	Normal position

He hits low-inside fastballs (.394) medium-deep and straightaway to all fields. By playing him correctly for this pitch, fielders could possibly catch some of his line-drive singles that now fall in front of them.

LOW-INSIDE FASTBALLS

BATTING AVERAGE .394
Play

Left	Medium-deep in straightaway left field
Center	Medium-deep in straightaway center field
Right	Medium-deep in straightaway right field
Short	Normal position
Second	Shifted toward first base

Wilkerson hits high-over-the-middle fastballs medium-deep down the left line and deep into right center.

BATTING AVERAGE .261
Play

Left	Medium-deep and shifted toward the left field line
Center	Medium-deep in straightaway center field
Right	Deep and shifted toward center field
Short	Up middle (shifted toward second base)
Second	Normal position

Wilkerson Against Curves And Sliders

Wilkerson's overall curve average of .212 against right-handed pitchers is weak. His low average against medium-high outside curves (.181) indicates that his hit balls in this location are probably just easy pop-ups and grounders.

MEDIUM-HIGH OUTSIDE CURVEBALLS

BATTING AVERAGE .181
Play

Left	Medium-deep in straightaway left field
Center	Short and shifted toward left field
Right	Medium-deep in straightaway right field
Short	Up middle (shifted toward second base)
Second	Shifted toward first base

He also has trouble with sliders thrown by right-handers (.241 overall). He hits low-inside sliders (.250) straightaway to all fields.

Wilkerson Against Left-Handed Pitchers

Wilkerson's overall average of .243 against left-handers would be even lower if not for his strong performance against medium-high inside fastballs (.363)

and low-outside fastballs (.500).

He pulls medium-high inside fastballs strongly to left field.

**MEDIUM-HIGH INSIDE FASTBALLS
(THROWN BY LEFT-HANDED PITCHERS)**

BATTING AVERAGE .363
Play

Left	Deep and shifted toward the left field line
Center	Deep and shifted toward left field
Right	*No instances recorded*
Short	Shifted toward third base
Second	Normal position

In contrast, he hits medium-high outside fastballs deep and straightaway to all field.

**MEDIUM-HIGH OUTSIDE FASTBALLS
(THROWN BY LEFT-HANDED PITCHERS)**

BATTING AVERAGE .117
Play

Left	Deep in straightaway left field
Center	Deep in straightaway center field
Right	Deep in straightaway right field
Short	Up middle (shifted toward second base)
Second	Normal position

Notice that Wilkerson has trouble with all fastballs thrown over the middle by left-handers (.222, .181 and .083, from high to low). This is indicative of his troubles in general when batting right-handed against left-handers.

Ahead And Behind In The Count Vs. RH

Ahead

Fastball Average .325

	Outside	Middle	Inside
High	2/ 0 /0	17/ 176 /3	8/ 500 /4
Med	51/ 313 /16	19/ 473 /9	28/ 250 /7
Low	5/ 400 /2	22/ 318 /7	17/ 411 /7

Curve Average .307

	Outside	Middle	Inside
High	0/ 0 /0	1/ 0 /0	1/ 1000 /1
Med	2/ 0 /0	1/ 1000 /1	4/ 250 /1
Low	0/ 0 /0	3/ 333 /1	1/ 0 /0

Behind

Fastball Average .338

	Outside	Middle	Inside
High	3/ 0 /0	13/ 384 /5	2/ 500 /1
Med	26/ 461 /12	4/ 500 /2	6/ 166 /1
Low	3/ 333 /1	9/ 222 /2	5/ 0 /0

Curve Average .066

	Outside	Middle	Inside
High	1/ 0 /0	3/ 0 /0	0/ 0 /0
Med	4/ 0 /0	1/ 0 /0	2/ 500 /1
Low	1/ 0 /0	3/ 0 /0	0/ 0 /0

Overall Evaluation

Against Right-Handed Pitchers

Overall Fastball	⚾⚾ ⚾⚾
Overall Curve	⚾⚾
Overall Slider	⚾⚾

Against Left-Handed Pitchers

Overall Fastball	⚾⚾
Overall Curve	⚾⚾
Overall Slider	Not enough information

Comments: Hits medium-outside fastballs well vs. RH.
Strengths: Medium-outside, medium-middle, high-inside and low-inside fastballs vs. RH, medium-inside curves vs.RH; medium-inside and low-outside fastballs vs. LH.
Weaknesses: Low- and high-outside fastballs, low- and high-middle fastballs, medium-inside fastballs vs. RH, outside curves vs. RH; medium-outside, low-middle and high-middle fastballs vs. LH, inside curves vs. LH.

Montreal Expos

Brooks, Hubie
Fitzgerald, Mike
Foley, Tom
Galarraga, Andres
Martinez, Dave
Owen, Spike
Raines, Tim
Wallach, Tim

Montreal Expos
BARS System
Hitting Analysis

Hubie Brooks Against Right-Handed Pitchers
Overall BARS Batting Average .290

Fastball Average .314

	Inside	Middle	Outside
High	42/ 261 /11	32/ 281 /9	25/ 160 /4
Med	60/ 283 /17	18/ 666 /12	71/ 408 /29
Low	27/ 148 /4	50/ 340 /17	34/ 294 /10

Curve Average .307

	Inside	Middle	Outside
High	2/ 0 /0	8/ 250 /2	3/ 333 /1
Med	10/ 300 /3	5/ 200 /1	26/ 461 /12
Low	4/ 250 /1	17/ 117 /2	39/ 333 /13

Slider Average .230

	Inside	Middle	Outside
High	0/ 0 /0	4/ 0 /0	3/ 666 /2
Med	4/ 500 /2	1/ 1000 /1	18/ 388 /7
Low	1/ 0 /0	8/ 0 /0	39/ 153 /6

Hubie Brooks Against Left-Handed Pitchers
Overall BARS Batting Average .272

Fastball Average .350

	Inside	Middle	Outside
High	11/ 181 /2	4/ 250 /1	11/ 272 /3
Med	12/ 250 /3	7/ 285 /2	33/ 363 /12
Low	6/ 166 /1	15/ 600 /9	15/ 466 /7

Curve Average .238

	Inside	Middle	Outside
High	0/ 0 /0	2/ 500 /1	3/ 0 /0
Med	6/ 500 /3	0/ 0 /0	6/ 333 /2
Low	9/ 222 /2	4/ 0 /0	12/ 166 /2

Slider Average .071

	Inside	Middle	Outside
High	0/ 0 /0	0/ 0 /0	1/ 0 /0
Med	4/ 250 /1	0/ 0 /0	2/ 0 /0
Low	4/ 0 /0	2/ 0 /0	1/ 0 /0

Right-handed hitter Hubie Brooks has a solid .314 overall fastball average against right-handed pitchers, an excellent .350 overall fastball average against left-handed pitchers. He hits curves very well against right-handers (.307 overall) but not as well against left-handers (.238 overall).

Brooks has an exceptional .408 average against medium-high outside fastballs thrown by right-handers. He hits this pitch into a corridor in left center field, deep and straightaway to right, and to the right side of the infield. By aligning themselves according to the following BARS fielding strategy for this pitch, fielders could prevent most of Brooks's base hits from this location.

MEDIUM-HIGH OUTSIDE FASTBALLS

BATTING AVERAGE .408
Play

Left	Medium-deep and shifted toward center field
Center	Deep and shifted toward left field
Right	Deep in straightaway right field
Short	Up middle (shifted toward second base)
Second	Shifted toward first base

He hits low-over-the-middle fastballs for a strong .340 average. He sends this pitch deep to all fields.

LOW-OVER-THE-MIDDLE FASTBALLS

BATTING AVERAGE .340
Play

Left	Deep in straightaway left field
Center	Deep and shifted toward left field
Right	Deep and shifted toward center field
Short	Normal position
Second	Shifted toward first base

His .283 against medium-high inside fastballs is adequate.

MEDIUM-HIGH INSIDE FASTBALLS

BATTING AVERAGE .283
Play

Left	Deep and shifted toward the left field line
Center	Medium-deep and shifted toward right field
Right	Medium-deep and shifted toward the right line
Short	Up middle (shifted toward second base)
Second	Normal position

Brooks has a .294 average in his low-outside fastball location. He hits this pitch straightaway to the outfield, but the shortstop needs to shift toward second and the second baseman toward first.

Brooks Against Curves And Sliders

Brooks has trouble with low-over-the-middle curves

against right-handers (.117) but he hits outside curves extremely well (.333, .461 and .333). He hits low-outside curves deep into the left- and right-center gaps and to the right side of the infield. He hits medium-high outside curves deep down the left line.

LOW-OUTSIDE CURVEBALLS

BATTING AVERAGE .333
Play

Left	Medium-deep in straightaway left field
Center	Deep and shifted toward left field
Right	Deep and shifted toward center field
Short	Up middle (shifted toward second base)
Second	Shifted toward first base

MEDIUM-HIGH OUTSIDE CURVEBALLS

BATTING AVERAGE .461
Play

Left	Deep and shifted toward the left field line
Center	Deep and shifted toward left field
Right	Deep in straightaway right field
Short	Up middle (shifted toward second base)
Second	Normal position

Brooks has trouble with low-outside sliders (.153) but hits medium-high outside sliders for a strong .388 average. He hits this pitch down both lines.

Brooks Against Left-Handed Pitchers

When facing left-handed pitchers, Brooks hits outside fastballs much better than inside fastballs. He hits a strong .363 in his medium-high outside fastball location and .466 against low-outside fastballs.

MEDIUM-HIGH OUTSIDE FASTBALLS (THROWN BY LEFT-HANDED PITCHERS)

BATTING AVERAGE .363
Play

Left	Medium-deep and shifted toward center field
Center	Deep and shifted toward right field
Right	Medium-deep and shifted toward the right line
Short	Up middle (shifted toward second base)
Second	Normal position

LOW-OUTSIDE FASTBALLS (THROWN BY LEFT-HANDED PITCHERS)

BATTING AVERAGE .466
Play

Left	*No instances recorded*
Center	Deep in straightaway center field
Right	Deep in straightaway right field
Short	Shifted toward third base
Second	Normal position

His .600 against low-over-the-middle fastballs is extremely strong.

LOW-OVER-THE-MIDDLE FASTBALLS (THROWN BY LEFT-HANDED PITCHERS)

BATTING AVERAGE .600
Play

Left	Deep and shifted toward the left field line
Center	Deep and shifted toward right field
Right	Medium-deep in straightaway right field
Short	Up middle (shifted toward second base)
Second	Shifted toward first base

Brooks has trouble with low curves thrown by left-handers. He seems to hit medium-high curves well.

Ahead And Behind In The Count Vs. RH

Ahead

Fastball Average .377

	Inside	Middle	Outside
High	20 / 250 / 5	11 / 272 / 3	10 / 100 / 1
Med	29 / 379 / 11	11 / 636 / 7	30 / 500 / 15
Low	13 / 230 / 3	23 / 434 / 10	12 / 416 / 5

Curve Average .518

	Inside	Middle	Outside
High	0 / 0 / 0	1 / 1000 / 1	1 / 0 / 0
Med	2 / 500 / 1	2 / 500 / 1	6 / 833 / 5
Low	0 / 0 / 0	6 / 166 / 1	9 / 555 / 5

Behind

Fastball Average .344

	Inside	Middle	Outside
High	6 / 333 / 2	5 / 200 / 1	4 / 500 / 2
Med	11 / 363 / 4	2 / 500 / 1	16 / 500 / 8
Low	3 / 333 / 1	8 / 125 / 1	6 / 166 / 1

Curve Average .405

	Inside	Middle	Outside
High	0 / 0 / 0	1 / 0 / 0	2 / 500 / 1
Med	4 / 500 / 2	2 / 0 / 0	11 / 636 / 7
Low	1 / 1000 / 1	2 / 500 / 1	14 / 214 / 3

Overall Evaluation

Against Right-Handed Pitchers

Overall Fastball	(3 baseballs)
Overall Curve	(4 baseballs)
Overall Slider	(1 baseball)

Against Left-Handed Pitchers

Overall Fastball	(4 baseballs)
Overall Curve	(1 baseball)
Overall Slider	Not enough information

Comments: Strong against outside curves vs. RH.
Strengths: Low-middle, medium-middle and medium-outside fastballs, medium-inside curves, all outside curves, medium-outside sliders vs. RH; low-middle, medium-outside and low-outside fastballs vs. LH.
Weaknesses: High-inside, low-inside and high-outside fastballs, over-the-middle curves, low sliders vs. RH; inside fastballs, high fastballs, low curves vs. LH.

Mike Fitzgerald Against Right-Handed Pitchers
Overall BARS Batting Average .258

Fastball Average .298

	Inside	Middle	Outside
High	9/ 222 /2	22/ 272 /6	10/ 400 /4
Med	16/ 375 /6	16/ 625 /10	45/ 222 /10
Low	11/ 181 /2	30/ 266 /8	25/ 280 /7

Curve Average .195

	Inside	Middle	Outside
High	2/ 0 /0	2/ 0 /0	1/ 0 /0
Med	7/ 285 /2	2/ 500 /1	12/ 250 /3
Low	2/ 0 /0	4/ 250 /1	14/ 142 /2

Slider Average .250

	Inside	Middle	Outside
High	1/ 0 /0	2/ 0 /0	1/ 0 /0
Med	1/ 0 /0	1/ 1000 /1	8/ 250 /2
Low	2/ 0 /0	1/ 1000 /1	11/ 272 /3

Mike Fitzgerald Against Left-Handed Pitchers
Overall BARS Batting Average .226

Fastball Average .282

	Inside	Middle	Outside
High	3/ 333 /1	11/ 363 /4	7/ 0 /0
Med	7/ 428 /3	1/ 0 /0	23/ 347 /8
Low	2/ 0 /0	19/ 263 /5	12/ 250 /3

Curve Average .272

	Inside	Middle	Outside
High	1/ 0 /0	3/ 333 /1	0/ 0 /0
Med	1/ 0 /0	0/ 0 /0	1/ 0 /0
Low	5/ 200 /1	4/ 500 /2	7/ 285 /2

Slider Average .000

	Inside	Middle	Outside
High	1/ 0 /0	0/ 0 /0	0/ 0 /0
Med	2/ 0 /0	0/ 0 /0	0/ 0 /0
Low	0/ 0 /0	3/ 0 /0	2/ 0 /0

Mike Fitzgerald, right-handed hitter, hits only .222 against medium-high outside fastballs. He hits .280, however, against low-outside fastballs. He send this pitch deep to the outfield.

LOW-OUTSIDE FASTBALLS

BATTING AVERAGE .280
Play

Left	Deep and shifted toward center field
Center	Deep in straightaway center field
Right	Deep and shifted toward center field
Short	Shifted toward third base
Second	*No instances recorded*

Fitzgerald has a fairly high number of recorded instances in his medium-over-the-middle fastball location against right-handers (16). This indicates that either pitchers are not throwing to Fitzgerald with caution or Fitzgerald is patient and waits for pitchers to come across the heart of the plate. Either way, he hits this pitch for an exceptionally strong .625 average, sending the ball deep down both lines.

MEDIUM-OVER-THE-MIDDLE FASTBALLS

BATTING AVERAGE .625
Play

Left	Deep and shifted toward the left field line
Center	Deep and shifted toward left field
Right	Deep and shifted toward the right field line
Short	Shifted toward third base
Second	Shifted toward first base

Fitzgerald has some problems with medium-high outside and low-outside curves against right-handers (.250 and .142). He also has some difficulty with medium-high outside sliders (.250). But he hits low-outside sliders fairly well (.272).

Fitzgerald Against Left-Handed Pitchers

Against left-handed pitchers, Fitzgerald has an excellent .347 average against medium-high outside fastballs. He hits this pitch deep to all fields.

**MEDIUM-HIGH OUTSIDE FASTBALLS
(THROWN BY LEFT-HANDED PITCHERS)**

BATTING AVERAGE .347
Play

Left	Deep in straightaway left field
Center	Deep in straightaway center field
Right	Deep and shifted toward the right field line
Short	Up middle (shifted toward second base)
Second	Normal position

He also hits high-over-the-middle fastballs (.363) and medium-high inside fastballs (.428) very well. He has problems with low fastballs and high-outside fastballs thrown by left-handers.

Medium-High Outside Fastballs Vs. LH

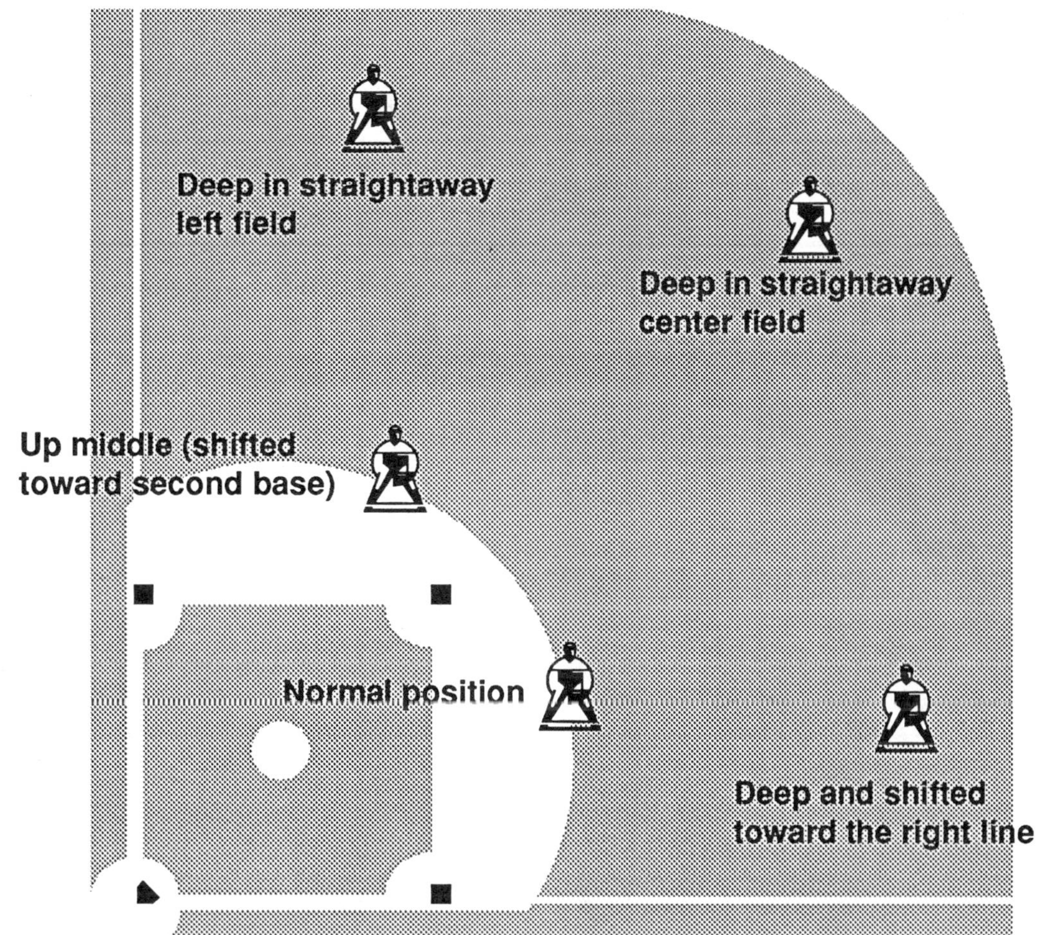

Ahead And Behind In The Count Vs. RH

Ahead

Fastball Average .372			Curve Average .400		
Inside	Middle	Outside	Inside	Middle	Outside
High 6/333 / 2	9/444 / 4	5/600 / 3	1/0 / 0	0/0 / 0	0/0 / 0
Med 11/363 / 4	12/666 / 8	22/272 / 6	3/666 / 2	0/0 / 0	3/0 / 0
Low 8/125 / 1	16/250 / 4	13/461 / 6	0/0 / 0	1/1000 / 1	2/500 / 1

Behind

Fastball Average .368			Curve Average .176		
Inside	Middle	Outside	Inside	Middle	Outside
High 1/0 / 0	1/0 / 0	1/1000 / 1	1/0 / 0	1/0 / 0	0/0 / 0
Med 1/0 / 0	2/500 / 1	4/250 / 1	2/0 / 0	1/0 / 0	5/400 / 2
Low 1/0 / 0	5/600 / 3	3/333 / 1	0/0 / 0	1/0 / 0	6/166 / 1

Overall Evaluation

Against Right-Handed Pitchers

Overall Fastball	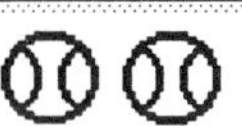 ⚾ ⚾
Overall Curve	⚾
Overall Slider	⚾ ⚾

Against Left-Handed Pitchers

Overall Fastball	⚾ ⚾
Overall Curve	⚾ ⚾
Overall Slider	Not enough information

Comments: Weak vs. outside curves vs. RH.
Strengths: Medium-inside, medium-middle and high-outside fastballs vs. RH; medium-inside, high-middle and medium-outside fastballs vs. LH.
Weaknesses: High-inside, low-inside, high-middle, low-middle, medium-outside fastballs, outside curves vs. RH; low fastballs and high-outside fastballs vs. LH.

Tom Foley (Left Handed) — *Montreal Expos*

Tom Foley Against Right-Handed Pitchers
Overall BARS Batting Average .224

Fastball Average .256

	Outside	Middle	Inside
High	20/ 200/4	26/ 269/7	19/ 263/5
Med	55/ 272/15	10/ 400/4	32/ 281/9
Low	14/ 214/3	25/ 360/9	29/ 103/3

Curve Average .250

	Outside	Middle	Inside
High	1/ 0/0	3/ 666/2	2/ 500/1
Med	8/ 250/2	1/ 0/0	2/ 0/0
Low	3/ 333/1	8/ 250/2	8/ 125/1

Slider Average .208

	Outside	Middle	Inside
High	0/ 0/0	2/ 500/1	4/ 0/0
Med	4/ 250/1	0/ 0/0	3/ 666/2
Low	0/ 0/0	4/ 0/0	7/ 142/1

Tom Foley Against Left-Handed Pitchers
Overall BARS Batting Average .326

Fastball Average .444

	Outside	Middle	Inside
High	0/ 0/0	3/ 333/1	3/ 666/2
Med	8/ 375/3	2/ 500/1	7/ 571/4
Low	1/ 0/0	2/ 0/0	1/ 1000/1

Curve Average .125

	Outside	Middle	Inside
High	0/ 0/0	0/ 0/0	0/ 0/0
Med	0/ 0/0	1/ 0/0	2/ 0/0
Low	4/ 250/1	0/ 0/0	1/ 0/0

Slider Average .375

	Outside	Middle	Inside
High	0/ 0/0	0/ 0/0	0/ 0/0
Med	3/ 333/1	0/ 0/0	0/ 0/0
Low	3/ 333/1	2/ 500/1	0/ 0/0

Left-handed hitter Tom Foley has trouble with outside fastballs and high fastballs against right-handed pitchers. He has a .272 average against medium-high outside fastballs thrown by right-handers. He hits this pitch medium-deep down the left line (his opposite field).

MEDIUM-HIGH OUTSIDE FASTBALLS

BATTING AVERAGE .272
Play

Left	Medium-deep and shifted toward the left field line
Center	Medium-deep in straightaway center field
Right	Deep in straightaway right field
Short	Up middle (shifted toward second base)
Second	Shifted toward first base

He has a .281 average against medium-high inside fastballs. He hits this pitch medium-deep to all fields.

MEDIUM-HIGH INSIDE FASTBALLS

BATTING AVERAGE .281
Play

Left	Medium-deep in straightaway left field
Center	Medium-deep in straightaway center field
Right	Medium-deep and shifted toward center field
Short	Normal position
Second	Normal position

Foley hits low-over-the-middle fastballs better when ahead in the count (.437 when ahead, .166 when behind). Fielders need to align themselves differently for this pitch when Foley is ahead and behind. The field diagram on the opposite page illustrates this.

**LOW-OVER-THE-MIDDLE FASTBALLS
(WHEN AHEAD IN THE COUNT)**

BATTING AVERAGE .437
Play

Left	Medium-deep in straightaway left field
Center	Medium-deep in straightaway center field
Right	Deep and shifted toward center field
Short	Shifted toward third base
Second	Shifted toward first base

**LOW-OVER-THE-MIDDLE FASTBALLS
(WHEN BEHIND IN THE COUNT)**

BATTING AVERAGE .166
Play

Left	Medium-deep and shifted toward center field
Center	Deep in straightaway center field
Right	Deep in straightaway right field
Short	Normal position
Second	Normal position

Low-Over-The-Middle Fastballs
Dark Fielders — Behind In The Count
Light Fielders — Ahead In The Count

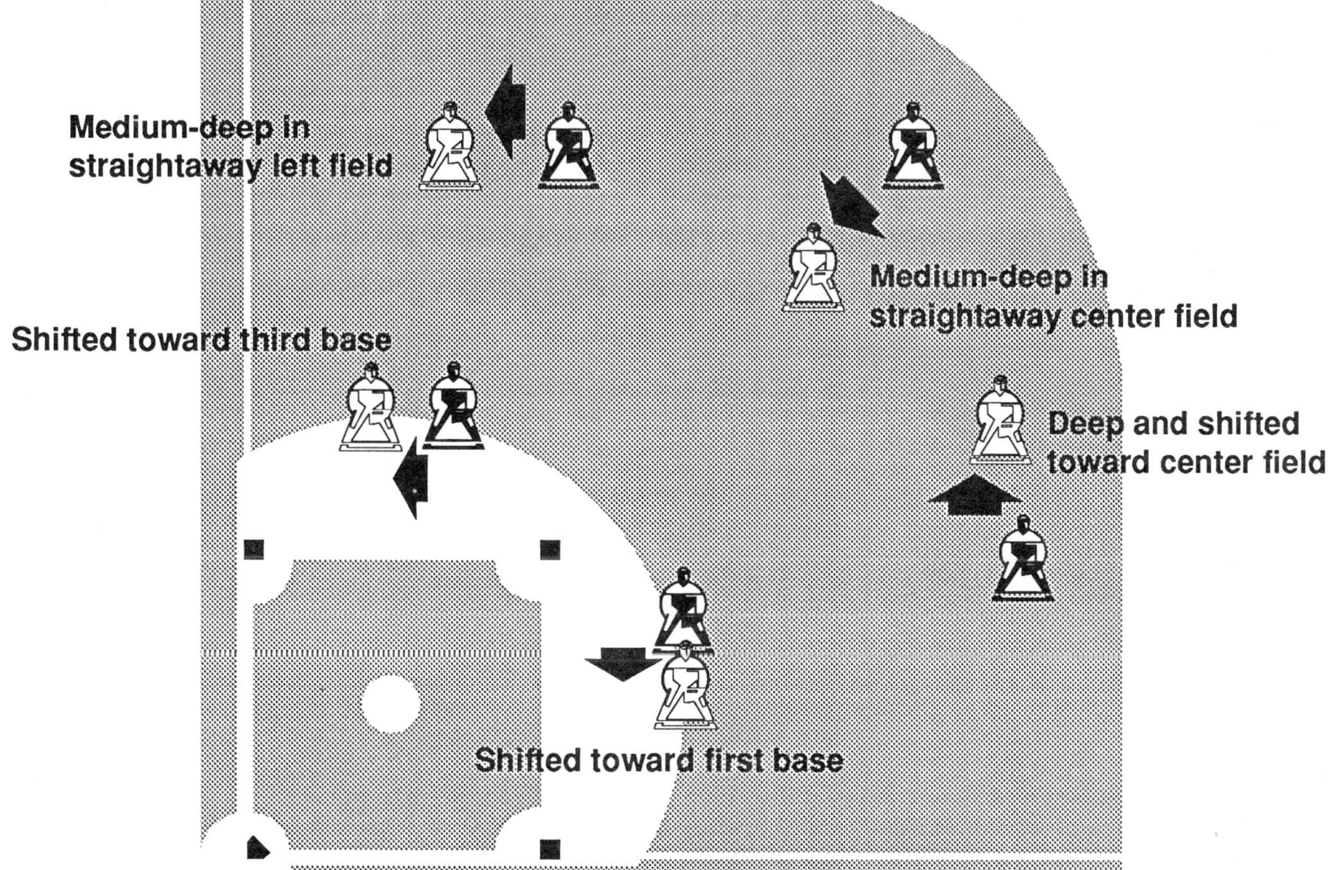

Ahead And Behind In The Count Vs. RH

Ahead

Fastball Average .284

	Outside	Middle	Inside
High	9/ 111 /1	20/ 250 /5	4/ 250 /1
Med	27/ 296 /8	6/ 500 /3	17/ 294 /5
Low	7/ 142 /1	16/ 437 /7	10/ 200 /2

Curve Average .600

	Outside	Middle	Inside
High	0/ 0 /0	1/ 1000 /1	2/ 500 /1
Med	2/ 500 /1	0/ 0 /0	0/ 0 /0
Low	0/ 0 /0	0/ 0 /0	0/ 0 /0

Behind

Fastball Average .333

	Outside	Middle	Inside
High	2/ 0 /0	3/ 666 /2	6/ 666 /4
Med	6/ 166 /1	3/ 333 /1	6/ 500 /3
Low	4/ 250 /1	6/ 166 /1	3/ 0 /0

Curve Average .333

	Outside	Middle	Inside
High	0/ 0 /0	1/ 0 /0	0/ 0 /0
Med	2/ 500 /1	1/ 0 /0	1/ 0 /0
Low	1/ 1000 /1	3/ 333 /1	0/ 0 /0

Overall Evaluation
Against Right-Handed Pitchers

Overall Fastball ⚾

Overall Curve ⚾ ⚾

Overall Slider ⚾

Against Left-Handed Pitchers

Overall Fastball ⚾ ⚾ ⚾ ⚾

Overall Curve — Not enough information

Overall Slider — Not enough information

Comments: Weak against outside fastballs and high fastballs vs. RH.

Strengths: Medium-middle and low-middle fastballs vs. RH; waist-high fastballs vs. LH.

Weaknesses: Outside fastballs, high fastballs, low-inside fastballs, low-inside curves and sliders vs. RH.

Andres Galarraga (Right Handed) — *Montreal Expos*

Andres Galarraga Against Right-Handed Pitchers
Overall BARS Batting Average .283

Fastball Average .294

	Inside	Middle	Outside
High	22/ 272 /6	13/ 153 /2	13/ 76 /1
Med	15/ 400 /6	2/ 1000/ 2	27/ 333 /9
Low	10/ 200 /2	15/ 333 /5	19/ 368 /7

Curve Average .325

	Inside	Middle	Outside
High	1/ 1000/ 1	2/ 0 /0	1/ 1000/ 1
Med	3/ 333 /1	0/ 0 /0	12/ 500 /6
Low	1/ 1000/ 1	2/ 500 /1	21/ 142 /3

Slider Average .264

	Inside	Middle	Outside
High	0/ 0 /0	0/ 0 /0	4/ 250 /1
Med	0/ 0 /0	2/ 500 /1	12/ 333 /4
Low	1/ 1000/ 1	1/ 0 /0	14/ 142 /2

Andres Galarraga Against Left-Handed Pitchers
Overall BARS Batting Average .291

Fastball Average .308

	Inside	Middle	Outside
High	4/ 500 /2	5/ 400 /2	6/ 166 /1
Med	10/ 200 /2	2/ 500 /1	13/ 384 /5
Low	5/ 0 /0	7/ 428 /3	16/ 312 /5

Curve Average .181

	Inside	Middle	Outside
High	1/ 0 /0	0/ 0 /0	1/ 1000/ 1
Med	2/ 0 /0	0/ 0 /0	2/ 1000/ 2
Low	0/ 0 /0	6/ 0 /0	10/ 100 /1

Slider Average .111

	Inside	Middle	Outside
High	0/ 0 /0	0/ 0 /0	0/ 0 /0
Med	1/ 0 /0	0/ 0 /0	1/ 0 /0
Low	3/ 0 /0	4/ 250 /1	0/ 0 /0

Right-handed hitter Andres Galarraga has trouble with high fastballs against right-handed pitchers (.272, .153 and .076, inside to outside). He hits waist-high fastballs excellently, however (.400, 1.000 and .333, inside to outside). He hits medium-high outside fastballs down both lines.

MEDIUM-HIGH OUTSIDE FASTBALLS

BATTING AVERAGE .333
Play
Left Deep and shifted toward the left field line
Center Medium-deep in straightaway center field
Right Medium-deep and shifted toward the right line
Short Normal position
Second Shifted toward first base

He hits medium-high inside fastballs deep to all fields.

MEDIUM-HIGH INSIDE FASTBALLS

BATTING AVERAGE .400
Play
Left Deep in straightaway left field
Center Deep and shifted toward right field
Right Deep in straightaway right field
Short Normal position
Second Normal position

His .368 average against low-outside fastballs is excellent.

LOW-OUTSIDE FASTBALLS

BATTING AVERAGE .368
Play
Left *No instances recorded*
Center Medium-deep in straightaway center field
Right Deep in straightaway right field
Short Up middle (shifted toward second base)
Second Shifted toward first base

His .333 against low-over-the-middle fastballs is also strong.

LOW-OVER-THE-MIDDLE FASTBALLS

BATTING AVERAGE .333
Play
Left Medium-deep and shifted toward the left field line
Center Medium-deep in straightaway center field
Right Medium-deep and shifted toward the right line
Short Normal position
Second Shifted toward first base

Galarraga hits high-inside fastballs (.272) straightaway to left and center and medium-deep down the right field line. It is not at all unusual for hitters (both right- and left-handed hitters) to hit high-inside fastballs down the opposite line.

Galarraga Against Curves And Sliders

Galarraga has trouble with low-outside curves and sliders (.142 in each location). But he hits medium-high outside curves and sliders excellently (.500 and .333).

MEDIUM-HIGH OUTSIDE CURVEBALLS

BATTING AVERAGE .500
Play

Left	Deep in straightaway left field
Center	Deep and shifted toward left field
Right	Deep and shifted toward center field
Short	Normal position
Second	*No instances recorded*

MEDIUM-HIGH OUTSIDE SLIDERS

BATTING AVERAGE .333
Play

Left	Deep in straightaway left field
Center	Medium-deep in straightaway center field
Right	Medium-deep and shifted toward center field
Short	Shifted toward third base
Second	*No instances recorded*

Galarraga Against Left-Handed Pitchers

Galarraga has some very strong fastball locations against left-handed pitchers. He hits .384 against medium-high outside fastballs. He hits this pitch deep down both lines.

MEDIUM-HIGH OUTSIDE FASTBALLS
(THROWN BY LEFT-HANDED PITCHERS)

BATTING AVERAGE .384
Play

Left	Deep and shifted toward the left field line
Center	Medium-deep in straightaway center field
Right	Deep and shifted toward the right field line
Short	Shifted toward third base
Second	Shifted toward first base

His .312 against low-outside fastballs is solid.

LOW-OUTSIDE FASTBALLS
(THROWN BY LEFT-HANDED PITCHERS)

BATTING AVERAGE .312
Play

Left	*No instances recorded*
Center	Medium-deep in straightaway center field
Right	Deep in straightaway right field
Short	Up middle (shifted toward second base)
Second	Normal position

His .428 against low-over-the-middle fastballs is very strong.

LOW-OVER-THE-MIDDLE FASTBALLS
(THROWN BY LEFT-HANDED PITCHERS)

BATTING AVERAGE .428
Play

Left	*No instances recorded*
Center	Deep in straightaway center field
Right	Deep and shifted toward the right field line
Short	Up middle (shifted toward second base)
Second	Normal position

Galarraga has problems with low-outside curves (.100) and low-over-the-middle curves (.000 on 0-for-6) against left-handers.

Ahead And Behind In The Count Vs. RH

Ahead

Fastball Average .333

	Inside	Middle	Outside
High	8/375/3	3/333/1	2/0/0
Med	8/500/4	2/1000/2	10/300/3
Low	3/0/0	7/142/1	8/375/3

Curve Average .875

	Inside	Middle	Outside
High	0/0/0	0/0/0	0/0/0
Med	0/0/0	0/0/0	4/750/3
Low	1/1000/1	1/1000/1	2/1000/2

Behind

Fastball Average .320

	Inside	Middle	Outside
High	5/200/1	3/0/0	2/500/1
Med	1/0/0	0/0/0	4/500/2
Low	1/0/0	4/500/2	5/400/2

Curve Average .625

	Inside	Middle	Outside
High	1/1000/1	2/0/0	1/1000/1
Med	1/1000/1	0/0/0	2/500/1
Low	0/0/0	0/0/0	1/1000/1

Overall Evaluation

Against Right-Handed Pitchers

Overall Fastball	⚾⚾ ⚾⚾
Overall Curve	⚾⚾ ⚾⚾ ⚾⚾ ⚾⚾
Overall Slider	⚾⚾ ⚾⚾

Against Left-Handed Pitchers

Overall Fastball	⚾ ⚾⚾ ⚾⚾
Overall Curve	⚾⚾
Overall Slider	Not enough information

Comments: Weak against high fastballs vs. RH.
Strengths: Medium-inside, low-middle, medium-outside and low-outside fastballs, medium-outside curves and medium-outside sliders vs. RH; over-the-middle fastballs, medium-outside and low-outside fastballs vs. LH.
Weaknesses: High fastballs, low-inside fastballs, low-outside curves and sliders vs. RH; medium-inside fastballs, low-outside and low-middle curves vs. LH.

Dave Martinez (Left Handed) — *Montreal Expos*

Dave Martinez Against Right-Handed Pitchers
Overall BARS Batting Average .223

Fastball Average .250

	Outside	Middle	Inside
High	27 / 37 / 1	30 / 300 / 9	34 / 205 / 7
Med	41 / 170 / 7	4 / 750 / 3	51 / 294 / 15
Low	35 / 200 / 7	66 / 348 / 23	59 / 254 / 15

Curve Average .196

	Outside	Middle	Inside
High	1 / 0 / 0	2 / 500 / 1	5 / 0 / 0
Med	2 / 1000 / 2	2 / 500 / 1	4 / 0 / 0
Low	13 / 76 / 1	8 / 500 / 4	24 / 125 / 3

Slider Average .302

	Outside	Middle	Inside
High	1 / 0 / 0	2 / 500 / 1	2 / 0 / 0
Med	1 / 0 / 0	0 / 0 / 0	8 / 250 / 2
Low	5 / 0 / 0	9 / 444 / 4	15 / 400 / 6

Dave Martinez Against Left-Handed Pitchers
Overall BARS Batting Average .226

Fastball Average .171

	Outside	Middle	Inside
High	1 / 0 / 0	3 / 333 / 1	6 / 166 / 1
Med	2 / 0 / 0	0 / 0 / 0	9 / 333 / 3
Low	3 / 0 / 0	4 / 0 / 0	7 / 142 / 1

Curve Average .300

	Outside	Middle	Inside
High	0 / 0 / 0	1 / 0 / 0	0 / 0 / 0
Med	1 / 1000 / 1	1 / 0 / 0	1 / 0 / 0
Low	1 / 0 / 0	2 / 0 / 0	3 / 666 / 2

Slider Average .400

	Outside	Middle	Inside
High	0 / 0 / 0	0 / 0 / 0	0 / 0 / 0
Med	2 / 500 / 1	0 / 0 / 0	0 / 0 / 0
Low	2 / 0 / 0	0 / 0 / 0	1 / 1000 / 1

Left-handed hitter Dave Martinez has a .294 average in his medium-high inside fastball location. He hits this pitch deep down the left line (his opposite field), into the left-center gap and straightaway to right.

MEDIUM-HIGH INSIDE FASTBALLS

BATTING AVERAGE .294
Play

Left	Deep and shifted toward the left field line
Center	Medium-deep and shifted toward left field
Right	Medium-deep in straightaway right field
Short	Up middle (shifted toward second base)
Second	Normal position

He hits low-over-the-middle fastballs better when ahead in the count (.384 when ahead, .200 when behind). When ahead, he hits this pitch deep to left and right fields.

LOW-OVER-THE-MIDDLE FASTBALLS
(WHEN AHEAD IN THE COUNT)

BATTING AVERAGE .384
Play

Left	Deep in straightaway left field
Center	Medium-deep in straightaway center field
Right	Deep and shifted toward center field
Short	Up middle (shifted toward second base)
Second	Shifted toward first base

LOW-OVER-THE-MIDDLE FASTBALLS
(WHEN BEHIND IN THE COUNT)

BATTING AVERAGE .200
Play

Left	Medium-deep and shifted toward the left line
Center	Medium-deep and shifted toward left field
Right	Medium-deep and shifted toward the right line
Short	Up middle (shifted toward second base)
Second	Normal position

He hits a solid .300 against high-over-the-middle fastballs.

HIGH-OVER-THE-MIDDLE FASTBALLS

BATTING AVERAGE .300
Play

Left	Medium-deep and shifted toward the left field line
Center	Deep and shifted toward left field
Right	Deep in straightaway right field
Short	Up middle (shifted toward second base)
Second	Normal position

Martinez has problems with all outside fastballs thrown by right-handers. He also has trouble with high-inside and low-inside fastballs. By pitching to his weak locations, right-handers can get an edge.

Martinez also has difficulties with low-outside and low-inside curves (.076 and .125). He hits low-inside and low-over-the-middle sliders excellently, however, (.400 and .444).

Low-Over-The-Middle Fastballs
Dark Fielders — Behind In The Count
Light Fielders — Ahead In The Count

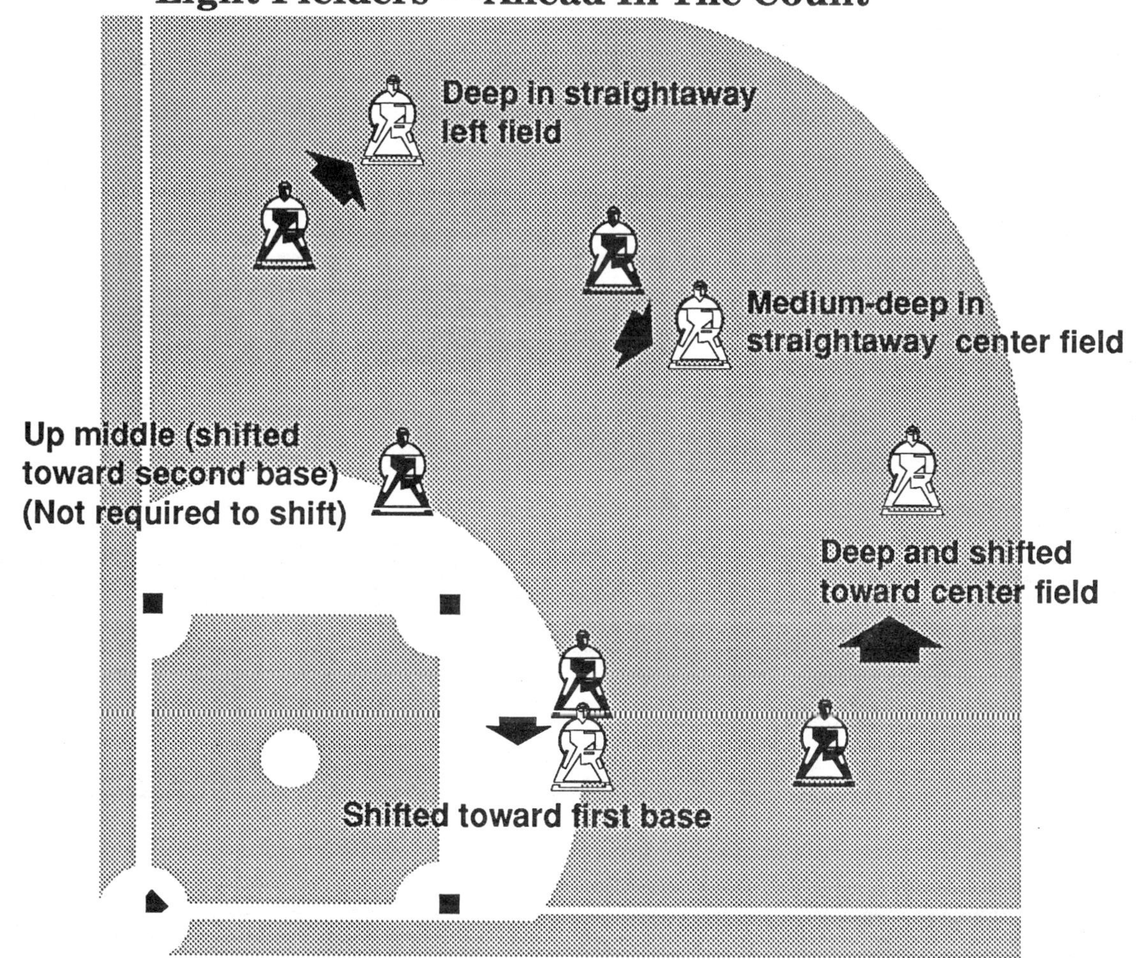

Ahead And Behind In The Count Vs. RH

Ahead

Fastball Average .302

	Outside	Middle	Inside
High	3/ 333 /1	17/ 294 /5	11/ 363 /4
Med	19/ 210 /4	3/ 666 /2	31/ 290 /9
Low	9/ 333 /3	39/ 384 /15	30/ 200 /6

Curve Average .400

	Outside	Middle	Inside
High	0/ 0 /0	0/ 0 /0	0/ 0 /0
Med	1/ 1000 /1	0/ 0 /0	2/ 0 /0
Low	1/ 0 /0	0/ 0 /0	1/ 1000 /1

Behind

Fastball Average .233

	Outside	Middle	Inside
High	3/ 0 /0	2/ 500 /1	7/ 285 /2
Med	6/ 0 /0	1/ 1000 /1	9/ 333 /3
Low	8/ 375 /3	15/ 200 /3	9/ 111 /1

Curve Average .384

	Outside	Middle	Inside
High	0/ 0 /0	2/ 500 /1	2/ 0 /0
Med	1/ 1000 /1	1/ 1000 /1	0/ 0 /0
Low	5/ 200 /1	8/ 500 /4	7/ 285 /2

Overall Evaluation

Against Right-Handed Pitchers

Overall Fastball	⚾
Overall Curve	⚾
Overall Slider	⚾ ⚾ ⚾ ⚾

Against Left-Handed Pitchers

Overall Fastball	⚾
Overall Curve	Not enough information
Overall Slider	Not enough information

Comments: Weak against outside fastballs vs. RH.

Strengths: Over-the-middle fastballs, medium-inside fastballs, over-the-middle curves, low-middle sliders and low-inside sliders vs. RH; medium-inside fastballs vs. LH.

Weaknesses: Outside fastballs, high-inside and low-inside fastballs, low-outside curves, inside curves, outside sliders vs. RH; low-inside and high inside fastballs vs. LH.

Spike Owen Against Right-Handed Pitchers
Overall BARS Batting Average .245

Fastball Average .267

	Outside	Middle	Inside
High	28 / 214/6	32 / 343/11	14 / 357/5
Med	139 / 266/37	23 / 391/9	54 / 277/15
Low	19 / 210/4	51 / 235/12	29 / 172/5

Curve Average .275

	Outside	Middle	Inside
High	3 / 333/1	3 / 666/2	0 / 0/0
Med	14 / 214/3	5 / 200/1	4 / 500/2
Low	3 / 0/0	2 / 500/1	6 / 166/1

Slider Average .200

	Outside	Middle	Inside
High	1 / 0/0	2 / 1000/2	1 / 1000/1
Med	4 / 0/0	0 / 0/0	6 / 0/0
Low	0 / 0/0	5 / 0/0	6 / 333/2

Spike Owen Against Left-Handed Pitchers
Overall BARS Batting Average .286

Fastball Average .328

	Inside	Middle	Outside
High	3 / 0/0	14 / 500/7	8 / 250/2
Med	18 / 388/7	9 / 333/3	53 / 339/18
Low	7 / 285/2	19 / 263/5	12 / 250/3

Curve Average .250

	Inside	Middle	Outside
High	0 / 0/0	3 / 666/2	0 / 0/0
Med	1 / 0/0	0 / 0/0	9 / 222/2
Low	5 / 0/0	4 / 500/2	6 / 166/1

Slider Average .333

	Inside	Middle	Outside
High	1 / 1000/1	0 / 0/0	0 / 0/0
Med	3 / 333/1	1 / 0/0	2 / 500/1
Low	4 / 0/0	1 / 1000/1	0 / 0/0

Switch-hitting Spike Owen hits fastballs much better when batting against left-handed pitchers. His .328 overall fastball average against left-handers is excellent. His .267 overall fastball average against right-handers leaves much room for improvement.

One of Owen's central problems against right-handers is his trouble with outside fastballs (.214, .266 and .210 from high to low). He also has trouble with low fastballs against right-handers (.210, .235 and .172, outside to inside).

Owen's Ahead and Behind charts on the opposite page show that he hits medium-high outside fastballs much better when behind in the count (.461) than when ahead (.230).

**MEDIUM-HIGH OUTSIDE FASTBALLS
(WHEN BEHIND IN THE COUNT)**

BATTING AVERAGE .461
> *Play*

Left	Medium-deep in straightaway left field
Center	Medium-deep in straightaway center field
Right	Deep and shifted toward center field
Short	Normal position
Second	Shifted toward first base

**MEDIUM-HIGH OUTSIDE FASTBALLS
(WHEN AHEAD IN THE COUNT)**

BATTING AVERAGE .230
> *Play*

Left	Deep and shifted toward the left field line
Center	Deep in straightaway center field
Right	Deep and shifted toward the right field line
Short	Up middle (shifted toward second base)
Second	Shifted toward first base

Owen pulls medium-high inside fastballs thrown by right-handers.

MEDIUM-HIGH INSIDE FASTBALLS

BATTING AVERAGE .277
> *Play*

Left	Medium-deep and shifted toward center field
Center	Deep in straightaway center field
Right	Medium-deep and shifted toward the right line
Short	Up middle (shifted toward second base)
Second	Shifted toward first base

In contrast to medium-high outside fastballs, Owen hits medium-high inside fastballs much better when ahead in the count (.142 when behind, .434 when ahead).

Owen has trouble with most curve locations against right-handers. His .214 in the highly pitched medium-high outside curve location is representative. He hits this pitch deep to all fields, but his low average indicates that he hits mostly easy fly balls.

MEDIUM-HIGH OUTSIDE CURVEBALLS

BATTING AVERAGE .214
Play

Left	Deep and shifted toward the left field line
Center	Deep in straightaway center field
Right	Deep in straightaway right field
Short	Normal position
Second	Shifted toward first base

Owen Against Left-Handed Pitchers

The switch-hitting Owen hits fastballs very well against left-handed pitchers. Other than his high-inside location, in which few instances are recorded, .250 is his lowest average.

The .339 in his medium-high outside and .388 in his medium-high inside location are excellent. He pulls medium-high outside fastballs deep to left and center fields.

MEDIUM-IIIGII OUTSIDE FASTBALLS (THROWN BY LEFT-HANDED PITCHERS)

BATTING AVERAGE .339
Play

Left	Deep and shifted toward the left field line
Center	Deep and shifted toward left field
Right	Medium-deep in straightaway right field

Short	Up middle (shifted toward second base)
Second	Normal position

Owen also pulls medium-high inside fastballs thrown by lefties down the left line, but he tends to hit the ball more toward right center and down the right line.

MEDIUM-HIGH INSIDE FASTBALLS (THROWN BY LEFT-HANDED PITCHERS)

BATTING AVERAGE .388
Play

Left	Deep and shifted toward the left field line
Center	Medium-deep and shifted toward right field
Right	Medium-deep and shifted toward the right line
Short	Normal position
Second	Normal position

When thrown high-over-the-middle fastballs by left-handers, Owen hits deep down both lines. Fielders are probably not playing him correctly for this pitch, hence his .500 average in this location.

HIGH-OVER-THE-MIDDLE FASTBALLS (THROWN BY LEFT-HANDED PITCHERS)

BATTING AVERAGE .500
Play

Left	Deep and shifted toward the left field line
Center	Deep in straightaway center field
Right	Deep and shifted toward the right field line
Short	Normal position
Second	Normal position

Ahead And Behind In The Count Vs. RH

Ahead

Fastball Average .281

	Outside	Middle	Inside
High	12/ 250 / 3	13/ 307 / 4	3/ 666 / 2
Med	65/ 230 / 15	10/ 300 / 3	23/ 434 / 10
Low	6/ 500 / 3	15/ 66 / 1	6/ 333 / 2

Curve Average .666

	Outside	Middle	Inside
High	0/ 0 / 0	0/ 0 / 0	0/ 0 / 0
Med	2/ 500 / 1	0/ 0 / 0	0/ 0 / 0
Low	0/ 0 / 0	1/ 1000 / 1	0/ 0 / 0

Behind

Fastball Average .287

	Outside	Middle	Inside
High	3/ 0 / 0	2/ 500 / 1	4/ 250 / 1
Med	26/ 461 / 12	3/ 333 / 1	14/ 142 / 2
Low	3/ 0 / 0	12/ 333 / 4	6/ 0 / 0

Curve Average .272

	Outside	Middle	Inside
High	2/ 500 / 1	2/ 1000 / 2	0/ 0 / 0
Med	7/ 142 / 1	4/ 250 / 1	1/ 0 / 0
Low	1/ 0 / 0	1/ 0 / 0	4/ 250 / 1

Overall Evaluation
Against Right-Handed Pitchers

Overall Fastball	⚾⚾
Overall Curve	⚾⚾ ⚾⚾ ⚾⚾
Overall Slider	⚾⚾

Against Left-Handed Pitchers

Overall Fastball	⚾ ⚾⚾ ⚾⚾ ⚾⚾
Overall Curve	⚾⚾ ⚾⚾
Overall Slider	⚾⚾ ⚾⚾ ⚾⚾ ⚾⚾

Comments: Owen hits fastballs better when batting RH against LH.

Strengths: High-middle, medium-middle and high-inside fastballs vs. RH; waist-high fastballs, high-middle fastballs vs. LH.

Weaknesses: All outside and all low fastballs, medium-outside curves vs. RH; low-middle and low-outside fastballs, outside curves vs. LH.

Tim Raines (Switch Hitter) — *Montreal Expos*

Tim Raines Against Right-Handed Pitchers
Overall BARS Batting Average .314

Fastball Average .345

	Outside	Middle	Inside
High	23/ 304 / 7	55/ 363 / 20	23/ 217 / 5
Med	65/ 369 / 24	22/ 363 / 8	72/ 347 / 25
Low	33/ 272 / 9	64/ 406 / 26	45/ 333 / 15

Curve Average .181

	Outside	Middle	Inside
High	3/ 0 / 0	2/ 500 / 1	1/ 0 / 0
Med	10/ 100 / 1	6/ 666 / 4	9/ 222 / 2
Low	3/ 333 / 1	11/ 0 / 0	10/ 100 / 1

Slider Average .312

	Outside	Middle	Inside
High	0/ 0 / 0	4/ 500 / 2	5/ 600 / 3
Med	3/ 333 / 1	1/ 1000 / 1	16/ 312 / 5
Low	1/ 0 / 0	9/ 333 / 3	9/ 0 / 0

Tim Raines Against Left-Handed Pitchers
Overall BARS Batting Average .306

Fastball Average .328

	Inside	Middle	Outside
High	6/ 166 / 1	17/ 352 / 6	12/ 416 / 5
Med	16/ 312 / 5	7/ 428 / 3	38/ 236 / 9
Low	6/ 666 / 4	30/ 333 / 10	20/ 350 / 7

Curve Average .166

	Inside	Middle	Outside
High	1/ 0 / 0	2/ 0 / 0	1/ 0 / 0
Med	7/ 142 / 1	2/ 500 / 1	8/ 250 / 2
Low	1/ 0 / 0	2/ 500 / 1	6/ 0 / 0

Slider Average .375

	Inside	Middle	Outside
High	2/ 500 / 1	0/ 0 / 0	0/ 0 / 0
Med	5/ 400 / 2	0/ 0 / 0	1/ 1000 / 1
Low	4/ 500 / 2	4/ 0 / 0	0/ 0 / 0

Switch-hitting Tim Raines is an excellent fastball hitter (.345 overall fastball average against right-handed pitchers, .328 overall against left-handed pitchers). Even so, he has distinct strengths and weaknesses.

Raines is very strong against all waist-high fastballs thrown by right-handers (.369, .363 and .347, outside to inside). He's also strong against over-the-middle fastballs (.363, .363 and .406, high to low). His weaknesses are in the high-inside and low-outside fastball locations (.217 and .272, respectively).

His .406 against low-over-the-middle fastballs is extremely strong. Batting left-handed against right-handed pitchers, he hits this ball to his opposite field (left field). But note that the shortstop needs to shift toward second for this pitch.

LOW-OVER-THE-MIDDLE FASTBALLS

BATTING AVERAGE .406
Play
Left Deep and shifted toward the left field line
Center Deep and shifted toward left field
Right Deep and shifted toward center field
Short Up middle (shifted toward second base)
Second Normal position

His .347 against medium-high inside fastballs is also excellent.

MEDIUM-HIGH INSIDE FASTBALLS

BATTING AVERAGE .347
Play
Left Deep in straightaway left field
Center Medium-deep in straightaway center field
Right Deep in straightaway right field
Short Up middle (shifted toward second base)
Second Shifted toward first base

Similarly, he is very strong against medium-high outside fastballs (.369) and high-over-the-middle fastballs (.363).

MEDIUM-HIGH OUTSIDE FASTBALLS

BATTING AVERAGE .369
Play
Left Medium-deep and shifted toward the left field line
Center Medium-deep in straightaway center field
Right Deep and shifted toward the right field line
Short Up middle (shifted toward second base)
Second Shifted toward first base

HIGH-OVER-THE-MIDDLE FASTBALLS

BATTING AVERAGE .363
Play
Left Deep in straightaway left field

Right	Deep in straightaway right field
Center	Deep in straightaway center field
Short	Normal position
Second	Normal position

It's interesting to see that Raines hits low-inside fastballs deep down the left line (his opposite field) and that the shortstop needs to play shifted toward third base. This emphasizes the point that fielders need to adjust for every type and location of pitch to maximize their chances of being correctly positioned.

LOW-INSIDE FASTBALLS

BATTING AVERAGE .333
Play

Left	Deep and shifted toward the left field line
Center	Medium-deep in straightaway center field
Right	Medium-deep in straightaway right field
Short	Shifted toward third base
Second	Shifted toward first base

Raines Against Curves And Sliders

Raines has a lot of trouble with medium-high inside curves (.222), low-inside curves (.100) and low-over-the-middle curves (.000 on 0-for-11). This sector gives right-handers a target for attack. Considering how well Raines hits fastballs, right-handers should try throwing him more curves.

He also has trouble with low-inside sliders (.000 on 0-for-9). But he hits low-over-the-middle and medium-high inside sliders very well (.333 and .312). He hits medium-high inside sliders deep down the left line.

MEDIUM-HIGH INSIDE SLIDERS

BATTING AVERAGE .312
Play

Left	Deep and shifted toward the left field line
Center	*No instances recorded*
Right	Deep in straightaway right field
Short	Shifted toward third base
Second	Shifted toward first base

Raines Against Left-Handed Pitchers

Raines has a low .236 average in his medium-high outside fastball location against left-handed pitchers. He hits the other two outside fastball locations excellently, however. He also hits all over-the-middle fastballs excellently (.352, .428 and .333, high to low). He hits low-over-the-middle fastballs deep down the left line and into medium-deep left center.

LOW-OVER-THE-MIDDLE FASTBALLS (THROWN BY LEFT-HANDED PITCHERS)

BATTING AVERAGE .333
Play

Left	Deep and shifted toward the left field line
Center	Medium-deep and shifted toward left field
Right	Medium-deep in straightaway right field
Short	Shifted toward third base
Second	Shifted toward first base

Raines has trouble with outside curves thrown by left-handers. His .142 average against medium-high inside curves also indicates a weakness.

Ahead And Behind In The Count Vs. RH

Ahead

Fastball Average .366

	Outside	Middle	Inside
High	13 / 384 / 5	34 / 382 / 13	11 / 181 / 2
Mod	37 / 405 / 15	14 / 428 / 6	33 / 303 / 10
Low	17 / 294 / 5	36 / 444 / 16	26 / 346 / 9

Curve Average .333

	Outside	Middle	Inside
High	0 / 0 / 0	1 / 1000 / 1	0 / 0 / 0
Mod	1 / 0 / 0	1 / 0 / 0	2 / 0 / 0
Low	0 / 0 / 0	0 / 0 / 0	1 / 1000 / 1

Behind

Fastball Average .413

	Outside	Middle	Inside
High	2 / 500 / 1	11 / 363 / 4	2 / 500 / 1
Med	11 / 363 / 4	0 / 0 / 0	14 / 571 / 8
Low	4 / 250 / 1	9 / 444 / 4	5 / 200 / 1

Curve Average .222

	Outside	Middle	Inside
High	2 / 0 / 0	0 / 0 / 0	0 / 0 / 0
Med	1 / 0 / 0	1 / 1000 / 1	5 / 400 / 2
Low	1 / 1000 / 1	7 / 0 / 0	1 / 0 / 0

Overall Evaluation

Against Right-Handed Pitchers

Overall Fastball	⚾ ⚾ ⚾ ⚾
Overall Curve	⚾
Overall Slider	⚾ ⚾ ⚾

Against Left-Handed Pitchers

Overall Fastball	⚾ ⚾ ⚾ ⚾
Overall Curve	⚾
Overall Slider	⚾ ⚾ ⚾

Comments: Excellent fastball hitter vs. both RH & LH. Strengths: Waist-high & all middle fastballs, high-outside & low-inside fastballs, medium-inside & all middle sliders vs. RH; all middle fastballs, medium-inside & high-outside fastballs, inside sliders vs. LH. Weaknesses: Low-outside & high-inside fastballs, inside curves, low-middle & medium-outside curves, low-inside sliders vs. RH; medium-outside fastballs, inside curves and outside curves vs. LH.

Tim Wallach (Right Handed)   *Montreal Expos*

Tim Wallach Against Right-Handed Pitchers
Overall BARS Batting Average .250

Fastball Average .296

	Inside	Middle	Outside
High	30/166/5	39/410/16	18/388/7
Med	28/214/6	25/240/6	95/294/28
Low	23/304/7	57/385/22	46/217/10

Curve Average .225

	Inside	Middle	Outside
High	5/200/1	6/166/1	6/0/0
Med	5/400/2	1/1000/1	21/238/5
Low	4/0/0	13/230/3	41/243/10

Slider Average .188

	Inside	Middle	Outside
High	1/0/0	6/166/1	3/0/0
Med	2/0/0	3/0/0	29/310/9
Low	7/142/1	11/90/1	44/181/8

Tim Wallach Against Left-Handed Pitchers
Overall BARS Batting Average .257

Fastball Average .302

	Inside	Middle	Outside
High	11/181/2	7/428/3	12/250/3
Med	10/300/3	1/0/0	38/342/13
Low	7/571/4	18/222/4	25/280/7

Curve Average .115

	Inside	Middle	Outside
High	1/0/0	0/0/0	1/0/0
Med	1/0/0	0/0/0	5/0/0
Low	6/333/2	4/250/1	8/0/0

Slider Average .285

	Inside	Middle	Outside
High	1/1000/1	0/0/0	0/0/0
Med	2/0/0	0/0/0	1/0/0
Low	2/0/0	1/1000/1	0/0/0

Right-handed hitter Tim Wallach has a fairly good .296 overall BARS fastball average against right-handed pitchers. Against left-handed pitchers his overall fastball average is .302. His curve averages are not as strong.

Starting with right-handers, note the contrasting strengths and weaknesses in Wallach's fastball chart. He hits .388 against high-outside fastballs, .410 against high-over-the-middle and .385 against low-over-the-middle. But he hits only .217 against low-outside, .214 against medium-high inside and .166 against high-inside.

Wallach hits medium-high outside fastballs much better when ahead in the count (.425 when ahead, .173 when behind). Fielders need to be aligned differently for this pitch when Wallach is ahead and behind.

**MEDIUM-HIGH OUTSIDE FASTBALLS
(WHEN AHEAD IN THE COUNT)**

BATTING AVERAGE .425
Play
Left	Deep in straightaway left field
Center	Deep in straightaway center field
Right	Medium-deep in straightaway right field
Short	Normal position
Second	Normal position

**MEDIUM-HIGH OUTSIDE FASTBALLS
(WHEN BEHIND IN THE COUNT)**

BATTING AVERAGE .173
Play
Left	Medium-deep in straightaway left field
Center	Deep and shifted toward left field
Right	Short in straightaway right field
Short	Shifted toward third base
Second	Normal position

His .385 against low-over-the-middle fastballs is very strong. His Ahead and Behind charts show that he hits this pitch better when behind in the count (.500 when behind, .346 when ahead). When ahead, he pulls the ball down the left line and into right center.

**LOW-OVER-THE-MIDDLE FASTBALLS
(WHEN BEHIND IN THE COUNT)**

BATTING AVERAGE .500
Play
Left	Deep in straightaway left field
Center	Medium-deep in straightaway center field
Right	Deep and shifted toward the right field line
Short	Up middle (shifted toward second base)
Second	*No instances recorded*

**LOW-OVER-THE-MIDDLE FASTBALLS
(WHEN AHEAD IN THE COUNT)**

BATTING AVERAGE .346
Play
Left	Deep and shifted toward the left field line

Center	Medium-deep in straightaway center field
Right	Deep and shifted toward center field
Short	Up middle (shifted toward second base)
Second	Normal position

His .410 against high-over-the-middle fastballs is exceptionally good.

HIGH-OVER-THE-MIDDLE FASTBALLS

BATTING AVERAGE .410
Play

Left	Deep and shifted toward the left field line
Center	Deep and shifted toward left field
Right	Medium-deep in straightaway right field
Short	Up middle (shifted toward second base)
Second	Normal position

Wallach has a lot of trouble with outside curves and low curves. These weak locations present ample targets for right-handers to attack.

He also has trouble with all low sliders. But he hits .310 against medium-high outside sliders.

MEDIUM-HIGH OUTSIDE SLIDERS

BATTING AVERAGE .310
Play

Left	Medium-deep and shifted toward the left field line
Center	Deep and shifted toward left field
Right	Deep in straightaway right field
Short	Shifted toward third base
Second	Normal position

Wallach Against Left-Handed Pitchers

As against right-handed pitchers, Wallach has many contrasting strong and weak locations against left-handed pitchers. He hits only .222 against low-over-the-middle fastballs and only .181 against high-inside fastballs.

He hits a strong .342 against medium-high outside fastballs. He pulls this pitch down the left line and into left center. But the shortstop needs to play shifted toward second base and the second baseman shifted toward first base.

MEDIUM-HIGH OUTSIDE FASTBALLS (THROWN BY LEFT-HANDED PITCHERS)

BATTING AVERAGE .342
Play

Left	Deep and shifted toward the left field line
Center	Deep and shifted toward left field
Right	Deep in straightaway right field
Short	Up middle (shifted toward second base)
Second	Shifted toward first base

He hits .280 against low-outside fastballs thrown by left-handers.

LOW-OUTSIDE FASTBALLS (THROWN BY LEFT-HANDED PITCHERS)

BATTING AVERAGE .280
Play

Left	Deep in straightaway left field
Center	Short and shifted toward right field
Right	Deep and shifted toward the right field line
Short	Up middle (shifted toward second base)
Second	*No instances recorded*

He has trouble with outside curves against left-handers. In general, he has trouble with curves thrown by lefties.

Ahead And Behind In The Count Vs. RH

Ahead

	Fastball Average .328			Curve Average .294		
	Inside	Middle	Outside	Inside	Middle	Outside
High	15/0 /0	15/400 /6	8/500 /4	1/1000 /1	0/0 /0	2/0 /0
Med	11/181 /2	10/300 /3	47/425 /20	1/0 /0	1/1000 /1	6/166 /1
Low	10/200 /2	26/346 /9	10/400 /4	0/0 /0	2/0 /0	4/500 /2

Behind

	Fastball Average .317			Curve Average .333		
	Inside	Middle	Outside	Inside	Middle	Outside
High	7/571 /4	10/600 /6	1/0 /0	2/0 /0	4/250 /1	1/0 /0
Med	8/250 /2	3/0 /0	23/173 /4	1/1000 /1	0/0 /0	5/600 /3
Low	4/500 /2	14/500 /7	15/133 /2	0/0 /0	5/400 /2	15/266 /4

Overall Evaluation

Against Right-Handed Pitchers

Overall Fastball ◯◯ ◯◯

Overall Curve ◯◯

Overall Slider ◯◯

Against Left-Handed Pitchers

Overall Fastball ◯◯ ◯◯ ◯◯

Overall Curve ◯◯

Overall Slider — Not enough information

Comments: Weak vs. outside & low curves vs. RH.
Strengths: Low-inside, high-middle, low-middle and high-outside fastballs, medium-outside sliders vs. RH; medium-inside, low-inside, high-middle and medium-outside fastballs vs. LH.
Weaknesses: High-inside, medium-inside, medium-middle and low-outside fastballs, outside and low curves, low sliders vs. RH; high-inside, high-outside and low-middle fastballs, outside curves vs. LH.

Carter, Gary
Dykstra, Lenny
Hernandez, Keith
Johnson, Howard
McReynolds, Kevin
Strawberry, Darryl
Teufel, Tim
Wilson, Mookie

New York Mets
BARS System
Hitting Analysis

Gary Carter Against Right-Handed Pitchers
Overall BARS Batting Average .256

Fastball Average .287

	Inside	Middle	Outside
High	30/ 166 /5	42/ 285 /12	31/ 258 /8
Med	39/ 487 /19	20/ 200 /4	103/ 233 /24
Low	23/ 217 /5	53/ 396 /21	55/ 290 /16

Curve Average .275

	Inside	Middle	Outside
High	5/ 200 /1	8/ 375 /3	6/ 166 /1
Med	4/ 500 /2	3/ 333 /1	43/ 302 /13
Low	0/ 0 /0	8/ 375 /3	32/ 187 /6

Slider Average .233

	Inside	Middle	Outside
High	4/ 250 /1	7/ 571 /4	4/ 500 /2
Med	5/ 0 /0	5/ 400 /2	32/ 125 /4
Low	5/ 0 /0	12/ 333 /4	33/ 242 /8

Gary Carter Against Left-Handed Pitchers
Overall BARS Batting Average .271

Fastball Average .306

	Inside	Middle	Outside
High	3/ 0 /0	9/ 444 /4	22/ 227 /5
Med	8/ 0 /0	3/ 333 /1	59/ 355 /21
Low	10/ 200 /2	27/ 444 /12	35/ 257 /9

Curve Average .275

	Inside	Middle	Outside
High	0/ 0 /0	5/ 400 /2	1/ 1000 /1
Med	3/ 333 /1	4/ 0 /0	2/ 500 /1
Low	5/ 200 /1	4/ 500 /2	5/ 0 /0

Slider Average .250

	Inside	Middle	Outside
High	2/ 0 /0	2/ 1000 /2	0/ 0 /0
Med	3/ 0 /0	2/ 500 /1	3/ 333 /1
Low	5/ 200 /1	5/ 200 /1	2/ 0 /0

Right-handed hitting Gary Carter has a .287 overall fastball average against right-handed pitchers, .306 against fastballs thrown by left-handed pitchers.

Against right-handers, Carter hits only .233 against medium-high outside fastballs. But he hits a sparkling .487 against medium-high inside fastballs. By positioning themselves according to the BARS fielding strategy for this pitch, fielders could prevent most of the base hits resulting from pitches to this location.

MEDIUM-HIGH INSIDE FASTBALLS

BATTING AVERAGE .487
Play
Left	Medium-deep and shifted toward the left field line
Center	Deep and shifted toward left field
Right	Medium-deep and shifted toward the right line
Short	Up middle (shifted toward second base)
Second	*No instances recorded*

His .396 against low-over-the-middle fastballs is also excellent. The field diagram on the opposite page shows how fielders should be positioned for this pitch.

LOW-OVER-THE-MIDDLE FASTBALLS

BATTING AVERAGE .396
Play
Left	Medium-deep and shifted toward the left field line
Center	Deep and shifted toward left field
Right	Deep and shifted toward the right field line

Short Shifted toward third base
Second Shifted toward first base

Carter has trouble with low-outside curves against right-handers (.187) but he hits medium-high outside curves very well (.302). He has trouble with low-outside sliders and with medium-high outside sliders against right-handers.

Carter Against Left-Handed Pitchers

Carter hits medium-high outside fastballs for a strong .355 average against left-handed pitchers. He pulls this pitch deep to all fields, but the second baseman needs to play shifted toward first base.

MEDIUM-HIGH OUTSIDE FASTBALLS
(THROWN BY LEFT-HANDED PITCHERS)

BATTING AVERAGE .355
Play
Left	Deep and shifted toward the left field line
Center	Deep and shifted toward left field
Right	Deep and shifted toward center field
Short	Normal position
Second	Shifted toward first base

Carter's .444 against low-over-the-middle fastballs is very strong. He hits this pitch medium-deep down the left line and straightaway to center and right.

Low-Over-The-Middle Fastballs

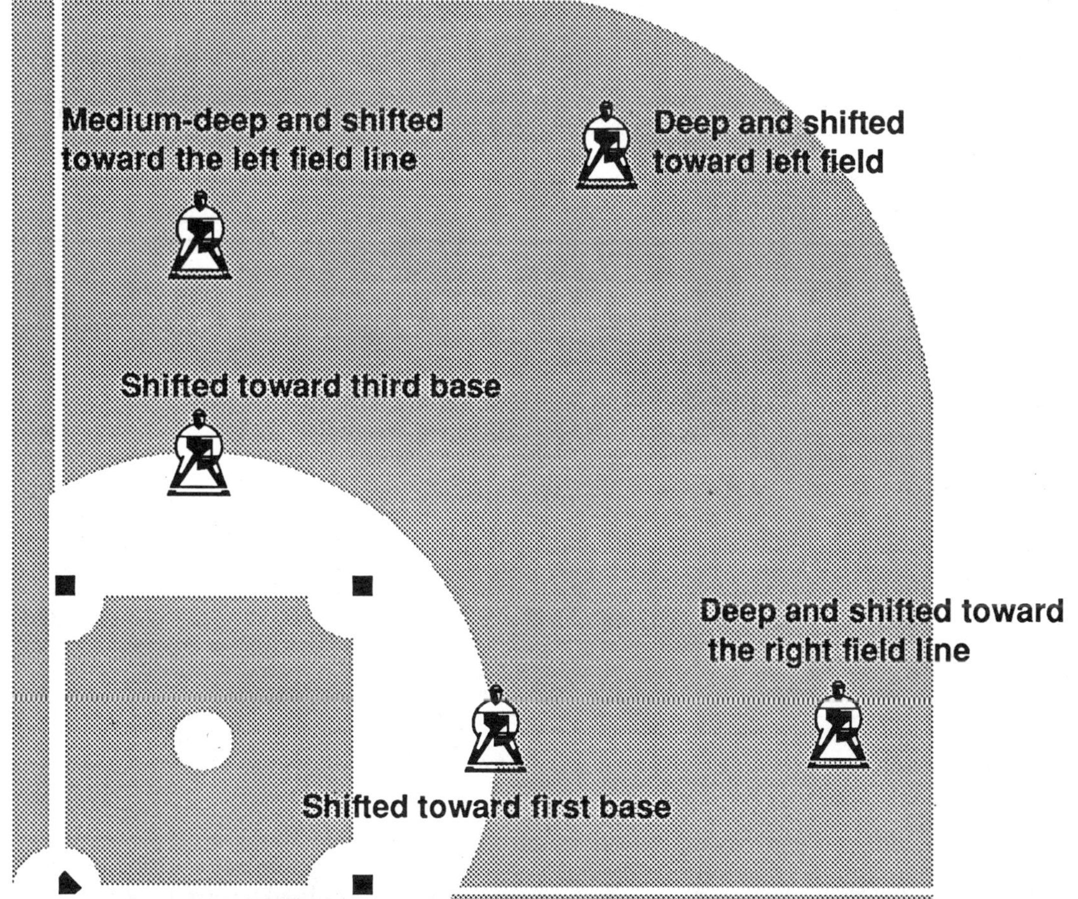

Ahead And Behind In The Count Vs. RH

Ahead

	Fastball Average .353			Curve Average .425		
	Inside	Middle	Outside	Inside	Middle	Outside
High	10 / 300 / 3	23 / 347 / 8	14 / 357 / 5	1 / 1000 / 1	4 / 750 / 3	4 / 250 / 1
Med	19 / 526 / 10	10 / 200 / 2	56 / 250 / 14	2 / 500 / 1	2 / 0 / 0	19 / 421 / 8
Low	10 / 200 / 2	28 / 535 / 15	25 / 400 / 10	0 / 0 / 0	2 / 500 / 1	6 / 333 / 2

Behind

	Fastball Average .303			Curve Average .210		
	Inside	Middle	Outside	Inside	Middle	Outside
High	7 / 0 / 0	5 / 600 / 3	3 / 333 / 1	1 / 0 / 0	1 / 0 / 0	2 / 0 / 0
Med	7 / 285 / 2	2 / 500 / 1	11 / 272 / 3	0 / 0 / 0	0 / 0 / 0	6 / 0 / 0
Low	7 / 428 / 3	6 / 333 / 2	8 / 250 / 2	0 / 0 / 0	2 / 500 / 1	7 / 428 / 3

Overall Evaluation
Against Right-Handed Pitchers

Overall Fastball 

Overall Curve

Overall Slider

Against Left-Handed Pitchers

Overall Fastball

Overall Curve

Overall Slider

Comments: Weak vs. medium-outside fastballs vs. RH.
Strengths: Medium-inside and low-middle fastballs, low-middle and medium-outside curves, over-the-middle sliders vs. RH; medium-outside and over-the-middle fastballs vs. LH.
Weaknesses: High-inside, low-inside, high-outside and medium-outside fastballs, low-outside curves, low-outside and low-inside sliders vs. RH; high-outside, low-outside and all inside fastballs vs. LH.

Lenny Dykstra Against Right-Handed Pitchers
Overall BARS Batting Average .273

Fastball Average .293

	Outside	Middle	Inside
High	33 / 242 / 8	42 / 333 / 14	42 / 238 / 10
Med	64 / 343 / 22	16 / 375 / 6	58 / 275 / 16
Low	17 / 176 / 3	54 / 370 / 20	45 / 222 / 10

Curve Average .258

	Outside	Middle	Inside
High	2 / 0 / 0	2 / 0 / 0	4 / 500 / 2
Med	9 / 222 / 2	3 / 0 / 0	5 / 400 / 2
Low	7 / 142 / 1	11 / 454 / 5	15 / 200 / 3

Slider Average .225

	Outside	Middle	Inside
High	3 / 0 / 0	2 / 0 / 0	2 / 0 / 0
Med	2 / 0 / 0	4 / 0 / 0	8 / 375 / 3
Low	3 / 0 / 0	5 / 200 / 1	11 / 454 / 5

Lenny Dykstra Against Left-Handed Pitchers
Overall BARS Batting Average .211

Fastball Average .257

	Outside	Middle	Inside
High	2 / 0 / 0	11 / 363 / 4	9 / 222 / 2
Med	6 / 166 / 1	1 / 0 / 0	18 / 333 / 6
Low	6 / 166 / 1	5 / 200 / 1	8 / 250 / 2

Curve Average .227

	Outside	Middle	Inside
High	2 / 0 / 0	2 / 0 / 0	0 / 0 / 0
Med	6 / 333 / 2	1 / 1000 / 1	0 / 0 / 0
Low	4 / 0 / 0	6 / 333 / 2	1 / 0 / 0

Slider Average .062

	Outside	Middle	Inside
High	3 / 0 / 0	0 / 0 / 0	1 / 0 / 0
Med	3 / 333 / 1	1 / 0 / 0	3 / 0 / 0
Low	3 / 0 / 0	0 / 0 / 0	2 / 0 / 0

Lenny Dykstra, left-handed hitter, has a much higher BARS average against right-handed pitchers (.273 overall against right-handers, .211 overall against left-handers).

Dykstra hits .293 overall against fastballs thrown by right-handers. His .343 medium-high outside average is excellent. He hits this pitch deep and straightaway to the outfield.

MEDIUM-HIGH OUTSIDE FASTBALLS

BATTING AVERAGE .343

Play

Left	Deep in straightaway left field
Center	Deep in straightaway center field
Right	Deep in straightaway right field
Short	Up middle (shifted toward second base)
Second	Normal position

He hits low-over-the-middle fastballs at a .370 clip. He hits this pitch medium-deep to all fields. If fielders adjusted properly, they could prevent most of his base hits from this location.

LOW-OVER-THE-MIDDLE FASTBALLS

BATTING AVERAGE .370

Play

Left	Medium-deep and shifted toward the left field line
Center	Medium-deep in straightaway center field
Right	Medium-deep in straightaway right field
Short	Shifted toward third base
Second	Shifted toward first base

Dykstra is strong against all over-the-middle fastballs against right-handers, but he is weak against all inside fastballs (.238, .275 and .222, high to low). His .275 against medium-high inside fastballs is barely adequate.

MEDIUM-HIGH INSIDE FASTBALLS

BATTING AVERAGE .275

Play

Left	Deep and shifted toward the left field line
Center	Medium-deep in straightaway center field
Right	Deep in straightaway right field
Short	Up middle (shifted toward second base)
Second	Shifted toward first base

His .333 against high-over-the-middle fastballs is excellent.

HIGH-OVER-THE-MIDDLE FASTBALLS

BATTING AVERAGE .333

Play

Left	Medium-deep and shifted toward the left field line
Center	Deep and shifted toward left field

Right   Deep in straightaway right field
Short   Up middle (shifted toward second base)
Second   Shifted toward first base

Dykstra Against Curves And Sliders

Dykstra has trouble with low-inside curves (.200) but he hits low-over-the-middle curves extremely well (.454). He pulls this pitch to right field and to the right side of the infield.

LOW-OVER-THE-MIDDLE CURVEBALLS

BATTING AVERAGE .454
  Play
Left   *No instances recorded*
Center   *No instances recorded*
Right   Medium-deep in straightaway right field
Short   Up middle (shifted toward second base)
Second   Shifted toward first base

He has an excellent .454 average against low-inside sliders. He scatters this pitch to all fields.

LOW-INSIDE SLIDERS

BATTING AVERAGE .454
  Play
Left   Medium-deep and shifted toward the left field line
Center   Medium-deep in straightaway center field
Right   Deep and shifted toward the right field line
Short   *No instances recorded*
Second   *No instances recorded*

Dykstra Against Left-Handed Pitchers

Dykstra has trouble with fastballs against left-handed pitchers. He has two strong fastball locations: medium-high inside and high-over-the-middle.

He goes down the left line (his opposite field) with medium-high inside fastballs. Fielders need to adjust properly for this pitch. It is a mistake to think that Dykstra automatically pulls inside fastballs.

MEDIUM-HIGH INSIDE FASTBALLS

BATTING AVERAGE .333
  Play
Left   Medium-deep and shifted toward the left field line
Center   *No instances recorded*
Right   Deep in straightaway right field
Short   Up middle (shifted toward second base)
Second   Normal position

He pulls high-over-the-middle fastballs.

HIGH-OVER-THE-MIDDLE FASTBALLS

BATTING AVERAGE .363
  Play
Left   Deep in straightaway left field
Center   Deep and shifted toward right field
Right   Medium-deep and shifted toward the right line
Short   *No instances recorded*
Second   Normal position

Ahead And Behind In The Count Vs. RH

Ahead

Fastball Average .360

	Outside	Middle	Inside
High	12/250 /3	24/500 /12	17/294 /5
Med	41/487 /20	12/416 /5	35/257 /9
Low	6/166 /1	31/387 /12	22/227 /5

Curve Average .400

	Outside	Middle	Inside
High	0/0 /0	1/0 /0	3/666 /2
Med	2/500 /1	1/0 /0	0/0 /0
Low	0/0 /0	0/0 /0	3/333 /1

Behind

Fastball Average .298

	Outside	Middle	Inside
High	7/142 /1	7/142 /1	11/272 /3
Med	7/285 /2	2/0 /0	10/400 /4
Low	2/1000 /2	8/500 /4	13/230 /3

Curve Average .333

	Outside	Middle	Inside
High	0/0 /0	1/0 /0	0/0 /0
Med	5/200 /1	2/0 /0	1/1000/1
Low	1/0 /0	7/428 /3	4/500 /2

Overall Evaluation

Against Right-Handed Pitchers

Overall Fastball ⚾⚾ ⚾⚾
Overall Curve ⚾⚾ ⚾⚾
Overall Slider ⚾

Against Left-Handed Pitchers

Overall Fastball ⚾⚾
Overall Curve ⚾⚾
Overall Slider ⚾⚾

Comments: Weak in the four fastball corners.
Strengths: Over-the-middle and medium-outside fastballs vs. RH, low-middle curves vs. RH, low-inside and medium-inside sliders vs. RH; medium-inside and high-middle fastballs vs. LH.
Weaknesses: Four fastball corners and medium-inside fastballs vs. RH, outside and low-inside curves vs. RH; low fastballs and high-inside fastballs vs. LH.

Keith Hernandez (Left Handed)   *New York Mets*

Keith Hernandez Against Right-Handed Pitchers
Overall BARS Batting Average .282

Fastball Average .340

	Outside	Middle	Inside
High	28/ 321/9	54/ 333/18	30/ 366/11
Med	81/ 345/28	32/ 281/9	65/ 384/25
Low	30/ 233/7	83/ 373/31	58/ 327/19

Curve Average .256

	Outside	Middle	Inside
High	3/ 333/1	14/ 142/2	5/ 400/2
Med	11/ 363/4	3/ 0/0	3/ 666/2
Low	13/ 76/1	14/ 428/6	16/ 187/3

Slider Average .166

	Outside	Middle	Inside
High	1/ 0/0	5/ 0/0	2/ 0/0
Med	4/ 500/2	3/ 0/0	11/ 181/2
Low	6/ 0/0	7/ 428/3	21/ 142/3

Keith Hernandez Against Left-Handed Pitchers
Overall BARS Batting Average .275

Fastball Average .317

	Outside	Middle	Inside
High	5/ 0/0	29/ 275/8	16/ 375/6
Med	27/ 296/8	8/ 625/5	53/ 396/21
Low	9/ 333/3	30/ 400/12	40/ 150/6

Curve Average .269

	Outside	Middle	Inside
High	1/ 1000/1	4/ 250/1	4/ 0/0
Med	11/ 272/3	3/ 666/2	8/ 250/2
Low	15/ 266/4	15/ 200/3	2/ 500/1

Slider Average .200

	Outside	Middle	Inside
High	1/ 1000/1	1/ 0/0	0/ 0/0
Med	5/ 200/1	2/ 0/0	2/ 500/1
Low	15/ 133/2	7/ 142/1	2/ 500/1

Left-handed hitting Keith Hernandez has an excellent BARS fastball average against right-handed pitchers (.340 overall). Against right-handers, he has only one weak fastball location (low outside, .233).

He hits medium-high outside fastballs for a strong .345 average. He hits this pitch straightaway to the outfield while pulling it to the right side of the infield.

MEDIUM-HIGH OUTSIDE FASTBALLS

BATTING AVERAGE .345
  Play
Left   Deep in straightaway left field
Center   Deep in straightaway center field
Right   Medium-deep in straightaway right field
Short   Up middle (shifted toward second base)
Second   Shifted toward first base

Hernandez hits medium-high inside fastballs for a sparkling .384 average, but his Ahead and Behind charts on the opposite page show that he hits medium-high inside fastballs very poorly when behind in the count (.100) and extremely well when ahead in the count (.600). He pulls this pitch sharply when ahead. The following charts show how vital it can be for fielders to adjust when the count on a batter changes.

MEDIUM-HIGH INSIDE FASTBALLS
(WHEN AHEAD IN THE COUNT)

BATTING AVERAGE .600
  Play
Left   Deep and shifted toward center field
Center   Deep in straightaway center field
Right   Deep and shifted toward the right field line
Short   Up middle (shifted toward second base)
Second   Shifted toward first base

MEDIUM-HIGH INSIDE FASTBALLS
(WHEN BEHIND IN THE COUNT)

BATTING AVERAGE .100
  Play
Left   Medium-deep in straightaway left field
Center   Deep and shifted toward left field
Right   Medium-deep in straightaway right field
Short   Normal position
Second   Normal position

Hernandez Against Curves And Sliders

Hernandez hits low-outside curves poorly against right-handers (.076), but he hits medium-high outside (.363) and low-over-the-middle curves (.428) very well.

He goes to his opposite field (left field) with low-over-the-middle curves. Note, however, that the shortstop needs to play shifted toward second base.

LOW-OVER-THE-MIDDLE CURVEBALLS

BATTING AVERAGE .428
Play

Left	Deep and shifted toward the left field line
Center	Deep and shifted toward left field
Right	Deep and shifted toward center field
Short	Up middle (shifted toward second base)
Second	Normal position

He has a lot of trouble with inside sliders thrown by right-handers. His .181 against medium-high inside sliders and .142 against low-inside sliders give a target for right-handers.

Hernandez Against Left-Handed Pitchers

Hernandez's BARS charts show that left-handed pitchers throw him more inside than outside fastballs. This is good strategy if pitchers keep the ball low (.150 against low-inside fastballs vs. left-handers); but it could be a disaster if they let the ball get up to the medium-high inside (.396) or high-inside (.375) fastball locations.

Hernandez hits medium-high inside fastballs in such a unique way against left-handers that fielders need to pay careful attention to the following BARS fielding strategy for this pitch.

MEDIUM-HIGH INSIDE FASTBALLS (THROWN BY LEFT-HANDED PITCHERS)

BATTING AVERAGE .396
Play

Left	Medium-deep and shifted toward center field
Center	Short in straightaway center field
Right	Deep and shifted toward the right field line
Short	Up middle (shifted toward second base)
Second	Shifted toward first base

His .400 against low-over-the-middle fastballs thrown by left-handers is also excellent.

LOW-OVER-THE-MIDDLE FASTBALLS (THROWN BY LEFT-HANDED PITCHERS)

BATTING AVERAGE .400
Play

Left	Deep and shifted toward the left field line
Center	Deep and shifted toward right field
Right	Deep in straightaway right field
Short	Up middle (shifted toward second base)
Second	Normal position

He has trouble with low-outside and low-over-the-middle curves against left-handers (.266 and .200 respectively). He also has trouble with sliders in these two locations against left-handers (.133 and .142 respectively).

Ahead And Behind In The Count Vs. RH

Ahead

Fastball Average .397

	Outside	Middle	Inside
High	9/ 222 /2	28/ 428 /12	11/ 636 /7
Med	36/ 416 /15	17/ 294 /5	30/ 600 /18
Low	12/ 250 /3	54/ 351 /19	32/ 312 /10

Curve Average .400

	Outside	Middle	Inside
High	0/ 0 /0	5/ 400 /2	0/ 0 /0
Med	0/ 0 /0	0/ 0 /0	0/ 0 /0
Low	1/ 1000 /1	3/ 333 /1	1/ 0 /0

Behind

Fastball Average .306

	Outside	Middle	Inside
High	4/ 750 /3	6/ 166 /1	11/ 272 /3
Med	19/ 421 /8	6/ 166 /1	10/ 100 /1
Low	3/ 666 /2	9/ 222 /2	7/ 285 /2

Curve Average .333

	Outside	Middle	Inside
High	0/ 0 /0	4/ 0 /0	2/ 500 /1
Med	4/ 500 /2	2/ 0 /0	2/ 1000 /2
Low	4/ 0 /0	4/ 500 /2	2/ 500 /1

Overall Evaluation

Against Right-Handed Pitchers

Overall Fastball	⚾ ⚾ ⚾ ⚾
Overall Curve	⚾ ⚾
Overall Slider	⚾

Against Left-Handed Pitchers

Overall Fastball	⚾ ⚾ ⚾
Overall Curve	⚾ ⚾
Overall Slider	⚾

Comments: Hits better when ahead in the count.
Strengths: All fastballs vs. RH (except low-outside), medium-outside and low-middle curves, low-middle sliders vs. RH; high-inside, medium-inside and low-middle fastballs vs. LH.
Weaknesses: Low-outside fastballs, low-outside, low-inside and high-middle curves, inside sliders vs. RH; low-inside fastballs, outside sliders vs. LH.

Howard Johnson (Switch Hitter) — *New York Mets*

Howard Johnson Against Right-Handed Pitchers
Overall BARS Batting Average .241

Fastball Average .307

	Outside	Middle	Inside
High	42 / 190 / 8	38 / 368 / 14	17 / 176 / 3
Med	100 / 330 / 33	20 / 550 / 11	30 / 233 / 7
Low	35 / 342 / 12	42 / 333 / 14	27 / 222 / 6

Curve Average .140

	Outside	Middle	Inside
High	11 / 181 / 2	9 / 111 / 1	4 / 750 / 3
Med	10 / 300 / 3	7 / 285 / 2	5 / 0 / 0
Low	25 / 40 / 1	13 / 230 / 3	23 / 0 / 0

Slider Average .225

	Outside	Middle	Inside
High	1 / 0 / 0	2 / 0 / 0	5 / 0 / 0
Med	1 / 0 / 0	7 / 285 / 2	4 / 250 / 1
Low	5 / 400 / 2	2 / 500 / 1	4 / 250 / 1

Howard Johnson Against Left-Handed Pitchers
Overall BARS Batting Average .244

Fastball Average .259

	Inside	Middle	Outside
High	7 / 142 / 1	9 / 0 / 0	12 / 416 / 5
Med	8 / 0 / 0	7 / 571 / 4	30 / 333 / 10
Low	5 / 400 / 2	11 / 454 / 5	19 / 52 / 1

Curve Average .263

	Inside	Middle	Outside
High	0 / 0 / 0	2 / 0 / 0	0 / 0 / 0
Med	2 / 500 / 1	1 / 1000 / 1	3 / 666 / 2
Low	2 / 0 / 0	3 / 333 / 1	6 / 0 / 0

Slider Average .000

	Inside	Middle	Outside
High	2 / 0 / 0	1 / 0 / 0	1 / 0 / 0
Med	0 / 0 / 0	0 / 0 / 0	0 / 0 / 0
Low	0 / 0 / 0	0 / 0 / 0	1 / 0 / 0

Switch-hitting Howard Johnson has a good .307 overall fastball average hitting left-handed against right-handed pitchers. His .259 overall fastball average against left-handed pitchers is weak.

Against right-handers, Johnson has trouble with high-outside fastballs (.190) and all inside fastballs (.176, .233 and .222, high to low). But he hits low-outside, medium-high outside and all over-the-middle fastballs excellently.

He hits medium-high outside fastballs straightaway to all fields.

MEDIUM-HIGH OUTSIDE FASTBALLS

BATTING AVERAGE .330
Play

Left	Deep in straightaway left field
Center	Medium-deep in straightaway center field
Right	Deep in straightaway right field
Short	Up middle (shifted toward second base)
Second	Normal position

His Ahead and Behind charts on the opposite page show that he hits low-over-the-middle fastballs for a much higher average when behind in the count (.454 when behind, .238 when ahead). The BARS fielding strategies show that fielders need to be positioned differently for this pitch when Johnson is ahead and behind in the count.

LOW-OVER-THE-MIDDLE FASTBALLS (WHEN BEHIND IN THE COUNT)

BATTING AVERAGE .454
Play

Left	Short in straightaway left field
Center	Medium-deep in straightaway center field
Right	*No instances recorded*
Short	Normal position
Second	Shifted toward first base

LOW-OVER-THE-MIDDLE FASTBALLS (WHEN AHEAD IN THE COUNT)

BATTING AVERAGE .238
Play

Left	Deep in straightaway left field
Center	Deep in straightaway center field
Right	Deep and shifted toward center field
Short	*No instances recorded*
Second	Normal position

He also hits high-over-the-middle fastballs excellently (.368). He scatters this pitch to all fields.

HIGH-OVER-THE-MIDDLE FASTBALLS

BATTING AVERAGE .368
Play

Left	Deep and shifted toward the left field line
Center	Deep and shifted toward left field

Right	Deep and shifted toward the right field line
Short	Up middle (shifted toward second base)
Second	Normal position

Johnson Against Curves And Sliders

Johnson has extreme difficulty with low curves thrown by right-handed pitchers. His .040, .230 and .000 (on 0-for-23) offer a target for right-handers. The high number of recorded instances in these locations show that pitchers are aware of this.

In contrast, he hits medium-high outside curves very well (.300).

Johnson Against Left-Handed Pitchers

Johnson has trouble with low-outside fastballs thrown by left-handed pitchers (.052 on 1-for-19) but he hits medium-high outside (.333), high-outside (.416), medium-over-the-middle (.571) and low-over-the-middle (.454) fastballs excellently.

He pulls medium-high outside fastballs deep down the left line.

MEDIUM-HIGH INSIDE FASTBALLS
(THROWN BY LEFT-HANDED PITCHERS)

BATTING AVERAGE .333
  Play

Left	Deep and shifted toward the left field line
Center	Deep in straightaway center field
Right	Medium-deep in straightaway right field
Short	Normal position
Second	Normal position

He pulls high-outside fastballs medium-deep down the left line.

HIGH-OUTSIDE FASTBALLS
(THROWN BY LEFT-HANDED PITCHERS)

BATTING AVERAGE .416
  Play

Left	Medium-deep and shifted toward the left field line
Center	Deep in straightaway center field
Right	*No instances recorded*
Short	Normal position
Second	Normal position

He hits low-over-the-middle fastballs deep down the left line and medium-deep into the right-center gap.

LOW-OVER-THE-MIDDLE FASTBALLS
(THROWN BY LEFT-HANDED PITCHERS)

BATTING AVERAGE .454
  Play

Left	Deep and shifted toward the left field line
Center	Deep in straightaway center field
Right	Medium-deep and shifted toward center field
Short	Up middle (shifted toward second base)
Second	Normal position

Taken together, the fielding strategies for these locations show how important it is for fielders to position themselves for different locations and counts on the batter.

Johnson has several poor fastball locations against left-handers. His 0-for-8 against medium-high inside and 0-for-9 against high-over-the-middle fastballs, sandwiching in his 1-for-7 against high-inside fastballs, make a target for left-handers to attack.

Ahead And Behind In The Count Vs. RH

Ahead

Fastball Average .329

	Outside	Middle	Inside
High	18 / 166 / 3	14 / 428 / 6	4 / 250 / 1
Med	48 / 375 / 18	8 / 375 / 3	15 / 266 / 4
Low	13 / 461 / 6	21 / 238 / 5	14 / 357 / 5

Curve Average .444

	Outside	Middle	Inside
High	1 / 1000 / 1	2 / 0 / 0	2 / 500 / 1
Med	3 / 666 / 2	2 / 1000 / 2	1 / 0 / 0
Low	0 / 0 / 0	3 / 666 / 2	4 / 0 / 0

Behind

Fastball Average .393

	Outside	Middle	Inside
High	10 / 300 / 3	6 / 333 / 2	0 / 0 / 0
Med	17 / 352 / 6	8 / 625 / 5	5 / 200 / 1
Low	7 / 571 / 4	11 / 454 / 5	2 / 0 / 0

Curve Average .200

	Outside	Middle	Inside
High	5 / 200 / 1	5 / 200 / 1	1 / 1000 / 1
Med	4 / 250 / 1	1 / 0 / 0	0 / 0 / 0
Low	7 / 142 / 1	1 / 0 / 0	1 / 0 / 0

Overall Evaluation
Against Right-Handed Pitchers

Overall Fastball	⚾⚾ ⚾⚾⚾
Overall Curve	⚾⚾
Overall Slider	⚾

Against Left-Handed Pitchers

Overall Fastball	⚾⚾
Overall Curve	⚾⚾ ⚾⚾
Overall Slider	Not enough information

Comments: Weak against inside fastballs and low curves vs. RH.

Strengths: Low-outside, medium-outside and over-the-middle fastballs, medium-outside curves vs. RH; high-outside, medium-outside, medium-middle and low-middle fastballs vs. LH.

Weaknesses: High-outside and all inside fastballs, low curves vs. RH; low-outside, high-middle, high-inside and medium-inside fastballs vs. LH.

Kevin McReynolds Against Right-Handed Pitchers
Overall BARS Batting Average .236

Fastball Average .253

	Inside	Middle	Outside
High	21 / 285 / 6	49 / 224 / 11	25 / 160 / 4
Med	36 / 194 / 7	14 / 714 / 10	87 / 287 / 25
Low	21 / 238 / 5	56 / 232 / 13	42 / 190 / 8

Curve Average .256

	Inside	Middle	Outside
High	6 / 333 / 2	12 / 416 / 5	4 / 250 / 1
Med	9 / 444 / 4	8 / 375 / 3	31 / 258 / 8
Low	2 / 0 / 0	21 / 285 / 6	51 / 156 / 8

Slider Average .287

	Inside	Middle	Outside
High	3 / 666 / 2	5 / 600 / 3	4 / 0 / 0
Med	2 / 500 / 1	2 / 0 / 0	26 / 346 / 9
Low	0 / 0 / 0	14 / 285 / 4	31 / 193 / 6

Kevin McReynolds Against Left-Handed Pitchers
Overall BARS Batting Average .236

Fastball Average .242

	Inside	Middle	Outside
High	10 / 100 / 1	12 / 166 / 2	17 / 235 / 4
Med	12 / 83 / 1	3 / 333 / 1	33 / 242 / 8
Low	7 / 571 / 4	27 / 333 / 9	15 / 200 / 3

Curve Average .344

	Inside	Middle	Outside
High	0 / 0 / 0	1 / 0 / 0	3 / 0 / 0
Med	1 / 1000 / 1	4 / 500 / 2	7 / 428 / 3
Low	2 / 500 / 1	7 / 428 / 3	4 / 0 / 0

Slider Average .333

	Inside	Middle	Outside
High	0 / 0 / 0	0 / 0 / 0	2 / 0 / 0
Med	6 / 500 / 3	1 / 1000 / 1	3 / 666 / 2
Low	4 / 0 / 0	5 / 200 / 1	3 / 333 / 1

Right-handed hitting Kevin McReynolds hits fastballs for a .253 BARS average against right-handed pitchers, .242 against left-handed pitchers.

Starting with his performance against right-handers, note that he hits .287 against medium-high outside fastballs. He hits this pitch to straightaway left and center and to the right-center gap. The shortstop needs to play shifted toward second and the second baseman shifted toward first.

MEDIUM-HIGH OUTSIDE FASTBALLS

BATTING AVERAGE .287
Play

Left	Medium-deep in straightaway left field
Center	Deep in straightaway center field
Right	Deep and shifted toward center field
Short	Up middle (shifted toward second base)
Second	Shifted toward first base

McReynolds has trouble with low fastballs thrown by right-handers (.238, .232 and .190, inside to outside).

He scatters low-outside fastballs. His .190 average suggests that most of his hit balls from this location are easy outs.

LOW-OUTSIDE FASTBALLS

BATTING AVERAGE .190
Play

Left	Deep and shifted toward the left field line
Center	Deep and shifted toward right field
Right	Medium-deep and shifted toward the right line
Short	Shifted toward third base
Second	*No instances recorded*

He hits high-inside fastballs for a .285 average. Shown below is the unusual fielding strategy required for McReynolds for this pitch. If fielders positioned themselves as suggested by the BARS strategy, they could prevent most of his hits resulting from this location.

HIGH-INSIDE FASTBALLS

BATTING AVERAGE .285
Play

Left	Medium-deep in straightaway left field
Center	Medium-deep and shifted toward left field
Right	Short and shifted toward center field
Short	Normal position
Second	Shifted toward first base

McReynolds Against Curves And Sliders

McReynolds has trouble with outside curves thrown by right-handers. His .156 average in the low-outside location is very weak. His .258 in the medium-high outside curve location is fair.

MEDIUM-HIGH OUTSIDE CURVEBALLS

BATTING AVERAGE .258

Play

Left	Deep in straightaway left field
Center	Medium-deep in straightaway center field
Right	Deep and shifted toward the right field line
Short	Up middle (shifted toward second base)
Second	Shifted toward first base

He also has trouble with low-outside sliders against right-handers (.193). He hits medium-high outside sliders very well (.346).

MEDIUM-HIGH OUTSIDE SLIDERS

BATTING AVERAGE .346

Play

Left	Deep in straightaway left field
Center	Medium-deep in straightaway center field
Right	Deep in straightaway right field
Short	Normal position
Second	Normal position

McReynolds Against Left-Handed Pitchers

McReynolds has trouble with outside fastballs thrown by left-handed pitchers (.235, .242 and .200, high to low). He hits medium-high outside fastballs deep to all fields.

MEDIUM-HIGH OUTSIDE FASTBALLS (THROWN BY LEFT-HANDED PITCHERS)

BATTING AVERAGE .242

Play

Left	Deep and shifted toward the left field line
Center	Deep and shifted toward left field
Right	Deep in straightaway right field
Short	Normal position
Second	*No instances recorded*

He also has trouble with medium-high inside and all high fastballs against left-handers. He hits low-over-the-middle fastballs very well, however, (.333).

LOW-OVER-THE-MIDDLE FASTBALLS (THROWN BY LEFT-HANDED PITCHERS)

BATTING AVERAGE .333

Play

Left	Deep in straightaway left field
Center	Deep and shifted toward left field
Right	Medium-deep and shifted toward the right line
Short	Normal position
Second	*No instances recorded*

McReynolds hits well against medium-high outside and low-over-the-middle curves thrown by left-handers. He hits low-over-the-middle curves into the left-center and right-center gaps.

Ahead And Behind In The Count Vs. RH

Ahead

Fastball Average .320

	Inside	Middle	Outside
High	7/714 /5	23/217 /5	11/181 /2
Med	15/266 /4	10/800 /8	38/342 /13
Low	5/200 /1	28/285 /8	16/187 /3

Curve Average .297

	Inside	Middle	Outside
High	0/0 /0	4/750 /3	2/500 /1
Med	0/0 /0	4/500 /2	9/333 /3
Low	0/0 /0	6/166 /1	12/83 /1

Behind

Fastball Average .253

	Inside	Middle	Outside
High	4/250 /1	7/285 /2	5/0 /0
Med	10/100 /1	2/1000 /2	18/333 /6
Low	4/250 /1	9/222 /2	4/250 /1

Curve Average .340

	Inside	Middle	Outside
High	2/0 /0	5/200 /1	1/0 /0
Med	5/600 /3	1/1000 /1	11/272 /3
Low	0/0 /0	9/333 /3	16/375 /6

Overall Evaluation

Against Right-Handed Pitchers

Overall Fastball	(1 ball)
Overall Curve	(2 balls)
Overall Slider	(3 balls)

Against Left-Handed Pitchers

Overall Fastball	(1 ball)
Overall Curve	(4 balls)
Overall Slider	(4 balls)

Comments: Weak against low fastballs vs. RH. Strengths: Medium-middle fastballs, medium-inside, high-middle and medium-middle curves, medium-high outside sliders vs. RH; low-inside and low-middle fastballs, medium-outside & low-middle curves vs. LH. Weaknesses: Low fastballs, medium-inside, high-middle and high-outside fastballs, outside curves and low-outside sliders vs. RH; high, outside and medium-inside fastballs vs. LH.

Darryl Strawberry Against Right-Handed Pitchers
Overall BARS Batting Average .294

	Fastball Average .319			Curve Average .250			Slider Average .346		
	Outside	Middle	Inside	Outside	Middle	Inside	Outside	Middle	Inside
High	44/ 295 /13	59/ 406 /24	31/ 129 /4	3/ 0 /0	9/ 666 /6	3/ 333 /1	1/ 1000 /1	5/ 0 /0	3/ 0 /0
Med	90/ 333 /30	28/ 464 /13	49/ 346 /17	13/ 461 /6	5/ 800 /4	8/ 125 /1	5/ 400 /2	1/ 1000 /1	8/ 625 /5
Low	45/ 200 /9	55/ 381 /21	31/ 225 /7	19/ 0 /0	26/ 153 /4	18/ 222 /4	4/ 0 /0	10/ 700 /7	15/ 133 /2

Darryl Strawberry Against Left-Handed Pitchers
Overall BARS Batting Average .211

	Fastball Average .255			Curve Average .209			Slider Average .095		
	Outside	Middle	Inside	Outside	Middle	Inside	Outside	Middle	Inside
High	10/ 100 /1	19/ 315 /6	18/ 55 /1	1/ 1000 /1	4/ 0 /0	1/ 0 /0	2/ 500 /1	1/ 0 /0	1/ 0 /0
Med	24/ 375 /9	10/ 400 /4	46/ 239 /11	7/ 285 /2	7/ 428 /3	10/ 400 /4	6/ 0 /0	2/ 0 /0	5/ 200 /1
Low	10/ 200 /2	20/ 450 /9	15/ 66 /1	18/ 111 /2	9/ 111 /1	5/ 0 /0	18/ 55 /1	5/ 0 /0	2/ 500 /1

Darryl Strawberry, left-handed hitter, has a much higher fastball average against right-handed than against left-handed pitchers. He has several weak fastball locations against right-handers but his other fastball averages are solid.

He hits a strong .333 against medium-high outside fastballs thrown by right-handed pitchers. He hits this pitch deep down the left line (Strawberry's opposite field).

MEDIUM-HIGH OUTSIDE FASTBALLS

BATTING AVERAGE .333
Play
Left   Deep and shifted toward the left field line
Center   Deep in straightaway center field
Right   Deep in straightaway right field
Short   Normal position
Second   Shifted toward first base

He also hits medium-high inside fastballs very well (.346), going down both lines.

MEDIUM-HIGH INSIDE FASTBALLS

BATTING AVERAGE .346
Play
Left   Medium-deep and shifted toward the left field line
Center   Deep and shifted toward right field
Right   Deep and shifted toward the right field line

Short   Normal position
Second   Shifted toward first base

Strawberry is exceptionally strong against all waist-high fastballs and all fastballs thrown down the middle, top to bottom, by right-handers. He hits high-over-the-middle fastballs deep and straightaway to all fields. He hits low-over-the-middle fastballs deep down the right line and to the right side of the infield.

LOW-OVER-THE-MIDDLE FASTBALLS

BATTING AVERAGE .381
Play
Left   Deep in straightaway left field
Center   Deep in straightaway center field
Right   Deep and shifted toward the right field line
Short   Up middle (shifted toward second base)
Second   Shifted toward first base

Strawberry goes to the opposite field with low-outside fastballs (.200) but pulls to the right side of the infield.

LOW-OUTSIDE FASTBALLS

BATTING AVERAGE .200
Play
Left   Deep and shifted toward the left field line
Center   Deep in straightaway center field
Right   Deep and shifted toward center field

| Short | Up middle (shifted toward second base) |
| Second | Shifted toward first base |

Strawberry Against Curves And Sliders

Strawberry hits medium-high outside curves very well against right-handers (.461) but he has considerable trouble with all low curves. His 0-for-19 against low-outside curves indicates a substantial weakness. Since he does not have a recorded base hit in this location, his hit balls are probably easy outs.

LOW-OUTSIDE CURVEBALLS

BATTING AVERAGE .000 (0 for 19)
Play

Left	Deep in straightaway left field
Center	*No instances recorded*
Right	Deep in straightaway right field
Short	Normal position
Second	Normal position

Strawberry hits very well against low-over-the-middle sliders and medium-inside sliders thrown by right-handers. He has a weakness in the low-inside slider location.

Strawberry Against Left-Handed Pitchers

Strawberry's overall average is considerably lower against left-handed pitchers than it is against right-handed pitchers. His fastball average is nearly 65 points less against left-handers. He has trouble with all four corner fastball locations against left-handers. He does, however, hit medium-outside fastballs well (.375).

MEDIUM-HIGH OUTSIDE FASTBALLS (THROWN BY LEFT-HANDED PITCHERS)

BATTING AVERAGE .375
Play

Left	Deep in straightaway left field
Center	Medium-deep in straightaway center field
Right	Deep and shifted toward center field
Short	Up middle (shifted toward second base)
Second	Normal position

In contrast, he hits medium-high inside fastballs for a low .239 average. He tends to go to his opposite field (left field) with this pitch against left-handers.

MEDIUM-HIGH INSIDE FASTBALLS (THROWN BY LEFT-HANDED PITCHERS)

BATTING AVERAGE .239
Play

Left	Deep and shifted toward the left field line
Center	Deep and shifted toward left field
Right	Deep and shifted toward center field
Short	Normal position
Second	Normal position

As against right-handers, Strawberry hits over-the-middle fastballs very well against left-handers (.315, .400 and .450, high to low).

He has trouble with all low curves against left-handers but hits all medium-high curves solidly. One glaring weakness in his charts against left-handers is in the low-outside slider location (.055). His 0-for-6 against medium-high outside sliders indicates that outside sliders are a problem for him in general.

Ahead And Behind In The Count Vs. RH

Ahead

Fastball Average .353

	Outside	Middle	Inside
High	7/ 428 /3	23/ 478 /11	15/ 266 /4
Med	46/ 369 /17	16/ 562 /9	22/ 272 /6
Low	16/ 125 /2	26/ 307 /8	13/ 384 /5

Curve Average .360

	Outside	Middle	Inside
High	0/ 0 /0	1/ 1000 /1	1/ 1000 /1
Med	4/ 500 /2	1/ 0 /0	4/ 250 /1
Low	3/ 0 /0	8/ 125 /1	3/ 1000 /3

Behind

Fastball Average .483

	Outside	Middle	Inside
High	9/ 666 /6	15/ 266 /4	2/ 0 /0
Med	13/ 461 /6	2/ 1000 /2	4/ 1000 /4
Low	6/ 333 /2	8/ 625 /5	3/ 333 /1

Curve Average .300

	Outside	Middle	Inside
High	2/ 0 /0	4/ 500 /2	1/ 0 /0
Med	5/ 800 /4	3/ 1000 /3	1/ 0 /0
Low	8/ 0 /0	4/ 0 /0	2/ 0 /0

Overall Evaluation

Against Right-Handed Pitchers

Overall Fastball	🅞🅞 🅞🅞🅞
Overall Curve	🅞🅞 🅞🅞
Overall Slider	🅞🅞 🅞🅞 🅞🅞

Against Left-Handed Pitchers

Overall Fastball	🅞🅞
Overall Curve	🅞🅞
Overall Slider	🅞🅞

Comments: Overall average is 83 points higher vs. RH. Strengths: All waist-high and over-the-middle fastballs vs. RH, medium-outside curves vs. RH, low-middle and medium-inside sliders vs. RH; over-the-middle fastballs, medium-outside fastballs and medium-inside curves vs. LH. Weaknesses: Fastball corners except high-outside, low curves, low-inside sliders vs. RH; four fastball corners, low curves and low sliders vs. LH.

Tim Teufel Against Right-Handed Pitchers
Overall BARS Batting Average .262

	Fastball Average .322			Curve Average .212			Slider Average .161		
	Inside	Middle	Outside	Inside	Middle	Outside	Inside	Middle	Outside
High	12/ 250 / 3	14/ 285 / 4	8/ 0 / 0	1/ 0 / 0	4/ 750 / 3	3/ 0 / 0	0/ 0 / 0	0/ 0 / 0	0/ 0 / 0
Med	26/ 346 / 9	11/ 363 / 4	31/ 483 / 15	2/ 500 / 1	2/ 500 / 1	5/ 0 / 0	3/ 0 / 0	4/ 0 / 0	9/ 111 / 1
Low	12/ 250 / 3	29/ 344 / 10	12/ 166 / 2	0/ 0 / 0	5/ 200 / 1	11/ 90 / 1	1/ 0 / 0	3/ 333 / 1	11/ 272 / 3

Tim Teufel Against Left-Handed Pitchers
Overall BARS Batting Average .233

	Fastball Average .231			Curve Average .181			Slider Average .470		
	Inside	Middle	Outside	Inside	Middle	Outside	Inside	Middle	Outside
High	8/ 125 / 1	16/ 312 / 5	16/ 187 / 3	0/ 0 / 0	0/ 0 / 0	1/ 0 / 0	0/ 0 / 0	1/ 1000 / 1	0/ 0 / 0
Med	11/ 181 / 2	12/ 333 / 4	35/ 228 / 8	1/ 0 / 0	1/ 0 / 0	5/ 400 / 2	2/ 500 / 1	0/ 0 / 0	2/ 500 / 1
Low	10/ 0 / 0	26/ 384 / 10	13/ 76 / 1	1/ 0 / 0	7/ 285 / 2	6/ 0 / 0	3/ 333 / 1	6/ 500 / 3	3/ 333 / 1

Right-handed hitting Tim Teufel hits fastballs very well against right-handed pitchers (.322) but poorly against left-handed pitchers (.231).

He is strong against all waist-high fastballs thrown by right-handers. His .483 against medium-high outside fastballs is top rate. The diagram on the opposite page shows where fielders need to be for this pitch.

MEDIUM-HIGH OUTSIDE FASTBALLS

BATTING AVERAGE .483
Play

Left	Deep and shifted toward the left field line
Center	Deep in straightaway center field
Right	Deep in straightaway right field
Short	Up middle (shifted toward second base)
Second	Shifted toward first base

His .346 against medium-high inside fastballs thrown by right-handers is also excellent.

MEDIUM-HIGH INSIDE FASTBALLS

BATTING AVERAGE .346
Play

Left	Medium-deep and shifted toward the left field line
Center	Deep and shifted toward left field
Right	Deep and shifted toward the right field line
Short	Shifted toward third base
Second	Normal position

His .344 against low-over-the-middle fastballs is almost as strong.

LOW-OVER-THE-MIDDLE FASTBALLS

BATTING AVERAGE .344
Play

Left	Deep in straightaway left field
Center	Deep and shifted toward left field
Right	Medium-deep and shifted toward center field
Short	Up middle (shifted toward second base)
Second	Normal position

Teufel Against Left-Handed Pitchers

Teufel is strong against fastballs thrown over-the-middle by left-handed pitchers. He hits low-over-the-middle fastballs deep to all fields.

LOW-OVER-THE-MIDDLE FASTBALLS
(THROWN BY LEFT-HANDED PITCHERS)

BATTING AVERAGE .384
Play

Left	Deep and shifted toward the left field line
Center	Deep and shifted toward left field
Right	Deep in straightaway right field
Short	Shifted toward third base
Second	*No instances recorded*

Against left-handers he is especially weak against inside and outside fastballs. By avoiding the middle of the plate, left-handers can gain an advantage.

Medium-High Outside Fastballs

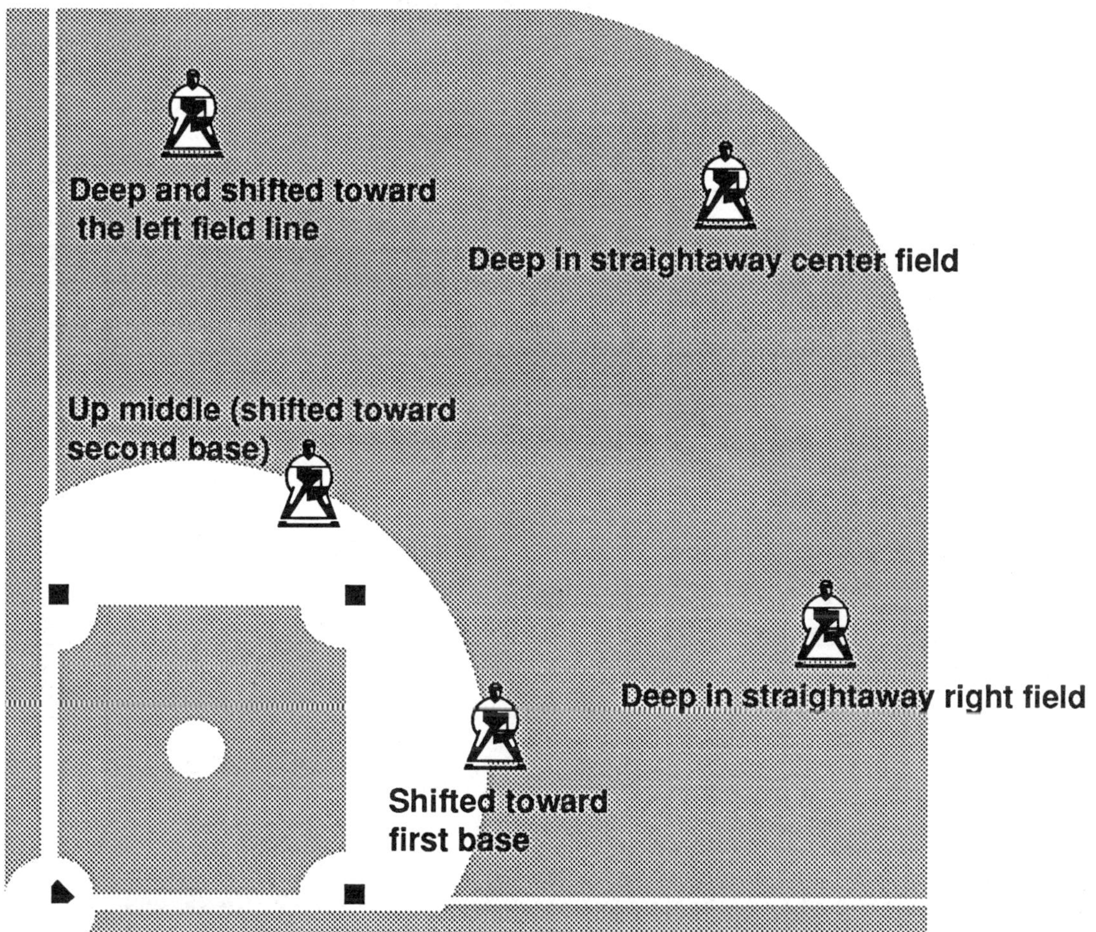

Ahead And Behind In The Count Vs. RH

Ahead

	Fastball Average .362			Curve Average .333		
	Inside	Middle	Outside	Inside	Middle	Outside
High	5/ 200 /1	8/ 250 /2	4/ 0 /0	0/ 0 /0	0/ 0 /0	1/ 0 /0
Med	12/ 333 /4	8/ 500 /4	16/ 562 /9	1/ 1000 /1	0/ 0 /0	0/ 0 /0
Low	7/ 142 /1	16/ 500 /8	4/ 0 /0	0/ 0 /0	1/ 0 /0	0/ 0 /0

Behind

	Fastball Average .281			Curve Average .272		
	Inside	Middle	Outside	Inside	Middle	Outside
High	3/ 666 /2	2/ 1000 /2	1/ 0 /0	0/ 0 /0	4/ 750 /3	1/ 0 /0
Med	6/ 0 /0	0/ 0 /0	8/ 500 /4	0/ 0 /0	1/ 0 /0	0/ 0 /0
Low	2/ 0 /0	7/ 0 /0	3/ 333 /1	0/ 0 /0	2/ 0 /0	3/ 0 /0

Overall Evaluation

Against Right-Handed Pitchers

Overall Fastball ⚾⚾ ⚾⚾ ⚾⚾
Overall Curve ⚾⚾
Overall Slider ⚾⚾

Against Left-Handed Pitchers

Overall Fastball ⚾⚾
Overall Curve ⚾⚾
Overall Slider ⚾⚾ ⚾⚾ ⚾⚾ ⚾⚾

Comments: Strong against waist-high fastballs vs. RH.
Strengths: Waist-high fastballs, low-middle fastballs vs. RH; over-the-middle fastballs vs. LH.
Weaknesses: High fastballs, low-outside and low-inside fastballs, low and outside curves, medium-outside sliders vs. RH; inside and outside fastballs vs. LH.

Mookie Wilson (Switch Hitter) — *New York Mets*

Mookie Wilson Against Right-Handed Pitchers
Overall BARS Batting Average .271

Fastball Average .296

	Outside	Middle	Inside
High	22/90 /2	24/375 /9	16/375 /6
Med	47/361 /17	21/238 /5	49/285 /14
Low	18/111 /2	57/368 /21	39/282 /11

Curve Average .226

	Outside	Middle	Inside
High	6/333 /2	3/333 /1	1/0 /0
Med	15/333 /5	4/500 /2	12/333 /4
Low	10/100 /1	19/105 /2	14/142 /2

Slider Average .390

	Outside	Middle	Inside
High	0/0 /0	3/0 /0	2/500 /1
Med	3/666 /2	6/333 /2	12/500 /6
Low	0/0 /0	4/500 /2	11/272 /3

Mookie Wilson Against Left-Handed Pitchers
Overall BARS Batting Average .267

Fastball Average .264

	Inside	Middle	Outside
High	14/285 /4	14/285 /4	15/200 /3
Med	9/111 /1	13/153 /2	48/291 /14
Low	17/235 /4	24/375 /9	35/257 /9

Curve Average .268

	Inside	Middle	Outside
High	0/0 /0	1/0 /0	0/0 /0
Med	4/0 /0	0/0 /0	9/444 /4
Low	3/333 /1	13/307 /4	11/181 /2

Slider Average .354

	Inside	Middle	Outside
High	3/666 /2	2/0 /0	1/0 /0
Med	4/250 /1	0/0 /0	3/333 /1
Low	8/250 /2	6/333 /2	4/750 /3

Switch-hitter Mookie Wilson hits .296 against fastballs when batting left-handed against right-handed pitchers but only .264 right-handed against left-handed pitchers.

Against right-handers he hits very poorly against low-outside and high-outside fastballs (.111 and .090 respectively). But he hits medium-high outside fastballs excellently (.361).

MEDIUM-HIGH OUTSIDE FASTBALLS

BATTING AVERAGE .361
Play
Left Deep and shifted toward the left field line
Center Medium-deep in straightaway center field
Right Medium-deep and shifted toward center field
Short Up middle (shifted toward second base)
Second Normal position

He hits high-over-the-middle and high-inside fastballs extremely well (.375 in both locations). Pitchers would do well to steer away from this sector.

His .368 against low-over-the-middle fastballs is very strong. Notice that this location has the highest number of recorded fastballs. Pitchers are trying to throw Wilson low fastballs, but he is hitting them well. If they throw him low, they should make sure it is outside.

LOW-OVER-THE-MIDDLE FASTBALLS

BATTING AVERAGE .368
Play
Left Medium-deep in straightaway left field
Center Medium-deep in straightaway center field
Right Deep in straightaway right field
Short Up middle (shifted toward second base)
Second Normal position

Wilson has problems with low curves (.100, .105 and .142, outside to inside). He hits all other curve locations excellently.

Wilson Against Left-Handed Pitchers

Wilson also hits low-over-the-middle fastballs well against left-handed pitchers (.375).

LOW-OVER-THE-MIDDLE FASTBALLS (THROWN BY LEFT-HANDED PITCHERS)

BATTING AVERAGE .375
Play
Left Medium-deep and shifted toward the left field line
Center Deep in straightaway center field
Right Deep and shifted toward center field
Short Up middle (shifted toward second base)
Second Normal position

Medium-High Outside Fastballs

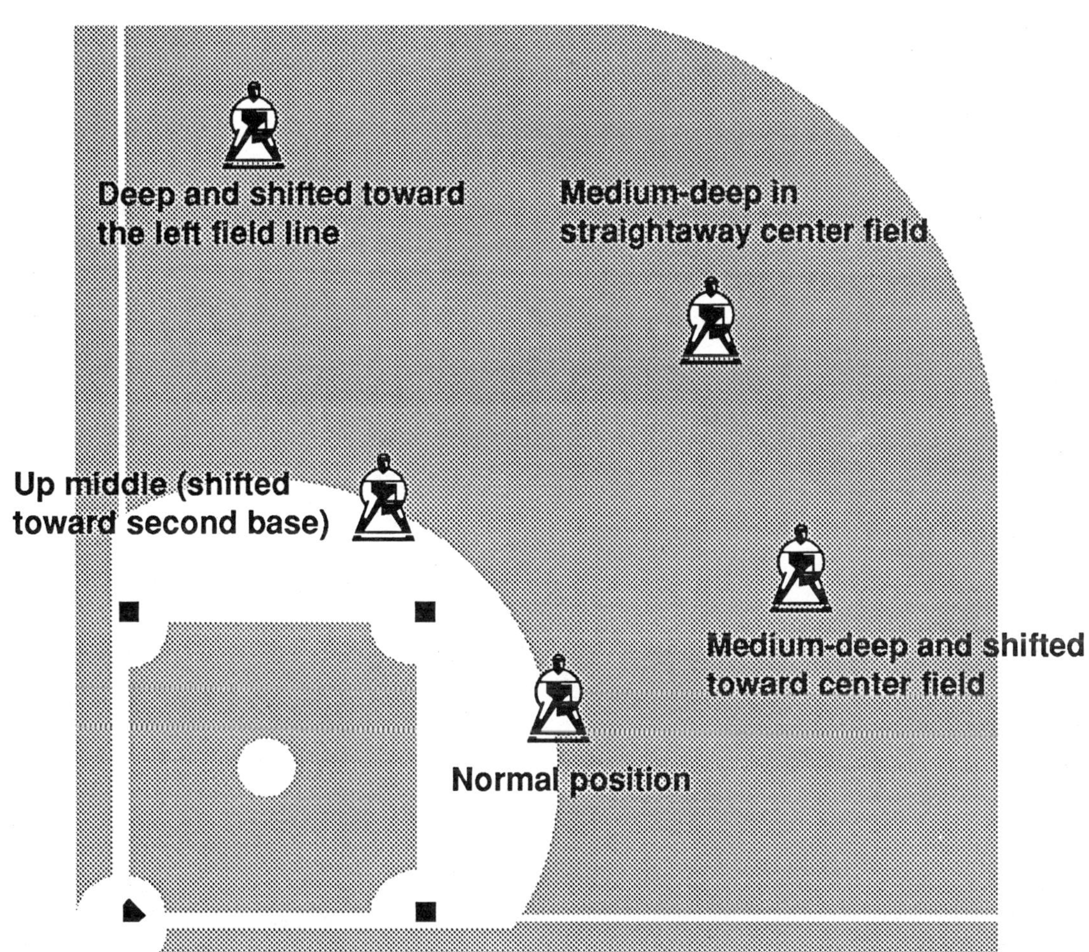

Ahead And Behind In The Count Vs. RH

Ahead

Fastball Average .343

	Outside	Middle	Inside
High	8/ 250 /2	13/ 384 /5	7/ 571 /4
Med	22/ 454 /10	15/ 266 /4	21/ 380 /8
Low	8/ 125 /1	23/ 391 /9	17/ 176 /3

Curve Average .409

	Outside	Middle	Inside
High	2/ 500 /1	0/ 0 /0	0/ 0 /0
Med	4/ 750 /3	3/ 666 /2	7/ 285 /2
Low	4/ 0 /0	1/ 0 /0	1/ 1000 /1

Behind

Fastball Average .313

	Outside	Middle	Inside
High	0/ 0 /0	2/ 500 /1	6/ 166 /1
Med	8/ 250 /2	3/ 333 /1	14/ 357 /5
Low	4/ 250 /1	6/ 333 /2	8/ 375 /3

Curve Average .208

	Outside	Middle	Inside
High	1/ 1000 /1	2/ 500 /1	0/ 0 /0
Med	5/ 0 /0	1/ 0 /0	2/ 500 /1
Low	2/ 0 /0	10/ 200 /2	1/ 0 /0

Overall Evaluation

Against Right-Handed Pitchers

Overall Fastball 
Overall Curve
Overall Slider

Against Left-Handed Pitchers

Overall Fastball
Overall Curve
Overall Slider

Comments: Weak against low curves vs. RH.
Strengths: Medium-outside, low-middle, high-middle and high-inside fastballs vs. RH, medium-outside and medium-inside curves vs. RH, medium-inside sliders vs. RH; low-middle fastballs, low-middle and medium-outside curves vs. LH.
Weaknesses: High-outside and low-outside fastballs and low curves vs. RH; high-outside, low-outside, low-inside fastballs vs. LH, low-outside curves vs. LH.

Philadelphia Phillies

Dernier, Bob
Hayes, Von
Herr, Tom
James, Chris
Jeltz, Steve
Samuel, Juan
Schmidt, Mike

Philadelphia Phillies
BARS System
Hitting Analysis

Bob Dernier (Right Handed)   *Philadelphia Phillies*

Bob Dernier Against Right-Handed Pitchers
Overall BARS Batting Average .221

Fastball Average .251

	Inside	Middle	Outside
High	31/ 96 /3	86/ 232 /20	30/ 100 /3
Med	43/ 232 /10	23/ 347 /8	154/ 318 /49
Low	31/ 129 /4	111/ 306 /34	64/ 203 /13

Curve Average .198

	Inside	Middle	Outside
High	5/ 200 /1	6/ 166 /1	2/ 0 /0
Med	10/ 400 /4	4/ 250 /1	43/ 186 /8
Low	2/ 0 /0	19/ 210 /4	40/ 175 /7

Slider Average .202

	Inside	Middle	Outside
High	0/ 0 /0	3/ 0 /0	6/ 0 /0
Med	1/ 0 /0	1/ 1000 /1	37/ 243 /9
Low	3/ 333 /1	8/ 250 /2	35/ 171 /6

Bob Dernier Against Left-Handed Pitchers
Overall BARS Batting Average .287

Fastball Average .329

	Inside	Middle	Outside
High	11/ 272 /3	31/ 290 /9	26/ 346 /9
Med	19/ 368 /7	7/ 428 /3	119/ 352 /42
Low	12/ 166 /2	39/ 410 /16	49/ 244 /12

Curve Average .269

	Inside	Middle	Outside
High	4/ 0 /0	2/ 0 /0	2/ 500 /1
Med	3/ 333 /1	1/ 0 /0	13/ 461 /6
Low	3/ 0 /0	14/ 357 /5	10/ 100 /1

Slider Average .000

	Inside	Middle	Outside
High	1/ 0 /0	0/ 0 /0	2/ 0 /0
Med	3/ 0 /0	0/ 0 /0	0/ 0 /0
Low	2/ 0 /0	1/ 0 /0	3/ 0 /0

Right-handed hitter Bob Dernier has a higher BARS overall fastball average against left-handed pitchers (.329 overall vs. left-handers, .251 vs. right-handers). He has three strong fastball locations against right-handers but he has half a dozen against left-handers.

Starting with right-handers, notice his problems against inside and high fastballs. These locations, along with his low-outside fastball location, give right-handers large sectors to attack.

His Ahead and Behind charts show that he hits medium-high outside fastballs better when he is ahead in the count (.333 when ahead, .240 when behind). When ahead he hits the ball medium-deep to straightaway left and center and into the right-center gap. When behind, he hits down both lines.

MEDIUM-HIGH OUTSIDE FASTBALLS (WHEN AHEAD IN THE COUNT)

BATTING AVERAGE .333
Play
Left   Medium-deep in straightaway left field
Center   Medium-deep in straightaway center field
Right   Deep and shifted toward center field
Short   Normal position
Second   Normal position

MEDIUM-HIGH OUTSIDE FASTBALLS (WHEN BEHIND IN THE COUNT)

BATTING AVERAGE .240
Play
Left   Deep and shifted toward the left line
Center   Deep and shifted toward left field
Right   Medium-deep and shifted toward the right line
Short   Up middle (shifted toward second base)
Second   Normal position

Right-handers throw him a lot of low fastballs. This is a mistake because he hits .306 in his low-over-the-middle location. Right-handers would be better off throwing him high fastballs.

LOW-OVER-THE-MIDDLE FASTBALLS

BATTING AVERAGE .306
Play
Left   Deep and shifted toward the left field line
Center   Deep and shifted toward left field
Right   Medium-deep in straightaway right field
Short   Normal position
Second   Shifted toward first base

Dernier has lots of problems against low curves and outside curves thrown by right-handed pitchers. These locations offer ample targets for right-handers. Similarly, he has problems with outside sliders thrown by right-handers. He hits medium-high outside sliders down both lines and to the right side of the infield.

MEDIUM-HIGH OUTSIDE SLIDERS

BATTING AVERAGE .243
Play

Left	Medium-deep and shifted toward the left field line
Center	Deep and shifted toward left field
Right	Deep and shifted toward the right field line
Short	Up middle (shifted toward second base)
Second	Shifted toward first base

Dernier Against Left-handed Pitchers

Dernier comes alive against fastballs thrown by left-handed pitchers. His .352 against medium-high outside fastballs is excellent.

MEDIUM-HIGH OUTSIDE FASTBALLS (THROWN BY LEFT-HANDED PITCHERS)

BATTING AVERAGE .352
Play

Left	Deep in straightaway left field
Center	Medium-deep in straightaway center field
Right	Deep in straightaway right field
Short	Shifted toward third base
Second	Shifted toward first base

He hits a very strong .410 against low-over-the-middle fastballs thrown by left-handers. If the outfielders played medium-deep and the infielders played in their normal positions as suggested by the following BARS fielding strategy, they could prevent most of his hit balls from this location.

LOW-OVER-THE-MIDDLE FASTBALLS

BATTING AVERAGE .410
Play

Left	Medium-deep and shifted toward the left field line
Center	Medium-deep in straightaway center field
Right	Medium-deep in straightaway right field
Short	Normal position
Second	Normal position

His .346 in the high-outside fastball location is also very strong. Again, the outfielders need to play medium-deep for this pitch.

HIGH-OUTSIDE FASTBALLS (THROWN BY LEFT-HANDED PITCHERS)

BATTING AVERAGE .346
Play

Left	Medium-deep and shifted toward the left field line
Center	Medium-deep in straightaway center field
Right	Medium-deep and shifted toward center field
Short	Up middle (shifted toward second base)
Second	Normal position

Dernier hits medium-high outside and low-middle curves excellently against left-handers (.461 and .357 respectively). He has trouble, however, with low-outside curves thrown by lefties (.100).

Ahead And Behind In The Count Vs. RH

Ahead

Fastball Average .268   Curve Average .083

	Inside	Middle	Outside	Inside	Middle	Outside
High	13/ **76** /1	42/ **333** /14	16/ **62** /1	2/ **0** /0	1/ **0** /0	0/ **0** /0
Med	20/ **200** /4	14/ **214** /3	84/ **333** /28	1/ **0** /0	1/ **0** /0	3/ **333** /1
Low	7/ **142** /1	64/ **281** /18	30/ **266** /8	0/ **0** /0	2/ **0** /0	2/ **0** /0

Behind

Fastball Average .247   Curve Average .270

	Inside	Middle	Outside	Inside	Middle	Outside
High	5/ **0** /0	7/ **285** /2	5/ **200** /1	3/ **333** /1	4/ **250** /1	1/ **0** /0
Med	9/ **444** /4	4/ **250** /1	25/ **240** /6	3/ **333** /1	0/ **0** /0	19/ **315** /6
Low	2/ **0** /0	20/ **350** /7	12/ **83** /1	0/ **0** /0	5/ **400** /2	13/ **153** /2

Overall Evaluation

Against Right-Handed Pitchers

Overall Fastball	⚾⚾
Overall Curve	⚾⚾
Overall Slider	⚾⚾

Against Left-Handed Pitchers

Overall Fastball	⚾⚾⚾⚾
Overall Curve	⚾⚾
Overall Slider	Not enough information

Comments: Weak vs. high and inside fastballs vs. RH. Strengths: Medium-middle, low-middle and medium-outside fastballs vs. RH; waist-high, over-the-middle and high-outside fastballs, medium-outside and low-middle curves vs. LH. Weaknesses: Inside and high fastballs, low-outside fastballs, low and outside curves, outside sliders vs. RH; low-outside, low-inside and high-inside fastballs, low-outside curves vs. LH.

Von Hayes Against Right-Handed Pitchers
Overall BARS Batting Average .324

Fastball Average .364

	Outside	Middle	Inside
High	31/354/11	49/285/14	32/250/8
Med	66/378/25	22/636/14	53/339/18
Low	27/407/11	61/393/24	38/342/13

Curve Average .288

	Outside	Middle	Inside
High	1/1000/1	3/333/1	5/600/3
Med	4/0/0	4/500/2	7/142/1
Low	9/222/2	15/133/2	11/454/5

Slider Average .212

	Outside	Middle	Inside
High	0/0/0	4/0/0	4/500/2
Med	4/250/1	4/0/0	7/428/3
Low	0/0/0	13/153/2	11/181/2

Von Hayes Against Left-Handed Pitchers
Overall BARS Batting Average .254

Fastball Average .296

	Outside	Middle	Inside
High	4/750/3	11/363/4	12/166/2
Med	17/176/3	4/250/1	31/258/8
Low	5/200/1	16/375/6	8/500/4

Curve Average .178

	Outside	Middle	Inside
High	2/0/0	4/0/0	1/1000/1
Med	3/0/0	2/500/1	3/0/0
Low	4/0/0	4/500/2	5/200/1

Slider Average .300

	Outside	Middle	Inside
High	2/500/1	3/666/2	1/0/0
Med	4/500/2	0/0/0	0/0/0
Low	5/0/0	2/0/0	3/333/1

Left-handed Von Hayes has an excellent .364 overall fastball average against right-handed pitchers. He has one weak fastball location (.250 high-inside) but his other locations are solid.

Against right-handers, he hits a fine .378 against medium-high outside fastballs. He hits this pitch deep to his opposite field (left field). But notice that the shortstop needs to shift toward second and the second baseman toward first.

MEDIUM-HIGH OUTSIDE FASTBALLS

BATTING AVERAGE .378
Play

Left	Deep and shifted toward the left field line
Center	Deep and shifted toward left field
Right	Deep and shifted toward center field
Short	Up middle (shifted toward second base)
Second	Shifted toward first base

His .393 average against low-over-the-middle fastballs is very strong.

LOW-OVER-THE-MIDDLE FASTBALLS

BATTING AVERAGE .393
Play

Left	Deep and shifted toward the left field line
Center	Medium-deep in straightaway center field
Right	Deep and shifted toward center field
Short	Normal position
Second	Shifted toward first base

He hits low-outside fastballs at a blistering .407 pace.

LOW-OUTSIDE FASTBALLS

BATTING AVERAGE .407
Play

Left	Medium-deep in straightaway left field
Center	Deep and shifted toward right field
Right	Deep in straightaway right field
Short	Up middle (shifted toward second base)
Second	Shifted toward first base

A right-hander would not want to throw Hayes a fastball down the pipe (.636). It's interesting to see how he hits this pitch.

MEDIUM-OVER-THE-MIDDLE FASTBALLS

BATTING AVERAGE .636
Play

Left	Deep and shifted toward the left line
Center	Deep and shifted toward left field
Right	Medium-deep and shifted toward the right line
Short	Up middle (shifted toward second base)
Second	Normal position

Hayes hits high-outside fastballs down both the left

and right lines. He hits low-inside fastballs down the left line and into the right-center gap.

HIGH-OUTSIDE FASTBALLS

BATTING AVERAGE .354
Play

Left	Medium-deep and shifted toward the left line
Center	Medium-deep in straightaway center field
Right	Medium-deep and shifted toward the right line
Short	Shifted toward third base
Second	Normal position

LOW-INSIDE FASTBALLS

BATTING AVERAGE .342
Play

Left	Medium-deep and shifted toward the left field line
Center	Medium-deep in straightaway center field
Right	Deep and shifted toward center field
Short	Shifted toward third base
Second	Shifted toward first base

Hayes has a lot of trouble with low-outside and low-over-the-middle curves (.222 and .133). He hits low-inside curves very well, however (.454)

His low-over-the-middle and low-inside slider averages are also low (.153 and .181). His weak curve and slider sectors give targets for right-handers.

Hayes Against Left-Handed Pitchers

Hayes has a fairly good .296 overall fastball average against left-handed pitchers. His .176 medium-high outside and .258 medium-high inside averages are poor but he hits low over-the-middle (.375) and high-over-the-middle (.363) fastballs very well.

LOW-OVER-THE-MIDDLE FASTBALLS
(THROWN BY LEFT-HANDED PITCHERS)

BATTING AVERAGE .375
Play

Left	Medium-deep in straightaway left field
Center	Medium-deep in straightaway center field
Right	Deep and shifted toward the right field line
Short	Normal position
Second	Shifted toward first base

HIGH-OVER-THE-MIDDLE FASTBALLS
(THROWN BY LEFT-HANDED PITCHERS)

BATTING AVERAGE .363
Play

Left	Deep and shifted toward the left field line
Center	Deep in straightaway center field
Right	Deep in straightaway right field
Short	Up middle (shifted toward second base)
Second	Shifted toward first base

He hits medium-high inside fastballs thrown by left-handers medium-deep to all fields. His low average in this location indicates that most of his hit balls probably are easy pop-ups or ground outs.

MEDIUM-HIGH INSIDE FASTBALLS
(THROWN BY LEFT-HANDED PITCHERS)

BATTING AVERAGE .258
Play

Left	Medium-deep in straightaway left field
Center	Medium-deep in straightaway center field
Right	Medium-deep and shifted toward the right line
Short	Up middle (shifted toward second base)
Second	Shifted toward first base

Ahead And Behind In The Count Vs. RH

Ahead

	Fastball Average .395			Curve Average .500		
	Outside	Middle	Inside	Outside	Middle	Inside
High	13/384/5	28/250/7	13/384/5	0/0/0	0/0/0	0/0/0
Med	32/437/14	11/636/7	34/352/12	0/0/0	0/0/0	0/0/0
Low	8/500/4	29/448/13	19/368/7	0/0/0	2/0/0	2/1000/2

Behind

	Fastball Average .397			Curve Average .384		
	Outside	Middle	Inside	Outside	Middle	Inside
High	6/500/3	7/714/5	8/125/1	1/1000/1	3/333/1	4/750/3
Med	12/416/5	3/666/2	7/285/2	2/0/0	2/500/1	1/1000/1
Low	9/444/4	14/285/4	2/500/1	4/0/0	5/0/0	4/750/3

Overall Evaluation
Against Right-Handed Pitchers

Overall Fastball	◯◯ ◯◯ ◯◯ ◯◯
Overall Curve	◯◯ ◯◯ ◯◯
Overall Slider	◯◯

Against Left-Handed Pitchers

Overall Fastball	◯◯ ◯◯
Overall Curve	◯◯
Overall Slider	◯◯ ◯◯ ◯◯ ◯◯

Comments: High-inside only fastball weakness vs. RH. Strengths: Fastballs except high-inside, low-inside curves and medium-inside sliders vs. RH; high-middle, low-middle and low-inside fastballs vs. LH. Weaknesses: High-inside fastballs, low-outside, low-middle and medium-inside curves, low sliders vs. RH; medium-outside, high-inside and medium-inside fastballs, outside curves vs. LH.

Tom Herr (Switch Hitter) — *Philadelphia Phillies*

Tom Herr Against Right-Handed Pitchers
Overall BARS Batting Average .242

Fastball Average .251

	Outside	Middle	Inside
High	23/ 260 / 6	40/ 400 / 16	21/ 142 / 3
Med	56/ 267 / 15	19/ 157 / 3	53/ 264 / 14
Low	25/ 80 / 2	66/ 287 / 19	55/ 218 / 12

Curve Average .208

	Outside	Middle	Inside
High	3/ 0 / 0	4/ 750 / 3	2/ 0 / 0
Med	7/ 285 / 2	3/ 0 / 0	10/ 300 / 3
Low	10/ 100 / 1	19/ 52 / 1	14/ 357 / 5

Slider Average .307

	Outside	Middle	Inside
High	0/ 0 / 0	1/ 0 / 0	3/ 0 / 0
Med	2/ 500 / 1	2/ 0 / 0	7/ 571 / 4
Low	3/ 0 / 0	8/ 375 / 3	13/ 307 / 4

Tom Herr Against Left-Handed Pitchers
Overall BARS Batting Average .285

Fastball Average .306

	Inside	Middle	Outside
High	17/ 235 / 4	21/ 380 / 8	14/ 357 / 5
Med	29/ 379 / 11	4/ 500 / 2	41/ 195 / 8
Low	16/ 437 / 7	21/ 238 / 5	20/ 300 / 6

Curve Average .424

	Inside	Middle	Outside
High	3/ 666 / 2	1/ 0 / 0	1/ 0 / 0
Med	5/ 200 / 1	1/ 1000 / 1	5/ 0 / 0
Low	2/ 500 / 1	11/ 545 / 6	4/ 750 / 3

Slider Average .241

	Inside	Middle	Outside
High	1/ 0 / 0	2/ 500 / 1	0/ 0 / 0
Med	4/ 500 / 2	1/ 0 / 0	4/ 250 / 1
Low	10/ 300 / 3	6/ 0 / 0	1/ 0 / 0

Switch-hitting Tom Herr has a higher BARS fastball average against left-handed pitchers (.306 overall fastball average vs. left-handers, .251 overall fastball average vs. right-handers). He has half a dozen strong fastball locations against left-handers, only one against right-handers.

His strong location against right-handers is in the high-over-the-middle location (.400). Batting left-handed, he hits this pitch down both lines and to the right side of the infield.

HIGH-OVER-THE-MIDDLE FASTBALLS

BATTING AVERAGE .400
Play

Left	Medium-deep and shifted toward the left field line
Center	Deep in straightaway center field
Right	Deep and shifted toward the right field line
Short	Up middle (shifted toward second base)
Second	Shifted toward first base

His .287 against low-over-the-middle fastballs thrown by right-handers is fair. He goes to his opposite field (left field) with this pitch. Notice, however, that the shortstop needs to play shifted toward second.

LOW-OVER-THE-MIDDLE FASTBALLS

BATTING AVERAGE .287

Play

Left	Medium-deep and shifted toward the left field line
Center	Deep and shifted toward left field
Right	Deep and shifted toward center field
Short	Up middle (shifted toward second base)
Second	Normal position

Herr is weak in his other fastball locations. By pitching him inside or outside fastballs, right-handers can get an edge.

Herr Against Curves And Sliders

He has a lot of trouble with low-outside and low-over-the-middle curves. This sector should be a target for right-handers. He hits medium-high inside and low-inside curves very well. The following strategy shows how fielders need to position themselves for low-inside curves.

LOW-INSIDE CURVEBALLS

BATTING AVERAGE .357
Play

Left	Medium-deep and shifted toward the left field line
Center	Deep and shifted toward left field
Right	Deep and shifted toward the right field line
Short	*No instances recorded*
Second	Shifted toward first base

He also hits medium-high inside and low-inside sliders very well. He goes deep down the left line with low-inside sliders. Since there are no recorded ground balls to the infield for this pitch to Herr, pitchers would not want to throw him this pitch with a runner on third and less than two outs, because a fly ball to any of the outfielders would drive in the runner. Pitchers often throw hitters low pitches to avoid long fly balls, but the following BARS fielding strategy shows that this is not always correct.

LOW-INSIDE SLIDERS

BATTING AVERAGE .307

Play	
Left	Deep and shifted toward the left field line
Center	Medium-deep in straightaway center field
Right	Deep in straightaway right field
Short	*No instances recorded*
Second	*No instances recorded*

Herr Against Left-Handed Pitchers

Batting right-handed against left-handed pitchers, Herr has a good .306 overall fastball average. Oddly enough he is very weak in the highly pitched medium-high outside fastball location (.195). Most of his hit balls from this location are probably easy fly balls and grounders.

MEDIUM-HIGH OUTSIDE FASTBALLS (THROWN BY LEFT-HANDED PITCHERS)

BATTING AVERAGE .195

Play	
Left	Deep and shifted toward center field
Center	Medium-deep in straightaway center field
Right	Deep in straightaway right field
Short	Normal position
Second	Normal position

He hits a strong .379 against medium-high inside fastballs thrown by left-handers.

MEDIUM-HIGH INSIDE FASTBALLS (THROWN BY LEFT-HANDED PITCHERS)

BATTING AVERAGE .379

Play	
Left	Deep and shifted toward the left field line
Center	Medium-deep in straightaway center field
Right	Medium-deep and shifted toward center field
Short	Shifted toward third base
Second	Shifted toward first base

His .380 against high-over-the-middle fastballs is also very strong. Notice that he hits this pitch medium-deep to all fields and down both lines.

HIGH-OVER-THE-MIDDLE FASTBALLS (THROWN BY LEFT-HANDED PITCHERS)

BATTING AVERAGE .380

Play	
Left	Medium-deep and shifted toward the left line
Center	Medium-deep in straightaway center field
Right	Medium-deep and shifted toward the right line
Short	Up middle (shifted toward second base)
Second	Normal position

Ahead And Behind In The Count Vs. RH

Ahead

	Fastball Average .289			Curve Average .181		
	Outside	Middle	Inside	Outside	Middle	Inside
High	15 / 266 / 4	23 / 391 / 9	6 / 166 / 1	0 / 0 / 0	1 / 1000 / 1	1 / 0 / 0
Med	25 / 320 / 8	5 / 200 / 1	27 / 296 / 8	1 / 1000 / 1	0 / 0 / 0	2 / 0 / 0
Low	11 / 90 / 1	35 / 314 / 11	22 / 272 / 6	2 / 0 / 0	3 / 0 / 0	1 / 0 / 0

Behind

	Fastball Average .344			Curve Average .173		
	Outside	Middle	Inside	Outside	Middle	Inside
High	1 / 0 / 0	9 / 333 / 3	9 / 222 / 2	1 / 0 / 0	0 / 0 / 0	1 / 0 / 0
Med	11 / 363 / 4	2 / 500 / 1	10 / 500 / 5	3 / 0 / 0	1 / 0 / 0	3 / 333 / 1
Low	3 / 333 / 1	8 / 375 / 3	8 / 250 / 2	4 / 250 / 1	8 / 125 / 1	2 / 500 / 1

Overall Evaluation

Against Right-Handed Pitchers

Overall Fastball	⚾⚾
Overall Curve	⚾⚾
Overall Slider	⚾⚾⚾⚾

Against Left-Handed Pitchers

Overall Fastball	⚾⚾⚾
Overall Curve	⚾⚾⚾⚾
Overall Slider	⚾

Comments: Weak vs. outside & inside fastballs vs. RH. Strengths: High-middle fastballs, medium-inside and low-inside curves, low-middle, low-inside and medium-inside sliders vs. RH; medium-inside, low-inside, high-middle and high-outside fastballs, low-middle curves, low-inside sliders vs. LH.
Weaknesses:Outside, inside and waist-high fastballs, low-outside and low-middle curves vs. RH; high-inside, low-middle & medium-outside fastballs vs. LH.

Chris James Against Right-Handed Pitchers
Overall BARS Batting Average .240

Fastball Average .256

	Inside	Middle	Outside
High	12/ 333 /4	4/ 250 /1	13/ 384 /5
Med	6/ 166 /1	1/ 0 /0	16/ 312 /5
Low	6/ 166 /1	9/ 111 /1	7/ 142 /1

Curve Average .228

	Inside	Middle	Outside
High	2/ 500 /1	0/ 0 /0	3/ 333 /1
Med	2/ 0 /0	1/ 0 /0	12/ 333 /4
Low	1/ 1000 /1	0/ 0 /0	14/ 71 /1

Slider Average .350

	Inside	Middle	Outside
High	0/ 0 /0	1/ 0 /0	1/ 0 /0
Med	2/ 0 /0	0/ 0 /0	5/ 800 /4
Low	0/ 0 /0	2/ 0 /0	9/ 333 /3

Chris James Against Left-Handed Pitchers
Overall BARS Batting Average .238

Fastball Average .311

	Inside	Middle	Outside
High	7/ 428 /3	5/ 400 /2	3/ 0 /0
Med	6/ 333 /2	0/ 0 /0	10/ 400 /4
Low	4/ 500 /2	4/ 0 /0	6/ 166 /1

Curve Average .111

	Inside	Middle	Outside
High	0/ 0 /0	1/ 0 /0	0/ 0 /0
Med	1/ 1000 /1	0/ 0 /0	1/ 0 /0
Low	3/ 0 /0	1/ 0 /0	2/ 0 /0

Slider Average .142

	Inside	Middle	Outside
High	0/ 0 /0	0/ 0 /0	0/ 0 /0
Med	2/ 0 /0	0/ 0 /0	1/ 0 /0
Low	1/ 0 /0	2/ 500 /1	1/ 0 /0

Right-handed hitter Chris James has problems with low fastballs thrown by right-handed pitchers (.166, .111 and .142). He hits medium-high outside fastballs (.312) and high-outside fastballs (.384) very well, however.

He hits medium-high outside fastballs straightaway to all fields.

MEDIUM-HIGH OUTSIDE FASTBALLS

BATTING AVERAGE .312
> *Play*

Left	Deep in straightaway left field
Center	Deep in straightaway center field
Right	Medium-deep in straightaway right
Short	Normal position
Second	Normal position

He also hits high-outside fastballs straightaway. But the center fielder needs to play medium-deep and the shortstop needs to play shifted toward third base.

HIGH-OUTSIDE FASTBALLS

BATTING AVERAGE .384
> *Play*

Left	Deep in straightaway left field
Center	Medium-deep in straightaway center field
Right	Medium-deep in straightaway right field
Short	Shifted toward third base
Second	Up middle (shifted toward second base)

James has trouble with low-outside curves thrown by right-handers (.071) but he hits medium-high outside curves excellently (.333).

MEDIUM-HIGH OUTSIDE CURVEBALLS

BATTING AVERAGE .333
> *Play*

Left	Medium-deep and shifted toward the left field line
Center	Deep and shifted toward left field
Right	Deep in straightaway right field
Short	Up middle (shifted toward second base)
Second	*No instances recorded*

James Against Left-Handed Pitchers

Facing left-handed pitchers, James has a solid .400 average against medium-high outside fastballs. He hits this pitch deep down the left line and deep into the right-center gap.

MEDIUM-HIGH OUTSIDE FASTBALLS
(THROWN BY LEFT-HANDED PITCHERS)

BATTING AVERAGE .400
> *Play*

Left	Deep and shifted toward the left field line
Center	Deep and shifted toward right field
Right	Medium-deep in straightaway right field
Short	Normal position
Second	*No instances recorded*

High-Outside Fastballs

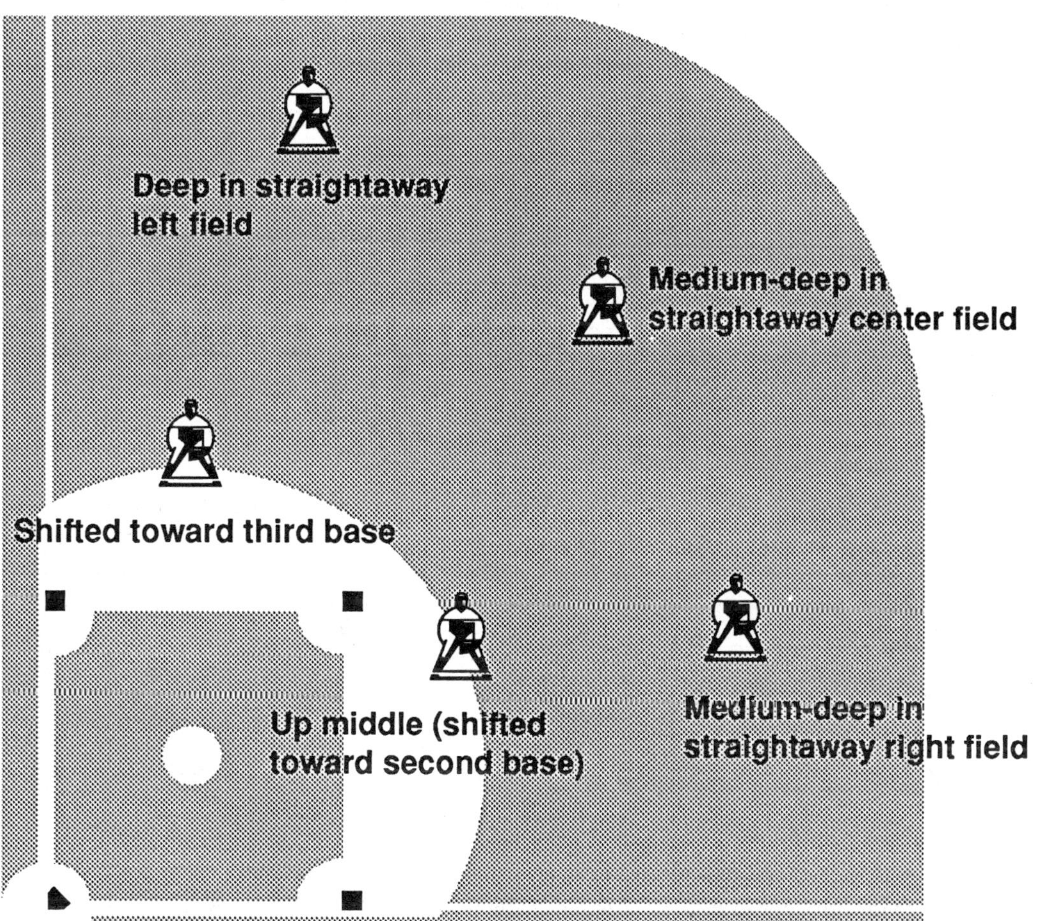

Ahead And Behind In The Count Vs. RH

Ahead

	Fastball Average .275			Curve Average .200		
	Inside	Middle	Outside	Inside	Middle	Outside
High	500 1/2	0 0/0	428 7/3	0 1/0	0 0/0	0 1/0
Med	0 2/0	0 1/0	333 3/1	0 0/0	0 0/0	200 5/1
Low	333 3/1	166 6/1	0 3/0	1000 1/1	0 0/0	0 2/0

Behind

	Fastball Average .411			Curve Average .222		
	Inside	Middle	Outside	Inside	Middle	Outside
High	500 4/2	1000 1/1	1000 1/1	1000 1/1	0 0/0	0 1/0
Med	333 3/1	0 0/0	333 3/1	0 0/0	0 0/0	0 2/0
Low	0 2/0	0 2/0	1000 1/1	0 0/0	0 0/0	200 5/1

Overall Evaluation

Against Right-Handed Pitchers

Overall Fastball 

Overall Curve

Overall Slider

Against Left-Handed Pitchers

Overall Fastball

Overall Curve — Not enough information

Overall Slider — Not enough information

Comments: Strong sector high-outside/medium-high outside fastballs against RH.

Strengths: High-outside and medium-high outside fastballs, medium-outside curves, low-outside and medium-outside sliders vs. RH; inside fastballs, medium-outside fastballs vs. LH.

Weaknesses: Low fastballs, low-outside curves vs. RH.

Steve Jeltz (Switch Hitter) — *Philadelphia Phillies*

Steve Jeltz Against Right-Handed Pitchers
Overall BARS Batting Average .194

Each cell shows: pitch count (top) / batting average / hits.

Fastball Average .229

	Outside	Middle	Inside
High	7 / 0 / 0	16 / 312 / 5	10 / 100 / 1
Med	32 / 437 / 14	9 / 444 / 4	21 / 190 / 4
Low	9 / 0 / 0	22 / 136 / 3	18 / 111 / 2

Curve Average .294

	Outside	Middle	Inside
High	3 / 0 / 0	0 / 0 / 0	3 / 666 / 2
Med	9 / 111 / 1	0 / 0 / 0	2 / 500 / 1
Low	6 / 166 / 1	5 / 400 / 2	6 / 500 / 3

Slider Average .166

	Outside	Middle	Inside
High	0 / 0 / 0	0 / 0 / 0	0 / 0 / 0
Med	2 / 0 / 0	0 / 0 / 0	0 / 0 / 0
Low	2 / 500 / 1	0 / 0 / 0	2 / 0 / 0

Steve Jeltz Against Left-Handed Pitchers
Overall BARS Batting Average .230

Fastball Average .254

	Inside	Middle	Outside
High	2 / 0 / 0	2 / 500 / 1	3 / 333 / 1
Med	5 / 200 / 1	1 / 0 / 0	19 / 210 / 4
Low	4 / 250 / 1	11 / 181 / 2	8 / 500 / 4

Curve Average .100

	Inside	Middle	Outside
High	0 / 0 / 0	1 / 0 / 0	0 / 0 / 0
Med	1 / 0 / 0	1 / 0 / 0	1 / 0 / 0
Low	1 / 0 / 0	3 / 333 / 1	2 / 0 / 0

Slider Average .125

	Inside	Middle	Outside
High	1 / 0 / 0	0 / 0 / 0	0 / 0 / 0
Med	2 / 0 / 0	0 / 0 / 0	1 / 0 / 0
Low	3 / 333 / 1	0 / 0 / 0	1 / 0 / 0

Switch-hitting Steve Jeltz has some very strong and some very weak fastball locations against right-handed pitchers. He is weak against all inside fastballs and low fastballs. By keeping fastballs inside or low to Jeltz, right-handers could have an advantage.

He hits medium-high outside fastballs extremely well, however (.437). The following fielding strategy and the field diagram on the opposite page show how fielders need to be positioned for fastballs to this location.

MEDIUM-HIGH OUTSIDE FASTBALLS

BATTING AVERAGE .437
Play

Left	Deep and shifted toward the left field line
Center	Medium-deep in straightaway center field
Right	Medium-deep and shifted toward center field
Short	Up middle (shifted toward second base)
Second	Normal position

He hits high-over-the-middle fastballs for a .312 average.

HIGH-OVER-THE-MIDDLE FASTBALLS

BATTING AVERAGE .312
Play

Left	Medium-deep and shifted toward the left field line
Center	Medium-deep in straightaway center field
Right	Deep and shifted toward center field
Short	Normal position
Second	*No instances recorded*

Jeltz has trouble against outside curves (.000, .111 and .166, high to low). He hits inside curves better.

Jeltz Against Left-Handed Pitchers

Jeltz has trouble with medium-high outside and low-over-the-middle fastballs against left-handers. These are his two most highly pitched locations and his low averages bring down his overall average.

He hits .210 against medium-high outside fastballs thrown by left-handers. Batting right-handed, he pulls this pitch deep down the left line. Note that the shortstop needs to play shifted toward second and the second baseman shifted toward first.

MEDIUM-HIGH OUTSIDE FASTBALLS
(THROWN BY LEFT-HANDED PITCHERS)

BATTING AVERAGE .210
Play

Left	Deep and shifted toward the left field line
Center	Medium-deep and shifted toward right field
Right	Deep in straightaway right field
Short	Up middle (shifted toward second base)
Second	Shifted toward first base

Medium-High Outside Fastballs

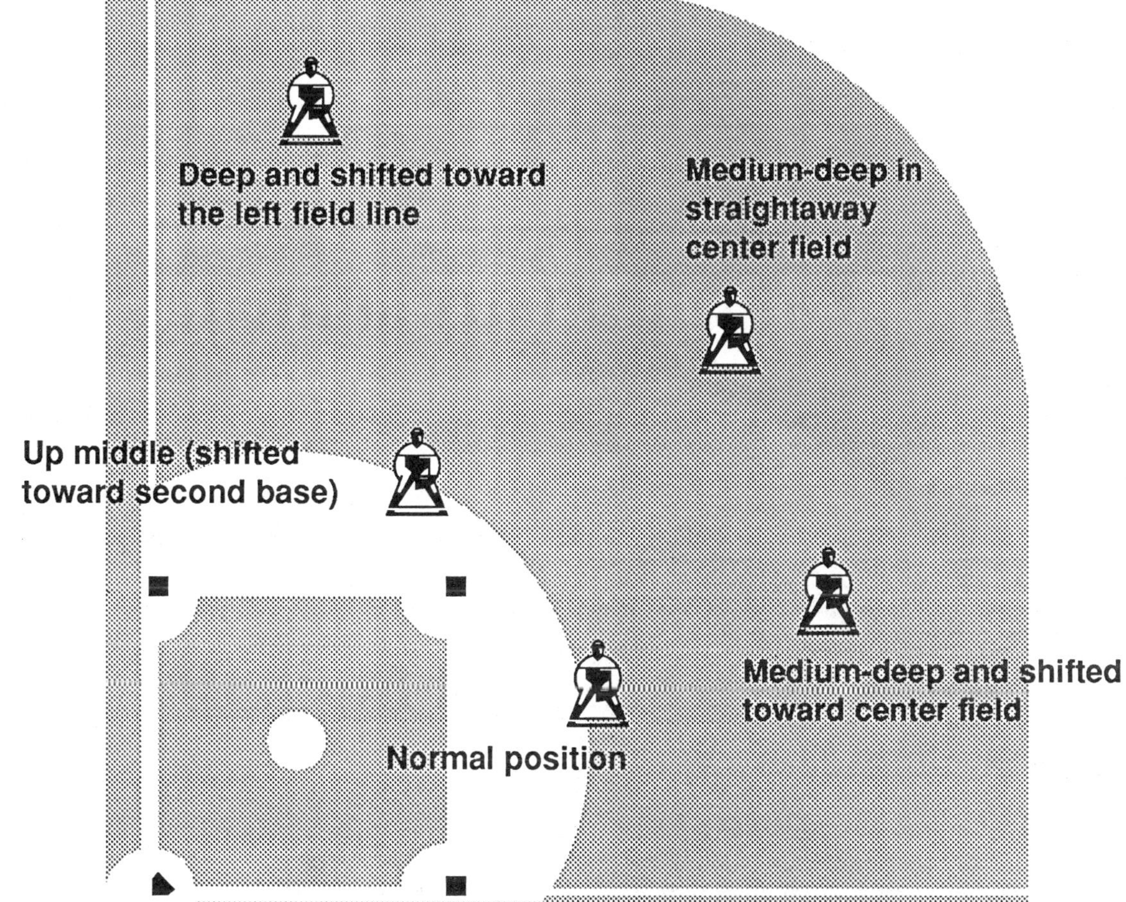

Ahead And Behind In The Count Vs. RH

Ahead

	Fastball Average .210			Curve Average .000		
	Outside	Middle	Inside	Outside	Middle	Inside
High	2/ 0 /0	7/ 285 /2	4/ 0 /0	0/ 0 /0	0/ 0 /0	0/ 0 /0
Med	13/ 461 /6	4/ 500 /2	8/ 125 /1	0/ 0 /0	0/ 0 /0	1/ 0 /0
Low	0/ 0 /0	10/ 0 /0	9/ 111 /1	0/ 0 /0	0/ 0 /0	0/ 0 /0

Behind

	Fastball Average .375			Curve Average .636		
	Outside	Middle	Inside	Outside	Middle	Inside
High	1/ 0 /0	4/ 500 /2	2/ 0 /0	0/ 0 /0	0/ 0 /0	1/ 1000 /1
Med	4/ 750 /3	2/ 500 /1	5/ 400 /2	4/ 250 /1	0/ 0 /0	1/ 1000 /1
Low	2/ 0 /0	1/ 0 /0	3/ 333 /1	1/ 1000 /1	2/ 500 /1	2/ 1000 /2

Overall Evaluation

Against Right-Handed Pitchers

Overall Fastball	
Overall Curve	
Overall Slider	Not enough information

Against Left-Handed Pitchers

Overall Fastball	(○)
Overall Curve	Not enough information
Overall Slider	Not enough information

Comments: Weak vs. inside and low fastballs vs. RH.

Strengths: Medium-outside, high-middle and medium-middle fastballs vs. RH; low-outside fastballs vs. LH.

Weaknesses: Inside fastballs, low fastballs, high-outside fastballs, outside curves vs. RH; medium-outside and low-middle fastballs vs. LH.

Juan Samuel (Right Handed)   *Philadelphia Phillies*

Juan Samuel Against Right-Handed Pitchers
Overall BARS Batting Average .268

Fastball Average .258

	Inside	Middle	Outside
High	20/100 /2	35/285 /10	34/294 /10
Med	29/172 /5	10/500 /5	59/305 /18
Low	14/285 /4	47/276 /13	42/190 /8

Curve Average .289

	Inside	Middle	Outside
High	1/1000 /1	7/142 /1	4/1000 /4
Med	7/285 /2	5/600 /3	38/342 /13
Low	6/0 /0	23/391 /9	47/148 /7

Slider Average .360

	Inside	Middle	Outside
High	0/0 /0	4/250 /1	2/0 /0
Med	5/400 /2	6/500 /3	30/500 /15
Low	3/666 /2	7/571 /4	43/209 /9

Juan Samuel Against Left-Handed Pitchers
Overall BARS Batting Average .275

Fastball Average .301

	Inside	Middle	Outside
High	9/0 /0	7/428 /3	5/0 /0
Med	15/133 /2	11/363 /4	17/647 /11
Low	7/285 /2	20/350 /7	15/200 /3

Curve Average .151

	Inside	Middle	Outside
High	2/0 /0	1/1000 /1	0/0 /0
Med	3/333 /1	2/0 /0	5/0 /0
Low	8/0 /0	7/285 /2	5/200 /1

Slider Average .269

	Inside	Middle	Outside
High	0/0 /0	1/1000 /1	1/1000 /1
Med	3/333 /1	0/0 /0	4/500 /2
Low	12/0 /0	2/1000 /2	3/0 /0

Right-handed hitter Juan Samuel hits .258 against fastballs thrown by right-handed pitchers. He has a solid .305 average against medium-high outside fastballs, sending the ball deep into the left-center gap and straightaway to center and right.

MEDIUM-HIGH OUTSIDE FASTBALLS

BATTING AVERAGE .305
Play

Left	Deep and shifted toward center field
Center	Deep in straightaway center field
Right	Medium-deep in straightaway right field
Short	Normal position
Second	Normal position

His .190 against low-outside fastballs and .276 against low-over-the-middle fastballs offer a weak sector for right-handers to attack. The same is true with his .100 high-inside and .172 medium-high inside sector.

He has a lot of problems with low-outside curves (.148) but he hits medium-high outside curves (.342) and low-over-the-middle curves (.391) excellently.

He also has problems with low-outside sliders (.209). But he hits an exceptional .500 against medium-high outside sliders.

MEDIUM-HIGH OUTSIDE SLIDERS

BATTING AVERAGE .500
Play

Left	Deep in straightaway left field
Center	Medium-deep in straightaway center field
Right	Deep and shifted toward center field
Short	Normal position
Second	Normal position

Samuel Against Left-Handed Pitchers

Samuel is very tough against all over-the-middle fastballs thrown by left-handed pitchers (.428, .363 and .350, high to low). In addition, he hits an outstanding .647 against medium-high outside fastballs against left-handers. The following strategy and the field diagram on the opposite page show how fielders need to play for this pitch.

**MEDIUM-HIGH OUTSIDE FASTBALLS
(THROWN BY LEFT-HANDED PITCHERS)**

BATTING AVERAGE .647
Play

Left	Deep and shifted toward the left field line
Center	Deep and shifted toward left field
Right	Medium-deep in straightaway right field
Short	Normal position
Second	Normal position

Samuel has problems against low-outside fastballs (.200), medium-high inside fastballs (.133) and high-inside fastballs (.000 on 0-for-9). Pinpointing these locations could give left-handers an added edge.

Medium-High Outside Fastballs Vs. LH

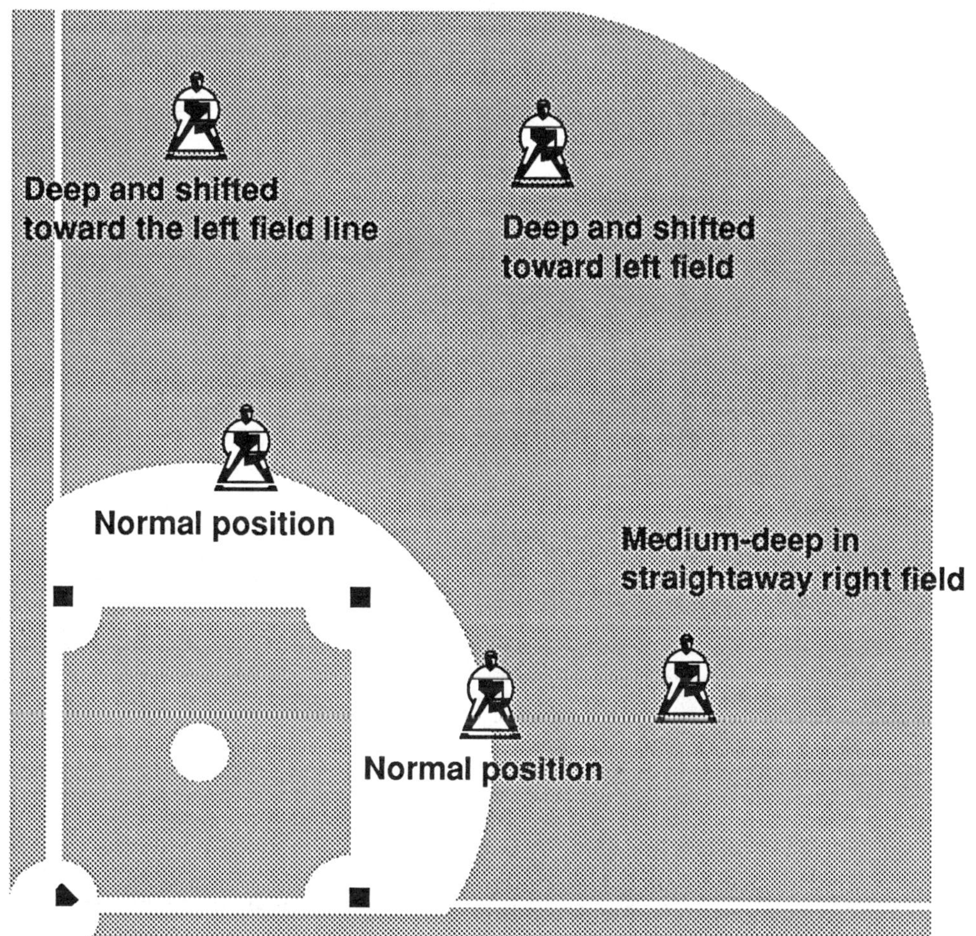

Ahead And Behind In The Count Vs. RH

Ahead

Fastball Average .329

	Inside	Middle	Outside
High	3 / 0 / 0	9 / 222 / 2	7 / 714 / 5
Med	10 / 100 / 1	6 / 500 / 3	22 / 454 / 10
Low	4 / 250 / 1	19 / 368 / 7	11 / 90 / 1

Curve Average .451

	Inside	Middle	Outside
High	0 / 0 / 0	3 / 0 / 0	0 / 0 / 0
Med	1 / 250 / 1	1 / 1000 / 1	11 / 363 / 1
Low	0 / 0 / 0	5 / 800 / 4	7 / 571 / 4

Behind

Fastball Average .391

	Inside	Middle	Outside
High	5 / 400 / 2	14 / 500 / 7	10 / 400 / 4
Med	11 / 272 / 3	0 / 0 / 0	8 / 625 / 5
Low	4 / 500 / 2	12 / 166 / 2	10 / 400 / 4

Curve Average .307

	Inside	Middle	Outside
High	1 / 1000 / 1	4 / 250 / 1	0 / 0 / 0
Med	0 / 0 / 0	3 / 333 / 1	12 / 500 / 6
Low	2 / 0 / 0	8 / 250 / 2	9 / 111 / 1

Overall Evaluation

Against Right-Handed Pitchers

Overall Fastball   (1 ball)

Overall Curve   (3 balls)

Overall Slider   (4 balls)

Against Left-Handed Pitchers

Overall Fastball   (3 balls)

Overall Curve   (1 ball)

Overall Slider   (2 balls)

Comments: Weak vs. low-outside pitches, strong vs. medium-outside pitches.

Strengths: Medium-middle and medium-outside fastballs, low-middle and medium-outside curves, low-middle and medium-outside sliders vs. RH; over-the-middle and medium-outside fastballs vs. LH.

Weaknesses: Inside and low fastballs, low-outside curves and sliders vs. RH; medium-inside and low-outside fastballs, low-inside curves and sliders vs. LH.

Mike Schmidt (Right Handed) — *Philadelphia Phillies*

Mike Schmidt Against Right-Handed Pitchers
Overall BARS Batting Average .239

Fastball Average .264

	Inside	Middle	Outside
High	18 / 55 / 1	17 / 470 / 8	21 / 142 / 3
Med	42 / 333 / 14	23 / 434 / 10	76 / 210 / 16
Low	26 / 346 / 9	68 / 279 / 19	57 / 210 / 12

Curve Average .253

	Inside	Middle	Outside
High	1 / 1000 / 1	4 / 500 / 2	4 / 0 / 0
Med	4 / 250 / 1	5 / 600 / 3	15 / 400 / 6
Low	4 / 250 / 1	10 / 400 / 4	28 / 35 / 1

Slider Average .229

	Inside	Middle	Outside
High	1 / 0 / 0	4 / 500 / 2	3 / 333 / 1
Med	2 / 0 / 0	1 / 1000 / 1	19 / 263 / 5
Low	7 / 428 / 3	13 / 153 / 2	37 / 162 / 6

Mike Schmidt Against Left-Handed Pitchers
Overall BARS Batting Average .335

Fastball Average .346

	Inside	Middle	Outside
High	6 / 500 / 3	5 / 400 / 2	8 / 125 / 1
Med	8 / 125 / 1	4 / 500 / 2	22 / 272 / 6
Low	11 / 363 / 4	21 / 428 / 9	13 / 461 / 6

Curve Average .391

	Inside	Middle	Outside
High	1 / 0 / 0	1 / 0 / 0	0 / 0 / 0
Med	2 / 0 / 0	2 / 1000 / 2	2 / 0 / 0
Low	3 / 666 / 2	5 / 400 / 2	7 / 428 / 3

Slider Average .285

	Inside	Middle	Outside
High	0 / 0 / 0	0 / 0 / 0	0 / 0 / 0
Med	1 / 0 / 0	0 / 0 / 0	0 / 0 / 0
Low	5 / 200 / 1	3 / 333 / 1	5 / 400 / 2

Mike Schmidt, right-handed hitter, has some very strong and some very weak locations in his fastball chart against right-handed pitchers. He has trouble with outside fastballs (.142, .210 and .210, high to low) but he hits medium-high inside (.333), high-over-the-middle (.470) and medium-over-the-middle (.434) fastballs excellently.

He hits medium-high inside fastballs deep to all fields.

MEDIUM-HIGH INSIDE FASTBALLS

BATTING AVERAGE .333

Play

Left   Deep in straightaway left field
Center   Deep in straightaway center field
Right   Deep in straightaway right field
Short   Normal position
Second   Shifted toward first base

He pulls high-over-the-middle fastballs deep down the left line and deep into the left-center gap. Notice that the shortstop needs to play shifted toward second base.

HIGH-OVER-THE-MIDDLE FASTBALLS

BATTING AVERAGE .470

Play

Left   Deep and shifted toward the left field line
Center   Deep and shifted toward left field

Right   Deep in straightaway right field
Short   Up middle (shifted toward second base)
Second   Normal position

Although Schmidt hits only .210 against medium-high outside fastballs, his Ahead and Behind charts show that he hits this pitch very well when ahead in the count (.315 when ahead, .000 on 0-for-10 when behind).

He hits this pitch deep to the outfield and into the hole between third and short when ahead. When behind, he has no recorded instances of hit balls to left field and the shortstop needs to play shifted toward second base.

MEDIUM-HIGH OUTSIDE FASTBALLS
(WHEN AHEAD IN THE COUNT)

BATTING AVERAGE .315

Play

Left   Deep in straightaway left field
Center   Deep and shifted toward left field
Right   Deep in straightaway right field
Short   Shifted toward third base
Second   Normal position

MEDIUM-HIGH OUTSIDE FASTBALLS
(WHEN BEHIND IN THE COUNT)

BATTING AVERAGE .000 (0 for 10)

Play

Left   *No instances recorded*
Center   Short and shifted toward right field

Right Deep in straightaway right field
Short Up middle (shifted toward second base)
Second Normal position

In contrast, he hits low-over-the-middle fastballs considerably better when behind in the count (.454 when behind, .263 when ahead).

LOW-OVER-THE-MIDDLE FASTBALLS
(WHEN BEHIND IN THE COUNT)

BATTING AVERAGE .454
Play
Left Medium-deep and shifted toward the left field line
Center Deep and shifted toward left field
Right Deep in straightaway right field
Short Shifted toward third base
Second Normal position

LOW-OVER-THE-MIDDLE FASTBALLS
(WHEN BEHIND IN THE COUNT)

BATTING AVERAGE .263
Play
Left Deep and shifted toward the left field line
Center Deep in straightaway center field
Right Deep and shifted toward center field
Short Shifted toward third base
Second Normal position

These instances emphasize the necessity of positioning fielders not only for the type and location of pitch, but for the count as well.

Schmidt has a lot of problems with low-outside curves thrown by right-handed pitchers (.035 on 1-for-28). This is a significant weakness right-handers can focus on. He hits medium-high outside and low-over-the-middle curves very well, however (.400 in each location).

He also has a lot of trouble with low-outside sliders (.162 on 6-for-37). In contrast to curves, he hits only .263 against medium-high outside sliders and .153 against low-over-the-middle sliders.

Schmidt Against Left-Handed Pitchers

Schmidt hits an excellent .346 overall against fastballs thrown by left-handed pitchers. His .428 against low-over-the-middle fastballs is exceptional.

LOW-OVER-THE-MIDDLE FASTBALLS
(THROWN BY LEFT-HANDED PITCHERS)

BATTING AVERAGE .428
Play
Left Deep and shifted toward the left field line
Center Deep in straightaway center field
Right Deep and shifted toward center field
Short Normal position
Second *No instances recorded*

His .461 against low-outside fastballs is also extremely good.

LOW-OUTSIDE FASTBALLS
(THROWN BY LEFT-HANDED PITCHERS)

BATTING AVERAGE .350
Play
Left Medium-deep and shifted toward the left field line
Center Deep in straightaway center field
Right Deep in straightaway right field
Short Normal position
Second *No instances recorded*

Ahead And Behind In The Count Vs. RH

Ahead

Fastball Average .333

	Inside	Middle	Outside
High	1/ 0 /0	10/ 400 /4	7/ 285 /2
Med	22/ 272 /6	11/ 545 /6	38/ 315 /12
Low	11/ 454 /5	38/ 263 /10	21/ 380 /8

Curve Average .400

	Inside	Middle	Outside
High	0/ 0 /0	3/ 666 /2	1/ 0 /0
Med	1/ 0 /0	2/ 500 /1	3/ 666 /2
Low	0/ 0 /0	1/ 1000 /1	4/ 0 /0

Behind

Fastball Average .274

	Inside	Middle	Outside
High	2/ 0 /0	5/ 400 /2	1/ 0 /0
Med	7/ 285 /2	4/ 500 /2	10/ 0 /0
Low	1/ 0 /0	11/ 454 /5	10/ 300 /3

Curve Average .357

	Inside	Middle	Outside
High	0/ 0 /0	0/ 0 /0	2/ 0 /0
Med	1/ 0 /0	2/ 1000 /2	3/ 666 /2
Low	1/ 0 /0	2/ 0 /0	3/ 333 /1

Overall Evaluation

Against Right-Handed Pitchers

Overall Fastball	⚾
Overall Curve	⚾ ⚾
Overall Slider	⚾

Against Left-Handed Pitchers

Overall Fastball	⚾ ⚾ ⚾ ⚾
Overall Curve	⚾ ⚾ ⚾ ⚾
Overall Slider	⚾ ⚾ ⚾

Comments: Weak against outside fastballs vs. RH.
Strengths: Medium-inside, low-inside, high-middle and medium-middle fastballs, over-the-middle and medium-outside curves, low-inside sliders vs. RH; over-the-middle and low fastballs, low curves vs. LH.
Weaknesses: Outside and high-inside fastballs, low-outside curves and sliders, low-middle sliders vs. RH; medium-outside, medium-inside and high-outside fastballs vs. LH.

Pittsburgh Pirates

Belliard, Rafael
Bonds, Barry
Bonilla, Bobby
Bream, Sid
Cangelosi, John
LaValliere, Mike
Oberkfell, Ken
Redus, Gary
Reynolds, R. J.
Van Slyke, Andy

Pittsburgh Pirates
BARS System
Hitting Analysis

Rafael Belliard (Right Handed)   *Pittsburgh Pirates*

Rafael Belliard Against Right-Handed Pitchers
Overall BARS Batting Average .221

Fastball Average .303

	Inside	Middle	Outside
High	10 / 400 / 4	10 / 300 / 3	4 / 0 / 0
Med	16 / 125 / 2	1 / 0 / 0	12 / 416 / 5
Low	5 / 200 / 1	11 / 636 / 7	10 / 200 / 2

Curve Average .153

	Inside	Middle	Outside
High	1 / 0 / 0	1 / 0 / 0	3 / 333 / 1
Med	1 / 0 / 0	4 / 0 / 0	6 / 166 / 1
Low	1 / 0 / 0	5 / 600 / 3	17 / 58 / 1

Slider Average .200

	Inside	Middle	Outside
High	0 / 0 / 0	3 / 0 / 0	1 / 0 / 0
Med	1 / 0 / 0	0 / 0 / 0	4 / 500 / 2
Low	1 / 0 / 0	5 / 400 / 2	10 / 100 / 1

Rafael Belliard Against Left-Handed Pitchers
Overall BARS Batting Average .169

Fastball Average .162

	Inside	Middle	Outside
High	3 / 0 / 0	3 / 0 / 0	4 / 0 / 0
Med	4 / 500 / 2	1 / 1000 / 1	13 / 0 / 0
Low	3 / 333 / 1	3 / 333 / 1	3 / 333 / 1

Curve Average .000

	Inside	Middle	Outside
High	1 / 0 / 0	0 / 0 / 0	0 / 0 / 0
Med	0 / 0 / 0	0 / 0 / 0	2 / 0 / 0
Low	1 / 0 / 0	2 / 0 / 0	3 / 0 / 0

Slider Average .500

	Inside	Middle	Outside
High	0 / 0 / 0	0 / 0 / 0	0 / 0 / 0
Med	0 / 0 / 0	0 / 0 / 0	0 / 0 / 0
Low	2 / 0 / 0	4 / 750 / 3	2 / 500 / 1

Rafael Belliard, right-handed hitter, has some very strong fastball locations against right-handed pitchers. These offset the weak locations to bring his BARS overall fastball average to a good .303.

He hits medium-high outside fastballs for a strong .416. He hits this pitch deep into the left-center gap, straightaway to center and right fields and up middle to the shortstop. The field diagram on the opposite page illustrates the BARS fielding strategy for this pitch.

MEDIUM-HIGH OUTSIDE FASTBALLS

BATTING AVERAGE .416
Play
Left   Deep and shifted toward center field
Center   Deep in straightaway center field
Right   Medium-deep in straightaway right field
Short   Up middle (shifted toward second base)
Second   Normal position

His .636 against low-over-the-middle fastballs thrown by right-handers is exceptional. Proper fielding alignment would prevent most of his base hits from this location.

LOW-OVER-THE-MIDDLE FASTBALLS

BATTING AVERAGE .636
Play
Left   Medium-deep in straightaway left field

Center   Medium-deep in straightaway center field
Right   Medium-deep and shifted toward the right line
Short   *No instances recorded*
Second   Normal position

His .400 against high-inside fastballs is also excellent. Notice the very unusual fielding strategy required for this pitch to Belliard.

HIGH-INSIDE FASTBALLS

BATTING AVERAGE .400
Play
Left   *No instances recorded*
Center   Short and shifted toward right field
Right   Short and shifted toward the right field line
Short   Up middle (shifted toward second base)
Second   Normal position

Belliard has trouble with low-outside and medium-high outside curves thrown by right-handers (.058 and .166). He also has trouble with low-outside sliders (.100).

Against left-handed pitchers, Belliard has a significant weakness in his medium-high outside fastball location (.000 on 0-for-13). This location and the adjacent high-outside fastball location are good targets for left-handers.

Medium-High Outside Fastballs

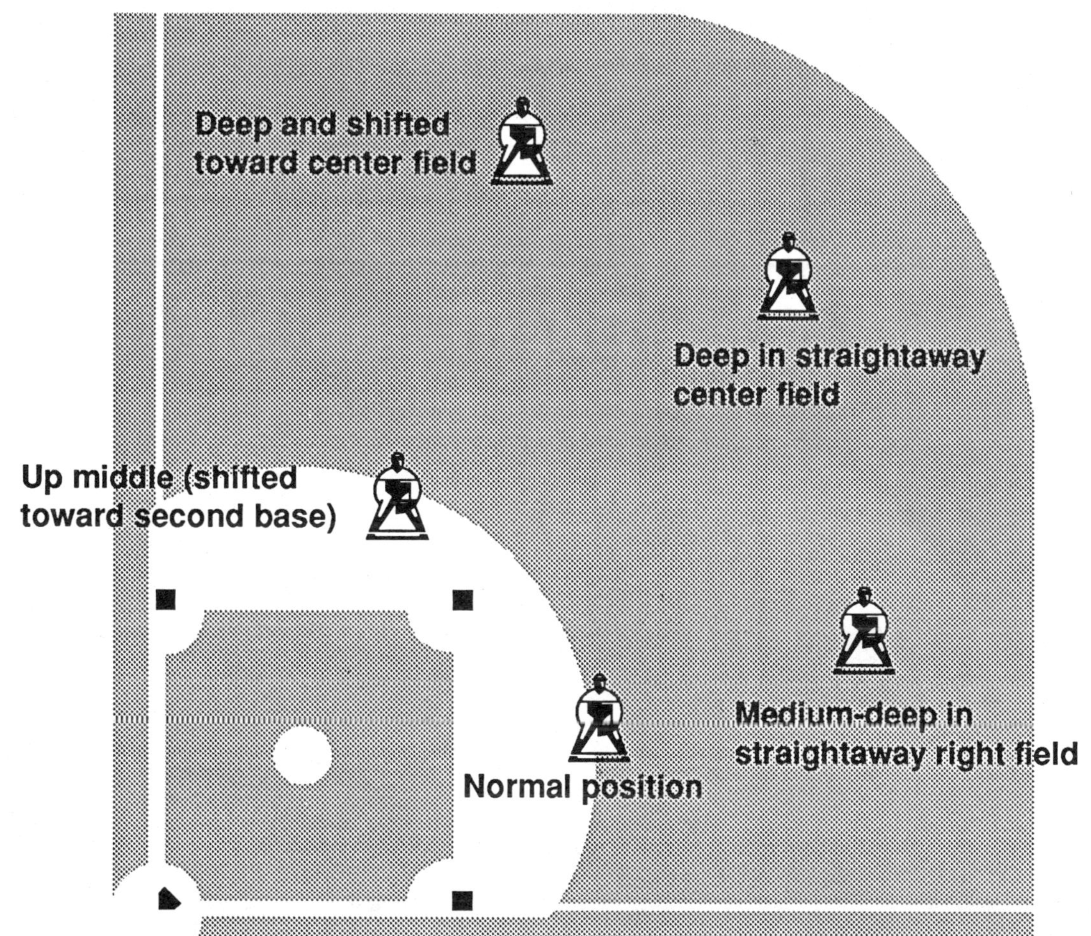

Ahead And Behind In The Count Vs. RH

Ahead

Fastball Average .400

	Inside	Middle	Outside
High	2 1000/2	5 600/3	2 0/0
Med	9 111/1	0 0/0	5 600/3
Low	2 0/0	5 800/4	5 200/1

Curve Average .500

	Inside	Middle	Outside
High	0 0/0	0 0/0	1 1000/1
Med	0 0/0	0 0/0	2 0/0
Low	0 0/0	1 1000/1	0 0/0

Behind

Fastball Average .214

	Inside	Middle	Outside
High	2 0/0	2 0/0	0 0/0
Med	2 0/0	0 0/0	2 500/1
Low	1 0/0	3 333/1	2 500/1

Curve Average .176

	Inside	Middle	Outside
High	1 0/0	1 0/0	1 0/0
Med	0 0/0	2 0/0	3 333/1
Low	1 0/0	2 1000/2	6 0/0

Overall Evaluation
Against Right-Handed Pitchers

Overall Fastball	
Overall Curve	
Overall Slider	

Against Left-Handed Pitchers

Overall Fastball	
Overall Curve	Not enough information
Overall Slider	Not enough information

Comments: Weak vs. medium-outside fastballs vs. LH.
Strengths: High-inside, high-middle, low middle and medium-outside fastballs, low-middle curves and sliders vs. RH.
Weaknesses: Medium-inside, low-inside, low-outside fastballs, medium-outside and low-outside curves, low-outside sliders vs. RH; high fastballs, medium-outside fastballs vs. LH.

Barry Bonds Against Right-Handed Pitchers
Overall BARS Batting Average .259

Fastball Average .286

	Outside	Middle	Inside
High	19 / 157 / 3	17 / 470 / 8	18 / 222 / 4
Med	29 / 275 / 8	7 / 428 / 3	20 / 250 / 5
Low	20 / 200 / 4	20 / 400 / 8	14 / 285 / 4

Curve Average .205

	Outside	Middle	Inside
High	3 / 0 / 0	2 / 0 / 0	3 / 333 / 1
Med	9 / 333 / 3	2 / 0 / 0	3 / 333 / 1
Low	4 / 0 / 0	5 / 200 / 1	3 / 333 / 1

Slider Average .193

	Outside	Middle	Inside
High	2 / 500 / 1	0 / 0 / 0	1 / 0 / 0
Med	7 / 142 / 1	1 / 0 / 0	7 / 285 / 2
Low	1 / 0 / 0	1 / 0 / 0	11 / 181 / 2

Barry Bonds Against Left-Handed Pitchers
Overall BARS Batting Average .259

Fastball Average .296

	Outside	Middle	Inside
High	2 / 0 / 0	3 / 1000 / 3	4 / 0 / 0
Med	13 / 307 / 4	0 / 0 / 0	14 / 357 / 5
Low	5 / 0 / 0	9 / 444 / 4	4 / 0 / 0

Curve Average .238

	Outside	Middle	Inside
High	0 / 0 / 0	1 / 0 / 0	1 / 0 / 0
Med	5 / 200 / 1	1 / 0 / 0	3 / 666 / 2
Low	5 / 0 / 0	2 / 500 / 1	3 / 333 / 1

Slider Average .277

	Outside	Middle	Inside
High	0 / 0 / 0	1 / 0 / 0	1 / 1000 / 1
Med	6 / 166 / 1	1 / 0 / 0	1 / 1000 / 1
Low	5 / 0 / 0	3 / 666 / 2	0 / 0 / 0

Left-handed hitter Barry Bonds has some problems with inside and outside fastballs against right-handed pitchers. He hits all over-the-middle fastballs exceptionally well, however.

He hits .275 against medium-high outside fastballs. He hits this pitch straightaway to left and center and into the deep right-center gap.

His .400 against low-over-the-middle fastballs is excellent. He hits this ball deep to all fields.

LOW-OVER-THE-MIDDLE FASTBALLS

BATTING AVERAGE .400

Play

Left	Deep in straightaway left field
Center	Deep and shifted toward left field
Right	Deep and shifted toward center field
Short	Up middle (shifted toward second base)
Second	Normal position

His .470 against high-over-the-middle fastballs is exceptionally strong. The following fielding strategy and the field diagram on the opposite page show how fielders need to be aligned for this pitch.

HIGH-OVER-THE-MIDDLE FASTBALLS

BATTING AVERAGE .470

Play

Left	Deep and shifted toward the left field line
Center	Deep and shifted toward left field
Right	Deep and shifted toward center field
Short	Up middle (shifted toward second base)
Second	Normal position

Bonds has a lot of trouble with low-inside sliders against right-handers (.181). He hits medium-high inside sliders fairly well, however (.285).

Against left-handed pitchers he hits medium-high outside fastballs (.307), low-over-the-middle fastballs (.444) and medium-high inside fastballs (.357) very well. He hits medium-high inside fastballs deep to all fields.

MEDIUM-HIGH INSIDE FASTBALLS
(THROWN BY LEFT-HANDED PITCHERS)

BATTING AVERAGE .357

Play

Left	Deep and shifted toward the left field line
Center	Deep in straightaway center field
Right	Deep in straightaway right field
Short	Shifted toward third base
Second	Shifted toward first base

High-Over-The-Middle Fastballs

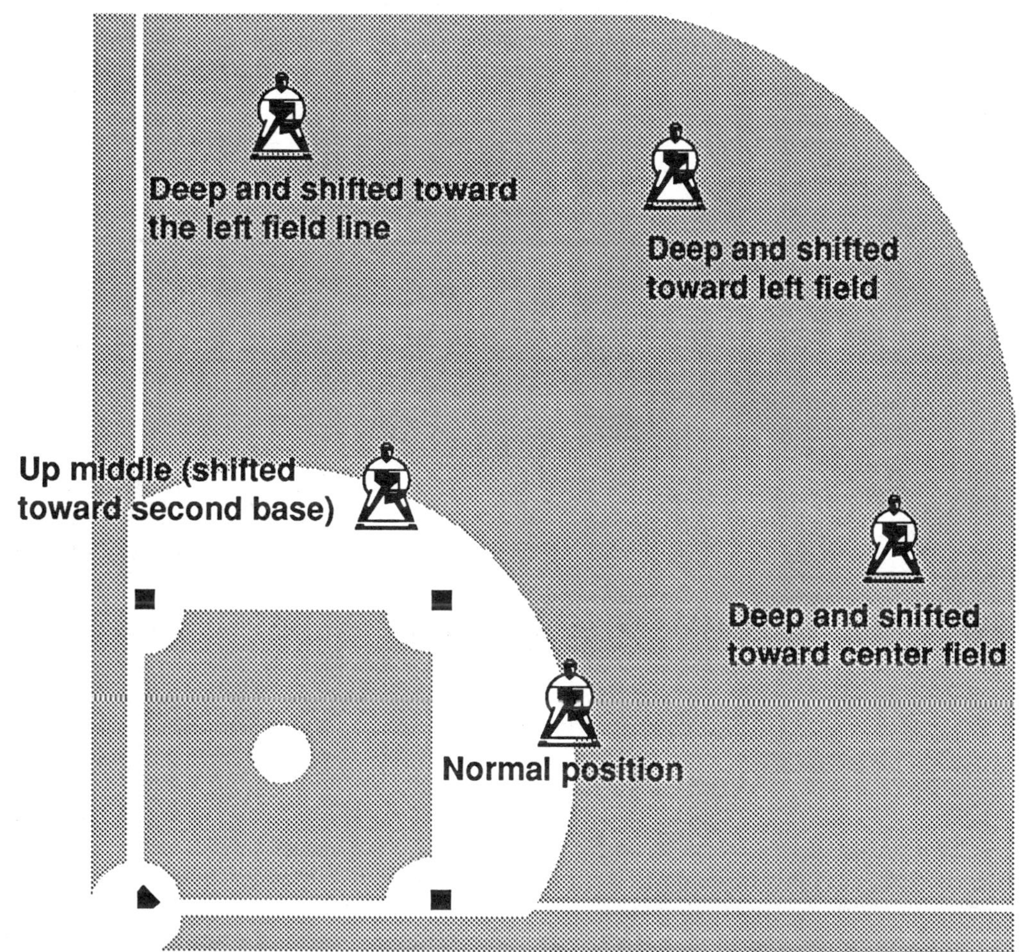

Ahead And Behind In The Count Vs. RH

Ahead

	Fastball Average .383			Curve Average .250		
	Outside	Middle	Inside	Outside	Middle	Inside
High	6/ 333 /2	5/ 600 /3	6/ 500 /3	0/ 0 /0	0/ 0 /0	1/ 0 /0
Med	17/ 352 /6	3/ 1000 /3	5/ 0 /0	1/ 0 /0	2/ 0 /0	1/ 1000 /1
Low	6/ 0 /0	15/ 533 /8	10/ 300 /3	0/ 0 /0	2/ 0 /0	1/ 1000 /1

Behind

	Fastball Average .233			Curve Average .333		
	Outside	Middle	Inside	Outside	Middle	Inside
High	3/ 333 /1	7/ 428 /3	7/ 142 /1	0/ 0 /0	0/ 0 /0	2/ 500 /1
Med	3/ 333 /1	0/ 0 /0	4/ 250 /1	2/ 500 /1	0/ 0 /0	1/ 0 /0
Low	2/ 0 /0	3/ 0 /0	1/ 0 /0	1/ 0 /0	2/ 500 /1	1/ 0 /0

Overall Evaluation

Against Right-Handed Pitchers

Overall Fastball  ⚾⚾ ⚾⚾

Overall Curve ⚾⚾

Overall Slider ⚾⚾

Against Left-Handed Pitchers

Overall Fastball ⚾⚾ ⚾⚾

Overall Curve ⚾⚾

Overall Slider ⚾⚾ ⚾⚾ ⚾⚾

Comments: Weak vs. outside and inside fastballs vs. RH.

Strengths: Over-the-middle fastballs, medium-outside curves vs. RH; medium-outside, low-middle and medium-inside fastballs vs. LH.

Weaknesses: Outside and inside fastballs, low sliders and medium-outside sliders vs. RH; outside curves, outside sliders vs. LH.

Bobby Bonilla (Switch Hitter) — *Pittsburgh Pirates*

Bobby Bonilla Against Right-Handed Pitchers
Overall BARS Batting Average .288

Fastball Average .362

	Outside	Middle	Inside
High	11/90/1	9/444/4	8/250/2
Med	32/281/9	5/400/2	26/423/11
Low	5/200/1	18/444/8	21/523/11

Curve Average .138

	Outside	Middle	Inside
High	5/200/1	2/500/1	0/0/0
Med	5/200/1	2/0/0	6/0/0
Low	6/0/0	5/400/2	5/0/0

Slider Average .133

	Outside	Middle	Inside
High	0/0/0	0/0/0	0/0/0
Med	2/0/0	0/0/0	4/0/0
Low	2/500/1	3/0/0	4/250/1

Bobby Bonilla Against Left-Handed Pitchers
Overall BARS Batting Average .274

Fastball Average .296

	Inside	Middle	Outside
High	7/285/2	10/400/4	6/166/1
Med	11/363/4	5/600/3	34/264/9
Low	9/222/2	11/454/5	15/133/2

Curve Average .388

	Inside	Middle	Outside
High	1/1000/1	2/500/1	2/500/1
Med	1/0/0	0/0/0	8/500/4
Low	0/0/0	4/0/0	0/0/0

Slider Average .133

	Inside	Middle	Outside
High	0/0/0	0/0/0	1/0/0
Med	5/400/2	1/0/0	1/0/0
Low	5/0/0	0/0/0	2/0/0

Switch-hitting Bobby Bonilla has a very strong sector in his fastball chart against right-handed pitchers (.423 medium-high inside, .523 low-inside and .444 low-over-the-middle). Right-handers would be better off to throw him outside fastballs rather than to chance the ball drifting into these strong locations.

He hits medium-high inside fastballs straightaway to left and center and into the medium-deep right-center gap.

MEDIUM-HIGH INSIDE FASTBALLS

BATTING AVERAGE .423
Play

Left	Deep in straightaway left field
Center	Medium-deep in straightaway center field
Right	Medium-deep and shifted toward center field
Short	Up middle (shifted toward second base)
Second	Normal position

He hits low-inside fastballs deep to all fields.

LOW-INSIDE FASTBALLS

BATTING AVERAGE .523
Play

Left	Deep in straightaway left field
Center	Deep in straightaway center field
Right	Deep and shifted toward center field
Short	Shifted toward third base
Second	Shifted toward first base

He pulls low-over-the-middle fastballs deep down the right line.

LOW-OVER-THE-MIDDLE FASTBALLS

BATTING AVERAGE .444
Play

Left	Deep in straightaway left field
Center	Medium-deep in straightaway center field
Right	Deep and shifted toward the right field line
Short	Shifted toward third base
Second	Normal position

He hits a fairly decent .281 against medium-high outside fastballs thrown by right-handers. He sends this pitch medium-deep into the left- and right-center gaps.

MEDIUM-HIGH OUTSIDE FASTBALLS

BATTING AVERAGE .281
Play

Left	Medium-deep and shifted toward center field
Center	Medium-deep in straightaway center field
Right	Medium-deep and shifted toward center field
Short	Normal position
Second	Normal position

Bonilla has some problems with inside and outside curves thrown by right-handers. Considering his strength against fastballs, right-handers should consider mixing in more breaking pitches to him.

Bonilla Against Left-Handed Pitchers

Bonilla doesn't hit fastballs as well overall against left-handed pitchers, but he has some strong locations. He hits medium-high inside fastballs for a solid .363 average.

MEDIUM-HIGH INSIDE FASTBALLS
(THROWN BY LEFT-HANDED PITCHERS)

BATTING AVERAGE .363
Play

Left	Deep in straightaway left field
Center	Short in straightaway center field
Right	Medium-deep in straightaway right field
Short	Normal position
Second	*No instances recorded*

His .454 against low-over-the-middle fastballs thrown by left-handers is exceptionally strong.

LOW-OVER-THE-MIDDLE FASTBALLS
(THROWN BY LEFT-HANDED PITCHERS)

BATTING AVERAGE .454
Play

Left	Deep and shifted toward the left field line
Center	Medium-deep in straightaway center field
Right	Deep and shifted toward the right field line
Short	Normal position
Second	*No instances recorded*

His .400 against high-over-the-middle fastballs is also excellent. He hits this pitch medium-deep to the outfield.

HIGH-OVER-THE-MIDDLE FASTBALLS
(THROWN BY LEFT-HANDED PITCHERS)

BATTING AVERAGE .400
Play

Left	Medium-deep in straightaway left field
Center	Medium-deep in straightaway center field
Right	Medium-deep in straightaway right field
Short	Shifted toward third base
Second	Shifted toward first base

Bonilla has trouble with outside fastballs thrown by left-handers (.166, .264 and .133). He hits medium-outside fastballs down both lines. His low average in this location indicates that most of his hit balls are easy pop-ups or ground balls.

MEDIUM-HIGH OUTSIDE FASTBALLS
(THROWN BY LEFT-HANDED PITCHERS)

BATTING AVERAGE .264
Play

Left	Medium-deep and shifted toward the left field line
Center	Medium-deep in straightaway center field
Right	Medium-deep and shifted toward the right line
Short	Normal position
Second	Shifted toward first base

Bonilla hits medium-high outside curves very well against left-handers (.500).

Ahead And Behind In The Count Vs. RH

Ahead

Fastball Average .462

	Outside	Middle	Inside
High	4/ 250 /1	2/ 500 /1	4/ 500 /2
Med	13/ 384 /5	1/ 1000 /1	7/ 571 /4
Low	2/ 0 /0	7/ 285 /2	14/ 642 /9

Curve Average .285

	Outside	Middle	Inside
High	1/ 1000 /1	0/ 0 /0	0/ 0 /0
Med	0/ 0 /0	1/ 0 /0	3/ 0 /0
Low	0/ 0 /0	2/ 500 /1	0/ 0 /0

Behind

Fastball Average .448

	Outside	Middle	Inside
High	0/ 0 /0	4/ 500 /2	0/ 0 /0
Med	9/ 222 /2	3/ 333 /1	5/ 400 /2
Low	1/ 1000 /1	6/ 833 /5	1/ 0 /0

Curve Average .100

	Outside	Middle	Inside
High	3/ 0 /0	2/ 500 /1	0/ 0 /0
Med	1/ 0 /0	0/ 0 /0	0/ 0 /0
Low	1/ 0 /0	1/ 0 /0	2/ 0 /0

Overall Evaluation

Against Right-Handed Pitchers

Overall Fastball	4
Overall Curve	1
Overall Slider	1

Against Left-Handed Pitchers

Overall Fastball	2
Overall Curve	4
Overall Slider	1

Comments: Strong vs. medium-inside, low-inside and all over-the-middle fastballs vs. RH.

Strengths: As above vs. RH; medium-inside and all over-the-middle fastballs, medium-outside curves vs. LH.

Weaknesses: High-outside fastballs, outside and inside curves vs. RH; low-inside fastballs, outside fastballs vs. LH.

Sid Bream Against Right-Handed Pitchers
Overall BARS Batting Average .222

Fastball Average .233

	Outside	Middle	Inside
High	13 / 307 / 4	21 / 285 / 6	20 / 250 / 5
Med	44 / 340 / 15	3 / 333 / 1	21 / 95 / 2
Low	13 / 0 / 0	19 / 210 / 4	13 / 153 / 2

Curve Average .153

	Outside	Middle	Inside
High	0 / 0 / 0	3 / 333 / 1	2 / 0 / 0
Med	5 / 0 / 0	4 / 250 / 1	6 / 166 / 1
Low	4 / 250 / 1	7 / 285 / 2	8 / 0 / 0

Slider Average .416

	Outside	Middle	Inside
High	2 / 0 / 0	2 / 1000 / 2	1 / 1000 / 1
Med	1 / 0 / 0	0 / 0 / 0	9 / 333 / 3
Low	2 / 0 / 0	3 / 666 / 2	4 / 500 / 2

Sid Bream Against Left-Handed Pitchers
Overall BARS Batting Average .213

Fastball Average .301

	Outside	Middle	Inside
High	6 / 0 / 0	7 / 714 / 5	8 / 375 / 3
Med	14 / 357 / 5	1 / 0 / 0	12 / 166 / 2
Low	6 / 166 / 1	1 / 1000 / 1	8 / 250 / 2

Curve Average .076

	Outside	Middle	Inside
High	4 / 0 / 0	2 / 0 / 0	1 / 0 / 0
Med	10 / 200 / 2	1 / 0 / 0	0 / 0 / 0
Low	5 / 0 / 0	1 / 0 / 0	2 / 0 / 0

Slider Average .142

	Outside	Middle	Inside
High	0 / 0 / 0	1 / 1000 / 1	0 / 0 / 0
Med	7 / 0 / 0	1 / 0 / 0	2 / 500 / 1
Low	7 / 142 / 1	3 / 0 / 0	0 / 0 / 0

Left-handed hitter Sid Bream has a lot of trouble with inside fastballs and low fastballs against right-handed pitchers. He has a strong sector in the four fastball locations consisting of high-outside/high-over-the-middle/medium-high outside/medium-over-the-middle. By staying away from this strong area, right-handers can gain an edge.

Bream hits medium-high outside fastballs deep down the left line (his opposite field) and medium-deep to straightaway center and right fields. Notice that the shortstop needs to be shifted toward second base. The field diagram on the opposite page illustrates the BARS fielding strategy for this pitch.

MEDIUM-HIGH OUTSIDE FASTBALLS

BATTING AVERAGE .340

Play

Left	Deep and shifted toward the left field line
Center	Medium-deep in straightaway center field
Right	Medium-deep in straightaway right field
Short	Up middle (shifted toward second base)
Second	Normal position

Bream also hits high-outside fastballs down the left line.

HIGH-OUTSIDE FASTBALLS

BATTING AVERAGE .307

Play

Left	Deep and shifted toward the left field line
Center	Deep in straightaway center field
Right	Deep and shifted toward center field
Short	*No instances recorded*
Second	Shifted toward first base

Bream seems to have problems with outside and inside curves thrown by right-handers. He hits very well against inside sliders.

Bream Against Left-Handed Pitchers

Bream hits medium-high outside fastballs very strongly against left-handed pitchers (.357). He hits this pitch straightaway to the outfield and to the right side of the infield.

MEDIUM-HIGH OUTSIDE FASTBALLS
(THROWN BY LEFT-HANDED PITCHERS)

BATTING AVERAGE .357

Play

Left	Deep in straightaway left field
Center	Deep in straightaway center field
Right	Medium-deep in straightaway right field
Short	Up middle (shifted toward second base)
Second	Shifted toward first base

He has trouble with outside curves and outside sliders against left-handers.

Medium-High Outside Fastballs

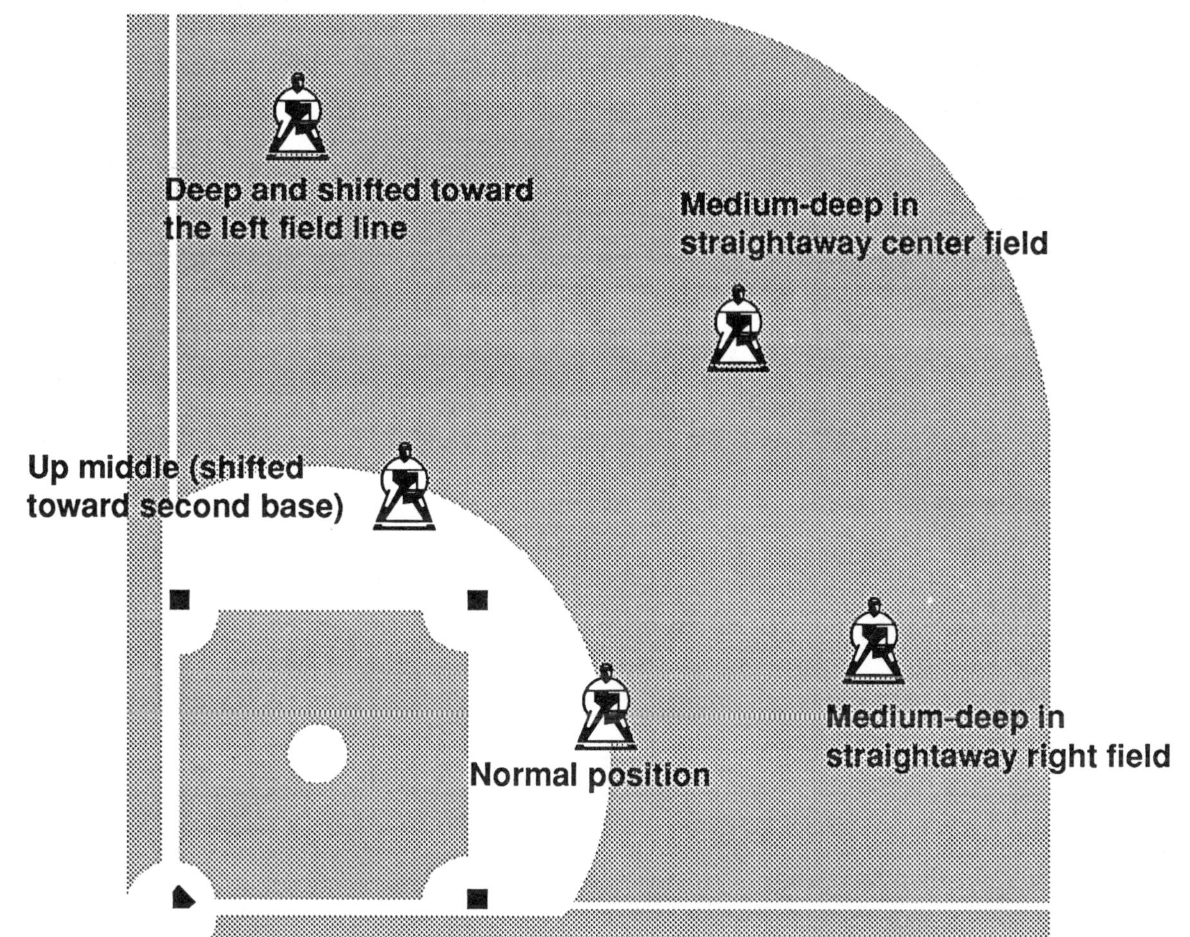

Ahead And Behind In The Count Vs. RH

Ahead

Fastball Average .240

	Outside	Middle	Inside
High	4/ 500 / 2	9/ 555 / 5	9/ 111 / 1
Med	28/ 307 / 8	2/ 500 / 1	7/ 0 / 0
Low	6/ 0 / 0	11/ 272 / 3	9/ 0 / 0

Curve Average .000

	Outside	Middle	Inside
High	0/ 0 / 0	1/ 0 / 0	1/ 0 / 0
Med	3/ 0 / 0	1/ 0 / 0	1/ 0 / 0
Low	0/ 0 / 0	2/ 0 / 0	1/ 0 / 0

Behind

Fastball Average .318

	Outside	Middle	Inside
High	2/ 0 / 0	3/ 333 / 1	4/ 250 / 1
Med	4/ 750 / 3	0/ 0 / 0	4/ 250 / 1
Low	2/ 0 / 0	2/ 500 / 1	1/ 0 / 0

Curve Average .307

	Outside	Middle	Inside
High	0/ 0 / 0	1/ 1000 / 1	0/ 0 / 0
Med	2/ 0 / 0	3/ 333 / 1	1/ 0 / 0
Low	2/ 500 / 1	3/ 333 / 1	1/ 0 / 0

Overall Evaluation

Against Right-Handed Pitchers

Overall Fastball ⚾⚾
Overall Curve ⚾⚾
Overall Slider ⚾⚾⚾⚾

Against Left-Handed Pitchers

Overall Fastball ⚾⚾⚾
Overall Curve ⚾⚾
Overall Slider ⚾

Comments: Weak against low fastballs and inside fastballs vs. RH.

Strengths: High-outside, high-middle and medium-outside fastballs, medium-inside sliders vs. RH; medium-outside, high-middle and high-inside fastballs vs. LH.

Weaknesses: Low and inside fastballs, inside curves, outside curves vs. RH; medium-inside and low-inside fastballs, outside curves and sliders vs. LH.

John Cangelosi (Switch Hitter) — *Pittsburgh Pirates*

John Cangelosi Against Right-Handed Pitchers
Overall BARS Batting Average .232

Fastball Average .257

	Outside	Middle	Inside
High	2 / 500 / 1	13 / 307 / 4	8 / 125 / 1
Med	43 / 209 / 9	8 / 500 / 4	25 / 400 / 10
Low	2 / 0 / 0	15 / 200 / 3	12 / 83 / 1

Curve Average .214

	Outside	Middle	Inside
High	0 / 0 / 0	1 / 0 / 0	0 / 0 / 0
Med	7 / 142 / 1	0 / 0 / 0	3 / 333 / 1
Low	0 / 0 / 0	2 / 500 / 1	1 / 0 / 0

Slider Average .222

	Outside	Middle	Inside
High	0 / 0 / 0	2 / 0 / 0	0 / 0 / 0
Med	1 / 0 / 0	0 / 0 / 0	1 / 1000 / 1
Low	1 / 0 / 0	0 / 0 / 0	4 / 250 / 1

John Cangelosi Against Left-Handed Pitchers
Overall BARS Batting Average .247

Fastball Average .276

	Inside	Middle	Outside
High	4 / 750 / 3	12 / 333 / 4	6 / 166 / 1
Med	9 / 333 / 3	2 / 500 / 1	29 / 275 / 8
Low	3 / 333 / 1	14 / 214 / 3	15 / 133 / 2

Curve Average .000

	Inside	Middle	Outside
High	0 / 0 / 0	0 / 0 / 0	1 / 0 / 0
Med	0 / 0 / 0	0 / 0 / 0	5 / 0 / 0
Low	0 / 0 / 0	0 / 0 / 0	1 / 0 / 0

Slider Average .000

	Inside	Middle	Outside
High	0 / 0 / 0	0 / 0 / 0	0 / 0 / 0
Med	0 / 0 / 0	1 / 0 / 0	1 / 0 / 0
Low	3 / 0 / 0	0 / 0 / 0	0 / 0 / 0

Switch-hitting John Cangelosi has problems with low fastballs against right-handed pitchers. He also has trouble with medium-high outside fastballs. He hits this pitch medium-deep to left and center and deep into the right-center gap.

MEDIUM-HIGH OUTSIDE FASTBALLS

BATTING AVERAGE .209
Play

Left	Medium-deep in straightaway left field
Center	Medium-deep in straightaway center field
Right	Deep and shifted toward center field
Short	Normal position
Second	Shifted toward first base

He hits medium-high inside fastballs extremely well (.400). The following fielding strategy and the field diagram on the opposite page show how fielders need to be positioned for this pitch.

MEDIUM-HIGH INSIDE FASTBALLS

BATTING AVERAGE .400
Play

Left	Medium-deep and shifted toward the left field line
Center	Deep in straightaway center field
Right	Deep and shifted toward center field
Short	Up middle (shifted toward second base)
Second	Normal position

He hits well against high-over-the-middle fastballs thrown by right-handers (.307).

HIGH-OVER-THE-MIDDLE FASTBALLS

BATTING AVERAGE .307
Play

Left	Medium-deep and shifted toward the left field line
Center	Medium-deep in straightaway center field
Right	Medium-deep and shifted toward center field
Short	Normal position
Second	*No instances recorded*

Against left-handed pitchers, Cangelosi hits .275 against medium-high outside fastballs. Batting right-handed, he pulls this pitch to the outfield.

MEDIUM-HIGH OUTSIDE FASTBALLS (THROWN BY LEFT-HANDED PITCHERS)

BATTING AVERAGE .275
Play

Left	Deep and shifted toward the left field line
Center	Deep and shifted toward left field
Right	Deep and shifted toward center field
Short	Up middle (shifted toward second base)
Second	Normal position

He hits a strong .333 against high-over-the-middle fastballs thrown by left-handers.

Medium-High Inside Fastballs

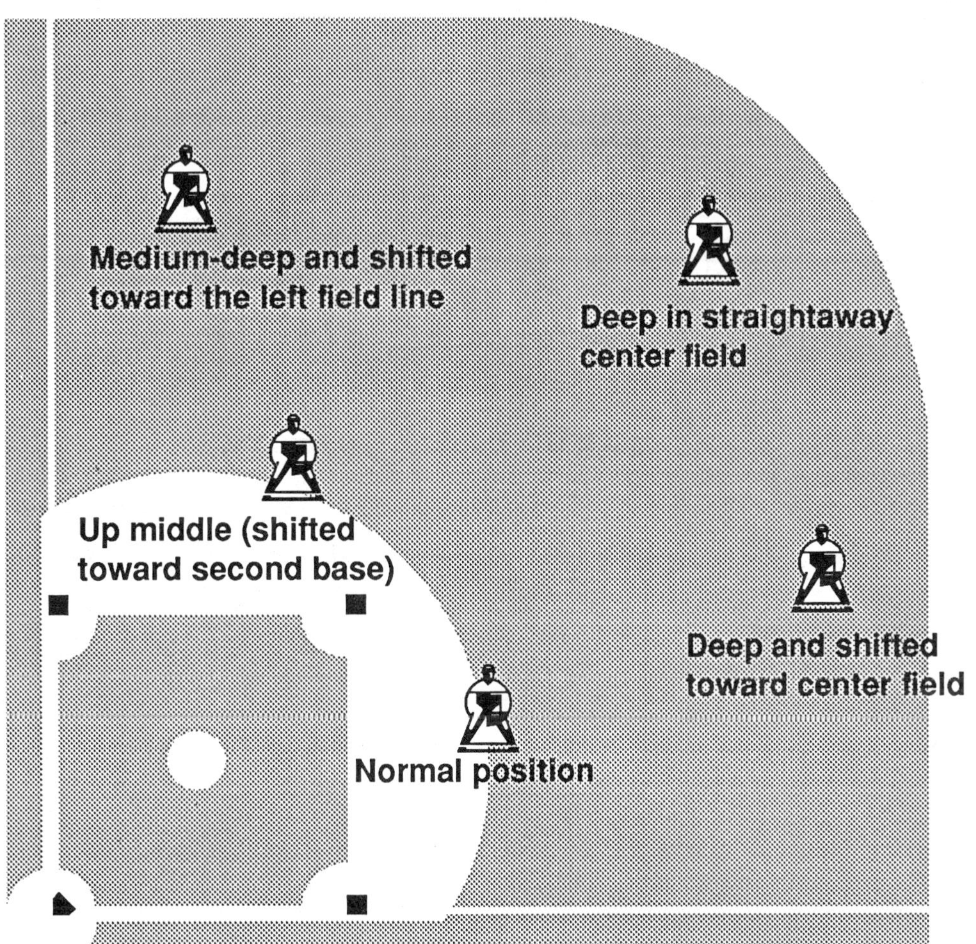

Ahead And Behind In The Count Vs. RH

Ahead

Fastball Average .310

	Outside	Middle	Inside
High	1 / 1000 / 1	11 / 363 / 4	3 / 333 / 1
Med	19 / 368 / 7	3 / 333 / 1	12 / 250 / 3
Low	0 / 0 / 0	5 / 0 / 0	4 / 250 / 1

Curve Average .333

	Outside	Middle	Inside
High	0 / 0 / 0	0 / 0 / 0	0 / 0 / 0
Med	1 / 0 / 0	0 / 0 / 0	1 / 0 / 0
Low	0 / 0 / 0	1 / 1000 / 1	0 / 0 / 0

Behind

Fastball Average .227

	Outside	Middle	Inside
High	0 / 0 / 0	0 / 0 / 0	2 / 0 / 0
Med	6 / 0 / 0	4 / 500 / 2	4 / 500 / 2
Low	1 / 0 / 0	4 / 250 / 1	1 / 0 / 0

Curve Average .250

	Outside	Middle	Inside
High	0 / 0 / 0	1 / 0 / 0	0 / 0 / 0
Med	0 / 0 / 0	0 / 0 / 0	2 / 500 / 1
Low	0 / 0 / 0	1 / 0 / 0	0 / 0 / 0

Overall Evaluation

Against Right-Handed Pitchers

Overall Fastball 

Overall Curve 

Overall Slider — Not enough information

Against Left-Handed Pitchers

Overall Fastball

Overall Curve — Not enough Information

Overall Slider — Not enough information

Comments: Weak against low fastballs and medium-outside fastballs vs. RH.

Strengths: High-middle and medium-inside fastballs vs. RH; inside fastballs & high-middle fastballs vs. LH.

Weaknesses: Low fastballs, medium-outside and high-inside fastballs, medium-outside curves vs. RH; outside fastballs, low-middle fastballs vs. LH.

Mike LaValliere (Left Handed) — *Pittsburgh Pirates*

Mike LaValliere Against Right-Handed Pitchers
Overall BARS Batting Average .258

Fastball Average .260

	Outside	Middle	Inside
High	10 / 300 /3	19 / 315 /6	12 / 83 /1
Med	23 / 304 /7	4 / 250 /1	23 / 217 /5
Low	13 / 76 /1	16 / 437 /7	18 / 277 /5

Curve Average .133

	Outside	Middle	Inside
High	0 / 0 /0	3 / 333 /1	4 / 250 /1
Med	5 / 0 /0	0 / 0 /0	5 / 200 /1
Low	1 / 0 /0	5 / 200 /1	7 / 0 /0

Slider Average .666

	Outside	Middle	Inside
High	1 / 1000 /1	0 / 0 /0	0 / 0 /0
Med	2 / 1000 /2	1 / 1000 /1	4 / 750 /3
Low	2 / 500 /1	0 / 0 /0	5 / 400 /2

Mike LaValliere Against Left-Handed Pitchers
Overall BARS Batting Average .133

Fastball Average .172

	Outside	Middle	Inside
High	2 / 0 /0	4 / 250 /1	2 / 1000 /2
Med	7 / 142 /1	1 / 0 /0	2 / 0 /0
Low	5 / 0 /0	4 / 250 /1	2 / 0 /0

Curve Average .000

	Outside	Middle	Inside
High	0 / 0 /0	0 / 0 /0	0 / 0 /0
Med	0 / 0 /0	0 / 0 /0	0 / 0 /0
Low	2 / 0 /0	3 / 0 /0	0 / 0 /0

Slider Average .111

	Outside	Middle	Inside
High	1 / 0 /0	1 / 0 /0	1 / 1000 /1
Med	1 / 0 /0	0 / 0 /0	0 / 0 /0
Low	3 / 0 /0	1 / 0 /0	1 / 0 /0

Left-handed hitting Mike LaValliere has trouble with inside fastballs and with low-outside fastballs against right-handed pitchers. But he hits medium-high outside fastballs at a .304 clip. He goes deep down the left line (his opposite field) with this pitch. The field diagram on the opposite page illustrates the BARS fielding strategy for this pitch to him.

MEDIUM-HIGH OUTSIDE FASTBALLS

BATTING AVERAGE .304
Play

Left	Deep and shifted toward the left field line
Center	Medium-deep and shifted toward right field
Right	Medium-deep in straightaway right field
Short	Up middle (shifted toward second base)
Second	Normal position

His .437 against low-over-the-middle fastballs is extremely high. He hits this pitch down both lines.

LOW-OVER-THE-MIDDLE FASTBALLS

BATTING AVERAGE .437
Play

Left	Medium-deep and shifted toward the left field line
Center	Medium-deep in straightaway center field
Right	Deep and shifted toward the right field line
Short	*No instances recorded*
Second	Shifted toward first base

His .315 against high-over-the-middle fastballs is good.

HIGH-OVER-THE-MIDDLE FASTBALLS

BATTING AVERAGE .315
Play

Left	Deep in straightaway left field
Center	Deep and shifted toward left field
Right	Deep in straightaway right field
Short	Up middle (shifted toward second base)
Second	Normal position

He goes to his opposite field with high-outside fastballs (.300).

HIGH-OUTSIDE FASTBALLS

BATTING AVERAGE .300
Play

Left	Medium-deep and shifted toward the left field line
Center	Deep and shifted toward left field
Right	Deep and shifted toward center field
Second	*No instances recorded*
Second	Normal position

LaValliere has trouble with low curves and outside curves thrown by right-handed pitchers. He also has trouble with outside fastballs thrown by left-handed pitchers.

Medium-High Outside Fastballs

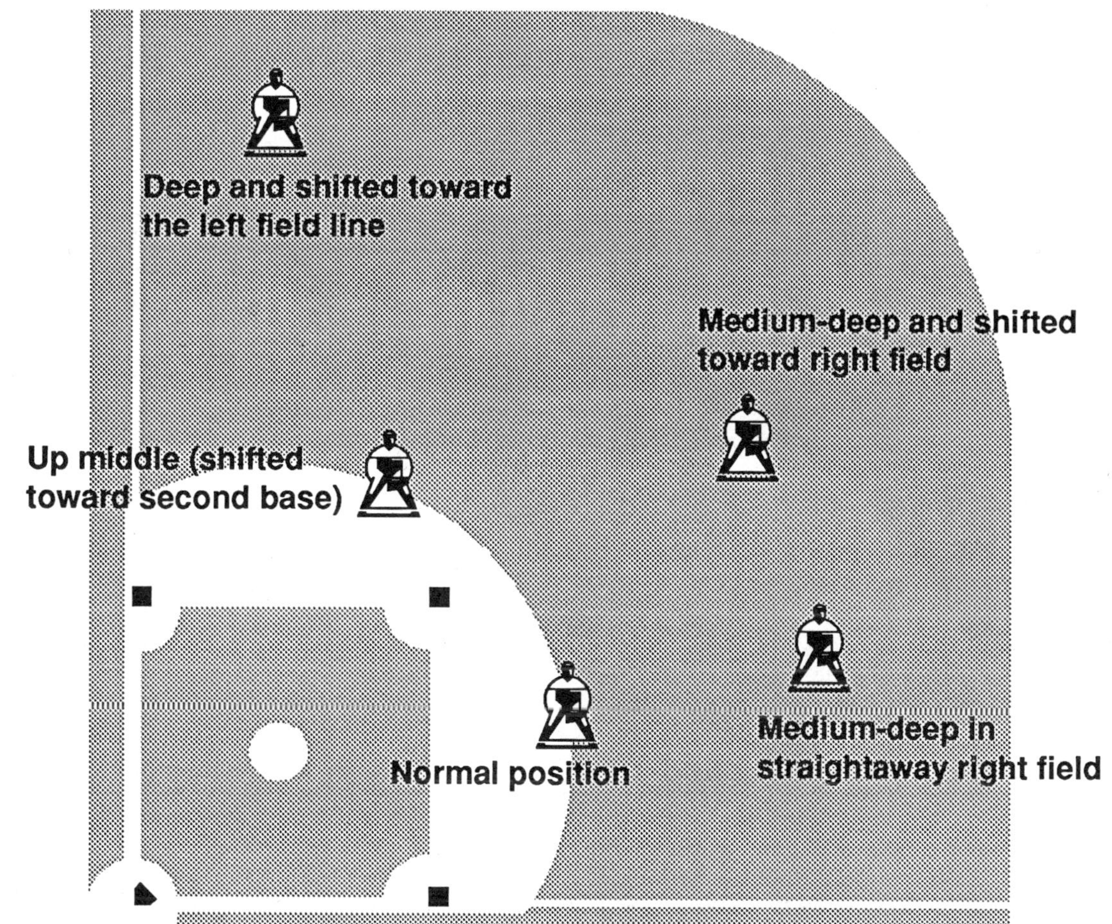

Ahead And Behind In The Count Vs. RH

Ahead

Fastball Average .294

	Outside	Middle	Inside
High	8/ 375 /3	9/ 333 /3	5/ 0 /0
Med	12/ 416 /5	3/ 333 /1	15/ 200 /3
Low	1/ 0 /0	9/ 444 /4	6/ 166 /1

Curve Average .000

	Outside	Middle	Inside
High	0/ 0 /0	0/ 0 /0	2/ 0 /0
Med	2/ 0 /0	0/ 0 /0	0/ 0 /0
Low	0/ 0 /0	0/ 0 /0	1/ 0 /0

Behind

Fastball Average .291

	Outside	Middle	Inside
High	1/ 0 /0	6/ 500 /3	4/ 0 /0
Med	7/ 285 /2	0/ 0 /0	2/ 0 /0
Low	1/ 0 /0	3/ 666 /2	0/ 0 /0

Curve Average .300

	Outside	Middle	Inside
High	0/ 0 /0	1/ 1000 /1	0/ 0 /0
Med	1/ 0 /0	0/ 0 /0	2/ 500 /1
Low	1/ 0 /0	3/ 333 /1	2/ 0 /0

Overall Evaluation
Against Right-Handed Pitchers

Overall Fastball 🟡🟡

Overall Curve 🟡🟡

Overall Slider 🟡🟡🟡🟡🟡

Against Left-Handed Pitchers

Overall Fastball 🟡🟡

Overall Curve — Not enough information

Overall Slider — Not enough information

Comments: Difficulties with inside fastballs and low-outside fastballs vs. RH.

Strengths: High-outside, medium-outside, high-middle and low-middle fastballs vs. RH.

Weaknesses: Low-outside, high-inside and medium-inside fastballs, low and inside curves vs. RH; fastballs in general vs. LH.

Ken Oberkfell (Left Handed) — *Pittsburgh Pirates*

Ken Oberkfell Against Right-Handed Pitchers
Overall BARS Batting Average .263

Fastball Average .293

	Outside	Middle	Inside
High	32 / 218 / 7	73 / 260 / 19	40 / 250 / 10
Med	137 / 291 / 40	37 / 459 / 17	102 / 313 / 32
Low	44 / 227 / 10	115 / 313 / 36	81 / 283 / 23

Curve Average .198

	Outside	Middle	Inside
High	5 / 200 / 1	8 / 500 / 4	2 / 500 / 1
Med	22 / 90 / 2	4 / 0 / 0	20 / 250 / 5
Low	14 / 142 / 2	16 / 187 / 3	20 / 200 / 4

Slider Average .324

	Outside	Middle	Inside
High	0 / 0 / 0	3 / 0 / 0	9 / 222 / 2
Med	7 / 571 / 4	4 / 500 / 2	18 / 555 / 10
Low	6 / 166 / 1	14 / 214 / 3	13 / 153 / 2

Ken Oberkfell Against Left-Handed Pitchers
Overall BARS Batting Average .291

Fastball Average .301

	Outside	Middle	Inside
High	7 / 285 / 2	10 / 700 / 7	11 / 181 / 2
Med	24 / 291 / 7	10 / 400 / 4	38 / 236 / 9
Low	18 / 222 / 4	25 / 360 / 9	13 / 230 / 3

Curve Average .333

	Outside	Middle	Inside
High	3 / 666 / 2	2 / 500 / 1	3 / 0 / 0
Med	12 / 416 / 5	3 / 333 / 1	6 / 333 / 2
Low	12 / 416 / 5	7 / 142 / 1	3 / 0 / 0

Slider Average .416

	Outside	Middle	Inside
High	0 / 0 / 0	0 / 0 / 0	1 / 1000 / 1
Med	4 / 250 / 1	3 / 0 / 0	1 / 1000 / 1
Low	6 / 666 / 4	8 / 250 / 2	1 / 1000 / 1

Left-handed hitter Ken Oberkfell has trouble with high fastballs (.218, .260 and .250, outside to inside) and with low-outside fastballs (.227) against right-handers. He hits waist-high fastballs very well.

His Ahead and Behind charts on the opposite page show that Oberkfell hits medium-high outside fastballs better when behind in the count (.312 when behind, .280 when ahead). Every fielder except the second baseman needs to be positioned differently for this pitch when Oberkfell is ahead and behind in the count.

**MEDIUM-HIGH OUTSIDE FASTBALLS
(WHEN BEHIND IN THE COUNT)**

BATTING AVERAGE .312
Play
Left   Medium-deep in straightaway left field
Center   Deep and shifted toward left field
Right   Deep and shifted toward center field
Short   Up middle (shifted toward second base)
Second   Shifted toward first base

**MEDIUM-HIGH OUTSIDE FASTBALLS
(WHEN AHEAD IN THE COUNT)**

BATTING AVERAGE .280
Play
Left   Deep in straightaway left field
Center   Deep in straightaway center field
Right   Medium-deep in straightaway right field
Short   Normal position
Second   Shifted toward first base

He also hits low-over-the-middle fastballs better when behind in the count (.363 when behind, .275 when ahead). He tends to pull the ball more when ahead.

**LOW-OVER-THE-MIDDLE FASTBALLS
(WHEN BEHIND IN THE COUNT)**

BATTING AVERAGE .363
Play
Left   Deep in straightaway left field
Center   Medium-deep in straightaway center field
Right   Deep and shifted toward center field
Short   Up middle (shifted toward second base)
Second   Normal position

**LOW-OVER-THE-MIDDLE FASTBALLS
(WHEN AHEAD IN THE COUNT)**

BATTING AVERAGE .275
Play
Left   Medium-deep in straightaway left field
Center   Deep and shifted toward right field
Right   Deep and shifted toward the right field line
Short   Up middle (shifted toward second base)
Second   Shifted toward first base

Right-handers throw Oberkfell more low than high

fastballs. This is a mistake because he hits low fastballs better than high fastballs. He's not a power hitter, so pitchers don't have to worry about him hitting home runs in the high fastball locations.

Oberkfell Against Curves And Sliders

Oberkfell has trouble against outside curves and low curves thrown by right-handed pitchers. These weaknesses give right-handers ample targets.

He also has trouble with low sliders thrown by right-handers. He hits medium-high inside sliders extremely well, however (.555).

MEDIUM-HIGH INSIDE SLIDERS

BATTING AVERAGE .555

Play	
Left	Deep and shifted toward the left field line
Center	Short and shifted toward right field
Right	Deep and shifted toward the right field line
Short	*No instances recorded*
Second	Normal position

Oberkfell Against Left-Handed Pitchers

Oberkfell has trouble with inside fastballs against left-handed pitchers (.181, .236 and .230, high to low). But he hits medium-high outside fastballs fairly well (.291).

**MEDIUM-HIGH OUTSIDE FASTBALLS
(THROWN BY LEFT-HANDED PITCHERS)**

BATTING AVERAGE .291

Play	
Left	Deep and shifted toward the left field line
Center	Medium-deep in straightaway center field
Right	Deep in straightaway right field
Short	Up middle (shifted toward second base)
Second	Normal position

He has a strong .360 average against low-over-the-middle fastballs.

**LOW-OVER-THE-MIDDLE FASTBALLS
(THROWN BY LEFT-HANDED PITCHERS)**

BATTING AVERAGE .360

Play	
Left	Deep and shifted toward the left field line
Center	Deep in straightaway center field
Right	Medium-deep in straightaway right field
Short	Up middle (shifted toward second base)
Second	Shifted toward first base

He crushes high-over-the-middle fastballs (.700).

**HIGH-OVER-THE-MIDDLE FASTBALLS
(THROWN BY LEFT-HANDED PITCHERS)**

BATTING AVERAGE .700

Play	
Left	Deep and shifted toward center field
Center	Medium-deep in straightaway center field
Right	Deep and shifted toward the right field line
Short	Up middle (shifted toward second base)
Second	Shifted toward first base

He hits very strongly against low-outside and medium-high outside curves thrown by left-handers (.416 in each).

Ahead And Behind In The Count Vs. RH

Ahead

Fastball Average .298

	Outside	Middle	Inside
High	9/222/2	38/263/10	16/312/5
Med	75/280/21	23/521/12	52/384/20
Low	20/50/1	58/275/16	44/295/13

Curve Average .214

	Outside	Middle	Inside
High	0/0/0	0/0/0	0/0/0
Med	3/0/0	0/0/0	3/666/2
Low	2/0/0	3/0/0	3/333/1

Behind

Fastball Average .303

	Outside	Middle	Inside
High	9/444/4	13/384/5	15/200/3
Med	32/312/10	4/250/1	12/250/3
Low	4/500/2	22/363/8	11/90/1

Curve Average .309

	Outside	Middle	Inside
High	1/0/0	4/750/3	1/1000/1
Med	10/200/2	3/0/0	8/375/3
Low	5/400/2	5/200/1	5/200/1

Overall Evaluation

Against Right-Handed Pitchers

Overall Fastball	⚾⚾ ⚾⚾
Overall Curve	⚾⚾
Overall Slider	⚾⚾ ⚾⚾ ⚾⚾ ⚾⚾

Against Left-Handed Pitchers

Overall Fastball	⚾⚾ ⚾⚾ ⚾⚾
Overall Curve	⚾⚾ ⚾⚾ ⚾⚾ ⚾⚾
Overall Slider	⚾⚾ ⚾⚾ ⚾⚾ ⚾⚾

Comments: Weak against high fastballs vs. RH.
Strengths: Waist-high and low-middle fastballs, high-middle curves, waist-high sliders vs. RH; over-the-middle fastballs, outside curves and low-outside sliders vs. LH.
Weaknesses: High fastballs, low-outside fastballs, outside and low curves, low sliders vs. RH; low-outside, high-inside and low-inside fastballs, low-middle and inside curves vs. LH.

Gary Redus Against Right-Handed Pitchers
Overall BARS Batting Average .240

Fastball Average .276

	Inside	Middle	Outside
High	12/ 166 / 2	17/ 294 / 5	19/ 105 / 2
Med	28/ 357 / 10	11/ 272 / 3	74/ 283 / 21
Low	10/ 300 / 3	30/ 333 / 10	20/ 250 / 5

Curve Average .219

	Inside	Middle	Outside
High	0/ 0 / 0	4/ 500 / 2	5/ 400 / 2
Med	3/ 333 / 1	4/ 0 / 0	24/ 291 / 7
Low	1/ 1000 / 1	10/ 300 / 3	31/ 64 / 2

Slider Average .265

	Inside	Middle	Outside
High	2/ 500 / 1	1/ 0 / 0	0/ 0 / 0
Med	0/ 0 / 0	1/ 1000 / 1	24/ 250 / 6
Low	2/ 0 / 0	5/ 400 / 2	29/ 241 / 7

Gary Redus Against Left-Handed Pitchers
Overall BARS Batting Average .237

Fastball Average .277

	Inside	Middle	Outside
High	6/ 166 / 1	0/ 0 / 0	10/ 300 / 3
Med	14/ 285 / 4	12/ 500 / 6	33/ 303 / 10
Low	5/ 0 / 0	12/ 333 / 4	9/ 0 / 0

Curve Average .272

	Inside	Middle	Outside
High	0/ 0 / 0	0/ 0 / 0	0/ 0 / 0
Med	5/ 400 / 2	2/ 0 / 0	10/ 400 / 4
Low	4/ 0 / 0	5/ 400 / 2	7/ 142 / 1

Slider Average .214

	Inside	Middle	Outside
High	3/ 666 / 2	0/ 0 / 0	0/ 0 / 0
Med	5/ 200 / 1	1/ 0 / 0	2/ 0 / 0
Low	9/ 222 / 2	4/ 0 / 0	4/ 250 / 1

Right-handed Gary Redus hits medium-high inside fastballs for a fine .357 average. He hits this pitch deep to left and center and medium-deep down the right line.

MEDIUM-HIGH INSIDE FASTBALLS

BATTING AVERAGE .357
Play

Left	Deep in straightaway left field
Center	Deep and shifted toward left field
Right	Medium-deep and shifted toward the right line
Short	Normal position
Second	Normal position

His .333 against low-over-the-middle fastballs is also excellent.

LOW-OVER-THE-MIDDLE FASTBALLS

BATTING AVERAGE .333
Play

Left	Deep in straightaway left field
Center	Deep in straightaway center field
Right	Deep and shifted toward center field
Short	Shifted toward third base
Second	Shifted toward first base

Redus hits a fairly good .283 against medium-high outside fastballs. He hits this pitch deep down the left line, deep into the right-center gap, and medium-deep to straightaway right.

MEDIUM-HIGH OUTSIDE FASTBALLS

BATTING AVERAGE .283
Play

Left	Deep and shifted toward the left field line
Center	Deep and shifted toward right field
Right	Medium-deep in straightaway right field
Short	Normal position
Second	Shifted toward first base

Redus Against Curves And Sliders

Redus has a lot of trouble with low-outside curves thrown by right-handers (.064 on 2-for-31). But he hits medium-high outside curves very well (.291).

MEDIUM-HIGH OUTSIDE CURVEBALLS

BATTING AVERAGE .291
Play

Left	Deep and shifted toward center field
Center	Medium-deep in straightaway center field
Right	Deep in straightaway right field
Short	Shifted toward third base
Second	Normal position

He hits low-over-the-middle curves excellently against right-handers (.300).

LOW-OVER-THE-MIDDLE CURVEBALLS

BATTING AVERAGE .300
Play

Left	Deep in straightaway left field
Center	Medium-deep in straightaway center field
Right	Medium-deep and shifted toward center field
Short	Normal position
Second	*No instances recorded*

Redus hits low-outside and medium-high outside sliders fairly well (.241 and .250). He pulls low-outside sliders medium-deep down the left line.

LOW-OUTSIDE SLIDERS

BATTING AVERAGE .241
Play

Left	Medium-deep and shifted toward the left field line
Center	Medium-deep in straightaway center field
Right	Deep and shifted toward center field
Short	Normal position
Second	*No instances recorded*

Redus Against Left-Handed Pitchers

Redus hits well against high-outside and medium-high outside fastballs thrown by left-handed pitchers (.300 and .303) but he has trouble with low-outside fastballs (0-for-9).

He hits medium-high outside fastballs straightaway to left and center and deep down the right line. The second baseman needs to shift toward first base.

MEDIUM-HIGH OUTSIDE FASTBALLS (THROWN BY LEFT-HANDED PITCHERS)

BATTING AVERAGE .303
Play

Left	Medium-deep in straightaway left field
Center	Deep in straightaway center field
Right	Deep and shifted toward the right field line
Short	Normal position
Second	Shifted toward first base

He hits high-outside fastballs straightaway to all fields.

HIGH-OUTSIDE FASTBALLS (THROWN BY LEFT-HANDED PITCHERS)

BATTING AVERAGE .300
Play

Left	Medium-deep in straightaway left field
Center	Deep in straightaway center field
Right	Deep in straightaway right field
Short	Up middle (shifted toward second base)
Second	*No instances recorded*

He hits a solid .333 against low-over-the-middle fastballs thrown by left-handers.

LOW-OVER-THE-MIDDLE FASTBALLS (THROWN BY LEFT-HANDED PITCHERS)

BATTING AVERAGE .333
Play

Left	Medium-deep in straightaway left field
Center	Deep in straightaway center field
Right	Medium-deep and shifted toward center field
Short	Normal position
Second	*No instances recorded*

Ahead And Behind In The Count Vs. RH

Ahead

Fastball Average .356

	Inside	Middle	Outside
High	2/ 0 / 0	8/ 250 / 2	5/ 200 / 1
Med	13/ 384 / 5	4/ 250 / 1	34/ 323 / 11
Low	0/ 0 / 0	14/ 500 / 7	7/ 571 / 4

Curve Average .333

	Inside	Middle	Outside
High	0/ 0 / 0	0/ 0 / 0	1/ 1000 / 1
Med	0/ 0 / 0	1/ 0 / 0	8/ 375 / 3
Low	0/ 0 / 0	2/ 500 / 1	3/ 0 / 0

Behind

Fastball Average .148

	Inside	Middle	Outside
High	2/ 0 / 0	3/ 0 / 0	3/ 333 / 1
Med	4/ 0 / 0	1/ 0 / 0	6/ 166 / 1
Low	3/ 666 / 2	5/ 0 / 0	0/ 0 / 0

Curve Average .409

	Inside	Middle	Outside
High	0/ 0 / 0	2/ 1000 / 2	2/ 500 / 1
Med	2/ 500 / 1	1/ 0 / 0	8/ 375 / 3
Low	0/ 0 / 0	3/ 333 / 1	4/ 250 / 1

Overall Evaluation

Against Right-Handed Pitchers

Overall Fastball	
Overall Curve	
Overall Slider	

Against Left-Handed Pitchers

Overall Fastball	
Overall Curve	
Overall Slider	

Comments: Weak vs. low-outside pitches vs. RH & LH.
Strengths: Medium-inside and low-middle fastballs, low-middle and medium-outside curves vs. RH; low-middle, high-outside and medium-outside fastballs, medium-outside curves vs. LH.
Weaknesses: High-inside, high-outside and low-outside fastballs, low-outside curves, outside sliders vs. RH; high-inside, low-inside, low-outside fastballs, low-outside curves & sliders, low-inside sliders vs. LH.

R. J. Reynolds (Switch Hitter) — *Pittsburgh Pirates*

R. J. Reynolds Against Right-Handed Pitchers
Overall BARS Batting Average .291

Fastball Average .336

	Outside	Middle	Inside
High	23/ 130 / 3	34/ 470 / 16	11/ 181 / 2
Med	35/ 342 / 12	7/ 571 / 4	17/ 352 / 6
Low	14/ 285 / 4	40/ 425 / 17	36/ 250 / 9

Curve Average .255

	Outside	Middle	Inside
High	2/ 0 / 0	2/ 1000 / 2	2/ 0 / 0
Med	7/ 142 / 1	3/ 333 / 1	9/ 444 / 4
Low	4/ 250 / 1	9/ 222 / 2	9/ 111 / 1

Slider Average .083

	Outside	Middle	Inside
High	1/ 0 / 0	0/ 0 / 0	0/ 0 / 0
Med	2/ 500 / 1	0/ 0 / 0	4/ 0 / 0
Low	1/ 0 / 0	4/ 250 / 1	12/ 0 / 0

R. J. Reynolds Against Left-Handed Pitchers
Overall BARS Batting Average .295

Fastball Average .307

	Inside	Middle	Outside
High	2/ 0 / 0	3/ 333 / 1	3/ 333 / 1
Med	3/ 0 / 0	4/ 500 / 2	7/ 142 / 1
Low	6/ 500 / 3	7/ 428 / 3	4/ 250 / 1

Curve Average .333

	Inside	Middle	Outside
High	0/ 0 / 0	1/ 0 / 0	1/ 1000 / 1
Med	2/ 0 / 0	0/ 0 / 0	2/ 500 / 1
Low	1/ 0 / 0	2/ 500 / 1	0/ 0 / 0

Slider Average .333

	Inside	Middle	Outside
High	0/ 0 / 0	0/ 0 / 0	0/ 0 / 0
Med	2/ 500 / 1	0/ 0 / 0	0/ 0 / 0
Low	1/ 0 / 0	1/ 0 / 0	2/ 500 / 1

Switch-hitting R.J. Reynolds has an excellent BARS overall fastball average against right-handed pitchers (.336). He's a little weak in the four fastball corners but his other locations are all solid.

He hits medium-high outside fastballs much better when ahead in the count (.545 when ahead, .200 when behind). The following strategy shows how vital it is for fielders to adjust not only for the pitch location and pitch type but also for the count.

MEDIUM-HIGH OUTSIDE FASTBALLS (WHEN AHEAD IN THE COUNT)

BATTING AVERAGE .545
Play

Left	Deep and shifted toward the left field line
Center	Medium-deep in straightaway center field
Right	Deep and shifted toward the right field line
Short	Shifted toward third base
Second	Shifted toward first base

MEDIUM-HIGH OUTSIDE FASTBALLS (WHEN BEHIND IN THE COUNT)

BATTING AVERAGE .200
Play

Left	Deep and shifted toward the left field line
Center	Deep in straightaway center field
Right	Deep and shifted toward center field
Short	Up middle (shifted toward second base)
Second	Normal position

His .425 average against low-over-the-middle fastballs is excellent.

LOW-OVER-THE-MIDDLE FASTBALLS

BATTING AVERAGE .425
Play

Left	Deep in straightaway left field
Center	Deep and shifted toward left field
Right	Medium-deep in straightaway right field
Short	Up middle (shifted toward second base)
Second	Shifted toward first base

His .470 against high-over-the-middle fastballs is exceptionally strong.

HIGH-OVER-THE-MIDDLE FASTBALLS

BATTING AVERAGE .470
Play

Left	Deep in straightaway left field
Center	Medium-deep in straightaway center field
Right	Deep and shifted toward center field
Short	Up middle (shifted toward second base)
Second	Shifted toward first base

Reynolds hits .352 against medium-high inside fastballs. He hits this straightaway to center and right fields and medium-deep down the left line.

He has problems with low curves and low sliders thrown by right-handers. In particular, his low-inside curve and slider locations are weak.

Medium-High Outside Fastballs
Dark Fielders — Ahead In The Count
Light Fielders — Behind In The Count

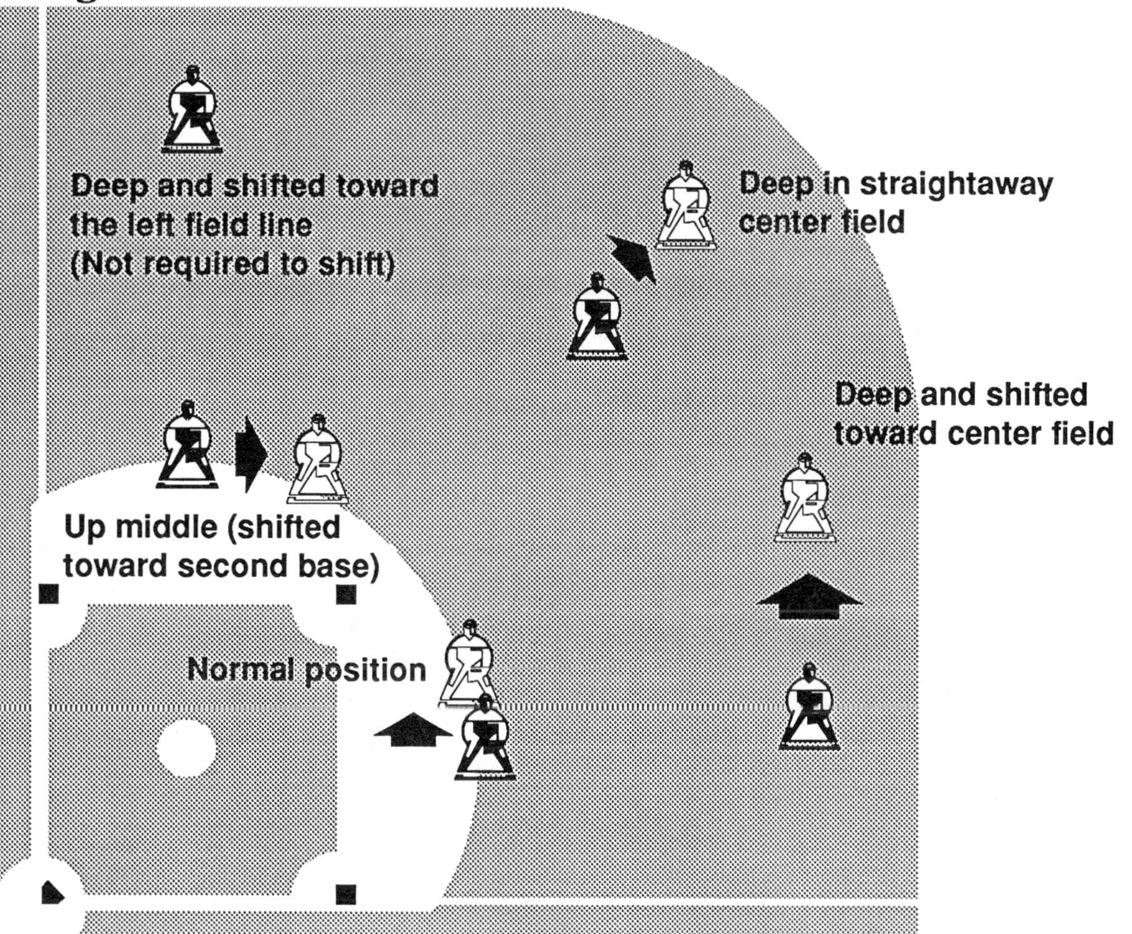

Ahead And Behind In The Count Vs. RH

Ahead

Fastball Average .386

	Outside	Middle	Inside
High	4/ 250 /1	15/ 466 /7	3/ 0 /0
Med	11/ 545 /6	2/ 500 /1	9/ 444 /4
Low	3/ 333 /1	24/ 416 /10	17/ 235 /4

Curve Average .384

	Outside	Middle	Inside
High	0/ 0 /0	1/ 1000 /1	2/ 0 /0
Med	2/ 500 /1	0/ 0 /0	3/ 333 /1
Low	2/ 500 /1	2/ 0 /0	1/ 1000 /1

Behind

Fastball Average .432

	Outside	Middle	Inside
High	3/ 0 /0	7/ 714 /5	1/ 0 /0
Med	10/ 200 /2	2/ 1000 /2	3/ 0 /0
Low	3/ 666 /2	6/ 500 /3	2/ 1000 /2

Curve Average .428

	Outside	Middle	Inside
High	0/ 0 /0	0/ 0 /0	0/ 0 /0
Med	1/ 0 /0	3/ 333 /1	2/ 1000 /2
Low	0/ 0 /0	1/ 0 /0	0/ 0 /0

Overall Evaluation
Against Right-Handed Pitchers

Overall Fastball 

Overall Curve

Overall Slider

Against Left-Handed Pitchers

Overall Fastball 

Overall Curve — Not enough information

Overall Slider — Not enough information

Comments: Excellent waist-high and over-the-middle fastball hitter vs. RH.

Strengths: Waist-high and over-the-middle fastballs, medium-inside curves vs. RH; low-inside and low-middle fastballs vs. LH.

Weaknesses: High-outside, high-inside and low-inside fastballs, outside curves, low curves, low sliders, inside sliders vs. RH; medium-outside fastballs vs. LH.

Andy Van Slyke (Left Handed) — *Pittsburgh Pirates*

Andy Van Slyke Against Right-Handed Pitchers
Overall BARS Batting Average .269

Fastball Average .298

	Outside	Middle	Inside
High	19 / 105 / 2	46 / 369 / 17	20 / 100 / 2
Med	65 / 261 / 17	28 / 178 / 5	47 / 340 / 16
Low	41 / 268 / 11	61 / 459 / 28	42 / 285 / 12

Curve Average .200

	Outside	Middle	Inside
High	3 / 0 / 0	4 / 250 / 1	0 / 0 / 0
Med	12 / 416 / 5	1 / 1000 / 1	10 / 200 / 2
Low	15 / 133 / 2	9 / 111 / 1	6 / 0 / 0

Slider Average .393

	Outside	Middle	Inside
High	2 / 0 / 0	1 / 1000 / 1	0 / 0 / 0
Med	4 / 0 / 0	1 / 1000 / 1	8 / 625 / 5
Low	3 / 0 / 0	9 / 555 / 5	5 / 200 / 1

Andy Van Slyke Against Left-Handed Pitchers
Overall BARS Batting Average .190

Fastball Average .198

	Outside	Middle	Inside
High	6 / 0 / 0	8 / 250 / 2	12 / 333 / 4
Med	15 / 133 / 2	5 / 200 / 1	20 / 350 / 7
Low	14 / 142 / 2	15 / 66 / 1	6 / 166 / 1

Curve Average .212

	Outside	Middle	Inside
High	0 / 0 / 0	3 / 333 / 1	2 / 0 / 0
Med	9 / 333 / 3	1 / 1000 / 1	2 / 0 / 0
Low	10 / 100 / 1	5 / 200 / 1	1 / 0 / 0

Slider Average .142

	Outside	Middle	Inside
High	0 / 0 / 0	0 / 0 / 0	1 / 0 / 0
Med	5 / 200 / 1	1 / 0 / 0	0 / 0 / 0
Low	10 / 100 / 1	1 / 0 / 0	3 / 333 / 1

Left-handed hitter Andy Van Slyke has a BARS overall fastball average of .298 against right-handed pitchers. Against left-handed pitchers his overall fastball average is .198 — 100 points less. Even so, he has a lot of trouble with outside fastballs thrown by right-handers (.105, .261 and .268, high to low).

In contrast, he hits medium-high inside fastballs for a solid .340 average. He pulls this pitch to the outfield, but the shortstop needs to shift toward third.

He hits high-over-the-middle fastballs for a very strong .369 average. He hits this pitch down both lines.

HIGH-OVER-THE-MIDDLE FASTBALLS

BATTING AVERAGE .369
Play
Left	Deep and shifted toward the left field line
Center	Deep in straightaway center field
Right	Deep and shifted toward the right field line
Short	Up middle (shifted toward second base)
Second	Shifted toward first base

He also hits low-over-the-middle fastballs down both lines. The field diagram on the opposite page shows how fielders need to align themselves for this pitch.

LOW-OVER-THE-MIDDLE FASTBALLS

BATTING AVERAGE .459

Play
Left	Deep and shifted toward the left field line
Center	Deep and shifted toward right field
Right	Deep and shifted toward the right field line
Short	Normal position
Second	Normal position

Van Slyke has trouble with low curves thrown by right-handers (.133, .111 and .000, outside to inside). He hits medium-high outside curves for an excellent .416, however.

Van Slyke Against Left-Handed Pitchers

Van Slyke also has trouble with outside fastballs thrown by left-handed pitchers (.000, .133 and .142, high to low). In addition, he has trouble with low fastballs and low curves against lefties. He hits medium-high inside fastballs very well (.350).

MEDIUM-HIGH INSIDE FASTBALLS
(THROWN BY LEFT-HANDED PITCHERS)

BATTING AVERAGE .350
Play
Left	Deep in straightaway left field
Center	Deep and shifted toward right field
Right	Deep and shifted toward the right field line
Short	Up middle (shifted toward second base)
Second	Normal position

Low-Over-The-Middle Fastballs

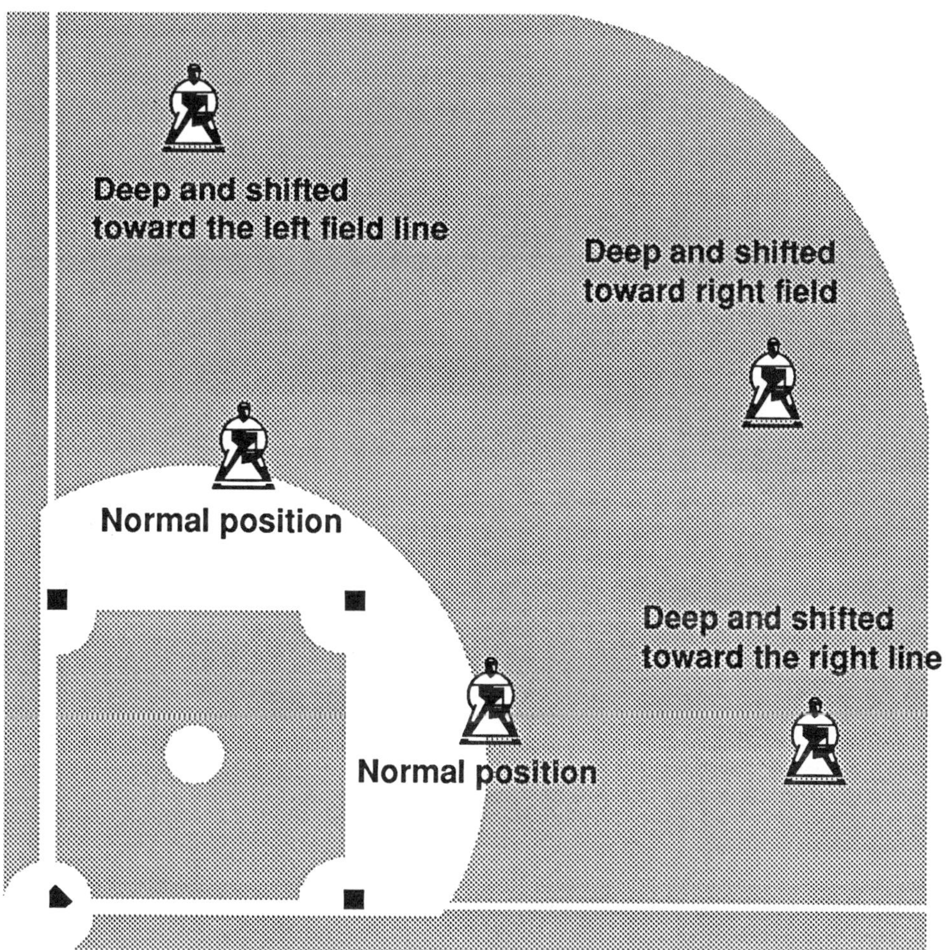

Ahead And Behind In The Count Vs. RH

Ahead

Fastball Average .287

	Outside	Middle	Inside
High	9 / 111 / 1	20 / 950 / 7	5 / 0 / 0
Med	36 / 222 / 8	20 / 250 / 5	29 / 344 / 10
Low	21 / 380 / 8	35 / 342 / 12	23 / 260 / 6

Curve Average .000

	Outside	Middle	Inside
High	0 / 0 / 0	0 / 0 / 0	0 / 0 / 0
Med	1 / 0 / 0	0 / 0 / 0	0 / 0 / 0
Low	0 / 0 / 0	0 / 0 / 0	1 / 0 / 0

Behind

Fastball Average .375

	Outside	Middle	Inside
High	2 / 500 / 1	6 / 666 / 4	8 / 125 / 1
Med	7 / 285 / 2	3 / 0 / 0	5 / 400 / 2
Low	2 / 0 / 0	9 / 666 / 6	6 / 333 / 2

Curve Average .368

	Outside	Middle	Inside
High	1 / 0 / 0	1 / 1000 / 1	0 / 0 / 0
Med	3 / 666 / 2	1 / 1000 / 1	2 / 0 / 0
Low	7 / 285 / 2	3 / 333 / 1	1 / 0 / 0

Overall Evaluation

Against Right-Handed Pitchers

Overall Fastball ○○ ○○
Overall Curve ○○
Overall Slider ○○ ○○○○

Against Left-Handed Pitchers

Overall Fastball ○○
Overall Curve ○○
Overall Slider ○○

Comments: Weak vs. outside fastballs vs. RH and LH. Strengths: High-middle, low-middle and medium-inside fastballs, medium-outside curves, low-middle and medium-inside sliders vs. RH; high-inside and medium-inside fastballs, medium-outside curves v. LH. Weaknesses: Outside fastballs, medium-middle and high-inside fastballs, low and inside curves, outside sliders vs. RH; outside, over-the-middle and low fastballs, low curves and outside sliders vs. LH.

Brunansky, Tom
Coleman, Vince
Guerrero, Pedro
McGee, Willie
Oquendo, Jose
Pena, Tony
Pendleton, Terry
Smith, Ozzie
Thompson, Milt

St. Louis Cardinals
BARS System
Hitting Analysis

Tom Brunansky Against Right-Handed Pitchers
Overall BARS Batting Average .245

Fastball Average .289

	Inside	Middle	Outside
High	13/ 230 /3	32/ 406 /13	15/ 266 /4
Med	39/ 282 /11	24/ 416 /10	104/ 250 /26
Low	16/ 187 /3	36/ 416 /15	35/ 171 /6

Curve Average .173

	Inside	Middle	Outside
High	3/ 333 /1	7/ 142 /1	5/ 200 /1
Med	4/ 500 /2	7/ 142 /1	24/ 208 /5
Low	5/ 200 /1	15/ 133 /2	22/ 90 /2

Slider Average .303

	Inside	Middle	Outside
High	1/ 0 /0	3/ 0 /0	2/ 0 /0
Med	1/ 0 /0	5/ 400 /2	20/ 400 /8
Low	2/ 0 /0	7/ 142 /1	25/ 360 /9

Tom Brunansky Against Left-Handed Pitchers
Overall BARS Batting Average .254

Fastball Average .301

	Inside	Middle	Outside
High	3/ 0 /0	9/ 666 /6	21/ 142 /3
Med	15/ 333 /5	11/ 181 /2	63/ 349 /22
Low	4/ 750 /3	18/ 222 /4	15/ 200 /3

Curve Average .218

	Inside	Middle	Outside
High	2/ 0 /0	3/ 0 /0	1/ 0 /0
Med	2/ 500 /1	1/ 1000 /1	9/ 222 /2
Low	3/ 333 /1	8/ 250 /2	3/ 0 /0

Slider Average .250

	Inside	Middle	Outside
High	1/ 0 /0	1/ 1000 /1	2/ 500 /1
Med	1/ 0 /0	6/ 500 /3	3/ 333 /1
Low	3/ 0 /0	7/ 142 /1	8/ 125 /1

Tom Brunansky, right-handed hitter, has some problems with outside fastballs against right-handed pitchers (.266, .250, .171, high to low). His strength is over-the-middle, top to bottom (.406, .416 and .416). By keeping fastballs inside or outside, right-handers could get an edge.

He pulls low-over-the-middle fastballs deep to all fields. But note that the shortstop needs to shift toward second and the second baseman toward first.

LOW-OVER-THE-MIDDLE FASTBALLS

BATTING AVERAGE .416
> *Play*

Left	Deep and shifted toward the left field line
Center	Deep and shifted toward left field
Right	Deep and shifted toward center field
Short	Up middle (shifted toward second base)
Second	Shifted toward first base

In contrast, he hits high-over-the-middle fastballs medium-deep to the outfield. This shows the value of aligning fielders according to the BARS fielding strategy for each type and location of pitch. The field diagram on the opposite page compares fielding strategies for these two over-the-middle pitches.

HIGH-OVER-THE-MIDDLE FASTBALLS

BATTING AVERAGE .406
> *Play*

Left	Medium-deep and shifted toward the left field line
Center	Medium-deep in straightaway center field
Right	Medium-deep and shifted toward center field
Short	Shifted toward third base
Second	Shifted toward first base

Brunansky has trouble with outside curves thrown by right-handers (.200, .208 and .090). He hits outside sliders exceptionally well, however (.400 against medium-high outside and .360 against low-outside).

He has a good .301 overall fastball average against left-handed pitchers. He hits a strong .349 against medium-high outside fastballs thrown by left-handers.

MEDIUM-HIGH OUTSIDE FASTBALLS
(THROWN BY LEFT-HANDED PITCHERS)

BATTING AVERAGE .349
> *Play*

Left	Deep in straightaway left field
Center	Deep in straightaway center field
Right	Deep in straightaway right field
Short	Normal position
Second	Shifted toward first base

Over-The-Middle Fastballs
Dark Fielders — Low-Over-The-Middle
Light Fielders — High-Over-The-Middle

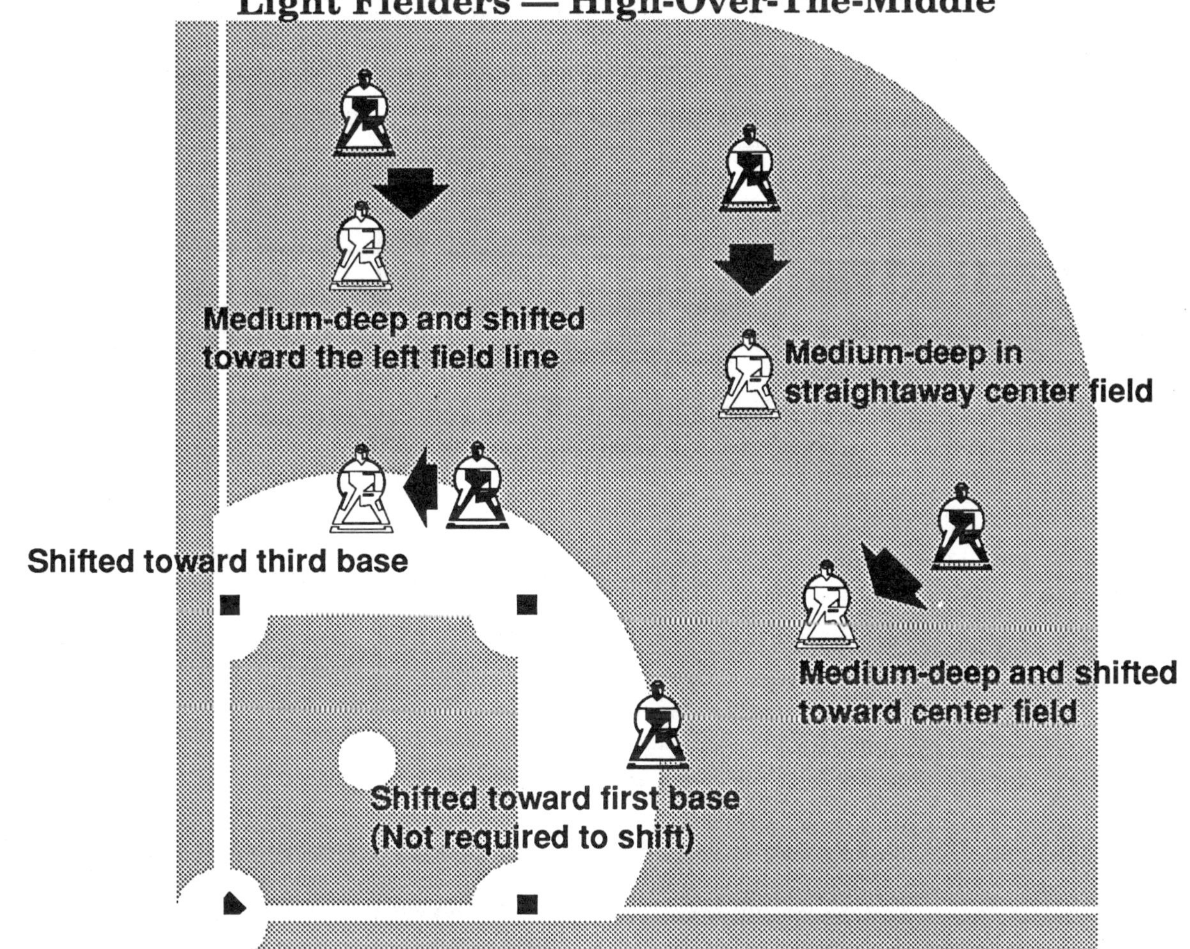

Ahead And Behind In The Count Vs. RH

Ahead

Fastball Average .357

	Inside	Middle	Outside
High	3 / 333 / 1	15 / 466 / 7	5 / 600 / 3
Med	19 / 315 / 6	15 / 533 / 8	47 / 276 / 13
Low	5 / 0 / 0	16 / 500 / 8	15 / 266 / 4

Curve Average .315

	Inside	Middle	Outside
High	0 / 0 / 0	2 / 0 / 0	1 / 0 / 0
Med	1 / 1000 / 1	1 / 0 / 0	5 / 400 / 2
Low	2 / 500 / 1	3 / 333 / 1	4 / 250 / 1

Behind

Fastball Average .363

	Inside	Middle	Outside
High	5 / 400 / 2	3 / 666 / 2	0 / 0 / 0
Med	6 / 166 / 1	2 / 500 / 1	14 / 285 / 4
Low	1 / 0 / 0	9 / 444 / 4	4 / 500 / 2

Curve Average .166

	Inside	Middle	Outside
High	2 / 500 / 1	3 / 0 / 0	1 / 0 / 0
Med	1 / 1000 / 1	3 / 0 / 0	8 / 250 / 2
Low	0 / 0 / 0	4 / 0 / 0	2 / 0 / 0

Overall Evaluation
Against Right-Handed Pitchers

Overall Fastball	⚾⚾
Overall Curve	⚾
Overall Slider	⚾⚾⚾⚾

Against Left-Handed Pitchers

Overall Fastball	⚾⚾⚾
Overall Curve	⚾
Overall Slider	⚾⚾

Comments: Weak against inside and outside fastballs, outside curves vs. RH.

Strengths: Over-the-middle fastballs, medium-outside and low-outside sliders vs. RH; medium-inside, high-middle and medium-outside fastballs vs. LH.

Weaknesses: Inside and outside fastballs, over-the-middle and outside curves vs. RH; high-outside, low-middle and low-outside fastballs, outside curves and low sliders vs. LH.

Vince Coleman (Switch Hitter) — *St. Louis Cardinals*

Vince Coleman Against Right-Handed Pitchers
Overall BARS Batting Average .293

Fastball Average .320

	Outside	Middle	Inside
High	22 / 227 / 5	47 / 319 / 15	36 / 250 / 9
Med	41 / 463 / 19	10 / 700 / 7	54 / 351 / 19
Low	17 / 176 / 3	58 / 362 / 21	39 / 153 / 6

Curve Average .349

	Outside	Middle	Inside
High	3 / 333 / 1	0 / 0 / 0	1 / 0 / 0
Med	9 / 0 / 0	0 / 0 / 0	8 / 500 / 4
Low	12 / 333 / 4	17 / 529 / 9	13 / 307 / 4

Slider Average .294

	Outside	Middle	Inside
High	1 / 0 / 0	0 / 0 / 0	3 / 333 / 1
Med	1 / 0 / 0	2 / 0 / 0	8 / 375 / 3
Low	0 / 0 / 0	4 / 500 / 2	15 / 266 / 4

Vince Coleman Against Left-Handed Pitchers
Overall BARS Batting Average .225

Fastball Average .226

	Inside	Middle	Outside
High	3 / 666 / 2	22 / 318 / 7	11 / 272 / 3
Med	19 / 210 / 4	1 / 0 / 0	35 / 200 / 7
Low	12 / 83 / 1	25 / 160 / 4	13 / 307 / 4

Curve Average .346

	Inside	Middle	Outside
High	1 / 0 / 0	2 / 1000 / 2	2 / 500 / 1
Med	0 / 0 / 0	2 / 500 / 1	3 / 0 / 0
Low	4 / 500 / 2	8 / 250 / 2	4 / 250 / 1

Slider Average .281

	Inside	Middle	Outside
High	2 / 0 / 0	1 / 1000 / 1	0 / 0 / 0
Med	7 / 571 / 4	3 / 0 / 0	4 / 500 / 2
Low	7 / 0 / 0	4 / 250 / 1	4 / 250 / 1

Switch-hitting Vince Coleman's overall fastball average is nearly 100 points higher against right-handed than against left-handed pitchers (.320 against right-handers, .226 against left-handers).

Coleman is exceptionally strong against waist-high fastballs thrown by right-handers (.463, .700 and .351, outside to inside). He's also strong down-the-middle from top to bottom (.319, .700 and .362). His weaknesses are in the four fastball corners.

His .351 against medium-high inside fastballs is excellent. Batting left-handed against right-handed pitchers, he hits this pitch medium-deep down both lines and to the right side of the infield. Fielders could prevent most of his base hits from this location by aligning themselves according to the following fielding strategy.

MEDIUM-HIGH INSIDE FASTBALLS

BATTING AVERAGE .351
Play

Left	Medium-deep and shifted toward the left line
Center	Medium-deep in straightaway center field
Right	Medium-deep and shifted toward the right line
Short	Up middle (shifted toward second base)
Second	Shifted toward first base

His .463 against medium-outside fastballs is exceptional. He also hits this pitch medium-deep to all fields.

MEDIUM-HIGH OUTSIDE FASTBALLS

BATTING AVERAGE .463
Play

Left	Medium-deep and shifted toward center field
Center	Medium-deep in straightaway center field
Right	Medium-deep and shifted toward center field
Short	Up middle (shifted toward second base)
Second	Normal position

He is very strong against low-over-the-middle fastballs. Notice in his Ahead and Behind charts that he hits this pitch better when ahead in the count (.476 when ahead, .357 when behind). He hits the ball deeper when ahead. This shows the necessity of adjusting fielders not only for the type of pitch but for the count.

LOW-OVER-THE-MIDDLE FASTBALLS
(WHEN AHEAD IN THE COUNT)

BATTING AVERAGE .476
Play

Left	Deep in straightaway left field
Center	Deep and shifted toward right field
Right	Deep in straightaway right field
Short	Up middle (shifted toward second base)
Second	Shifted toward first base

LOW-OVER-THE-MIDDLE FASTBALLS
(WHEN BEHIND IN THE COUNT)

BATTING AVERAGE .357
Play

Left   *No instances recorded*
Center   Medium-deep in straightaway center field
Right   Medium-deep in straightaway right field
Short   Up middle (shifted toward second base)
Second   Shifted toward first base

Coleman Against Curves And Sliders

Coleman hits unusually well against low curves thrown by right-handed pitchers. His .333, .529 and .307, outside to inside, are as consistently strong as any player's in baseball. He hits low-over-the-middle curves straightaway to the outfield but to the right side of the infield.

LOW-OVER-THE-MIDDLE CURVEBALLS

BATTING AVERAGE .529
Play

Left   Medium-deep in straightaway left field
Center   Medium-deep in straightaway center field
Right   Deep in straightaway right field
Short   Up middle (shifted toward second base)
Second   Shifted toward first base

He hits sliders fairly well overall against right-handers. His .266 against low-inside sliders is adequate.

Coleman Against Left-Handed Pitchers

Coleman's fastball locations are much spottier against left-handed pitchers. He hits high-over-the-middle and low-outside fastballs pretty well (.318 and .307) but has trouble in most of his other locations.

Batting right-handed against left-handers, he pulls high-over-the-middle fastballs deep down the left line and into the left-center gap.

HIGH-OVER-THE-MIDDLE FASTBALLS (THROWN BY LEFT-HANDED PITCHERS)

BATTING AVERAGE .318
Play

Left   Deep and shifted toward the left field line
Center   Medium-deep and shifted toward left field
Right   Deep in straightaway right field
Short   Shifted toward third base
Second   Shifted toward first base

He goes down the right line with low-outside fastballs thrown by lefties. But notice that the shortstop needs to play shifted toward third base.

LOW-OUTSIDE FASTBALLS (THROWN BY LEFT-HANDED PITCHERS)

BATTING AVERAGE .307
Play

Left   Deep and shifted toward center field
Center   Deep in straightaway center field
Right   Deep and shifted toward the right field line
Short   Shifted toward third base
Second   Normal position

Ahead And Behind In The Count Vs. RH

Ahead

	Fastball Average .374			Curve Average .555		
	Outside	Middle	Inside	Outside	Middle	Inside
High	8/250 /2	23/347 /8	13/153 /2	1/1000 /1	0/0 /0	0/0 /0
Med	13/615 /8	6/833 /5	24/333 /8	0/0 /0	0/0 /0	2/1000 /2
Low	6/333 /2	21/476 /10	17/235 /4	0/0 /0	0/0 /0	6/333 /2

Behind

	Fastball Average .333			Curve Average .481		
	Outside	Middle	Inside	Outside	Middle	Inside
High	3/666 /2	10/300 /3	8/125 /1	0/0 /0	0/0 /0	1/0 /0
Med	8/500 /4	2/0 /0	15/400 /6	4/0 /0	0/0 /0	3/666 /2
Low	0/0 /0	14/357 /5	6/166 /1	7/571 /4	11/545 /6	1/1000 /1

Overall Evaluation

Against Right-Handed Pitchers

Overall Fastball   ◯◯ ◯◯ ◯◯
Overall Curve   ◯◯ ◯◯ ◯◯ ◯◯
Overall Slider   ◯◯ ◯◯ ◯◯

Against Left-Handed Pitchers

Overall Fastball   ◯◯
Overall Curve   ◯◯ ◯◯ ◯◯ ◯◯
Overall Slider   ◯◯ ◯◯ ◯◯

Comments: Exceptional waist-high and over-the-middle fastball hitter vs. RH. Also very strong vs. low curves against RH.

Strengths: As above, medium-inside curves and sliders vs. RH; high-middle and low-outside fastballs, medium-inside sliders vs. LH.

Weaknesses: Four fastball corners vs. RH; medium-high inside, low-inside, high-outside and medium-outside fastballs, low-inside sliders vs. LH.

Pedro Guerrero (Right Handed)   *St. Louis Cardinals*

Pedro Guerrero Against Right-Handed Pitchers
Overall BARS Batting Average .287

Fastball Average .340

	Inside	Middle	Outside
High	18 / 277 / 5	31 / 354 / 11	14 / 214 / 3
Med	34 / 205 / 7	16 / 375 / 6	50 / 340 / 17
Low	20 / 400 / 8	37 / 486 / 18	27 / 333 / 9

Curve Average .343

	Inside	Middle	Outside
High	3 / 0 / 0	5 / 800 / 4	3 / 333 / 1
Med	5 / 0 / 0	6 / 500 / 3	17 / 411 / 7
Low	4 / 500 / 2	10 / 200 / 2	14 / 285 / 4

Slider Average .203

	Inside	Middle	Outside
High	0 / 0 / 0	1 / 0 / 0	2 / 500 / 1
Med	2 / 0 / 0	5 / 600 / 3	18 / 166 / 3
Low	1 / 0 / 0	11 / 272 / 3	24 / 125 / 3

Pedro Guerrero Against Left-Handed Pitchers
Overall BARS Batting Average .310

Fastball Average .341

	Inside	Middle	Outside
High	2 / 0 / 0	4 / 750 / 3	10 / 300 / 3
Med	8 / 375 / 3	7 / 714 / 5	24 / 333 / 8
Low	7 / 0 / 0	15 / 466 / 7	8 / 0 / 0

Curve Average .250

	Inside	Middle	Outside
High	0 / 0 / 0	0 / 0 / 0	1 / 1000 / 1
Med	5 / 200 / 1	1 / 0 / 0	5 / 200 / 1
Low	2 / 0 / 0	6 / 500 / 3	4 / 0 / 0

Slider Average .363

	Inside	Middle	Outside
High	0 / 0 / 0	1 / 1000 / 1	2 / 0 / 0
Med	3 / 666 / 2	1 / 0 / 0	3 / 1000 / 3
Low	5 / 200 / 1	1 / 1000 / 1	6 / 0 / 0

Right-handed hitter Pedro Guerrero is an outstanding fastball hitter. He hits curves very well against right-handed pitchers, but has problems with curves against left-handers.

Starting with Guerrero's fastball chart against right-handers, notice his strength against low fastballs (.400, .486 and .333, inside to outside). He hits low-over-the-middle fastballs deep to all fields.

LOW-OVER-THE-MIDDLE FASTBALLS

BATTING AVERAGE .486
Play
Left   Deep in straightaway left field
Center   Deep in straightaway center field
Right   Deep and shifted toward the right field line
Short   Up middle (shifted toward second base)
Second   Normal position

His .400 against low-inside fastballs is very strong. He hits this pitch deep down the left line and into the right-center gap.

LOW-INSIDE FASTBALLS

BATTING AVERAGE .400
Play
Left   Deep and shifted toward the left field line
Center   Deep and shifted toward right field
Right   Medium-deep in straightaway right field
Short   Shifted toward third base
Second   *No instances recorded*

His .333 against low-outside fastballs is excellent.

LOW-OUTSIDE FASTBALLS

BATTING AVERAGE .333
Play
Left   Deep and shifted toward center field
Center   Deep in straightaway center field
Right   Deep in straightaway right field
Short   Shifted toward third base
Second   Normal position

His .340 against medium-high outside fastballs shows his effectiveness against outside pitches . He pulls this pitch deep down the left line and into the right-center gap.

MEDIUM-HIGH OUTSIDE FASTBALLS

BATTING AVERAGE .340
Play
Left   Deep and shifted toward the left field line
Center   Medium-deep in straightaway center field
Right   Deep and shifted toward center field
Short   Normal position
Second   Normal position

Guerrero is weak against high-outside fastballs

thrown by right-handers (.214) but he hits high-over-the-middle fastballs for an excellent .354 average.

HIGH-OVER-THE-MIDDLE FASTBALLS

BATTING AVERAGE .354
Play

Left	Deep and shifted toward center field
Center	Deep and shifted toward right field
Right	Deep in straightaway right field
Short	Normal position
Second	*No instances recorded*

Guerrero hits outside curves very well against right-handers. He hits medium-high outside curves down the left line and straightaway to center and right.

MEDIUM-HIGH OUTSIDE CURVEBALLS

BATTING AVERAGE .411
Play

Left	Medium-deep and shifted toward the left field line
Center	Medium-deep in straightaway center field
Right	Deep in straightaway right field
Short	Normal position
Second	*No instances recorded*

He hits low-outside curves deep to all fields. Note that there are no recorded instances of Guerrero hitting this pitch to the infield. In fact, the BARS System has not recorded an instance in which Guerrero, against right-handers, has hit a curve to the second baseman.

LOW-OUTSIDE CURVEBALLS

BATTING AVERAGE .285
Play

Left	Deep and shifted toward center field

Center	Deep in straightaway center field
Right	Deep in straightaway right field
Short	*No instances recorded*
Second	*No instances recorded*

Guerrero is weak against sliders overall. He hits low-over-the-middle sliders fairly well (.272) but has trouble with low-outside (.125) and medium-outside (.166) sliders.

Guerrero Against Left-Handed Pitchers

Guerrero has a sparkling .341 overall fastball average against left-handed pitchers. He hits .333 against medium-outside fastballs.

MEDIUM-HIGH OUTSIDE FASTBALLS (THROWN BY LEFT-HANDED PITCHERS)

BATTING AVERAGE .333
Play

Left	Deep in straightaway left field
Center	Deep and shifted toward left field
Right	Deep in straightaway right field
Short	Up middle (shifted toward second base)
Second	Normal position

He hits low-over-the-middle fastballs very well.

LOW-OVER-THE-MIDDLE FASTBALLS

BATTING AVERAGE .466
Play

Left	Medium-deep in straightaway left field
Center	Deep and shifted toward left field
Right	Medium-deep in straightaway right field
Short	Normal position
Second	*No instances recorded*

Ahead And Behind In The Count Vs. RH

Ahead

Fastball Average .371

	Inside	Middle	Outside
High	8/ 375 /3	16/ 250 /4	8/ 250 /2
Med	14/ 285 /4	9/ 444 /4	22/ 363 /8
Low	11/ 454 /5	22/ 409 /9	11/ 545 /6

Curve Average .470

	Inside	Middle	Outside
High	1/ 0 /0	3/ 666 /2	0/ 0 /0
Med	1/ 0 /0	1/ 1000 /1	6/ 333 /2
Low	0/ 0 /0	3/ 333 /1	2/ 1000 /2

Behind

Fastball Average .416

	Inside	Middle	Outside
High	4/ 250 /1	8/ 375 /3	3/ 333 /1
Med	8/ 250 /2	1/ 0 /0	10/ 500 /5
Low	3/ 666 /2	6/ 666 /4	5/ 400 /2

Curve Average .388

	Inside	Middle	Outside
High	1/ 0 /0	1/ 1000 /1	0/ 0 /0
Med	3/ 0 /0	1/ 1000 /1	6/ 500 /3
Low	2/ 1000 /2	3/ 0 /0	1/ 0 /0

Overall Evaluation

Against Right-Handed Pitchers

Overall Fastball	⚾⚾⚾⚾
Overall Curve	⚾⚾⚾⚾
Overall Slider	⚾

Against Left-Handed Pitchers

Overall Fastball	⚾⚾⚾⚾
Overall Curve	⚾⚾
Overall Slider	⚾⚾⚾⚾

Comments: Strong against low fastballs vs. RH. Strengths: Low fastballs, over-the-middle fastballs, medium-outside fastballs, medium-outside curves vs. RH; waist-high and over-the-middle fastballs vs. LH. Weaknesses: High-inside, medium-inside and high-outside fastballs, low-middle curves, low-outside and medium-outside sliders vs. RH; low-inside and low-outside fastballs vs. LH.

Willie McGee Against Right-Handed Pitchers
Overall BARS Batting Average .283

Fastball Average .333

	Outside	Middle	Inside
High	18 / 111 / 2	32 / 312 / 10	31 / 258 / 8
Med	63 / 349 / 22	15 / 466 / 7	67 / 298 / 20
Low	24 / 250 / 6	44 / 500 / 22	42 / 357 / 15

Curve Average .265

	Outside	Middle	Inside
High	6 / 166 / 1	13 / 230 / 3	6 / 0 / 0
Med	23 / 391 / 9	9 / 444 / 4	20 / 300 / 6
Low	14 / 71 / 1	33 / 393 / 13	34 / 147 / 5

Slider Average .270

	Outside	Middle	Inside
High	1 / 0 / 0	4 / 250 / 1	7 / 0 / 0
Med	1 / 0 / 0	0 / 0 / 0	16 / 250 / 4
Low	4 / 500 / 2	17 / 470 / 8	24 / 208 / 5

Willie McGee Against Left-Handed Pitchers
Overall BARS Batting Average .263

Fastball Average .280

	Inside	Middle	Outside
High	12 / 83 / 1	10 / 400 / 4	12 / 333 / 4
Med	26 / 269 / 7	4 / 750 / 3	39 / 358 / 14
Low	17 / 176 / 3	24 / 250 / 6	13 / 153 / 2

Curve Average .270

	Inside	Middle	Outside
High	1 / 0 / 0	4 / 250 / 1	1 / 1000 / 1
Med	6 / 500 / 3	2 / 0 / 0	8 / 375 / 3
Low	12 / 166 / 2	9 / 222 / 2	5 / 200 / 1

Slider Average .227

	Inside	Middle	Outside
High	5 / 400 / 2	1 / 0 / 0	0 / 0 / 0
Med	9 / 333 / 3	1 / 0 / 0	1 / 0 / 0
Low	15 / 133 / 2	7 / 142 / 1	5 / 400 / 2

Switch-hitting Willie McGee has an excellent .333 overall fastball average against right-handed pitchers. His .280 fastball average against left-handed pitchers is not as strong.

Notice that right-handers throw McGee more inside than outside fastballs, but he hits high-inside and low-inside fastballs better than the corresponding outside fastball locations.

McGee's .349 against medium-high outside fastballs is excellent. He hits this pitch deep to all fields.

MEDIUM-HIGH OUTSIDE FASTBALLS

BATTING AVERAGE .349
Play
Left   Deep and shifted toward the left field line
Center   Deep in straightaway center field
Right   Deep in straightaway right field
Short   Up middle (shifted toward second base)
Second   Normal position

His .298 against medium-high inside fastballs is fairly good.

MEDIUM-HIGH INSIDE FASTBALLS

BATTING AVERAGE .298
Play
Left   Medium-deep and shifted toward the left field line

Center   Deep in straightaway center field
Right   Medium-deep in straightaway right field
Short   Up middle (shifted toward second base)
Second   Normal position

Right-handers also tend to throw McGee more low than high fastballs. This is a big mistake because he hits low fastballs very well overall. The .500 and .357 in his low-over-the-middle and low-inside fastball locations are very solid. Notice that he hits both these pitches medium-deep down the left line. By aligning themselves properly, fielders could prevent most of McGee's base hits from pitches to these locations.

LOW-OVER-THE-MIDDLE FASTBALLS

BATTING AVERAGE .500
Play
Left   Medium-deep and shifted toward the left field line
Center   Medium-deep in straightaway center field
Right   Deep and shifted toward the right field line
Short   Up middle (shifted toward second base)
Second   Normal position

LOW-INSIDE FASTBALLS

BATTING AVERAGE .357
Play
Left   Medium-deep and shifted toward the left field line

Center	Deep in straightaway center field
Right	Deep in straightaway right field
Short	Up middle (shifted toward second base)
Second	Normal position

McGee Against Curves And Sliders

McGee has some very strong and some very weak curve and slider locations. He is weak against low-outside curves (.071) but very strong against medium-high outside (.391) and low-over-the-middle (.393) curves. His .147 against low-inside curves is also weak. In general, pitchers need to keep curves down and in or down and away.

He hits low-over-the-middle curves medium-deep down the left line (sound familiar?) and deep into the right-center gap.

LOW-OVER-THE-MIDDLE CURVEBALLS

BATTING AVERAGE .393
Play

Left	Medium-deep and shifted toward the left field line
Center	Medium-deep in straightaway center field
Right	Deep and shifted toward center field
Short	Normal position
Second	Shifted toward first base

McGee has a lot of trouble with inside sliders against right-handers (.000, .250 and .208, high to low). He hits low-over-the-middle sliders for an excellent .470 average, however.

McGee Against Left-Handed Pitchers

Batting right-handed, McGee has trouble with inside fastballs thrown by left-handed pitchers (.083, .269 and .176). He hits medium-high outside fastballs for an excellent .358 average.

MEDIUM-HIGH OUTSIDE FASTBALLS (THROWN BY LEFT-HANDED PITCHERS)

BATTING AVERAGE .358
Play

Left	Deep and shifted toward the left field line
Center	Deep and shifted toward right field
Right	Medium-deep in straightaway right field
Short	Shifted toward third base
Second	Shifted toward first base

His .333 against high-outside fastballs is also strong.

HIGH-OUTSIDE FASTBALLS (THROWN BY LEFT-HANDED PITCHERS)

BATTING AVERAGE .333
Play

Left	Medium-deep and shifted toward the left field line
Center	Deep in straightaway center field
Right	Deep and shifted toward the right field line
Short	*No instances recorded*
Second	*No instances recorded*

McGee has trouble with low curves and most low sliders against left-handers. This, along with his weakness against low fastballs and inside fastballs, gives ample targets for lefties.

Ahead And Behind In The Count Vs. RH

Ahead

Fastball Average .435

	Outside	Middle	Inside
High	3/ 333 /1	17/ 352 /6	13/ 461 /6
Med	26/ 500 /13	6/ 500 /3	27/ 296 /8
Low	3/ 333 /1	21/ 476 /10	24/ 541 /13

Curve Average .346

	Outside	Middle	Inside
High	1/ 0 /0	5/ 600 /3	2/ 0 /0
Med	5/ 100 /2	6/ 333 /2	9/ 444 /4
Low	4/ 0 /0	10/ 500 /5	10/ 200 /2

Behind

Fastball Average .287

	Outside	Middle	Inside
High	4/ 0 /0	6/ 166 /1	9/ 111 /1
Med	13/ 153 /2	6/ 500 /3	18/ 277 /5
Low	5/ 400 /2	11/ 727 /8	8/ 125 /1

Curve Average .294

	Outside	Middle	Inside
High	3/ 333 /1	3/ 0 /0	2/ 0 /0
Med	11/ 272 /3	1/ 1000 /1	5/ 200 /1
Low	6/ 166 /1	15/ 400 /6	5/ 400 /2

Overall Evaluation

Against Right-Handed Pitchers

Overall Fastball	⚾ ⚾ ⚾ ⚾
Overall Curve	⚾ ⚾
Overall Slider	⚾ ⚾

Against Left-Handed Pitchers

Overall Fastball	⚾ ⚾
Overall Curve	⚾ ⚾
Overall Slider	⚾

Comments: Hits over-the-middle fastballs well vs. RH.
Strengths: Medium-outside, low-inside and over-the-middle fastballs, waist-high curves, low-middle curves and low-middle sliders vs. RH; high-middle, high-outside and medium-outside fastballs, medium-inside curves and sliders, medium-outside curves vs. LH.
Weaknesses: High-outside, high-inside and low-outside fastballs, low-outside and low-inside curves, inside sliders vs. RH; inside fastballs vs. LH.

Jose Oquendo (Switch Hitter) — St. Louis Cardinals

Jose Oquendo Against Right-Handed Pitchers
Overall BARS Batting Average .242

Fastball Average .264

	Outside	Middle	Inside
High	11/ 90 /1	12/ 500 /6	10/ 400 /4
Med	22/ 318 /7	18/ 166 /3	16/ 187 /3
Low	7/ 142 /1	18/ 388 /7	26/ 192 /5

Curve Average .270

	Outside	Middle	Inside
High	1/ 0 /0	4/ 500 /2	0/ 0 /0
Med	5/ 200 /1	4/ 0 /0	5/ 800 /4
Low	2/ 500 /1	6/ 166 /1	10/ 100 /1

Slider Average .166

	Outside	Middle	Inside
High	0/ 0 /0	0/ 0 /0	2/ 500 /1
Med	1/ 0 /0	2/ 0 /0	1/ 0 /0
Low	3/ 0 /0	0/ 0 /0	3/ 333 /1

Jose Oquendo Against Left-Handed Pitchers
Overall BARS Batting Average .252

Fastball Average .212

	Inside	Middle	Outside
High	2/ 0 /0	6/ 166 /1	5/ 0 /0
Med	7/ 285 /2	3/ 0 /0	8/ 250 /2
Low	2/ 0 /0	7/ 428 /3	7/ 285 /2

Curve Average .238

	Inside	Middle	Outside
High	1/ 0 /0	1/ 1000 /1	3/ 0 /0
Med	3/ 666 /2	0/ 0 /0	4/ 250 /1
Low	3/ 0 /0	4/ 250 /1	2/ 0 /0

Slider Average .500

	Inside	Middle	Outside
High	0/ 0 /0	1/ 1000 /1	0/ 0 /0
Med	4/ 500 /2	0/ 0 /0	2/ 500 /1
Low	0/ 0 /0	3/ 333 /1	0/ 0 /0

Switch-hitting Jose Oquendo hits medium-high outside fastballs at a .318 clip against right-handed pitchers. Batting left-handed, he hits this pitch medium-deep down both lines.

MEDIUM-HIGH OUTSIDE FASTBALLS

BATTING AVERAGE .318
Play

Left	Medium-deep and shifted toward the left line
Center	Medium-deep and shifted toward right field
Right	Medium-deep and shifted toward the right line
Short	Normal position
Second	Shifted toward first base

He hits low-over-the-middle fastballs for an excellent .388 average. By aligning themselves according to the following fielding strategy and the field diagram on the opposite page, fielders could prevent most of his base hits from this location.

LOW-OVER-THE-MIDDLE FASTBALLS

BATTING AVERAGE .388
Play

Left	Medium-deep and shifted toward the left field line
Center	Medium-deep in straightaway center field
Right	Short in straightaway right field
Short	Up middle (shifted toward second base)
Second	Shifted toward first base

Oquendo's .500 against high-over-the-middle fastballs is also very strong.

HIGH-OVER-THE-MIDDLE FASTBALLS

BATTING AVERAGE .500
Play

Left	Medium-deep in straightaway left field
Center	Medium-deep in straightaway center field
Right	Deep and shifted toward the right field line
Short	Shifted toward third base
Second	Shifted toward first base

He has trouble with medium-high inside (.187) and low-inside (.192) fastballs. By keeping fastballs in this sector, right-handers can get an edge. His .400 against high-inside fastballs is excellent, however.

HIGH-INSIDE FASTBALLS

BATTING AVERAGE .400
Play

Left	Deep and shifted toward the left field line
Center	Deep in straightaway center field
Right	*No instances recorded*
Short	Normal position
Second	*No instances recorded*

Oquendo's 1-for-10 against low-inside curves indicates a weakness.

Low-Over-The-Middle Fastballs

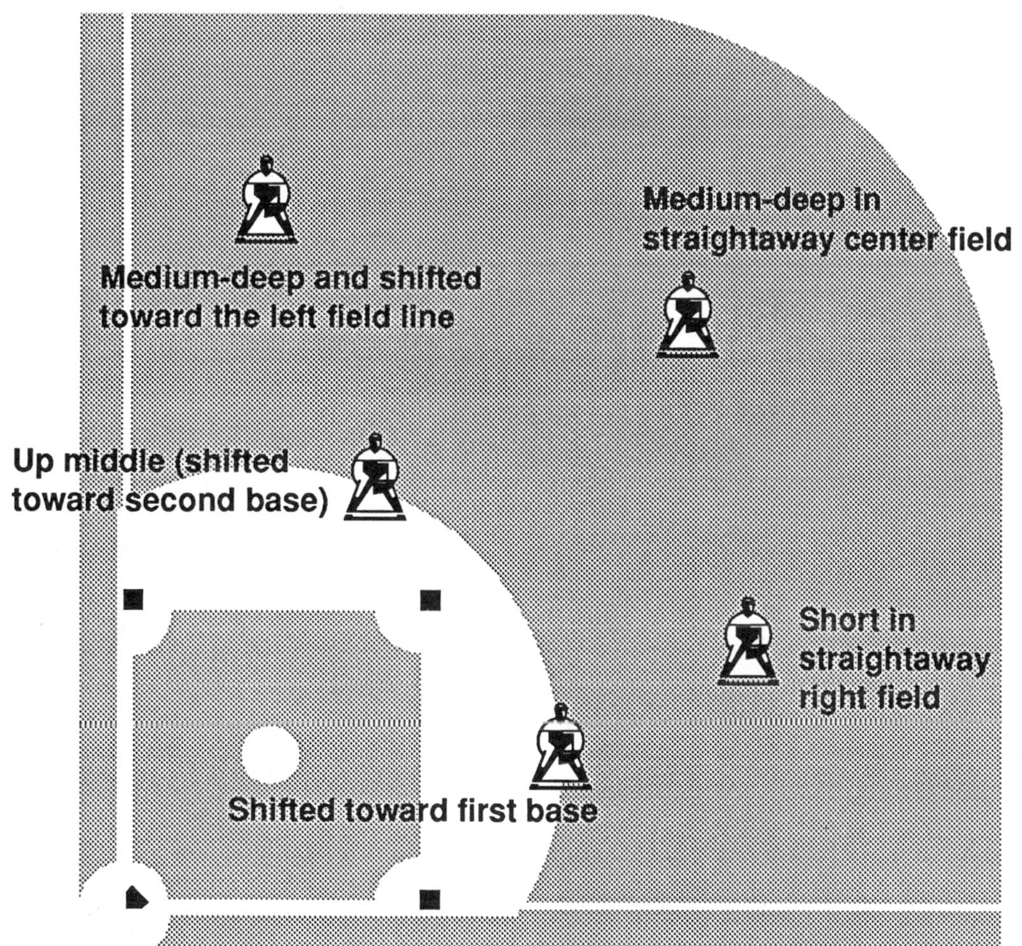

Ahead And Behind In The Count Vs. RH

Ahead

Fastball Average .225

	Outside	Middle	Inside
High	5/ 200 /1	5/ 600 /3	8/ 250 /2
Med	16/ 312 /5	13/ 0 /0	11/ 181 /2
Low	6/ 166 /1	10/ 300 /3	19/ 210 /4

Curve Average .666

	Outside	Middle	Inside
High	0/ 0 /0	2/ 500 /1	0/ 0 /0
Med	0/ 0 /0	0/ 0 /0	0/ 0 /0
Low	0/ 0 /0	0/ 0 /0	1/ 1000 /1

Behind

Fastball Average .312

	Outside	Middle	Inside
High	1/ 0 /0	2/ 500 /1	1/ 1000 /1
Med	2/ 0 /0	2/ 500 /1	4/ 250 /1
Low	0/ 0 /0	2/ 500 /1	2/ 0 /0

Curve Average .285

	Outside	Middle	Inside
High	0/ 0 /0	1/ 1000 /1	0/ 0 /0
Med	1/ 1000 /1	3/ 0 /0	2/ 500 /1
Low	0/ 0 /0	4/ 250 /1	3/ 0 /0

Overall Evaluation

Against Right-Handed Pitchers

Overall Fastball 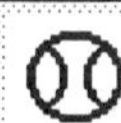

Overall Curve

Overall Slider — Not enough information

Against Left-Handed Pitchers

Overall Fastball 

Overall Curve 

Overall Slider — Not enough information

Comments: Weak sector against medium-inside and low-inside fastballs vs. RH.

Strengths: High-middle, high-inside, medium-outside and low-middle fastballs, medium-inside curves vs. RH; low-middle fastballs vs. LH.

Weaknesses: High-outside, medium-middle, low-outside, medium-inside and low-inside fastballs, low-inside and low-middle curves vs. RH; high fastballs vs. LH.

Tony Pena Against Right-Handed Pitchers
Overall BARS Batting Average .273

Fastball Average .325

	Inside	Middle	Outside
High	25/200 /5	38/447 /17	15/266 /4
Med	42/190 /8	12/500 /6	39/512 /20
Low	14/214 /3	52/269 /14	33/333 /11

Curve Average .237

	Inside	Middle	Outside
High	5/0 /0	10/400 /4	3/0 /0
Med	4/250 /1	3/666 /2	30/233 /7
Low	4/250 /1	7/428 /3	35/171 /6

Slider Average .250

	Inside	Middle	Outside
High	0/0 /0	3/666 /2	5/0 /0
Med	0/0 /0	3/0 /0	23/304 /7
Low	1/0 /0	7/285 /2	30/233 /7

Tony Pena Against Left-Handed Pitchers
Overall BARS Batting Average .302

Fastball Average .352

	Inside	Middle	Outside
High	3/0 /0	5/0 /0	5/400 /2
Med	4/500 /2	5/600 /3	23/347 /8
Low	6/166 /1	19/473 /9	18/333 /6

Curve Average .384

	Inside	Middle	Outside
High	1/0 /0	1/0 /0	0/0 /0
Med	2/500 /1	2/500 /1	5/600 /3
Low	1/0 /0	6/500 /3	8/250 /2

Slider Average .411

	Inside	Middle	Outside
High	1/0 /0	0/0 /0	0/0 /0
Med	0/0 /0	1/0 /0	3/666 /2
Low	3/0 /0	4/1000 /4	5/200 /1

Right-handed hitting Tony Pena has an excellent .325 overall fastball average against right-handed pitchers. He hits a dazzling .512 against medium-high outside fastballs.

MEDIUM-HIGH OUTSIDE FASTBALLS

BATTING AVERAGE .512
Play
Left Deep in straightaway left field
Center Medium-deep in straightaway center field
Right Medium-deep in straightaway right field
Short Up middle (shifted toward second base)
Second Normal position

His .447 against high-over-the-middle fastballs is almost as impressive. He hits this pitch into a corridor in left-center field. By aligning themselves according to the following unusual fielding strategy, fielders could get to most of Pena's hits that are now falling in.

HIGH-OVER-THE-MIDDLE FASTBALLS

BATTING AVERAGE .447
Play
Left Medium-deep and shifted toward center field
Center Deep and shifted toward left field
Right Deep in straightaway right field
Short Up middle (shifted toward second base)
Second Shifted toward first base

Pena is weak against inside fastballs and low-over-the-middle fastballs thrown by right-handers. He is also weak against outside curves (.000, .233 and .171). He has trouble with low-outside sliders (.233) but hits medium-high outside sliders excellently (.304).

Pena hits a vibrant .352 against fastballs thrown by left-handed pitchers. He hits medium-outside fastballs (.347) deep to all fields.

MEDIUM-HIGH OUTSIDE FASTBALLS
(THROWN BY LEFT-HANDED PITCHERS)

BATTING AVERAGE .347
Play
Left Deep in straightaway left field
Center Deep and shifted toward left field
Right Deep and shifted toward center field
Short Up middle (shifted toward second base
Second Normal position

He hits low-over-the-middle fastballs deep into the right-center gap for a very high .473 average.

LOW-OVER-THE-MIDDLE FASTBALLS
(THROWN BY LEFT-HANDED PITCHERS)

BATTING AVERAGE .473
Play
Left Deep in straightaway left field
Center Medium-deep in straightaway center field
Right Deep and shifted toward center field
Short Up middle (shifted toward second base)
Second *No instances recorded*

High-Over-The-Middle Fastballs

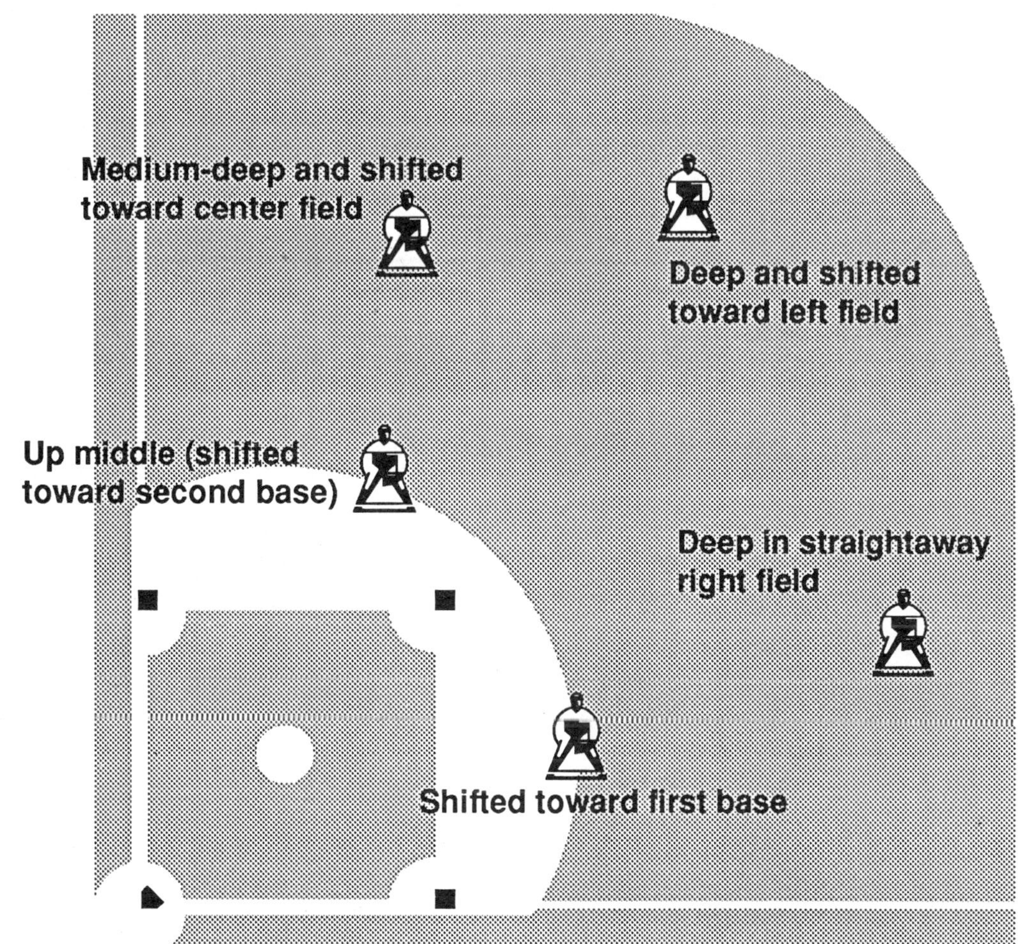

Ahead And Behind In The Count Vs. RH

Ahead

Fastball Average .313

	Inside	Middle	Outside
High	10 / 300 / 3	20 / 400 / 8	7 / 0 / 0
Med	25 / 160 / 4	7 / 428 / 3	20 / 650 / 13
Low	6 / 166 / 1	29 / 206 / 6	10 / 400 / 4

Curve Average .258

	Inside	Middle	Outside
High	2 / 0 / 0	5 / 400 / 2	0 / 0 / 0
Med	3 / 0 / 0	0 / 0 / 0	10 / 200 / 2
Low	3 / 333 / 1	2 / 500 / 1	6 / 333 / 2

Behind

Fastball Average .479

	Inside	Middle	Outside
High	7 / 142 / 1	9 / 777 / 7	4 / 500 / 2
Med	7 / 285 / 2	3 / 666 / 2	3 / 666 / 2
Low	3 / 666 / 2	6 / 500 / 3	6 / 333 / 2

Curve Average .266

	Inside	Middle	Outside
High	1 / 0 / 0	1 / 0 / 0	2 / 0 / 0
Med	1 / 1000 / 1	0 / 0 / 0	11 / 272 / 3
Low	0 / 0 / 0	2 / 500 / 1	12 / 250 / 3

Overall Evaluation

Against Right-Handed Pitchers

Overall Fastball	⚾⚾⚾⚾
Overall Curve	⚾
Overall Slider	⚾⚾

Against Left-Handed Pitchers

Overall Fastball	⚾⚾⚾⚾
Overall Curve	⚾⚾⚾⚾
Overall Slider	⚾⚾⚾⚾

Comments: Weak against inside fastballs vs. RH.
Consistent hitter vs. LH (especially outside fastballs).
Strengths: High-middle, medium-middle, medium-outside and low-outside fastballs, over-the-middle curves, medium-outside sliders vs. RH; waist-high, outside and low-middle fastballs vs. LH.
Weaknesses: Inside fastballs, low-middle fastballs, outside and inside curves, low-outside sliders vs. RH.

Terry Pendleton (Switch Hitter) — *St. Louis Cardinals*

Terry Pendleton Against Right-Handed Pitchers
Overall BARS Batting Average .240

Fastball Average .261

	Outside	Middle	Inside
High	17/ 58 /1	62/ 241 /15	18/ 222 /4
Med	46/ 282 /13	14/ 500 /7	43/ 279 /12
Low	19/ 105 /2	49/ 326 /16	34/ 264 /9

Curve Average .212

	Outside	Middle	Inside
High	3/ 0 /0	4/ 250 /1	4/ 250 /1
Med	12/ 166 /2	2/ 0 /0	13/ 384 /5
Low	4/ 0 /0	11/ 545 /6	27/ 74 /2

Slider Average .344

	Outside	Middle	Inside
High	1/ 0 /0	0/ 0 /0	4/ 500 /2
Med	2/ 0 /0	1/ 1000 /1	3/ 333 /1
Low	2/ 0 /0	5/ 400 /2	11/ 363 /4

Terry Pendleton Against Left-Handed Pitchers
Overall BARS Batting Average .283

Fastball Average .333

	Inside	Middle	Outside
High	7/ 285 /2	13/ 384 /5	12/ 333 /4
Med	19/ 210 /4	3/ 333 /1	29/ 310 /9
Low	10/ 200 /2	27/ 481 /13	15/ 333 /5

Curve Average .178

	Inside	Middle	Outside
High	1/ 0 /0	0/ 0 /0	3/ 333 /1
Med	2/ 0 /0	1/ 0 /0	9/ 333 /3
Low	5/ 200 /1	4/ 0 /0	3/ 0 /0

Slider Average .277

	Inside	Middle	Outside
High	1/ 0 /0	0/ 0 /0	0/ 0 /0
Med	1/ 0 /0	1/ 0 /0	1/ 0 /0
Low	3/ 333 /1	7/ 428 /3	4/ 250 /1

Right-handed hitting Terry Pendleton hits .261 overall against fastballs thrown by right-handed pitchers. He hits an excellent .326 in his low-over-the-middle location. The left fielder needs to shift toward the left line for this pitch but the shortstop needs to shift toward second and the second baseman toward first.

LOW-OVER-THE-MIDDLE FASTBALLS

BATTING AVERAGE .326
Play

Left	Deep and shifted toward the left field line
Center	Medium-deep in straightaway center field
Right	Deep in straightaway right field
Short	Up middle (shifted toward second base)
Second	Shifted toward first base

He has a lot of trouble with high fastballs thrown by right-handers (.058, .241 and .222, outside to inside). If right-handers keep their fastballs up, they'll have an edge on him.

Pendleton has two strong curve locations against right-handers — .545 low-over-the-middle and .384 medium-high inside. He hits medium-high inside curves very unusually. The following fielding strategy and the field diagram on the opposite page show how fielders need to play to prevent most of Pendleton's base hits from pitches to this location.

MEDIUM-HIGH INSIDE CURVEBALLS

BATTING AVERAGE .384
Play

Left	Short and shifted toward the left line
Center	Medium-deep and shifted toward left field
Right	Medium-deep and shifted toward the right line
Short	Up middle (shifted toward second base)
Second	Normal position

Pendleton has an excellent .333 overall fastball average against left-handed pitchers. He hits a lot of low-over-the-middle fastballs and has a very high average in this location (.481). Batting right-handed, he goes to the opposite field (left field) with this pitch.

LOW-OVER-THE-MIDDLE FASTBALLS
(THROWN BY LEFT-HANDED PITCHERS)

BATTING AVERAGE .481
Play

Left	Deep and shifted toward the left field line
Center	Medium-deep in straightaway center field
Right	Deep and shifted toward center field
Short	Normal position
Second	Normal position

Medium-High Inside Curveballs

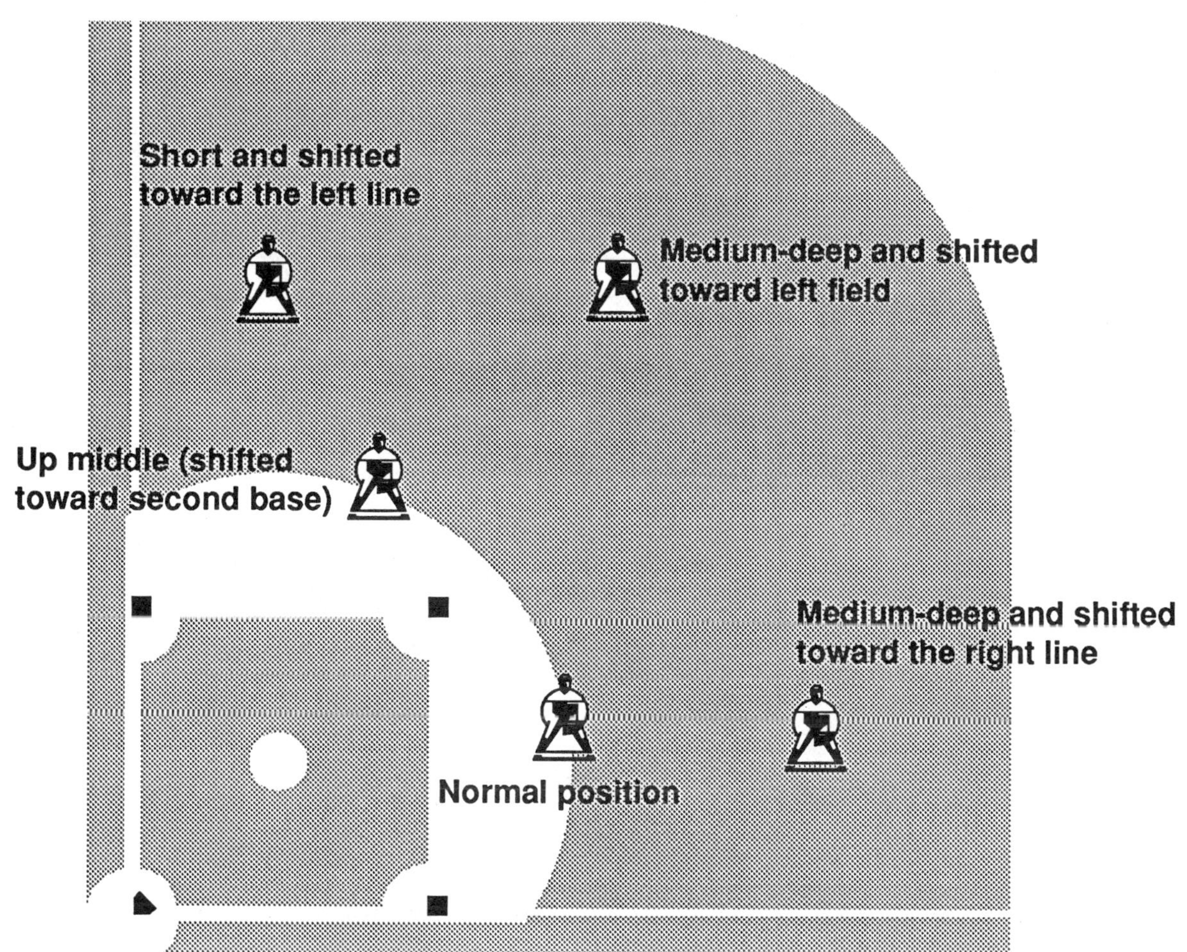

Ahead And Behind In The Count Vs. RH

Ahead

Fastball Average .272

	Outside	Middle	Inside
High	7/ 142 /1	27/ 333 /9	7/ 142 /1
Med	23/ 347 /8	5/ 800 /4	23/ 217 /5
Low	5/ 0 /0	29/ 241 /7	17/ 235 /4

Curve Average .200

	Outside	Middle	Inside
High	1/ 0 /0	1/ 0 /0	1/ 1000 /1
Med	1/ 0 /0	1/ 0 /0	2/ 500 /1
Low	0/ 0 /0	0/ 0 /0	3/ 0 /0

Behind

Fastball Average .377

	Outside	Middle	Inside
High	2/ 0 /0	11/ 272 /3	7/ 428 /3
Med	9/ 333 /3	2/ 500 /1	6/ 333 /2
Low	1/ 0 /0	9/ 777 /7	6/ 166 /1

Curve Average .370

	Outside	Middle	Inside
High	1/ 0 /0	0/ 0 /0	1/ 0 /0
Med	5/ 400 /2	1/ 0 /0	6/ 333 /2
Low	1/ 0 /0	4/ 1000 /4	8/ 250 /2

Overall Evaluation

Against Right-Handed Pitchers

Overall Fastball

Overall Curve

Overall Slider

Against Left-Handed Pitchers

Overall Fastball

Overall Curve

Overall Slider

Comments: Weak vs, high, outside and inside fastballs vs. RH. Strong vs. outside fastballs vs. LH.
Strengths: Medium-middle and low-middle fastballs, low-middle and medium-inside curves, inside sliders vs. RH; over-the-middle and outside fastballs, medium-outside curves and low-middle sliders vs. LH.
Weaknesses: High, outside and inside fastballs, outside curves, low-inside curves vs. RH; medium-inside and low-inside fastballs, low curves vs. LH.

Ozzie Smith (Switch Hitter) — St. Louis Cardinals

Ozzie Smith Against Right-Handed Pitchers
Overall BARS Batting Average .291

Fastball Average .334

	Outside	Middle	Inside
High	25/ 320 / 8	65/ 338 / 22	36/ 416 / 15
Med	61/ 311 / 19	33/ 333 / 11	76/ 302 / 23
Low	30/ 333 / 10	60/ 350 / 21	47/ 340 / 16

Curve Average .241

	Outside	Middle	Inside
High	4/ 0 / 0	9/ 222 / 2	5/ 200 / 1
Med	12/ 166 / 2	3/ 333 / 1	9/ 555 / 5
Low	4/ 250 / 1	10/ 100 / 1	6/ 333 / 2

Slider Average .205

	Outside	Middle	Inside
High	0/ 0 / 0	3/ 0 / 0	2/ 0 / 0
Med	5/ 200 / 1	1/ 0 / 0	11/ 454 / 5
Low	2/ 500 / 1	3/ 0 / 0	12/ 83 / 1

Ozzie Smith Against Left-Handed Pitchers
Overall BARS Batting Average .250

Fastball Average .266

	Inside	Middle	Outside
High	7/ 571 / 4	17/ 235 / 4	20/ 300 / 6
Med	10/ 400 / 4	11/ 272 / 3	48/ 250 / 12
Low	9/ 444 / 4	33/ 212 / 7	25/ 160 / 4

Curve Average .192

	Inside	Middle	Outside
High	3/ 0 / 0	3/ 333 / 1	2/ 0 / 0
Med	2/ 500 / 1	1/ 0 / 0	4/ 250 / 1
Low	0/ 0 / 0	6/ 166 / 1	5/ 200 / 1

Slider Average .227

	Inside	Middle	Outside
High	3/ 333 / 1	2/ 500 / 1	1/ 0 / 0
Med	1/ 0 / 0	2/ 0 / 0	3/ 0 / 0
Low	4/ 0 / 0	3/ 666 / 2	3/ 333 / 1

Switch-hitting Ozzie Smith has consistent averages throughout his fastball chart against right-handed pitchers. Not one of his locations is under .300.

Notice that right-handers throw him more inside than outside fastballs. His consistent averages make this incidental. If anything, he hits inside fastballs better than outside fastballs. The .302 in his medium-high inside fastball location is solid enough. He hits this pitch medium-deep to all fields.

MEDIUM-HIGH INSIDE FASTBALLS

BATTING AVERAGE .302
Play
Left | Medium-deep and shifted toward the left field line
Center | Medium-deep in straightaway center field
Right | Medium-deep in straightaway right field
Short | Up middle (shifted toward second base)
Second | Normal position

He hits .311 against medium-high outside fastballs.

MEDIUM-HIGH OUTSIDE FASTBALLS

BATTING AVERAGE .311
Play
Left | Medium-deep and shifted toward the left field line
Center | Deep in straightaway center field

Right | Medium-deep and shifted toward center field
Short | Up middle (shifted toward second base)
Second | Normal position

He hits high-over-the-middle fastballs (.338) medium-deep down both lines and to the right side of the infield.

HIGH-OVER-THE-MIDDLE FASTBALLS

BATTING AVERAGE .338
Play
Left | Medium-deep and shifted toward the left line
Center | Deep and shifted toward left field
Right | Medium-deep and shifted toward the right line
Short | Up middle (shifted toward second base)
Second | Shifted toward first base

He hits high-inside fastballs down both lines for a very strong .416 average.

HIGH-INSIDE FASTBALLS

BATTING AVERAGE .416
Play
Left | Medium-deep and shifted toward the left field line
Center | Medium-deep in straightaway center field
Right | Deep and shifted toward the right field line
Short | Normal position
Second | Shifted toward first base

His .350 average against low-over-the-middle fastballs is also strong. He hits this pitch deep to left and right fields.

LOW-OVER-THE-MIDDLE FASTBALLS

BATTING AVERAGE .350
Play

Left	Deep in straightaway left field
Center	Medium-deep in straightaway center field
Right	Deep and shifted toward center field
Short	Up middle (shifted toward second base)
Second	Normal position

Smith Against Curves And Sliders

Smith has some problems with outside curves and low-over-the-middle curves thrown by right-handed pitchers. These weaknesses are in such contrast to his fastball strengths that right-handers should try throwing Smith more curves than they do.

He has trouble with low-inside sliders (.083) but he hits medium-high inside sliders very well (.454). He hits this pitch medium-deep down both lines.

Smith Against Left-Handed Pitchers

Smith's fastball chart against left-handed pitchers shows less consistency. He hits inside fastballs very well but has some problems with over-the-middle and outside fastballs. He hits only .250 against medium-high outside fastballs thrown by left-handers.

MEDIUM-HIGH OUTSIDE FASTBALLS
(THROWN BY LEFT-HANDED PITCHERS)

BATTING AVERAGE .250
Play

Left	Deep and shifted toward the left field line
Center	Medium-deep and shifted toward right field
Right	Deep in straightaway right field
Short	Up middle (shifted toward second base)
Second	Normal position

He hits .300 against high-outside fastballs thrown by left-handers.

HIGH-OUTSIDE FASTBALLS
(THROWN BY LEFT-HANDED PITCHERS)

BATTING AVERAGE .300
Play

Left	Deep and shifted toward the left field line
Center	Medium-deep in straightaway center field
Right	Deep in straightaway right field
Short	Up middle (shifted toward second base)
Second	Normal position

He pulls medium-high inside fastballs when he hits to the outfield but he goes to the opposite side (right side) of the infield when he hits grounders.

MEDIUM-HIGH INSIDE FASTBALLS
(THROWN BY LEFT-HANDED PITCHERS)

BATTING AVERAGE .400
Play

Left	Deep and shifted toward the left field line
Center	Deep and shifted toward left field
Right	*No instances recorded*
Short	Up middle (shifted toward second base)
Second	Shifted toward first base

Ahead And Behind In The Count Vs. RH

Ahead

Fastball Average .368

	Outside	Middle	Inside
High	17/ 235 /4	30/ 500 /15	24/ 458 /11
Med	37/ 324 /12	13/ 384 /5	38/ 342 /13
Low	19/ 368 /7	31/ 322 /10	27/ 370 /10

Curve Average .375

	Outside	Middle	Inside
High	1/ 0 /0	0/ 0 /0	2/ 500 /1
Med	1/ 0 /0	0/ 0 /0	1/ 1000 /1
Low	0/ 0 /0	1/ 0 /0	2/ 500 /1

Behind

Fastball Average .256

	Outside	Middle	Inside
High	3/ 666 /2	10/ 100 /1	6/ 166 /1
Med	6/ 166 /1	11/ 272 /3	18/ 333 /6
Low	3/ 666 /2	10/ 200 /2	7/ 142 /1

Curve Average .250

	Outside	Middle	Inside
High	3/ 0 /0	5/ 200 /1	2/ 0 /0
Med	5/ 200 /1	2/ 0 /0	4/ 750 /3
Low	3/ 333 /1	3/ 0 /0	1/ 1000 /1

Overall Evaluation
Against Right-Handed Pitchers

Overall Fastball	⚾⚾ ⚾⚾ ⚾⚾ ⚾⚾
Overall Curve	⚾⚾
Overall Slider	⚾⚾

Against Left-Handed Pitchers

Overall Fastball	⚾⚾
Overall Curve	⚾⚾
Overall Slider	⚾⚾

Comments: No weak fastball locations vs. RH.
Strengths: Fastballs in general, medium-inside and low-inside curves, medium-inside sliders vs. RH; inside fastballs, high-outside fastballs vs. LH.
Weaknesses: Outside curves, high curves, low-middle curves, low-inside sliders vs. RH; over-the-middle fastballs, medium-outside and low-outside fastballs vs. LH.

Milt Thompson Against Right-Handed Pitchers
Overall BARS Batting Average .274

Fastball Average .363

	Outside	Middle	Inside
High	14/ 285 / 4	23/ 391 / 9	13/ 461 / 6
Med	43/ 465 / 20	12/ 666 / 8	33/ 303 / 10
Low	14/ 285 / 4	26/ 269 / 7	34/ 264 / 9

Curve Average .098

	Outside	Middle	Inside
High	1/ 0 / 0	3/ 0 / 0	1/ 1000/ 1
Med	7/ 0 / 0	2/ 0 / 0	7/ 428 / 3
Low	10/ 0 / 0	5/ 0 / 0	15/ 66 / 1

Slider Average .200

	Outside	Middle	Inside
High	0/ 0 / 0	0/ 0 / 0	1/ 0 / 0
Med	4/ 500 / 2	2/ 500 / 1	7/ 0 / 0
Low	1/ 0 / 0	2/ 0 / 0	13/ 230 / 3

Milt Thompson Against Left-Handed Pitchers
Overall BARS Batting Average .250

Fastball Average .214

	Outside	Middle	Inside
High	2/ 0 / 0	3/ 333 / 1	2/ 0 / 0
Med	2/ 0 / 0	0/ 0 / 0	8/ 375 / 3
Low	3/ 0 / 0	4/ 250 / 1	4/ 250 / 1

Curve Average .333

	Outside	Middle	Inside
High	1/ 1000/ 1	1/ 1000/ 1	0/ 0 / 0
Med	1/ 0 / 0	1/ 0 / 0	1/ 0 / 0
Low	2/ 500 / 1	1/ 0 / 0	1/ 0 / 0

Slider Average .250

	Outside	Middle	Inside
High	0/ 0 / 0	0/ 0 / 0	0/ 0 / 0
Med	1/ 0 / 0	0/ 0 / 0	0/ 0 / 0
Low	3/ 333 / 1	0/ 0 / 0	0/ 0 / 0

Left-handed hitter Milt Thompson has two weak low fastball locations against right-handed pitchers (.269 low-over-the-middle and .264 low-inside) but the rest of his fastball locations are solid.

He hits an excellent .465 against medium-high outside fastballs. The following fielding strategy and the field diagram on the opposite page show how fielders need to be positioned for this pitch.

MEDIUM-HIGH OUTSIDE FASTBALLS

BATTING AVERAGE .465
Play

Left	Medium-deep and shifted toward the left field line
Center	Medium-deep in straightaway center field
Right	Deep in straightaway right field
Short	Up middle (shifted toward second base)
Second	Normal position

He hits medium-high inside fastballs (.303) down both lines.

MEDIUM-HIGH INSIDE FASTBALLS

BATTING AVERAGE .303
Play

Left	Medium-deep and shifted toward the left field line
Center	Medium-deep in straightaway center field
Right	Deep and shifted toward the right field line
Short	Up middle (shifted toward second base)
Second	Normal position

His .391 against high-over-the-middle fastballs is extremely good.

HIGH-OVER-THE-MIDDLE FASTBALLS

BATTING AVERAGE .391
Play

Left	Medium-deep and shifted toward the left field line
Center	Deep in straightaway center field
Right	*No instances recorded*
Short	Up middle (shifted toward second base)
Second	Normal position

Thompson has trouble with low-inside fastballs. He hits this pitch short to center field and to the right side of the infield.

LOW-INSIDE FASTBALLS

BATTING AVERAGE .264
Play

Left	Deep in straightaway left field
Center	Short in straightaway center field
Right	*No instances recorded*
Short	Up middle (shifted toward second base)
Second	Shifted toward first base

Thompson is very weak against outside curves, low curves, low sliders and inside sliders. Considering his overall strength against fastballs, right-handers should mix in more breaking pitches to him.

Medium-High Outside Fastballs

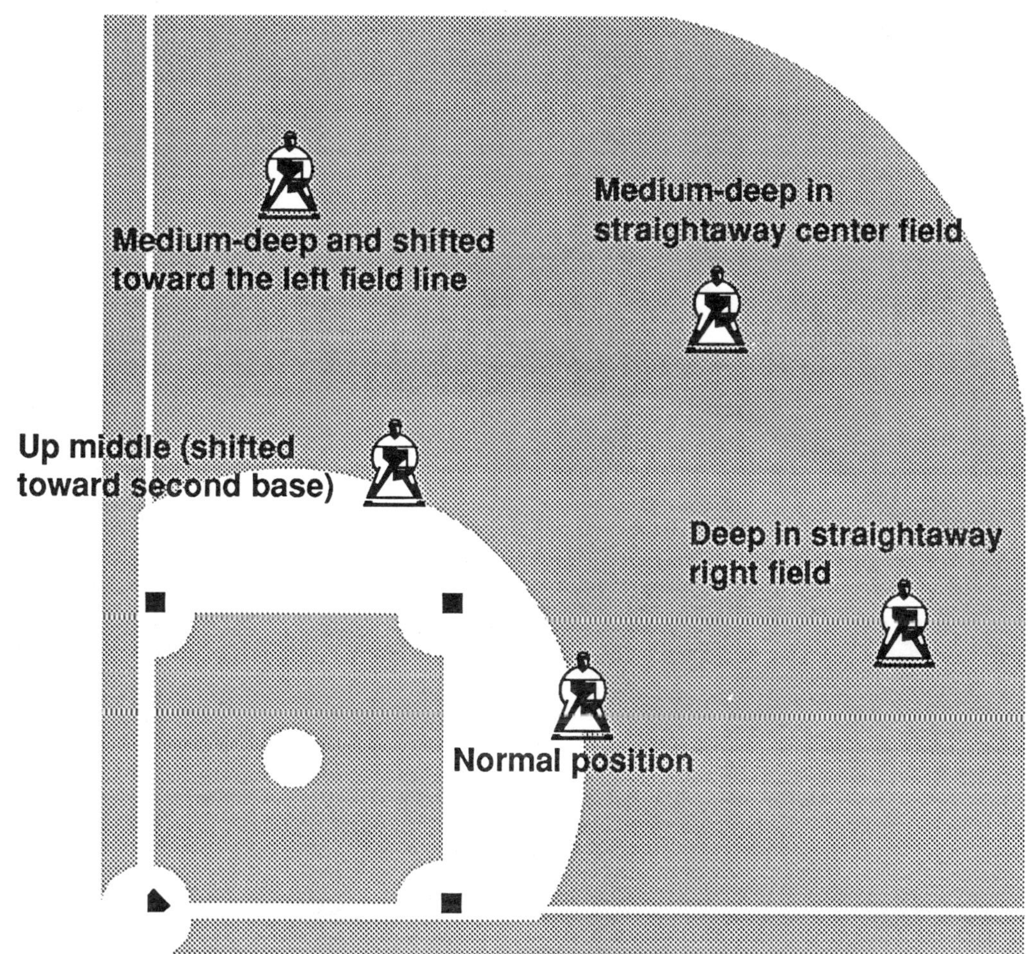

Ahead And Behind In The Count Vs. RH

Ahead

Fastball Average .404

	Outside	Middle	Inside
High	4/250 /1	9/444 /4	7/714 /5
Med	21/571 /12	6/666 /4	13/153 /2
Low	8/250 /2	13/230 /3	13/384 /5

Curve Average .125

	Outside	Middle	Inside
High	0/0 /0	1/0 /0	0/0 /0
Med	2/0 /0	0/0 /0	2/500 /1
Low	1/0 /0	1/0 /0	1/0 /0

Behind

Fastball Average .446

	Outside	Middle	Inside
High	2/500 /1	6/666 /4	1/0 /0
Med	12/333 /4	1/1000 /1	5/800 /4
Low	3/666 /2	5/400 /2	12/250 /3

Curve Average .142

	Outside	Middle	Inside
High	1/0 /0	1/0 /0	0/0 /0
Med	1/0 /0	1/0 /0	1/1000 /1
Low	2/0 /0	0/0 /0	0/0 /0

Overall Evaluation

Against Right-Handed Pitchers

Overall Fastball ⚾⚾⚾⚾

Overall Curve ⚾

Overall Slider ⚾

Against Left-Handed Pitchers

Overall Fastball ⚾

Overall Curve — Not enough information

Overall Slider — Not enough information

Comments: Very weak against low curves and low sliders vs. RH.

Strengths: Waist-high fastballs, high-middle fastballs, medium-inside curves vs. RH; medium-inside fastballs vs. LH.

Weaknesses: Low-middle and low-inside fastballs, outside curves, low curves, inside sliders, low sliders vs. RH.

Benedict, Bruce
Davis, Jody
Evans, Darrell
Gant, Ron
James, Dion
Murphy, Dale
Perry, Gerald
Smith, Lonnie
Thomas, Andres

Atlanta Braves
BARS System
Hitting Analysis

Bruce Benedict Against Right-Handed Pitchers
Overall BARS Batting Average .256

Fastball Average .273

	Inside	Middle	Outside
High	15 / 133 / 2	39 / 307 / 12	19 / 105 / 2
Med	31 / 193 / 6	48 / 375 / 18	100 / 250 / 25
Low	12 / 250 / 3	60 / 300 / 18	52 / 326 / 17

Curve Average .265

	Inside	Middle	Outside
High	2 / 1000 / 2	0 / 0 / 0	0 / 0 / 0
Med	4 / 500 / 2	8 / 500 / 4	17 / 58 / 1
Low	1 / 0 / 0	16 / 187 / 3	31 / 290 / 9

Slider Average .339

	Inside	Middle	Outside
High	0 / 0 / 0	1 / 0 / 0	2 / 0 / 0
Med	1 / 0 / 0	1 / 0 / 0	15 / 266 / 4
Low	2 / 0 / 0	7 / 285 / 2	27 / 481 / 13

Bruce Benedict Against Left-Handed Pitchers
Overall BARS Batting Average .223

Fastball Average .244

	Inside	Middle	Outside
High	8 / 0 / 0	7 / 428 / 3	13 / 0 / 0
Med	10 / 100 / 1	5 / 200 / 1	46 / 326 / 15
Low	4 / 250 / 1	25 / 320 / 8	25 / 240 / 6

Curve Average .242

	Inside	Middle	Outside
High	1 / 0 / 0	0 / 0 / 0	3 / 333 / 1
Med	0 / 0 / 0	0 / 0 / 0	8 / 250 / 2
Low	2 / 0 / 0	9 / 222 / 2	10 / 300 / 3

Slider Average .444

	Inside	Middle	Outside
High	0 / 0 / 0	0 / 0 / 0	0 / 0 / 0
Med	1 / 0 / 0	1 / 0 / 0	4 / 750 / 3
Low	0 / 0 / 0	1 / 1000 / 1	2 / 0 / 0

Right-handed Bruce Benedict hits .273 overall against fastballs thrown by right-handed pitchers, .244 overall against fastballs thrown by left-handed pitchers. He hits curves fairly well against right-handers (.265 overall) and hits sliders excellently (.339 overall).

Notice that he hits only .250 against fastballs thrown by right-handers in the highly pitched medium-high outside location. He hits this pitch medium-deep to all fields.

MEDIUM-HIGH OUTSIDE FASTBALLS

BATTING AVERAGE .250
Play

Left	Medium-deep and shifted toward center field
Center	Medium-deep in straightaway center field
Right	Medium-deep in straightaway right field
Short	Normal position
Second	Normal position

His Ahead and Behind charts show that he hits medium-high outside fastballs for a higher average when ahead in the count (.296 when ahead, .166 when behind).

The high number of recorded instances in Benedict's low-over-the-middle and low-outside fastball locations shows that right-handed pitchers are throwing him a lot of low pitches. But his high average in each of these locations indicates that this is a mistake. His .326 against low-outside fastballs is excellent.

LOW-OUTSIDE FASTBALLS

BATTING AVERAGE .326
Play

Left	Medium-deep in straightaway left field
Center	Deep in straightaway center field
Right	Medium-deep in straightaway right field
Short	Up middle (shifted toward second base)
Second	Normal position

His .300 in the low-over-the-middle fastball location is solid enough.

LOW-OVER-THE-MIDDLE FASTBALLS

BATTING AVERAGE .300
Play

Left	Deep and shifted toward the left field line
Center	Medium-deep in straightaway center field
Right	Deep and shifted toward center field
Short	Up middle (shifted toward second base)
Second	Normal position

He is very weak against inside fastballs thrown by right-handers. The three inside locations are a better target for pitchers than low fastballs.

Benedict has some very weak curve locations against right-handers but he hits a solid .290 against low-outside curves. In fact, Benedict hits low-outside pitches very well against right-handers. This shows that not all hitters have trouble with low-outside pitches.

By following the BARS fielding strategy for low-outside fastballs, fielders could prevent most of Benedict's hits that are now falling in.

LOW-OUTSIDE CURVEBALLS

BATTING AVERAGE .290

Play	
Left	Deep and shifted toward the left field line
Center	Short in straightaway center field
Right	Medium-deep and shifted toward center field
Short	Up middle (shifted toward second base)
Second	Normal position

Benedict also hits low-outside sliders very well (.481). Notice in the following strategy that he pulls this pitch when hitting ground balls to the infield.

LOW-OUTSIDE SLIDERS

BATTING AVERAGE .481

Play	
Left	Medium-deep in straightaway left field
Center	Medium-deep in straightaway center field
Right	Medium-deep and shifted toward center field
Short	Shifted toward third base
Second	*No instances recorded*

Against left-handed pitchers, Benedict is strong against medium-high outside fastballs (.326) and low-over-the-middle fastballs (.320). He is weak against low-outside fastballs (.240) and high-outside fastballs (.000 on 0-for-13).

He pulls medium-high outside fastballs deep down the left line. But he hits this pitch medium-deep straightaway to center and right and up the middle to the shortstop.

MEDIUM-HIGH OUTSIDE FASTBALLS (THROWN BY LEFT-HANDED PITCHERS)

BATTING AVERAGE .326

Play	
Left	Deep and shifted toward the left field line
Center	Medium-deep in straightaway center field
Right	Medium-deep in straightaway right field
Short	Up middle (shifted toward second base)
Second	Normal position

He pulls low-over-the-middle fastballs.

LOW-OVER-THE-MIDDLE FASTBALLS (THROWN BY LEFT-HANDED PITCHERS)

BATTING AVERAGE .320

Play	
Left	Medium-deep and shifted toward the left field line
Center	Medium-deep and shifted toward left field
Right	Medium-deep and shifted toward center field
Short	Normal position
Second	Normal position

Ahead And Behind In The Count Vs. RH

Ahead

Fastball Average .274	Inside	Middle	Outside	Curve Average .400	Inside	Middle	Outside
High	8/ 0 /0	24/ 375 /9	8/ 125 /1		0/ 0 /0	0/ 0 /0	0/ 0 /0
Med	11/ 90 /1	32/ 375 /12	54/ 296 /16		1/ 1000 /1	1/ 1000 /1	3/ 0 /0
Low	3/ 333 /1	38/ 263 /10	26/ 230 /6		0/ 0 /0	5/ 200 /1	5/ 600 /3

Behind

Fastball Average .369	Inside	Middle	Outside	Curve Average .392	Inside	Middle	Outside
High	3/ 0 /0	2/ 500 /1	2/ 0 /0		1/ 1000 /1	0/ 0 /0	0/ 0 /0
Med	3/ 666 /2	7/ 428 /3	12/ 166 /2		3/ 333 /1	4/ 750 /3	4/ 0 /0
Low	0/ 0 /0	8/ 375 /3	9/ 666 /6		0/ 0 /0	3/ 333 /1	13/ 384 /5

Overall Evaluation

Against Right-Handed Pitchers

Overall Fastball   (2 balls)
Overall Curve   (4 balls)
Overall Slider   (6 balls)

Against Left-Handed Pitchers

Overall Fastball   (2 balls)
Overall Curve   (2 balls)
Overall Slider   Not enough information

Comments: Weak vs. inside fastballs, strong vs. low-middle and low-outside fastballs vs. RH.

Strengths: Low-outside and all over-the-middle fastballs, low-outside curves and sliders vs. RH; medium-outside and low-middle fastballs, low-outside curves vs. LH.

Weaknesses: Inside fastballs, medium-outside and high-outside fastballs, medium-outside and low-middle curves vs. RH; all inside, high-outside fastballs vs. LH.

Jody Davis Against Right-Handed Pitchers
Overall BARS Batting Average .251

Fastball Average .295

	Inside	Middle	Outside
High	55 / 200 / 11	95 / 315 / 30	53 / 150 / 8
Med	80 / 262 / 21	42 / 476 / 20	209 / 315 / 66
Low	48 / 333 / 16	161 / 378 / 61	107 / 168 / 18

Curve Average .229

	Inside	Middle	Outside
High	2 / 0 / 0	17 / 176 / 3	13 / 153 / 2
Med	19 / 421 / 8	3 / 0 / 0	79 / 329 / 26
Low	8 / 125 / 1	34 / 323 / 11	95 / 115 / 11

Slider Average .245

	Inside	Middle	Outside
High	3 / 333 / 1	3 / 333 / 1	9 / 222 / 2
Med	5 / 400 / 2	4 / 500 / 2	71 / 281 / 20
Low	3 / 0 / 0	23 / 347 / 8	87 / 172 / 15

Jody Davis Against Left-Handed Pitchers
Overall BARS Batting Average .250

Fastball Average .275

	Inside	Middle	Outside
High	12 / 166 / 2	26 / 192 / 5	22 / 227 / 5
Med	20 / 250 / 5	11 / 454 / 5	75 / 266 / 20
Low	12 / 250 / 3	57 / 421 / 24	70 / 214 / 15

Curve Average .283

	Inside	Middle	Outside
High	3 / 333 / 1	3 / 333 / 1	1 / 1000 / 1
Med	5 / 600 / 3	2 / 500 / 1	11 / 545 / 6
Low	12 / 0 / 0	20 / 100 / 2	17 / 352 / 6

Slider Average .218

	Inside	Middle	Outside
High	1 / 0 / 0	0 / 0 / 0	1 / 0 / 0
Med	4 / 750 / 3	0 / 0 / 0	5 / 400 / 2
Low	9 / 111 / 1	6 / 0 / 0	6 / 166 / 1

Right-handed hitting Jody Davis hits fastballs at a .295 overall clip against right-handed pitchers. He has trouble with curves and sliders against right-handers, although he does have some strong locations in these charts.

He hits a fine .315 against medium-high outside fastballs. He hits this pitch deep and straightaway to all fields.

MEDIUM-HIGH OUTSIDE FASTBALLS

BATTING AVERAGE .315
Play

Left	Deep in straightaway left field
Center	Deep in straightaway center field
Right	Deep in straightaway right field
Short	Shifted toward third base
Second	Normal position

Davis's fastball charts show that right-handers throw him more low than high fastballs. This is all right if they keep the ball low and outside. He has excellent averages in his other two low fastball locations.

He hits .378 against low-over-the-middle fastballs. He hits this pitch deep down the left line, straightaway to center and right, and into the hole between third and short.

LOW-OVER-THE-MIDDLE FASTBALLS

BATTING AVERAGE .378
Play

Left	Deep and shifted toward the left field line
Center	Medium-deep in straightaway center field
Right	Deep in straightaway right field
Short	Shifted toward third base
Second	Normal position

His .315 against high-over-the-middle fastballs is good.

HIGH-OVER-THE-MIDDLE FASTBALLS

BATTING AVERAGE .315
Play

Left	Deep in straightaway left field
Center	Medium-deep in straightaway center field
Right	Deep and shifted toward center field
Short	Normal position
Second	Normal position

Davis Against Curves And Sliders

Davis has trouble with high curves and low-outside curves against right-handed pitchers. He hits medium-high outside curves excellently.

MEDIUM-HIGH OUTSIDE CURVEBALLS

BATTING AVERAGE .329
Play

Left	Deep in straightaway left field
Center	Medium-deep in straightaway center field
Right	Deep and shifted toward center field
Short	Shifted toward third base
Second	Normal position

He also has trouble with low-outside sliders (.172). But he hits low-over-the-middle sliders very well (.347).

LOW-OVER-THE-MIDDLE SLIDERS

BATTING AVERAGE .347
Play

Left	Deep in straightaway left field
Center	Medium-deep in straightaway center field
Right	Deep and shifted toward center field
Short	Up middle (shifted toward second base)
Second	*No instances recorded*

Davis Against Left-Handed Pitchers

Davis's .275 overall fastball average against left-handed pitchers is only fair. He has two strong locations: medium-over-the-middle (.454) and low-over-the-middle (.421).

He hits low-over-the-middle fastballs medium-deep down the left line and deep into the left-center gap.

LOW-OVER-THE-MIDDLE FASTBALLS
(THROWN BY LEFT-HANDED PITCHERS)

BATTING AVERAGE .421
Play

Left	Medium-deep and shifted toward the left field line
Center	Deep and shifted toward left field
Right	Deep in straightaway right field
Short	Shifted toward third base
Second	Normal position

He hits medium-high outside fastballs (.266) deep to all fields.

MEDIUM-HIGH OUTSIDE FASTBALLS
(THROWN BY LEFT-HANDED PITCHERS)

BATTING AVERAGE .266
Play

Left	Deep in straightaway left field
Center	Deep and shifted toward left field
Right	Deep and shifted toward center field
Short	Normal position
Second	Normal position

He hits low-outside curves and medium-high outside curves excellently against left-handers. He drives medium-high outside curves (.545) deep to all fields.

MEDIUM-HIGH OUTSIDE CURVEBALLS
(THROWN BY LEFT-HANDED PITCHERS)

BATTING AVERAGE .545
Play

Left	Deep in straightaway left field
Center	Deep in straightaway center field
Right	Deep and shifted toward center field
Short	Normal position
Second	Normal position

Ahead And Behind In The Count Vs. RH

Ahead

Fastball Average .332

	Inside	Middle	Outside
High	17/ 176 /3	36/ 444 /16	20/ 200 /4
Med	32/ 218 /7	23/ 521 /12	99/ 414 /41
Low	22/ 363 /8	81/ 345 /28	49/ 142 /7

Curve Average .342

	Inside	Middle	Outside
High	0/ 0 /0	6/ 166 /1	6/ 166 /1
Med	8/ 625 /5	0/ 0 /0	19/ 263 /5
Low	2/ 0 /0	10/ 500 /5	19/ 368 /7

Behind

Fastball Average .326

	Inside	Middle	Outside
High	10/ 300 /3	20/ 300 /6	8/ 125 /1
Med	20/ 300 /6	7/ 428 /3	31/ 322 /10
Low	6/ 333 /2	29/ 482 /14	13/ 153 /2

Curve Average .281

	Inside	Middle	Outside
High	0/ 0 /0	3/ 333 /1	1/ 0 /0
Med	4/ 500 /2	0/ 0 /0	22/ 409 /9
Low	1/ 1000 /1	12/ 416 /5	28/ 71 /2

Overall Evaluation

Against Right-Handed Pitchers

Overall Fastball ⚾⚾⚾⚾

Overall Curve ⚾⚾

Overall Slider ⚾

Against Left-Handed Pitchers

Overall Fastball ⚾⚾⚾⚾

Overall Curve ⚾⚾⚾⚾⚾⚾

Overall Slider ⚾⚾

Comments: Vulnerable to low-outside pitches vs. RH. Strengths: Over-the-middle, low-inside and medium-outside fastballs, low-middle, medium-inside and medium-outside curves, low-middle sliders vs. RH; low-middle fastballs, outside curves vs. LH. Weaknesses: High-inside, medium-inside, high-outside and low-outside fastballs, high curves, low-outside curves and sliders vs. RH; inside, high and outside fastballs, low-inside & low-middle curves v. LH.

Darrell Evans (Left Handed) — *Atlanta Braves*

Darrell Evans Against Right-Handed Pitchers
Overall BARS Batting Average .241

Fastball Average .279

	Outside	Middle	Inside
High	23 / 173 / 4	28 / 321 / 9	13 / 230 / 3
Med	114 / 298 / 34	22 / 227 / 5	63 / 396 / 25
Low	25 / 200 / 5	83 / 265 / 22	51 / 215 / 11

Curve Average .194

	Outside	Middle	Inside
High	1 / 0 / 0	3 / 0 / 0	3 / 333 / 1
Med	28 / 142 / 4	13 / 230 / 3	14 / 285 / 4
Low	12 / 83 / 1	14 / 357 / 5	20 / 150 / 3

Slider Average .230

	Outside	Middle	Inside
High	0 / 0 / 0	4 / 750 / 3	2 / 0 / 0
Med	7 / 428 / 3	5 / 400 / 2	6 / 166 / 1
Low	3 / 0 / 0	9 / 111 / 1	16 / 125 / 2

Darrell Evans Against Left-Handed Pitchers
Overall BARS Batting Average .238

Fastball Average .266

	Outside	Middle	Inside
High	2 / 500 / 1	5 / 200 / 1	6 / 0 / 0
Med	34 / 117 / 4	9 / 444 / 4	34 / 411 / 14
Low	6 / 0 / 0	25 / 320 / 8	14 / 285 / 4

Curve Average .250

	Outside	Middle	Inside
High	0 / 0 / 0	2 / 0 / 0	2 / 500 / 1
Med	22 / 227 / 5	3 / 666 / 2	13 / 307 / 4
Low	12 / 83 / 1	6 / 500 / 3	4 / 0 / 0

Slider Average .250

	Outside	Middle	Inside
High	0 / 0 / 0	2 / 500 / 1	0 / 0 / 0
Med	4 / 0 / 0	3 / 666 / 2	5 / 200 / 1
Low	5 / 200 / 1	5 / 200 / 1	0 / 0 / 0

Left-handed hitting Darrell Evans has three strong fastball locations against right-handed pitchers (.298 medium-high outside, .321 high-over-the-middle and .396 medium-high inside). He has very weak averages in his three low fastball locations (.200, .265 and .215 from outside to inside). If pitchers could keep their fastballs low, they would have an edge on Evans.

He hits medium-high outside fastballs straight-away to the outfield. But he pulls this pitch to the right side of the infield.

MEDIUM-HIGH OUTSIDE FASTBALLS

BATTING AVERAGE .298
Play
Left — Medium-deep in straightaway left field
Center — Deep in straightaway center field
Right — Deep in straightaway right field
Short — Up middle (shifted toward second base)
Second — Shifted toward first base

He hits medium-high inside fastballs better when he is ahead in the count (.406 when ahead, .285 when behind). He pulls this pitch to the outfield when ahead.

MEDIUM-HIGH INSIDE FASTBALLS
(WHEN AHEAD IN THE COUNT)

BATTING AVERAGE .406
Play
Left — Short and shifted toward center field
Center — Deep and shifted toward right field
Right — Deep and shifted toward the right field line
Short — Shifted toward third base
Second — Normal position

When behind, the left-handed Evans goes down the left field line with this pitch.

MEDIUM-HIGH INSIDE FASTBALLS
(WHEN BEHIND IN THE COUNT)

BATTING AVERAGE .285
Play
Left — Medium-deep and shifted toward the left field line
Center — Medium-deep and shifted toward right field
Right — Deep in straightaway right field
Short — Normal position
Second — Shifted toward first base

He also hits low-over-the-middle fastballs better when ahead (.133 when behind, .255 when ahead). When ahead, he pulls this pitch more than when behind.

LOW-OVER-THE-MIDDLE FASTBALLS
(WHEN AHEAD IN THE COUNT)

BATTING AVERAGE .255
Play
Left — Deep and shifted toward center field
Center — Deep in straightaway center field

Right	Deep and shifted toward the right field line
Short	Up middle (shifted toward second base)
Second	Shifted toward first base

LOW-OVER-THE-MIDDLE FASTBALLS (WHEN BEHIND IN THE COUNT)

BATTING AVERAGE .133
Play

Left	Medium-deep in straightaway left field
Center	Deep and shifted toward left field
Right	Deep and shifted toward center field
Short	Shifted toward third base
Second	*No instances recorded*

Evans has trouble with all curves except those thrown to the medium-high inside (.285) and low-over-the-middle locations (.357).

LOW-OVER-THE-MIDDLE CURVEBALLS

BATTING AVERAGE .357
Play

Left	Deep and shifted toward center field
Center	Medium-deep in straightaway center field
Right	Deep in straightaway right field
Short	Up middle (shifted toward second base)
Second	Shifted toward first base

He has trouble with all low sliders thrown by right-handed pitchers.

Evans Against Left-Handed Pitchers

Evans hits medium-high inside fastballs extremely well against left-handed pitchers (.411). As against right-handers, he hits this pitch much better when ahead in the count (.333 when behind, .529 when ahead).

MEDIUM-HIGH INSIDE FASTBALLS (THROWN BY LEFT-HANDED PITCHERS WHEN EVANS IS BEHIND IN THE COUNT)

BATTING AVERAGE .333
Play

Left	Medium-deep and shifted toward center field
Center	Medium-deep in straightaway center field
Right	Deep in straightaway right field
Short	Shifted toward third base
Second	Shifted toward first base

MEDIUM-HIGH INSIDE FASTBALLS (THROWN BY LEFT-HANDED PITCHERS WHEN EVANS IS AHEAD IN THE COUNT)

BATTING AVERAGE .529
Play

Left	Short and shifted toward the left field line
Center	Medium-deep in straightaway center field
Right	Medium-deep and shifted toward the right line
Short	Up middle (shifted toward second base)
Second	Shifted toward first base

He has a weakness against medium-high outside fastballs thrown by left-handers (.117).

He hits medium-high outside and low-outside curves very poorly against left-handers (.227 and .083 respectively). But he hits medium-high inside curves excellently (.307).

Ahead And Behind In The Count Vs. RH

Ahead

Fastball Average .302

	Outside	Middle	Inside
High	6/166/1	10/400/4	3/333/1
Med	51/274/14	10/300/3	32/406/13
Low	11/272/3	43/255/11	19/315/6

Curve Average .277

	Outside	Middle	Inside
High	0/0/0	0/0/0	1/0/0
Med	4/500/2	5/0/0	3/666/2
Low	0/0/0	2/500/1	3/0/0

Behind

Fastball Average .255

	Outside	Middle	Inside
High	2/0/0	11/454/5	3/0/0
Med	18/333/6	4/0/0	14/285/4
Low	5/400/2	15/133/2	14/214/3

Curve Average .307

	Outside	Middle	Inside
High	1/0/0	1/0/0	0/0/0
Med	10/200/2	1/1000/1	4/250/1
Low	4/250/1	1/0/0	4/750/3

Overall Evaluation

Against Right-Handed Pitchers

Overall Fastball	
Overall Curve	
Overall Slider	

Against Left-Handed Pitchers

Overall Fastball	
Overall Curve	
Overall Slider	

Comments: Has problems with low fastballs vs. RH. Strengths: Medium-inside and high-middle fastballs, low-middle curves vs. RH; medium-inside and low-middle fastballs, medium-inside curves vs. LH. Weaknesses: Low fastballs, high-outside, high-inside and medium-middle fastballs, outside curves, low sliders and inside sliders, low-inside curves vs. RH; medium-outside fastballs, outside curves and sliders vs. LH.

Ron Gant Against Right-Handed Pitchers
Overall BARS Batting Average .246

Fastball Average .275

	Inside	Middle	Outside
High	17 / 176 / 3	14 / 142 / 2	12 / 250 / 3
Med	9 / 333 / 3	6 / 500 / 3	27 / 333 / 9
Low	5 / 400 / 2	8 / 625 / 5	11 / 0 / 0

Curve Average .250

	Inside	Middle	Outside
High	2 / 500 / 1	3 / 333 / 1	7 / 428 / 3
Med	1 / 1000 / 1	2 / 500 / 1	11 / 181 / 2
Low	1 / 0 / 0	0 / 0 / 0	9 / 0 / 0

Slider Average .320

	Inside	Middle	Outside
High	3 / 0 / 0	3 / 0 / 0	5 / 600 / 3
Med	0 / 0 / 0	1 / 1000 / 1	7 / 428 / 3
Low	0 / 0 / 0	0 / 0 / 0	6 / 166 / 1

Ron Gant Against Left-Handed Pitchers
Overall BARS Batting Average .232

Fastball Average .309

	Inside	Middle	Outside
High	4 / 250 / 1	3 / 333 / 1	5 / 600 / 3
Med	5 / 0 / 0	2 / 500 / 1	10 / 300 / 3
Low	4 / 250 / 1	3 / 666 / 2	6 / 166 / 1

Curve Average .133

	Inside	Middle	Outside
High	1 / 0 / 0	1 / 0 / 0	2 / 0 / 0
Med	0 / 0 / 0	1 / 0 / 0	0 / 0 / 0
Low	2 / 0 / 0	3 / 333 / 1	5 / 200 / 1

Slider Average .000

	Inside	Middle	Outside
High	0 / 0 / 0	0 / 0 / 0	0 / 0 / 0
Med	0 / 0 / 0	0 / 0 / 0	0 / 0 / 0
Low	0 / 0 / 0	0 / 0 / 0	2 / 0 / 0

Right-handed Ron Gant hits medium-high outside fastballs excellently against right-handed pitchers (.333). He hits this pitch deep down the left line and medium-deep to center and right. By following the fielding strategy shown below and in the field diagram on the opposite page, fielders could get an edge on Gant.

MEDIUM-HIGH OUTSIDE FASTBALLS

BATTING AVERAGE .333
Play
Left Deep and shifted toward the left field line
Center Medium-deep in straightaway center field
Right Medium-deep and shifted toward center field
Short Normal position
Second Normal position

Gant is weak against low-outside fastballs thrown by right-handers (.000 on 0-for-11). He's also weak against high fastballs (.176, .142 and .250, inside to outside). By keeping fastballs to Gant up or low and away, right-handers should have little problem with him.

He hits high-outside fastballs straightaway to left, into the right-center gap and down the right line. Note that although the center and right fielders need to play Gant to go to his opposite field (right field) the shortstop needs to play shifted toward third base for this pitch.

HIGH-OUTSIDE FASTBALLS

BATTING AVERAGE .250
Play
Left Deep in straightaway left field
Center Medium-deep and shifted toward right field
Right Deep and shifted toward the right field line
Short Shifted toward third base
Second Normal position

Gant has trouble with medium-high outside curves (.181) and low-outside curves (.000 on 0-for-9) against right-handers. He hits high-outside curves very well (.428) but, by keeping curves down and away to him, right-handers can stay away from his strength.

Gant Against Left-Handed Pitchers

Gant hits medium-high outside fastballs well against left-handed pitchers (.300).

**MEDIUM-HIGH OUTSIDE FASTBALLS
(THROWN BY LEFT-HANDED PITCHERS)**

BATTING AVERAGE .300
Play
Left *No instances recorded*
Center Deep in straightaway center field
Right Deep and shifted toward the right field line
Short Normal position
Second Normal position

Medium-High Outside Fastballs

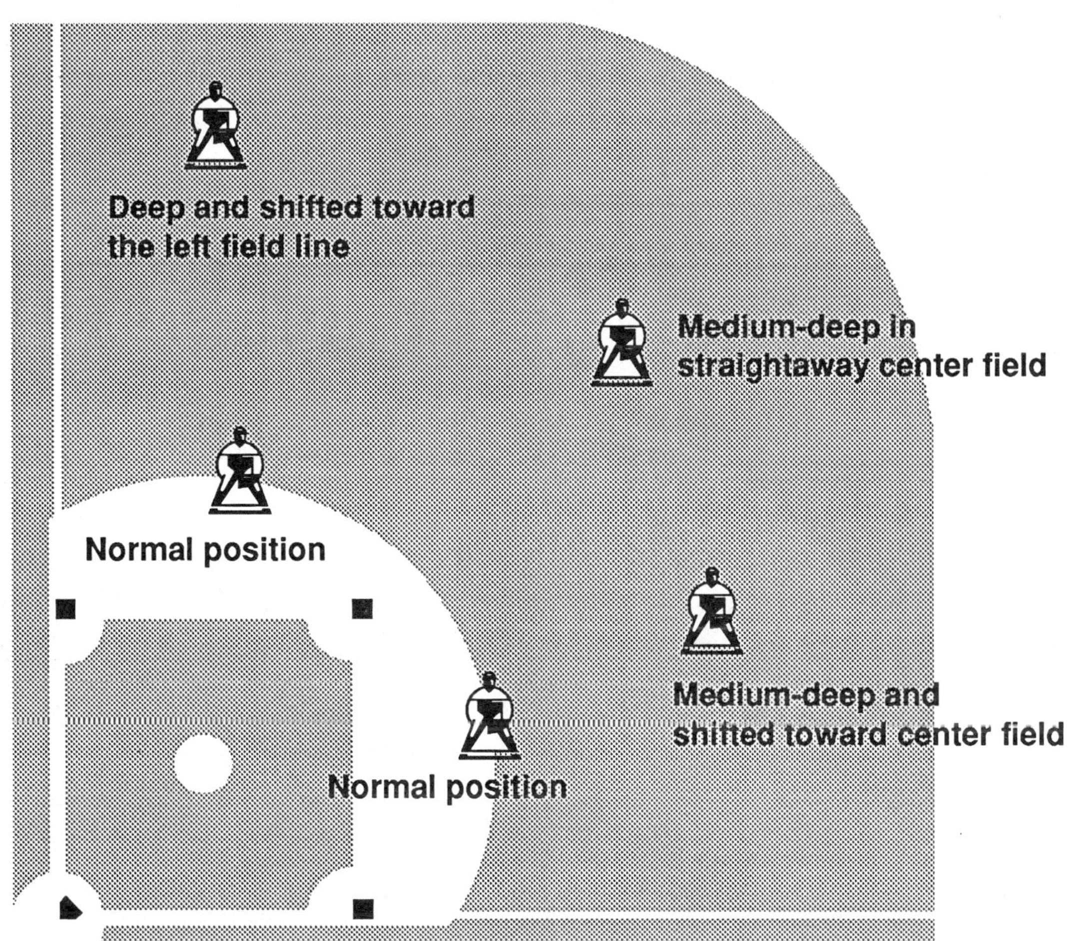

Ahead And Behind In The Count Vs. RH

Ahead

	Fastball Average .274			Curve Average .500		
	Inside	Middle	Outside	Inside	Middle	Outside
High	9/ 222 / 2	10/ 0 / 0	6/ 166 / 1	1/ 1000 / 1	2/ 0 / 0	2/ 500 / 1
Med	2/ 500 / 1	2/ 500 / 1	10/ 400 / 4	1/ 1000 / 1	0/ 0 / 0	4/ 500 / 2
Low	3/ 666 / 2	5/ 600 / 3	4/ 0 / 0	0/ 0 / 0	0/ 0 / 0	0/ 0 / 0

Behind

	Fastball Average .411			Curve Average .142		
	Inside	Middle	Outside	Inside	Middle	Outside
High	1/ 0 / 0	1/ 1000 / 1	1/ 0 / 0	1/ 0 / 0	0/ 0 / 0	2/ 500 / 1
Med	1/ 0 / 0	3/ 666 / 2	7/ 428 / 3	0/ 0 / 0	1/ 0 / 0	2/ 0 / 0
Low	1/ 0 / 0	1/ 1000 / 1	1/ 0 / 0	0/ 0 / 0	0/ 0 / 0	1/ 0 / 0

Overall Evaluation

Against Right-Handed Pitchers

Overall Fastball	 ⚾⚾
Overall Curve	⚾⚾
Overall Slider	⚾⚾⚾⚾

Against Left-Handed Pitchers

Overall Fastball	⚾⚾⚾
Overall Curve	⚾
Overall Slider	Not enough information

Comments: Weak vs. high fastballs against RH.
Strengths: Waist-high fastballs, low-middle fastballs, high-outside curves, medium-outside and high-outside sliders vs. RH; medium-outside fastballs vs. LH.
Weaknesses: High fastballs, low-outside fastballs, medium-outside and low-outside curves vs. RH.

Dion James (Left Handed)   *Atlanta Braves*

Dion James Against Right-Handed Pitchers
Overall BARS Batting Average .284

Fastball Average .304

	Outside	Middle	Inside
High	23 / 217 / 5	26 / 346 / 9	22 / 181 / 4
Med	81 / 320 / 26	27 / 555 / 15	35 / 342 / 12
Low	32 / 93 / 3	56 / 339 / 19	30 / 266 / 8

Curve Average .235

	Outside	Middle	Inside
High	2 / 500 / 1	3 / 0 / 0	0 / 0 / 0
Med	9 / 444 / 4	1 / 1000 / 1	4 / 0 / 0
Low	7 / 142 / 1	1 / 0 / 0	7 / 142 / 1

Slider Average .388

	Outside	Middle	Inside
High	1 / 0 / 0	1 / 1000 / 1	1 / 1000 / 1
Med	1 / 0 / 0	1 / 1000 / 1	3 / 666 / 2
Low	4 / 250 / 1	4 / 250 / 1	2 / 0 / 0

Dion James Against Left-Handed Pitchers
Overall BARS Batting Average .300

Fastball Average .373

	Outside	Middle	Inside
High	3 / 666 / 2	5 / 600 / 3	5 / 0 / 0
Med	13 / 307 / 4	5 / 600 / 3	22 / 363 / 8
Low	6 / 166 / 1	7 / 571 / 4	1 / 0 / 0

Curve Average .250

	Outside	Middle	Inside
High	3 / 0 / 0	0 / 0 / 0	0 / 0 / 0
Med	4 / 250 / 1	1 / 0 / 0	3 / 333 / 1
Low	4 / 500 / 2	2 / 500 / 1	3 / 0 / 0

Slider Average .000

	Outside	Middle	Inside
High	0 / 0 / 0	1 / 0 / 0	1 / 0 / 0
Med	2 / 0 / 0	0 / 0 / 0	0 / 0 / 0
Low	3 / 0 / 0	0 / 0 / 0	0 / 0 / 0

Left-handed hitter Dion James hits a solid .304 overall against fastballs thrown by right-handed pitchers and a sparkling .373 overall against fastballs thrown by left-handed pitchers.

His .342 against medium-high inside fastballs thrown by right-handers is excellent. By positioning themselves according the BARS fielding strategy for this pitch, fielders could prevent most of James's hits from this location.

MEDIUM-HIGH INSIDE FASTBALLS

BATTING AVERAGE .342

Play

Left	Medium-deep and shifted toward the left field line
Center	Medium-deep in straightaway center field
Right	Short and shifted toward center field
Short	Up middle (shifted toward second base)
Second	Normal position

His .320 against medium-high outside fastballs thrown by right-handers is more than adequate. He hits this pitch deep down both lines. The chart below and the field diagram on the opposite page show how fielders need to play for fastballs to this location.

MEDIUM-HIGH OUTSIDE FASTBALLS

BATTING AVERAGE .320

Play

Left	Deep and shifted toward the left field line
Center	Medium-deep in straightaway center field
Right	Deep and shifted toward the right field line
Short	Up middle (shifted toward second base)
Second	Shifted toward first base

James has weaknesses in the four fastball corners. He also has trouble with low curves against right-handers.

James Against Left-Handed Pitchers

James hits all waist-high and over-the-middle fastballs well against left-handed pitchers. His .363 against medium-high inside fastballs is excellent.

MEDIUM-HIGH INSIDE FASTBALLS
(THROWN BY LEFT-HANDED PITCHERS)

BATTING AVERAGE .363

Play

Left	Medium-deep in straightaway left field
Center	Deep and shifted toward left field
Right	Deep and shifted toward the right field line
Short	Normal position
Second	Shifted toward first base

He hits .307 against medium-high outside fastballs thrown by left-handers.

Medium-High Outside Fastballs

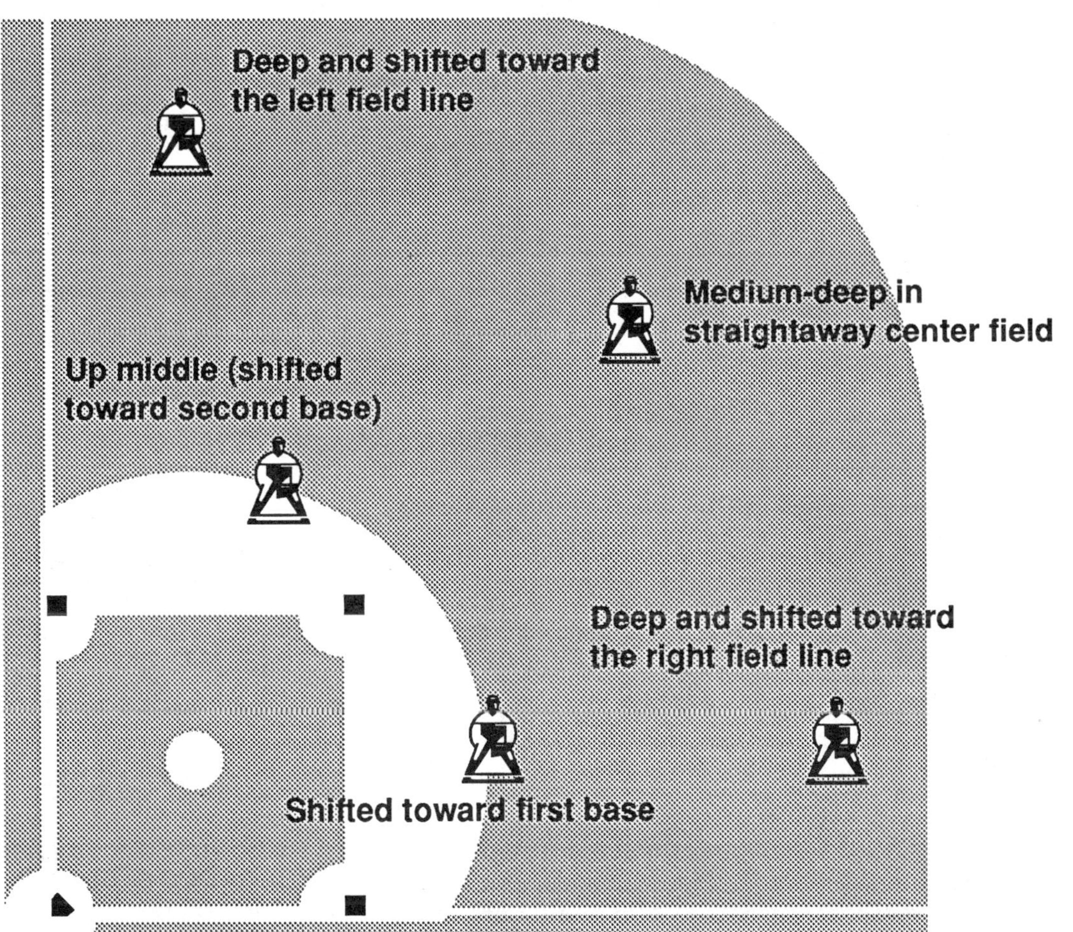

Ahead And Behind In The Count Vs. RH

Ahead

Fastball Average .351

	Outside	Middle	Inside
High	11/ 181 / 2	12/ 333 / 4	8/ 250 / 2
Med	43/ 395 / 17	13/ 615 / 8	22/ 409 / 9
Low	14/ 71 / 1	33/ 363 / 12	12/ 333 / 4

Curve Average .250

	Outside	Middle	Inside
High	0/ 0 / 0	0/ 0 / 0	0/ 0 / 0
Med	1/ 1000 / 1	0/ 0 / 0	2/ 0 / 0
Low	1/ 0 / 0	0/ 0 / 0	0/ 0 / 0

Behind

Fastball Average .295

	Outside	Middle	Inside
High	4/ 250 / 1	4/ 750 / 3	6/ 166 / 1
Med	18/ 277 / 5	6/ 500 / 3	4/ 0 / 0
Low	6/ 333 / 2	9/ 222 / 2	4/ 250 / 1

Curve Average .357

	Outside	Middle	Inside
High	1/ 0 / 0	2/ 0 / 0	0/ 0 / 0
Med	4/ 750 / 3	1/ 1000 / 1	1/ 0 / 0
Low	4/ 250 / 1	0/ 0 / 0	1/ 0 / 0

Overall Evaluation

Against Right-Handed Pitchers

	Rating
Overall Fastball	3 balls
Overall Curve	1 ball
Overall Slider	4 balls

Against Left-Handed Pitchers

	Rating
Overall Fastball	4 balls
Overall Curve	2 balls
Overall Slider	Not enough information

Comments: Strong vs. waist-high and over-the-middle fastballs vs. both RH and LH.

Strengths: Waist-high and over-the-middle fastballs, medium-outside curves vs. RH; waist-high and over-the-middle fastballs vs. LH.

Weaknesses: The four fastball corners, low curves vs. RH.

Dale Murphy Against Right-Handed Pitchers
Overall BARS Batting Average .270

Fastball Average .323

	Inside	Middle	Outside
High	40 / 125 / 5	71 / 366 / 26	63 / 285 / 18
Med	98 / 336 / 33	71 / 394 / 28	194 / 355 / 69
Low	45 / 244 / 11	148 / 371 / 55	92 / 228 / 21

Curve Average .219

	Inside	Middle	Outside
High	0 / 0 / 0	15 / 533 / 8	12 / 416 / 5
Med	7 / 428 / 3	19 / 421 / 8	54 / 203 / 11
Low	11 / 181 / 2	42 / 142 / 6	104 / 144 / 15

Slider Average .276

	Inside	Middle	Outside
High	1 / 0 / 0	11 / 454 / 5	6 / 333 / 2
Med	10 / 100 / 1	7 / 571 / 4	45 / 333 / 15
Low	9 / 111 / 1	32 / 406 / 13	74 / 175 / 13

Dale Murphy Against Left-Handed Pitchers
Overall BARS Batting Average .276

Fastball Average .310

	Inside	Middle	Outside
High	7 / 142 / 1	27 / 333 / 9	40 / 300 / 12
Med	25 / 200 / 5	19 / 421 / 8	78 / 474 / 37
Low	17 / 176 / 3	44 / 250 / 11	59 / 203 / 12

Curve Average .246

	Inside	Middle	Outside
High	1 / 1000 / 1	4 / 500 / 2	3 / 0 / 0
Med	11 / 90 / 1	2 / 0 / 0	14 / 428 / 6
Low	13 / 76 / 1	12 / 250 / 3	13 / 307 / 4

Slider Average .314

	Inside	Middle	Outside
High	1 / 0 / 0	2 / 0 / 0	1 / 0 / 0
Med	10 / 400 / 4	0 / 0 / 0	8 / 625 / 5
Low	11 / 90 / 1	11 / 272 / 3	10 / 400 / 4

Dale Murphy's BARS records are examined in detail in the second chapter of this book. The examination on these two pages uses slightly updated BARS records for Murphy. The BARS System continually updates its records, and the statistics shown here are the latest available at the time of publication.

A right-handed hitter, Murphy hits .323 overall against fastballs thrown by right-handed pitchers. His .355 average against medium-high outside fastballs is excellent. When ahead (.461, see his Ahead and Behind charts on the opposite page), he tends to pull medium-high outside fastballs down the left line. When behind (.354) he hits the same pitch into the left-center and right-center gaps. This shows the importance of positioning fielders not only for the type and location of pitch, but for the count when the pitch is delivered.

MEDIUM-HIGH OUTSIDE FASTBALLS
(WHEN AHEAD IN THE COUNT)

BATTING AVERAGE .461
Play

Left	Deep and shifted toward the left field line
Center	Deep and shifted toward right field
Right	Deep in straightaway right field
Short	Normal position
Second	Shifted toward first base

MEDIUM-HIGH OUTSIDE FASTBALLS
(WHEN BEHIND IN THE COUNT)

BATTING AVERAGE .354
Play

Left	Deep and shifted toward center field
Center	Deep in straightaway center field
Right	Deep and shifted toward center field
Short	Normal position
Second	Normal position

Notice in Murphy's Ahead and Behind charts that he hits high-over-the-middle fastballs considerably better when ahead in the count (.600 when ahead, .266 when behind). By positioning themselves properly according to the count for this pitch, fielders could prevent most of his base hits resulting from this location.

HIGH-OVER-THE-MIDDLE FASTBALLS
(WHEN AHEAD IN THE COUNT)

BATTING AVERAGE .600
Play

Left	Deep in straightaway left field
Center	Medium-deep in straightaway center field
Right	Deep and shifted toward center field
Short	Shifted toward third base
Second	*No instances recorded*

HIGH-OVER-THE-MIDDLE FASTBALLS
(WHEN BEHIND IN THE COUNT)

BATTING AVERAGE .266
Play

Left	Deep in straightaway left field
Center	Deep in straightaway center field
Right	Deep and shifted toward center field
Short	Normal position
Second	Normal position

Murphy hits a resounding .371 against low-over-the-middle fastballs thrown by right-handers. He hits this pitch deep to all fields.

LOW-OVER-THE-MIDDLE FASTBALLS

BATTING AVERAGE .371
Play

Left	Deep in straightaway left field
Center	Deep and shifted toward right field
Right	Deep in straightaway right field
Short	Normal position
Second	Normal position

Murphy has weaknesses against low-outside fastballs (.228), low-inside fastballs (.244) and high-inside fastballs (.125).

IIe is also weak against medium-high outside curves and all low curves. This gives a target for right-handers. His weakness against low-outside sliders and all inside sliders also presents a target for right-handers. He has some very strong locations in his curve and slider charts, but by looking at his BARS records, pitchers can gain an edge.

Murphy Against Left-Handed Pitchers

Murphy has an outstanding fastball sector consisting of his high-middle/high-outside/medium-middle/medium-outside locations. Left-handed pitchers need to stay away from this sector. He hits medium-high outside fastballs deep to the outfield.

MEDIUM-HIGH OUTSIDE FASTBALLS
(THROWN BY LEFT-HANDED PITCHERS)

BATTING AVERAGE .474
Play

Left	Deep and shifted toward center field
Center	Deep in straightaway center field
Right	Deep in straightaway right field
Short	Normal position
Second	Normal position

He has trouble with low-over-the-middle and all inside curves. He hits low-outside and medium-high outside curves excellently, however.

MEDIUM-HIGH OUTSIDE CURVEBALLS
(THROWN BY LEFT-HANDED PITCHERS)

BATTING AVERAGE .428
Play

Left	Deep and shifted toward the left field line
Center	Short in straightaway center field
Right	*No instances recorded*
Short	Normal position
Second	*No instances recorded*

He has trouble with low-inside sliders but hits medium-high inside and all outside sliders very well.

Ahead And Behind In The Count Vs. RH

Ahead

Fastball Average .411

	Inside	Middle	Outside
High	13/ 153 /2	30/ 600 /18	24/ 375 /9
Med	39/ 461 /18	30/ 400 /12	91/ 461 /42
Low	20/ 250 /5	73/ 383 /28	30/ 333 /10

Curve Average .343

	Inside	Middle	Outside
High	0/ 0 /0	7/ 571 /4	5/ 400 /2
Med	2/ 1000 /2	7/ 428 /3	14/ 285 /4
Low	2/ 500 /1	5/ 0 /0	22/ 272 /6

Behind

Fastball Average .340

	Inside	Middle	Outside
High	4/ 250 /1	15/ 266 /4	15/ 200 /3
Med	24/ 291 /7	19/ 473 /9	31/ 354 /11
Low	4/ 0 /0	19/ 526 /10	13/ 307 /4

Curve Average .305

	Inside	Middle	Outside
High	0/ 0 /0	4/ 250 /1	3/ 333 /1
Med	0/ 0 /0	7/ 571 /4	17/ 294 /5
Low	2/ 0 /0	8/ 375 /3	18/ 222 /4

Overall Evaluation
Against Right-Handed Pitchers

Overall Fastball ⚾ ⚾ ⚾ ⚾

Overall Curve ⚾ ⚾

Overall Slider ⚾ ⚾

Against Left-Handed Pitchers

Overall Fastball ⚾ ⚾ ⚾ ⚾

Overall Curve ⚾ ⚾

Overall Slider ⚾ ⚾ ⚾ ⚾ ⚾

Comments: Weak against low curves vs. RH.
Strengths: Waist-high and over-the-middle fastballs, medium-middle and high curves, over-the-middle and medium-outside sliders vs. RH; medium-outside fastballs, curves and sliders, low outside curves vs. LH.
Weaknesses: Four fastball corners except high-outside, medium-outside and low curves, low-outside and inside sliders vs. RH; low fastballs and inside curves vs. LH.

Gerald Perry (Left Handed) — *Atlanta Braves*

Gerald Perry Against Right-Handed Pitchers
Overall BARS Batting Average .243

Fastball Average .268

	Outside	Middle	Inside
High	32 / 250 / 8	66 / 333 / 22	33 / 303 / 10
Med	118 / 279 / 33	20 / 400 / 8	61 / 327 / 20
Low	25 / 120 / 3	61 / 245 / 15	39 / 76 / 3

Curve Average .256

	Outside	Middle	Inside
High	7 / 285 / 2	14 / 500 / 7	10 / 100 / 1
Med	10 / 100 / 1	12 / 416 / 5	30 / 233 / 7
Low	5 / 400 / 2	12 / 166 / 2	13 / 153 / 2

Slider Average .326

	Outside	Middle	Inside
High	1 / 0 / 0	7 / 428 / 3	5 / 400 / 2
Med	5 / 400 / 2	3 / 0 / 0	10 / 300 / 3
Low	4 / 250 / 1	3 / 666 / 2	11 / 272 / 3

Gerald Perry Against Left-Handed Pitchers
Overall BARS Batting Average .233

Fastball Average .236

	Outside	Middle	Inside
High	12 / 166 / 2	9 / 333 / 3	18 / 111 / 2
Med	17 / 176 / 3	0 / 0 / 0	19 / 263 / 5
Low	11 / 0 / 0	8 / 125 / 1	14 / 571 / 8

Curve Average .227

	Outside	Middle	Inside
High	3 / 333 / 1	11 / 272 / 3	7 / 285 / 2
Med	12 / 250 / 3	1 / 1000 / 1	1 / 0 / 0
Low	13 / 0 / 0	3 / 333 / 1	4 / 0 / 0

Slider Average .333

	Outside	Middle	Inside
High	0 / 0 / 0	1 / 0 / 0	1 / 0 / 0
Med	5 / 600 / 3	1 / 0 / 0	4 / 500 / 2
Low	2 / 0 / 0	4 / 250 / 1	0 / 0 / 0

Left-handed hitter Gerald Perry has some strong fastball, curve and slider locations in his charts, but he has several distinct sectors of weakness.

Against right-handed pitchers, Perry hits medium-high outside fastballs for a fairly good .279 average. He hits this pitch deep down the left line, straightaway to center and right, and to the right side of the infield. In contrast, he hits an excellent .327 against medium-high inside fastballs. If fielders adjusted properly for this pitch, as indicated by the BARS fielding strategy shown below and in the field diagram on the opposite page, they could take away most of his base hits resulting from this location.

MEDIUM-HIGH INSIDE FASTBALLS

BATTING AVERAGE .327
Play

Left	Medium-deep in straightaway left field
Center	Medium-deep in straightaway center field
Right	Deep and shifted toward center field
Short	Up middle (shifted toward second base)
Second	Shifted toward first base

He hits high-over-the-middle fastballs (.333) deep to all fields.

HIGH-OVER-THE-MIDDLE FASTBALLS

BATTING AVERAGE .333
Play

Left	Deep and shifted toward the left field line
Center	Deep and shifted toward right field
Right	Deep in straightaway right field
Short	Normal position
Second	Normal position

Perry is weak against low fastballs thrown by right-handers (.120, .245 and .076, outside to inside). If right-handers keep their fastballs to him low, they will have an edge.

Perry has weaknesses in many of his curve and slider locations against right-handers. He is especially vulnerable in his inside curve locations. He hits only .100 in his high-inside curve location, but he hits high-over-the-middle curves for a .500 average. And his .300 against medium-high inside sliders is excellent.

Perry Against Left-Handed Pitchers

Perry is weak against outside fastballs thrown by left-handed pitchers (.166, .176 and .000, high to low). He is also weak against low-outside curves and medium-high outside curves thrown by left-handers (.000 and .250, respectively).

His strongest location against left-handers is for low-inside fastballs (.571).

Medium-High Inside Fastballs

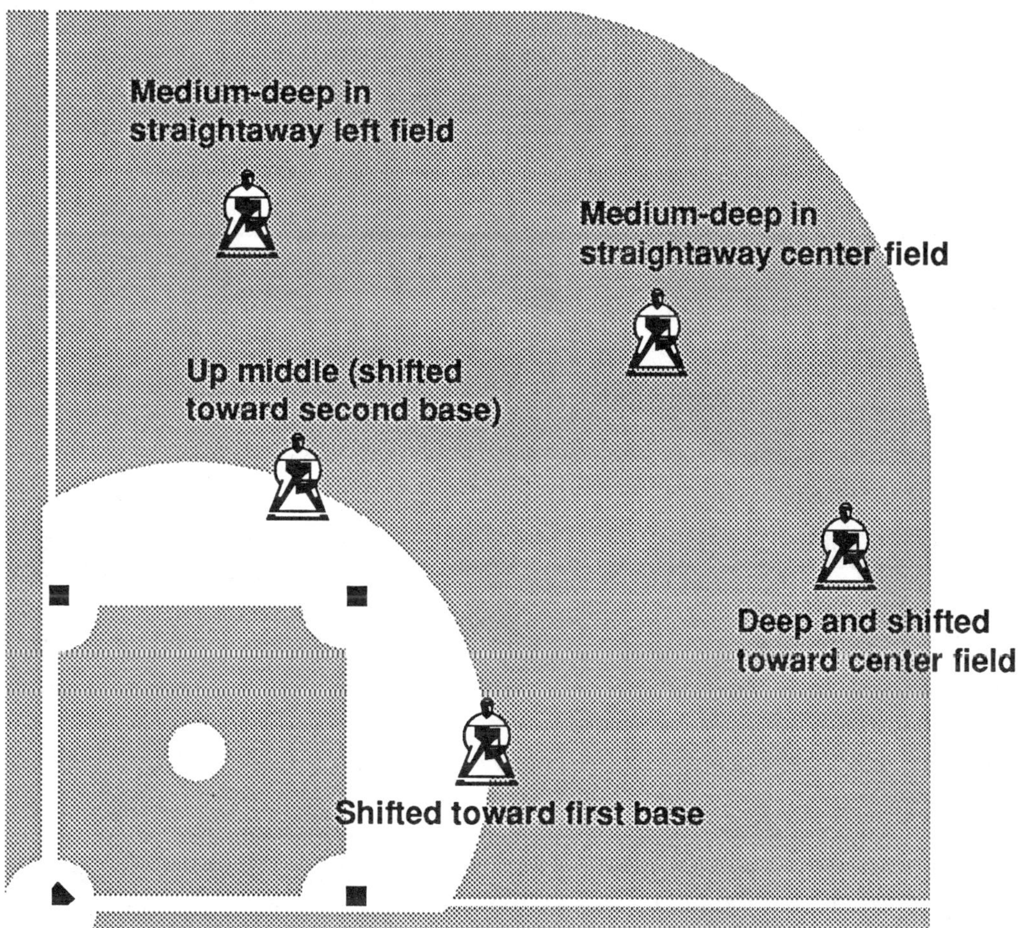

Ahead And Behind In The Count Vs. RH

Ahead

Fastball Average .304

	Outside	Middle	Inside
High	15/ 200 / 3	42/ 357 / 15	20/ 150 / 3
Med	65/ 292 / 19	9/ 666 / 6	34/ 441 / 15
Low	7/ 142 / 1	39/ 307 / 12	19/ 105 / 2

Curve Average .210

	Outside	Middle	Inside
High	2/ 0 / 0	5/ 600 / 3	4/ 0 / 0
Med	3/ 333 / 1	6/ 166 / 1	9/ 111 / 1
Low	2/ 500 / 1	6/ 166 / 1	1/ 0 / 0

Behind

Fastball Average .320

	Outside	Middle	Inside
High	2/ 500 / 1	11/ 363 / 4	4/ 1000 / 4
Med	23/ 304 / 7	3/ 333 / 1	14/ 357 / 5
Low	6/ 0 / 0	7/ 285 / 2	5/ 0 / 0

Curve Average .322

	Outside	Middle	Inside
High	4/ 500 / 2	2/ 500 / 1	2/ 0 / 0
Med	1/ 0 / 0	5/ 600 / 3	10/ 200 / 2
Low	2/ 500 / 1	0/ 0 / 0	5/ 200 / 1

Overall Evaluation

Against Right-Handed Pitchers

Overall Fastball ⚾⚾

Overall Curve ⚾⚾ ⚾⚾

Overall Slider ⚾⚾ ⚾⚾ ⚾⚾ ⚾⚾

Against Left-Handed Pitchers

Overall Fastball ⚾⚾

Overall Curve ⚾⚾

Overall Slider ⚾⚾ ⚾⚾ ⚾⚾ ⚾⚾

Comments: RH pitchers should keep fastballs away from the sector consisting of medium-middle, high-middle, high-inside and medium-high inside.

Strengths: As above, high-middle and medium-middle curves, medium-inside sliders vs. RH; high-middle fastballs vs. LH.

Weaknesses: Low fastballs, outside fastballs, inside curves, low-middle curves vs. RH; outside fastballs, inside fastballs except low, low-outside curves vs. LH.

Lonnie Smith Against Right-Handed Pitchers
Overall BARS Batting Average .255

Fastball Average .275

	Inside	Middle	Outside
High	26 / 115 / 3	30 / 233 / 7	3 / 333 / 1
Med	87 / 379 / 33	41 / 365 / 15	80 / 325 / 26
Low	45 / 200 / 9	67 / 253 / 17	38 / 105 / 4

Curve Average .240

	Inside	Middle	Outside
High	3 / 333 / 1	10 / 300 / 3	6 / 333 / 2
Med	17 / 235 / 4	17 / 294 / 5	31 / 290 / 9
Low	7 / 142 / 1	15 / 266 / 4	19 / 52 / 1

Slider Average .268

	Inside	Middle	Outside
High	1 / 0 / 0	5 / 400 / 2	0 / 0 / 0
Med	5 / 0 / 0	10 / 600 / 6	15 / 266 / 4
Low	7 / 142 / 1	14 / 214 / 3	25 / 240 / 6

Lonnie Smith Against Left-Handed Pitchers
Overall BARS Batting Average .237

Fastball Average .237

	Inside	Middle	Outside
High	7 / 0 / 0	17 / 176 / 3	10 / 100 / 1
Med	29 / 275 / 8	17 / 235 / 4	50 / 300 / 15
Low	13 / 307 / 4	46 / 239 / 11	17 / 176 / 3

Curve Average .250

	Inside	Middle	Outside
High	1 / 1000 / 1	4 / 500 / 2	0 / 0 / 0
Med	3 / 0 / 0	6 / 333 / 2	8 / 375 / 3
Low	7 / 0 / 0	14 / 214 / 3	1 / 0 / 0

Slider Average .241

	Inside	Middle	Outside
High	1 / 0 / 0	3 / 0 / 0	1 / 0 / 0
Med	8 / 375 / 3	1 / 1000 / 1	1 / 0 / 0
Low	9 / 0 / 0	5 / 600 / 3	0 / 0 / 0

Right-handed Lonnie Smith is very strong against waist-high fastballs thrown by right-handed pitchers. But he is weak against low fastballs. In fact, he has trouble with all low pitches thrown by right-handers.

His .325 medium-high outside fastball average against right-handers is excellent. He hits this pitch into the deep left-center gap and straightaway to the other fields.

MEDIUM-HIGH OUTSIDE FASTBALLS

BATTING AVERAGE .325

Play

Left	Deep and shifted toward center field
Center	Medium-deep in straightaway center field
Right	Medium-deep in straightaway right field
Short	Up middle (shifted toward second base)
Second	Normal position

Pitchers throw him a lot of inside fastballs, as indicated by the high number of recorded instances in his medium-high inside location (87). It's all right to throw him inside if the pitch is high or low, but he hits a very strong .379 against medium-high inside fastballs.

Note that if outfielders play Smith medium-deep and straightaway, and if infielders play him in their normal positions, they will prevent most of his base hits from the medium-high inside fastball location.

MEDIUM-HIGH INSIDE FASTBALLS

BATTING AVERAGE .379

Play

Left	Medium-deep in straightaway left field
Center	Medium-deep in straightaway center field
Right	Medium-deep in straightaway right field
Short	Normal position
Second	Normal position

His .253 against low-over-the-middle fastballs is poor. He hits this pitch deep to the outfield and to the right side of the infield.

LOW-OVER-THE-MIDDLE FASTBALLS

BATTING AVERAGE .253

Play

Left	Deep in straightaway left field
Center	Deep in straightaway center field
Right	Deep and shifted toward center field
Short	Up middle (shifted toward second base)
Second	Shifted toward first base

Smith Against Curves And Sliders

Smith has a lot of trouble with low curves thrown by right-handed pitchers. His .052 average against low-outside curves is very weak. He hits medium-high outside curves well, however (.290).

MEDIUM-HIGH OUTSIDE CURVEBALLS

BATTING AVERAGE .290
Play

Left	Deep and shifted toward the left field line
Center	Medium-deep in straightaway center field
Right	Medium-deep in straightaway right field
Short	Normal position
Second	Shifted toward first base

His trouble with low pitches continues in his slider chart. His .240 against low-outside sliders is weak. His .266 against medium-high outside sliders is just fair.

Notice the strong .600 against medium-over-the-middle sliders. In general, right-handed pitchers need to avoid giving Smith any pitch through the heart of the plate.

Smith Against Left-Handed Pitchers

Overall, Smith is weaker against left-handed than against right-handed pitchers. This is somewhat unusual for a right-handed hitter.

He has trouble with fastballs in general, having only two strong locations (.300 against medium-high outside, .307 against low-inside).

He hits medium-high outside fastballs straightaway to left and center and deep down the right line.

**MEDIUM-HIGH OUTSIDE FASTBALLS
(THROWN BY LEFT-HANDED PITCHERS)**

BATTING AVERAGE .300
Play

Left	Medium-deep in straightaway left field
Center	Deep in straightaway center field
Right	Deep and shifted toward the right field line
Short	Normal position
Second	Normal position

In contrast, he pulls low-inside fastballs deep down the left line. But note that he hits this pitch medium-deep down the right line. By positioning themselves properly, fielders could take away a lot of his hits from this location.

**LOW-INSIDE FASTBALLS
(THROWN BY LEFT-HANDED PITCHERS)**

BATTING AVERAGE .307
Play

Left	Deep and shifted toward the left field line
Center	Deep in straightaway center field
Right	Medium-deep and shifted toward the right line
Short	Normal position
Second	*No instances recorded*

Smith is weak against low curves thrown by left-handers. His 0-for-7 against low-inside curves and 3-for-14 against low-over-the-middle curves give a target for left-handers, especially since these locations are adjacent.

Ahead And Behind In The Count Vs. RH

Ahead

Fastball Average .342

	Inside	Middle	Outside
High	9/111 / 1	13/384 / 5	0/0 / 0
Med	46/456 / 21	22/454 / 10	45/355 / 16
Low	27/222 / 6	36/305 / 11	9/111 / 1

Curve Average .225

	Inside	Middle	Outside
High	0/0 / 0	3/333 / 1	4/250 / 1
Med	7/142 / 1	6/166 / 1	12/250 / 3
Low	0/0 / 0	5/400 / 2	3/0 / 0

Behind

Fastball Average .362

	Inside	Middle	Outside
High	4/250 / 1	4/250 / 1	1/1000 / 1
Med	16/500 / 8	6/333 / 2	7/285 / 2
Low	8/250 / 2	10/400 / 4	2/0 / 0

Curve Average .418

	Inside	Middle	Outside
High	0/0 / 0	3/666 / 2	2/500 / 1
Med	6/500 / 3	7/571 / 4	12/416 / 5
Low	3/333 / 1	5/200 / 1	5/200 / 1

Overall Evaluation
Against Right-Handed Pitchers

- **Overall Fastball** — 4 baseballs
- **Overall Curve** — 2 baseballs
- **Overall Slider** — 4 baseballs

Against Left-Handed Pitchers

- **Overall Fastball** — 2 baseballs
- **Overall Curve** — 4 baseballs
- **Overall Slider** — 2 baseballs

Comments: Strong vs. waist-high fastballs vs. RH.
Strengths: Waist-high fastballs, medium-middle, high-middle and medium-outside curves vs. RH; medium-outside and low-inside fastballs vs. LH.
Weaknesses: Low fastballs, high-inside and high-middle fastballs, low curves, medium-inside curves, low sliders vs. RH; low-outside and high fastballs, low curves and low-inside sliders vs. LH.

Andres Thomas Against Right-Handed Pitchers
Overall BARS Batting Average .228

Fastball Average .237

	Inside	Middle	Outside
High	24/ 166/4	24/ 291/7	23/ 173/4
Med	26/ 115/3	6/ 333/2	63/ 253/16
Low	14/ 428/6	19/ 315/6	20/ 200/4

Curve Average .256

	Inside	Middle	Outside
High	3/ 0/0	8/ 250/2	7/ 142/1
Med	5/ 200/1	4/ 500/2	27/ 407/11
Low	0/ 0/0	3/ 0/0	21/ 142/3

Slider Average .274

	Inside	Middle	Outside
High	1/ 1000/1	2/ 1000/2	5/ 200/1
Med	0/ 0/0	1/ 0/0	16/ 187/3
Low	2/ 500/1	7/ 428/3	17/ 176/3

Andres Thomas Against Left-Handed Pitchers
Overall BARS Batting Average .201

Fastball Average .239

	Inside	Middle	Outside
High	8/ 0/0	7/ 142/1	7/ 142/1
Med	16/ 250/4	4/ 500/2	27/ 333/9
Low	4/ 0/0	12/ 333/4	11/ 181/2

Curve Average .225

	Inside	Middle	Outside
High	1/ 0/0	0/ 0/0	4/ 250/1
Med	2/ 0/0	1/ 0/0	7/ 428/3
Low	4/ 0/0	8/ 375/3	4/ 0/0

Slider Average .333

	Inside	Middle	Outside
High	0/ 0/0	2/ 500/1	1/ 0/0
Med	0/ 0/0	0/ 0/0	1/ 1000/1
Low	2/ 500/1	4/ 250/1	2/ 0/0

Andres Thomas, right-handed hitter, has relatively low BARS fastball and curve averages against right- and left-handed pitchers.

He has a couple of strong fastball locations against right-handers, but in general his averages are weak throughout the chart. He has trouble with all outside fastballs. His .253 against medium-high outside fastballs is poor. He hits this pitch deep into the left-center gap and straightaway to the other fields.

MEDIUM-HIGH OUTSIDE FASTBALLS

BATTING AVERAGE .253
Play

Left	Deep and shifted toward center field
Center	Medium-deep in straightaway center field
Right	Deep in straightaway right field
Short	Up middle (shifted toward second base)
Second	Normal position

He hits only .173 against high-outside fastballs, but his .291 against high-over-the-middle fastballs is fairly good.

HIGH-OVER-THE-MIDDLE FASTBALLS

BATTING AVERAGE .291
Play

Left	Deep in straightaway left field
Center	Medium-deep in straightaway center field
Right	Deep and shifted toward center field
Short	Up middle (shifted toward second base)
Second	Normal position

He hits .315 against low-over-the-middle fastballs, and his .428 against low-inside fastballs is excellent. He hits low-inside fastballs to medium-deep left and right fields and to short center field. By positioning themselves according to the BARS strategy for this pitch, fielders could catch most of his line drives resulting from pitches to this location, drives that are now falling in for base hits.

LOW-INSIDE FASTBALLS

BATTING AVERAGE .428
Play

Left	Medium-deep and shifted toward the left field line
Center	Short in straightaway center field
Right	Medium-deep in straightaway right field
Short	Normal position
Second	Normal position

Thomas is very weak against high-inside and medium-high inside fastballs thrown by right-handers. This sector and his outside fastball locations offer targets for right-handers to attack.

Thomas Against Curves And Sliders

Thomas hits medium-high outside curves extremely well against right-handers (.407).

MEDIUM-HIGH OUTSIDE CURVEBALLS

BATTING AVERAGE .407
Play

Left	Deep in straightaway left field
Center	Medium-deep in straightaway center field
Right	Medium-deep in straightaway right field
Short	Up middle (shifted toward second base)
Second	Normal position

In contrast, he hits low-outside curves very poorly (.142).

He has trouble with outside sliders thrown by right-handers (.200, .187 and .176, high to low). He hits low-outside sliders medium-deep to all fields, but his low average in this location indicates that most of his hit balls are easy outs.

Thomas Against Left-Handed Pitchers

Against left-handed pitchers, Thomas hits medium-high outside fastballs for a solid .333. He pulls this pitch deep down the left line.

**MEDIUM-HIGH OUTSIDE FASTBALLS
(THROWN BY LEFT-HANDED PITCHERS)**

BATTING AVERAGE .333
Play

Left	Deep and shifted toward the left field line
Center	Deep in straightaway center field
Right	Medium-deep in straightaway right field
Short	Normal position
Second	Shifted toward first base

He also hits low-over-the-middle fastballs for a .333 average. He pulls this pitch deep down the left line, into the left-center gap and to the left side of the infield.

**LOW-OVER-THE-MIDDLE FASTBALLS
(THROWN BY LEFT-HANDED PITCHERS)**

BATTING AVERAGE .333
Play

Left	Deep and shifted toward the left field line
Center	Medium-deep and shifted toward left field
Right	Deep in straightaway right field
Short	Shifted toward third base
Second	*No instances recorded*

Thomas is weak against low-outside fastballs, all high fastballs, and all inside fastballs thrown by left-handers. His fielding strategy for medium-high inside fastballs shows that he hits the ball to all fields. His .250 average in this location indicates that he is not hitting this pitch hard.

**MEDIUM-HIGH INSIDE FASTBALLS
(THROWN BY LEFT-HANDED PITCHERS)**

BATTING AVERAGE .250
Play

Left	Medium-deep in straightaway left field
Center	Short and shifted toward left field
Right	Deep and shifted toward the right field line
Short	Up middle (shifted toward second base)
Second	*No instances recorded*

Ahead And Behind In The Count Vs. RH

Ahead

Fastball Average .305

	Inside	Middle	Outside
High	9/222/2	15/266/4	9/333/3
Med	11/181/2	4/500/2	31/258/8
Low	8/625/5	13/307/4	8/375/3

Curve Average .294

	Inside	Middle	Outside
High	0/0/0	2/500/1	2/0/0
Med	3/0/0	1/0/0	8/500/4
Low	0/0/0	0/0/0	1/0/0

Behind

Fastball Average .250

	Inside	Middle	Outside
High	2/0/0	2/1000/2	6/166/1
Med	4/0/0	0/0/0	12/250/3
Low	0/0/0	5/400/2	1/0/0

Curve Average .318

	Inside	Middle	Outside
High	0/0/0	2/500/1	2/0/0
Med	0/0/0	1/0/0	8/500/4
Low	0/0/0	2/0/0	7/285/2

Overall Evaluation

Against Right-Handed Pitchers

Overall Fastball	1
Overall Curve	2
Overall Slider	2

Against Left-Handed Pitchers

Overall Fastball	1
Overall Curve	1
Overall Slider	4

Comments: Weak against outside fastballs vs. RH.
Strengths: Low-inside and low-middle fastballs, medium-outside curves, low-middle sliders vs. RH; medium-outside and low-middle fastballs, medium-outside curves vs. LH.
Weaknesses: Outside fastballs, medium-inside and high-inside fastballs, low-outside curves, outside sliders vs. RH; low-outside fastballs, all high and inside fastballs vs. LH.

Benzinger, Todd
Daniels, Kal
Davis, Eric
Larkin, Barry
Oester, Ron
Reed, Jeff
Trillo, Manny
Youngblood, Joel

Cincinnati Reds
BARS System
Hitting Analysis

Todd Benzinger Against Right-Handed Pitchers
Overall BARS Batting Average .254

Fastball Average .293

	Outside	Middle	Inside
High	13/ 0/0	14/ 428/6	3/ 0/0
Med	64/ 343/22	4/ 250/1	6/ 0/0
Low	6/ 0/0	9/ 555/5	7/ 428/3

Curve Average .142

	Outside	Middle	Inside
High	0/ 0/0	0/ 0/0	1/ 0/0
Med	6/ 0/0	1/ 0/0	2/ 500/1
Low	1/ 0/0	0/ 0/0	3/ 333/1

Slider Average .333

	Outside	Middle	Inside
High	0/ 0/0	0/ 0/0	0/ 0/0
Med	0/ 0/0	1/ 1000/1	0/ 0/0
Low	0/ 0/0	0/ 0/0	2/ 0/0

Todd Benzinger Against Left-Handed Pitchers
Overall BARS Batting Average .207

Fastball Average .272

	Inside	Middle	Outside
High	2/ 0/0	4/ 200/1	9/ 222/2
Med	2/ 500/1	0/ 0/0	23/ 217/5
Low	5/ 400/2	5/ 200/1	5/ 600/3

Curve Average .111

	Inside	Middle	Outside
High	2/ 0/0	0/ 0/0	1/ 0/0
Med	0/ 0/0	0/ 0/0	3/ 333/1
Low	1/ 0/0	0/ 0/0	2/ 0/0

Slider Average .000

	Inside	Middle	Outside
High	1/ 0/0	0/ 0/0	0/ 0/0
Med	0/ 0/0	0/ 0/0	1/ 0/0
Low	1/ 0/0	0/ 0/0	0/ 0/0

Switch-hitting Todd Benzinger has an unusual record against right-handed pitchers in that his fastball chart is so heavily skewed toward outside pitches. His 64 instances in the medium-high outside fastball location are more than the total number of instances in his other fastball locations combined.

He hits this pitch excellently (.343), driving the ball deep to all fields. The shortstop needs to shift toward second base and the second baseman toward first base. The following BARS fielding strategy and the field diagram on the opposite page show where fielders need to play to prevent most of Benzinger's hits from pitches to this location.

MEDIUM-HIGH OUTSIDE FASTBALLS

BATTING AVERAGE .343

Play

Left	Deep in straightaway left field
Center	Deep in straightaway center field
Right	Deep and shifted toward center field
Short	Up middle (shifted toward second base)
Second	Shifted toward first base

In contrast, he hits .000 on 0-for-13 in his high-outside fastball location. His 0-for-6 against low-outside fastballs also indicates a weakness.

He hits an excellent .428 against high-over-the-middle fastballs thrown by right-handers.

HIGH-OVER-THE-MIDDLE FASTBALLS

BATTING AVERAGE .428

Play

Left	Deep in straightaway left field
Center	Deep and shifted toward left field
Right	Deep and shifted toward the right field line
Short	Normal position
Second	*No instances recorded*

Benzinger has a sparkling .555 average against low-over-the-middle fastballs. He hits this pitch deep down the left line, medium-deep to straightaway center, and deep into the right-center gap.

Benzinger Against Left-Handed Pitchers

Benzinger hits .272 overall against fastballs thrown by left-handed pitchers. He hits only .217 in the highly pitched medium-high outside fastball location.

MEDIUM-HIGH OUTSIDE FASTBALLS (THROWN BY LEFT-HANDED PITCHERS)

BATTING AVERAGE .217

Play

Left	Deep and shifted toward center field
Center	Medium-deep in straightaway center field
Right	Deep in straightaway right field
Short	Up middle (shifted toward second base)
Second	Normal position

Medium-High Outside Fastballs

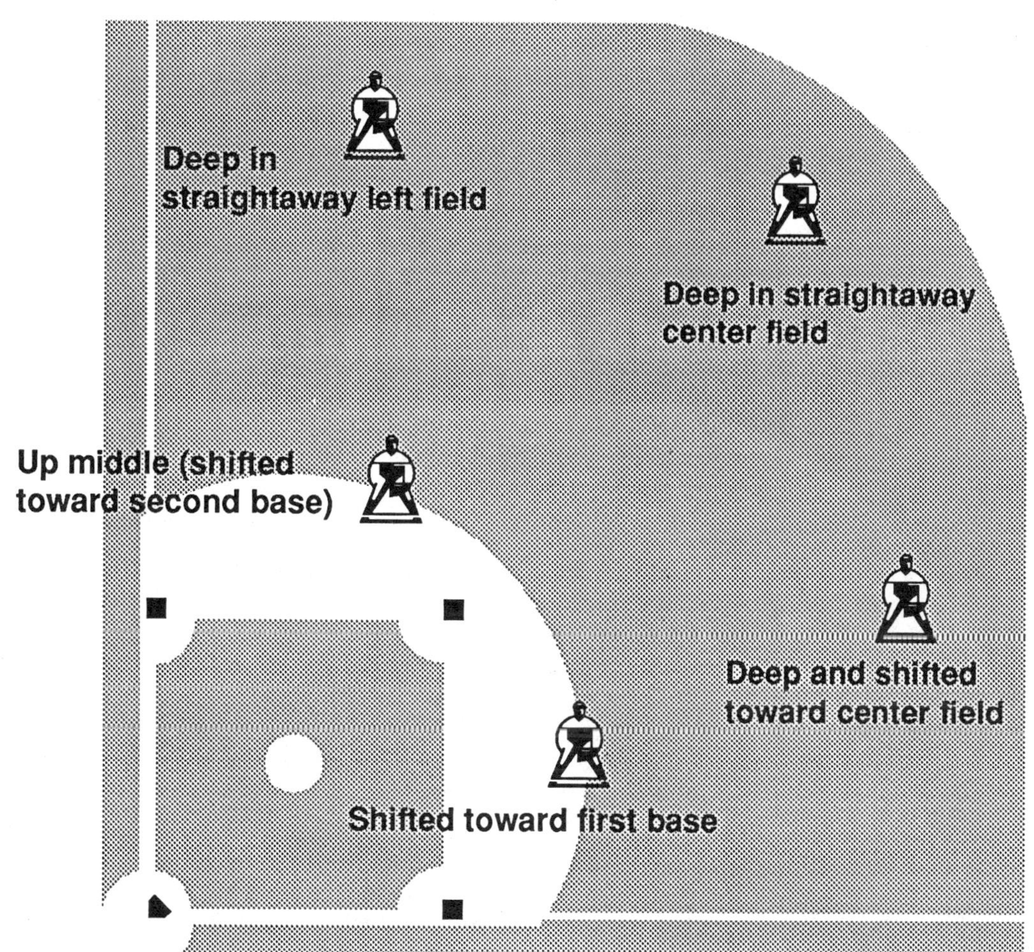

Ahead And Behind In The Count Vs. RH

Ahead

Fastball Average .370

	Outside	Middle	Inside
High	4/ 0/0	6/ 000/2	0/ 0/0
Med	33/ 333/11	3/ 333/1	1/ 0/0
Low	0/ 0/0	4/ 750/3	3/ 1000/3

Curve Average 1.000

	Outside	Middle	Inside
High	0/ 0/0	0/ 0/0	1/ 0/0
Med	0/ 0/0	0/ 0/0	1/ 1000/1
Low	0/ 0/0	0/ 0/0	0/ 0/0

Behind

Fastball Average .272

	Outside	Middle	Inside
High	4/ 0/0	6/ 500/3	0/ 0/0
Med	13/ 461/6	1/ 0/0	2/ 0/0
Low	4/ 0/0	2/ 0/0	1/ 0/0

Curve Average .000

	Outside	Middle	Inside
High	0/ 0/0	0/ 0/0	0/ 0/0
Med	0/ 0/0	0/ 0/0	0/ 0/0
Low	0/ 0/0	0/ 0/0	0/ 0/0

Overall Evaluation

Against Right-Handed Pitchers

Overall Fastball	
Overall Curve	
Overall Slider	Not enough information

Against Left-Handed Pitchers

Overall Fastball	(1 ball)
Overall Curve	Not enough information
Overall Slider	Not enough information

Comments: RH throw him an extraordinary number of medium-high outside fastballs (which he hits excellently).

Strengths: Medium-high outside, high-middle, low-middle and low-inside fastballs vs. RH.

Weaknesses: High-outside and low-outside fastballs, outside curves vs. RH; high fastballs, medium-outside fastballs vs. LH.

Kal Daniels Against Right-Handed Pitchers
Overall BARS Batting Average .309

Fastball Average .376

	Outside	Middle	Inside
High	5 / 200 / 1	11 / 727 / 8	8 / 125 / 1
Med	34 / 382 / 13	1 / 0 / 0	16 / 562 / 9
Low	8 / 125 / 1	11 / 272 / 3	7 / 285 / 2

Curve Average .409

	Outside	Middle	Inside
High	2 / 500 / 1	0 / 0 / 0	0 / 0 / 0
Med	3 / 333 / 1	1 / 1000 / 1	4 / 500 / 2
Low	5 / 0 / 0	3 / 666 / 2	4 / 500 / 2

Slider Average .230

	Outside	Middle	Inside
High	1 / 0 / 0	0 / 0 / 0	3 / 0 / 0
Med	2 / 1000 / 2	0 / 0 / 0	2 / 500 / 1
Low	1 / 0 / 0	1 / 0 / 0	3 / 0 / 0

Kal Daniels Against Left-Handed Pitchers
Overall BARS Batting Average .173

Fastball Average .260

	Outside	Middle	Inside
High	4 / 500 / 2	1 / 0 / 0	3 / 0 / 0
Med	7 / 285 / 2	1 / 1000 / 1	4 / 250 / 1
Low	1 / 0 / 0	1 / 0 / 0	1 / 0 / 0

Curve Average .076

	Outside	Middle	Inside
High	1 / 0 / 0	1 / 0 / 0	0 / 0 / 0
Med	3 / 333 / 1	1 / 0 / 0	2 / 0 / 0
Low	3 / 0 / 0	2 / 0 / 0	0 / 0 / 0

Slider Average .111

	Outside	Middle	Inside
High	0 / 0 / 0	0 / 0 / 0	0 / 0 / 0
Med	3 / 333 / 1	0 / 0 / 0	1 / 0 / 0
Low	4 / 0 / 0	0 / 0 / 0	1 / 0 / 0

Left-handed hitter Kal Daniels has an excellent .376 overall BARS fastball average against right-handed pitchers. He is especially strong against medium-high outside fastballs (.382), high-over-the-middle fastballs (.727) and medium-high inside fastballs (.562).

He goes deep to all fields with medium-high outside fastballs.

MEDIUM-HIGH OUTSIDE FASTBALLS

BATTING AVERAGE .382
> *Play*

Left	Deep and shifted toward the left field line
Center	Deep in straightaway center field
Right	Deep in straightaway right field
Short	Normal position
Second	Normal position

His .727 against high-over-the-middle fastballs sounds more like an airplane than a batting average. He hits this pitch into the left-center gap and straightaway to right. Proper positioning of fielders would prevent most of Daniels's hits from this location.

HIGH-OVER-THE-MIDDLE FASTBALLS

BATTING AVERAGE .727
> *Play*

Left	Medium-deep and shifted toward center field
Center	Deep and shifted toward left field
Right	Deep in straightaway right field
Short	Normal position
Second	Shifted toward first base

He hits medium-high inside fastballs medium-deep to left and center fields and deep down the right line. The field diagram on the opposite page shows how fielders need to be positioned for this pitch.

MEDIUM-HIGH INSIDE FASTBALLS

BATTING AVERAGE .562
> *Play*

Left	Medium-deep in straightaway left field
Center	Medium-deep in straightaway center field
Right	Deep and shifted toward the right field line
Short	Up middle (shifted toward second base)
Second	Normal position

Daniels hits .272 against low-over-the-middle fastballs.

LOW-OVER-THE-MIDDLE FASTBALLS

BATTING AVERAGE .272
> *Play*

Left	Deep and shifted toward the left field line
Center	Medium-deep in straightaway center field
Right	Medium-deep and shifted toward center field
Short	Up middle (shifted toward second base)
Second	Normal position

Medium-High Inside Fastballs

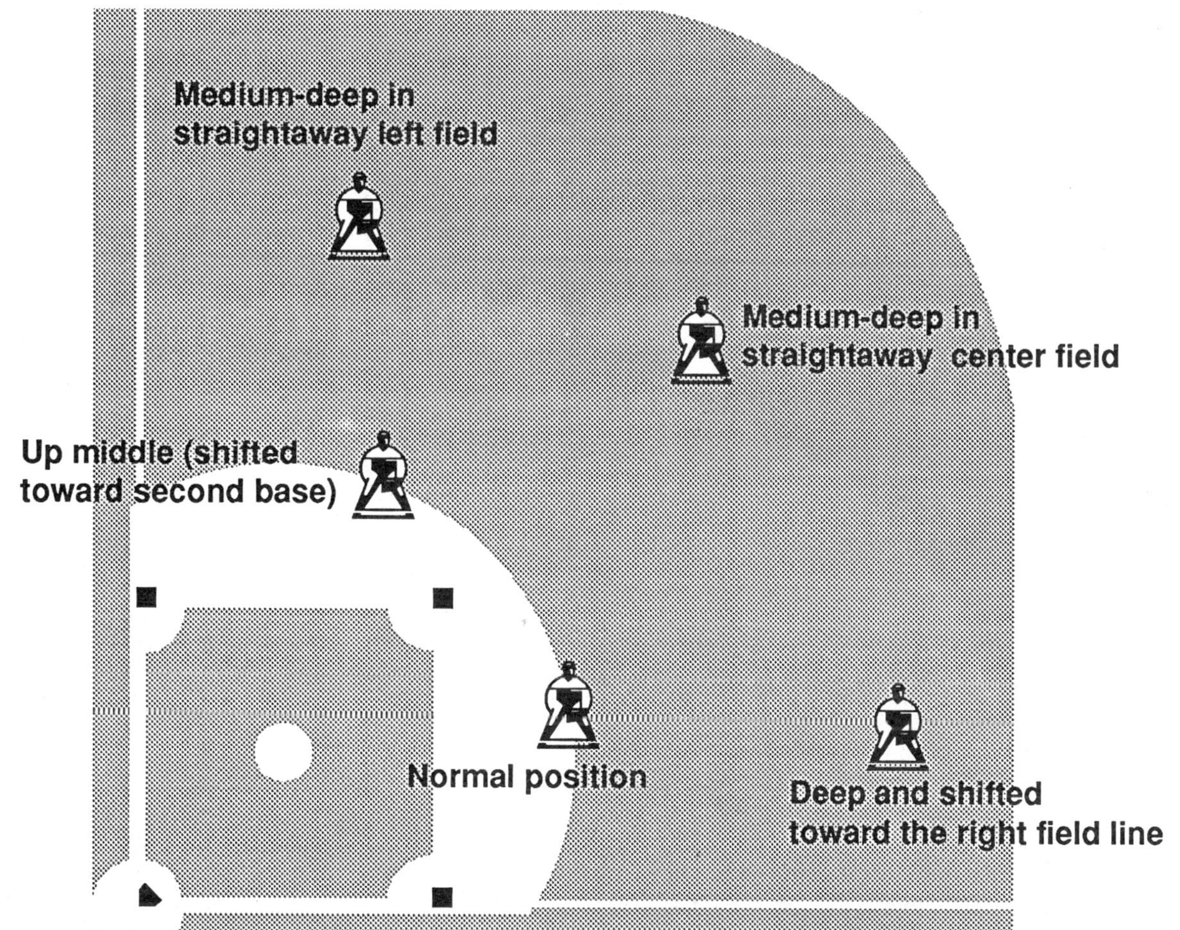

Ahead And Behind In The Count Vs. RH

Ahead

Fastball Average .428

	Outside	Middle	Inside
High	2/ 500 /1	4/ 1000 /4	3/ 333 /1
Med	17/ 411 /7	0/ 0 /0	13/ 538 /7
Low	2/ 0 /0	6/ 166 /1	2/ 0 /0

Curve Average .333

	Outside	Middle	Inside
High	0/ 0 /0	0/ 0 /0	0/ 0 /0
Med	1/ 0 /0	0/ 0 /0	1/ 1000 /1
Low	2/ 0 /0	0/ 0 /0	2/ 500 /1

Behind

Fastball Average .375

	Outside	Middle	Inside
High	1/ 0 /0	3/ 666 /2	3/ 0 /0
Med	5/ 600 /3	0/ 0 /0	1/ 0 /0
Low	2/ 500 /1	0/ 0 /0	1/ 0 /0

Curve Average .800

	Outside	Middle	Inside
High	0/ 0 /0	0/ 0 /0	0/ 0 /0
Med	1/ 1000 /1	0/ 0 /0	2/ 500 /1
Low	0/ 0 /0	1/ 1000 /1	1/ 1000 /1

Overall Evaluation

Against Right-Handed Pitchers

Overall Fastball
Overall Curve
Overall Slider — Not enough information

Against Left-Handed Pitchers

Overall Fastball
Overall Curve — Not enough information
Overall Slider — Not enough information

Comments: Has three very strong fastball locations against RH.

Strengths: Medium-outside, high-middle and medium-inside fastballs vs. RH.

Weaknesses: Low-outside, low-middle and high-inside fastballs vs. RH.

Eric Davis Against Right-Handed Pitchers
Overall BARS Batting Average .237

Fastball Average .233

	Inside	Middle	Outside
High	13 / 0/0	15 / 266/4	7 / 0/0
Med	19 / 421/8	7 / 285/2	29 / 206/6
Low	13 / 307/4	14 / 357/5	16 / 125/2

Curve Average .382

	Inside	Middle	Outside
High	0 / 0/0	3 / 333/1	6 / 666/4
Med	1 / 0/0	3 / 333/1	14 / 642/9
Low	0 / 0/0	0 / 0/0	20 / 150/3

Slider Average .181

	Inside	Middle	Outside
High	0 / 0/0	0 / 0/0	4 / 0/0
Med	0 / 0/0	1 / 0/0	8 / 125/1
Low	1 / 0/0	0 / 0/0	8 / 375/3

Eric Davis Against Left-Handed Pitchers
Overall BARS Batting Average .327

Fastball Average .407

	Inside	Middle	Outside
High	2 / 0/0	5 / 400/2	3 / 666/2
Med	3 / 333/1	0 / 0/0	20 / 500/10
Low	4 / 250/1	9 / 444/4	8 / 250/2

Curve Average .350

	Inside	Middle	Outside
High	1 / 0/0	0 / 0/0	1 / 0/0
Med	1 / 0/0	0 / 0/0	5 / 0/0
Low	1 / 0/0	7 / 714/5	4 / 500/2

Slider Average .375

	Inside	Middle	Outside
High	0 / 0/0	0 / 0/0	0 / 0/0
Med	1 / 1000/1	0 / 0/0	3 / 333/1
Low	0 / 0/0	3 / 333/1	1 / 0/0

Right-handed hitter Eric Davis hits .233 overall against fastballs thrown by right-handed pitchers, but his .407 overall fastball average against left-handed pitchers is excellent. He hits curves extremely well overall against both right- and left-handers.

Starting with his fastball performance against right-handers, notice his weakness against high fastballs (.000 on 0-for-13, .266 and .000 on 0-for-7, inside to outside). He also has trouble with outside fastballs (.000, .206 and .125, high to low). These areas offer targets for right-handers to attack.

Davis's strong fastball sector consists of the four remaining locations: medium-high inside (.421), medium-over-the-middle (.285), low-inside (.307), and low-over-the-middle (.357). By staying away from this sector, right-handers can get an edge.

Davis hits medium-high inside fastballs deep down the left line.

MEDIUM-HIGH INSIDE FASTBALLS

BATTING AVERAGE .421
Play

Left	Deep and shifted toward the left field line
Center	Medium-deep in straightaway center field
Right	Deep in straightaway right field
Short	Shifted toward third base
Second	*No instances recorded*

He pulls low-over-the-middle fastballs deep to all fields.

LOW-OVER-THE-MIDDLE FASTBALLS

BATTING AVERAGE .357
Play

Left	Deep and shifted toward the left field line
Center	Deep and shifted toward left field
Right	Deep and shifted toward center field
Short	Normal position
Second	*No instances recorded*

He also hits low-inside fastballs deep to the outfield.

LOW-INSIDE FASTBALLS

BATTING AVERAGE .307
Play

Left	Deep and shifted toward the left field line
Center	*No instances recorded*
Right	Deep in straightaway right field
Short	Up middle (shifted toward second base)
Second	Normal position

Davis Against Curves And Sliders

Right-handed pitchers throw Davis a lot of outside

curves. The fact that they throw him outside means that they are pitching him carefully. Nonetheless, he hits medium-high outside curves exceptionally well (.642). He pulls this pitch to all fields.

MEDIUM-HIGH OUTSIDE CURVEBALLS

BATTING AVERAGE .642
Play

Left	Deep and shifted toward the left field line
Center	Deep and shifted toward left field
Right	Deep and shifted toward center field
Short	Shifted toward third base
Second	*No instances recorded*

If right-handers throw him outside curves, they should keep the ball low. His .150 average against low-outside curves is weak.

He has trouble with medium-high outside sliders (.125) but hits low-outside sliders excellently (.375). Notice that there are no recorded instances of Davis hitting this pitch to the infield. That means, with a man on third and less than two outs, pitchers should avoid throwing Davis this pitch since he is likely to hit it deep to the outfield and drive in the runner.

LOW-OUTSIDE SLIDERS

BATTING AVERAGE .375
Play

Left	Deep in straightaway left field
Center	Deep and shifted toward left field
Right	Deep in straightaway right field
Short	*No instances recorded*
Second	*No instances recorded*

Davis Against Left-Handed Pitchers

Davis hits a sparkling .500 against medium-high outside fastballs thrown by left-handed pitchers. He hits this pitch deep to the outfield.

MEDIUM-HIGH OUTSIDE FASTBALLS (THROWN BY LEFT-HANDED PITCHERS)

BATTING AVERAGE .500
Play

Left	Deep in straightaway left field
Center	Deep and shifted toward left field
Right	Deep in straightaway right field
Short	Up middle (shifted toward second base)
Second	*No instances recorded*

He hits a strong .444 against low-over-the-middle fastballs thrown by left-handers.

LOW-OVER-THE-MIDDLE FASTBALLS (THROWN BY LEFT-HANDED PITCHERS)

BATTING AVERAGE .444
Play

Left	Medium-deep and shifted toward the left field line
Center	*No instances recorded*
Right	Deep in straightaway right field
Short	Up middle (shifted toward second base)
Second	*No instances recorded*

Against left-handers, Davis hits an exceptional .714 against low-over-the-middle curves and .500 against low-outside curves. Left-handers should consider this a strong sector and avoid throwing to it.

Ahead And Behind In The Count Vs. RH

Ahead

Fastball Average .326

	Inside	Middle	Outside
High	4/0 / 0	2/500 / 1	3/0 / 0
Med	7/571 / 4	4/500 / 2	10/200 / 2
Low	6/333 / 2	6/333 / 2	4/500 / 2

Curve Average .333

	Inside	Middle	Outside
High	0/0 / 0	0/0 / 0	3/666 / 2
Med	0/0 / 0	0/0 / 0	5/400 / 2
Low	0/0 / 0	0/0 / 0	4/0 / 0

Behind

Fastball Average .300

	Inside	Middle	Outside
High	3/0 / 0	5/600 / 3	0/0 / 0
Med	2/500 / 1	0/0 / 0	5/0 / 0
Low	3/666 / 2	1/0 / 0	1/0 / 0

Curve Average .583

	Inside	Middle	Outside
High	0/0 / 0	0/0 / 0	2/1000 / 2
Med	0/0 / 0	2/500 / 1	4/750 / 3
Low	0/0 / 0	0/0 / 0	4/250 / 1

Overall Evaluation

Against Right-Handed Pitchers

Overall Fastball	⚾
Overall Curve	⚾ ⚾ ⚾ ⚾
Overall Slider	⚾

Against Left-Handed Pitchers

Overall Fastball	⚾ ⚾ ⚾ ⚾
Overall Curve	⚾ ⚾ ⚾ ⚾
Overall Slider	Not enough information

Comments: Weak vs. high & outside fastballs vs. RH.
Strengths: Medium-inside, low-inside and low-middle fastballs, medium-outside curves and low-outside sliders vs. RH; low-middle and medium-outside fastballs, low-middle curves vs. LH.
Weaknesses: High fastballs, outside fastballs, low-outside curves, medium-outside sliders vs. RH.

Barry Larkin (Right Handed) — *Cincinnati Reds*

Barry Larkin Against Right-Handed Pitchers
Overall BARS Batting Average .227

Fastball Average .289

	Inside	Middle	Outside
High	13/ 153/2	8/ 250/2	9/ 444/4
Med	16/ 375/6	1/ 1000/1	20/ 200/4
Low	8/ 125/1	17/ 411/7	15/ 266/4

Curve Average .125

	Inside	Middle	Outside
High	0/ 0/0	1/ 1000/1	1/ 0/0
Med	0/ 0/0	1/ 0/0	3/ 0/0
Low	0/ 0/0	2/ 0/0	8/ 125/1

Slider Average .173

	Inside	Middle	Outside
High	0/ 0/0	1/ 0/0	0/ 0/0
Med	2/ 500/1	0/ 0/0	7/ 142/1
Low	2/ 500/1	1/ 0/0	10/ 100/1

Barry Larkin Against Left-Handed Pitchers
Overall BARS Batting Average .301

Fastball Average .275

	Inside	Middle	Outside
High	2/ 500/1	5/ 400/2	5/ 400/2
Med	6/ 0/0	2/ 1000/2	7/ 285/2
Low	3/ 0/0	6/ 333/2	4/ 0/0

Curve Average .250

	Inside	Middle	Outside
High	0/ 0/0	0/ 0/0	1/ 0/0
Med	1/ 0/0	0/ 0/0	0/ 0/0
Low	1/ 1000/1	1/ 0/0	0/ 0/0

Slider Average .000

	Inside	Middle	Outside
High	0/ 0/0	0/ 0/0	0/ 0/0
Med	0/ 0/0	0/ 0/0	0/ 0/0
Low	0/ 0/0	0/ 0/0	0/ 0/0

Barry Larkin, right-handed hitter, has a .289 BARS overall fastball average against right-handed pitchers. He has scattered weak and strong locations throughout his fastball chart. His .200 against medium-high outside fastballs is weak, but he hits a strong .375 against medium-high inside fastballs. The following fielding strategy and the field diagram on the opposite page show how fielders need to play for this pitch.

MEDIUM-HIGH INSIDE FASTBALLS

BATTING AVERAGE .375
Play
Left	Medium-deep in straightaway left field
Center	Medium-deep and shifted toward left field
Right	Medium-deep and shifted toward the right line
Short	Up middle (shifted toward second base)
Second	Normal position

His .411 against low-over-the-middle fastballs thrown by right-handers is very strong.

LOW-OVER-THE-MIDDLE FASTBALLS

BATTING AVERAGE .411
Play
Left	Medium-deep in straightaway left field
Center	Deep in straightaway center field
Right	Deep and shifted toward the right field line
Short	Up middle (shifted toward second base)
Second	Normal position

He hits high-outside fastballs for a .444 average.

HIGH-OUTSIDE FASTBALLS

BATTING AVERAGE .444
Play
Left	Medium-deep and shifted toward the left field line
Center	Deep in straightaway center field
Right	Deep and shifted toward center field
Short	Shifted toward third base
Second	Normal position

The two best fastball sectors for right-handers to attack are those consisting of the high-inside/high-over-the-middle locations and the medium-high outside/low-outside locations. By throwing to these sectors right-handers have the best chance of hitting one of Larkin's weak locations.

Other areas of weakness are outside curves and outside sliders against right-handers. Against left-handed pitchers, Larkin hits medium-high outside fastballs for a .285 average but has problems with medium-high inside fastballs (.000 on 0-for-6).

Medium-High Inside Fastballs

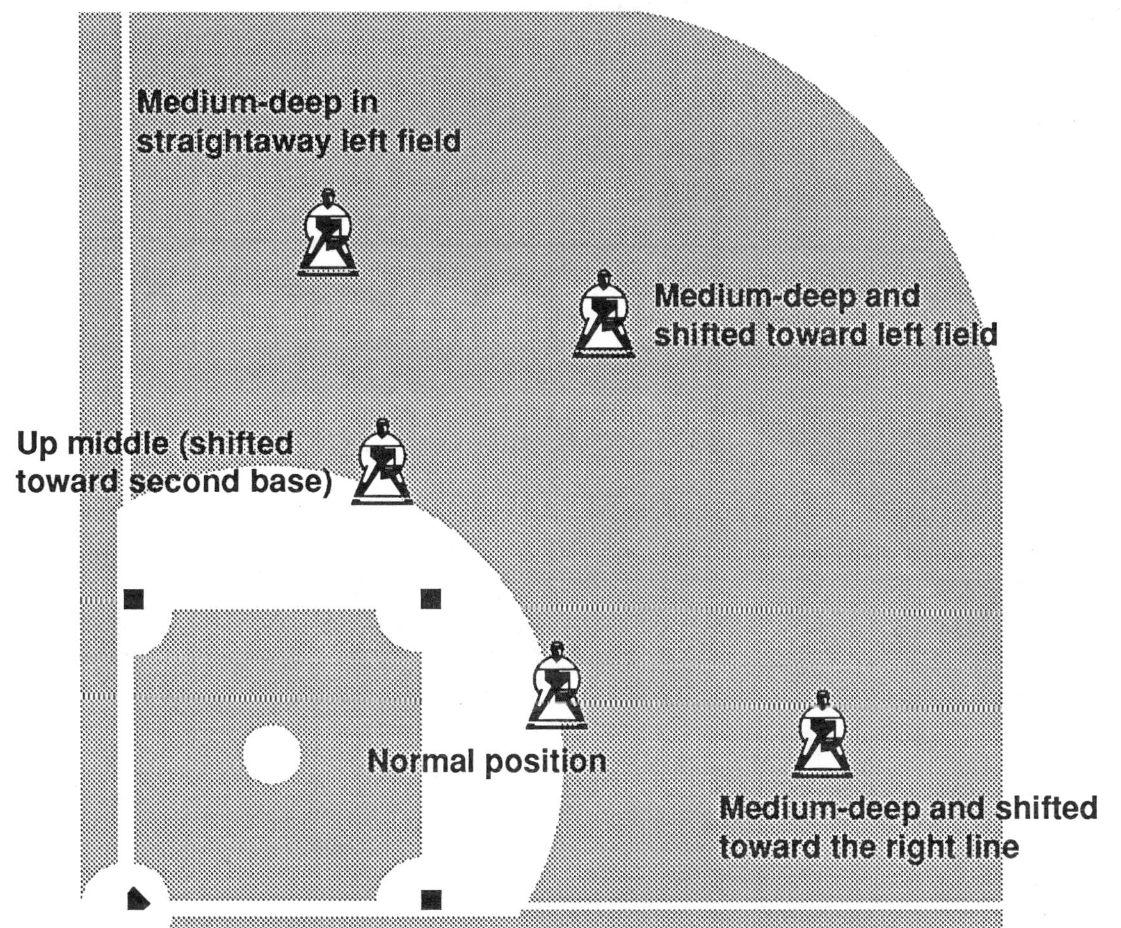

Ahead And Behind In The Count Vs. RH

Ahead

Fastball Average .244

	Inside	Middle	Outside
High	8/ 125 /1	3/ 0 /0	0/ 0 /0
Med	9/ 333 /3	0/ 0 /0	12/ 333 /4
Low	5/ 200 /1	9/ 222 /2	3/ 333 /1

Curve Average .000

	Inside	Middle	Outside
High	0/ 0 /0	0/ 0 /0	0/ 0 /0
Med	0/ 0 /0	0/ 0 /0	2/ 0 /0
Low	0/ 0 /0	0/ 0 /0	0/ 0 /0

Behind

Fastball Average .217

	Inside	Middle	Outside
High	3/ 333 /1	3/ 333 /1	4/ 250 /1
Med	2/ 500 /1	0/ 0 /0	6/ 0 /0
Low	1/ 0 /0	0/ 0 /0	4/ 250 /1

Curve Average 1.000

	Inside	Middle	Outside
High	0/ 0 /0	1/ 1000 /1	0/ 0 /0
Med	0/ 0 /0	0/ 0 /0	0/ 0 /0
Low	0/ 0 /0	0/ 0 /0	1/ 1000 /1

Overall Evaluation

Against Right-Handed Pitchers

Overall Fastball	
Overall Curve	
Overall Slider	

Against Left-Handed Pitchers

Overall Fastball	
Overall Curve	Not enough information
Overall Slider	Not enough information

Comments: Weak in the low-outside/medium-outside fastball sector vs. RH.

Strengths: Medium-inside, low-middle and high-outside fastballs vs. RH.

Weaknesses: High-inside, low-inside, medium-outside and low-outside fastballs, outside curves and outside sliders vs. RH.

Ron Oester (Switch Hitter) — Cincinnati Reds

Ron Oester Against Right-Handed Pitchers
Overall BARS Batting Average .250

Fastball Average .297

	Outside	Middle	Inside
High	17/ 352 / 6	36/ 305 / 11	12/ 166 / 2
Med	58/ 293 / 17	10/ 400 / 4	36/ 305 / 11
Low	19/ 210 / 4	38/ 342 / 13	23/ 260 / 6

Curve Average .241

	Outside	Middle	Inside
High	4/ 250 / 1	6/ 166 / 1	2/ 1000 / 2
Med	14/ 500 / 7	2/ 0 / 0	4/ 250 / 1
Low	7/ 142 / 1	10/ 100 / 1	9/ 0 / 0

Slider Average .176

	Outside	Middle	Inside
High	1/ 0 / 0	1/ 1000 / 1	2/ 0 / 0
Med	1/ 0 / 0	0/ 0 / 0	3/ 0 / 0
Low	0/ 0 / 0	2/ 0 / 0	7/ 285 / 2

Ron Oester Against Left-Handed Pitchers
Overall BARS Batting Average .137

Fastball Average .144

	Inside	Middle	Outside
High	4/ 250 / 1	3/ 0 / 0	6/ 0 / 0
Med	9/ 222 / 2	6/ 333 / 2	18/ 111 / 2
Low	8/ 0 / 0	14/ 214 / 3	15/ 133 / 2

Curve Average .153

	Inside	Middle	Outside
High	0/ 0 / 0	0/ 0 / 0	1/ 0 / 0
Med	1/ 0 / 0	1/ 0 / 0	2/ 0 / 0
Low	2/ 500 / 1	5/ 200 / 1	1/ 0 / 0

Slider Average .150

	Inside	Middle	Outside
High	0/ 0 / 0	1/ 0 / 0	1/ 0 / 0
Med	2/ 500 / 1	1/ 1000 / 1	3/ 0 / 0
Low	4/ 0 / 0	7/ 142 / 1	1/ 0 / 0

Switch-hitting Ron Oester hits a solid .297 overall against fastballs thrown by right-handed pitchers. He has three weak fastball locations: low-outside (.210), high-inside (.166) and low-inside (.260). The rest of his fastball locations are solid.

He hits .293 against medium-high outside fastballs. He hits this pitch deep into the left-center gap and deep down the right line. The shortstop needs to play shifted toward second base and the second baseman shifted toward first base.

MEDIUM-HIGH OUTSIDE FASTBALLS

BATTING AVERAGE .293
Play

Left	Deep in straightaway left field
Center	Deep and shifted toward left field
Right	Deep and shifted toward the right field line
Short	Up middle (shifted toward second base)
Second	Shifted toward first base

He hits a strong .342 against low-over-the-middle fastballs.

LOW-OVER-THE-MIDDLE FASTBALLS

BATTING AVERAGE .342
Play

Left	Deep in straightaway left field

Center	Medium-deep and shifted toward right field
Right	Medium-deep in straightaway right field
Short	Up middle (shifted toward second base)
Second	Normal position

He hits .305 against both medium-high inside fastballs and high-over-the-middle fastballs. Fielders need to align themselves quite differently for these two pitches, however.

MEDIUM-HIGH INSIDE FASTBALLS

BATTING AVERAGE .305
Play

Left	Short and shifted toward the left field line
Center	Medium-deep in straightaway center field
Right	Deep and shifted toward the right field line
Short	Shifted toward third base
Second	Shifted toward first base

HIGH-OVER-THE-MIDDLE FASTBALLS

BATTING AVERAGE .305
Play

Left	Medium-deep in straightaway left field
Center	Medium-deep in straightaway center field
Right	Deep in straightaway right field
Short	Up middle (shifted toward second base)
Second	Normal position

Oester's .352 against high-outside fastballs is outstanding. He goes medium-deep down the left line with this pitch.

HIGH-OUTSIDE FASTBALLS

BATTING AVERAGE .352
Play

Left	Medium-deep and shifted toward the left field line
Center	Deep and shifted toward right field
Right	Medium-deep in straightaway right field
Short	Up middle (shifted toward second base)
Second	Normal position

Oester Against Curves And Sliders

Oester has a lot of problems with low curves thrown by right-handed pitchers (.142, .100 and .000 on 0-for-9, outside to inside). By keeping curves low, right-handers can get an edge on him.

He hits medium-high outside curves very well, however (.500). He hits this pitch deep into the left-center gap and deep down the right line.

MEDIUM-HIGH OUTSIDE CURVEBALLS

BATTING AVERAGE .500
Play

Left	Deep in straightaway left field
Center	Deep and shifted toward left field
Right	Deep and shifted toward the right field line
Short	Normal position
Second	Shifted toward first base

Oester's .285 against low-inside sliders is pretty good. He has trouble in most of his other slider locations.

Oester Against Left-Handed Pitchers

Oester has a terrible time against left-handed pitchers. His overall .144 against fastballs is weak.

He hits only .214 against low-over-the-middle fastballs thrown by left-handers. His low average indicates that most of his hit balls in this location are easy pop-ups and grounders.

LOW-OVER-THE-MIDDLE FASTBALLS

BATTING AVERAGE .214
Play

Left	Medium-deep in straightaway left field
Center	Medium-deep in straightaway center field
Right	Deep and shifted toward the right field line
Short	Up middle (shifted toward second base)
Second	Shifted toward first base

He has even more trouble against low-outside fastballs (.133) and medium-high outside fastballs (.111).

Against left-handers Oester has a .153 overall curve average and a .150 overall slider average. He has few strong locations in these charts.

Ahead And Behind In The Count Vs. RH

Ahead

Fastball Average .391

	Outside	Middle	Inside
High	7/428 /3	18/333 /6	6/333 /2
Med	26/346 /9	6/500 /3	22/454 /10
Low	6/500 /3	21/333 /7	8/500 /4

Curve Average .428

	Outside	Middle	Inside
High	0/0 /0	1/0 /0	0/0 /0
Med	5/1000 /5	2/0 /0	2/500 /1
Low	0/0 /0	3/0 /0	1/0 /0

Behind

Fastball Average .342

	Outside	Middle	Inside
High	4/750 /3	6/333 /2	3/0 /0
Med	8/500 /4	1/1000 /1	5/0 /0
Low	3/0 /0	4/500 /2	4/250 /1

Curve Average .210

	Outside	Middle	Inside
High	3/0 /0	2/500 /1	1/1000 /1
Med	4/500 /2	0/0 /0	1/0 /0
Low	1/0 /0	4/0 /0	3/0 /0

Overall Evaluation
Against Right-Handed Pitchers

Overall Fastball	
Overall Curve	
Overall Slider	

Against Left-Handed Pitchers

Overall Fastball	
Overall Curve	
Overall Slider	

Comments: Difficulty with low curves vs. RH.
Strengths: Waist-high fastballs, over-the-middle fastballs, high-outside fastballs, medium-outside curves vs. RH.
Weaknesses: Low-outside, high-inside and low-inside fastballs, low curves vs. RH; fastballs, curves and sliders in general vs. LH.

Jeff Reed Against Right-Handed Pitchers
Overall BARS Batting Average .196

Fastball Average .209

	Outside	Middle	Inside
High	3 / 0 / 0	9 / 111 / 1	13 / 307 / 4
Med	19 / 315 / 6	3 / 0 / 0	15 / 200 / 3
Low	8 / 125 / 1	10 / 200 / 2	6 / 166 / 1

Curve Average .200

	Outside	Middle	Inside
High	0 / 0 / 0	1 / 1000 / 1	0 / 0 / 0
Med	0 / 0 / 0	1 / 0 / 0	0 / 0 / 0
Low	1 / 0 / 0	2 / 0 / 0	5 / 200 / 1

Slider Average .000

	Outside	Middle	Inside
High	1 / 0 / 0	0 / 0 / 0	2 / 0 / 0
Med	0 / 0 / 0	0 / 0 / 0	1 / 0 / 0
Low	0 / 0 / 0	2 / 0 / 0	1 / 0 / 0

Jeff Reed Against Left-Handed Pitchers
Overall BARS Batting Average .214

Fastball Average .250

	Outside	Middle	Inside
High	1 / 1000 / 1	0 / 0 / 0	1 / 0 / 0
Med	1 / 1000 / 1	0 / 0 / 0	3 / 0 / 0
Low	0 / 0 / 0	1 / 0 / 0	1 / 0 / 0

Curve Average .000

	Outside	Middle	Inside
High	0 / 0 / 0	0 / 0 / 0	0 / 0 / 0
Med	0 / 0 / 0	0 / 0 / 0	0 / 0 / 0
Low	1 / 0 / 0	0 / 0 / 0	0 / 0 / 0

Slider Average .250

	Outside	Middle	Inside
High	0 / 0 / 0	0 / 0 / 0	0 / 0 / 0
Med	0 / 0 / 0	0 / 0 / 0	0 / 0 / 0
Low	2 / 0 / 0	1 / 1000 / 1	1 / 0 / 0

Left-handed hitter Jeff Reed has a .315 average against medium-high outside fastballs thrown by right-handed pitchers. He hits this pitch deep down the left line (his opposite field) and straightaway to center and right. Notice, however, that the shortstop needs to play shifted toward second and the second baseman shifted toward first. The field diagram on the opposite page illustrates the BARS fielding strategy for this pitch.

MEDIUM-HIGH OUTSIDE FASTBALLS

BATTING AVERAGE .315
Play
Left	Deep and shifted toward the left field line
Center	Medium-deep in straightaway center field
Right	Deep in straightaway right field
Short	Up middle (shifted toward second base)
Second	Shifted toward first base

He hits a fine .307 against high-inside fastballs thrown by right-handers. He hits this pitch medium-deep to left and center. Proper alignment would allow fielders to prevent most of Reed's base hits from this location.

HIGH-INSIDE FASTBALLS

BATTING AVERAGE .307
Play
Left	Medium-deep in straightaway left field
Center	Medium-deep in straightaway center field
Right	*No instances recorded*
Short	Up middle (shifted toward second base)
Second	Shifted toward first base

He has no other strong fastball locations against right-handers. He is weak in all of his low fastball locations (.125, .200 and .166, outside to inside). His .200 against medium-high inside fastballs is also weak. His low average indicates that most of his hit balls in this location are easy outs.

MEDIUM-HIGH INSIDE FASTBALLS

BATTING AVERAGE .200
Play
Left	Short and shifted toward the left field line
Center	Medium-deep in straightaway center field
Right	Medium-deep in straightaway right field
Short	Up middle (shifted toward second base)
Second	Shifted toward first base

Medium-High Outside Fastballs

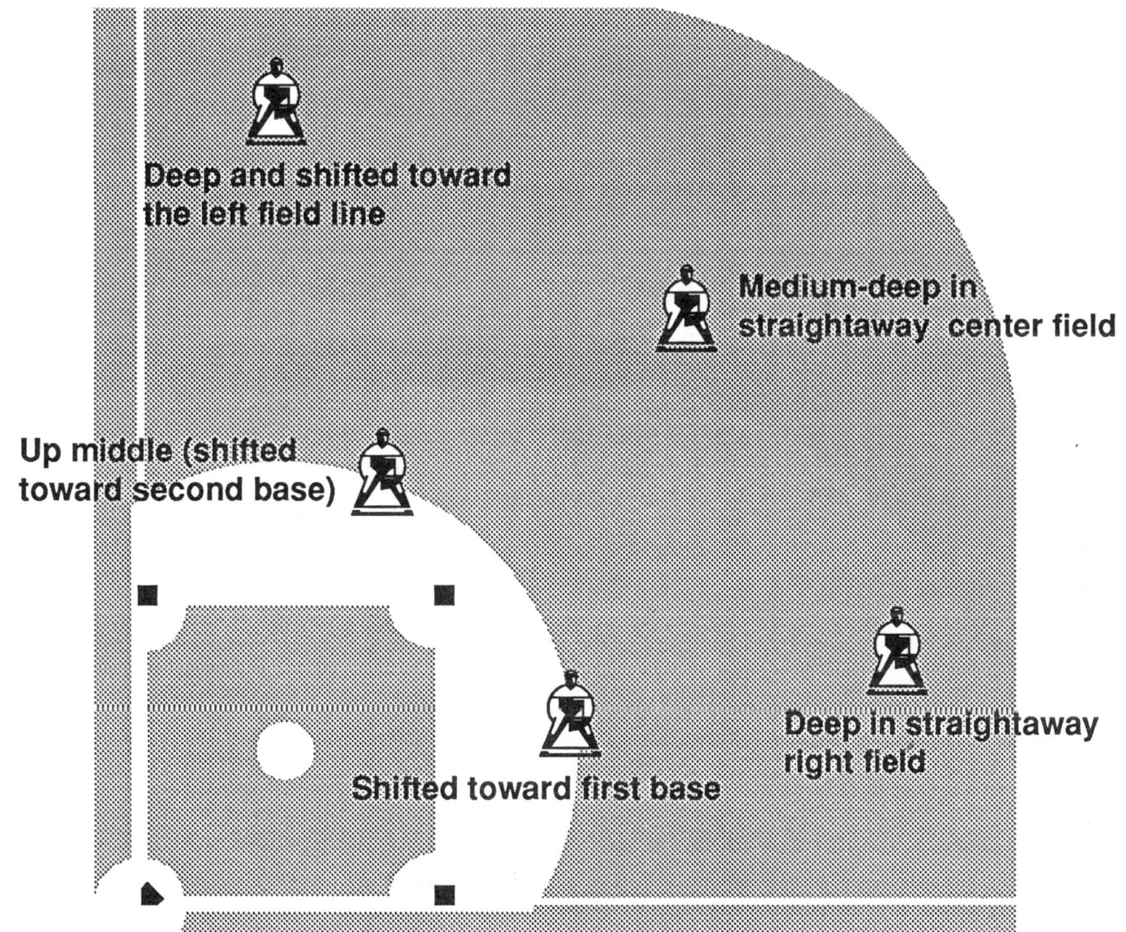

Ahead And Behind In The Count Vs. RH

Ahead

Fastball Average .219

	Outside	Middle	Inside
High	0/ 0/0	4/ 0/0	5/ 600/3
Med	13/ 307/4	2/ 0/0	4/ 0/0
Low	5/ 200/1	4/ 0/0	4/ 250/1

Curve Average .000

	Outside	Middle	Inside
High	0/ 0/0	0/ 0/0	0/ 0/0
Med	0/ 0/0	1/ 0/0	0/ 0/0
Low	0/ 0/0	1/ 0/0	0/ 0/0

Behind

Fastball Average .411

	Outside	Middle	Inside
High	0/ 0/0	3/ 333/1	1/ 0/0
Med	4/ 500/2	0/ 0/0	6/ 500/3
Low	1/ 0/0	1/ 1000/1	1/ 0/0

Curve Average .400

	Outside	Middle	Inside
High	0/ 0/0	1/ 1000/1	0/ 0/0
Med	0/ 0/0	0/ 0/0	0/ 0/0
Low	0/ 0/0	1/ 0/0	3/ 333/1

Overall Evaluation
Against Right-Handed Pitchers

Overall Fastball 

Overall Curve Not enough information

Overall Slider Not enough information

Against Left-Handed Pitchers

Overall Fastball Not enough information

Overall Curve Not enough information

Overall Slider Not enough information

Comments: Weak against low fastballs and medium-inside fastballs vs. RH.

Strengths: Medium-outside and high-inside fastballs vs. RH.

Weaknesses: Low fastballs, high-middle fastballs and medium-inside fastballs vs. RH.

Manny Trillo (Right Handed) — *Cincinnati Reds*

Manny Trillo Against Right-Handed Pitchers
Overall BARS Batting Average .250

Fastball Average .297

	Inside	Middle	Outside
High	25 / 240 / 6	23 / 130 / 3	11 / 181 / 2
Med	33 / 272 / 9	7 / 714 / 5	48 / 354 / 17
Low	16 / 312 / 5	45 / 400 / 18	37 / 216 / 8

Curve Average .218

	Inside	Middle	Outside
High	3 / 0 / 0	1 / 0 / 0	1 / 0 / 0
Med	3 / 666 / 2	9 / 555 / 5	14 / 142 / 2
Low	5 / 200 / 1	2 / 500 / 1	17 / 58 / 1

Slider Average .157

	Inside	Middle	Outside
High	1 / 1000 / 1	2 / 0 / 0	0 / 0 / 0
Med	1 / 0 / 0	2 / 500 / 1	23 / 217 / 5
Low	2 / 0 / 0	7 / 285 / 2	19 / 0 / 0

Manny Trillo Against Left-Handed Pitchers
Overall BARS Batting Average .289

Fastball Average .278

	Inside	Middle	Outside
High	5 / 200 / 1	6 / 0 / 0	12 / 166 / 2
Med	15 / 333 / 5	2 / 0 / 0	25 / 320 / 8
Low	13 / 384 / 5	19 / 421 / 8	18 / 166 / 3

Curve Average .310

	Inside	Middle	Outside
High	3 / 333 / 1	2 / 500 / 1	1 / 1000 / 1
Med	1 / 1000 / 1	1 / 0 / 0	3 / 333 / 1
Low	3 / 0 / 0	7 / 142 / 1	8 / 375 / 3

Slider Average .384

	Inside	Middle	Outside
High	2 / 500 / 1	1 / 1000 / 1	0 / 0 / 0
Med	1 / 1000 / 1	0 / 0 / 0	2 / 1000 / 2
Low	1 / 0 / 0	3 / 0 / 0	3 / 0 / 0

Right-handed Manny Trillo has a solid .297 BARS fastball average against right-handed pitchers. He hits a very strong .354 against medium-high outside fastballs. The fielding strategy below and the field diagram on the opposite page show how fielders need to be positioned for this pitch to Trillo.

MEDIUM-HIGH OUTSIDE FASTBALLS

BATTING AVERAGE .354
Play

Left	Deep and shifted toward center field
Center	Medium-deep in straightaway center field
Right	Medium-deep in straightaway right field
Short	Shifted toward third base
Second	Shifted toward first base

He also hits excellently against low-over-the-middle fastballs thrown by right-handers (.400).

LOW-OVER-THE-MIDDLE FASTBALLS

BATTING AVERAGE .400
Play

Left	Deep and shifted toward the left field line
Center	Deep and shifted toward right field
Right	Deep in straightaway right field
Short	Up middle (shifted toward second base)
Second	Normal position

Trillo has trouble with high fastballs thrown by right-handers (.240, .130 and .181, inside to outside). He is also weak against outside curves and outside sliders.

Trillo has some very strong and some very weak fastball locations against left-handed pitchers. He hits a fine .320 against medium-high outside fastballs.

MEDIUM-HIGH OUTSIDE FASTBALLS (THROWN BY LEFT-HANDED PITCHERS)

BATTING AVERAGE .320
Play

Left	Deep and shifted toward center field
Center	Deep in straightaway center field
Right	Medium-deep and shifted toward the right line
Short	Shifted toward third base
Second	Normal position

He hits an outstanding .421 against low-over-the-middle fastballs.

LOW-OVER-THE-MIDDLE FASTBALLS (THROWN BY LEFT-HANDED PITCHERS)

BATTING AVERAGE .421
Play

Left	Medium-deep and shifted toward center field
Center	Medium-deep in straightaway center field
Right	Medium-deep and shifted toward the right line
Short	*No instances recorded*
Second	*No instances recorded*

Medium-High Outside Fastballs

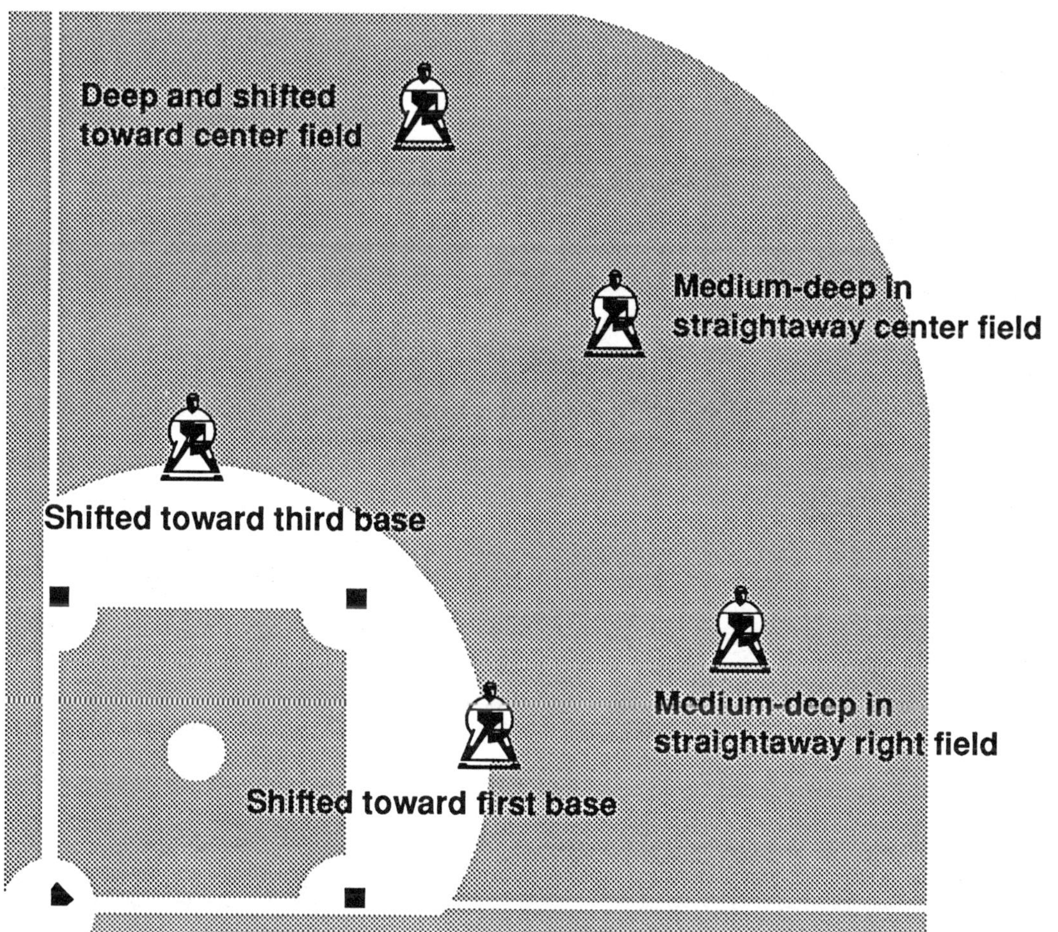

Ahead And Behind In The Count Vs. RH

Ahead

	Fastball Average .354			Curve Average .333		
	Inside	Middle	Outside	Inside	Middle	Outside
High	9/ 333 /3	10/ 200 /2	4/ 250 /1	0/ 0 /0	0/ 0 /0	0/ 0 /0
Med	17/ 470 /8	1/ 0 /0	18/ 277 /5	0/ 0 /0	0/ 0 /0	1/ 0 /0
Low	3/ 333 /1	20/ 550 /11	11/ 181 /2	0/ 0 /0	0/ 0 /0	2/ 500 /1

Behind

	Fastball Average .327			Curve Average .260		
	Inside	Middle	Outside	Inside	Middle	Outside
High	7/ 285 /2	6/ 166 /1	2/ 0 /0	1/ 0 /0	0/ 0 /0	1/ 0 /0
Med	7/ 0 /0	2/ 1000 /2	14/ 357 /5	2/ 500 /1	4/ 1000 /4	7/ 0 /0
Low	4/ 250 /1	6/ 500 /3	10/ 500 /5	0/ 0 /0	1/ 1000 /1	7/ 0 /0

Overall Evaluation

Against Right-Handed Pitchers

Overall Fastball — 2 baseballs
Overall Curve — 1 baseball
Overall Slider — 1 baseball

Against Left-Handed Pitchers

Overall Fastball — 2 baseballs
Overall Curve — 4 baseballs
Overall Slider — 4 baseballs

Comments: Weak against high fastballs, outside curves and outside sliders vs. RH.

Strengths: Medium-outside, low-middle and low-inside fastballs vs. RH; medium-outside, low-middle, low-inside and medium-inside fastballs, outside curves vs. LH.

Weaknesses: High fastballs, medium-inside and low-outside fastballs, outside curves and sliders vs. RH; low-outside and high-outside fastballs vs. LH.

Joel Youngblood (Right Handed) — *Cincinnati Reds*

Joel Youngblood Against Right-Handed Pitchers
Overall BARS Batting Average .267

Fastball Average .322

	Inside	Middle	Outside
High	5/ 200 /1	16/ 437 /7	7/ 285 /2
Med	31/ 290 /9	17/ 352 /6	34/ 352 /12
Low	7/ 285 /2	21/ 333 /7	14/ 214 /3

Curve Average .277

	Inside	Middle	Outside
High	2/ 500 /1	2/ 1000 /2	3/ 333 /1
Med	2/ 0 /0	2/ 500 /1	7/ 0 /0
Low	0/ 0 /0	6/ 666 /4	12/ 83 /1

Slider Average .062

	Inside	Middle	Outside
High	0/ 0 /0	4/ 250 /1	1/ 0 /0
Med	0/ 0 /0	1/ 0 /0	4/ 0 /0
Low	1/ 0 /0	1/ 0 /0	4/ 0 /0

Joel Youngblood Against Left-Handed Pitchers
Overall BARS Batting Average .213

Fastball Average .210

	Inside	Middle	Outside
High	4/ 0 /0	6/ 333 /2	6/ 0 /0
Med	6/ 333 /2	3/ 1000 /3	17/ 117 /2
Low	5/ 200 /1	9/ 222 /2	1/ 0 /0

Curve Average .217

	Inside	Middle	Outside
High	1/ 0 /0	1/ 1000 /1	1/ 0 /0
Med	3/ 333 /1	3/ 0 /0	4/ 0 /0
Low	3/ 0 /0	5/ 400 /2	2/ 500 /1

Slider Average .333

	Inside	Middle	Outside
High	0/ 0 /0	0/ 0 /0	0/ 0 /0
Med	2/ 0 /0	2/ 1000 /2	0/ 0 /0
Low	2/ 0 /0	3/ 333 /1	0/ 0 /0

Right-handed hitting Joel Youngblood has a strong .322 overall average against fastballs thrown by right-handed pitchers. Against right-handers, he hits curves for a .277 average.

Starting with fastballs, Youngblood hits an excellent .352 in his medium-high outside location. He hits this pitch deep to all fields, as shown in the field diagram on the opposite page.

MEDIUM-HIGH OUTSIDE FASTBALLS

BATTING AVERAGE .352
Play

Left	Deep in straightaway left field
Center	Deep in straightaway center field
Right	Deep and shifted toward center field
Short	Normal position
Second	Normal position

He hits over-the-middle fastballs very well (.437, .352 and .333, high to low). He pulls high-over-the-middle fastballs deep down the left line and into the right-center gap.

HIGH-OVER-THE-MIDDLE FASTBALLS

BATTING AVERAGE .437
Play

Left	Deep and shifted toward the left field line
Center	Deep in straightaway center field
Right	Deep and shifted toward center field
Short	Normal position
Second	*No instances recorded*

He also pulls low-over-the-middle fastballs deep down the left line.

LOW-OVER-THE-MIDDLE FASTBALLS

BATTING AVERAGE .333
Play

Left	Deep and shifted toward the left field line
Center	Deep in straightaway center field
Right	Medium-deep in straightaway right field
Short	Shifted toward third base
Second	*No instances recorded*

Youngblood has a relatively high number of recorded instances in his medium-over-the-middle fastball location. This high number of instances probably means that he is a patient hitter: he waits for pitchers to throw over the plate. He has a weakness against medium-high outside and low-outside curves thrown by right-handed pitchers. As well as he hits fastballs, right-handers should consider attacking his weak curve locations.

Youngblood's .117 against medium-high outside fastballs thrown by left-handed pitchers shows that he has a tendency toward weakness in that location.

Medium-High Outside Fastballs

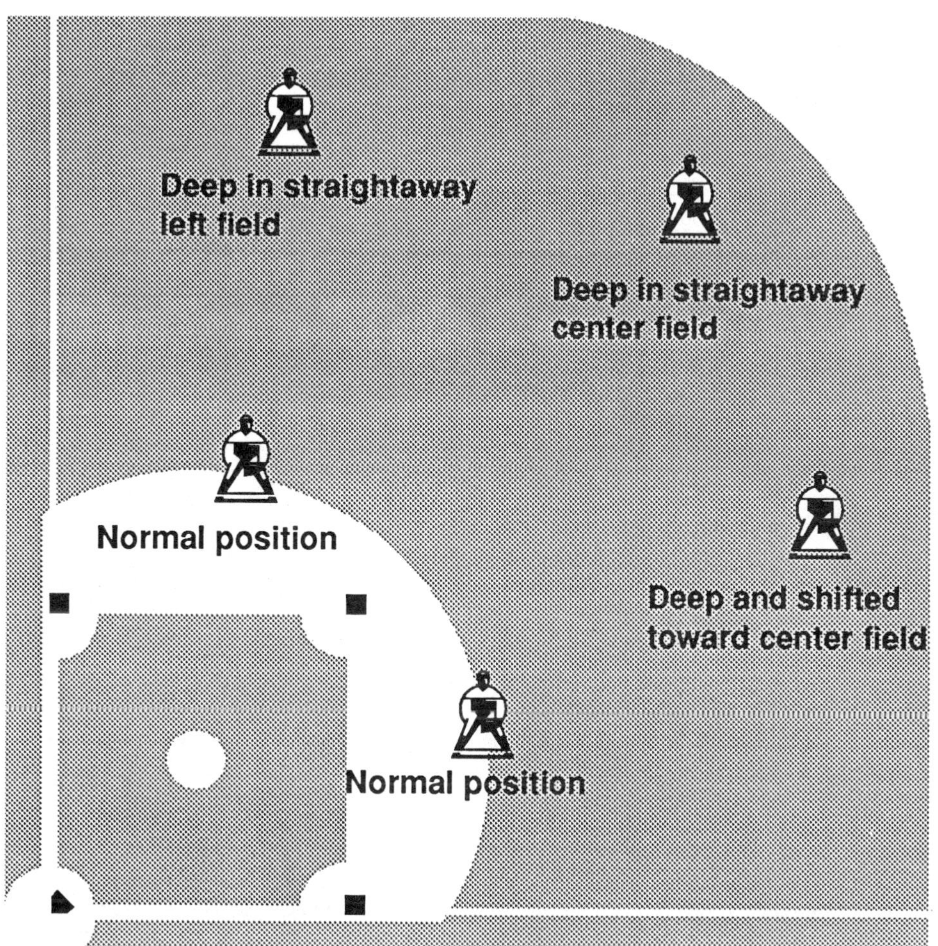

Ahead And Behind In The Count Vs. RH

Ahead

Fastball Average .297

	Inside	Middle	Outside
High	3/ 333/1	7/ 428/3	4/ 0/0
Med	14/ 285/4	12/ 250/3	14/ 428/6
Low	2/ 0/0	13/ 307/4	5/ 200/1

Curve Average .400

	Inside	Middle	Outside
High	1/ 0/0	0/ 0/0	1/ 1000/1
Med	0/ 0/0	1/ 1000/1	2/ 0/0
Low	0/ 0/0	0/ 0/0	0/ 0/0

Behind

Fastball Average .592

	Inside	Middle	Outside
High	0/ 0/0	2/ 1000/2	2/ 1000/2
Med	7/ 285/2	1/ 1000/1	8/ 500/4
Low	2/ 1000/2	4/ 500/2	1/ 1000/1

Curve Average .250

	Inside	Middle	Outside
High	0/ 0/0	0/ 0/0	2/ 0/0
Med	0/ 0/0	1/ 0/0	3/ 0/0
Low	0/ 0/0	4/ 500/2	2/ 500/1

Overall Evaluation

Against Right-Handed Pitchers

Overall Fastball	⚾ ⚾ ⚾
Overall Curve	⚾ ⚾ ⚾
Overall Slider	⚾

Against Left-Handed Pitchers

Overall Fastball	⚾
Overall Curve	⚾
Overall Slider	Not enough information

Comments: Weak against outside fastballs vs. LH.
Strengths: Fastballs over-the-middle, medium-outside fastballs, curves down the middle vs. RH.
Weaknesses: Low-outside fastballs, low-outside and medium-outside curves, outside sliders vs. RH; outside and low fastballs vs. LH.

Houston Astros

Ashby, Alan
Bass, Kevin
Davis, Glenn
Doran, Bill
Hatcher, Billy
Lombardozzi, Steve
Puhl, Terry
Ramirez, Rafael
Reynolds, Craig

Houston Astros
BARS System
Hitting Analysis

Alan Ashby (Switch Hitter)   *Houston Astros*

Alan Ashby Against Right-Handed Pitchers
Overall BARS Batting Average .245

Fastball Average .284

	Outside	Middle	Inside
High	20/200/4	35/314/11	15/66/1
Med	75/293/22	19/263/5	25/400/10
Low	22/136/3	36/388/14	17/294/5

Curve Average .183

	Outside	Middle	Inside
High	4/250/1	1/0/0	2/500/1
Med	23/217/5	2/0/0	6/333/2
Low	9/111/1	16/187/3	8/0/0

Slider Average .230

	Outside	Middle	Inside
High	0/0/0	3/333/1	2/0/0
Med	2/500/1	2/0/0	5/600/3
Low	2/0/0	7/142/1	3/0/0

Alan Ashby Against Left-Handed Pitchers
Overall BARS Batting Average .204

Fastball Average .254

	Inside	Middle	Outside
High	5/200/1	12/250/3	13/230/3
Med	9/444/4	9/111/1	47/212/10
Low	3/0/0	13/461/6	11/272/3

Curve Average .100

	Inside	Middle	Outside
High	0/0/0	3/333/1	1/0/0
Med	3/0/0	2/0/0	5/200/1
Low	3/0/0	14/71/1	9/111/1

Slider Average .312

	Inside	Middle	Outside
High	1/1000/1	0/0/0	0/0/0
Med	2/500/1	2/0/0	2/0/0
Low	5/200/1	3/333/1	1/1000/1

Switch-hitter Alan Ashby hits .284 overall against fastballs thrown by right-handed pitchers, .254 overall against fastballs thrown by left-handed pitchers.

Starting with right-handers, notice his .293 average against medium-high outside fastballs. He hits this pitch medium-deep to left and center and deep down the right line.

MEDIUM-HIGH OUTSIDE FASTBALLS

BATTING AVERAGE .293
> *Play*

Left	Medium-deep in straightaway left field
Center	Medium-deep and shifted toward left field
Right	Deep and shifted toward the right field line
Short	Up middle (shifted toward second base)
Second	Normal position

He hits a very strong .400 against medium-high inside fastballs. Batting left-handed against right-handers, he hits this pitch deep down the left line (his opposite field).

MEDIUM-HIGH INSIDE FASTBALLS

BATTING AVERAGE .400
> *Play*

Left	Deep and shifted toward the left field line
Center	Deep in straightaway center field
Right	Medium-deep in straightaway right field
Short	Normal position
Second	Normal position

His .388 in his low-over-the-middle fastball location is also excellent. He hits this pitch down both lines. The strategy below and the field diagram on the opposite page show how fielders need to play for pitches to this location.

LOW-OVER-THE-MIDDLE FASTBALLS

BATTING AVERAGE .388
> *Play*

Left	Medium-deep and shifted toward the left line
Center	Medium-deep in straightaway center field
Right	Medium-deep and shifted toward the right line
Short	Up middle (shifted toward second base)
Second	Shifted toward first base

Ashby has trouble with outside and low curves against right- and left-handers. Since these are adjacent locations pitchers don't need pinpoint control to take advantage of these weaknesses.

Batting right-handed against left-handed pitchers, Ashby has trouble with fastballs (.254 overall). His .212 in the highly pitched medium-high outside location is weak. He hits very well, however, in his low-over-the-middle fastball location (.461).

Low-Over-The-Middle Fastballs

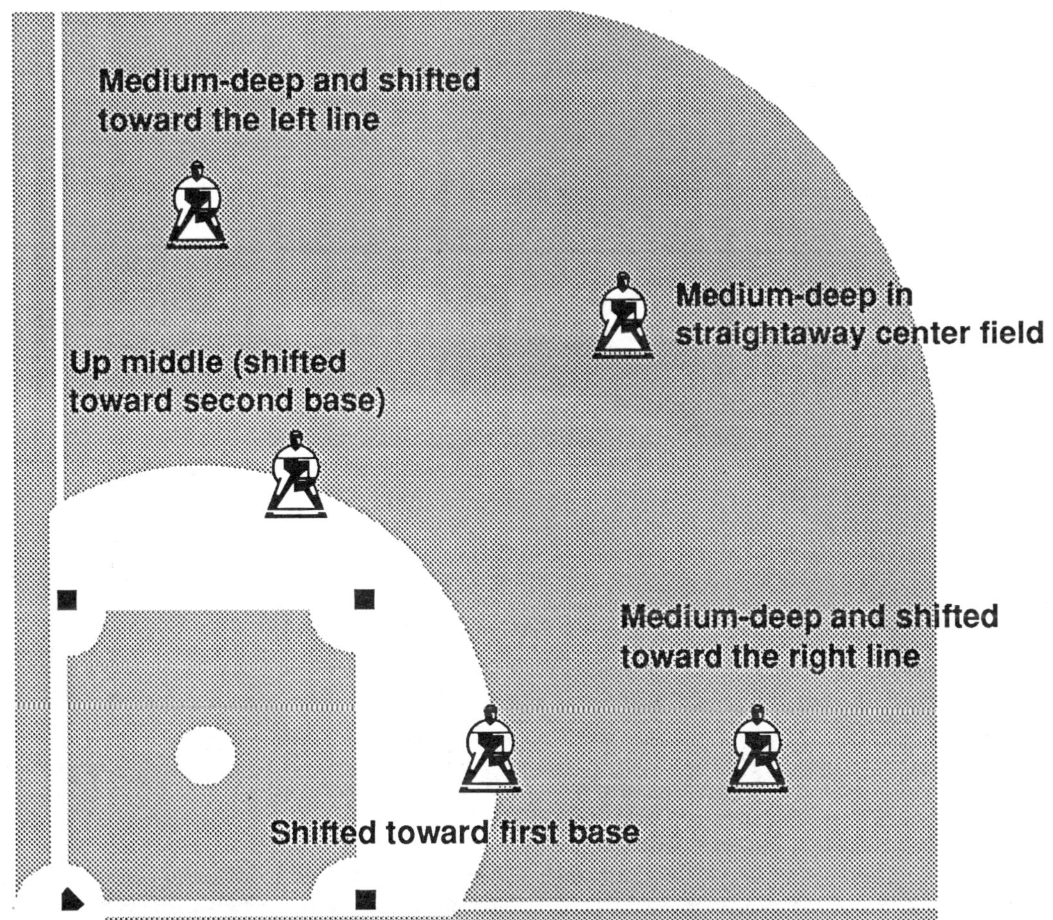

Ahead And Behind In The Count Vs. RH

Ahead

	Fastball Average .291			Curve Average .250		
	Outside	Middle	Inside	Outside	Middle	Inside
High	3/ 0/0	14/ 214/3	6/ 166/1	1/ 0/0	1/ 0/0	2/ 500/1
Med	41/ 317/13	15/ 333/5	13/ 384/5	10/ 500/5	2/ 0/0	5/ 200/1
Low	11/ 90/1	24/ 416/10	7/ 142/1	1/ 0/0	7/ 142/1	3/ 0/0

Behind

	Fastball Average .513			Curve Average .200		
	Outside	Middle	Inside	Outside	Middle	Inside
High	5/ 200/1	10/ 600/6	1/ 0/0	3/ 333/1	0/ 0/0	0/ 0/0
Med	10/ 500/5	1/ 0/0	1/ 1000/1	6/ 0/0	0/ 0/0	1/ 1000/1
Low	2/ 500/1	3/ 666/2	4/ 750/3	3/ 333/1	2/ 0/0	0/ 0/0

Overall Evaluation

Against Right-Handed Pitchers

Overall Fastball 

Overall Curve 

Overall Slider 

Against Left-Handed Pitchers

Overall Fastball 

Overall Curve 

Overall Slider 

Comments: Weak against low and outside curves vs. RH and LH.

Strengths: High-middle, low-middle and medium-inside fastballs vs. RH; medium-inside and low-middle fastballs vs. LH.

Weaknesses: High-outside, low-outside, medium-middle and high-inside fastballs, outside and low curves, low sliders vs. RH; high fastballs and outside fastballs, low and outside curves vs. LH.

Kevin Bass Against Right-Handed Pitchers
Overall BARS Batting Average .275

Fastball Average .299

	Outside	Middle	Inside
High	37/ 270 /10	52/ 307 /16	30/ 333 /10
Med	104/ 298 /31	30/ 233 /7	49/ 326 /16
Low	15/ 466 /7	52/ 250 /13	35/ 314 /11

Curve Average .238

	Outside	Middle	Inside
High	3/ 333 /1	4/ 250 /1	0/ 0 /0
Med	14/ 428 /6	7/ 142 /1	12/ 166 /2
Low	13/ 307 /4	28/ 214 /6	24/ 166 /4

Slider Average .230

	Outside	Middle	Inside
High	2/ 500 /1	3/ 333 /1	5/ 0 /0
Med	3/ 333 /1	4/ 250 /1	6/ 166 /1
Low	4/ 500 /2	6/ 500 /3	19/ 105 /2

Kevin Bass Against Left-Handed Pitchers
Overall BARS Batting Average .300

Fastball Average .334

	Inside	Middle	Outside
High	13/ 153 /2	31/ 516 /16	26/ 269 /7
Med	25/ 400 /10	18/ 500 /9	85/ 282 /24
Low	11/ 272 /3	28/ 428 /12	35/ 228 /8

Curve Average .296

	Inside	Middle	Outside
High	4/ 0 /0	5/ 400 /2	1/ 0 /0
Med	5/ 200 /1	2/ 0 /0	14/ 571 /8
Low	9/ 0 /0	10/ 500 /5	14/ 214 /3

Slider Average .321

	Inside	Middle	Outside
High	1/ 0 /0	1/ 1000 /1	1/ 0 /0
Med	11/ 545 /6	1/ 0 /0	1/ 0 /0
Low	6/ 0 /0	2/ 500 /1	4/ 250 /1

Switch-hitting Kevin Bass hits better batting right-handed against left-handed pitchers (.300 overall against left-handers, .275 overall against right-handers). He hits fastballs well against right-handers (.299) but excellently against left-handers (.334).

Starting with right-handers, notice that Bass has many solid fastball locations. He hits medium-high outside fastballs (.298) deep to all fields.

MEDIUM-HIGH OUTSIDE FASTBALLS

BATTING AVERAGE .298

Play

Left	Deep in straightaway left field
Center	Deep in straightaway center field
Right	Deep and shifted toward center field
Short	Up middle (shifted toward second base)
Second	Normal position

He hits medium-high inside fastballs extremely well when ahead in the count (.366 when ahead, .142 when behind). When ahead, he hits this pitch deep down both lines and to the right side of the infield.

MEDIUM-HIGH INSIDE FASTBALLS
(WHEN AHEAD IN THE COUNT)

BATTING AVERAGE .366

Play

Left	Deep and shifted toward the left field line
Center	Deep in straightaway center field
Right	Deep and shifted toward the right field line
Short	Up middle (shifted toward second base)
Second	Shifted toward first base

When behind, he hits it to his opposite field (left field, batting left handed).

MEDIUM-HIGH OUTSIDE FASTBALLS
(WHEN BEHIND IN THE COUNT)

BATTING AVERAGE .142

Play

Left	Medium-deep and shifted toward the left field line
Center	Deep and shifted toward left field
Right	Deep and shifted toward center field
Short	Up middle (shifted toward second base)
Second	*No instances recorded*

He hits high-over-the-middle fastballs for a solid .307 average.

HIGH-OVER-THE-MIDDLE FASTBALLS

BATTING AVERAGE .307

Play

Left	Deep and shifted toward the left field line

Center	Deep and shifted toward left field
Right	Deep in straightaway right field
Short	Up middle (shifted toward second base)
Second	Normal position

Bass Against Curves And Sliders

Bass hits curves and sliders poorly overall against right-handed pitchers. He is very weak against inside curves and sliders. He is strong, however, against outside curves (.333, .428 and .307, high to low).

He hits medium-high outside curves down the left line and into the deep left-center gap.

MEDIUM-HIGH OUTSIDE CURVEBALLS

BATTING AVERAGE .428
Play

Left	Medium-deep and shifted toward the left field line
Center	Deep and shifted toward left field
Right	Medium-deep in straightaway right field
Short	Shifted toward third base
Second	Normal position

Bass Against Left-Handed Pitchers

Bass hits fastballs excellently overall against left-handed pitchers (.334). He is slightly weak against outside fastballs (.269, .282 and .228, high to low), but he has very strong averages over the center of the plate and medium-high inside.

Batting right-handed against left-handers, he pulls medium-high outside fastballs deep down the left line.

MEDIUM-HIGH OUTSIDE FASTBALLS (THROWN BY LEFT-HANDED PITCHERS)

BATTING AVERAGE .282
Play

Left	Deep and shifted toward the left field line
Center	Deep in straightaway center field
Right	Deep in straightaway right field
Short	Normal position
Second	Normal position

He hits a brilliant .516 against high-over-the-middle fastballs thrown by left-handers. He also pulls this pitch deep down the left line.

HIGH-OVER-THE-MIDDLE FASTBALLS (THROWN BY LEFT-HANDED PITCHERS)

BATTING AVERAGE .516
Play

Left	Deep and shifted toward the left field line .
Center	Deep in straightaway center field
Right	Medium-deep in straightaway right field
Short	Normal position
Second	*No instances recorded*

He has trouble with low-outside curves against left-handers, but he hits medium-high outside (.571) and low-middle curves (.500) extremely well. He hits medium-high outside curves straightaway to left and right and into the left-center gap.

Ahead And Behind In The Count Vs. RH

Ahead

Fastball Average .329

	Outside	Middle	Inside
High	16/ 250 /4	26/ 307 /8	7/ 285 /2
Med	50/ 320 /16	18/ 333 /6	30/ 366 /11
Low	9/ 555 /5	25/ 360 /9	16/ 250 /4

Curve Average .363

	Outside	Middle	Inside
High	0/ 0 /0	1/ 0 /0	0/ 0 /0
Med	3/ 666 /2	4/ 0 /0	5/ 0 /0
Low	2/ 1000 /2	3/ 666 /2	4/ 500 /2

Behind

Fastball Average .343

	Outside	Middle	Inside
High	1/ 1000 /1	10/ 600 /6	10/ 400 /4
Med	19/ 315 /6	5/ 200 /1	7/ 142 /1
Low	0/ 0 /0	7/ 0 /0	5/ 600 /3

Curve Average .228

	Outside	Middle	Inside
High	1/ 0 /0	2/ 500 /1	0/ 0 /0
Med	1/ 0 /0	3/ 333 /1	3/ 333 /1
Low	6/ 333 /2	14/ 214 /3	5/ 0 /0

Overall Evaluation
Against Right-Handed Pitchers

Overall Fastball	⚾ ⚾⚾ ⚾⚾
Overall Curve	⚾
Overall Slider	⚾

Against Left-Handed Pitchers

Overall Fastball	⚾⚾ ⚾⚾ ⚾⚾ ⚾⚾
Overall Curve	⚾⚾ ⚾⚾ ⚾⚾
Overall Slider	⚾⚾ ⚾⚾ ⚾⚾ ⚾⚾

Comments: Strong vs. inside fastballs vs. RH. Strengths: Inside fastballs, high-middle and low-outside fastballs, outside curves vs. RH; over-the-middle and medium-inside fastballs, medium-outside and low-middle curves, medium-inside sliders vs. LH. Weaknesses: Low-middle, medium-middle and high-outside fastballs, inside and over-the-middle curves, inside sliders vs. RH; four fastballs corners vs. LH, inside and low-outside curves vs. LH.

Glenn Davis (Right Handed)   *Houston Astros*

Glenn Davis Against Right-Handed Pitchers
Overall BARS Batting Average .264

Fastball Average .307

	Inside	Middle	Outside
High	23/ 260 /6	41/ 292 /12	26/ 538 /14
Med	34/ 264 /9	16/ 562 /9	75/ 280 /21
Low	12/ 250 /3	28/ 357 /10	31/ 129 /4

Curve Average .238

	Inside	Middle	Outside
High	1/ 0 /0	6/ 500 /3	3/ 333 /1
Med	2/ 0 /0	1/ 1000 /1	32/ 218 /7
Low	0/ 0 /0	12/ 333 /4	31/ 161 /5

Slider Average .271

	Inside	Middle	Outside
High	1/ 0 /0	4/ 0 /0	8/ 375 /3
Med	0/ 0 /0	1/ 1000 /1	29/ 310 /9
Low	0/ 0 /0	3/ 666 /2	24/ 166 /4

Glenn Davis Against Left-Handed Pitchers
Overall BARS Batting Average .254

Fastball Average .294

	Inside	Middle	Outside
High	8/ 125 /1	19/ 263 /5	11/ 363 /4
Med	9/ 444 /4	8/ 500 /4	52/ 346 /18
Low	8/ 250 /2	19/ 263 /5	19/ 105 /2

Curve Average .200

	Inside	Middle	Outside
High	1/ 1000 /1	4/ 750 /3	5/ 400 /2
Med	4/ 500 /2	6/ 0 /0	10/ 200 /2
Low	9/ 0 /0	7/ 0 /0	4/ 0 /0

Slider Average .400

	Inside	Middle	Outside
High	3/ 666 /2	0/ 0 /0	0/ 0 /0
Med	5/ 600 /3	1/ 1000 /1	3/ 333 /1
Low	2/ 0 /0	4/ 250 /1	2/ 0 /0

Glenn Davis, right-handed hitter, has fairly strong overall fastball averages against both right- and left-handed pitchers (.307 overall vs. right-handers, .294 vs. left-handers). In contrast, he has low curve averages.

Starting with right-handers, notice Davis's trouble with inside fastballs (.260, .264 and .250, high to low). He hits very well against all fastballs down the middle of the plate and against high-outside and medium-high outside fastballs. He has trouble with low-outside fastballs.

Davis hits medium-high outside fastballs much better when ahead in the count (.351 when ahead, .235 when behind). When ahead, he hits this pitch more down the right line.

MEDIUM-HIGH OUTSIDE FASTBALLS (WHEN AHEAD IN THE COUNT)

BATTING AVERAGE .351
Play

Left	Deep in straightaway left field
Center	Deep and shifted toward left field
Right	Deep and shifted toward the right field line
Short	Normal position
Second	*No instances recorded*

MEDIUM-HIGH OUTSIDE FASTBALLS (WHEN BEHIND IN THE COUNT)

BATTING AVERAGE .235
Play

Left	Deep in straightaway left field
Center	Deep and shifted toward left field
Right	Deep in straightaway right field
Short	Up middle (shifted toward second base)
Second	*No instances recorded*

His .538 against high-outside fastballs deserves attention. He hits this pitch deep to all fields.

HIGH-OUTSIDE FASTBALLS

BATTING AVERAGE .538
Play

Left	Deep in straightaway left field
Center	Deep and shifted toward left field
Right	Deep in straightaway right field
Short	Up middle (shifted toward second base)
Second	*No instances recorded*

His .357 against low-over-the-middle fastballs is also excellent.

LOW-OVER-THE-MIDDLE FASTBALLS

BATTING AVERAGE .357
Play

Left	Deep and shifted toward the left field line

Center	Medium-deep in straightaway center field	
Right	Deep and shifted toward center field	
Short	Normal position	
Second	Normal position	

Davis Against Curves And Sliders

Davis has trouble with curves against right-handed pitchers. He is weak in the low-outside (.161) and medium-high outside (.218) curve locations. He hits low-over-the-middle curves at a .333 clip, however.

He has trouble with low-outside sliders (.166) but hits medium-high outside sliders very well (.310). He hits this pitch deep down the left line and medium-deep to center and right. Notice that the shortstop needs to play shifted toward third base.

MEDIUM-HIGH OUTSIDE SLIDERS

BATTING AVERAGE .310

Play

Left	Deep and shifted toward the left field line
Center	Medium-deep in straightaway center field
Right	Medium-deep in straightaway right field
Short	Shifted toward third base
Second	Normal position

Davis Against Left-Handed Pitchers

Davis hits high-outside and medium-high outside fastballs strongly against left-handed pitchers. As against right-handers, he hits medium-high outside fastballs better when ahead in the count (.400 when ahead, .294 when behind).

When ahead, he goes down the right line with this pitch, as he does against right-handers.

MEDIUM-HIGH OUTSIDE FASTBALLS (THROWN BY LEFT-HANDED PITCHERS WHEN DAVIS IS AHEAD IN THE COUNT)

BATTING AVERAGE .400

Play

Left	Deep in straightaway left field
Center	Deep and shifted toward left field
Right	Medium-deep and shifted toward the right line
Short	Up middle (shifted toward second base)
Second	Normal position

MEDIUM-HIGH OUTSIDE FASTBALLS (THROWN BY LEFT-HANDED PITCHERS WHEN DAVIS IS BEHIND IN THE COUNT)

BATTING AVERAGE .294

Play

Left	Deep and shifted toward the left field line
Center	Deep in straightaway center field
Right	Deep and shifted toward center field
Short	Up middle (shifted toward second base)
Second	Shifted toward first base

The medium-high and high-outside fastball locations form his strongest fastball sector against left-handed pitchers. Left-handers should steer away from these and attack the low fastball locations, in which Davis is weak.

He is also weak against medium-high outside curves (.200) and all low curves against left-handers. Left-handed pitchers throw Davis few curves in comparison to fastballs; they should throw more because of these weaknesses.

Ahead And Behind In The Count Vs. RH

Ahead

Fastball Average .345				Curve Average .269		
	Inside	Middle	Outside	Inside	Middle	Outside
High	9/ 333 /3	22/ 318 /7	9/ 666 /6	0/ 0 /0	3/ 666 /2	2/ 0 /0
Med	18/ 277 /5	9/ 444 /4	37/ 351 /13	1/ 0 /0	0/ 0 /0	11/ 181 /2
Low	6/ 333 /2	16/ 375 /6	10/ 100 /1	0/ 0 /0	2/ 0 /0	7/ 428 /3

Behind

Fastball Average .350				Curve Average .291		
	Inside	Middle	Outside	Inside	Middle	Outside
High	4/ 500 /2	7/ 285 /2	8/ 500 /4	0/ 0 /0	1/ 1000 /1	1/ 1000 /1
Med	4/ 250 /1	2/ 1000 /2	17/ 235 /4	0/ 0 /0	0/ 0 /0	11/ 181 /2
Low	1/ 0 /0	5/ 400 /2	9/ 333 /3	0/ 0 /0	5/ 200 /1	6/ 333 /2

Overall Evaluation

Against Right-Handed Pitchers

Overall Fastball	⚾⚾ ⚾⚾ ⚾
Overall Curve	⚾
Overall Slider	⚾ ⚾

Against Left-Handed Pitchers

Overall Fastball	⚾ ⚾
Overall Curve	⚾
Overall Slider	⚾ ⚾ ⚾

Comments: Weak vs. inside fastballs vs. RH.

Strenghts: Low-middle, medium-middle and high-outside fastballs, low-middle curves and medium-outside sliders vs. RH; medium-outside and high-outside fastballs vs. LH.

Weaknesses: Inside fastballs, low-outside fastballs, low-outside and medium-outside curves, low-outside sliders vs. RH; low fastballs, high-middle fastballs, low and medium-outside curves vs. LH.

Bill Doran (Switch Hitter) — *Houston Astros*

Bill Doran Against Right-Handed Pitchers
Overall BARS Batting Average .270

Fastball Average .302

	Outside	Middle	Inside
High	45/ 222/10	65/ 261/17	17/ 117/2
Med	151/ 331/50	43/ 348/15	47/ 319/15
Low	33/ 181/6	87/ 379/33	48/ 291/14

Curve Average .273

	Outside	Middle	Inside
High	8/ 250/2	6/ 166/1	4/ 500/2
Med	23/ 260/6	5/ 800/4	11/ 363/4
Low	15/ 66/1	12/ 416/5	11/ 90/1

Slider Average .271

	Outside	Middle	Inside
High	1/ 0/0	6/ 166/1	7/ 142/1
Med	4/ 250/1	4/ 500/2	16/ 250/4
Low	5/ 800/4	7/ 428/3	9/ 0/0

Bill Doran Against Left-Handed Pitchers
Overall BARS Batting Average .306

Fastball Average .348

	Inside	Middle	Outside
High	7/ 428/3	27/ 333/9	28/ 321/9
Med	22/ 272/6	25/ 400/10	82/ 402/33
Low	9/ 222/2	38/ 368/14	32/ 250/8

Curve Average .320

	Inside	Middle	Outside
High	1/ 0/0	9/ 444/4	2/ 500/1
Med	8/ 125/1	3/ 0/0	10/ 300/3
Low	7/ 0/0	6/ 666/4	4/ 750/3

Slider Average .228

	Inside	Middle	Outside
High	1/ 0/0	3/ 333/1	1/ 0/0
Med	3/ 333/1	4/ 0/0	5/ 200/1
Low	6/ 333/2	10/ 300/3	2/ 0/0

Switch-hitting Bill Doran hits a solid .302 against fastballs thrown by right-handed pitchers, .348 against fastballs thrown by left-handed pitchers.

Against right-handers, he has a strong .331 average against medium-high outside fastballs. By positioning themselves properly for this type and location of pitch, fielders could prevent most of Doran's base hits that are now dropping in.

MEDIUM-HIGH OUTSIDE FASTBALLS

BATTING AVERAGE .331
> *Play*

Left	Medium-deep in straightaway left field
Center	Medium-deep in straightaway center field
Right	Medium-deep in straightaway right field
Short	Up middle (shifted toward second base)
Second	Normal position

Notice that Doran is thrown more low than high fastballs by right-handers. This is a mistake because he hits low-over-the-middle and low-inside fastballs very well while being weak in his three high fastball locations (.222, .261 and .117, outside to inside).

He hits low-over-the-middle fastballs (.379) straight-away to left and right fields, into the deep left-center gap and to the right side of the infield.

LOW-OVER-THE-MIDDLE FASTBALLS

BATTING AVERAGE .379
> *Play*

Left	Deep in straightaway left field
Center	Deep and shifted toward left field
Right	Medium-deep in straightaway right field
Short	Up middle (shifted toward second base)
Second	Shifted toward first base

Batting left-handed against right-handed pitchers, Doran goes down the left line (his opposite field) with medium-high inside fastballs.

MEDIUM-HIGH INSIDE FASTBALLS

BATTING AVERAGE .319
> *Play*

Left	Medium-deep and shifted toward the left field line
Center	Medium-deep in straightaway center field
Right	Deep in straightaway right field
Short	Up middle (shifted toward second base)
Second	Normal position

Doran Against Curves And Sliders

Doran has trouble with outside curves thrown by right-handed pitchers (.250, .260 and .066, high to low). He hits low-over-the-middle curves very well, however.

LOW-OVER-THE-MIDDLE CURVEBALLS

BATTING AVERAGE .416
Play

Left	Medium-deep and shifted toward center field
Center	Medium-deep in straightaway center field
Right	Medium-deep and shifted toward center field
Short	Shifted toward third base
Second	*No instances recorded*

His .363 against medium-high inside curves is also excellent.

MEDIUM-HIGH INSIDE CURVEBALLS

BATTING AVERAGE .363
Play

Left	Deep and shifted toward center field
Center	Short and shifted toward right field
Right	Deep and shifted toward the right field line
Short	Shifted toward third base
Second	Shifted toward first base

Doran Against Left-Handed Pitchers

Doran's .348 overall fastball average against left-handed pitchers is very strong. He hits a brilliant .402 against medium-high outside fastballs thrown by left-handers. Batting right-handed, he pulls this pitch down the left line. Notice also that the shortstop needs to play shifted toward third base.

MEDIUM-HIGH OUTSIDE FASTBALLS
(THROWN BY LEFT-HANDED PITCHERS)

BATTING AVERAGE .402

Play

Left	Medium-deep and shifted toward the left field line
Center	Deep in straightaway center field
Right	Deep and shifted toward center field
Short	Shifted toward third base
Second	Normal position

His .368 against low-over-the-middle fastballs is also strong.

LOW-OVER-THE-MIDDLE FASTBALLS
(THROWN BY LEFT-HANDED PITCHERS)

BATTING AVERAGE .368
Play

Left	Deep and shifted toward the left field line
Center	Deep in straightaway center field
Right	Medium-deep and shifted toward center field
Short	Up middle (shifted toward second base)
Second	Shifted toward first base

He hits .333 vs. high-over-the-middle fastballs.

HIGH-OVER-THE-MIDDLE FASTBALLS
(THROWN BY LEFT-HANDED PITCHERS)

BATTING AVERAGE .333
Play

Left	Deep and shifted toward the left field line
Center	Deep in straightaway center field
Right	Medium-deep in straightaway right field
Short	Up middle (shifted toward second base)
Second	Normal position

Doran hits a fine .300 against medium-high outside curves thrown by left-handers. He hits this pitch medium-deep down the left line and into short right-center.

Ahead And Behind In The Count Vs. RH

Ahead

Fastball Average .323 — Curve Average .312

	Outside	Middle	Inside	Outside	Middle	Inside
High	16/375 /6	40/275 /11	6/166 /1	2/500 /1	0/0 /0	1/0 /0
Med	79/329 /26	31/322 /10	31/387 /12	2/0 /0	4/750 /3	4/0 /0
Low	14/142 /2	54/370 /20	26/307 /8	1/1000 /1	1/0 /0	1/0 /0

Behind

Fastball Average .323 — Curve Average .344

	Outside	Middle	Inside	Outside	Middle	Inside
High	9/222 /2	4/500 /2	3/0 /0	3/0 /0	4/250 /1	2/500 /1
Med	18/555 /10	4/250 /1	2/500 /1	8/500 /4	1/1000 /1	1/1000 /1
Low	7/285 /2	11/181 /2	7/142 /1	4/0 /0	5/400 /2	1/0 /0

Overall Evaluation
Against Right-Handed Pitchers

Overall Fastball	3
Overall Curve	2
Overall Slider	2

Against Left-Handed Pitchers

Overall Fastball	4
Overall Curve	4
Overall Slider	1

Comments: Weak against high fastballs vs. RH.
Strengths: Waist-high fastballs, low-middle fastballs, low-middle and medium-inside curves vs. RH; high fastballs, over-the-middle fastballs, medium-outside fastballs and curves, low-middle sliders vs. LH.
Weaknesses: High fastballs, low-outside fastballs, outside curves, low-inside curves, inside sliders vs. RH; medium-inside, low-inside and low-outside fastballs, inside curves vs. LH.

Billy Hatcher (Right Handed)   *Houston Astros*

Billy Hatcher Against Right-Handed Pitchers
Overall BARS Batting Average .265

Fastball Average .302

	Inside	Middle	Outside
High	30/366/11	44/386/17	19/315/6
Med	22/272/6	8/250/2	69/260/18
Low	11/363/4	31/258/8	24/250/6

Curve Average .258

	Inside	Middle	Outside
High	5/200/1	9/444/4	5/600/3
Med	5/200/1	2/0/0	29/275/8
Low	0/0/0	6/166/1	28/178/5

Slider Average .241

	Inside	Middle	Outside
High	0/0/0	3/333/1	3/0/0
Med	2/0/0	2/0/0	27/333/9
Low	0/0/0	2/0/0	19/210/4

Billy Hatcher Against Left-Handed Pitchers
Overall BARS Batting Average .286

Fastball Average .282

	Inside	Middle	Outside
High	11/272/3	12/333/4	17/352/6
Med	15/266/4	1/0/0	51/333/17
Low	7/142/1	18/166/3	13/230/3

Curve Average .192

	Inside	Middle	Outside
High	3/333/1	0/0/0	1/0/0
Med	2/500/1	1/0/0	4/0/0
Low	6/166/1	4/250/1	5/200/1

Slider Average .478

	Inside	Middle	Outside
High	1/1000/1	1/0/0	0/0/0
Med	5/600/3	0/0/0	4/750/3
Low	6/333/2	4/0/0	2/1000/2

Billy Hatcher, right-handed hitter, has a good .302 overall fastball average against right-handed pitchers. Against left-handed pitchers he hits .282 overall against fastballs.

Starting with his performance against right-handers, notice that Hatcher has trouble with medium-high outside fastballs (.260). Since this is his most highly pitched fastball location, it brings his overall average down.

He hits this pitch straightaway to all fields. But note that the shortstop needs to play shifted toward second and the second baseman shifted toward first.

MEDIUM-HIGH OUTSIDE FASTBALLS

BATTING AVERAGE .260
Play

Left Deep in straightaway left field
Center Medium-deep in straightaway center field
Right Medium-deep in straightaway right field
Short Up middle (shifted toward second base)
Second Shifted toward first base

Hatcher is strong against all high fastballs thrown by right-handers. He hits a splendid .386 against high-over-the-middle fastballs. The strategy below and the field diagram on the opposite page show where fielders need to play to prevent most of Hatcher's hits from this location.

HIGH-OVER-THE-MIDDLE FASTBALLS

BATTING AVERAGE .386
Play

Left Deep and shifted toward the left field line
Center Medium-deep in straightaway center field
Right Deep in straightaway right field
Short Shifted toward third base
Second Shifted toward first base

Hatcher has trouble with low-outside curves and sliders (.178 and .210, respectively). He hits medium-high outside curves and sliders well (.275 and .333).

Hatcher Against Left-Handed Pitchers

Hatcher hits a strong .333 against medium-high outside fastballs thrown by left-handed pitchers. He pulls this pitch medium-deep down the left line.

MEDIUM-HIGH OUTSIDE FASTBALLS
(THROWN BY LEFT-HANDED PITCHERS)

BATTING AVERAGE .333
Play

Left Medium-deep and shifted toward the left field line
Center Deep in straightaway center field
Right Medium-deep in straightaway right field
Short Shifted toward third base
Second Shifted toward first base

High-Over-The-Middle Fastballs

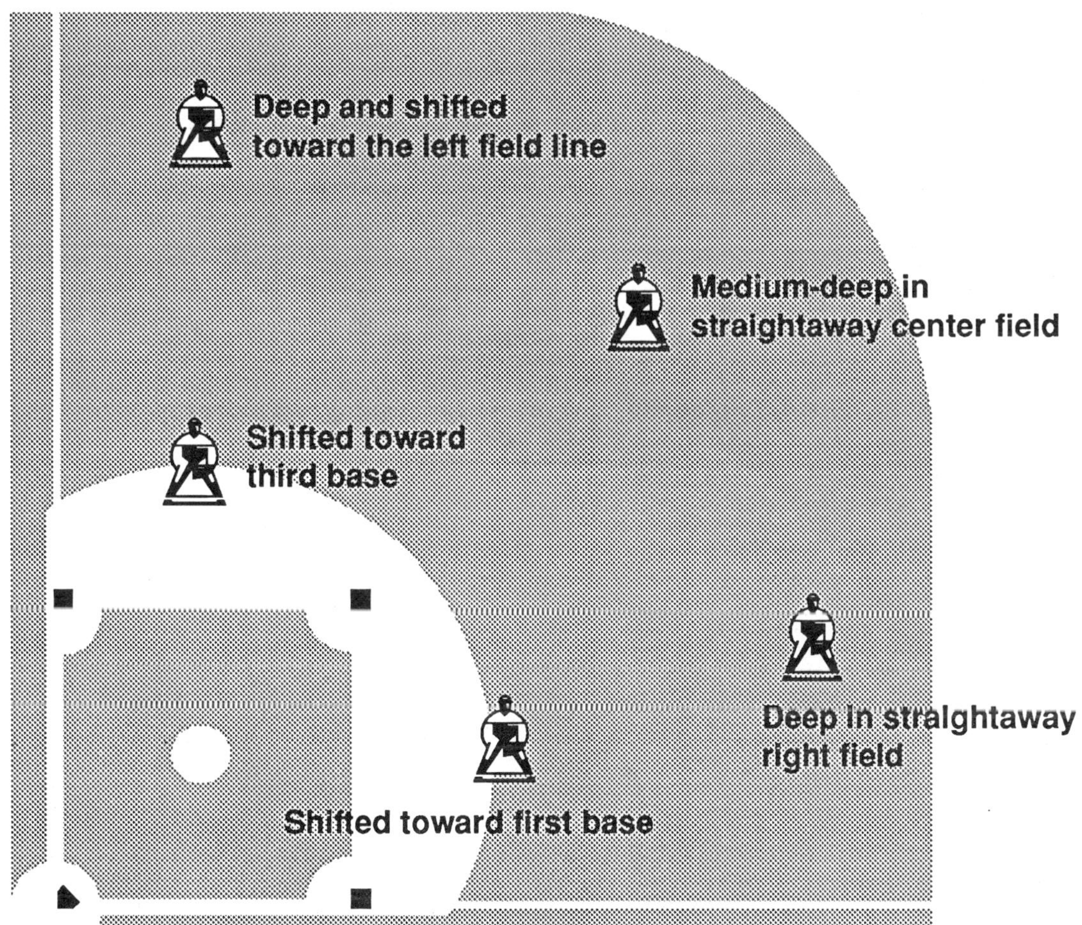

Ahead And Behind In The Count Vs. RH

Ahead

Fastball Average .389

	Inside	Middle	Outside
High	14/ 500 /7	22/ 454 /10	9/ 222 /2
Med	13/ 461 /6	8/ 250 /2	37/ 324 /12
Low	4/ 750 /3	14/ 357 /5	10/ 400 /4

Curve Average .500

	Inside	Middle	Outside
High	2/ 500 /1	2/ 500 /1	1/ 1000 /1
Med	1/ 0 /0	0/ 0 /0	6/ 500 /3
Low	0/ 0 /0	1/ 0 /0	1/ 1000 /1

Behind

Fastball Average .350

	Inside	Middle	Outside
High	4/ 500 /2	8/ 625 /5	6/ 333 /2
Med	3/ 0 /0	0/ 0 /0	7/ 428 /3
Low	3/ 333 /1	8/ 125 /1	1/ 0 /0

Curve Average .344

	Inside	Middle	Outside
High	2/ 0 /0	4/ 500 /2	1/ 1000 /1
Med	2/ 500 /1	0/ 0 /0	9/ 333 /3
Low	0/ 0 /0	2/ 500 /1	9/ 222 /2

Overall Evaluation

Against Right-Handed Pitchers

Overall Fastball 

Overall Curve

Overall Slider

Against Left-Handed Pitchers

Overall Fastball

Overall Curve

Overall Slider

Comments: Strong vs. high fastballs vs. RH.
Strenghts: High fastballs, low-inside fastballs, medium-outside sliders vs. RH; high-middle, high-outside and medium-outside fastballs vs. LH.
Weaknesses: Waist-high fastballs, low-middle and low-outside fastballs, low-outside curves and sliders vs. RH; low fastballs and inside fastballs, low curves vs. LH.

Steve Lombardozzi (Right Handed) — *Houston Astros*

Steve Lombardozzi Against Right-Handed Pitchers
Overall BARS Batting Average .204

Fastball Average .228

	Inside	Middle	Outside
High	19/105 / 2	12/333 / 4	6/166 / 1
Med	32/187 / 6	8/375 / 3	58/258 / 15
Low	7/142 / 1	9/333 / 3	11/181 / 2

Curve Average .160

	Inside	Middle	Outside
High	0/0 / 0	2/0 / 0	0/0 / 0
Med	1/0 / 0	2/0 / 0	6/333 / 2
Low	1/0 / 0	3/333 / 1	10/100 / 1

Slider Average .111

	Inside	Middle	Outside
High	0/0 / 0	1/0 / 0	0/0 / 0
Med	0/0 / 0	0/0 / 0	9/111 / 1
Low	0/0 / 0	1/0 / 0	7/142 / 1

Steve Lombardozzi Against Left-Handed Pitchers
Overall BARS Batting Average .200

Fastball Average .263

	Inside	Middle	Outside
High	2/500 / 1	9/111 / 1	4/0 / 0
Med	7/142 / 1	1/0 / 0	28/357 / 10
Low	5/0 / 0	7/428 / 3	9/333 / 3

Curve Average .066

	Inside	Middle	Outside
High	0/0 / 0	0/0 / 0	2/0 / 0
Med	1/0 / 0	0/0 / 0	2/500 / 1
Low	5/0 / 0	2/0 / 0	3/0 / 0

Slider Average .090

	Inside	Middle	Outside
High	1/0 / 0	0/0 / 0	0/0 / 0
Med	3/0 / 0	0/0 / 0	2/0 / 0
Low	4/250 / 1	1/0 / 0	0/0 / 0

Right-handed hitter Steve Lombardozzi has a low .228 overall fastball average against right-handed pitchers. He hits .263 overall against fastballs thrown by left-handers, bolstered mainly by the strong .357 in his medium-high outside fastball location.

Against right-handers, Lombardozzi hits .258 against medium-high outside fastballs. He hits this pitch straightaway to the outfield and to his opposite side (right side) of the infield.

MEDIUM-HIGH OUTSIDE FASTBALLS

BATTING AVERAGE .258
> *Play*

Left	Deep in straightaway left field
Center	Deep in straightaway center field
Right	Medium-deep in straightaway right field
Short	Up middle (shifted toward second base)
Second	Shifted toward first base

Lombardozzi hits weakly against all inside fastballs thrown by right-handers. He hits only .187 against medium-high inside fastballs. His low average in this location indicates that most of his hit balls are easy outs. Since he hits medium-deep and short to the outfield, he probably doesn't get good wood on the ball.

MEDIUM-HIGH INSIDE FASTBALLS

BATTING AVERAGE .187

> *Play*

Left	Medium-deep in straightaway left field
Center	Short in straightaway center field
Right	Short in straightaway right field
Short	Normal position
Second	Shifted toward first base

Lombardozzi Against Left-Handed Pitchers

Lombardozzi's .357 against medium-high outside fastballs is one of the strongest locations in his charts. He hits this pitch deep down the left line, into medium-deep center field, and deep into the right-center gap. The field diagram on the opposite page shows how fielders need to be positioned when Lombardozzi is thrown this pitch by a left-hander.

MEDIUM-HIGH OUTSIDE FASTBALLS (THROWN BY LEFT-HANDED PITCHERS)

BATTING AVERAGE .357
> *Play*

Left	Deep and shifted toward the left field line
Center	Medium-deep in straightaway center field
Right	Deep and shifted toward center field
Short	Normal position
Second	Normal position

Medium-High Outside Fastballs Vs. LH

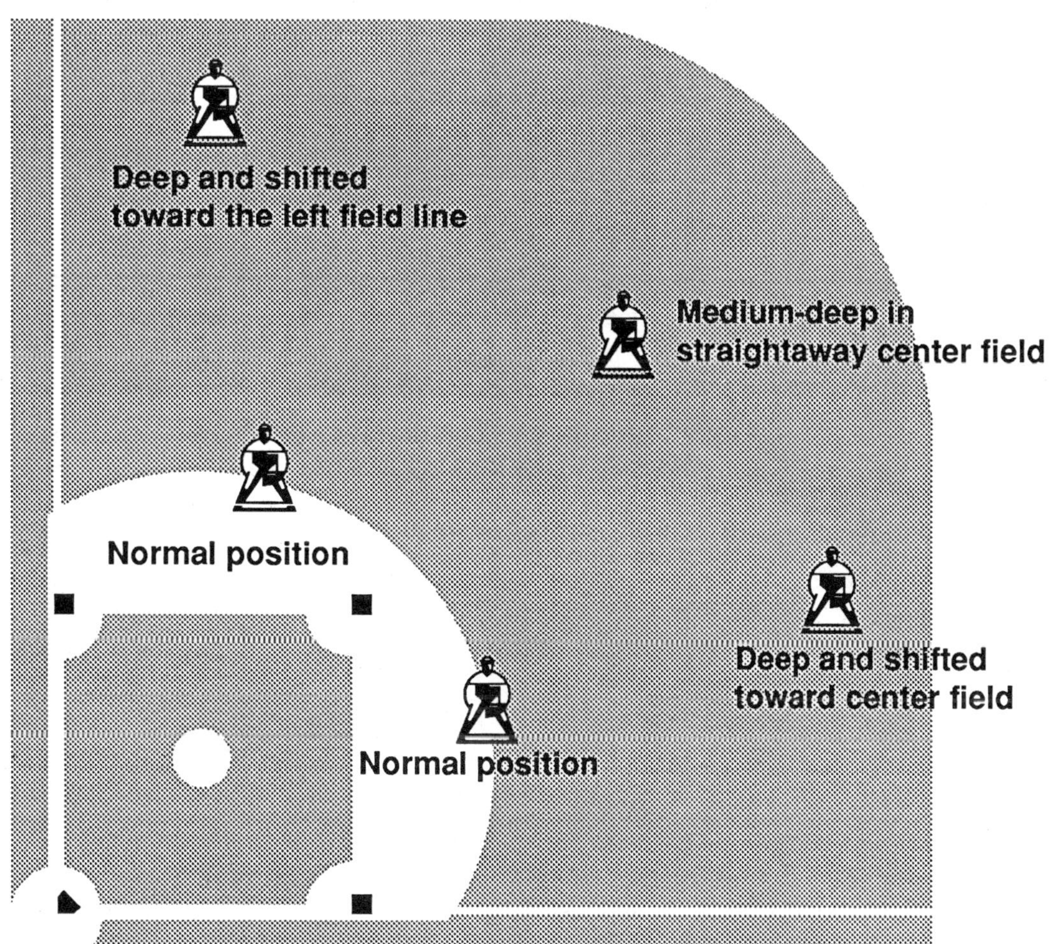

Ahead And Behind In The Count Vs. RH

Ahead

Fastball Average .277

	Inside	Middle	Outside
High	9 / 111 / 1	6 / 333 / 2	1 / 0 / 0
Med	15 / 66 / 1	8 / 375 / 3	33 / 333 / 11
Low	0 / 0 / 0	6 / 500 / 3	5 / 400 / 2

Curve Average .000

	Inside	Middle	Outside
High	0 / 0 / 0	0 / 0 / 0	0 / 0 / 0
Med	0 / 0 / 0	1 / 0 / 0	1 / 0 / 0
Low	0 / 0 / 0	0 / 0 / 0	0 / 0 / 0

Behind

Fastball Average .291

	Inside	Middle	Outside
High	3 / 333 / 1	3 / 333 / 1	2 / 500 / 1
Med	5 / 200 / 1	0 / 0 / 0	8 / 375 / 3
Low	2 / 0 / 0	0 / 0 / 0	1 / 0 / 0

Curve Average .500

	Inside	Middle	Outside
High	0 / 0 / 0	0 / 0 / 0	0 / 0 / 0
Med	1 / 0 / 0	0 / 0 / 0	1 / 1000 / 1
Low	0 / 0 / 0	1 / 1000 / 1	3 / 333 / 1

Overall Evaluation

Against Right-Handed Pitchers

Overall Fastball 

Overall Curve

Overall Slider

Against Left-Handed Pitchers

Overall Fastball 

Overall Curve — Not enough Information

Overall Slider — Not enough information

Comments: If RH pitchers keep fastballs outside or inside, they'll have an advantage on Lombardozzi.
Strengths: Over-the-middle fastballs vs. RH; medium-outside and low-middle fastballs vs. LH.
Weaknesses: Inside fastballs, outside fastballs, low-outside curves, outside sliders vs. RH; high-middle fastballs vs. LH.

Terry Puhl (Left Handed) — *Houston Astros*

Terry Puhl Against Right-Handed Pitchers
Overall BARS Batting Average .316

Fastball Average .358

	Outside	Middle	Inside
High	14/ 285 /4	37/ 378 /14	21/ 476 /10
Med	60/ 350 /21	30/ 366 /11	48/ 375 /18
Low	17/ 58 /1	45/ 444 /20	29/ 310 /9

Curve Average .250

	Outside	Middle	Inside
High	5/ 0 /0	7/ 142 /1	2/ 500 /1
Med	8/ 250 /2	3/ 666 /2	9/ 222 /2
Low	8/ 375 /3	11/ 272 /3	7/ 142 /1

Slider Average .281

	Outside	Middle	Inside
High	1/ 0 /0	2/ 0 /0	2/ 0 /0
Med	3/ 333 /1	1/ 0 /0	5/ 600 /3
Low	4/ 250 /1	7/ 428 /3	7/ 142 /1

Terry Puhl Against Left-Handed Pitchers
Overall BARS Batting Average .231

Fastball Average .219

	Outside	Middle	Inside
High	1/ 0 /0	13/ 153 /2	13/ 307 /4
Med	16/ 187 /3	11/ 454 /5	17/ 235 /4
Low	1/ 0 /0	7/ 142 /1	12/ 83 /1

Curve Average .275

	Outside	Middle	Inside
High	0/ 0 /0	2/ 1000 /2	1/ 0 /0
Med	8/ 250 /2	1/ 0 /0	7/ 285 /2
Low	5/ 200 /1	5/ 200 /1	0/ 0 /0

Slider Average .333

	Outside	Middle	Inside
High	0/ 0 /0	1/ 0 /0	0/ 0 /0
Med	3/ 666 /2	0/ 0 /0	2/ 0 /0
Low	3/ 333 /1	1/ 0 /0	2/ 500 /1

Left-handed hitter Terry Puhl is an excellent fastball hitter against right-handed pitchers (.358 overall fastball average). He has only one weak location, low-outside (.058).

He hits medium-high outside fastballs at a strong .350 clip. He hits this pitch deep to the outfield and to the right side of the infield.

MEDIUM-HIGH OUTSIDE FASTBALLS

BATTING AVERAGE .350

Play

Left	Deep in straightaway left field
Center	Deep and shifted toward left field
Right	Deep in straightaway right field
Short	Up middle (shifted toward second base)
Second	Shifted toward first base

He also hits medium-high inside fastballs excellently (.375). Note where the shortstop needs to be positioned for this inside fastball.

MEDIUM-HIGH INSIDE FASTBALLS

BATTING AVERAGE .375

Play

Left	Deep in straightaway left field
Center	Medium-deep and shifted toward right field
Right	Deep in straightaway right field
Short	Shifted toward third base
Second	*No instances recorded*

Pitchers throw Puhl a lot of low pitches. This is OK if they keep the ball down and away, but right-handers who throw him low fastballs need to stay away from the low-over-the-middle/low-inside fastball sector.

The following fielding strategy and the field chart on the opposite page show where fielders need to play for this pitch. If positioned correctly, they could prevent almost all of the hits now resulting from pitches to this location.

LOW-OVER-THE-MIDDLE FASTBALLS

BATTING AVERAGE .444

Play

Left	Medium-deep and shifted toward the left field line
Center	Medium-deep in straightaway center field
Right	Deep and shifted toward center field
Short	Normal position
Second	Normal position

Puhl hits curves fairly well overall (.250) against right-handers. He hits sliders for a solid .281 average overall.

Against left-handed pitchers, Puhl has trouble with fastballs. He hits well only against fastballs through the heart of the plate (.454). He hits curves fairly well (.275) and sliders excellently (.333) vs. left-handers.

Low-Over-The-Middle Fastballs

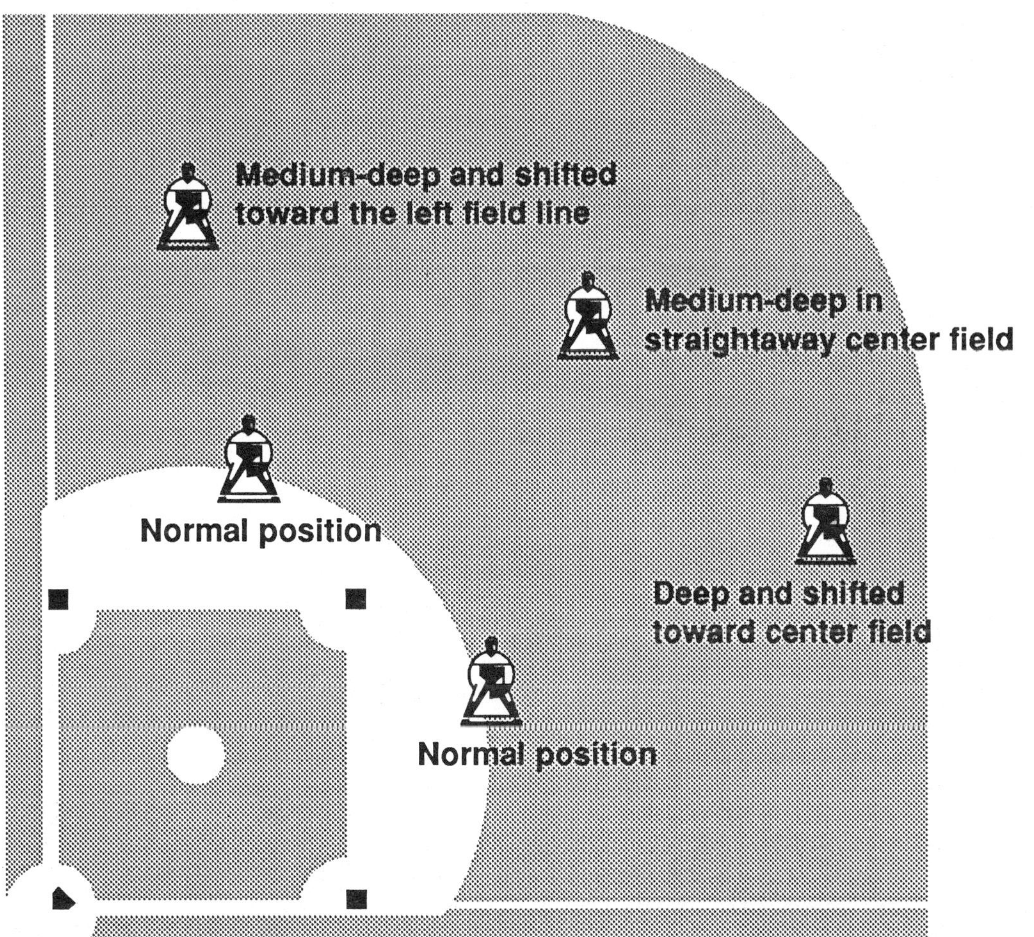

Ahead And Behind In The Count Vs. RH

Ahead

Fastball Average .416

	Outside	Middle	Inside
High	6/500/3	17/352/6	9/555/5
Med	28/428/12	21/476/10	32/375/12
Low	11/90/1	29/482/14	15/466/7

Curve Average .300

	Outside	Middle	Inside
High	1/0/0	2/500/1	0/0/0
Med	1/0/0	0/0/0	2/0/0
Low	1/1000/1	1/0/0	2/500/1

Behind

Fastball Average .319

	Outside	Middle	Inside
High	3/333/1	7/142/1	7/571/4
Med	10/500/5	4/0/0	6/500/3
Low	1/0/0	5/200/1	4/0/0

Curve Average .117

	Outside	Middle	Inside
High	4/0/0	2/0/0	1/0/0
Med	3/0/0	1/0/0	3/0/0
Low	1/1000/1	2/500/1	0/0/0

Overall Evaluation

Against Right-Handed Pitchers

Overall Fastball ⚾⚾⚾⚾

Overall Curve ⚾⚾

Overall Slider ⚾⚾⚾

Against Left-Handed Pitchers

Overall Fastball ⚾

Overall Curve ⚾⚾⚾

Overall Slider ⚾⚾⚾⚾

Comments: Excellent fastball hitter vs. RH.
Strengths: All fastballs except low-outside vs. RH; medium-middle and high-inside fastballs vs. LH.
Weaknesses: Low-outside fastballs, low-inside and medium-inside curves, low-inside sliders vs. RH; all fastballs except medium-middle and high-inside, medium-outside and low-outside curves vs. LH.

Rafael Ramirez Against Right-Handed Pitchers
Overall BARS Batting Average .256

Fastball Average .285

	Inside	Middle	Outside
High	33/ 242 /8	81/ 222 /18	23/ 260 /6
Med	97/ 288 /28	64/ 359 /23	114/ 324 /37
Low	41/ 195 /8	134/ 313 /42	79/ 253 /20

Curve Average .216

	Inside	Middle	Outside
High	7/ 285 /2	16/ 437 /7	3/ 0 /0
Med	8/ 125 /1	17/ 117 /2	49/ 224 /11
Low	3/ 333 /1	31/ 258 /8	78/ 179 /14

Slider Average .253

	Inside	Middle	Outside
High	0/ 0 /0	10/ 0 /0	3/ 666 /2
Med	5/ 400 /2	7/ 428 /3	31/ 290 /9
Low	3/ 333 /1	23/ 260 /6	56/ 214 /12

Rafael Ramirez Against Left-Handed Pitchers
Overall BARS Batting Average .264

Fastball Average .317

	Inside	Middle	Outside
High	17/ 294 /5	28/ 285 /8	10/ 200 /2
Med	37/ 378 /14	22/ 318 /7	57/ 280 /16
Low	15/ 400 /6	56/ 321 /18	48/ 333 /16

Curve Average .293

	Inside	Middle	Outside
High	1/ 0 /0	6/ 166 /1	3/ 333 /1
Med	3/ 666 /2	5/ 400 /2	19/ 315 /6
Low	6/ 166 /1	19/ 315 /6	13/ 230 /3

Slider Average .193

	Inside	Middle	Outside
High	0/ 0 /0	0/ 0 /0	0/ 0 /0
Med	4/ 0 /0	2/ 1000 /2	5/ 200 /1
Low	10/ 100 /1	8/ 125 /1	2/ 500 /1

Right-handed Rafael Ramirez hits fastballs fairly well against right-handed pitchers (.285 overall) and very well against left-handed pitchers (.317 overall). He has a lot of trouble with curves and sliders against right-handers (.216 and .253 respectively) but he hits curves well against left-handers (.293).

Starting with his performance against right-handers, notice how many low-over-the-middle fastballs Ramirez receives. Right-handers would be better off to throw him more high fastballs since he's weak in his three high locations (.242, .222 and .260, inside to outside).

Ramirez's Ahead and Behind charts on the opposite page show that he hits low-over-the-middle fastballs much better when ahead in the count (.378 when ahead, .133 when behind). The following BARS fielding strategies show that each of the outfielders needs to shift for this pitch when Ramirez is ahead and behind in the count.

LOW-OVER-THE-MIDDLE FASTBALLS (WHEN AHEAD IN THE COUNT)

BATTING AVERAGE .378

Play

Left	Deep in straightaway left field
Center	Medium-deep in straightaway center field
Right	Medium-deep in straightaway right field
Short	Up middle (shifted toward second base)
Second	Normal position

LOW-OVER-THE-MIDDLE FASTBALLS (WHEN BEHIND IN THE COUNT)

BATTING AVERAGE .133

Play

Left	Deep and shifted toward the left field line
Center	Deep in straightaway center field
Right	Medium-deep and shifted toward center field
Short	Up middle (shifted toward second base)
Second	Normal position

Ramirez also hits medium-high outside fastballs excellently (.324). He hits this pitch deep down both lines.

MEDIUM-HIGH OUTSIDE FASTBALLS

BATTING AVERAGE .324

Play

Left	Deep and shifted toward the left field line
Center	Medium-deep in straightaway center field
Right	Deep and shifted toward the right field line
Short	Normal position
Second	Shifted toward first base

He pulls medium-high inside fastballs (.288) deep

down the left line and deep into the left-center gap.

MEDIUM-HIGH INSIDE FASTBALLS

BATTING AVERAGE .288
Play

Left	Deep and shifted toward the left field line
Center	Deep and shifted toward left field
Right	Medium-deep in straightaway right field
Short	Up middle (shifted toward second base)
Second	Normal position

Ramirez Against Curves And Sliders

Ramirez has a low overall curve average against right-handed pitchers (.216). He is especially weak against outside and low-over-the-middle curves.

He is also weak against low-outside and low-over-the-middle sliders. But he hits medium-high outside sliders well (.290). He hits this pitch medium-deep to the outfield.

MEDIUM-HIGH OUTSIDE SLIDERS

BATTING AVERAGE .290
Play

Left	Medium-deep and shifted toward the left field line
Center	Medium-deep and shifted toward left field
Right	Medium-deep in straightaway right field
Short	Up middle (shifted toward second base)
Second	Normal position

Ramirez Against Left-Handed Pitchers

Left-handed pitchers also throw Ramirez more low than high fastballs. This is a big mistake because he hits low fastballs extremely well against lefties (.400, .321 and .333, inside to outside).

Ramirez's .321 average against low-over-the-middle fastballs is very good.

LOW-OVER-THE-MIDDLE FASTBALLS (THROWN BY LEFT-HANDED PITCHERS)

BATTING AVERAGE .321
Play

Left	Medium-deep and shifted toward center field
Center	Medium-deep in straightaway center field
Right	Deep and shifted toward center field
Short	Normal position
Second	Shifted toward first base

One of the most interesting things in Ramirez's charts is the way he hits medium-high inside fastballs against left-handers (.378). The following BARS fielding strategy shows how fielders should position themselves for this pitch. If they did, they could take away most of his hits that are dropping in front of the outfielders.

MEDIUM-HIGH INSIDE FASTBALLS (THROWN BY LEFT-HANDED PITCHERS)

BATTING AVERAGE .378
Play

Left	Medium-deep and shifted toward the left field line
Center	Short in straightaway center field
Right	Short in straightaway right field
Short	Normal position
Second	Normal position

Ahead And Behind In The Count Vs. RH

Ahead

Fastball Average .316

	Inside	Middle	Outside
High	13/ 200 /3	44/ 204 /9	7/ 571 /4
Med	37/ 243 /9	38/ 315 /12	49/ 460 /23
Low	13/ 153 /2	66/ 378 /25	39/ 256 /10

Curve Average .310

	Inside	Middle	Outside
High	1/ 0 /0	2/ 500 /1	2/ 0 /0
Med	2/ 500 /1	0/ 0 /0	8/ 375 /3
Low	0/ 0 /0	4/ 500 /2	10/ 200 /2

Behind

Fastball Average .301

	Inside	Middle	Outside
High	10/ 100 /1	16/ 312 /5	5/ 200 /1
Med	18/ 277 /5	11/ 545 /6	22/ 454 /10
Low	12/ 333 /4	30/ 133 /4	12/ 416 /5

Curve Average .222

	Inside	Middle	Outside
High	3/ 333 /1	8/ 500 /4	1/ 0 /0
Med	3/ 0 /0	8/ 125 /1	16/ 125 /2
Low	1/ 1000 /1	8/ 125 /1	24/ 250 /6

Overall Evaluation

Against Right-Handed Pitchers

Overall Fastball	⚾⚾
Overall Curve	⚾
Overall Slider	⚾⚾

Against Left-Handed Pitchers

Overall Fastball	⚾⚾⚾
Overall Curve	⚾⚾⚾
Overall Slider	⚾

Comments: Weak vs. high fastballs against RH. Strengths: Low-middle, medium-middle and medium-outside fastballs, waist-high sliders vs. RH; low and waist-high fastballs, waist-high and low-middle curves vs. LH. Weaknesses: High fastballs, low-inside and low-outside fastballs, outside curves and low-outside sliders vs. RH; high-outside fastballs, low-outside curves and low-inside sliders vs. LH.

Craig Reynolds (Left Handed)   *Houston Astros*

Craig Reynolds Against Right-Handed Pitchers
Overall BARS Batting Average .267

Fastball Average .291

	Outside	Middle	Inside
High	48/ 354 /17	81/ 308 /25	34/ 117 /4
Med	136/ 272 /37	35/ 428 /15	48/ 354 /17
Low	27/ 111 /3	57/ 368 /21	31/ 193 /6

Curve Average .272

	Outside	Middle	Inside
High	5/ 0 /0	8/ 375 /3	2/ 0 /0
Med	9/ 222 /2	3/ 333 /1	12/ 416 /5
Low	9/ 222 /2	18/ 388 /7	11/ 90 /1

Slider Average .277

	Outside	Middle	Inside
High	3/ 0 /0	2/ 500 /1	3/ 333 /1
Med	3/ 333 /1	3/ 333 /1	6/ 333 /2
Low	5/ 400 /2	5/ 200 /1	6/ 166 /1

Craig Reynolds Against Left-Handed Pitchers
Overall BARS Batting Average .283

Fastball Average .305

	Outside	Middle	Inside
High	2/ 0 /0	6/ 0 /0	9/ 444 /4
Med	10/ 300 /3	4/ 250 /1	11/ 272 /3
Low	2/ 500 /1	8/ 375 /3	7/ 428 /3

Curve Average .352

	Outside	Middle	Inside
High	2/ 500 /1	3/ 333 /1	1/ 0 /0
Med	10/ 200 /2	5/ 600 /3	5/ 600 /3
Low	3/ 0 /0	5/ 400 /2	0/ 0 /0

Slider Average .090

	Outside	Middle	Inside
High	0/ 0 /0	2/ 500 /1	1/ 0 /0
Med	2/ 0 /0	0/ 0 /0	2/ 0 /0
Low	4/ 0 /0	0/ 0 /0	0/ 0 /0

Craig Reynolds, left-handed hitter, has strong fastball averages against right- and left-handed pitchers (.291 overall against right-handers, .305 overall against left-handers). He hits curves fairly well against right-handers (.272 overall) and excellently against left-handers (.352).

Notice how well Reynolds hits fastballs when ahead in the count against right-handers (.340 overall). When ahead, he hits medium-high inside fastballs at a .468 pace. If fielders adjusted properly for this pitch according to the count, they could prevent most of his hits resulting from this location.

MEDIUM-HIGH INSIDE FASTBALLS (WHEN AHEAD IN THE COUNT)

BATTING AVERAGE .468
Play
Left   Medium-deep in straightaway left field
Center   Medium-deep and shifted toward right field
Right   Medium-deep and shifted toward the right line
Short   Up middle (shifted toward second base)
Second   Normal position

He also hits low-over-the-middle fastballs much better when ahead (.483 when ahead, .181 when behind). Every fielder needs to shift for this pitch when Reynolds is ahead and behind. The following strategies and the field chart on the opposite page show how

fielders need to be positioned.

LOW-OVER-THE-MIDDLE FASTBALLS (WHEN AHEAD IN THE COUNT)

BATTING AVERAGE .483
Play
Left   Medium-deep in straightaway left field
Center   Deep in straightaway center field
Right   Medium-deep in straightaway right field
Short   Up middle (shifted toward second base)
Second   Normal position

LOW-OVER-THE-MIDDLE FASTBALLS (WHEN BEHIND IN THE COUNT)

BATTING AVERAGE .181
Play
Left   Medium-deep and shifted toward the left field line
Center   Deep and shifted toward right field
Right   Deep and shifted toward the right field line
Short   Normal position
Second   Shifted toward first base

Reynolds is weak against low-inside and all outside curves against right-handers. He is very strong, however, against medium-inside and low-over-the-middle curves.

Against left-handed pitchers, Reynolds hits medium-high outside fastballs well (.300).

Low-Over-The-Middle Fastballs
Dark Fielders — Behind In The Count
Light Fielders — Ahead In The Count

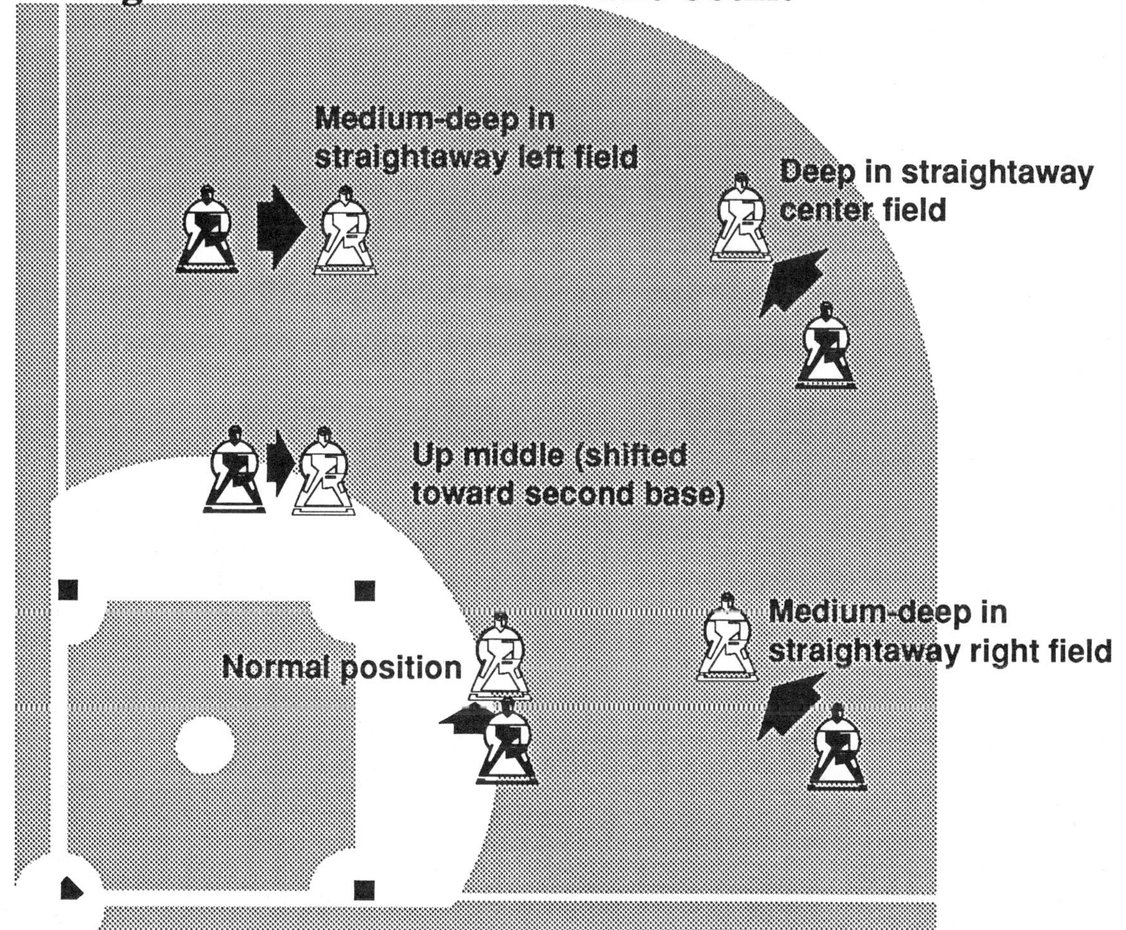

Ahead And Behind In The Count Vs. RH

Ahead

Fastball Average .340

	Outside	Middle	Inside
High	28/ 357 /10	48/ 375 /18	19/ 157 /3
Med	68/ 294 /20	25/ 400 /10	32/ 468 /15
Low	6/ 0 /0	31/ 483 /15	16/ 125 /2

Curve Average .473

	Outside	Middle	Inside
High	3/ 0 /0	3/ 333 /1	1/ 0 /0
Med	1/ 1000 /1	1/ 1000 /1	6/ 666 /4
Low	1/ 0 /0	3/ 666 /2	0/ 0 /0

Behind

Fastball Average .281

	Outside	Middle	Inside
High	8/ 625 /5	8/ 250 /2	5/ 0 /0
Med	22/ 318 /7	4/ 500 /2	5/ 0 /0
Low	3/ 333 /1	11/ 181 /2	5/ 200 /1

Curve Average .333

	Outside	Middle	Inside
High	1/ 0 /0	3/ 333 /1	1/ 0 /0
Med	3/ 0 /0	1/ 0 /0	1/ 0 /0
Low	3/ 666 /2	10/ 400 /4	1/ 1000 /1

Overall Evaluation
Against Right-Handed Pitchers

Overall Fastball 

Overall Curve

Overall Slider

Against Left-Handed Pitchers

Overall Fastball

Overall Curve

Overall Slider — Not enough information

Comments: Strong vs. over-the-middle, high-outside and medium-inside fastballs vs. RH.

Strengths: Over-the-middle fastballs, medium-inside and high-outside fastballs, over-the-middle and medium-inside curves vs. RH; medium-outside and low-middle fastballs vs. LH.

Weaknesses: Four fastball corners except high-outside, low-inside and all outside curves vs. RH; medium-inside fastballs, medium-outside curves v. LH.

Los Angeles Dodgers

Anderson, Dave
Dempsey, Rick
Gibson, Kirk
Griffin, Alfredo
Hatcher, Mickey
Marshall, Mike
Murray, Eddie
Randolph, Willie
Scioscia, Mike
Shelby, John
Stubbs, Franklin

Los Angeles Dodgers
BARS System
Hitting Analysis

Dave Anderson (Right Handed) — *Los Angeles Dodgers*

Dave Anderson Against Right-Handed Pitchers
Overall BARS Batting Average .210

Fastball Average .241

	Inside	Middle	Outside
High	12 / 333 / 4	30 / 166 / 5	7 / 142 / 1
Med	20 / 250 / 5	15 / 333 / 5	43 / 232 / 10
Low	5 / 200 / 1	26 / 307 / 8	20 / 200 / 4

Curve Average .181

	Inside	Middle	Outside
High	1 / 0 / 0	0 / 0 / 0	2 / 1000 / 2
Med	3 / 0 / 0	0 / 0 / 0	8 / 125 / 1
Low	0 / 0 / 0	8 / 250 / 2	11 / 90 / 1

Slider Average .115

	Inside	Middle	Outside
High	0 / 0 / 0	1 / 0 / 0	1 / 0 / 0
Med	1 / 0 / 0	0 / 0 / 0	6 / 166 / 1
Low	0 / 0 / 0	3 / 333 / 1	14 / 71 / 1

Dave Anderson Against Left-Handed Pitchers
Overall BARS Batting Average .227

Fastball Average .264

	Inside	Middle	Outside
High	2 / 0 / 0	7 / 285 / 2	5 / 0 / 0
Med	4 / 0 / 0	1 / 0 / 0	13 / 307 / 4
Low	2 / 0 / 0	14 / 500 / 7	5 / 200 / 1

Curve Average .333

	Inside	Middle	Outside
High	0 / 0 / 0	0 / 0 / 0	0 / 0 / 0
Med	0 / 0 / 0	0 / 0 / 0	2 / 0 / 0
Low	2 / 500 / 1	1 / 0 / 0	1 / 1000 / 1

Slider Average .100

	Inside	Middle	Outside
High	0 / 0 / 0	0 / 0 / 0	1 / 0 / 0
Med	1 / 0 / 0	1 / 0 / 0	1 / 0 / 0
Low	4 / 250 / 1	1 / 0 / 0	1 / 0 / 0

Right-handed hitter Dave Anderson has three strong fastball locations against right-handed pitchers (.333 high-inside, .307 low-over-the-middle, and .333 medium-over-the-middle).

He hits low-over-the-middle fastballs straightaway to left and center fields and medium-deep into the right-center gap.

LOW-OVER-THE-MIDDLE FASTBALLS

BATTING AVERAGE .307

Play

Left	Medium-deep in straightaway left field
Center	Deep in straightaway center field
Right	Medium-deep and shifted toward center field
Short	Shifted toward third base
Second	Shifted toward first base

He has weaknesses in his three outside fastball locations against right-handers (.142, .232 and .200, high to low). He pulls medium-high outside fastballs medium-deep down the left line. The following fielding strategy and the field diagram on the opposite page show how fielders should position themselves for this pitch to Anderson.

MEDIUM-HIGH OUTSIDE FASTBALLS

BATTING AVERAGE .232

Play

Left	Medium-deep and shifted toward the left field line
Center	Deep and shifted toward left field
Right	Deep in straightaway right field
Short	Shifted toward third base
Second	Normal position

Anderson is also weak against medium-high inside fastballs (.250). He hits this pitch deep down the left line.

MEDIUM-HIGH INSIDE FASTBALLS

BATTING AVERAGE .250

Play

Left	Deep and shifted toward the left field line
Center	Medium-deep in straightaway center field
Right	Medium-deep in straightaway right field
Short	Shifted toward third base
Second	Shifted toward first base

Anderson has problems with medium-high outside and low-outside curves and sliders thrown by right-handed pitchers. These locations offer targets for right-handers and give Anderson an indication of where his performance can be improved.

Against left-handed pitchers, Anderson hits medium-high outside fastballs (.307) and low-over-the-middle fastballs (.500) well. He has problems in his inside fastball locations.

Medium-High Outside Fastballs

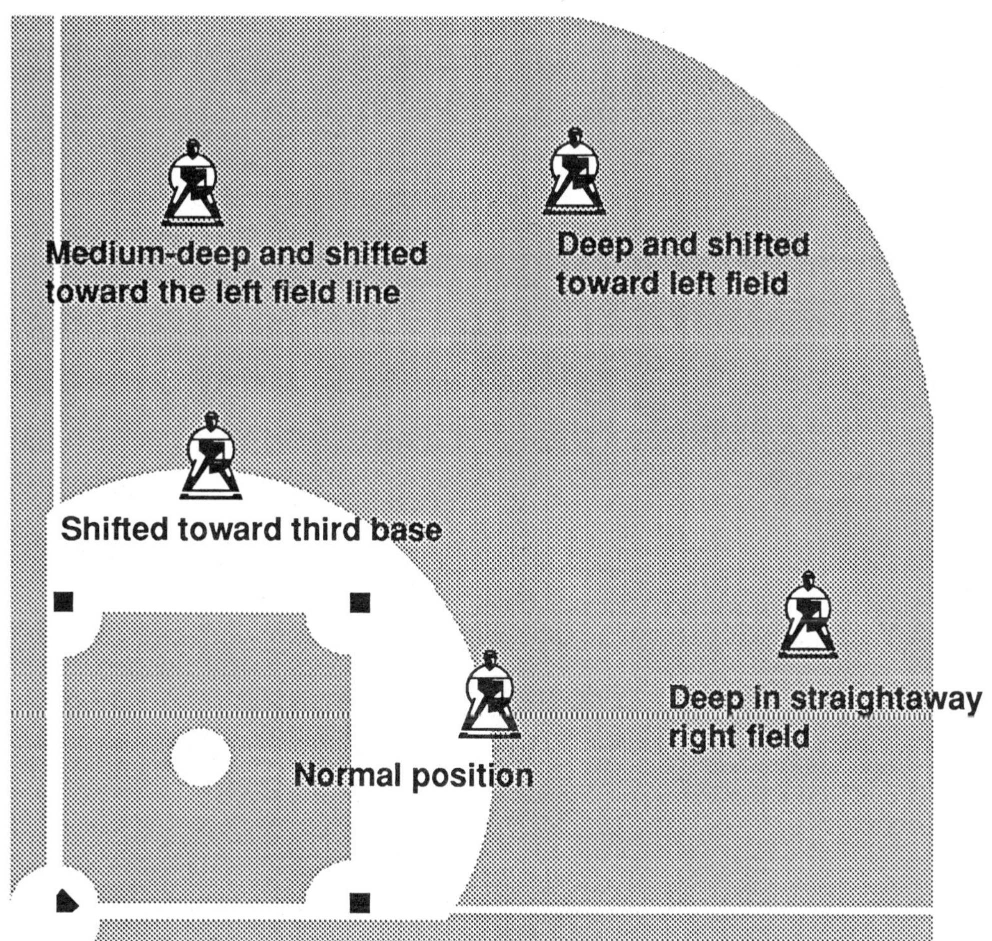

Ahead And Behind In The Count Vs. RH

Ahead

	Fastball Average .316			Curve Average .000		
	Inside	Middle	Outside	Inside	Middle	Outside
High	4/ 250 /1	11/ 272 /3	2/ 500 /1	0/ 0 /0	0/ 0 /0	0/ 0 /0
Med	9/ 555 /5	7/ 142 /1	21/ 238 /5	1/ 0 /0	0/ 0 /0	1/ 0 /0
Low	3/ 333 /1	16/ 312 /5	6/ 500 /3	0/ 0 /0	1/ 0 /0	2/ 0 /0

Behind

	Fastball Average .300			Curve Average .375		
	Inside	Middle	Outside	Inside	Middle	Outside
High	1/ 1000/1	8/ 250 /2	1/ 0 /0	0/ 0 /0	0/ 0 /0	2/ 1000/2
Med	2/ 0 /0	1/ 1000/1	7/ 428 /3	0/ 0 /0	0/ 0 /0	4/ 0 /0
Low	2/ 0 /0	3/ 333 /1	5/ 200 /1	0/ 0 /0	1/ 1000/1	1/ 0 /0

Overall Evaluation

Against Right-Handed Pitchers

Overall Fastball ⚾⚾
Overall Curve ⚾⚾
Overall Slider ⚾

Against Left-Handed Pitchers

Overall Fastball ⚾⚾
Overall Curve — Not enough information
Overall Slider — Not enough information

Comments: Weak against outside fastballs, curves and sliders thrown by RH.

Strengths: High-inside, medium-middle and low-middle fastballs vs. RH; low-middle and medium-outside fastballs vs. LH.

Weaknesses: All fastballs except as above against both RH and LH; outside and low curves, outside sliders vs. RH.

Rick Dempsey Against Right-Handed Pitchers
Overall BARS Batting Average .208

Fastball Average .208

	Inside	Middle	Outside
High	9 / 111 / 1	23 / 304 / 7	9 / 333 / 3
Med	29 / 206 / 6	26 / 153 / 4	67 / 283 / 19
Low	14 / 214 / 3	24 / 83 / 2	20 / 50 / 1

Curve Average .196

	Inside	Middle	Outside
High	2 / 0 / 0	0 / 0 / 0	3 / 0 / 0
Med	2 / 500 / 1	8 / 500 / 4	17 / 176 / 3
Low	3 / 333 / 1	6 / 166 / 1	20 / 100 / 2

Slider Average .294

	Inside	Middle	Outside
High	2 / 0 / 0	1 / 0 / 0	2 / 0 / 0
Med	3 / 0 / 0	3 / 333 / 1	15 / 533 / 8
Low	1 / 0 / 0	7 / 571 / 4	17 / 117 / 2

Rick Dempsey Against Left-Handed Pitchers
Overall BARS Batting Average .227

Fastball Average .251

	Inside	Middle	Outside
High	4 / 250 / 1	12 / 250 / 3	11 / 272 / 3
Med	5 / 0 / 0	13 / 461 / 6	56 / 267 / 15
Low	7 / 142 / 1	17 / 235 / 4	14 / 142 / 2

Curve Average .294

	Inside	Middle	Outside
High	1 / 0 / 0	2 / 0 / 0	2 / 500 / 1
Med	3 / 333 / 1	2 / 0 / 0	20 / 300 / 6
Low	5 / 200 / 1	8 / 500 / 4	8 / 250 / 2

Slider Average .150

	Inside	Middle	Outside
High	0 / 0 / 0	2 / 500 / 1	0 / 0 / 0
Med	5 / 200 / 1	3 / 0 / 0	3 / 0 / 0
Low	2 / 500 / 1	1 / 0 / 0	4 / 0 / 0

Rick Dempsey, right-handed hitter, has a lot of trouble with fastballs thrown by right-handed pitchers (.208 overall). He has trouble with all low fastballs and all inside fastballs thrown by right-handers. He also hits poorly against medium-over-the-middle fastballs (.153). This is unusual because most hitters have a good average against this pitch.

He hits medium-high outside fastballs fairly well (.283). He hits this pitch straightaway to left and center and into the deep right-center gap.

MEDIUM-HIGH OUTSIDE FASTBALLS

BATTING AVERAGE .283
Play

Left	Deep in straightaway left field
Center	Medium-deep in straightaway center field
Right	Deep and shifted toward center field
Short	Normal position
Second	Shifted toward first base

His .304 average against high-over-the-middle fastballs is sound. The following strategy and the field diagram on the opposite page show how fielders need to position themselves for fastballs to this location

HIGH-OVER-THE-MIDDLE FASTBALLS

BATTING AVERAGE .304
Play

Left	Medium-deep and shifted toward the left field line
Center	Deep and shifted toward left field
Right	Medium-deep and shifted toward the right line
Short	Shifted toward third base
Second	Normal position

In addition to being weak against all low and all inside fastballs, Dempsey has trouble with outside curves (.000, .176 and .100, high to low). He also has trouble with low-outside sliders (.117), although he hits medium-high outside sliders very well (.533).

Dempsey Against Left-Handed Pitchers

Dempsey has only one strong location in his fastball chart against left-handed pitchers (.461 medium-over-the-middle). He hits .267 against medium-high outside fastballs.

His .300 against medium-high outside curves is excellent. He pulls this pitch deep down the left line.

MEDIUM-HIGH OUTSIDE CURVEBALLS

BATTING AVERAGE .300
Play

Left	Deep and shifted toward the left field line
Center	Deep in straightaway center field
Right	Medium-deep in straightaway right field
Short	Shifted toward third base
Second	Shifted toward first base

High-Over-The-Middle Fastballs

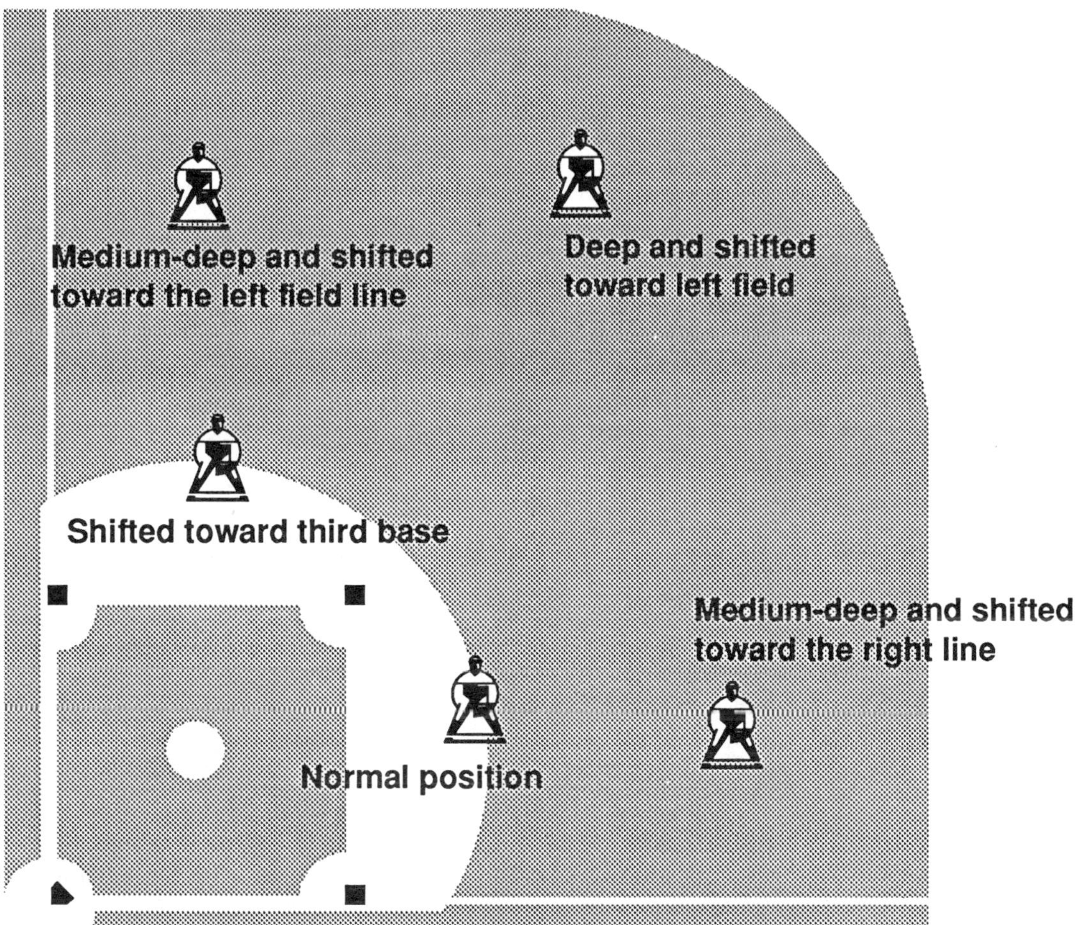

Ahead And Behind In The Count Vs. RH

Ahead

Fastball Average .222   Curve Average .200

	Inside	Middle	Outside	Inside	Middle	Outside
High	3/ 0 / 0	7/ 428 / 3	1/ 0 / 0	2/ 0 / 0	0/ 0 / 0	0/ 0 / 0
Med	13/ 230 / 3	15/ 133 / 2	23/ 304 / 7	0/ 0 / 0	2/ 500 / 1	5/ 200 / 1
Low	7/ 285 / 2	7/ 0 / 0	5/ 200 / 1	0/ 0 / 0	3/ 333 / 1	3/ 0 / 0

Behind

Fastball Average .277   Curve Average .260

	Inside	Middle	Outside	Inside	Middle	Outside
High	1/ 1000 / 1	4/ 0 / 0	4/ 750 / 3	0/ 0 / 0	0/ 0 / 0	1/ 0 / 0
Med	8/ 250 / 2	1/ 0 / 0	11/ 363 / 4	1/ 1000 / 1	5/ 400 / 2	4/ 0 / 0
Low	1/ 0 / 0	3/ 0 / 0	3/ 0 / 0	2/ 500 / 1	2/ 0 / 0	8/ 250 / 2

Overall Evaluation

Against Right-Handed Pitchers

Overall Fastball 

Overall Curve

Overall Slider

Against Left-Handed Pitchers

Overall Fastball 

Overall Curve

Overall Slider

Comments: Weak vs. inside and low fastballs vs. RH.
Strengths: High-middle and high-outside fastballs, medium-outside and low-middle sliders vs. RH; medium-middle fastballs, medium-outside and low-middle curves vs. LH.
Weaknesses: Inside, low and medium-middle fastballs, outside curves and low-outside sliders vs. RH; all fastballs except medium-middle against LH.

Kirk Gibson Against Right-Handed Pitchers
Overall BARS Batting Average .250

Fastball Average .265

	Outside	Middle	Inside
High	26 / 192 / 5	25 / 200 / 5	14 / 285 / 4
Med	118 / 211 / 25	35 / 457 / 16	45 / 311 / 14
Low	44 / 204 / 9	55 / 309 / 17	33 / 303 / 10

Curve Average .250

	Outside	Middle	Inside
High	5 / 400 / 2	6 / 500 / 3	1 / 1000 / 1
Med	25 / 280 / 7	10 / 400 / 4	6 / 166 / 1
Low	23 / 217 / 5	23 / 86 / 2	21 / 238 / 5

Slider Average .296

	Outside	Middle	Inside
High	1 / 0 / 0	3 / 0 / 0	1 / 1000 / 1
Med	8 / 250 / 2	1 / 1000 / 1	6 / 500 / 3
Low	10 / 100 / 1	5 / 200 / 1	19 / 368 / 7

Kirk Gibson Against Left-Handed Pitchers
Overall BARS Batting Average .268

Fastball Average .305

	Outside	Middle	Inside
High	7 / 142 / 1	10 / 400 / 4	12 / 250 / 3
Med	33 / 363 / 12	12 / 333 / 4	48 / 208 / 10
Low	12 / 166 / 2	16 / 437 / 7	17 / 470 / 8

Curve Average .189

	Outside	Middle	Inside
High	4 / 0 / 0	0 / 0 / 0	1 / 0 / 0
Med	27 / 148 / 4	4 / 0 / 0	8 / 500 / 4
Low	24 / 208 / 5	9 / 222 / 2	2 / 0 / 0

Slider Average .306

	Outside	Middle	Inside
High	1 / 1000 / 1	1 / 0 / 0	1 / 0 / 0
Med	11 / 272 / 3	5 / 600 / 3	5 / 200 / 1
Low	15 / 133 / 2	6 / 666 / 4	4 / 250 / 1

Left-handed hitter Kirk Gibson has numerous strong locations in his BARS charts. But he has specific areas of weakness on which pitchers can focus.

His charts against right-handed pitchers show that he has problems with outside fastballs (.192, .211 and .204, high to low). The high number of recorded instances in these locations indicates that pitchers are aware of this. By working on fastballs to these locations, or by holding off on them until he has two strikes, Gibson could improve his overall effectiveness.

He hits very well in several other fastball locations. His .309 against low-over-the-middle fastballs is good. He hits this pitch straightaway to the outfield and to the right side of the infield.

LOW-OVER-THE-MIDDLE FASTBALLS

BATTING AVERAGE .309
Play

Left	Medium-deep in straightaway left field
Center	Deep in straightaway center field
Right	Deep in straightaway right field
Short	Up middle (shifted toward second base)
Second	Shifted toward first base

His .311 against medium-high inside fastballs is also good. He hits this pitch straightaway to the outfield, but notice that both the left and center fielders need to play short. By positioning themselves according to the following strategy, fielders could take away most of Gibson's hits resulting from pitches to this location.

MEDIUM-HIGH INSIDE FASTBALLS

BATTING AVERAGE .311
Play

Left	Short in straightaway left field
Center	Short in straightaway center field
Right	Deep in straightaway right field
Short	Normal position
Second	Shifted toward first base

Gibson Against Curves And Sliders

Gibson has trouble with all low curves thrown by right-handed pitchers (.217, .086 and .238, outside to inside) but he hits medium-high outside curves pretty well (.280). He hits this pitch medium-deep into the left-center and right-center gaps and to the right side of the infield.

MEDIUM-HIGH OUTSIDE CURVEBALLS

BATTING AVERAGE .280
Play

Left	Medium-deep and shifted toward center field
Center	Medium-deep and shifted toward right field

Gibson has trouble with low-outside sliders thrown by right-handers but he hits low-inside sliders extremely well (.368). The fielding strategy for this pitch is unusual; by positioning themselves properly, fielders could take away most of Gibson's line drives that apparently are falling in for base hits.

LOW-INSIDE SLIDERS

BATTING AVERAGE .368
Play

Left   Medium-deep and shifted toward center field
Center   Short and shifted toward right field
Right   Deep in straightaway right field
Short   Up middle (shifted toward second base)
Second   *No instances recorded*

Gibson Against Left-Handed Pitchers

Left-handed pitchers are attacking Gibson with inside fastballs, as indicated by the high number of recorded instances in his inside fastball locations. This strategy is all right if they keep the ball away from Gibson's strong low-inside fastball location (.470). The BARS fielding strategy shows that Gibson goes down the left line (his opposite field) with this inside pitch.

LOW-INSIDE FASTBALLS
(THROWN BY LEFT-HANDED PITCHERS)

BATTING AVERAGE .470
Play

Left   Medium-deep and shifted toward the left field line
Center   Deep in straightaway center field
Right   *No instances recorded*
Short   Normal position
Second   Normal position

He also hits medium-high outside and low-over-the-middle fastballs very well against left-handers (.363 and .437). He hits medium-high outside fastballs straightaway to the outfield. Notice that the center fielder needs to play short.

MEDIUM-HIGH OUTSIDE FASTBALLS
(THROWN BY LEFT-HANDED PITCHERS)

BATTING AVERAGE .363
Play

Left   Deep in straightaway left field
Center   Short in straightaway center field
Right   Deep in straightaway right field
Short   Up middle (shifted toward second base)
Second   Shifted toward first base

He has a lot of trouble with all outside curves and low curves against lefties. These locations, along with his weak low-outside slider location, offer targets for left-handers.

Ahead And Behind In The Count Vs. RH

Ahead

	Fastball Average .363			Curve Average .357		
	Outside	Middle	Inside	Outside	Middle	Inside
High	1 · 750/3	10 · 500/5	5 · 400/2	0 · 0/0	3 · 1000/3	0 · 0/0
Med	48 · 291/14	17 · 529/9	18 · 333/6	3 · 333/1	6 · 333/2	3 · 0/0
Low	19 · 368/7	33 · 242/8	11 · 545/6	1 · 0/0	7 · 142/1	5 · 600/3

Behind

	Fastball Average .295			Curve Average .378		
	Outside	Middle	Inside	Outside	Middle	Inside
High	6 · 166/1	5 · 0/0	4 · 500/2	3 · 666/2	2 · 0/0	0 · 0/0
Med	18 · 222/4	3 · 666/2	12 · 416/5	11 · 454/5	3 · 333/1	1 · 0/0
Low	2 · 0/0	7 · 428/3	4 · 250/1	9 · 333/3	5 · 200/1	3 · 666/2

Overall Evaluation
Against Right-Handed Pitchers

Overall Fastball
Overall Curve
Overall Slider

Against Left-Handed Pitchers

Overall Fastball
Overall Curve
Overall Slider 

Comments: Weak against outside fastballs vs. RH. Strengths: Low-middle, medium-middle, medium-inside and low-inside fastballs, low-inside sliders vs. RH; over-the-middle, medium-outside and low-inside fastballs vs. LH. Weaknesses: Outside and high-middle fastballs, low curves, outside sliders vs. RH; low-outside, high-outside, high-inside and medium-inside fastballs, all low and outside curves, low-outside sliders vs. LH.

Alfredo Griffin Against Right-Handed Pitchers
Overall BARS Batting Average .203

Fastball Average .235

	Outside	Middle	Inside
High	10 / 200 / 2	22 / 363 / 8	18 / 166 / 3
Med	54 / 148 / 8	21 / 142 / 3	45 / 288 / 13
Low	16 / 312 / 5	51 / 313 / 16	39 / 179 / 7

Curve Average .169

	Outside	Middle	Inside
High	0 / 0 / 0	1 / 1000 / 1	0 / 0 / 0
Med	12 / 83 / 1	4 / 500 / 2	10 / 0 / 0
Low	1 / 0 / 0	15 / 266 / 4	10 / 100 / 1

Slider Average .173

	Outside	Middle	Inside
High	1 / 0 / 0	2 / 500 / 1	1 / 1000 / 1
Med	5 / 0 / 0	4 / 500 / 2	2 / 0 / 0
Low	1 / 0 / 0	1 / 0 / 0	6 / 0 / 0

Alfredo Griffin Against Left-Handed Pitchers
Overall BARS Batting Average .309

Fastball Average .345

	Inside	Middle	Outside
High	3 / 666 / 2	15 / 266 / 4	14 / 357 / 5
Med	18 / 388 / 7	8 / 500 / 4	44 / 318 / 14
Low	12 / 416 / 5	16 / 250 / 4	9 / 333 / 3

Curve Average .312

	Inside	Middle	Outside
High	2 / 0 / 0	1 / 0 / 0	1 / 0 / 0
Med	4 / 250 / 1	2 / 500 / 1	6 / 500 / 3
Low	3 / 333 / 1	9 / 333 / 3	4 / 250 / 1

Slider Average .296

	Inside	Middle	Outside
High	1 / 0 / 0	1 / 0 / 0	0 / 0 / 0
Med	6 / 166 / 1	1 / 1000 / 1	6 / 166 / 1
Low	6 / 333 / 2	3 / 333 / 1	3 / 666 / 2

Switch-hitting Alfredo Griffin has a much higher overall BARS fastball average against left-handed pitchers (.345 against left-handers, .235 against right-handers). He has many weak locations scattered through his fastball chart against right-handers, but he does have several fastball strengths. The .288 in his medium-high inside fastball location is adequate.

MEDIUM-HIGH INSIDE FASTBALLS

BATTING AVERAGE .288

Play

Left	Medium-deep in straightaway left field
Center	Deep and shifted toward left field
Right	Medium-deep and shifted toward center field
Short	Shifted toward third base
Second	Shifted toward first base

The .313 in his low-over-the-middle fastball location is good.

LOW-OVER-THE-MIDDLE FASTBALLS

BATTING AVERAGE .313

Play

Left	Medium-deep and shifted toward center field
Center	Medium-deep in straightaway center field
Right	Deep in straightaway right field
Short	Up middle (shifted toward second base)
Second	Shifted toward first base

Griffin is very weak against curves and sliders thrown by right-handers.

Griffin really comes alive against left-handed pitchers. His overall .345 fastball average is excellent. He hits .318 against medium-high outside fastballs. The following fielding strategy and the field diagram on the opposite page show where fielders need to be positioned for this pitch.

MEDIUM-HIGH OUTSIDE FASTBALLS (THROWN BY LEFT-HANDED PITCHERS)

BATTING AVERAGE .318

Play

Left	Medium-deep in straightaway left field
Center	Medium-deep in straightaway center field
Right	Medium-deep in straightaway right field
Short	Normal position
Second	Shifted toward first base

He hits .388 against medium-high inside fastballs thrown by left-handers.

MEDIUM-HIGH INSIDE FASTBALLS (THROWN BY LEFT-HANDED PITCHERS)

BATTING AVERAGE .388

Play

Left	*No instances recorded*
Center	Medium-deep and shifted toward left field
Right	Medium-deep and shifted toward center field
Short	Normal position
Second	Shifted toward second base

Medium-High Outside Fastballs Vs. LH

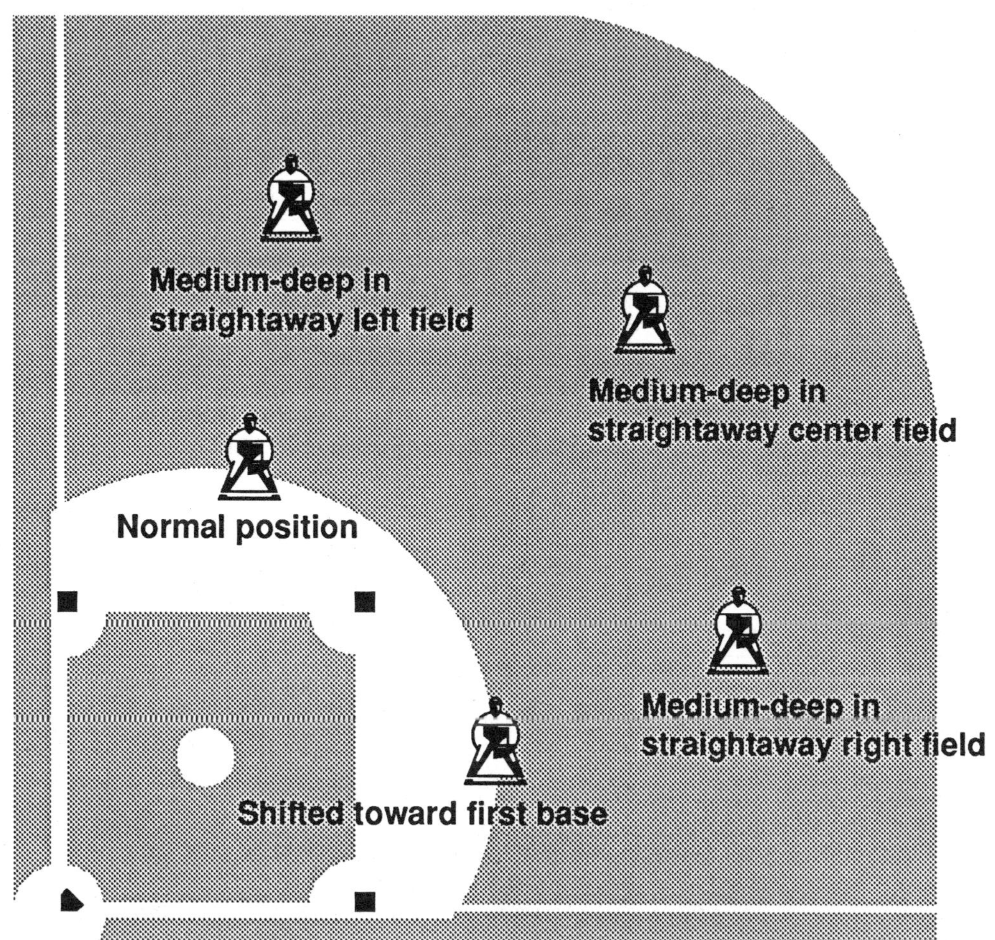

Ahead And Behind In The Count Vs. RH

Ahead

Fastball Average .242

	Outside	Middle	Inside
High	5/ 0 / 0	8/ 250 / 2	6/ 0 / 0
Med	22/ 181 / 4	13/ 230 / 3	20/ 400 / 8
Low	6/ 333 / 2	33/ 303 / 10	19/ 157 / 3

Curve Average .444

	Outside	Middle	Inside
High	0/ 0 / 0	0/ 0 / 0	0/ 0 / 0
Med	3/ 333 / 1	1/ 1000 / 1	1/ 0 / 0
Low	0/ 0 / 0	3/ 666 / 2	1/ 0 / 0

Behind

Fastball Average .328

	Outside	Middle	Inside
High	4/ 500 / 2	4/ 500 / 2	5/ 400 / 2
Med	19/ 157 / 3	4/ 0 / 0	9/ 333 / 3
Low	5/ 400 / 2	10/ 500 / 5	7/ 428 / 3

Curve Average .074

	Outside	Middle	Inside
High	0/ 0 / 0	1/ 1000 / 1	0/ 0 / 0
Med	7/ 0 / 0	3/ 333 / 1	5/ 0 / 0
Low	0/ 0 / 0	7/ 0 / 0	4/ 0 / 0

Overall Evaluation

Against Right-Handed Pitchers

Overall Fastball 

Overall Curve

Overall Slider

Against Left-Handed Pitchers

Overall Fastball

Overall Curve

Overall Slider

Comments: Weak overall against curves vs. RH.
Strengths: High-middle, low-outside and low-middle fastballs vs. RH; all fastballs except low-middle and high-middle, low-middle curves vs. LH.
Weaknesses: High-outside, high-inside, medium-outside, medium-middle and low-inside fastballs, curves in general vs. RH; high-middle and low-middle fastballs vs. LH.

Mickey Hatcher Against Right-Handed Pitchers
Overall BARS Batting Average .241

Fastball Average .230

	Inside	Middle	Outside
High	10/ 200 /2	8/ 125 /1	5/ 200 /1
Med	27/ 148 /4	17/ 411 /7	55/ 218 /12
Low	11/ 90 /1	31/ 322 /10	14/ 214 /3

Curve Average .322

	Inside	Middle	Outside
High	2/ 0 /0	5/ 400 /2	2/ 0 /0
Med	1/ 0 /0	4/ 500 /2	9/ 333 /3
Low	0/ 0 /0	0/ 0 /0	8/ 375 /3

Slider Average .269

	Inside	Middle	Outside
High	0/ 0 /0	1/ 0 /0	2/ 0 /0
Med	3/ 333 /1	3/ 0 /0	3/ 666 /2
Low	4/ 500 /2	1/ 0 /0	9/ 222 /2

Mickey Hatcher Against Left-Handed Pitchers
Overall BARS Batting Average .344

Fastball Average .369

	Inside	Middle	Outside
High	3/ 666 /2	12/ 500 /6	9/ 111 /1
Med	18/ 388 /7	6/ 500 /3	24/ 291 /7
Low	7/ 428 /3	20/ 450 /9	20/ 300 /6

Curve Average .375

	Inside	Middle	Outside
High	0/ 0 /0	0/ 0 /0	2/ 500 /1
Med	1/ 0 /0	1/ 0 /0	10/ 400 /4
Low	3/ 666 /2	4/ 250 /1	3/ 333 /1

Slider Average .500

	Inside	Middle	Outside
High	0/ 0 /0	1/ 0 /0	0/ 0 /0
Med	4/ 750 /3	2/ 500 /1	0/ 0 /0
Low	3/ 666 /2	5/ 400 /2	1/ 0 /0

Right-handed hitter Mickey Hatcher has trouble in all but a few fastball locations against right-handed pitchers. His inside, outside and high locations offer targets for right-handers. He hits a fine .322 against low-over-the-middle fastballs, however. He pulls this pitch deep down the left line and deep into the right center gap.

LOW-OVER-THE-MIDDLE FASTBALLS

BATTING AVERAGE .322
   Play

Left	Deep and shifted toward the left field line
Center	Deep in straightaway center field
Right	Deep and shifted toward center field
Short	Normal position
Second	Normal position

Hatcher's performance against left-handed pitchers is another story. His .369 overall fastball average is excellent. He hits all low fastballs very solidly. The following strategy and the field diagram on the opposite page show how fielders need to position themselves for low-over-the-middle fastballs (.450).

LOW-OVER-THE-MIDDLE FASTBALLS
(THROWN BY LEFT-HANDED PITCHERS)

BATTING AVERAGE .450
   Play

Left	Deep and shifted toward the left field line
Center	Deep and shifted toward left field
Right	Deep in straightaway right field
Short	Shifted toward third base
Second	Normal position

His .388 against medium-high inside fastballs thrown by left-handers is very strong. Notice that he hits this inside pitch to the right side of the infield (his opposite field) but deep down the left line and medium-deep into right-center.

MEDIUM-HIGH INSIDE FASTBALLS
(THROWN BY LEFT-HANDED PITCHERS)

BATTING AVERAGE .388
   Play

Left	Deep and shifted toward the left field line
Center	Medium-deep in straightaway center field
Right	Medium-deep and shifted toward center field
Short	Up middle (shifted toward second base)
Second	Shifted toward first base

He hits medium-high outside curves at a .400 clip against lefties.

Low-Over-The-Middle Fastballs Vs. LH

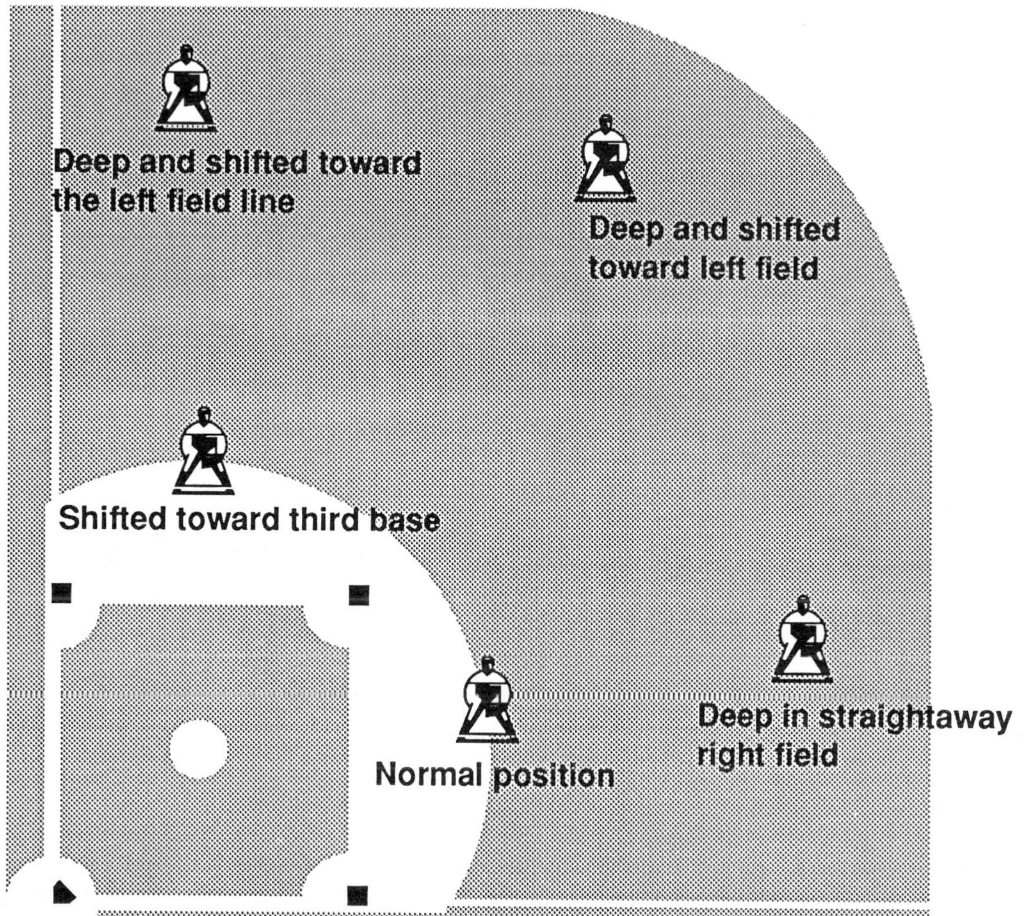

Ahead And Behind In The Count Vs. RH

Ahead

Fastball Average .268

	Inside	Middle	Outside
High	3/ 0 /0	4/ 250 /1	2/ 500 /1
Med	15/ 133 /2	12/ 416 /5	30/ 233 /7
Low	4/ 0 /0	17/ 411 /7	6/ 333 /2

Curve Average .357

	Inside	Middle	Outside
High	1/ 0 /0	2/ 500 /1	0/ 0 /0
Med	0/ 0 /0	3/ 666 /2	7/ 285 /2
Low	0/ 0 /0	0/ 0 /0	1/ 0 /0

Behind

Fastball Average .222

	Inside	Middle	Outside
High	3/ 666 /2	2/ 0 /0	1/ 0 /0
Med	6/ 166 /1	2/ 500 /1	14/ 214 /3
Low	3/ 0 /0	2/ 500 /1	3/ 0 /0

Curve Average .500

	Inside	Middle	Outside
High	0/ 0 /0	2/ 500 /1	0/ 0 /0
Med	0/ 0 /0	0/ 0 /0	1/ 1000 /1
Low	0/ 0 /0	0/ 0 /0	1/ 0 /0

Overall Evaluation

Against Right-Handed Pitchers

Overall Fastball: 1 baseball
Overall Curve: 4 baseballs
Overall Slider: 2 baseballs

Against Left-Handed Pitchers

Overall Fastball: 4 baseballs
Overall Curve: 4 baseballs
Overall Slider: 4 baseballs

Comments: Very strong overall against LH.
Strengths: Medium-middle and low-middle fastballs, medium-outside and low-outside curves vs. RH; fastballs except high-outside, outside curves vs. LH.
Weaknesses: High, inside and outside fastballs, low-outside sliders vs. RH; high-outside fastballs vs. LH.

Mike Marshall (Right Handed) *Los Angeles Dodgers*

Mike Marshall Against Right-Handed Pitchers
Overall BARS Batting Average .269

Fastball Average .335

	Inside	Middle	Outside
High	16 / 312 / 5	25 / 280 / 7	18 / 277 / 5
Med	34 / 294 / 10	16 / 437 / 7	61 / 409 / 25
Low	28 / 285 / 8	46 / 391 / 18	30 / 233 / 7

Curve Average .247

	Inside	Middle	Outside
High	1 / 0 / 0	9 / 111 / 1	6 / 166 / 1
Med	6 / 333 / 2	11 / 363 / 4	19 / 315 / 6
Low	5 / 0 / 0	19 / 421 / 8	37 / 162 / 6

Slider Average .227

	Inside	Middle	Outside
High	0 / 0 / 0	2 / 0 / 0	6 / 333 / 2
Med	1 / 0 / 0	1 / 0 / 0	20 / 250 / 5
Low	3 / 0 / 0	15 / 400 / 6	31 / 161 / 5

Mike Marshall Against Left-Handed Pitchers
Overall BARS Batting Average .239

Fastball Average .291

	Inside	Middle	Outside
High	5 / 200 / 1	10 / 400 / 4	10 / 300 / 3
Med	9 / 111 / 1	5 / 200 / 1	16 / 437 / 7
Low	6 / 166 / 1	17 / 529 / 9	18 / 55 / 1

Curve Average .194

	Inside	Middle	Outside
High	0 / 0 / 0	1 / 0 / 0	1 / 0 / 0
Med	3 / 333 / 1	1 / 0 / 0	4 / 250 / 1
Low	15 / 133 / 2	6 / 166 / 1	5 / 400 / 2

Slider Average .200

	Inside	Middle	Outside
High	1 / 0 / 0	1 / 1000 / 1	2 / 500 / 1
Med	5 / 400 / 2	2 / 500 / 1	4 / 0 / 0
Low	11 / 90 / 1	4 / 0 / 0	5 / 200 / 1

Mike Marshall, right-handed hitter, has an excellent .335 overall fastball average against right-handed pitchers. He is strong against all waist-high fastballs.

Notice in Marshall's Ahead and Behind charts on the opposite page that he hits medium-high outside fastballs for an astounding .692 average when behind in the count. When behind, he pulls this pitch to all fields. When ahead, he hits more straightaway and to the right side of the infield. The following strategies and the field diagram on the opposite page show how vital it is for fielders to adjust not only for the type and location of pitch, but for the count.

**MEDIUM-HIGH OUTSIDE FASTBALLS
(WHEN BEHIND IN THE COUNT)**

BATTING AVERAGE .692
Play
Left   Medium-deep and shifted toward the left field line
Center   Deep and shifted toward left field
Right   Deep and shifted toward center field
Short   Shifted toward third base
Second   Normal position

**MEDIUM-HIGH OUTSIDE FASTBALLS
(WHEN AHEAD IN THE COUNT)**

BATTING AVERAGE .333
Play
Left   Deep in straightaway left field

Center   Medium-deep in straightaway center field
Right   Deep and shifted toward center field
Short   Up middle (shifted toward second base)
Second   Shifted toward first base

Marshall's .391 against low-over-the-middle fastballs is also very strong.

LOW-OVER-THE-MIDDLE FASTBALLS

BATTING AVERAGE .391
Play
Left   Medium-deep in straightaway left field
Center   Deep in straightaway center field
Right   Deep and shifted toward center field
Short   Normal position
Second   *No instances recorded*

Marshall has a lot of trouble with low-outside curves thrown by right-handers, although he hits medium-outside curves (.315) and low-over-the-middle curves (.421) excellently. He also has trouble with low-outside sliders, while hitting medium-high outside sliders (.250) and low-over-the-middle sliders (.400) well.

Against left-handed pitchers, Marshall hits medium-high outside fastballs and low-over-the-middle fastballs extremely effectively (.437 and .529). He pulls low-over-the-middle fastballs medium-deep down the left line and into the deep right-center gap.

Medium-High Outside Fastballs

Dark Fielders — Behind In The Count
Light Fielders — Ahead In The Count

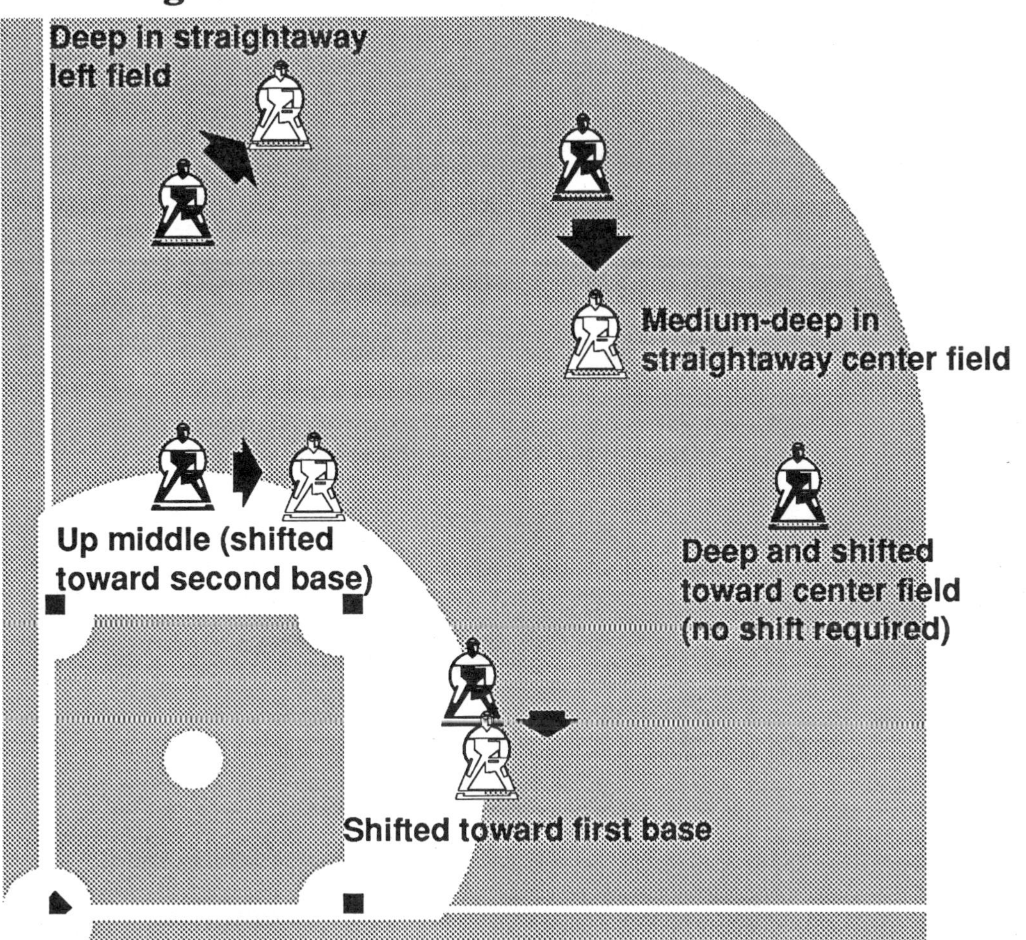

Ahead And Behind In The Count Vs. RH

Ahead

Fastball Average .386

	Inside	Middle	Outside
High	4 / 500 / 2	9 / 222 / 2	5 / 200 / 1
Med	18 / 444 / 8	12 / 416 / 5	24 / 333 / 8
Low	10 / 400 / 4	26 / 500 / 13	11 / 272 / 3

Curve Average .416

	Inside	Middle	Outside
High	0 / 0 / 0	4 / 0 / 0	2 / 500 / 1
Med	2 / 500 / 1	5 / 200 / 1	10 / 600 / 6
Low	0 / 0 / 0	7 / 428 / 3	6 / 500 / 3

Behind

Fastball Average .468

	Inside	Middle	Outside
High	2 / 500 / 1	6 / 500 / 3	5 / 600 / 3
Med	3 / 0 / 0	1 / 1000 / 1	13 / 692 / 9
Low	4 / 250 / 1	7 / 142 / 1	6 / 500 / 3

Curve Average .296

	Inside	Middle	Outside
High	1 / 0 / 0	4 / 250 / 1	0 / 0 / 0
Med	4 / 250 / 1	3 / 666 / 2	2 / 0 / 0
Low	0 / 0 / 0	4 / 750 / 3	9 / 111 / 1

Overall Evaluation

Against Right-Handed Pitchers

Overall Fastball — 4 balls
Overall Curve — 1 ball
Overall Slider — 1 ball

Against Left-Handed Pitchers

Overall Fastball — 2 balls
Overall Curve — 1 ball
Overall Slider — 1 ball

Comments: Weak against low-outside pitches vs. RH.
Strengths: Waist-high, high-inside and low-middle fastballs, waist-high and low-middle curves, low-middle sliders vs. RH; medium-outside fastballs vs. LH.
Weaknesses: Low-outside fastballs, curves and sliders, high-middle curves and medium-outside sliders vs. RH; inside fastballs, low-outside fastballs, low-inside curves and low sliders vs. LH.

Eddie Murray (Switch Hitter)   *Los Angeles Dodgers*

Eddie Murray Against Right-Handed Pitchers
Overall BARS Batting Average .287

Fastball Average .310

	Outside	Middle	Inside
High	49/ 163/8	35/ 285/10	16/ 250/4
Med	221/ 321/71	48/ 562/27	77/ 220/17
Low	41/ 219/9	62/ 338/21	40/ 400/16

Curve Average .238

	Outside	Middle	Inside
High	11/ 363/4	11/ 454/5	3/ 333/1
Med	40/ 275/11	11/ 272/3	16/ 125/2
Low	11/ 272/3	31/ 129/4	13/ 153/2

Slider Average .290

	Outside	Middle	Inside
High	5/ 600/3	4/ 500/2	2/ 500/1
Med	6/ 333/2	4/ 0/0	8/ 375/3
Low	4/ 0/0	10/ 200/2	12/ 250/3

Eddie Murray Against Left-Handed Pitchers
Overall BARS Batting Average .303

Fastball Average .298

	Inside	Middle	Outside
High	16/ 125/2	20/ 250/5	20/ 200/4
Med	23/ 391/9	21/ 380/8	111/ 297/33
Low	11/ 181/2	23/ 478/11	20/ 250/5

Curve Average .367

	Inside	Middle	Outside
High	3/ 0/0	6/ 333/2	4/ 0/0
Med	2/ 500/1	8/ 500/4	27/ 444/12
Low	6/ 333/2	15/ 400/6	8/ 250/2

Slider Average .371

	Inside	Middle	Outside
High	1/ 0/0	2/ 0/0	1/ 0/0
Med	9/ 555/5	4/ 500/2	13/ 307/4
Low	3/ 333/1	1/ 1000/1	1/ 0/0

Murray's .310 overall fastball average against right-handed pitchers is good but his .238 overall curve average is mediocre. His .298 overall fastball average against left-handed pitchers is respectable; his .367 overall curve average and .371 overall slider averages are outstanding.

Hitting left-handed against right-handers, Murray goes deep down both lines with medium-high outside fastballs.

MEDIUM-HIGH OUTSIDE FASTBALLS

BATTING AVERAGE .321
Play

Left	Deep and shifted toward the left field line
Center	Medium-deep in straightaway center field
Right	Deep and shifted toward the right field line
Short	Up middle (shifted toward second base)
Second	Normal position

Although a pitcher would not want to throw Murray a medium-over-the-middle fastball (.562), it is interesting to note that the BARS fielding strategy for this type of pitch is almost exactly similar to the above strategy for a medium-high outside fastball. The only difference is that the center fielder needs to play deep instead of of medium-deep.

Murray also hits low-inside fastballs well (.400). He hits these pitches deep into the left-center gap and deep down the right field line.

LOW-INSIDE FASTBALLS

BATTING AVERAGE .400
Play

Left	Deep in straightaway left field
Center	Deep and shifted toward left field
Right	Deep and shifted toward the right field line
Short	Up middle (shifted toward second base)
Second	Shifted toward first base

His fastball weaknesses are medium-high inside (.220), low-outside (.219) and high-outside (.163). He hits medium-high inside fastballs deep down the left line and straightaway to the other fields.

Murray hits outside curves fairly well against right-handers (.363, .275 and .272, high to low) but he has considerable trouble with low-over-the-middle, low-inside and medium-high inside curves. He hits medium-high outside curves deep down the left line and into the right-center gap.

MEDIUM-HIGH OUTSIDE CURVEBALLS

BATTING AVERAGE .275
Play

Left	Deep and shifted toward the left field line
Center	Medium-deep in straightaway center field
Right	Deep and shifted toward center field
Short	Up middle (shifted toward second base)
Second	Shifted toward first base

He hits high-outside curves deep down both lines.

HIGH-OUTSIDE CURVEBALLS

BATTING AVERAGE .363
Play

Left	Deep and shifted toward the left field line
Center	Deep and shifted toward left field
Right	Deep and shifted toward the right field line
Short	Normal position
Second	Shifted toward first base

Murray Against Left-Handed Pitchers

Hitting right-handed against left-handed pitchers, Murray has distinct strong and weak fastball locations. His .478 against low-over-the-middle fastballs is outstanding, as is his .391 against medium-high inside fastballs. His .297 against medium-high outside is also fairly strong, but his .181, .125, .200 and .250 in the four fastball corners are weak.

He hits medium-high outside fastballs straightaway against left-handers.

MEDIUM-HIGH OUTSIDE FASTBALLS
(THROWN BY LEFT-HANDED PITCHERS)

BATTING AVERAGE .297
Play

Left	Deep in straightaway left field
Center	Deep in straightaway center field
Right	Medium-deep in straightaway right field
Short	Up middle (shifted toward second base)
Second	Normal position

Every fielder is required to shift for medium-high inside as compared to medium-high outside fastballs thrown by left-handed pitchers.

He hits low-over-the-middle fastballs much differently.

LOW-OVER-THE-MIDDLE FASTBALLS
(THROWN BY LEFT-HANDED PITCHERS)

BATTING AVERAGE .478
Play

Left	Deep and shifted toward the left field line
Center	Medium-deep in straightaway center field
Right	Deep in straightaway right field
Short	Normal position
Short	Up middle (shifted toward second base)

Against left-handers, Murray hits curves very well overall. He hits medium-high outside curves extremely well (.444).

MEDIUM-HIGH OUTSIDE CURVEBALLS
(THROWN BY LEFT-HANDED PITCHERS)

BATTING AVERAGE .444
Play

Left	Medium-deep in straightaway left field
Center	Deep in straightaway center field
Right	Deep and shifted toward the right field line
Short	Normal position
Second	Normal position

Ahead And Behind In The Count Vs. RH

Ahead

Fastball Average .339

	Outside	Middle	Inside
High	18/166 /3	14/142 /2	4/0 /0
Med	95/336 /32	30/533 /16	42/190 /8
Low	12/416 /5	34/441 /15	19/526 /10

Curve Average .228

	Outside	Middle	Inside
High	4/250 /1	7/571 /1	1/0 /0
Med	13/76 /1	5/400 /2	8/125 /1
Low	3/333 /1	11/181 /2	5/200 /1

Behind

Fastball Average .349

	Outside	Middle	Inside
High	10/200 /2	5/400 /2	7/428 /3
Med	42/428 /18	4/750 /3	15/400 /6
Low	8/250 /2	7/0 /0	5/0 /0

Curve Average .361

	Outside	Middle	Inside
High	4/250 /1	2/500 /1	0/0 /0
Med	13/538 /7	3/333 /1	4/0 /0
Low	3/666 /2	5/200 /1	2/0 /0

Overall Evaluation
Against Right-Handed Pitchers

Overall Fastball	⚾⚾⚾
Overall Curve	⚾
Overall Slider	⚾⚾

Against Left-Handed Pitchers

Overall Fastball	⚾⚾
Overall Curve	⚾⚾⚾⚾
Overall Slider	⚾⚾⚾⚾

Comments: Hits fastballs well against RH and LH but hits curves and sliders better against LH.

Strengths: Medium-outside, low-middle, medium-middle and low-inside fastballs vs. RH; waist-high and low-middle fastballs vs. LH, medium-outside curves and sliders vs. LH.

Weaknesses: Low- and high-outside fastballs vs. RH, low and inside curves vs. RH; the four fastball corners vs. LH.

Willie Randolph (Right Handed) *Los Angeles Dodgers*

Willie Randolph Against Right-Handed Pitchers
Overall BARS Batting Average .242

Fastball Average .264

	Inside	Middle	Outside
High	16 / 312 / 5	52 / 307 / 16	14 / 285 / 4
Med	64 / 296 / 19	40 / 425 / 17	159 / 238 / 38
Low	13 / 153 / 2	80 / 275 / 22	58 / 137 / 8

Curve Average .204

	Inside	Middle	Outside
High	0 / 0 / 0	4 / 250 / 1	1 / 0 / 0
Med	8 / 0 / 0	9 / 111 / 1	22 / 318 / 7
Low	0 / 0 / 0	13 / 230 / 3	26 / 192 / 5

Slider Average .206

	Inside	Middle	Outside
High	4 / 250 / 1	4 / 250 / 1	1 / 0 / 0
Med	6 / 0 / 0	8 / 0 / 0	27 / 296 / 8
Low	4 / 0 / 0	12 / 333 / 4	31 / 193 / 6

Willie Randolph Against Left-Handed Pitchers
Overall BARS Batting Average .295

Fastball Average .326

	Inside	Middle	Outside
High	6 / 666 / 4	20 / 300 / 6	14 / 428 / 6
Med	26 / 307 / 8	29 / 413 / 12	85 / 270 / 23
Low	15 / 333 / 5	51 / 352 / 18	42 / 285 / 12

Curve Average .265

	Inside	Middle	Outside
High	0 / 0 / 0	1 / 0 / 0	2 / 0 / 0
Med	7 / 285 / 2	7 / 714 / 5	9 / 222 / 2
Low	6 / 0 / 0	9 / 222 / 2	8 / 250 / 2

Slider Average .208

	Inside	Middle	Outside
High	0 / 0 / 0	1 / 1000 / 1	2 / 500 / 1
Med	6 / 333 / 2	0 / 0 / 0	5 / 200 / 1
Low	3 / 0 / 0	1 / 0 / 0	6 / 0 / 0

Willie Randolph has trouble against right-handed pitchers. His .264 overall fastball average is low, and his curve and slider averages of .204 and .206 respectively show profound weaknesses. Nevertheless, he has at least one strong location in each of these charts.

His fastball strengths are medium-over-the-middle (.425), high-inside (.312) and high-over-the-middle (.307). He has weaknesses in the highly pitched medium-high outside and low-outside fastball locations (.238 and .137 respectively).

One of Randolph's stronger overall fastball locations is high-over-the-middle (.307). Notice in the Ahead and Behind grids at the bottom of the opposite page that he hits .266 in this location when behind, .434 when ahead.

The charts below show how differently fielders need to play for this pitch when he is ahead and behind.

MEDIUM-HIGH OUTSIDE FASTBALLS

BATTING AVERAGE .238
Play

Left	Deep and shifted toward center field
Center	Medium-deep in straightaway center field
Right	Medium-deep in straightaway right field
Short	Up middle (shifted toward second base)
Second	Normal position

LOW-OUTSIDE FASTBALLS

BATTING AVERAGE .137
Play

Left	*No instances recorded*
Center	Deep and shifted toward right field
Right	Deep in straightaway right field
Short	Normal position
Second	Normal position

HIGH-OVER-THE-MIDDLE FASTBALLS (WHEN RANDOLPH IS BEHIND IN THE COUNT)

BATTING AVERAGE .266
Play

Left	Medium-deep and shifted toward the left field line
Center	Deep and shifted toward left field
Right	Deep and shifted toward the right field line
Short	Normal position
Second	Normal position

HIGH-OVER-THE-MIDDLE FASTBALLS (WHEN RANDOLPH IS AHEAD IN THE COUNT)

BATTING AVERAGE .434
Play

Left	Deep and shifted toward the left field line
Center	Deep and shifted toward right field
Right	Medium-deep in straightaway right field
Short	Up middle (shifted toward second base)
Second	Shifted toward first base

Randolph Against Curves And Sliders

Randolph has many curve and slider weaknesses. He does, however, hit these two pitches well in the medium-high outside locations (.318 against curves, .296 against sliders). He has weaknesses in both low-outside locations.

The differences in fielding strategy required when Randolph is thrown low-outside curves and medium-high outside curves emphasize the necessity for fielders to adjust on every pitch.

LOW-OUTSIDE CURVEBALLS

BATTING AVERAGE .192
Play

Left	Medium-deep and shifted toward the left field line
Center	Deep in straightaway center field
Right	Deep and shifted toward center field
Short	Up middle (shifted toward second base)
Second	*No instances recorded*

MEDIUM-HIGH OUTSIDE CURVEBALLS

BATTING AVERAGE .318
Play

Left	Medium-deep and shifted toward the left field line
Center	Medium-deep in straightaway center field
Right	Deep in straightaway right field
Short	Normal position
Second	Shifted toward first base

Randolph Against Left-Handed Pitchers

Randolph has an excellent overall fastball average against left-handers (.326). His chart does not have what could be called a truly weak fastball location. The closest would be his medium-high outside location (.270). He hits very strongly in the high-outside (.428), low-over-the-middle (.352) and medium-over-the-middle (.413) fastball locations.

He hits low-over-the-middle fastballs deep to straightaway left, medium-deep to straightaway center, and into the right-center gap.

LOW-OVER-THE-MIDDLE FASTBALLS
(THROWN BY LEFT-HANDED PITCHERS)

BATTING AVERAGE .352
Play

Left	Deep in straightaway left field
Center	Medium-deep in straightaway center field
Right	Deep and shifted toward center field
Short	Normal position
Second	*No instances recorded*

He hits medium-high outside fastballs deep to all fields.

MEDIUM-HIGH OUTSIDE FASTBALLS
(THROWN BY LEFT-HANDED PITCHERS)

BATTING AVERAGE .270
Play

Left	Deep and shifted toward center field
Center	Deep in straightaway center field
Right	Deep in straightaway right field
Short	Up middle (shifted toward second base)
Second	Normal position

Ahead And Behind In The Count Vs. RH

Ahead

Fastball Average .313

	Inside	Middle	Outside
High	3/ 333/1	23/ 434/10	8/ 375/3
Med	26/ 346/9	22/ 545/12	90/ 288/26
Low	4/ 250/1	44/ 250/11	26/ 153/4

Curve Average .352

	Inside	Middle	Outside
High	0/ 0/0	0/ 0/0	0/ 0/0
Med	2/ 0/0	2/ 0/0	5/ 400/2
Low	0/ 0/0	3/ 666/2	5/ 100/2

Behind

Fastball Average .266

	Inside	Middle	Outside
High	6/ 500/3	15/ 266/4	5/ 200/1
Med	11/ 363/4	3/ 333/1	27/ 222/6
Low	3/ 0/0	11/ 272/3	9/ 222/2

Curve Average .166

	Inside	Middle	Outside
High	0/ 0/0	4/ 250/1	0/ 0/0
Med	4/ 0/0	5/ 0/0	8/ 375/3
Low	0/ 0/0	5/ 0/0	10/ 200/2

Overall Evaluation

Against Right-Handed Pitchers

Overall Fastball	(1 ball)
Overall Curve	(1 ball)
Overall Slider	(1 ball)

Against Left-Handed Pitchers

Overall Fastball	(4 balls)
Overall Curve	(2 balls)
Overall Slider	(1 ball)

Comments: Has problems against curves and sliders. Hits fastballs excellently against LH.

Strengths: Medium-middle fastballs, medium-outside curves and medium-outside sliders vs. RH; high-outside, low-inside, medium-middle and low-over-the-middle fastballs vs. LH.

Weaknesses: Low and outside fastballs vs. RH, low-outside curves and sliders vs. RH; medium-outside fastballs vs. LH, all outside and low curves vs. LH.

Mike Scioscia Against Right-Handed Pitchers
Overall BARS Batting Average .262

Fastball Average .319

	Outside	Middle	Inside
High	34 / 235 / 8	39 / 256 / 10	21 / 380 / 8
Med	73 / 301 / 22	9 / 555 / 5	41 / 439 / 18
Low	21 / 190 / 4	44 / 431 / 19	22 / 136 / 3

Curve Average .158

	Outside	Middle	Inside
High	1 / 0 / 0	8 / 125 / 1	2 / 0 / 0
Med	12 / 250 / 3	4 / 250 / 1	7 / 285 / 2
Low	6 / 0 / 0	16 / 187 / 3	7 / 0 / 0

Slider Average .166

	Outside	Middle	Inside
High	1 / 0 / 0	1 / 0 / 0	6 / 166 / 1
Med	2 / 0 / 0	0 / 0 / 0	5 / 200 / 1
Low	1 / 1000 / 1	7 / 142 / 1	7 / 142 / 1

Mike Scioscia Against Left-Handed Pitchers
Overall BARS Batting Average .198

Fastball Average .271

	Outside	Middle	Inside
High	2 / 500 / 1	10 / 400 / 4	4 / 250 / 1
Med	14 / 357 / 5	2 / 500 / 1	23 / 173 / 4
Low	4 / 250 / 1	4 / 250 / 1	7 / 142 / 1

Curve Average .066

	Outside	Middle	Inside
High	0 / 0 / 0	1 / 0 / 0	0 / 0 / 0
Med	5 / 0 / 0	0 / 0 / 0	2 / 0 / 0
Low	5 / 0 / 0	2 / 500 / 1	0 / 0 / 0

Slider Average .083

	Outside	Middle	Inside
High	0 / 0 / 0	3 / 333 / 1	1 / 0 / 0
Med	3 / 0 / 0	1 / 0 / 0	1 / 0 / 0
Low	2 / 0 / 0	0 / 0 / 0	1 / 0 / 0

Left-handed hitter Mike Scioscia has a strong .319 overall fastball average against right-handed pitchers. He has areas of weakness, but these are offset by areas of great strength. He hits medium-outside fastballs fairly well (.301).

MEDIUM-HIGH OUTSIDE FASTBALLS

BATTING AVERAGE .301

Play

Left	Medium-deep in straightaway left field
Center	Deep in straightaway center field
Right	Deep and shifted toward center field
Short	Up middle (shifted toward second base)
Second	Shifted toward first base

He hits an excellent .439 against medium-high inside fastballs. The following strategy and the field diagram on the opposite page show how fielders need to be positioned for this pitch.

MEDIUM-HIGH INSIDE FASTBALLS

BATTING AVERAGE .439

Play

Left	Medium-deep in straightaway left field
Center	Deep and shifted toward left field
Right	Deep and shifted toward the right field line
Short	Up middle (shifted toward second base)
Second	Normal position

His .431 against low-over-the-middle fastballs is also extremely strong.

LOW-OVER-THE-MIDDLE FASTBALLS

BATTING AVERAGE .431

Play

Left	Medium-deep in straightaway left field
Center	Medium-deep and shifted toward left field
Right	Deep in straightaway right field
Short	Up middle (shifted toward second base)
Second	Shifted toward first base

Scioscia's fastball weaknesses are high-outside (.235), high-middle (.256), low-outside (.190) and low-inside (.136). He has a lot of trouble against all outside and low curves thrown by right-handers.

Against left-handed pitchers, Scioscia has weaknesses in his inside fastball locations (.250, .173 and .142, high to low). The fact that there are more recorded inside than outside fastball instances shows that left-handers are aware of his troubles with these pitches. He does, however, hit medium-high outside fastballs very well against left-handers (.357).

MEDIUM-HIGH OUTSIDE FASTBALLS
(THROWN BY LEFT-HANDED PITCHERS)

BATTING AVERAGE .357

Play

Left	Short and shifted toward the left field line
Center	Deep and shifted toward left field
Right	Deep and shifted toward center field
Short	Up middle (shifted toward second base)
Second	Normal position

Medium-High Inside Fastballs

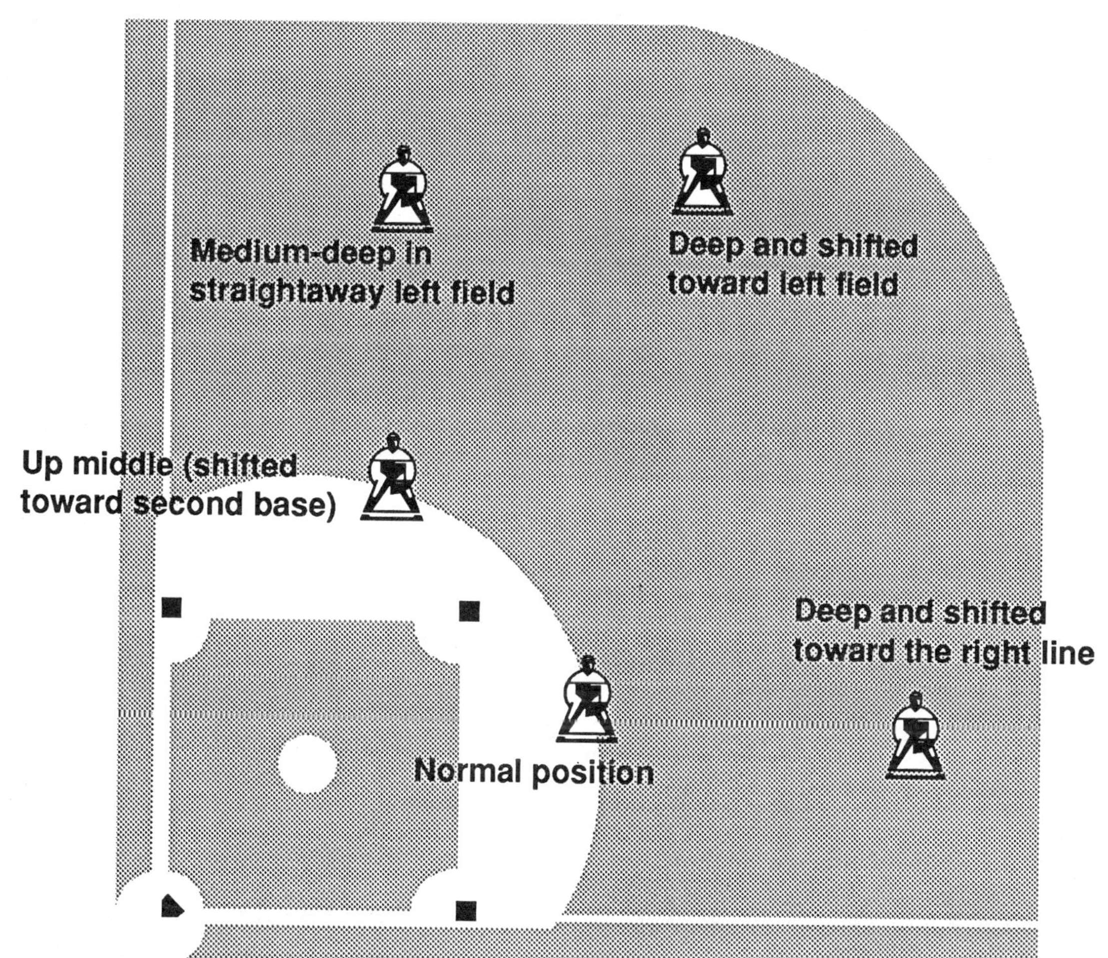

Ahead And Behind In The Count Vs. RH

Ahead

	Fastball Average .335			Curve Average .153		
	Outside	Middle	Inside	Outside	Middle	Inside
High	14/ **285** / 4	19/ **263** / 5	8/ **375** / 3	0/ **0** / 0	1/ **0** / 0	1/ **0** / 0
Mod	42/ **333** / 14	6/ **333** / 2	16/ **500** / 8	1/ **0** / 0	1/ **0** / 0	4/ **250** / 1
Low	10/ **100** / 1	27/ **407** / 11	7/ **285** / 2	0/ **0** / 0	5/ **200** / 1	0/ **0** / 0

Behind

	Fastball Average .360			Curve Average .214		
	Outside	Middle	Inside	Outside	Middle	Inside
High	7/ **285** / 2	12/ **333** / 4	4/ **500** / 2	1/ **0** / 0	3/ **0** / 0	1/ **0** / 0
Med	12/ **500** / 6	2/ **1000** / 2	9/ **222** / 2	4/ **500** / 2	2/ **500** / 1	2/ **500** / 1
Low	3/ **333** / 1	6/ **333** / 2	6/ **166** / 1	5/ **0** / 0	6/ **333** / 2	4/ **0** / 0

Overall Evaluation

Against Right-Handed Pitchers

Overall Fastball	⚾ ⚾ ⚾
Overall Curve	⚾
Overall Slider	⚾

Against Left-Handed Pitchers

Overall Fastball	⚾
Overall Curve	⚾
Overall Slider	Not enough information

Comments: Weak vs. outside and low curves vs. RH.

Strengths: Waist-high, high-inside and low-middle fastballs vs. RH; medium-outside and high-middle fastballs vs. LH.

Weaknesses: High-outside and high-middle fastballs, low-outside and low-inside fastballs, outside curves and low curves, inside sliders vs. RH; low and inside fastballs, outside curves vs. LH.

John Shelby (Switch Hitter) — Los Angeles Dodgers

John Shelby Against Right-Handed Pitchers
Overall BARS Batting Average .206

Fastball Average .230

	Outside	Middle	Inside
High	38 / 210 / 8	33 / 212 / 7	8 / 250 / 2
Med	95 / 210 / 20	29 / 275 / 8	28 / 250 / 7
Low	16 / 187 / 3	41 / 317 / 13	16 / 125 / 2

Curve Average .190

	Outside	Middle	Inside
High	5 / 600 / 3	2 / 0 / 0	1 / 0 / 0
Med	18 / 166 / 3	7 / 285 / 2	6 / 166 / 1
Low	8 / 0 / 0	10 / 300 / 3	6 / 0 / 0

Slider Average .212

	Outside	Middle	Inside
High	0 / 0 / 0	0 / 0 / 0	2 / 0 / 0
Med	7 / 428 / 3	0 / 0 / 0	6 / 500 / 3
Low	0 / 0 / 0	5 / 200 / 1	13 / 0 / 0

John Shelby Against Left-Handed Pitchers
Overall BARS Batting Average .203

Fastball Average .229

	Inside	Middle	Outside
High	7 / 0 / 0	14 / 214 / 3	17 / 117 / 2
Med	9 / 222 / 2	15 / 466 / 7	48 / 354 / 17
Low	11 / 181 / 2	24 / 125 / 3	12 / 0 / 0

Curve Average .214

	Inside	Middle	Outside
High	1 / 0 / 0	1 / 0 / 0	4 / 500 / 2
Med	2 / 0 / 0	2 / 500 / 1	11 / 363 / 4
Low	5 / 0 / 0	11 / 181 / 2	5 / 0 / 0

Slider Average .076

	Inside	Middle	Outside
High	0 / 0 / 0	0 / 0 / 0	0 / 0 / 0
Med	2 / 0 / 0	4 / 0 / 0	3 / 0 / 0
Low	7 / 285 / 2	7 / 0 / 0	3 / 0 / 0

Switch-hitting John Shelby has low fastball averages against both right- and left-handed pitchers (.230 overall against right-handers, .229 overall against left-handers). He has only one strong fastball location against right-handers (.317 low-over-the-middle). He hits this pitch deep and straightaway to all fields.

LOW-OVER-THE-MIDDLE FASTBALLS

BATTING AVERAGE .317

Play

Left	Deep in straightaway left field
Center	Deep in straightaway center field
Right	Deep in straightaway right field
Short	Normal position
Second	Normal position

His .210 against medium-high outside fastballs is weak. His low average indicates that most of his hit balls from this location are probably easy outs.

MEDIUM-HIGH OUTSIDE FASTBALLS

BATTING AVERAGE .210

Play

Left	Deep and shifted toward the left field line
Center	Deep in straightaway center field
Right	Deep and shifted toward center field
Short	Up middle (shifted toward second base)
Second	Shifted toward first base

Shelby is weak against curves and sliders thrown by right-handers. His .166 medium-high outside curve and .000 low-outside curve averages are poor. He hits .300 against low-over-the-middle curves, however.

His 0-for-13 against low-inside sliders is an additional target for right-handers.

Shelby Against Left-Handed Pitchers

Against left-handed pitchers, Shelby hits medium-high outside fastballs excellently (.354). By positioning themselves according to the following fielding strategy and the field diagram on the opposite page, fielders could prevent most of Shelby's hits from this location.

MEDIUM-HIGH OUTSIDE FASTBALLS (THROWN BY LEFT-HANDED PITCHERS)

BATTING AVERAGE .354

Play

Left	Deep in straightaway left field
Center	Medium-deep in straightaway center field
Right	Medium-deep in straightaway right field
Short	Normal position
Second	Normal position

Shelby is weak against low curves (.000, .181 and .000, inside to outside). He hits medium-high outside curves very well against lefties (.363).

Medium-High Outside Fastballs Vs. LH

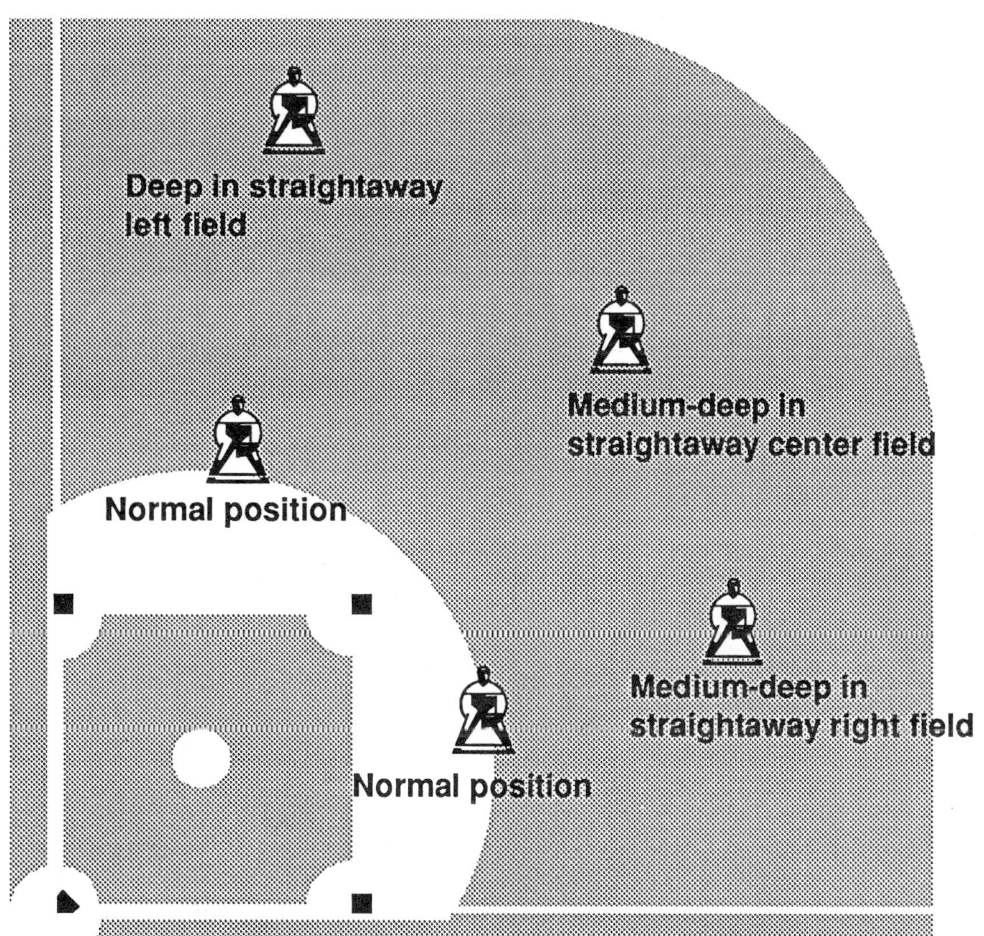

Ahead And Behind In The Count Vs. RH

Ahead

Fastball Average .280

	Outside	Middle	Inside
High	12/ 333 / 4	9/ 111 / 1	4/ 250 / 1
Med	42/ 261 / 11	13/ 153 / 2	14/ 357 / 5
Low	9/ 333 / 3	22/ 409 / 9	7/ 142 / 1

Curve Average .285

	Outside	Middle	Inside
High	0/ 0 / 0	0/ 0 / 0	0/ 0 / 0
Med	4/ 0 / 0	2/ 500 / 1	2/ 500 / 1
Low	2/ 0 / 0	3/ 666 / 2	1/ 0 / 0

Behind

Fastball Average .380

	Outside	Middle	Inside
High	7/ 428 / 3	5/ 200 / 1	3/ 333 / 1
Med	12/ 250 / 3	4/ 1000 / 4	2/ 500 / 1
Low	0/ 0 / 0	8/ 375 / 3	1/ 0 / 0

Curve Average .250

	Outside	Middle	Inside
High	3/ 666 / 2	0/ 0 / 0	1/ 0 / 0
Med	6/ 333 / 2	2/ 0 / 0	3/ 0 / 0
Low	0/ 0 / 0	1/ 0 / 0	0/ 0 / 0

Overall Evaluation

Against Right-Handed Pitchers

Overall Fastball ⚾⚾
Overall Curve ⚾⚾
Overall Slider ⚾

Against Left-Handed Pitchers

Overall Fastball ⚾
Overall Curve ⚾⚾
Overall Slider ⚾⚾

Comments: Weak against all outside and all high fastballs vs. RH.

Strengths: Low-middle fastballs, low-middle curves, medium-outside and medium-inside sliders vs. RH; medium-middle and medium-outside fastballs, medium-outside curves vs. LH.

Weaknesses: High, outside and inside fastballs, curves in general, low sliders vs. RH; high, inside and low fastballs, low curves vs. LH.

Franklin Stubbs Against Right-Handed Pitchers
Overall BARS Batting Average .221

Fastball Average .240

	Outside	Middle	Inside
High	17/117 /2	22/227 /5	12/0 /0
Med	60/350 /21	7/571 /4	20/200 /4
Low	19/157 /3	28/321 /9	19/52 /1

Curve Average .250

	Outside	Middle	Inside
High	3/333 /1	0/0 /0	1/0 /0
Med	6/500 /3	0/0 /0	6/500 /3
Low	4/0 /0	5/0 /0	7/142 /1

Slider Average .250

	Outside	Middle	Inside
High	0/0 /0	0/0 /0	2/500 /1
Med	1/0 /0	0/0 /0	3/333 /1
Low	0/0 /0	0/0 /0	6/166 /1

Franklin Stubbs Against Left-Handed Pitchers
Overall BARS Batting Average .218

Fastball Average .163

	Outside	Middle	Inside
High	2/500 /1	7/142 /1	7/142 /1
Med	18/111 /2	1/1000 /1	8/125 /1
Low	2/0 /0	7/285 /2	3/0 /0

Curve Average .421

	Outside	Middle	Inside
High	2/1000 /2	0/0 /0	0/0 /0
Med	4/500 /2	1/0 /0	4/250 /1
Low	4/250 /1	2/500 /1	2/500 /1

Slider Average .285

	Outside	Middle	Inside
High	0/0 /0	0/0 /0	0/0 /0
Med	4/250 /1	0/0 /0	0/0 /0
Low	2/500 /1	0/0 /0	1/0 /0

Franklin Stubbs, left-handed hitter, has low overall fastball averages against both right- and left-handed pitchers. He does, however, have some strong fastball locations against right-handed pitchers. He hits an excellent .350 in his medium-high outside fastball location. He hits this pitch deep to all fields.

MEDIUM-HIGH OUTSIDE FASTBALLS

BATTING AVERAGE .350
Play

Left	Deep and shifted toward center field
Center	Deep in straightaway center field
Right	Deep in straightaway right field
Short	Up middle (shifted toward second base)
Second	Normal position

Stubbs hits .321 against low-over-the-middle fastballs thrown by right-handers. Stubbs's fielding strategy is very unusual for this pitch. The following strategy and the field diagram on the opposite page show that Stubbs hits to a sector in center field. Proper positioning of the fielders could prevent most of his base hits resulting from this pitch.

LOW-OVER-THE-MIDDLE FASTBALLS

BATTING AVERAGE .321
Play

Left	Short and shifted toward center field
Center	Deep in straightaway center field
Right	Medium-deep and shifted toward center field
Short	Up middle (shifted toward second base)
Second	Shifted toward first base

Stubbs is very weak against high fastballs and inside fastballs thrown by right-handers. These weak locations offer wide targets for pitchers to focus on.

He is also weak against low curves thrown by right-handers. He has trouble getting his bat on the ball when pitches are thrown to his low curve locations.

Stubbs Against Left-Handed Pitchers

Stubbs has problems with fastballs thrown by left-handed pitchers. His .111 against medium-high outside fastballs is very weak. His low average indicates that most of his hit balls in this location are probably easy pop flies or ground outs.

MEDIUM-HIGH OUTSIDE FASTBALLS
(THROWN BY LEFT-HANDED PITCHERS)

BATTING AVERAGE .111
Play

Left	Deep and shifted toward the left field line
Center	*No instances recorded*
Right	Medium-deep in straightaway right field
Short	Shifted toward third base
Second	Shifted toward first base

Low-Over-The-Middle Fastballs

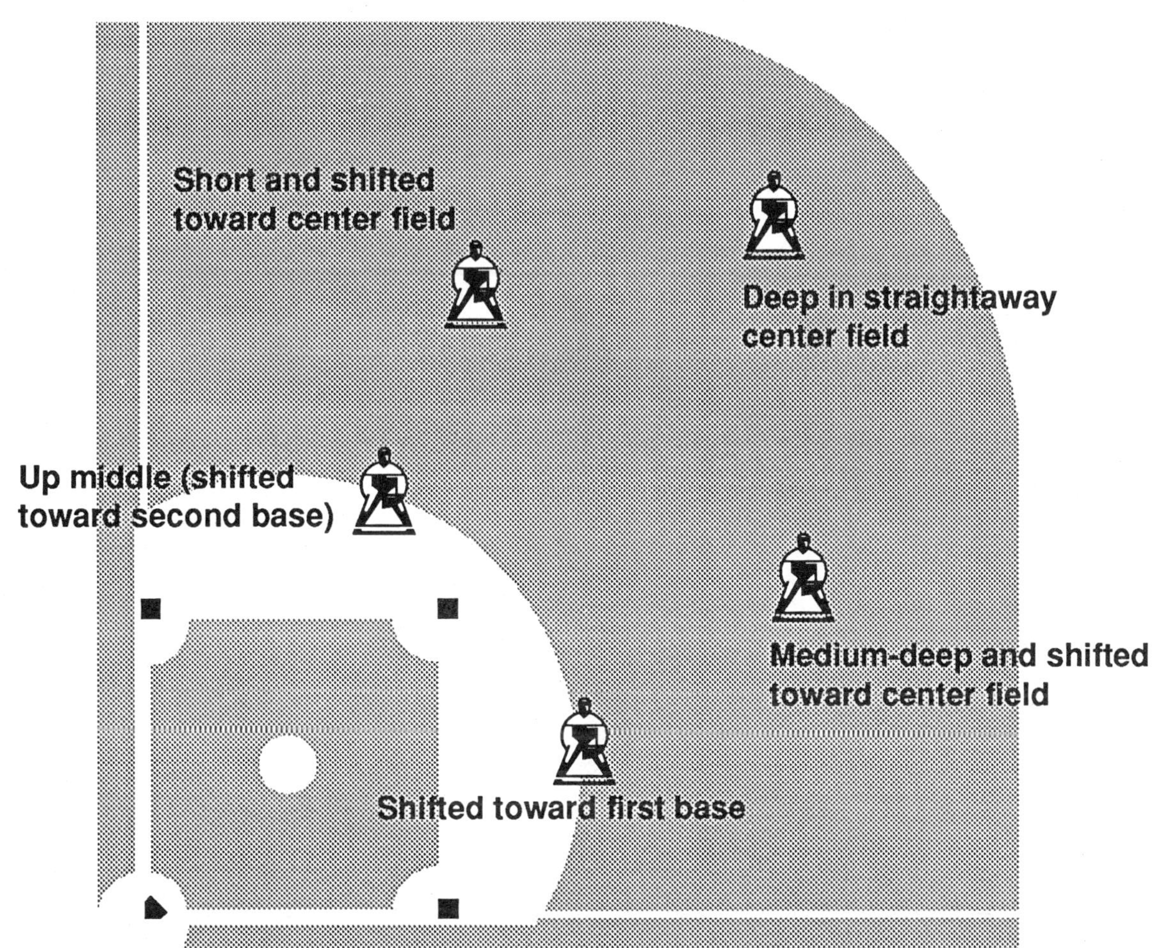

Ahead And Behind In The Count Vs. RH

Ahead

Fastball Average .333

	Outside	Middle	Inside
High	4/250 /1	3/333 /1	2/0 /0
Med	29/370 /11	4/500 /2	6/333 /2
Low	5/400 /2	13/307 /4	6/166 /1

Curve Average .444

	Outside	Middle	Inside
High	2/500 /1	0/0 /0	0/0 /0
Med	0/0 /0	0/0 /0	4/500 /2
Low	0/0 /0	2/0 /0	1/1000 /1

Behind

Fastball Average .187

	Outside	Middle	Inside
High	3/0 /0	3/666 /2	1/0 /0
Med	10/100 /1	0/0 /0	4/250 /1
Low	4/0 /0	4/500 /2	3/0 /0

Curve Average .333

	Outside	Middle	Inside
High	0/0 /0	0/0 /0	0/0 /0
Med	2/500 /1	0/0 /0	2/500 /1
Low	0/0 /0	0/0 /0	2/0 /0

Overall Evaluation

Against Right-Handed Pitchers

Overall Fastball	⚾
Overall Curve	⚾ ⚾
Overall Slider	⚾ ⚾

Against Left-Handed Pitchers

Overall Fastball	⚾
Overall Curve	⚾ ⚾ ⚾ ⚾
Overall Slider	⚾ ⚾ ⚾

Comments: Strong vs. medium-outside fastballs vs. RH.

Strengths: Medium-outside, medium-middle and low-middle fastballs vs. RH.

Weaknesses: High, inside, and low-outside fastballs, low curves vs. RH; medium-outside and all inside fastballs vs. LH.

  # *San Diego Padres*

Clark, Jack
Flannery, Tim
Gwynn, Tony
Kruk, John
Martinez, Carmelo
Ready, Randy
Santiago, Benito
Templeton, Garry
Wynne, Marvell

San Diego Padres
BARS System
Hitting Analysis

Jack Clark Against Right-Handed Pitchers
Overall BARS Batting Average .271

Fastball Average .318

	Inside	Middle	Outside
High	20/150/3	41/292/12	23/304/7
Med	27/370/10	20/650/13	75/333/25
Low	8/0/0	47/382/18	34/176/6

Curve Average .206

	Inside	Middle	Outside
High	1/0/0	4/250/1	1/0/0
Med	7/285/2	5/0/0	25/280/7
Low	5/200/1	12/250/3	32/156/5

Slider Average .303

	Inside	Middle	Outside
High	0/0/0	5/200/1	6/500/3
Med	2/500/1	1/1000/1	23/304/7
Low	0/0/0	8/250/2	21/238/5

Jacl Clark Against Left-Handed Pitchers
Overall BARS Batting Average .294

Fastball Average .396

	Inside	Middle	Outside
High	2/0/0	11/363/4	13/307/4
Med	6/166/1	7/571/4	28/428/12
Low	3/0/0	18/555/10	18/388/7

Curve Average .235

	Inside	Middle	Outside
High	0/0/0	2/500/1	6/166/1
Med	1/1000/1	3/333/1	6/166/1
Low	3/0/0	4/500/2	9/111/1

Slider Average .055

	Inside	Middle	Outside
High	1/0/0	2/0/0	0/0/0
Med	2/0/0	0/0/0	1/0/0
Low	7/142/1	4/0/0	1/0/0

Right-handed hitter Jack Clark hits fastballs at a .318 clip against right-handed pitchers. Against left-handed pitchers he hits a sparkling .396 against fastballs.

Starting with his performance against right-handers, he hits an excellent .333 against medium-high outside fastballs. His Ahead and Behind Charts on the opposite page show that he hits this pitch better when ahead in the count (.481 when ahead, .227 when behind). Notice that Clark tends to hit this pitch deep into the left-center and right-center gaps when he is ahead and straightaway when he is behind. This shows the necessity of aligning fielders for the count of the pitch as well as for the type and location of pitch.

**MEDIUM-HIGH OUTSIDE FASTBALLS
(WHEN AHEAD IN THE COUNT)**

BATTING AVERAGE .481
Play
Left	Deep in straightaway left field
Center	Deep and shifted toward left field
Right	Deep and shifted toward center field
Short	Normal position
Second	Normal position

**MEDIUM-HIGH OUTSIDE FASTBALLS
(WHEN BEHIND IN THE COUNT)**

BATTING AVERAGE .227
Play

Left	Medium-deep in straightaway left field
Center	Deep in straightaway center field
Right	Deep in straightaway right field
Short	Normal position
Second	Normal position

He hits low-over-the-middle fastballs for a strong .382 average. He hits this pitch deep into the left- and right-center gaps.

LOW-OVER-THE-MIDDLE FASTBALLS

BATTING AVERAGE .382
Play
Left	Deep in straightaway left field
Center	Deep and shifted toward left field
Right	Deep and shifted toward center field
Short	Normal position
Second	Normal position

He hits medium-high inside fastballs (.370) into the left-center gap and down the right field line.

MEDIUM-HIGH INSIDE FASTBALLS

BATTING AVERAGE .370
Play
Left	Medium-deep in straightaway left field
Center	Medium-deep and shifted toward left field
Right	Deep and shifted toward the right field line
Short	Shifted toward third base
Second	Shifted toward first base

Clark has an exceptional .650 average against medium-over-the-middle fastballs.

MEDIUM-OVER-THE-MIDDLE FASTBALLS

BATTING AVERAGE .650
Play

Left	Deep and shifted toward the left field line
Center	Deep and shifted toward left field
Right	Deep and shifted toward center field
Short	Normal position
Second	Normal position

Clark has a lot of trouble with low curves thrown by right-handed pitchers (.200, .250 and .156, inside to outside). He hits a fine .280 against medium-high outside curves.

He also has trouble with low sliders thrown by right-handers. His .304 against medium-high outside sliders is excellent.

MEDIUM-HIGH OUTSIDE SLIDERS

BATTING AVERAGE .304
Play

Left	Medium-deep in straightaway left field
Center	Deep in straightaway center field
Right	Deep and shifted toward center field
Short	Shifted toward third base
Second	*No instances recorded*

Clark Against Left-Handed Pitchers

Clark really comes alive against fastballs thrown by left-handed pitchers. He hits a strong .428 in the medium-high outside fastball location.

MEDIUM-HIGH OUTSIDE FASTBALLS
(THROWN BY LEFT-HANDED PITCHERS)

BATTING AVERAGE .428
Play

Left	Deep and shifted toward the left field line
Center	Deep in straightaway center field
Right	Deep and shifted toward center field
Short	Shifted toward third base
Second	*No instances recorded*

His .555 against low-over-the-middle fastballs is even more impressive.

LOW-OVER-THE-MIDDLE FASTBALLS

BATTING AVERAGE .555
Play

Left	Deep and shifted toward the left field line
Center	Medium-deep in straightaway center field
Right	Deep in straightaway right field
Short	Up middle (shifted toward second base)
Second	*No instances recorded*

Against left-handers, Clark pulls almost every fastball location down the left field line. An exception is the low-outside location.

LOW-OUTSIDE FASTBALLS
(THROWN BY LEFT-HANDED PITCHERS)

BATTING AVERAGE .388
Play

Left	Deep and shifted toward center field
Center	Deep in straightaway center field
Right	Deep and shifted toward center field
Short	Normal position
Second	*No instances recorded*

Ahead And Behind In The Count Vs. RH

Ahead

Fastball Average .466				Curve Average .291		
	Inside	Middle	Outside	Inside	Middle	Outside
High	5/ 400 /2	9/ 555 /5	9/ 222 /2	0/ 0 /0	1/ 0 /0	0/ 0 /0
Med	11/ 636 /7	11/ 636 /7	27/ 481 /13	2/ 500 /1	2/ 0 /0	10/ 300 /3
Low	4/ 0 /0	20/ 450 /9	9/ 444 /4	0/ 0 /0	3/ 333 /1	6/ 333 /2

Behind

Fastball Average .290				Curve Average .380		
	Inside	Middle	Outside	Inside	Middle	Outside
High	4/ 0 /0	9/ 111 /1	6/ 666 /4	0/ 0 /0	1/ 1000 /1	0/ 0 /0
Med	4/ 250 /1	3/ 1000 /3	22/ 227 /5	1/ 1000 /1	2/ 0 /0	8/ 375 /3
Low	0/ 0 /0	7/ 428 /3	7/ 142 /1	1/ 1000 /1	0/ 0 /0	8/ 250 /2

Overall Evaluation
Against Right-Handed Pitchers

Overall Fastball  (3 balls)

Overall Curve (1 ball)

Overall Slider (4 balls)

Against Left-Handed Pitchers

Overall Fastball  (4 balls)

Overall Curve (1 ball)

Overall Slider (1 ball)

Comments: Strong vs. waist-high fastballs vs. RH, over-the-middle and outside fastballs vs. LH.
Strengths: Waist-high fastballs, low-middle and high-outside fastballs, medium-outside curves and sliders vs. RH; over-the-middle and outside fastballs vs. LH.
Weaknesses: High-inside and low-outside fastballs, low curves and low sliders vs. RH; inside fastballs, outside curves and inside sliders vs. LH.

Tim Flannery (Left Handed) — *San Diego Padres*

Tim Flannery Against Right-Handed Pitchers
Overall BARS Batting Average .284

Fastball Average .303

	Outside	Middle	Inside
High	12 / 250 / 3	27 / 185 / 5	13 / 307 / 4
Med	35 / 371 / 13	14 / 142 / 2	62 / 338 / 21
Low	12 / 83 / 1	45 / 355 / 16	37 / 351 / 13

Curve Average .270

	Outside	Middle	Inside
High	2 / 0 / 0	1 / 0 / 0	5 / 400 / 2
Med	9 / 111 / 1	1 / 0 / 0	3 / 333 / 1
Low	1 / 0 / 0	6 / 500 / 3	9 / 333 / 3

Slider Average .166

	Outside	Middle	Inside
High	0 / 0 / 0	1 / 1000 / 1	0 / 0 / 0
Med	0 / 0 / 0	0 / 0 / 0	7 / 0 / 0
Low	1 / 1000 / 1	1 / 0 / 0	14 / 142 / 2

Tim Flannery Against Left-Handed Pitchers
Overall BARS Batting Average .100

Fastball Average .090

	Outside	Middle	Inside
High	0 / 0 / 0	3 / 0 / 0	1 / 0 / 0
Med	2 / 0 / 0	3 / 333 / 1	5 / 0 / 0
Low	2 / 0 / 0	4 / 250 / 1	2 / 0 / 0

Curve Average .142

	Outside	Middle	Inside
High	1 / 1000 / 1	0 / 0 / 0	1 / 0 / 0
Med	0 / 0 / 0	0 / 0 / 0	2 / 0 / 0
Low	2 / 0 / 0	1 / 0 / 0	0 / 0 / 0

Slider Average .000

	Outside	Middle	Inside
High	0 / 0 / 0	0 / 0 / 0	0 / 0 / 0
Med	1 / 0 / 0	0 / 0 / 0	1 / 0 / 0
Low	2 / 0 / 0	0 / 0 / 0	0 / 0 / 0

Left-handed hitter Tim Flannery has a good .303 overall fastball average against right-handed pitchers. He hits an impressive .371 against medium-high outside fastballs. He hits this pitch deep into the left-center gap and medium-deep to center and right.

MEDIUM-HIGH OUTSIDE FASTBALLS

BATTING AVERAGE .371

Play

Left	Deep and shifted toward center field
Center	Medium-deep in straightaway center field
Right	Medium-deep in straightaway right field
Short	Up middle (shifted toward second base)
Second	Shifted toward first base

Flannery hits inside fastballs extremely well. He has a solid .338 average against medium-high inside fastballs. His Ahead and Behind charts show that he hits medium-high inside pitches better when ahead in the count (.433 when ahead, .222 when behind). He hits this pitch medium-deep to all fields when ahead. The field diagram on the opposite page illustrates the BARS fielding strategy for this pitch when Flannery is ahead and behind in the count.

MEDIUM-HIGH INSIDE FASTBALLS
(WHEN AHEAD IN THE COUNT)

BATTING AVERAGE .433

Play

Left	Medium-deep and shifted toward the left field line
Center	Medium-deep in straightaway center field
Right	Medium-deep in straightaway right field
Short	Up middle (shifted toward second base)
Second	Normal position

MEDIUM-HIGH INSIDE FASTBALLS
(WHEN BEHIND IN THE COUNT)

BATTING AVERAGE .222

Play

Left	Deep and shifted toward the left field line
Center	Deep in straightaway center field
Right	Medium-deep in straightaway right field
Short	Up middle (shifted toward second base)
Second	Shifted toward first base

In contrast, Flannery hits low-inside fastballs better when he is behind in the count (.571 when behind, .277 when ahead).

Flannery has trouble with medium-high outside curves thrown by right-handed pitchers (.111) but he hits inside curves very well (.400, .333 and .333, high to low).

He has trouble with inside sliders against right-handers. His .142 against low-inside sliders and .000 on 0-for-7 against medium-high inside sliders give targets for pitchers.

Medium-High Inside Fastballs

Dark Fielders — Behind In The Count

Light Fielders — Ahead In The Count

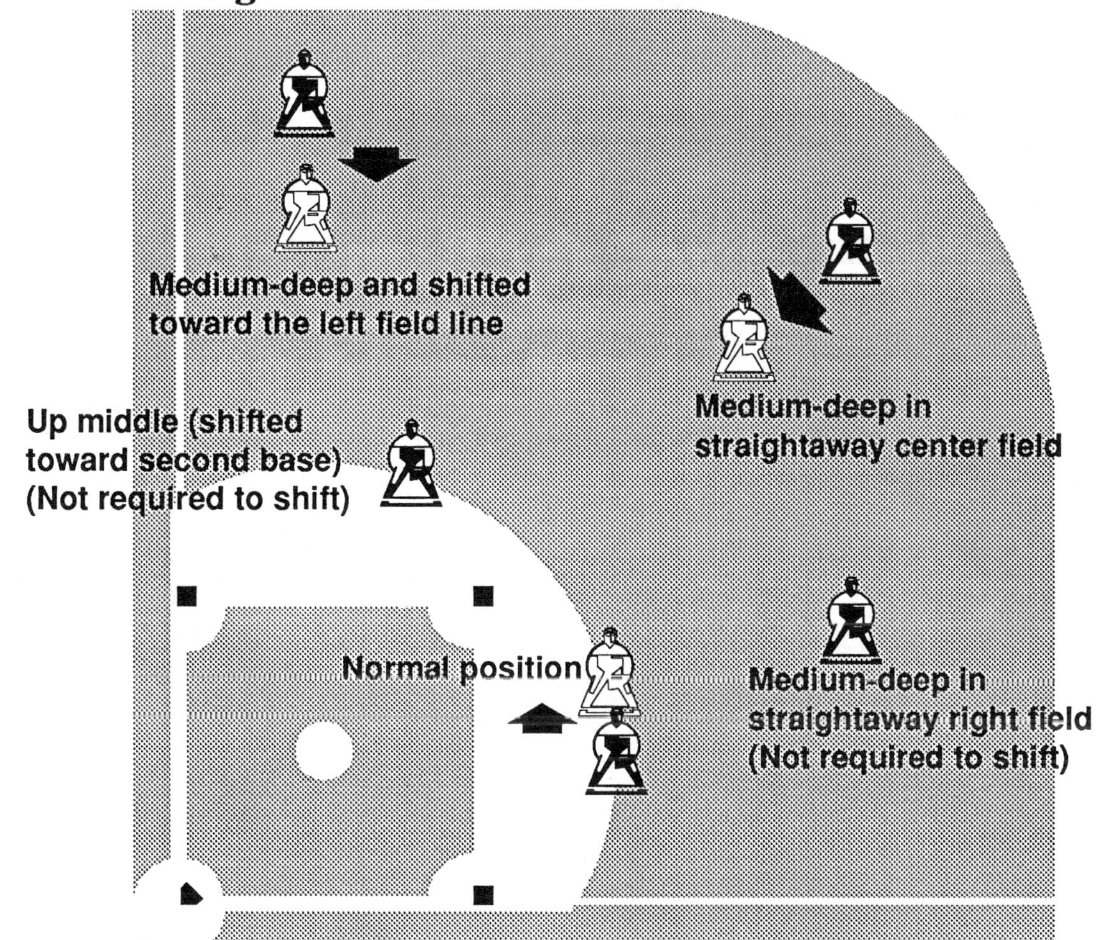

Ahead And Behind In The Count Vs. RH

Ahead

Fastball Average .362

	Outside	Middle	Inside
High	2/500/1	19/203/5	10/400/4
Med	17/470/8	6/166/1	30/133/13
Low	5/0/0	20/450/9	18/277/5

Curve Average .285

	Outside	Middle	Inside
High	0/0/0	0/0/0	2/500/1
Med	2/0/0	1/0/0	0/0/0
Low	0/0/0	1/1000/1	1/0/0

Behind

Fastball Average .230

	Outside	Middle	Inside
High	4/0/0	3/0/0	1/0/0
Med	2/0/0	2/0/0	9/222/2
Low	3/333/1	8/250/2	7/571/4

Curve Average .428

	Outside	Middle	Inside
High	0/0/0	0/0/0	2/500/1
Med	2/500/1	0/0/0	1/1000/1
Low	1/0/0	4/250/1	4/500/2

Overall Evaluation

Against Right-Handed Pitchers

Overall Fastball	
Overall Curve	
Overall Slider	

Against Left-Handed Pitchers

Overall Fastball

Overall Curve — Not enough information

Overall Slider — Not enough information

Comments: Strong against inside fastballs vs. RH.

Strengths: Medium-outside, low-middle and all inside fastballs, inside curves vs. RH.

Weaknesses: High-outside, low-outside, high-middle and medium-middle fastballs, outside curves and inside sliders vs. RH; fastballs in general vs. LH.

Tony Gwynn (Left Handed) — *San Diego Padres*

Tony Gwynn Against Right-Handed Pitchers
Overall BARS Batting Average .362

Fastball Average .392

	Outside	Middle	Inside
High	22 / 545 / 12	41 / 512 / 21	30 / 333 / 10
Med	69 / 333 / 23	23 / 478 / 11	62 / 290 / 18
Low	17 / 470 / 8	38 / 473 / 18	50 / 340 / 17

Curve Average .400

	Outside	Middle	Inside
High	2 / 500 / 1	5 / 600 / 3	8 / 250 / 2
Med	14 / 285 / 4	6 / 500 / 3	15 / 466 / 7
Low	5 / 200 / 1	15 / 400 / 6	15 / 466 / 7

Slider Average .382

	Outside	Middle	Inside
High	1 / 0 / 0	3 / 666 / 2	6 / 333 / 2
Med	0 / 0 / 0	1 / 0 / 0	9 / 222 / 2
Low	2 / 1000 / 2	7 / 571 / 4	18 / 333 / 6

Tony Gwynn Against Left-Handed Pitchers
Overall BARS Batting Average .323

Fastball Average .357

	Outside	Middle	Inside
High	1 / 0 / 0	12 / 416 / 5	15 / 333 / 5
Med	16 / 437 / 7	2 / 500 / 1	32 / 218 / 7
Low	8 / 250 / 2	21 / 380 / 8	16 / 562 / 9

Curve Average .214

	Outside	Middle	Inside
High	0 / 0 / 0	1 / 0 / 0	1 / 0 / 0
Med	1 / 0 / 0	3 / 333 / 1	2 / 0 / 0
Low	8 / 250 / 2	9 / 222 / 2	3 / 333 / 1

Slider Average .260

	Outside	Middle	Inside
High	0 / 0 / 0	0 / 0 / 0	2 / 0 / 0
Med	4 / 250 / 1	1 / 1000 / 1	2 / 500 / 1
Low	7 / 142 / 1	7 / 285 / 2	0 / 0 / 0

Left-handed hitter Tony Gwynn has exceptionally high overall fastball, curve and slider averages against right-handed pitchers. His overall fastball average of .392 is one of the highest recorded by the BARS System.

He hits a solid .333 against medium-high outside fastballs thrown by right-handers. He hits this pitch medium-deep down the left line and straightaway to center and left. Note that the shortstop needs to play shifted toward second and the second baseman shifted toward first.

MEDIUM-HIGH OUTSIDE FASTBALLS

Batting Average .333
Play

Left	Medium-deep and shifted toward the left field line
Center	Medium-deep in straightaway center field
Right	Deep in straightaway right field
Short	Up middle (shifted toward second base)
Second	Shifted toward first base

Gwynn hits medum-high inside fastballs for a .290 average. This is his 'weakest' fastball location against right-handers.

MEDIUM-HIGH INSIDE FASTBALLS

Batting Average .290
Play

Left	Medium-deep and shifted toward the left field line
Center	Medium-deep in straightaway center field
Right	Deep in straightaway right field
Short	Normal position
Second	Normal position

His .512 average against high-over-the-middle fastballs is extraordinary.

HIGH-OVER-THE-MIDDLE FASTBALLS

BATTING AVERAGE .512
Play

Left	Deep in straightaway left field
Center	Medium-deep in straightaway center field
Right	Deep and shifted toward center field
Short	Up middle (shifted toward second base)
Second	Normal position

His .473 average against low-over-the-middle fastballs is also extremely strong. He hits this pitch more to his opposite field (left field) when he is ahead in the count. But note that the shortstop needs to play toward second and the second baseman toward first for this pitch when Gwynn is ahead.

LOW-OVER-THE-MIDDLE FASTBALLS
(WHEN AHEAD IN THE COUNT)

BATTING AVERAGE .500
Play

Left	Deep and shifted toward the left field line
Center	Deep and shifted toward left field
Right	Deep and shifted toward center field
Short	Up middle (shifted toward second base)
Second	Shifted toward first base

LOW-OVER-THE-MIDDLE FASTBALLS
(WHEN BEHIND IN THE COUNT)

BATTING AVERAGE .416

Play

Left	Medium-deep in straightaway left field
Center	Medium-deep in straightaway center field
Right	Medium-deep in straightaway right field
Short	Normal position
Second	Normal position

He even hits low-outside fastballs excellently (.470). He goes deep down the left line and deep into the left-center gap with low-outside fastballs.

Gwynn hits low-inside and medium-high inside curves very well (.466 in each location). Right-handers would do better to throw him outside curves, especially low-outside. Gwynn pulls low-inside curves.

LOW-INSIDE CURVEBALLS

BATTING AVERAGE .466

Play

Left	*No instances recorded*
Center	Deep and shifted toward right field
Right	Deep and shifted toward the right field line
Short	Up middle (shifted toward second base)
Second	Normal position

He hits low sliders very well (1.000, .571 and .333). He has some trouble with medium-high inside sliders (.222).

Gwynn Against Left-Handed Pitchers

Gwynn's overall .357 fastball average against left-handed pitchers is excellent. He hits over-the-middle fastballs very strongly (.416, .500 and .380, high to low). He has a few isolated weak locations (.250 low-outside, .218 medium-high inside) but overall his locations are solid. He hits low-over-the-middle fastballs straightaway against left-handers.

LOW-OVER-THE-MIDDLE FASTBALLS
(THROWN BY LEFT-HANDED PITCHERS)

BATTING AVERAGE .380

Play

Left	Deep in straightaway left field
Center	Medium-deep in straightaway center field
Right	Deep in straightaway right field
Short	Up middle (shifted toward second base)
Second	Normal position

He hits an excellent .437 against medium-high outside fastballs thrown by lefties.

MEDIUM-HIGH OUTSIDE FASTBALLS
(THROWN BY LEFT-HANDED PITCHERS)

BATTING AVERAGE .437

Play

Left	*No instances recorded*
Center	Medium-deep in straightaway center field
Right	Medium-deep in straightaway right field
Short	Up middle (shifted toward second base)
Second	Shifted toward first base

Gwynn has some trouble with low-outside and low-over-the-middle curves against left-handers (.250 and .222 respectively). Considering his overall excellence against fastballs, left-handers should mix in more breaking pitches to him.

Ahead And Behind In The Count Vs. RH

Ahead

Fastball Average .406

	Outside	Middle	Inside
High	11/636/7	21/619/13	10/300/3
Med	28/285/8	12/416/5	31/322/10
Low	10/500/5	18/500/9	19/263/5

Curve Average .476

	Outside	Middle	Inside
High	0/0/0	1/1000/1	2/0/0
Med	3/333/1	1/0/0	5/600/3
Low	1/0/0	5/600/3	3/666/2

Behind

Fastball Average .281

	Outside	Middle	Inside
High	5/600/3	4/0/0	12/333/4
Med	11/363/4	2/0/0	8/0/0
Low	2/500/1	12/416/5	8/125/1

Curve Average .419

	Outside	Middle	Inside
High	2/500/1	2/500/1	2/500/1
Med	5/200/1	3/666/2	2/500/1
Low	2/0/0	8/375/3	5/600/3

Overall Evaluation

Against Right-Handed Pitchers

	Rating
Overall Fastball	4 baseballs
Overall Curve	4 baseballs
Overall Slider	4 baseballs

Against Left-Handed Pitchers

	Rating
Overall Fastball	4 baseballs
Overall Curve	1 baseball
Overall Slider	2 baseballs

Comments: Consistent excellence vs. fastballs vs. RH. Strengths: All fastballs, over-the-middle curves, medium-inside and low-inside curves, low sliders vs. RH; medium-outside, high-inside, low-inside and all over-the-middle fastballs vs. LH. Weaknesses: High-inside curves and medium-inside sliders vs. RH; medium-inside fastballs, low-outside and low-middle curves, outside sliders vs. LH.

John Kruk Against Right-Handed Pitchers
Overall BARS Batting Average .244

Fastball Average .325

	Outside	Middle	Inside
High	9/ 444 /4	15/ 266 /4	10/ 300 /3
Med	31/ 290 /9	4/ 250 /1	15/ 400 /6
Low	14/ 285 /4	10/ 400 /4	15/ 333 /5

Curve Average .200

	Outside	Middle	Inside
High	1/ 0 /0	0/ 0 /0	4/ 250 /1
Med	6/ 333 /2	2/ 0 /0	7/ 142 /1
Low	3/ 333 /1	5/ 200 /1	7/ 142 /1

Slider Average .150

	Outside	Middle	Inside
High	2/ 0 /0	0/ 0 /0	1/ 0 /0
Med	4/ 0 /0	0/ 0 /0	6/ 333 /2
Low	0/ 0 /0	2/ 0 /0	5/ 200 /1

John Kruk Against Left-Handed Pitchers
Overall BARS Batting Average .254

Fastball Average .250

	Outside	Middle	Inside
High	0/ 0 /0	3/ 666 /2	5/ 400 /2
Med	4/ 250 /1	0/ 0 /0	8/ 125 /1
Low	3/ 0 /0	3/ 333 /1	2/ 0 /0

Curve Average .357

	Outside	Middle	Inside
High	3/ 333 /1	1/ 1000 /1	1/ 0 /0
Med	3/ 333 /1	0/ 0 /0	1/ 1000 /1
Low	3/ 333 /1	1/ 0 /0	1/ 0 /0

Slider Average .000

	Outside	Middle	Inside
High	0/ 0 /0	0/ 0 /0	0/ 0 /0
Med	1/ 0 /0	0/ 0 /0	0/ 0 /0
Low	2/ 0 /0	0/ 0 /0	0/ 0 /0

Left-handed hitter John Kruk has a solid .325 overall fastball average against right-handed pitchers. He falls off considerably against curves and sliders (.200 and .150 overall, respectively).

He hits .290 against medium-high outside fastballs thrown by right-handers. He goes deep down the left line and medium-deep into the right-center gap with this pitch. Note that the shortstop needs to play shifted toward second base. The field diagram on the opposite page illustrates the BARS fielding strategy for this pitch.

MEDIUM-HIGH OUTSIDE FASTBALLS

BATTING AVERAGE .290
Play

Left	Deep and shifted toward the left field line
Center	Medium-deep in straightaway center field
Right	Medium-deep and shifted toward center field
Short	Up middle (shifted toward second base)
Second	Normal position

Kruk is strong against inside fastballs thrown by right-handers. He hits .400 against medium-high inside fastballs.

MEDIUM-HIGH INSIDE FASTBALLS

BATTING AVERAGE .400
Play

Left	Deep in straightaway left field
Center	*No instances recorded*
Right	Deep in straightaway right field
Short	Up middle (shifted toward second base)
Second	Shifted toward first base

He hits a solid .333 against low-inside fastballs. For this pitch, the left fielder needs to play short in straightaway left, the center fielder medium-deep and shifted toward right field, and the right fielder medium-deep and shifted toward the right line.

Note how differently the outfielders should play when Kruk is thrown a low-over-the-middle fastball.

LOW-OVER-THE-MIDDLE FASTBALLS

BATTING AVERAGE .400
Play

Left	Deep and shifted toward the left line
Center	Deep in straightaway center field
Right	Deep and shifted toward the right line
Short	Shifted toward third base
Second	Shifted toward first base

Kruk has trouble with inside curves against right-handers. He hits outside curves somewhat better.

Medium-High Outside Fastballs

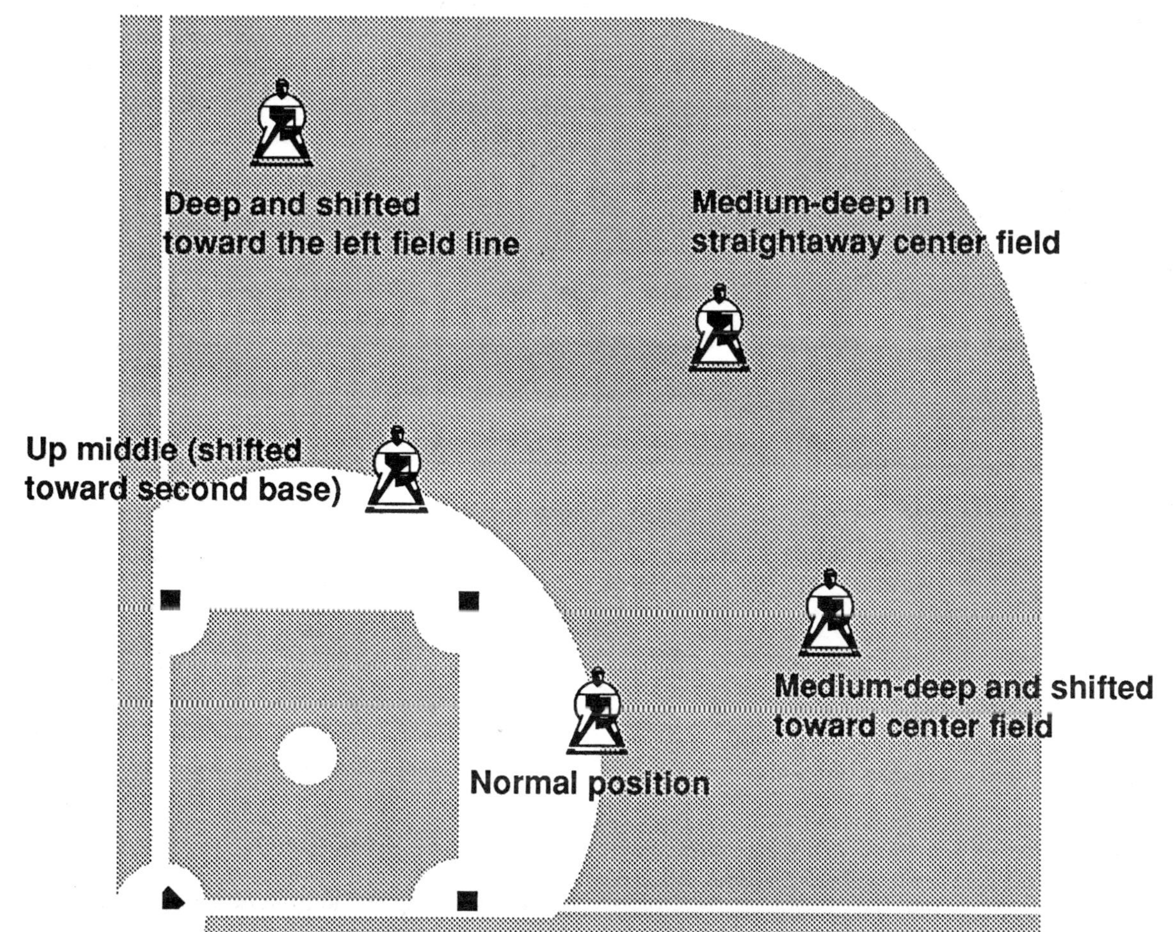

Ahead And Behind In The Count Vs. RH

Ahead

Fastball Average .411

	Outside	Middle	Inside
High	3/ 333 /1	7/ 428 /3	2/ 500 /1
Med	12/ 333 /4	3/ 333 /1	9/ 333 /3
Low	3/ 333 /1	7/ 571 /4	5/ 600 /3

Curve Average .090

	Outside	Middle	Inside
High	0/ 0 /0	0/ 0 /0	1/ 0 /0
Med	1/ 0 /0	1/ 0 /0	4/ 250 /1
Low	1/ 0 /0	1/ 0 /0	2/ 0 /0

Behind

Fastball Average .461

	Outside	Middle	Inside
High	1/ 1000 /1	1/ 0 /0	2/ 500 /1
Med	2/ 500 /1	0/ 0 /0	2/ 1000 /2
Low	3/ 333 /1	1/ 0 /0	1/ 0 /0

Curve Average .300

	Outside	Middle	Inside
High	0/ 0 /0	0/ 0 /0	1/ 0 /0
Med	3/ 333 /1	0/ 0 /0	1/ 0 /0
Low	1/ 1000 /1	2/ 0 /0	2/ 500 /1

Overall Evaluation
Against Right-Handed Pitchers

Overall Fastball	⚾ ⚾ ⚾ ⚾
Overall Curve	⚾
Overall Slider	⚾

Against Left-Handed Pitchers

Overall Fastball	⚾
Overall Curve	⚾ ⚾ ⚾ ⚾
Overall Slider	Not enough information

Comments: Strong against inside fastballs vs. RH.
Strengths: High-outside, medium-outside, low-middle and all inside fastballs vs. RH.
Weaknesses: High-middle fastballs and inside curves vs. RH; outside fastballs, medium-inside fastballs vs. LH.

Carmelo Martinez (Right Handed) — *San Diego Padres*

Carmelo Martinez Against Right-Handed Pitchers
Overall BARS Batting Average .231

Fastball Average .287

	Inside	Middle	Outside
High	3 / 333 / 1	23 / 217 / 5	11 / 90 / 1
Med	25 / 400 / 10	19 / 368 / 7	55 / 272 / 15
Low	5 / 800 / 4	24 / 250 / 6	16 / 187 / 3

Curve Average .233

	Inside	Middle	Outside
High	2 / 500 / 1	3 / 333 / 1	4 / 0 / 0
Med	0 / 0 / 0	3 / 333 / 1	18 / 333 / 6
Low	1 / 0 / 0	7 / 142 / 1	22 / 181 / 4

Slider Average .140

	Inside	Middle	Outside
High	1 / 0 / 0	2 / 0 / 0	3 / 0 / 0
Med	1 / 0 / 0	4 / 0 / 0	13 / 76 / 1
Low	0 / 0 / 0	5 / 200 / 1	21 / 238 / 5

Carmelo Martinez Against Left-Handed Pitchers
Overall BARS Batting Average .234

Fastball Average .313

	Inside	Middle	Outside
High	4 / 0 / 0	5 / 400 / 2	9 / 111 / 1
Med	3 / 666 / 2	2 / 500 / 1	22 / 363 / 8
Low	4 / 250 / 1	8 / 375 / 3	10 / 300 / 3

Curve Average .263

	Inside	Middle	Outside
High	1 / 0 / 0	1 / 0 / 0	2 / 500 / 1
Med	1 / 1000 / 1	0 / 0 / 0	5 / 600 / 3
Low	3 / 0 / 0	3 / 0 / 0	3 / 0 / 0

Slider Average .300

	Inside	Middle	Outside
High	1 / 0 / 0	0 / 0 / 0	0 / 0 / 0
Med	2 / 0 / 0	1 / 1000 / 1	1 / 0 / 0
Low	2 / 0 / 0	3 / 666 / 2	0 / 0 / 0

Right-handed hitter Carmelo Martinez hits well against fastballs (.287 overall against right-handed pitchers, .313 overall against left-handed pitchers). His curve averages, however, fall off considerably (.233 vs. right-handers, .263 vs. left-handers).

Starting with right-handers, notice his difficulty with all outside fastballs (.090, .272 and .187, high to low). He hits medium-high outside fastballs deep down the left line and deep into the left-center gap. The right fielder, however, needs to play short and straightaway, and the shortstop needs to shift toward second base.

MEDIUM-HIGH OUTSIDE FASTBALLS

BATTING AVERAGE .272

    Play

Left	Deep and shifted toward the left field line
Center	Deep and shifted toward left field
Right	Short in straightaway right field
Short	Up middle (shifted toward second base)
Second	Normal position

In contrast, he hits medium-high inside fastballs for a very strong .400 average. For this pitch, the right fielder needs to play medium-deep and the shortstop needs to play shifted toward third base.

MEDIUM-HIGH INSIDE FASTBALLS

BATTING AVERAGE .400

    Play

Left	Deep and shifted toward the left field line
Center	Deep and shifted toward left field
Right	Medium-deep in straightaway right field
Short	Shifted toward third base
Second	*No instances recorded*

Martinez Against Curves And Sliders

Martinez has trouble with low-over-the-middle curves (.142) and low-outside curves (.181) against right-handed pitchers, but he hits medium-high outside curves very well (.333). He hits this pitch medium-deep to the outfield. If fielders aligned themselves as indicated by the BARS fielding strategy for this pitch, they could prevent a lot of his line drives that are now falling in.

MEDIUM-HIGH OUTSIDE CURVEBALLS

BATTING AVERAGE .333

    Play

Left	Medium-deep and shifted toward center field
Center	Medium-deep in straightaway center field
Right	Medium-deep and shifted toward the right line
Short	Normal position
Second	Shifted toward first base

He has trouble with low-middle sliders (.200), low-outside sliders (.238) and medium-high outside sliders (.076). He pulls low-outside sliders deep down the left line and deep into left center. The shortstop needs to play shifted toward second base.

LOW-OUTSIDE SLIDERS

BATTING AVERAGE .238
Play
Left	Deep and shifted toward the left field line
Center	Deep and shifted toward left field
Right	Medium-deep in straightaway right field
Short	Up middle (shifted toward second base)
Second	*No instances recorded*

Martinez Against Left-Handed Pitchers

Martinez hits .363 against medium-high outside fastballs thrown by left-handed pitchers. The BARS fielding strategy for this pitch shows that the center fielder needs to play shifted toward left field and the right fielder shifted toward center. The shortstop, however, needs to play shifted toward second and the second baseman shifted toward first.

**MEDIUM-HIGH OUTSIDE FASTBALLS
(THROWN BY LEFT-HANDED PITCHERS)**

BATTING AVERAGE .363
Play
Left	Medium-deep in straightaway left field
Center	Deep and shifted toward left field
Right	Deep and shifted toward center field
Short	Up middle (shifted toward second base)
Second	Shifted toward first base

He hits .300 against low-outside fastballs thrown by left-handers.

LOW-OUTSIDE FASTBALLS

BATTING AVERAGE .300
Play
Left	Medium-deep and shifted toward the left field line
Center	Deep in straightaway center field
Right	Medium-deep in straightaway right field
Short	Up middle (shifted toward second base)
Second	*No instances recorded*

His .111 against high-outside fastballs thrown by left-handers indicates a weakness. Most of his hit balls in this location are probably easy pop-ups or ground-outs.

**HIGH-OUTSIDE FASTBALLS
(THROWN BY LEFT-HANDED PITCHERS)**

BATTING AVERAGE .111
Play
Left	Deep and shifted toward the left field line
Center	Medium-deep and shifted toward left field
Right	Deep and shifted toward the right field line
Short	Normal position
Second	*No instances recorded*

Ahead And Behind In The Count Vs. RH

Ahead

Fastball Average .367

	Inside	Middle	Outside
High	0/ 0/0	7/ 428/3	4/ 250/1
Med	15/ 466/7	11/ 454/5	20/ 250/5
Low	2/ 1000/2	16/ 250/4	4/ 500/2

Curve Average .230

	Inside	Middle	Outside
High	0/ 0/0	2/ 500/1	1/ 0/0
Med	0/ 0/0	0/ 0/0	6/ 166/1
Low	0/ 0/0	2/ 500/1	2/ 0/0

Behind

Fastball Average .241

	Inside	Middle	Outside
High	0/ 0/0	8/ 0/0	3/ 0/0
Med	5/ 400/2	0/ 0/0	9/ 444/4
Low	1/ 1000/1	1/ 0/0	2/ 0/0

Curve Average .153

	Inside	Middle	Outside
High	1/ 1000/1	0/ 0/0	2/ 0/0
Med	0/ 0/0	0/ 0/0	3/ 0/0
Low	1/ 0/0	2/ 0/0	4/ 250/1

Overall Evaluation

Against Right-Handed Pitchers

Overall Fastball	
Overall Curve	
Overall Slider	

Against Left-Handed Pitchers

Overall Fastball	
Overall Curve	
Overall Slider	Not enough information

Comments: Weak against outside fastballs vs. RH.
Strengths: Inside fastballs, medium-middle fastballs, medium-outside curves vs. RH; all waist-high and all over-the-middle fastballs, low-outside fastballs, medium-outside curves vs. LH.
Weaknesses: High-middle and low-middle fastballs, all outside fastballs, low curves and low sliders, outside sliders vs. RH; high-outside fastballs vs. LH.

Randy Ready (Right Handed) — *San Diego Padres*

Randy Ready Against Right-Handed Pitchers
Overall BARS Batting Average .269

Fastball Average .312

	Inside	Middle	Outside
High	8/375/3	3/333/1	6/0/0
Med	12/500/6	7/428/3	15/266/4
Low	10/100/1	11/363/4	8/375/3

Curve Average .181

	Inside	Middle	Outside
High	1/0/0	3/0/0	1/1000/1
Med	1/0/0	2/0/0	8/375/3
Low	4/250/1	2/0/0	11/90/1

Slider Average .461

	Inside	Middle	Outside
High	0/0/0	0/0/0	1/1000/1
Med	2/1000/2	1/0/0	4/500/2
Low	1/0/0	2/500/1	2/0/0

Randy Ready Against Left-Handed Pitchers
Overall BARS Batting Average .315

Fastball Average .372

	Inside	Middle	Outside
High	0/0/0	4/250/1	1/1000/1
Med	6/333/2	5/600/3	11/363/4
Low	4/0/0	5/200/1	7/571/4

Curve Average .200

	Inside	Middle	Outside
High	0/0/0	0/0/0	1/0/0
Med	0/0/0	1/0/0	3/333/1
Low	1/0/0	4/250/1	0/0/0

Slider Average .400

	Inside	Middle	Outside
High	0/0/0	0/0/0	0/0/0
Med	2/500/1	0/0/0	0/0/0
Low	1/0/0	1/0/0	1/1000/1

Randy Ready, right-handed hitter, has a fine overall .312 fastball average against right-handed pitchers. He hits all over-the-middle fastballs well (.333, .428 and .363, high to low) but he has scattered weak and strong locations through the rest of his fastball chart.

He hits medium-high inside fastballs for an excellent .500 average. He hits this pitch straightaway to left and center fields and down the right field line.

MEDIUM-HIGH INSIDE FASTBALLS

BATTING AVERAGE .500
Play

Left	Deep in straightaway left field
Center	Medium-deep in straightaway center field
Right	Medium-deep and shifted toward the right line
Short	Shifted toward third base
Second	*No instances recorded*

He has an excellent .363 average against low-over-the-middle fastballs. He pulls this pitch to the outfield, but note that the shortstop needs to play shifted toward second base. The field diagram on the opposite page illustrates the BARS fielding strategy for this pitch.

LOW-OVER-THE-MIDDLE FASTBALLS

BATTING AVERAGE .363
Play

Left	Deep and shifted toward the left field line
Center	Deep and shifted toward left field

Right	Short and shifted toward center field
Short	Up middle (shifted toward second base)
Second	Normal position

Ready has trouble with low-outside curves (.090) but he hits medium-high outside curves for a .375 average.

Ready Against Left-Handed Pitchers

Ready is very effective against fastballs thrown by left-handed pitchers. His .363 against medium-high outside fastballs is excellent. He pulls this pitch.

MEDIUM-HIGH OUTSIDE FASTBALLS (THROWN BY LEFT-HANDED PITCHERS)

BATTING AVERAGE .363
Play

Left	Deep and shifted toward the left field line
Center	Deep and shifted toward left field
Right	Deep and shifted toward center field
Short	Normal position
Second	*No instances recorded*

His .571 against low-outside fastballs is very strong. He hits this pitch deep and straightaway to the outfield, but the shortstop needs to play shifted toward second and the second baseman shifted toward first for this pitch.

Low-Over-The-Middle Fastballs

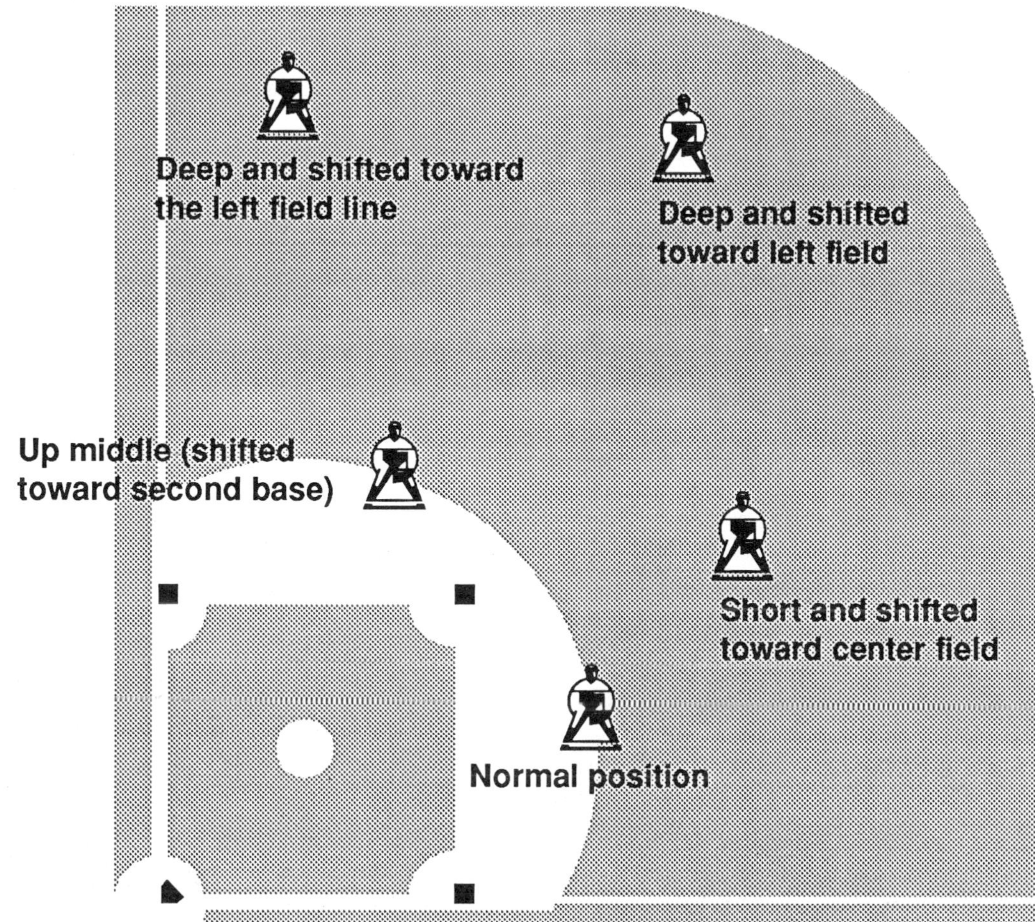

Ahead And Behind In The Count Vs. RH

Ahead

Fastball Average .300

	Inside	Middle	Outside
High	4/ 250 / 1	1/ 0 / 0	3/ 0 / 0
Med	4/ 750 / 3	3/ 666 / 2	4/ 250 / 1
Low	6/ 166 / 1	4/ 250 / 1	1/ 0 / 0

Curve Average .285

	Inside	Middle	Outside
High	1/ 0 / 0	1/ 0 / 0	1/ 1000 / 1
Med	0/ 0 / 0	0/ 0 / 0	4/ 250 / 1
Low	0/ 0 / 0	0/ 0 / 0	0/ 0 / 0

Behind

Fastball Average .312

	Inside	Middle	Outside
High	2/ 500 / 1	0/ 0 / 0	1/ 0 / 0
Med	4/ 500 / 2	1/ 0 / 0	4/ 250 / 1
Low	0/ 0 / 0	2/ 0 / 0	2/ 500 / 1

Curve Average .750

	Inside	Middle	Outside
High	0/ 0 / 0	0/ 0 / 0	0/ 0 / 0
Med	0/ 0 / 0	0/ 0 / 0	3/ 666 / 2
Low	0/ 0 / 0	0/ 0 / 0	1/ 1000 / 1

Overall Evaluation

Against Right-Handed Pitchers

Overall Fastball 

Overall Curve 🔵

Overall Slider 

Against Left-Handed Pitchers

Overall Fastball 🔵🔵🔵🔵

Overall Curve — Not enough information

Overall Slider — Not enough information

Comments: Strong against outside fastballs vs. LH.
Strengths: High-inside, medium-inside, low-outside and all over-the-middle fastballs, medium-outside curves vs. RH; waist-high fastballs, low-outside fastballs vs. LH.
Weaknesses: Low-inside, high-outside and medium-outside fastballs, low-outside curves vs. RH.

Benito Santiago (Right Handed) — *San Diego Padres*

Benito Santiago Against Right-Handed Pitchers
Overall BARS Batting Average .232

Fastball Average .257

	Inside	Middle	Outside
High	14 / 214 / 3	7 / 285 / 2	6 / 0 / 0
Med	16 / 250 / 4	3 / 333 / 1	29 / 344 / 10
Low	6 / 333 / 2	8 / 375 / 3	16 / 125 / 2

Curve Average .133

	Inside	Middle	Outside
High	1 / 0 / 0	2 / 500 / 1	4 / 250 / 1
Med	1 / 0 / 0	1 / 0 / 0	8 / 125 / 1
Low	0 / 0 / 0	1 / 0 / 0	12 / 83 / 1

Slider Average .187

	Inside	Middle	Outside
High	0 / 0 / 0	0 / 0 / 0	2 / 0 / 0
Med	0 / 0 / 0	0 / 0 / 0	5 / 200 / 1
Low	0 / 0 / 0	2 / 500 / 1	7 / 142 / 1

Benito Santiago Against Left-Handed Pitchers
Overall BARS Batting Average .304

Fastball Average .294

	Inside	Middle	Outside
High	2 / 0 / 0	3 / 333 / 1	0 / 0 / 0
Med	1 / 0 / 0	1 / 0 / 0	1 / 0 / 0
Low	4 / 500 / 2	3 / 666 / 2	2 / 0 / 0

Curve Average .333

	Inside	Middle	Outside
High	0 / 0 / 0	0 / 0 / 0	1 / 1000 / 1
Med	1 / 0 / 0	1 / 1000 / 1	0 / 0 / 0
Low	4 / 250 / 1	1 / 0 / 0	1 / 0 / 0

Slider Average .500

	Inside	Middle	Outside
High	0 / 0 / 0	1 / 0 / 0	0 / 0 / 0
Med	1 / 1000 / 1	0 / 0 / 0	1 / 1000 / 1
Low	1 / 0 / 0	0 / 0 / 0	0 / 0 / 0

Right-handed hitter Benito Santiago has several strong fastball locations against right-handed pitchers but his overall BARS fastball average is only .257.

He hits medium-high outside fastballs for a strong .344 average. He hits this pitch medium-deep and straightaway to left and center and deep down the right field line. The field diagram on the opposite page illustrates the following BARS fielding strategy for this pitch.

MEDIUM-HIGH OUTSIDE FASTBALLS

BATTING AVERAGE .344

Play

Left	Medium-deep in straightaway left field
Center	Medium-deep in straightaway center field
Right	Deep and shifted toward the right field line
Short	Shifted toward third base
Second	Shifted toward first base

He has a lot of trouble with low-outside fastballs thrown by right-handers (.125) but he hits low-over-the-middle fastballs extremely well (.375).

LOW-OVER-THE-MIDDLE FASTBALLS

BATTING AVERAGE .375

Play

Left	Deep and shifted toward the left field line
Center	Deep in straightaway center field
Right	Deep and shifted toward center field
Short	Up middle (shifted toward second base)
Second	*No instances recorded*

His .250 average against medium-high inside fastballs is weak. This, in conjunction with his .214 in the adjacent high-inside location, gives a target for pitchers.

MEDIUM-HIGH INSIDE FASTBALLS

BATTING AVERAGE .250

Play

Left	Deep and shifted toward the left field line
Center	Medium-deep in straightaway center field
Right	Deep and shifted toward center field
Short	Normal position
Second	*No instances recorded*

Santiago Against Curves And Sliders

Santiago has a lot of trouble with outside curves thrown by right-handed pitchers (.250, .125 and .083, high to low). These locations, along with his outside slider locations (.000, .200 and .142, high to low), offer areas of weakness for pitchers.

Medium-High Outside Fastballs

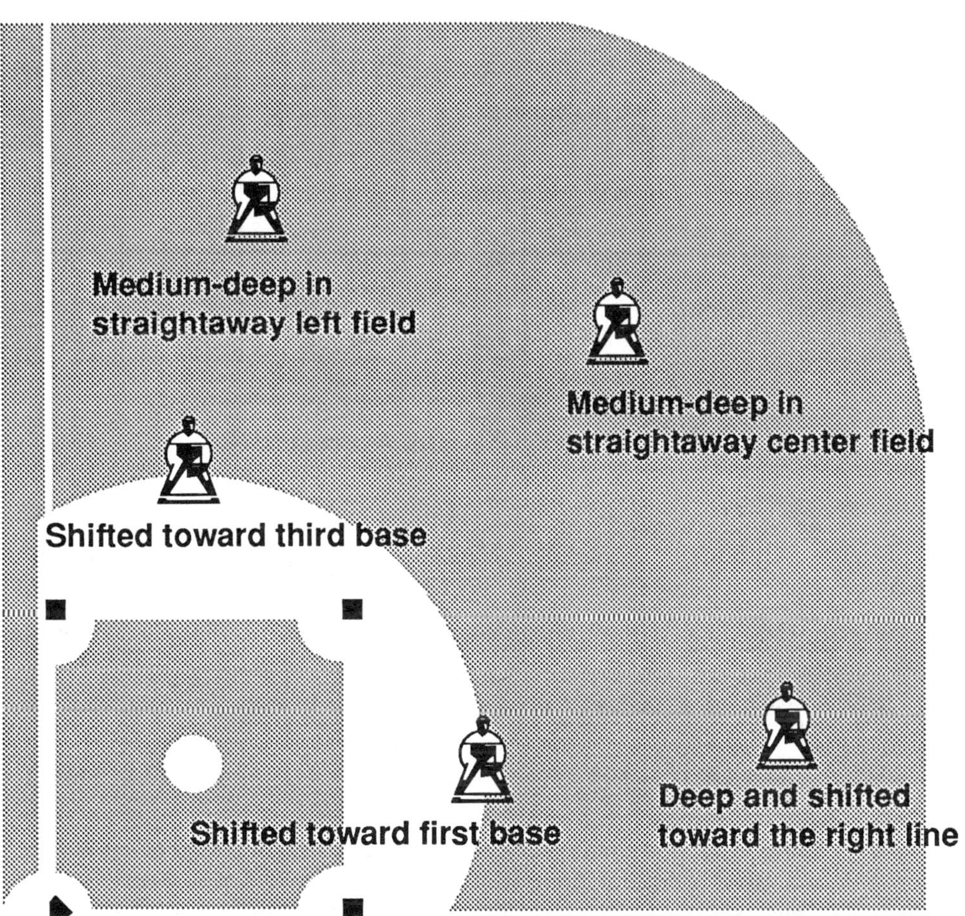

Ahead And Behind In The Count Vs. RH

Ahead

Fastball Average .179

	Inside	Middle	Outside
High	6/ 166 /1	3/ 0 /0	0/ 0 /0
Med	9/ 111 /1	2/ 0 /0	11/ 363 /4
Low	1/ 1000 /1	4/ 0 /0	3/ 0 /0

Curve Average .000

	Inside	Middle	Outside
High	1/ 0 /0	1/ 0 /0	1/ 0 /0
Med	1/ 0 /0	0/ 0 /0	4/ 0 /0
Low	0/ 0 /0	0/ 0 /0	3/ 0 /0

Behind

Fastball Average .642

	Inside	Middle	Outside
High	1/ 1000 /1	0/ 0 /0	1/ 0 /0
Med	0/ 0 /0	1/ 1000 /1	7/ 571 /4
Low	1/ 1000 /1	1/ 1000 /1	2/ 500 /1

Curve Average .285

	Inside	Middle	Outside
High	0/ 0 /0	0/ 0 /0	1/ 1000 /1
Med	0/ 0 /0	1/ 0 /0	1/ 0 /0
Low	0/ 0 /0	1/ 0 /0	3/ 333 /1

Overall Evaluation

Against Right-Handed Pitchers

Overall Fastball 

Overall Curve 

Overall Slider ⚾

Against Left-Handed Pitchers

Overall Fastball ⚾⚾

Overall Curve — Not enough information

Overall Slider — Not enough information

Comments: Difficulties with outside curves and sliders vs. RH.

Strengths: Low-inside, low-middle and medium-outside fastballs vs. RH.

Weaknesses: High-inside, medium-inside and low-outside fastballs, outside curves and outside sliders vs. RH.

Garry Templeton (Switch Hitter) — *San Diego Padres*

Garry Templeton Against Right-Handed Pitchers
Overall BARS Batting Average .255

Fastball Average .286

	Outside	Middle	Inside
High	31/ 129 /4	30/ 300 /9	11/ 363 /4
Med	77/ 272 /21	16/ 500 /8	30/ 200 /6
Low	26/ 115 /3	47/ 382 /18	46/ 369 /17

Curve Average .273

	Outside	Middle	Inside
High	6/ 333 /2	6/ 333 /2	0/ 0 /0
Med	15/ 266 /4	4/ 250 /1	13/ 230 /3
Low	4/ 750 /3	18/ 388 /7	18/ 55 /1

Slider Average .285

	Outside	Middle	Inside
High	1/ 0 /0	0/ 0 /0	2/ 0 /0
Med	3/ 333 /1	0/ 0 /0	9/ 222 /2
Low	3/ 0 /0	7/ 428 /3	10/ 400 /4

Garry Templeton Against Left-Handed Pitchers
Overall BARS Batting Average .216

Fastball Average .234

	Inside	Middle	Outside
High	1/ 0 /0	4/ 0 /0	8/ 125 /1
Med	6/ 166 /1	5/ 600 /3	13/ 307 /4
Low	12/ 83 /1	13/ 307 /4	19/ 263 /5

Curve Average .242

	Inside	Middle	Outside
High	0/ 0 /0	0/ 0 /0	5/ 600 /3
Med	2/ 1000 /2	3/ 0 /0	9/ 111 /1
Low	3/ 666 /2	4/ 0 /0	7/ 0 /0

Slider Average .230

	Inside	Middle	Outside
High	1/ 0 /0	1/ 1000 /1	0/ 0 /0
Med	1/ 0 /0	0/ 0 /0	0/ 0 /0
Low	4/ 250 /1	5/ 200 /1	·1/ 0 /0

Switch-hitting Garry Templeton has some very strong and some very weak fastball locations against right-handed pitchers. He has trouble with outside fastballs (.129, .272 and .115, high to low). He also has trouble with medium-high inside fastballs (.200). But his other fastball locations are solid.

He hits medium-high outside fastballs better when he is ahead in the count (.277 when ahead, .090 when behind). The following fielding strategies show how vital it is for fielders to adjust for the count of a pitch, not just for the type and location.

MEDIUM-HIGH OUTSIDE FASTBALLS
(WHEN AHEAD IN THE COUNT)

BATTING AVERAGE .277
   Play
Left   Medium-deep in straightaway left field
Center   Deep and shifted toward left field
Right   Deep in straightaway right field
Short   Up middle (shifted toward second base)
Second   Normal position

MEDIUM-HIGH OUTSIDE FASTBALLS
(WHEN BEHIND IN THE COUNT)

BATTING AVERAGE .090
   Play
Left   Medium-deep and shifted toward the left field line

Center   Deep in straightaway center field
Right   *No instances recorded*
Short   Up middle (shifted toward second base)
Second   Shifted toward first base

Templeton hits over-the-middle fastballs extremely well (.300, .500 and .382, high to low). He hits low-over-the-middle fastballs better when behind in the count (.500 when behind, .333 when ahead). When behind, he hits this pitch down both lines.

LOW-OVER-THE-MIDDLE FASTBALLS
(WHEN BEHIND IN THE COUNT)

BATTING AVERAGE .500
   Play
Left   Medium-deep and shifted toward the left field line
Center   Deep and shifted toward right field
Right   Deep and shifted toward the right field line
Short   Normal position
Second   *No instances recorded*

LOW-OVER-THE-MIDDLE FASTBALLS
(WHEN AHEAD IN THE COUNT)

BATTING AVERAGE .333
   Play
Left   Deep in straightaway left field
Center   Medium-deep and shifted toward left field
Right   Deep and shifted toward the right field line

Short   Normal position
Second   Normal position

His .369 against low-inside fastballs is excellent. He also hits this pitch down both lines.

LOW-INSIDE FASTBALLS

BATTING AVERAGE .369

Play

Left	Medium-deep and shifted toward the left field line
Center	Deep in straightaway center field
Right	Deep and shifted toward the right field line
Short	Normal position
Second	Normal position

Templeton Against Curves And Sliders

Against right-handed pitchers, Templeton has a lot of trouble with medium-inside and low-inside curves (.230 and .055), but he has an excellent .388 average against low-over-the-middle curves. He hits this pitch medium-deep to all fields. By aligning themselves according to the BARS fielding strategy for this pitch, fielders could prevent most of Templeton's line drives that fall in.

LOW-OVER-THE-MIDDLE CURVEBALLS

BATTING AVERAGE .388

Play

Left	Medium-deep in straightaway left field
Center	Medium-deep and shifted toward right field
Right	Medium-deep and shifted toward the right line
Short	Normal position
Second	Normal position

He hits very well against low-over-the-middle sliders (.428) and low-inside sliders (.400). He has trouble with medium-inside sliders (.222).

Templeton Against Left-Handed Pitchers

Templeton has trouble with inside fastballs thrown by left-handed pitchers. He hits very well against medium-high outside fastballs (.307) and low-over-the-middle fastballs (.307).

MEDIUM-HIGH OUTSIDE FASTBALLS (THROWN BY LEFT-HANDED PITCHERS)

BATTING AVERAGE .307

Play

Left	*No instances recorded*
Center	Medium-deep in straightaway center field
Right	Deep in straightaway right field
Short	Normal position
Second	Normal position

LOW-OVER-THE-MIDDLE FASTBALLS (THROWN BY LEFT-HANDED PITCHERS)

BATTING AVERAGE .307

Play

Left	*No instances recorded*
Center	Deep in straightaway center field
Right	Medium-deep in straightaway right field
Short	Normal position
Second	Normal position

Against curves thrown by left-handers, he has trouble in the sector consisting of the low-outside and three adjacent curve locations. This is the area for left-handers to attack.

Ahead And Behind In The Count Vs. RH

Ahead

Fastball Average .326

	Outside	Middle	Inside
High	10 / 200 / 2	13 / 384 / 5	3 / 333 / 1
Med	36 / 277 / 10	12 / 500 / 6	10 / 100 / 1
Low	9 / 111 / 1	27 / 333 / 9	24 / 500 / 12

Curve Average .384

	Outside	Middle	Inside
High	2 / 500 / 1	1 / 1000 / 1	0 / 0 / 0
Med	7 / 428 / 3	3 / 333 / 1	4 / 250 / 1
Low	0 / 0 / 0	5 / 400 / 2	4 / 250 / 1

Behind

Fastball Average .346

	Outside	Middle	Inside
High	5 / 400 / 2	3 / 333 / 1	3 / 333 / 1
Med	11 / 90 / 1	2 / 500 / 1	6 / 333 / 2
Low	5 / 200 / 1	12 / 500 / 6	5 / 600 / 3

Curve Average .400

	Outside	Middle	Inside
High	0 / 0 / 0	1 / 0 / 0	0 / 0 / 0
Med	2 / 0 / 0	1 / 0 / 0	3 / 333 / 1
Low	3 / 1000 / 3	4 / 500 / 2	1 / 0 / 0

Overall Evaluation

Against Right-Handed Pitchers

Overall Fastball	⚾⚾
Overall Curve	⚾⚾
Overall Slider	⚾⚾⚾

Against Left-Handed Pitchers

Overall Fastball	⚾
Overall Curve	⚾
Overall Slider	 Not enough information

Comments: Weak against outside fastballs vs. RH.

Strengths: High-inside and low-inside fastballs, all over-the-middle fastballs, low-middle curves and sliders, low-inside sliders vs. RH; low-middle and medium-outside fastballs vs. LH.

Weaknesses: Outside fastballs, medium-inside fastballs, inside curves, medium-inside sliders vs. RH; inside fastballs, high-outside fastballs, medium-outside and low-outside curves vs. LH.

Marvell Wynne (Left Handed) — *San Diego Padres*

Marvell Wynne Against Right-Handed Pitchers
Overall BARS Batting Average .258

Fastball Average .284

	Outside	Middle	Inside
High	15 / 200 / 3	29 / 310 / 9	14 / 214 / 3
Med	45 / 244 / 11	19 / 368 / 7	43 / 255 / 11
Low	23 / 86 / 2	38 / 447 / 17	24 / 333 / 8

Curve Average .244

	Outside	Middle	Inside
High	1 / 0 / 0	3 / 333 / 1	5 / 0 / 0
Med	7 / 571 / 4	0 / 0 / 0	14 / 285 / 4
Low	4 / 250 / 1	10 / 200 / 2	5 / 0 / 0

Slider Average .269

	Outside	Middle	Inside
High	0 / 0 / 0	3 / 333 / 1	3 / 666 / 2
Med	1 / 0 / 0	1 / 0 / 0	3 / 0 / 0
Low	0 / 0 / 0	3 / 333 / 1	12 / 250 / 3

Marvell Wynne Against Left-Handed Pitchers
Overall BARS Batting Average .216

Fastball Average .292

	Outside	Middle	Inside
High	0 / 0 / 0	2 / 0 / 0	2 / 500 / 1
Med	4 / 250 / 1	4 / 750 / 3	14 / 142 / 2
Low	1 / 1000 / 1	5 / 400 / 2	9 / 222 / 2

Curve Average .185

	Outside	Middle	Inside
High	1 / 1000 / 1	3 / 0 / 0	0 / 0 / 0
Med	3 / 333 / 1	2 / 500 / 1	4 / 250 / 1
Low	7 / 0 / 0	4 / 250 / 1	3 / 0 / 0

Slider Average .230

	Outside	Middle	Inside
High	1 / 1000 / 1	2 / 0 / 0	0 / 0 / 0
Med	3 / 333 / 1	0 / 0 / 0	1 / 0 / 0
Low	3 / 333 / 1	1 / 0 / 0	2 / 0 / 0

Left-handed hitter Marvell Wynne has trouble with outside fastballs thrown by right-handed pitchers (.200, .244 and .086, high to low). He hits over-the-middle and low-inside fastballs excellently, however.

His .447 average against low-over-the-middle fastballs is outstanding. He hits this pitch medium-deep to all fields. By aligning themselves according to the BARS fielding strategy for this pitch, fielders could prevent most of Wynne's base hits resulting from this location. The field diagram on the opposite page illustrates this strategy.

LOW-OVER-THE-MIDDLE FASTBALLS

BATTING AVERAGE .447
Play

Left	Medium-deep in straightaway left field
Center	Medium-deep in straightaway center field
Right	Medium-deep and shifted toward the right line
Short	Up middle (shifted toward second base)
Second	Shifted toward first base

His .333 against low-inside fastballs is also excellent.

LOW-INSIDE FASTBALLS

BATTING AVERAGE .333
Play

Left	Deep and shifted toward center field
Center	Medium-deep in straightaway center field
Right	Deep and shifted toward the right line
Short	Up middle (shifted toward second base)
Second	Shifted toward first base

Wynne hits a lot of medium-over-the-middle fastballs (.368). This shows that he is a patient hitter and waits for pitchers to come over the plate.

He pulls high-over-the-middle fastballs deep down the right field line.

HIGH-OVER-THE-MIDDLE FASTBALLS

BATTING AVERAGE .310
Play

Left	Deep in straightaway left field
Center	Deep and shifted toward right field
Right	Deep and shifted toward the right field line
Short	Up middle (shifted toward second base)
Second	Normal position

Wynne has trouble with low curves thrown by right-handed pitchers (.250, .200 and .000 on 0-for-5, outside to inside). He hits medium-high inside curves for a good .285 average.

He has trouble with low-inside sliders against right-handers (.250).

Against left-handed pitchers, Wynne has trouble with low-inside fastballs (.222) and medium-inside fastballs (.142).

Low-Over-The-Middle Fastballs

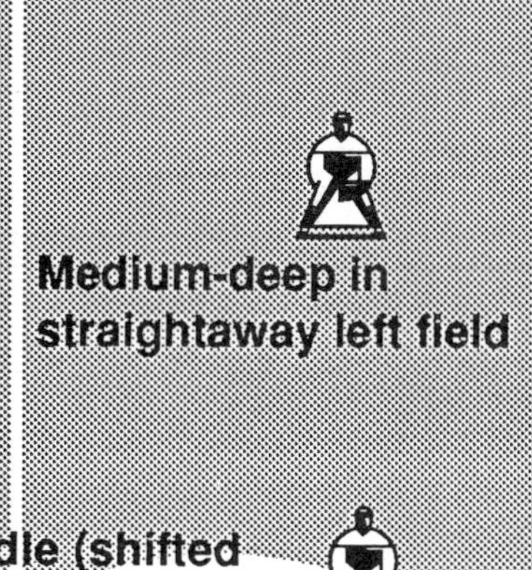

Ahead And Behind In The Count Vs. RH

Ahead

Each cell shows at-bats (top), batting average and hits (bottom, as average/hits).

Fastball Average .330

	Outside	Middle	Inside
High	4 / 250/1	10 / 500/5	7 / 142/1
Med	20 / 300/6	11 / 363/4	22 / 318/7
Low	11 / 0/0	27 / 481/13	12 / 333/4

Curve Average .285

	Outside	Middle	Inside
High	0 / 0/0	1 / 0/0	1 / 0/0
Med	2 / 1000/2	0 / 0/0	2 / 0/0
Low	0 / 0/0	1 / 0/0	0 / 0/0

Behind

Fastball Average .333

	Outside	Middle	Inside
High	3 / 333/1	6 / 166/1	4 / 500/2
Med	11 / 272/3	1 / 1000/1	11 / 272/3
Low	5 / 400/2	3 / 0/0	7 / 571/4

Curve Average .210

	Outside	Middle	Inside
High	0 / 0/0	1 / 1000/1	1 / 0/0
Med	3 / 333/1	0 / 0/0	6 / 166/1
Low	0 / 0/0	5 / 200/1	3 / 0/0

Overall Evaluation

Against Right-Handed Pitchers

Overall Fastball	
Overall Curve	
Overall Slider	(two balls)

Against Left-Handed Pitchers

Overall Fastball	
Overall Curve	
Overall Slider	Not enough information

Comments: Weak against outside fastballs vs. RH.
Strengths: Low-inside fastballs and all over-the-middle fastballs, medium-outside curves vs. RH.
Weaknesses: Outside fastballs, high-inside and medium-inside fastballs, low curves and low-inside sliders vs. RH; medium-inside and low-inside fastballs, low curves vs. LH.

Butler, Brett
Clark, Will
Gerhart, Ken
Kennedy, Terry
Maldonado, Candy
Mitchell, Kevin
Speier, Chris
Thompson, Rob
Uribe, Jose

San Francisco Giants
BARS System
Hitting Analysis

Brett Butler Against Right-Handed Pitchers
Overall BARS Batting Average .281

Fastball Average .292

	Outside	Middle	Inside
High	18 / 166 / 3	35 / 457 / 16	12 / 416 / 5
Med	117 / 341 / 40	49 / 224 / 11	112 / 267 / 30
Low	35 / 142 / 5	77 / 298 / 23	51 / 294 / 15

Curve Average .295

	Outside	Middle	Inside
High	5 / 200 / 1	2 / 1000 / 2	2 / 0 / 0
Med	9 / 444 / 4	6 / 166 / 1	15 / 400 / 6
Low	4 / 250 / 1	14 / 214 / 3	14 / 214 / 3

Slider Average .318

	Outside	Middle	Inside
High	0 / 0 / 0	0 / 0 / 0	0 / 0 / 0
Med	0 / 0 / 0	3 / 666 / 2	16 / 250 / 4
Low	7 / 142 / 1	7 / 285 / 2	11 / 454 / 5

Brett Butler Against Left-Handed Pitchers
Overall BARS Batting Average .274

Fastball Average .346

	Outside	Middle	Inside
High	8 / 375 / 3	13 / 461 / 6	15 / 266 / 4
Med	32 / 312 / 10	12 / 416 / 5	50 / 320 / 16
Low	9 / 222 / 2	25 / 480 / 12	18 / 277 / 5

Curve Average .153

	Outside	Middle	Inside
High	1 / 0 / 0	3 / 0 / 0	1 / 0 / 0
Med	7 / 285 / 2	6 / 0 / 0	8 / 250 / 2
Low	5 / 200 / 1	5 / 200 / 1	3 / 0 / 0

Slider Average .166

	Outside	Middle	Inside
High	0 / 0 / 0	3 / 0 / 0	0 / 0 / 0
Med	4 / 250 / 1	4 / 0 / 0	7 / 142 / 1
Low	4 / 250 / 1	0 / 0 / 0	2 / 500 / 1

Left-handed hitter Brett Butler hits fastballs well against right-handed pitchers (.292 overall) and excellently against left-handed pitchers (.346 overall). He hits curves very well against right-handers but poorly against left-handers.

Starting with right-handers, Butler hits a very sound .341 against medium-high outside fastballs. He hits this pitch medium-deep down the left line and deep into the left-center gap (going to his opposite field). Note, however, that the shortstop needs to play shifted toward second base for this pitch.

MEDIUM-HIGH OUTSIDE FASTBALLS

BATTING AVERAGE .341
Play

Left	Medium-deep and shifted toward the left field line
Center	Deep and shifted toward left field
Right	Deep in straightaway right field
Short	Up middle (shifted toward second base)
Second	Normal position

The Ahead and Behind charts on the opposite page show that Butler hits medium-high inside fastballs for a higher average when he is ahead in the count (.278 when ahead, .150 when behind). His fielding strategies show that he pulls this pitch more when he is ahead than when behind. This is not uncommon; many hitters tend to pull the ball more when they are ahead.

MEDIUM-HIGH INSIDE FASTBALLS
(WHEN AHEAD IN THE COUNT)

BATTING AVERAGE .278
Play

Left	Medium-deep and shifted toward center field
Center	Medium-deep in straightaway center field
Right	Deep and shifted toward the right field line
Short	Up middle (shifted toward second base)
Second	Normal position

MEDIUM-HIGH INSIDE FASTBALLS
(WHEN BEHIND IN THE COUNT)

BATTING AVERAGE .150
Play

Left	Medium-deep and shifted toward the left field line
Center	Medium-deep and shifted toward left field
Right	Deep in straightaway right field
Short	Normal position
Second	Shifted toward first base

Butler's .457 against high-over-the-middle fastballs is excellent.

HIGH-OVER-THE-MIDDLE FASTBALLS

BATTING AVERAGE .457
Play

Left	Medium-deep in straightaway left field

Center	Deep and shifted toward right field
Right	Deep in straightaway right field
Short	Normal position
Second	*No instances recorded*

Butler Against Curves And Sliders

Butler has a lot of trouble with low curves against right-handed pitchers (.250, .214 and .214, outside to inside). He hits .400 against medium-high inside curves, however. He pulls this pitch deep down the right line.

MEDIUM-HIGH INSIDE CURVEBALLS

BATTING AVERAGE .400

Play

Left	*No instances recorded*
Center	Medium-deep in straightaway center field
Right	Deep and shifted toward the right field line
Short	Normal position
Second	Shifted toward first base

Butler also hits very well against low-inside sliders (.454).

Butler Against Left-Handed Pitchers

Butler has a strong .346 overall fastball average against left-handed pitchers. His over-the-middle fastball averages are especially high (.461, .416 and .480, high to low).

He hits low-over-the-middle fastballs to his opposite field. Note that the shortstop needs to play shifted toward second base.

LOW-OVER-THE-MIDDLE FASTBALLS
(THROWN BY LEFT-HANDED PITCHERS)

BATTING AVERAGE .480

Play

Left	Medium-deep and shifted toward the left field line
Center	Deep and shifted toward left field
Right	Deep and shifted toward center field
Short	Up middle (shifted toward second base)
Second	Normal position

He also goes down the left line with medium-high inside fastballs.

MEDIUM-HIGH INSIDE FASTBALLS
(THROWN BY LEFT-HANDED PITCHERS)

BATTING AVERAGE .320

Play

Left	Medium-deep and shifted toward the left field line
Center	Medium-deep and shifted toward left field
Right	Deep in straightaway right field
Short	Normal position
Second	Shifted toward first base

His .312 against medium-high outside fastballs is good. He goes to his opposite field with this pitch also.

MEDIUM-HIGH OUTSIDE FASTBALLS
(THROWN BY LEFT-HANDED PITCHERS)

BATTING AVERAGE .312

Play

Left	Deep and shifted toward the left field line
Center	Deep and shifted toward left field
Right	Deep in straightaway right field
Short	Up middle (shifted toward second base)
Second	Normal position

Ahead And Behind In The Count Vs. RH

Ahead

Fastball Average .309 | Curve Average .777

	Outside	Middle	Inside	Outside	Middle	Inside
High	6/ 333/2	18/ 444/8	8/ 500/4	1/ 1000/1	2/ 1000/2	0/ 0/0
Med	60/ 350/21	31/ 258/8	61/ 278/17	1/ 1000/1	0/ 0/0	3/ 666/2
Low	9/ 111/1	32/ 281/9	24/ 291/7	0/ 0/0	0/ 0/0	2/ 500/1

Behind

Fastball Average .244 | Curve Average .312

	Outside	Middle	Inside	Outside	Middle	Inside
High	4/ 250/1	7/ 285/2	2/ 500/1	1/ 0/0	0/ 0/0	1/ 0/0
Med	21/ 380/8	6/ 0/0	20/ 150/3	4/ 500/2	3/ 333/1	7/ 428/3
Low	10/ 200/2	14/ 214/3	10/ 300/3	1/ 0/0	9/ 222/2	6/ 333/2

Overall Evaluation
Against Right-Handed Pitchers

Overall Fastball	⚾⚾
Overall Curve	⚾ ⚾ ⚾
Overall Slider	⚾ ⚾ ⚾ ⚾

Against Left-Handed Pitchers

Overall Fastball	⚾ ⚾ ⚾ ⚾
Overall Curve	⚾
Overall Slider	⚾

Comments: Thrown few curves compared to fastballs. Strengths: High-middle, high-inside, medium-outside fastballs, medium-inside curves, low-inside sliders vs. RH; over-the-middle and waist-high fastballs vs. LH. Weaknesses: High-outside, low-outside and medium-middle fastballs, low curves, vs. RH; low-outside and high-inside fastballs, inside curves vs. LH.

Will Clark Against Right-Handed Pitchers
Overall BARS Batting Average .272

Fastball Average .308

	Outside	Middle	Inside
High	14 / 285 / 4	10 / 200 / 2	9 / 222 / 2
Med	45 / 400 / 18	5 / 0 / 0	15 / 333 / 5
Low	16 / 375 / 6	16 / 187 / 3	16 / 312 / 5

Curve Average .326

	Outside	Middle	Inside
High	4 / 250 / 1	5 / 400 / 2	2 / 1000 / 2
Med	4 / 250 / 1	1 / 0 / 0	8 / 500 / 4
Low	5 / 0 / 0	4 / 250 / 1	13 / 307 / 4

Slider Average .187

	Outside	Middle	Inside
High	0 / 0 / 0	0 / 0 / 0	1 / 0 / 0
Med	1 / 0 / 0	0 / 0 / 0	5 / 400 / 2
Low	4 / 0 / 0	2 / 500 / 1	3 / 0 / 0

Will Clark Against Left-Handed Pitchers
Overall BARS Batting Average .273

Fastball Average .367

	Outside	Middle	Inside
High	0 / 0 / 0	6 / 333 / 2	7 / 142 / 1
Med	9 / 555 / 5	1 / 1000 / 1	9 / 333 / 3
Low	6 / 166 / 1	7 / 428 / 3	4 / 500 / 2

Curve Average .289

	Outside	Middle	Inside
High	3 / 333 / 1	2 / 1000 / 2	1 / 1000 / 1
Med	10 / 200 / 2	1 / 1000 / 1	4 / 0 / 0
Low	9 / 333 / 3	6 / 166 / 1	2 / 0 / 0

Slider Average .100

	Outside	Middle	Inside
High	2 / 0 / 0	0 / 0 / 0	0 / 0 / 0
Med	8 / 125 / 1	2 / 500 / 1	0 / 0 / 0
Low	5 / 0 / 0	3 / 0 / 0	0 / 0 / 0

Will Clark, left-handed hitter, has a solid .308 overall fastball average against right-handed pitchers. He hits an impressive .400 in his medium-high outside fastball location. The following fielding strategy and the field diagram on the opposite page show how fielders need to play for this pitch.

MEDIUM-HIGH OUTSIDE FASTBALLS

BATTING AVERAGE .400

Play

Left	Deep in straightaway left field
Center	Medium-deep in straightaway center field
Right	Deep and shifted toward center field
Short	Up middle (shifted toward second base)
Second	Normal position

His .375 against low-outside fastballs thrown by right-handers is also very strong.

LOW-OUTSIDE FASTBALLS

BATTING AVERAGE .375

Play

Left	Deep and shifted toward the left field line
Center	Medium-deep and shifted toward left field
Right	Medium-deep in straightaway right field
Short	Normal position
Second	Shifted toward first base

Clark is strong against medium-high inside fastballs thrown by right-handers (.333).

MEDIUM-HIGH INSIDE FASTBALLS

BATTING AVERAGE .333

Play

Left	Medium-deep and shifted toward the left field line
Center	Deep and shifted toward right field
Right	Deep in straightaway right field
Short	Shifted toward third base
Second	Normal position

Clark hits inside curves better than outside curves against right-handers. For this reason right-handers should throw him more outside curves than they now do. He hits low-inside curves for a .307 average.

LOW-INSIDE CURVES

BATTING AVERAGE .307

Play

Left	*No instances recorded*
Center	Medium-deep and shifted toward left field
Right	*No instances recorded*
Short	Shifted toward third base
Second	Shifted toward first base

Fewer instances have been recorded for Clark against left-handed pitchers. It is evident, however, that he hits waist-high fastballs and all over-the-middle fastballs very well.

Medium-High Outside Fastballs

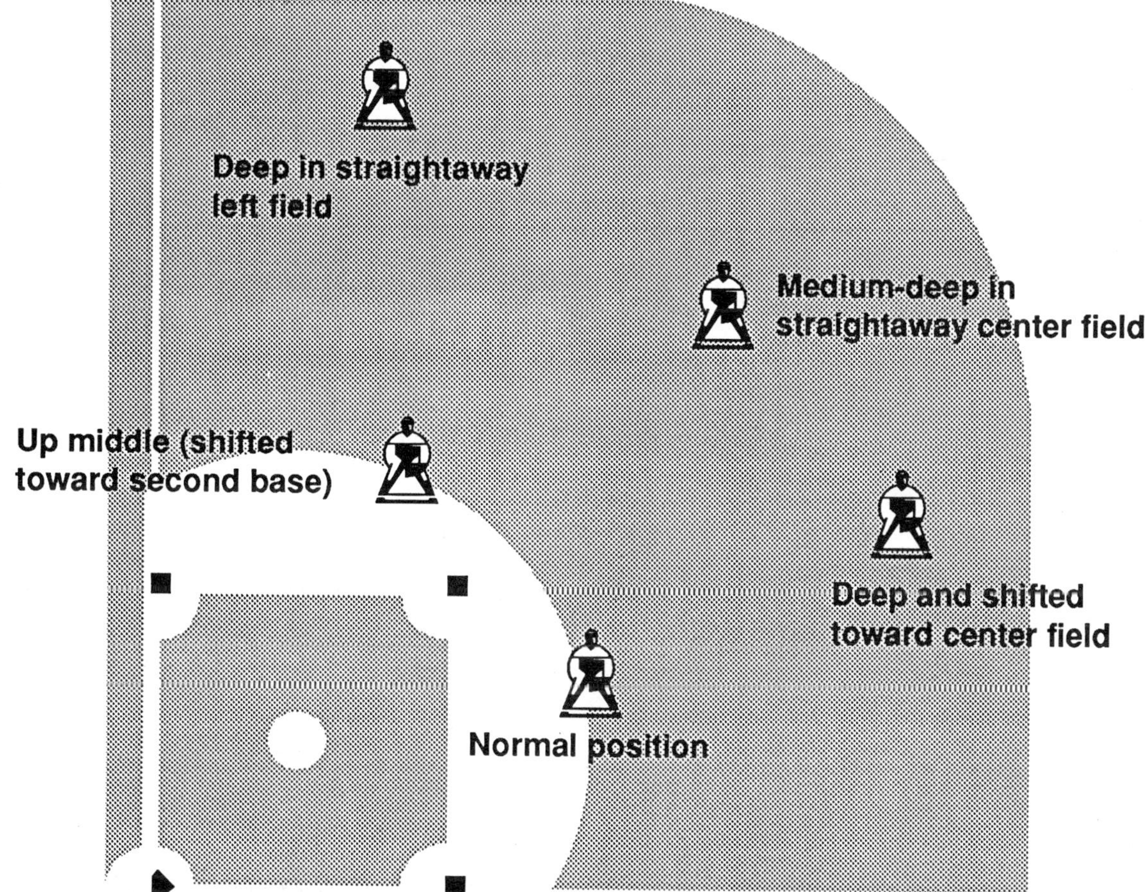

Ahead And Behind In The Count Vs. RH

Ahead

	Fastball Average .363			Curve Average .333		
	Outside	Middle	Inside	Outside	Middle	Inside
High	3/ 0/0	2/ 500/1	2/ 0/0	0/ 0/0	1/ 0/0	0/ 0/0
Med	31/ 451/14	2/ 0/0	6/ 333/2	0/ 0/0	0/ 0/0	4/ 500/2
Low	8/ 375/3	9/ 222/2	3/ 666/2	0/ 0/0	2/ 500/1	2/ 0/0

Behind

	Fastball Average .571			Curve Average .444		
	Outside	Middle	Inside	Outside	Middle	Inside
High	4/ 500/2	1/ 1000/1	2/ 1000/2	0/ 0/0	0/ 0/0	1/ 1000/1
Med	3/ 666/2	0/ 0/0	3/ 666/2	0/ 0/0	1/ 0/0	2/ 500/1
Low	4/ 250/1	2/ 500/1	2/ 500/1	0/ 0/0	1/ 0/0	4/ 500/2

Overall Evaluation

Against Right-Handed Pitchers

Overall Fastball ⚾ ⚾ ⚾

Overall Curve ⚾ ⚾ ⚾ ⚾

Overall Slider ⚾

Against Left-Handed Pitchers

Overall Fastball ⚾ ⚾ ⚾ ⚾

Overall Curve ⚾ ⚾ ⚾

Overall Slider ⚾

Comments: Strong against outside fastballs vs. RH.
Strengths: Outside fastballs, inside curves vs. RH; all waist-high and over-the-middle fastballs vs. LH.
Weaknesses: High-middle, high-inside and low-middle fastballs vs. RH; low-outside and high-inside fastballs, medium-outside curves, outside sliders vs. LH.

Ken Gerhart (Right Handed)   *San Francisco Giants*

Ken Gerhart Against Right-Handed Pitchers
Overall BARS Batting Average .195

Fastball Average .232

	Inside	Middle	Outside
High	3/ 0/0	3/ 333/1	4/ 250/1
Med	7/ 142/1	1/ 1000/1	40/ 200/8
Low	2/ 500/1	3/ 333/1	10/ 300/3

Curve Average .083

	Inside	Middle	Outside
High	0/ 0/0	0/ 0/0	0/ 0/0
Med	0/ 0/0	1/ 0/0	6/ 166/1
Low	1/ 0/0	1/ 0/0	3/ 0/0

Slider Average .187

	Inside	Middle	Outside
High	0/ 0/0	2/ 500/1	1/ 0/0
Med	1/ 0/0	0/ 0/0	7/ 142/1
Low	1/ 0/0	0/ 0/0	4/ 250/1

Ken Gerhart Against Left-Handed Pitchers
Overall BARS Batting Average .204

Fastball Average .238

	Inside	Middle	Outside
High	1/ 0/0	2/ 0/0	6/ 0/0
Med	6/ 0/0	1/ 1000/1	54/ 259/14
Low	3/ 333/1	5/ 600/3	6/ 166/1

Curve Average .428

	Inside	Middle	Outside
High	1/ 1000/1	0/ 0/0	0/ 0/0
Med	0/ 0/0	2/ 500/1	2/ 0/0
Low	0/ 0/0	2/ 500/1	0/ 0/0

Slider Average .166

	Inside	Middle	Outside
High	0/ 0/0	2/ 500/1	0/ 0/0
Med	1/ 0/0	0/ 0/0	2/ 500/1
Low	5/ 0/0	1/ 0/0	1/ 0/0

Right-handed Ken Gerhart has problems with fastballs thrown by right-handed pitchers. His .200 in the medium-high outside location is very weak.

MEDIUM-HIGH OUTSIDE FASTBALLS

BATTING AVERAGE .200

Play

Left	Medium-deep in straightaway left field
Center	Deep and shifted toward left field
Right	Short in straightaway right field
Short	Normal position
Second	*No instances recorded*

He hits low-outside fastballs well (.300). Not many instances have been recorded for Gerhart in this location, but the BARS fielding strategy indicates that he hits to straightaway center and deep right center.

LOW-OUTSIDE FASTBALLS

BATTING AVERAGE .300

Play

Left	*No instances recorded*
Center	Medium-deep in straightaway center field
Right	Deep and shifted toward center field
Short	Normal position
Second	Shifted toward first base

Gerhart's medium-high inside strategy indicates that he pulls this pitch to left and center fields.

MEDIUM-HIGH INSIDE FASTBALLS

BATTING AVERAGE .142

Play

Left	Deep and shifted toward the left field line
Center	Medium-deep and shifted toward left field
Right	Medium-deep in straightaway right field
Short	Normal position
Second	Normal position

Gerhart Against Left-Handed Pitchers

Gerhart hits medium-high outside fastballs better against left-handers than he does against right-handers, but his average in this location is still low (.259 vs. lefties). He hits pitches to this location better when he is ahead in the count.

**MEDIUM-HIGH OUTSIDE FASTBALLS
(THROWN BY LEFT-HANDED PITCHERS
WHEN GERHART IS AHEAD IN THE COUNT)**

BATTING AVERAGE .321 (9 for 28)

Play

Left	Deep and shifted toward the left field line
Center	Deep and shifted toward left field
Right	Deep and shifted toward the right field line
Short	Up middle (shifted toward second base)
Second	Normal position

MEDIUM-HIGH OUTSIDE FASTBALLS (THROWN BY LEFT-HANDED PITCHERS WHEN GERHART IS BEHIND IN THE COUNT)

BATTING AVERAGE .272 (3 for 11)

Play

Left   Deep and shifted toward the left field line
Center   Deep in straightaway center field
Right   Medium-deep in straightaway right field

The diagram below shows how fielders need to shift to be properly positioned for medium-high outside fastballs when Gerhart is ahead (dark men) and behind (light men) in the count against left-handers.

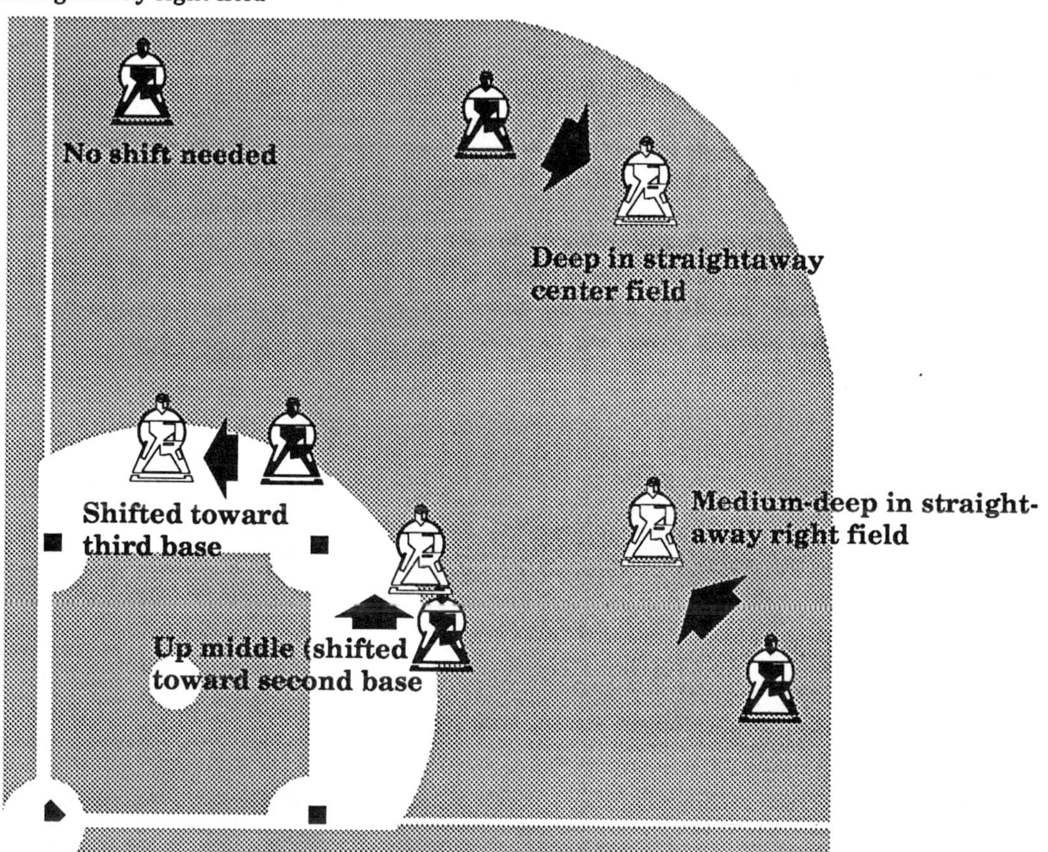

Ahead And Behind In The Count Vs. RH

Ahead

Fastball Average .242

	Inside	Middle	Outside
High	0 (1/0)	0 (1/0)	500 (2/1)
Med	250 (4/1)	1000 (1/1)	210 (19/4)
Low	0 (0/0)	0 (2/0)	333 (3/1)

Curve Average .000

	Inside	Middle	Outside
High	0 (0/0)	0 (0/0)	0 (0/0)
Med	0 (0/0)	0 (0/0)	0 (3/0)
Low	0 (0/0)	0 (1/0)	0 (0/0)

Behind

Fastball Average .357

	Inside	Middle	Outside
High	0 (1/0)	0 (0/0)	0 (0/0)
Med	0 (2/0)	0 (0/0)	375 (8/3)
Low	1000 (1/1)	0 (0/0)	500 (2/1)

Curve Average .000

	Inside	Middle	Outside
High	0 (0/0)	0 (0/0)	0 (0/0)
Med	0 (0/0)	0 (0/0)	0 (1/0)
Low	0 (0/0)	0 (0/0)	0 (0/0)

Overall Evaluation

Against Right-Handed Pitchers

Overall Fastball 
Overall Curve   Not enough information
Overall Slider   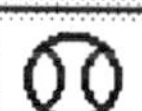

Against Left-Handed Pitchers

Overall Fastball
Overall Curve   Not enough information
Overall Slider   Not enough information

Comments: Since most fastballs to Gerhart are thrown in the medium-high outside location, he could focus on improving his performance against these pitches. Strengths: Low-outside fastballs thrown by RH. Weaknesses: Medium-outside and medium-inside fastballs vs. RH, medium-high outside curves and sliders vs. RH; outside fastballs vs. LH.

Terry Kennedy Against Right-Handed Pitchers
Overall BARS Batting Average .262

Fastball Average .289

	Outside	Middle	Inside
High	31/161 /5	39/384 /15	16/250 /4
Med	128/265 /34	19/368 /7	52/307 /16
Low	27/185 /5	64/375 /24	25/240 /6

Curve Average .320

	Outside	Middle	Inside
High	2/500 /1	4/1000 /4	4/750 /3
Med	15/266 /4	15/466 /7	4/500 /2
Low	9/0 /0	14/214 /3	14/142 /2

Slider Average .279

	Outside	Middle	Inside
High	2/1000 /2	4/250 /1	2/500 /1
Med	3/0 /0	1/1000 /1	6/500 /3
Low	3/0 /0	9/333 /3	13/76 /1

Terry Kennedy Against Left-Handed Pitchers
Overall BARS Batting Average .246

Fastball Average .323

	Outside	Middle	Inside
High	10/0 /0	9/555 /5	11/272 /3
Med	50/360 /18	5/400 /2	21/333 /7
Low	7/285 /2	12/333 /4	11/272 /3

Curve Average .105

	Outside	Middle	Inside
High	2/0 /0	4/0 /0	0/0 /0
Med	7/142 /1	2/0 /0	4/750 /3
Low	10/0 /0	8/0 /0	1/0 /0

Slider Average .133

	Outside	Middle	Inside
High	0/0 /0	1/0 /0	0/0 /0
Med	9/333 /3	2/0 /0	1/0 /0
Low	10/0 /0	4/250 /1	3/0 /0

Left-handed hitting Terry Kennedy is very strong against fastballs thrown over the middle part of the plate by right-handed pitchers (.384, .368 and .375 from high to low). He hits low-over-the-middle fastballs to the opposite field (left field) when ahead.

**LOW-OVER-THE-MIDDLE FASTBALLS
(WHEN AHEAD IN THE COUNT)**

BATTING AVERAGE .432
Play
Left　Deep and shifted toward the left field line
Center　Deep and shifted toward left field
Right　Medium-deep in straightaway right field
Short　Up middle (shifted toward second base)
Second　Normal position

**LOW-OVER-THE-MIDDLE FASTBALLS
(WHEN BEHIND IN THE COUNT)**

BATTING AVERAGE .333
Play
Left　Deep in straightaway left field
Center　Medium-deep in straightaway center field
Right　Medium-deep in straightaway right field
Short　Up middle (shifted toward second base)
Second　Normal position

He hits high-over-the-middle fastballs, however, straightaway to all fields.

HIGH-OVER-THE-MIDDLE FASTBALLS

BATTING AVERAGE .384
Play
Left　Medium-deep in straightaway left field
Center　Medium-deep in straightaway center field
Right　Deep in straightaway right field
Short　Up middle (shifted toward second base)
Second　Normal position

Kennedy hits medium-high outside fastballs straightaway but he hits medium-high inside fastballs into the right-center gap and down the right-field line.

MEDIUM-HIGH OUTSIDE FASTBALLS

BATTING AVERAGE .265
Play
Left　Medium-deep in straightaway left field
Center　Medium-deep in straightaway center field
Right　Deep in straightaway right field
Short　Up middle (shifted toward second base)
Second　Normal position

MEDIUM-HIGH INSIDE FASTBALLS

BATTING AVERAGE .307
Play
Left　Deep in straightaway left field
Center　Deep and shifted toward right field
Right　Deep and shifted toward the right field line

Short   Up middle (shifted toward second base)
Second   Normal position

Kennedy has low averages in his low-inside, high-inside, and outside fastball locations.   His strengths top to bottom down the middle of the plate and in the medium-high inside location keep his overall fastball average at a respectable .289 against right-handers.

Kennedy Against Curves And Sliders

Although Kennedy's overall curve average against right-handed pitchers is an excellent .320, he has definite problems with low curves. His 0-for-9 against low-outside curves, .214 against low-over-the-middle curves and .142 against low-inside curves present a weakness for pitchers to attack.

He hits medium-over-the-middle curves very well (.466). Pitchers want to avoid medium-over-the-middle curves to Kennedy, but it's interesting to know that he hits them down both lines and to the right side of the infield.

He hits medium-high outside curves into deep left center and medium-deep right center.

MEDIUM-HIGH OUTSIDE CURVEBALLS

BATTING AVERAGE .266

Play

Left   Deep in straightaway left field
Center   Deep and shifted toward left field
Right   Medium-deep and shifted toward center field
Short   Up middle (shifted toward second base)
Second   Normal position

Kennedy's weakness against low-inside sliders (.076) brings his overall slider average down sharply.

Kennedy Against Left-Handed Pitchers

Kennedy is also strong down the middle against left-handed pitchers (.555, .400 and .333, high to low). His most pitched location is medium-high outside, in which he hits a fine .360. He hits this pitch to short left and into the deep right-center gap. Fielders could probably cut off a lot of his hits if they followed the BARS fielding strategy for this pitch.

MEDIUM-HIGH OUTSIDE FASTBALLS (THROWN BY LEFT-HANDED PITCHERS)

BATTING AVERAGE .360

Play

Left   Short in straightaway left field
Center   Medium-deep in straightaway center field
Right   Deep and shifted toward center field
Short   Up middle (shifted toward second base)
Second   Shifted toward first base

Kennedy's high-outside fastball location is a real weakness for left-handers to attack. He seems to get his bat on the ball when this pitch is thrown, but mostly he hits easy fly balls and grounders.

Also notice his weakness against low curves and low sliders against left-handers. He has trouble getting the ball out of the infield against low-outside curves and low-outside sliders.

Ahead And Behind In The Count Vs. RH

Ahead

Fastball Average .329

	Outside	Middle	Inside
High	3/ 333 /1	14/ 428 /6	6/ 500 /3
Med	59/ 186 /1	12/ 416 /5	29/ 413 /12
Low	12/ 333 /4	37/ 432 /16	13/ 230 /3

Curve Average .357

	Outside	Middle	Inside
High	0/ 0 /0	3/ 1000 /3	2/ 500 /1
Med	4/ 250 /1	3/ 333 /1	3/ 666 /2
Low	3/ 0 /0	6/ 333 /2	4/ 0 /0

Behind

Fastball Average .309

	Outside	Middle	Inside
High	4/ 250 /1	7/ 428 /3	3/ 0 /0
Med	27/ 370 /10	3/ 333 /1	9/ 333 /3
Low	4/ 0 /0	9/ 333 /3	5/ 200 /1

Curve Average .400

	Outside	Middle	Inside
High	2/ 500 /1	1/ 1000 /1	1/ 1000 /1
Med	7/ 428 /3	10/ 400 /4	0/ 0 /0
Low	2/ 0 /0	3/ 333 /1	4/ 250 /1

Overall Evaluation

Against Right-Handed Pitchers

Overall Fastball   ⚾ ⚾
Overall Curve   ⚾ ⚾ ⚾ ⚾
Overall Slider   ⚾ ⚾ ⚾

Against Left-Handed Pitchers

Overall Fastball   ⚾ ⚾ ⚾
Overall Curve   ⚾
Overall Slider   ⚾

Comments: Kennedy hits fastballs better against LH; curves better against RH.

Strengths: Over-the-middle fastballs, medium-inside fastballs, medium-middle curves, low-middle sliders vs. RH; over-the-middle and waist-high fastballs, medium-outside sliders vs. LH.

Weaknesses: The four fastball corners vs. RH, all low curves, low-inside sliders vs. RH; high-outside fastballs, all low curves and all low sliders vs. LH.

Candy Maldonado Against Right-Handed Pitchers
Overall BARS Batting Average .249

Fastball Average .279

	Inside	Middle	Outside
High	16 / 312 / 5	15 / 400 / 6	10 / 300 / 3
Med	18 / 166 / 3	6 / 500 / 3	35 / 285 / 10
Low	16 / 62 / 1	21 / 285 / 6	24 / 333 / 8

Curve Average .190

	Inside	Middle	Outside
High	0 / 0 / 0	0 / 0 / 0	2 / 0 / 0
Med	1 / 0 / 0	1 / 0 / 0	5 / 400 / 2
Low	0 / 0 / 0	3 / 0 / 0	9 / 222 / 2

Slider Average .236

	Inside	Middle	Outside
High	1 / 0 / 0	1 / 0 / 0	2 / 500 / 1
Med	2 / 500 / 1	0 / 0 / 0	12 / 250 / 3
Low	2 / 0 / 0	4 / 500 / 2	14 / 142 / 2

Candy Maldonado Against Left-Handed Pitchers
Overall BARS Batting Average .291

Fastball Average .309

	Inside	Middle	Outside
High	8 / 0 / 0	11 / 363 / 4	8 / 250 / 2
Med	10 / 300 / 3	4 / 0 / 0	28 / 464 / 13
Low	4 / 500 / 2	13 / 384 / 5	24 / 208 / 5

Curve Average .250

	Inside	Middle	Outside
High	0 / 0 / 0	1 / 1000 / 1	1 / 1000 / 1
Med	4 / 500 / 2	0 / 0 / 0	4 / 250 / 1
Low	3 / 333 / 1	7 / 0 / 0	4 / 0 / 0

Slider Average .304

	Inside	Middle	Outside
High	0 / 0 / 0	0 / 0 / 0	1 / 0 / 0
Med	3 / 333 / 1	2 / 0 / 0	5 / 600 / 3
Low	3 / 333 / 1	6 / 166 / 1	3 / 333 / 1

Right-handed hitter Candy Maldonado hits fastballs fairly well against right-handed pitchers (.279 overall) and very well against left-handed pitchers (.309 overall).

Starting with right-handers, Maldonado hits .285 against medium-high outside fastballs. He hits this pitch down both lines, as shown on the opposite page.

MEDIUM-HIGH OUTSIDE FASTBALLS

BATTING AVERAGE .285
Play

Left	Medium-deep and shifted toward the left field line
Center	Deep in straightaway center field
Right	Deep and shifted toward the right field line
Short	Up middle (shifted toward second base)
Second	Normal position

If right-handers are going to throw low or medium-high, they should keep the ball inside against Maldonado. He hits a strong .333 against low-outside fastballs.

LOW-OUTSIDE FASTBALLS

BATTING AVERAGE .333
Play

Left	Deep in straightaway left field
Center	Deep and shifted toward left field
Right	Deep and shifted toward center field
Short	Normal position
Second	Normal position

Maldonado Against Left-Handed Pitchers

Maldonado hits medium-high outside fastballs for an exceptional .464 average against left-handers.

**MEDIUM-HIGH OUTSIDE FASTBALLS
(THROWN BY LEFT-HANDED PITCHERS)**

BATTING AVERAGE .464
Play

Left	Medium-deep and shifted toward the left field line
Center	Medium-deep in straightaway center field
Right	Deep in straightaway right field
Short	Normal position
Second	*No instances recorded*

His .384 against low-over-the-middle fastballs thrown by left-handers is also very strong.

**LOW-OVER-THE-MIDDLE FASTBALLS
(THROWN BY LEFT-HANDED PITCHERS)**

BATTING AVERAGE .384
Play

Left	Deep and shifted toward the left field line
Center	Medium-deep and shifted toward left field
Right	Medium-deep in straightaway right field
Short	Normal position
Second	Normal position

Medium-High Outside Fastballs

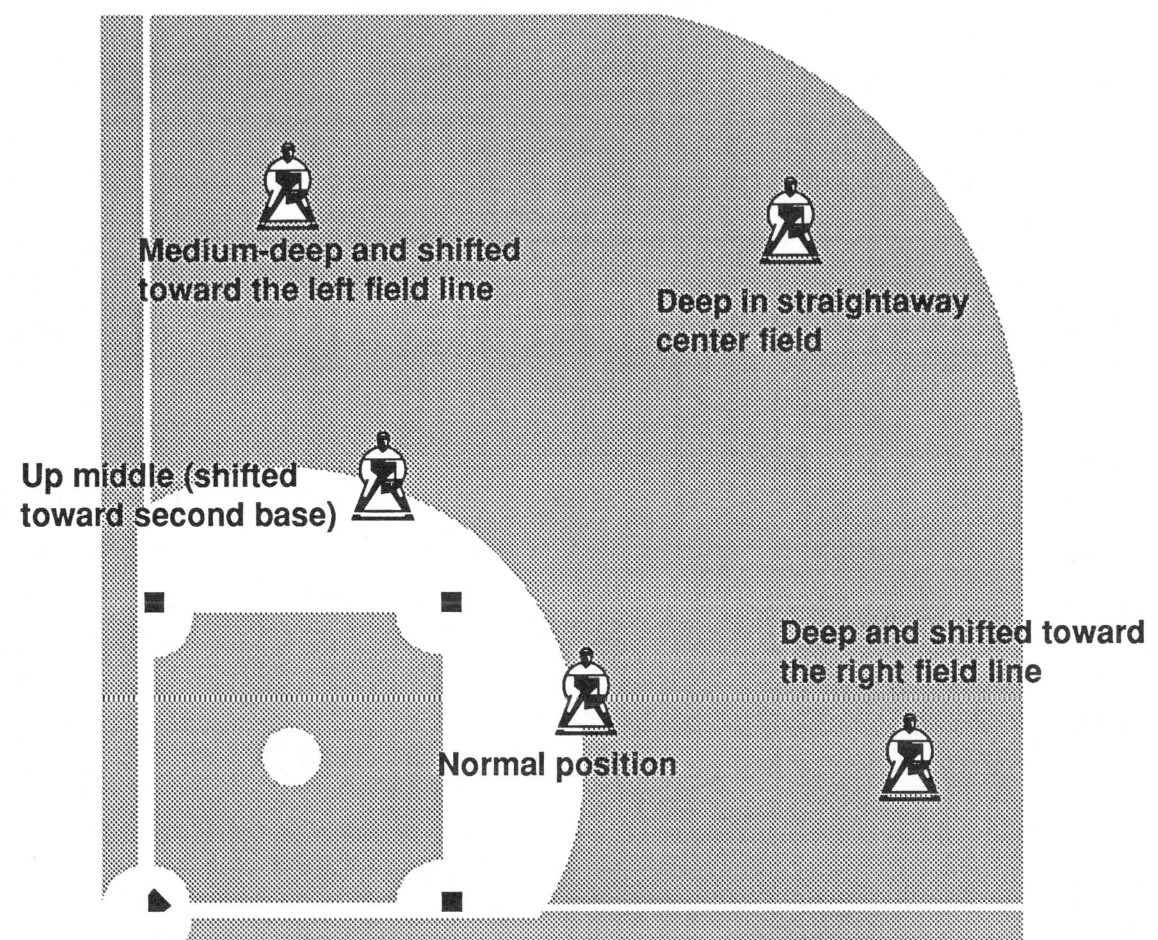

Ahead And Behind In The Count Vs. RH

Ahead

	Fastball Average .367			Curve Average .400		
	Inside	Middle	Outside	Inside	Middle	Outside
High	4/ 250 /1	7/ 428 /3	5/ 200 /1	0/ 0 /0	0/ 0 /0	1/ 0 /0
Med	10/ 200 /2	2/ 500 /1	15/ 466 /7	0/ 0 /0	0/ 0 /0	2/ 1000/2
Low	4/ 250 /1	11/ 363 /4	10/ 500 /5	0/ 0 /0	0/ 0 /0	2/ 0 /0

Behind

	Fastball Average .375			Curve Average .142		
	Inside	Middle	Outside	Inside	Middle	Outside
High	4/ 500 /2	5/ 600 /3	2/ 1000 /2	0/ 0 /0	0/ 0 /0	1/ 0 /0
Med	0/ 0 /0	2/ 500 /1	5/ 0 /0	0/ 0 /0	1/ 0 /0	2/ 0 /0
Low	5/ 0 /0	5/ 400 /2	4/ 500 /2	0/ 0 /0	0/ 0 /0	3/ 333 /1

Overall Evaluation

Against Right-Handed Pitchers

Overall Fastball   ⚾ ⚾

Overall Curve   ⚾

Overall Slider   ⚾

Against Left-Handed Pitchers

Overall Fastball   ⚾ ⚾ ⚾

Overall Curve   ⚾ ⚾

Overall Slider   ⚾ ⚾ ⚾ ⚾ ⚾

Comments: Hits medium-outside fastballs down both lines, high-outside fastballs down the right line vs. RH.

Strengths: Low-outside fastballs vs. RH; high-middle and low-middle fastballs, medium-outside and medium-inside fastballs vs. LH.

Weaknesses: Medium-inside and low-inside fastballs, low-outside curves, medium-outside and low-outside sliders vs. RH; low-outside fastballs, low-middle curves vs. LH.

Kevin Mitchell (Right Handed)   *San Francisco Giants*

Kevin Mitchell Against Right-Handed Pitchers
Overall BARS Batting Average .275

Fastball Average .355

	Inside	Middle	Outside
High	13/ 153 / 2	8/ 625 / 5	12/ 333 / 4
Med	25/ 360 / 9	2/ 500 / 1	37/ 405 / 15
Low	16/ 250 / 4	20/ 350 / 7	16/ 375 / 6

Curve Average .102

	Inside	Middle	Outside
High	4/ 0 / 0	0/ 0 / 0	3/ 0 / 0
Med	4/ 250 / 1	2/ 0 / 0	8/ 125 / 1
Low	2/ 1000 / 2	3/ 0 / 0	13/ 0 / 0

Slider Average .233

	Inside	Middle	Outside
High	0/ 0 / 0	1/ 0 / 0	2/ 0 / 0
Med	3/ 333 / 1	1/ 1000 / 1	9/ 333 / 3
Low	2/ 0 / 0	1/ 0 / 0	11/ 181 / 2

Kevin Mitchell Against Left-Handed Pitchers
Overall BARS Batting Average .298

Fastball Average .382

	Inside	Middle	Outside
High	11/ 272 / 3	2/ 0 / 0	10/ 100 / 1
Med	4/ 500 / 2	5/ 400 / 2	21/ 523 / 11
Low	3/ 0 / 0	14/ 571 / 8	11/ 363 / 4

Curve Average .222

	Inside	Middle	Outside
High	1/ 0 / 0	2/ 0 / 0	1/ 1000 / 1
Med	5/ 200 / 1	1/ 0 / 0	5/ 400 / 2
Low	5/ 200 / 1	5/ 200 / 1	2/ 0 / 0

Slider Average .333

	Inside	Middle	Outside
High	2/ 1000 / 2	2/ 0 / 0	0/ 0 / 0
Med	3/ 0 / 0	0/ 0 / 0	0/ 0 / 0
Low	1/ 0 / 0	0/ 0 / 0	1/ 1000 / 1

Kevin Mitchell, right-handed hitter, has excellent fastball averages against both right- and left-handed pitchers. Starting with right-handers, notice he has only two weak fastball locations (.153 high-inside, .250 low-inside). Every other fastball location is excellent. He hits .405 against medium-high outside fastballs.

MEDIUM-HIGH OUTSIDE FASTBALLS

BATTING AVERAGE .405
> *Play*

Left	Medium-deep in straightaway left field
Center	Deep in straightaway center field
Right	Deep in straightaway right field
Short	Normal position
Second	Shifted toward first base

His .360 against medium-high inside fastballs is also excellent.

MEDIUM-HIGH INSIDE FASTBALLS

BATTING AVERAGE .360
> *Play*

Left	Medium-deep and shifted toward the left field line
Center	Medium-deep in straightaway center field
Right	Medium-deep in straightaway right field
Short	Up middle (shifted toward second base)
Second	*No instances recorded*

Right-handers should be advised to try mixing in more curves and sliders to Mitchell considering how well he hits fastballs. He is especially weak against outside curves.

LOW-OUTSIDE CURVEBALLS

BATTING AVERAGE .000 (0 for 13)
> *Play*

Left	*No instances recorded*
Center	*No instances recorded*
Right	*No instances recorded*
Short	Normal position
Second	*No instances recorded*

Similarly, he has trouble with low-outside sliders thrown by right-handers (.181).

Against left-handed pitchers, Mitchell hits medium-high outside fastballs (.523), low-outside fastballs (.363) and low-over-the-middle fastballs (.571) very well.

He pulls medium-high outside fastballs deep to all fields.

**MEDIUM-HIGH OUTSIDE FASTBALLS
(THROWN BY LEFT-HANDED PITCHERS)**

BATTING AVERAGE .523
> *Play*

Left	Deep and shifted toward the left field line
Center	Deep and shifted toward left field
Right	Deep and shifted toward center field
Short	Normal position
Second	Normal position

Medium-High Outside Fastballs

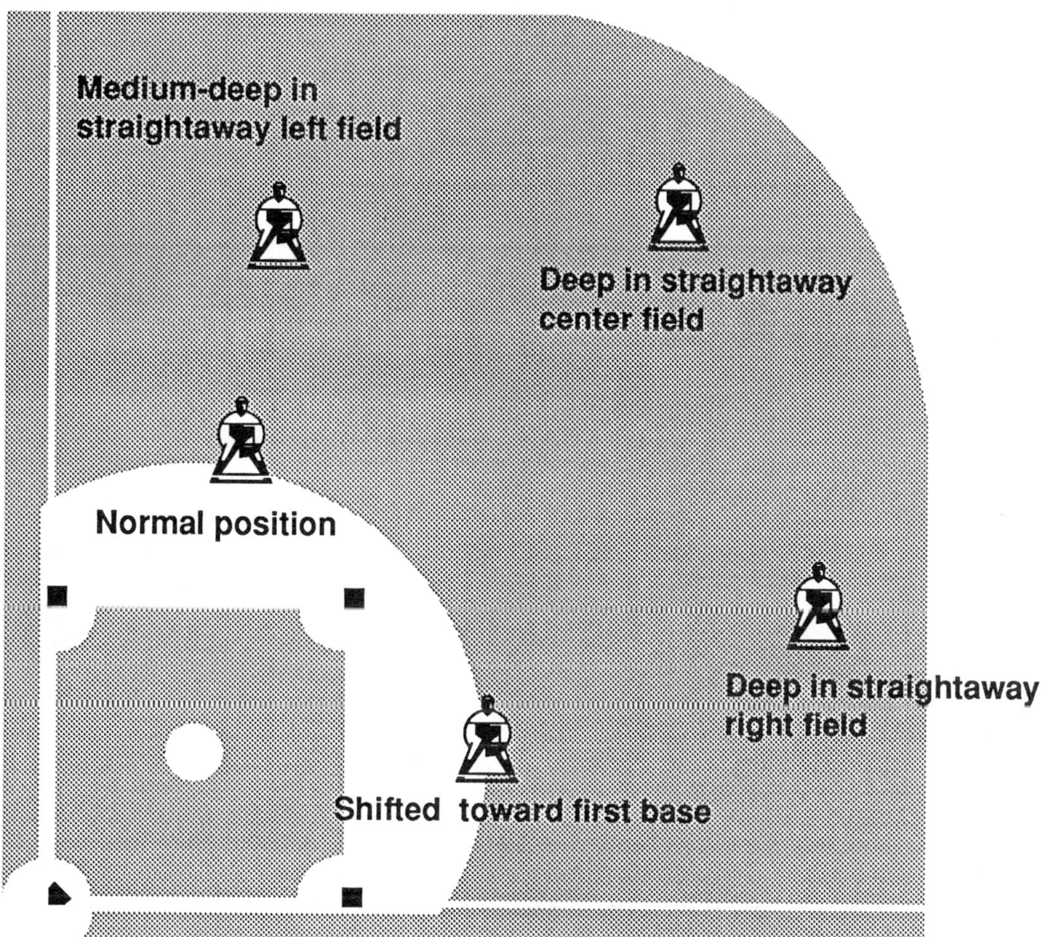

Ahead And Behind In The Count Vs. RH

Ahead

Fastball Average .363

	Inside	Middle	Outside
High	1/ 0 /0	5/ 600 /3	3/ 333 /1
Med	14/ 357 /5	1/ 0 /0	21/ 333 /7
Low	4/ 250 /1	11/ 363 /4	6/ 500 /3

Curve Average .181

	Inside	Middle	Outside
High	1/ 0 /0	0/ 0 /0	0/ 0 /0
Med	1/ 0 /0	0/ 0 /0	4/ 0 /0
Low	2/ 1000 /2	1/ 0 /0	2/ 0 /0

Behind

Fastball Average .500

	Inside	Middle	Outside
High	5/ 200 /1	2/ 1000 /2	3/ 666 /2
Med	3/ 666 /2	0/ 0 /0	6/ 500 /3
Low	5/ 400 /2	3/ 333 /1	5/ 600 /3

Curve Average .111

	Inside	Middle	Outside
High	0/ 0 /0	0/ 0 /0	1/ 0 /0
Med	0/ 0 /0	0/ 0 /0	3/ 333 /1
Low	0/ 0 /0	1/ 0 /0	4/ 0 /0

Overall Evaluation

Against Right-Handed Pitchers

Overall Fastball ⚾⚾⚾⚾
Overall Curve ⚾
Overall Slider ⚾

Against Left-Handed Pitchers

Overall Fastball ⚾⚾⚾⚾
Overall Curve ⚾
Overall Slider Not enough information

Comments: Strong vs. outside fastballs vs. RH.
Strengths: Outside fastballs, over-the-middle fastballs, medium-inside fastballs, medium-outside sliders vs. RH; waist-high and low-middle fastballs vs. LH.
Weaknesses: High-inside and low-inside fastballs, outside curves, low-outside sliders vs. RH; high fastballs vs. LH.

Chris Speier (Right Handed) San Francisco Giants

Chris Speier Against Right-Handed Pitchers
Overall BARS Batting Average .241

Fastball Average .283

	Inside	Middle	Outside
High	12/ 250 /3	31/ 322 /10	12/ 250 /3
Med	27/ 222 /6	13/ 461 /6	68/ 264 /18
Low	9/ 222 /2	43/ 325 /14	25/ 240 /6

Curve Average .181

	Inside	Middle	Outside
High	0/ 0 /0	2/ 500 /1	3/ 333 /1
Med	2/ 0 /0	0/ 0 /0	9/ 222 /2
Low	2/ 0 /0	3/ 0 /0	12/ 166 /2

Slider Average .200

	Inside	Middle	Outside
High	1/ 0 /0	0/ 0 /0	3/ 333 /1
Med	1/ 0 /0	2/ 0 /0	14/ 285 /4
Low	0/ 0 /0	7/ 142 /1	12/ 166 /2

Chris Speier Against Left-Handed Pitchers
Overall BARS Batting Average .228

Fastball Average .269

	Inside	Middle	Outside
High	5/ 0 /0	9/ 111 /1	2/ 0 /0
Med	4/ 0 /0	4/ 250 /1	23/ 434 /10
Low	3/ 0 /0	16/ 375 /6	12/ 250 /3

Curve Average .312

	Inside	Middle	Outside
High	1/ 1000 /1	1/ 1000 /1	2/ 0 /0
Med	1/ 0 /0	1/ 0 /0	3/ 1000 /3
Low	2/ 0 /0	3/ 0 /0	2/ 0 /0

Slider Average .111

	Inside	Middle	Outside
High	0/ 0 /0	1/ 0 /0	0/ 0 /0
Med	2/ 0 /0	0/ 0 /0	0/ 0 /0
Low	2/ 0 /0	4/ 250 /1	0/ 0 /0

Chris Speier, right-handed hitter, hits all over-the-middle fastballs well against right-handed pitchers (.322, .461 and .325, high to low). He has trouble with inside and outside fastballs.

His .325 against low-over-the-middle fastballs is excellent. He hits this pitch deep down the left line and deep into the right-center gap. The following fielding strategy and the field diagram on the opposite page show how fielders need to play for this pitch.

LOW-OVER-THE-MIDDLE FASTBALLS

BATTING AVERAGE .325
Play
Left Deep and shifted toward the left field line
Center Medium-deep in straightaway center field
Right Deep and shifted toward center field
Short Normal position
Second Shifted toward first base

His .322 against high-over-the-middle fastballs is strong.

HIGH-OVER-THE-MIDDLE FASTBALLS

BATTING AVERAGE .322
Play
Left Deep in straightaway left field
Center Deep and shifted toward right field
Right Medium-deep in straightaway right field
Short Shifted toward third base

Second Shifted toward first base

He is weak in the highly pitched medium-high outside fastball location (.264).

MEDIUM-HIGH OUTSIDE FASTBALLS

BATTING AVERAGE .264
Play
Left Medium-deep and shifted toward the left field line
Center Deep and shifted toward right field
Right Deep in straightaway right field
Short Normal position
Second Shifted toward first base

Speier is thrown a lot of outside curves and outside sliders. He has trouble with both types of pitches in his low-outside location (.166 against both) but he hits medium-high outside sliders well (.285).

Against left-handed pitchers, Speier hits medium-high outside fastballs excellently (.434).

MEDIUM-HIGH OUTSIDE FASTBALLS
(THROWN BY LEFT-HANDED PITCHERS)

BATTING AVERAGE .434
Play
Left Deep in straightaway left field
Center Deep and shifted toward right field
Right Medium-deep in straightaway right field
Short Up middle (shifted toward second base)
Second *No instances recorded*

Low-Over-The-Middle Fastballs

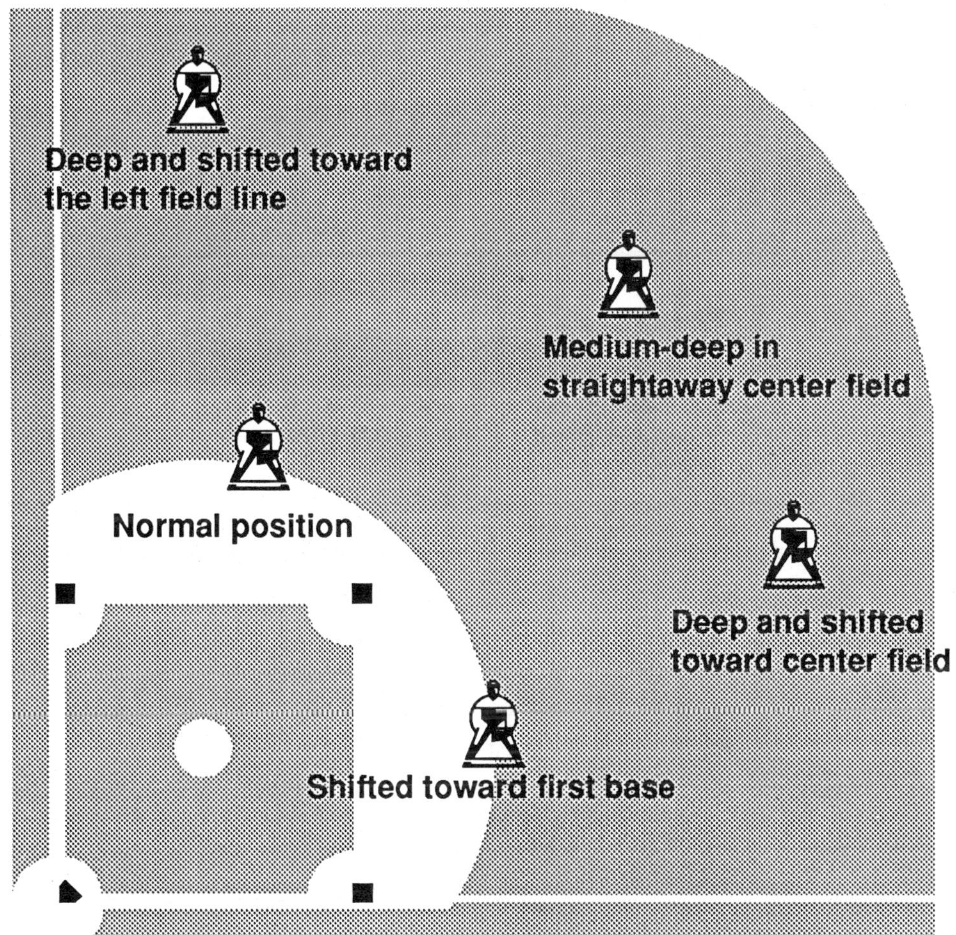

Ahead And Behind In The Count Vs. RH

Ahead

	Fastball Average .327			Curve Average .000		
	Inside	Middle	Outside	Inside	Middle	Outside
High	3/ 333 / 1	13/ 153 / 2	2/ 500 / 1	0/ 0 / 0	0/ 0 / 0	0/ 0 / 0
Med	7/ 142 / 1	8/ 500 / 4	44/ 363 / 16	0/ 0 / 0	0/ 0 / 0	1/ 0 / 0
Low	5/ 200 / 1	25/ 360 / 9	9/ 333 / 3	0/ 0 / 0	0/ 0 / 0	1/ 0 / 0

Behind

	Fastball Average .324			Curve Average .400		
	Inside	Middle	Outside	Inside	Middle	Outside
High	2/ 500 / 1	6/ 500 / 3	1/ 0 / 0	0/ 0 / 0	1/ 1000 / 1	2/ 500 / 1
Med	9/ 444 / 4	2/ 0 / 0	6/ 0 / 0	0/ 0 / 0	0/ 0 / 0	3/ 0 / 0
Low	1/ 0 / 0	7/ 285 / 2	3/ 666 / 2	0/ 0 / 0	1/ 0 / 0	3/ 666 / 2

Overall Evaluation

Against Right-Handed Pitchers

Overall Fastball 

Overall Curve

Overall Slider 

Against Left-Handed Pitchers

Overall Fastball

Overall Curve — Not enough information

Overall Slider — Not enough information

Comments: Weak vs. outside & inside fastballs vs. RH.
Strengths: Over-the-middle fastballs, medium-outside sliders vs. RH; medium-outside and low-middle fastballs vs. LH.
Weaknesses: Inside and outside fastballs, low-outside and medium-outside curves, low sliders vs. RH; low-outside, high-middle and all inside fastballs vs. LH.

Rob Thompson (Right Handed) — *San Francisco Giants*

Rob Thompson Against Right-Handed Pitchers
Overall BARS Batting Average .218

Fastball Average .256

	Inside	Middle	Outside
High	18 / 55 /1	19 / 473 /9	10 / 100 /1
Med	21 / 285 /6	9 / 222 /2	41 / 146 /6
Low	8 / 250 /2	28 / 428 /12	25 / 280 /7

Curve Average .132

	Inside	Middle	Outside
High	4 / 0 /0	7 / 142 /1	2 / 0 /0
Med	3 / 0 /0	5 / 400 /2	14 / 214 /3
Low	2 / 0 /0	1 / 0 /0	15 / 66 /1

Slider Average .058

	Inside	Middle	Outside
High	0 / 0 /0	0 / 0 /0	1 / 0 /0
Med	2 / 0 /0	0 / 0 /0	6 / 0 /0
Low	0 / 0 /0	2 / 0 /0	6 / 166 /1

Rob Thompson Against Left-Handed Pitchers
Overall BARS Batting Average .333

Fastball Average .390

	Inside	Middle	Outside
High	2 / 0 /0	4 / 500 /2	6 / 666 /4
Med	5 / 200 /1	6 / 333 /2	10 / 500 /5
Low	4 / 250 /1	12 / 416 /5	15 / 333 /5

Curve Average .333

	Inside	Middle	Outside
High	3 / 0 /0	2 / 1000 /2	0 / 0 /0
Med	2 / 500 /1	1 / 0 /0	1 / 1000 /1
Low	0 / 0 /0	1 / 0 /0	2 / 0 /0

Slider Average .142

	Inside	Middle	Outside
High	1 / 0 /0	0 / 0 /0	0 / 0 /0
Med	2 / 500 /1	0 / 0 /0	2 / 0 /0
Low	2 / 0 /0	0 / 0 /0	0 / 0 /0

Right-handed hitter Rob Thompson has two very strong fastball locations against right-handed pitchers (.473 high-over-the-middle and .428 low-over-the-middle). He hits high-over-the-middle fastballs straight-away to left and center and short toward the right line.

HIGH-OVER-THE-MIDDLE FASTBALLS

BATTING AVERAGE .473

Play

Left	Medium-deep in straightaway left field
Center	Deep in straightaway center field
Right	Short and shifted toward the right field line
Short	Shifted toward third base
Second	Normal position

He hits low-over-the-middle fastballs deep down the left line and straightaway to center and right.

LOW-OVER-THE-MIDDLE FASTBALLS

BATTING AVERAGE .428

Play

Left	Deep and shifted toward the left field line
Center	Medium-deep in straightaway center field
Right	Deep in straightaway right field
Short	Normal position
Second	Normal position

He has a lot of trouble with medium-high outside fastballs (.146) but he hits low-outside fastballs for a .280 average. He goes to his opposite field (right field) with this pitch.

LOW-OUTSIDE FASTBALLS

BATTING AVERAGE .280

Play

Left	*No instances recorded*
Center	Deep and shifted toward right field
Right	Medium-deep and shifted toward the right line
Short	Up middle (shifted toward second base)
Second	Normal position

Thompson has trouble with outside curves. His .214 against medium-high outside curves and .066 against low-outside curves give pitchers targets for attack.

Thompson hits outside fastballs very well against left-handed pitchers. He pulls medium-high outside fastballs. The following fielding strategy and the field diagram on the opposite page shows how fielders need to play him for this pitch.

MEDIUM-HIGH OUTSIDE FASTBALLS
(THROWN BY LEFT-HANDED PITCHERS)

BATTING AVERAGE .500

Play

Left	Medium-deep and shifted toward the left field line
Center	Deep and shifted toward left field
Right	Deep and shifted toward center field
Short	Normal position
Second	Normal position

Medium-High Outside Fastballs Vs. LH

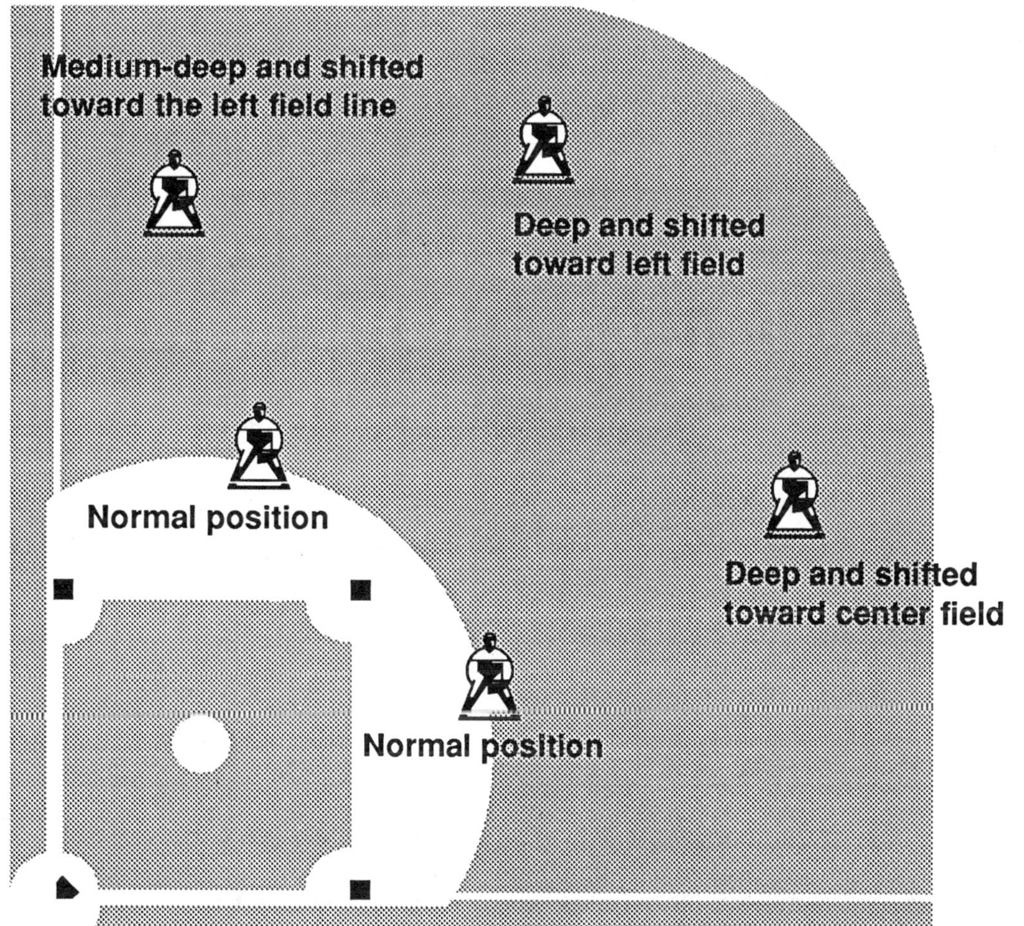

Ahead And Behind In The Count Vs. RH

Ahead

Fastball Average .360

	Inside	Middle	Outside
High	6 / 166 / 1	8 / 625 / 5	4 / 250 / 1
Med	13 / 307 / 4	8 / 250 / 2	16 / 250 / 4
Low	5 / 200 / 1	15 / 533 / 8	11 / 454 / 5

Curve Average .222

	Inside	Middle	Outside
High	1 / 0 / 0	4 / 0 / 0	0 / 0 / 0
Med	0 / 0 / 0	0 / 0 / 0	2 / 500 / 1
Low	0 / 0 / 0	0 / 0 / 0	2 / 500 / 1

Behind

Fastball Average .277

	Inside	Middle	Outside
High	2 / 0 / 0	0 / 0 / 0	0 / 0 / 0
Med	4 / 250 / 1	0 / 0 / 0	3 / 333 / 1
Low	1 / 0 / 0	5 / 400 / 2	3 / 333 / 1

Curve Average .133

	Inside	Middle	Outside
High	1 / 0 / 0	3 / 333 / 1	1 / 0 / 0
Med	1 / 0 / 0	0 / 0 / 0	4 / 250 / 1
Low	0 / 0 / 0	0 / 0 / 0	5 / 0 / 0

Overall Evaluation

Against Right-Handed Pitchers

Overall Fastball 
Overall Curve
Overall Slider 

Against Left-Handed Pitchers

Overall Fastball 
Overall Curve Not enough information
Overall Slider Not enough information

Comments: Weak against outside curves vs. RH. Strengths: High-middle and low-middle fastballs vs. RH; all over-the-middle and outside fastballs vs. LH. Weaknesses: The four fastball corners except low-outside (.280), medium-outside fastballs, outside curves and sliders vs. RH.

Jose Uribe (Switch Hitter)   *San Francisco Giants*

Jose Uribe Against Right-Handed Pitchers
Overall BARS Batting Average .269

Fastball Average .343

	Outside	Middle	Inside
High	16/ 125 / 2	41/ 292 / 12	13/ 384 / 5
Med	43/ 441 / 19	13/ 384 / 5	34/ 500 / 17
Low	23/ 173 / 4	25/ 160 / 4	16/ 562 / 9

Curve Average .272

	Outside	Middle	Inside
High	3/ 666 / 2	1/ 0 / 0	1/ 1000/ 1
Med	6/ 166 / 1	1/ 0 / 0	5/ 400 / 2
Low	2/ 500 / 1	9/ 222 / 2	5/ 0 / 0

Slider Average .047

	Outside	Middle	Inside
High	0/ 0 / 0	0/ 0 / 0	2/ 0 / 0
Med	1/ 0 / 0	0/ 0 / 0	4/ 0 / 0
Low	1/ 0 / 0	2/ 0 / 0	11/ 90 / 1

Jose Uribe Against Left-Handed Pitchers
Overall BARS Batting Average .298

Fastball Average .368

	Inside	Middle	Outside
High	5/ 200 / 1	10/ 400 / 4	7/ 428 / 3
Med	6/ 333 / 2	2/ 1000/ 2	14/ 428 / 6
Low	6/ 333 / 2	15/ 333 / 5	11/ 272 / 3

Curve Average .083

	Inside	Middle	Outside
High	1/ 0 / 0	0/ 0 / 0	1/ 0 / 0
Med	0/ 0 / 0	0/ 0 / 0	3/ 0 / 0
Low	5/ 0 / 0	2/ 500 / 1	0/ 0 / 0

Slider Average .200

	Inside	Middle	Outside
High	2/ 0 / 0	2/ 500 / 1	1/ 1000 / 1
Med	3/ 0 / 0	1/ 0 / 0	2/ 0 / 0
Low	2/ 0 / 0	2/ 500 / 1	0/ 0 / 0

Switch-hitting Jose Uribe has excellent fastball averages against both right- and left-handed pitchers (.343 overall against right-handers, .368 overall against left-handers). In comparison to the number of recorded fastball instances, he has very few recorded curve and slider instances. As well as he hits fastballs, pitchers should consider mixing in more breaking pitches to him.

Starting with right-handers, notice Uribe's strength against waist-high and inside fastballs. He hits medium-high outside fastballs for a brilliant .441 average. He hits this pitch medium-deep to all fields. By aligning themselves as indicated below, fielders could prevent most of his hits resulting from pitches to this location.

MEDIUM-HIGH OUTSIDE FASTBALLS

BATTING AVERAGE .441
Play

Left	Medium-deep in straightaway left field
Center	Medium-deep in straightaway center field
Right	Medium-deep and shifted toward center field
Short	Up middle (shifted toward second base)
Second	Normal position

He hits medium-high inside fastballs for a stunning .500 average. The following fielding strategy and the field diagram on the opposite page show how vital it is for fielders to shift for inside and outside pitches.

Every fielder except the second baseman needs to shift for a medium-high inside as compared to a medium-high outside fastball.

MEDIUM-HIGH INSIDE FASTBALLS

BATTING AVERAGE .500
Play

Left	Deep and shifted toward center field
Center	Deep in straightaway center field
Right	Medium-deep in straightaway right field
Short	Normal position
Second	Normal position

Uribe is weak against low curves and outside sliders against right-handers. These are the areas pitchers need to attack.

Batting right-handed against left-handed pitchers, Uribe hits medium-high outside fastballs excellently.

MEDIUM-HIGH OUTSIDE FASTBALLS
(THROWN BY LEFT-HANDED PITCHERS)

BATTING AVERAGE .428
Play

Left	Deep and shifted toward center field
Center	Deep and shifted toward right field
Right	Medium-deep in straightaway right field
Short	Up middle (shifted toward second base)
Second	Normal position

Medium-High Outside And Inside Fastballs
Medium-high outside fastballs — dark fielders
Medium high inside fastballs — light fielders

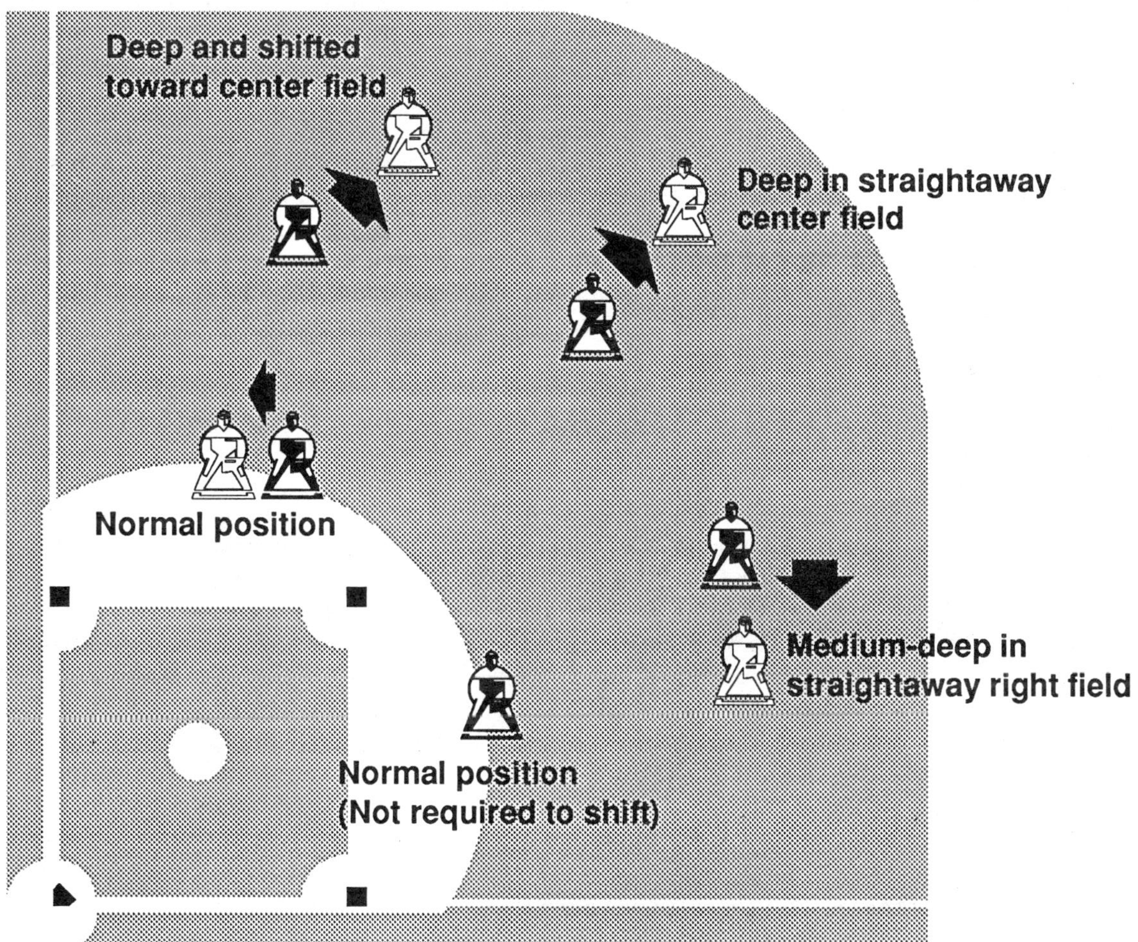

Ahead And Behind In The Count Vs. RH

Ahead

Fastball Average .384

	Outside	Middle	Inside
High	8/ 0/0	22/ 272/6	7/ 571/4
Med	30/ 500/15	6/ 666/4	15/ 466/7
Low	13/ 153/2	11/ 272/3	5/ 800/4

Curve Average .500

	Outside	Middle	Inside
High	1/ 1000/1	0/ 0/0	0/ 0/0
Med	0/ 0/0	0/ 0/0	0/ 0/0
Low	0/ 0/0	1/ 0/0	0/ 0/0

Behind

Fastball Average .343

	Outside	Middle	Inside
High	3/ 666/2	8/ 250/2	2/ 0/0
Med	4/ 250/1	1/ 1000/1	4/ 750/3
Low	5/ 200/1	3/ 0/0	2/ 500/1

Curve Average .500

	Outside	Middle	Inside
High	2/ 500/1	1/ 0/0	1/ 1000/1
Med	1/ 0/0	0/ 0/0	1/ 1000/1
Low	0/ 0/0	2/ 500/1	0/ 0/0

Overall Evaluation
Against Right-Handed Pitchers

Overall Fastball ⚾⚾⚾⚾

Overall Curve ⚾⚾

Overall Slider ⚾

Against Left-Handed Pitchers

Overall Fastball ⚾⚾⚾⚾

Overall Curve ⚾

Overall Slider ⚾

Comments: Strong against inside fastballs vs. RH.
Strengths: Inside fastballs and waist-high fastballs vs. RH; over-the-middle and waist-high fastballs vs. LH.
Weaknesses: High-outside, low-outside, low-middle fastballs, low-middle curves and inside sliders vs. RH; low-outside fastballs vs. LH.

Updating The BARS Records

The BARS System gathers information continually throughout the year. During the season, many games are scouted live on TV, but many are taped for later scouting. Most games for a particular season are recorded into the BARS computer by October or November. Some scouts, however, work through the winter catching up on games they did not have time to scout during the season.

This continual updating of information adds to the statistics of every player in the majors. Information for a certain year (such as the 1987 season or the 1988 season) is final when all available games for that year have been scouted, but the cumulative BARS statistics for hitters and pitchers are ongoing — they are never absolutely final.

It is interesting to look at how hitters' cumulative averages change as information is added from year to year. Several chapters in *The Tenth Man* compare numerous players' single-season BARS records from one year to the next. In this chapter, we'll compare several cumulative BARS batting records, showing how players' records change as additional information is gathered.

Darryl Strawberry, New York Mets

The following two fastball grids for Darryl Strawberry show how his records have progressed as information has been gathered over the last few years.

Fastball Average .320

Previous

	Outside	Middle	Inside
High	24/ 208 / 5	43/ 418 / 18	19/ 157 / 3
Med	64/ 312 / 20	26/ 423 / 11	35/ 342 / 12
Low	31/ 193 / 6	44/ 386 / 17	17/ 294 / 5

Fastball Average .319

Recent

	Outside	Middle	Inside
High	44/ 295 / 13	59/ 406 / 24	31/ 129 / 4
Med	90/ 333 / 30	28/ 464 / 13	49/ 346 / 17
Low	45/ 200 / 9	55/ 381 / 21	31/ 225 / 7

Note that there are many more recorded instances in Strawberry's latest chart, which contains the complete BARS fastball record for Strawberry at the end of the 1988 season. His recorded instances have increased from 64 to 90 in his medium-high outside location, from 35 to 49 in his medium-high inside location, from 24 to 44 in his high-outside location, etc.

His average has changed slightly in each location. This is inevitable as additional at-bats and base hits are recorded. In some locations his average has increased, in some his average has decreased. His overall fastball average, however, stayed about the same (.320 and .319).

Even though his averages in the nine locations changed, they remained fairly relative to each other. For instance, he is weak against low-outside fastballs in each chart, (.193 and .200). And he is strong against medium-high inside fastballs (.342 and .346).

The only significant change is the increase in his high-outside location (.208 and .295). In his earlier chart he was 5 for 24 in this location. In his latest chart he is 13 for 44. This means that in the 20 additional instances recorded he got 8 hits. Several years ago it was a good bet to throw him a high-outside fastball. It seems that now he's learned to hit it.

The BARS fielding strategy may also change slightly for hitters over the years. The following fielding charts compare the strategy for Strawberry's medium-high outside fastball locations.

MEDIUM-HIGH OUTSIDE FASTBALLS

Batting Average .312
> *Play*

Left	Deep and shifted toward the left field line
Center	Medium-deep in straightaway center field
Right	Deep in straightaway right field
Short	Normal position
Second	Normal position

MEDIUM-HIGH OUTSIDE FASTBALLS

Batting Average .333
> *Play*

Left	Deep and shifted toward the left field line
Center	Deep in straightaway center field
Right	Deep in straightaway right field
Short	Normal position
Second	Shifted toward first base

The fielding strategies for the centerfielder and the second baseman have changed. The strategies for the other fielders have stayed the same.

George Brett, Kansas City Royals

The BARS System has a lot of information for players like George Brett, who has been active for a number of years.

Brett's most recent fastball and curve charts are compared below with his charts of several years ago.

Previous

Fastball Average .370

	Outside	Middle	Inside
High	24 / 166 / 4	62 / 274 / 17	14 / 428 / 6
Med	110 / 400 / 44	82 / 500 / 41	57 / 315 / 18
Low	33 / 333 / 11	86 / 360 / 31	18 / 444 / 8

Curve Average .308

	Outside	Middle	Inside
High	4 / 250 / 1	4 / 500 / 2	2 / 0 / 0
Med	27 / 444 / 12	17 / 352 / 6	20 / 400 / 8
Low	7 / 0 / 0	26 / 153 / 4	13 / 307 / 4

Recent

Fastball Average .358

	Outside	Middle	Inside
High	46 / 239 / 11	91 / 318 / 29	20 / 350 / 7
Med	175 / 382 / 67	91 / 494 / 45	80 / 275 / 22
Low	53 / 320 / 17	116 / 362 / 42	23 / 391 / 9

Curve Average .304

	Outside	Middle	Inside
High	8 / 250 / 2	9 / 666 / 6	2 / 0 / 0
Med	37 / 351 / 13	19 / 421 / 8	21 / 380 / 8
Low	10 / 0 / 0	29 / 137 / 4	16 / 312 / 5

Note that, for the most part, Brett's strengths and weaknesses remain the same in the charts. For example, his medium-high outside fastball average fell slightly (.400 to .382), his high-outside fastballs average rose (.166 to .239), and his medium-high inside average fell (.315 to .275). Overall, his fastball average stayed about the same (.370 and .358).

His curve charts are very similar: he remains hitless against low-outside curves, is still weak against low-over-the-middle curves, and is still strong against low-inside curves. His overall curve averages were .308 and .304.

The more information that the BARS System has for a player, the more stable his cumulative fielding strategy is from year to year. The following charts show the fielding strategies for Brett's medium-high outside locations in the two charts.

MEDIUM-HIGH OUTSIDE FASTBALLS

Batting Average .400

Play

Left	Deep and shifted toward the left field line
Center	Deep in straightaway center field
Right	Deep and shifted toward center field
Short	Up middle (shifted toward second base)
Second	Shifted toward first base

MEDIUM-HIGH OUTSIDE FASTBALLS

Batting Average .382

Play

Left	Deep and shifted toward the left field line
Center	Deep in straightaway center field
Right	Deep and shifted toward center field
Short	Up middle (shifted toward second base)
Second	Shifted toward first base

BARS Records For Every Player

The BARS System has complete records for every player in the majors. This information is constantly updated so that the most complete records can be generated.

The BARS System itself is progressing. Soon we will have an additional statistic in each location of the batting grids. This will indicate the number of home runs hit off pitches to that particular location. This will increase the practical value of the BARS batting records because if a hitter has a low average in a certain location but has a high number of home runs, pitchers will be able to adjust accordingly. The BARS fielding strategy is right over 90 percent of the time, but if a hit ball doesn't stay in the park, even the most accurate strategy will be useless.

The Increasing Precision In Modern Sports

Everything evolves and changes. It's the nature of men and women to try to improve their performances — whatever they're involved in. A person who has a hobby like golf or bowling is continually trying to improve. The same is true with professional sports. It's not so much the money involved; people just want to do better each time they try something.

Athletes have become bigger, stronger and faster over the years. Some of this is due to training techniques, some to general trends in the population. In every sport that has fixed measurements of achievement, such as the number of seconds it takes to run a mile or swim 100 meters, the general performance of athletes has improved over the years. Twelve-year-olds today swim faster than Johnny Weissmuller did at his peak. Even high-school pole vaulters go over sixteen feet, although for years the fifteen-foot mark was considered unreachable.

The same is true of all track and field events. It is only in sports such as football and baseball, in which there are no direct measurements of performance, that any argument still exists that old-time athletes may be superior to the stars of today. The natural talents of a Babe Ruth, Ty Cobb, or Joe DiMaggio would make them stars in any era, but if the performance of track and field athletes is any indication, the average ballplayer of today is superior to the average ballplayer of thirty or forty years ago.

A lot of this is due to training and conditioning techniques. The scientific knowledge focussed on sports performance today allows an athlete to develop himself to a higher level, and to maintain his peak for a greater number of years.

The overall strategy of sports evolves also. The strategies involved in sports such as golf, skiing, basketball, football and others are much more sophisticated today than they were even ten years ago. How many set shots do you see in basketball today? Even quick jump shots are often blocked. The pace is faster, the scouting more complex and accurate, and the strategy of team coordination much more effective.

Increasing Precision In Football

During the last decade people have begun to realize that football is a precision game that loses a lot when played in less than ideal conditions. Fans used to think that football was at its best when two teams slogged it out on a field that was so muddy runners couldn't cut, quarterbacks couldn't grip the ball properly to pass, and receivers couldn't hold on to the ball if it did get to them. Fans used to say that such conditions gave the

better team a chance to excel.

But gradually people realized that playing in bad weather doesn't really give the better team an edge: it throws both teams into a survival-type offense and defense and takes away much of the refinement of the game. During the last decade this has been generally accepted by everyone, especially with the increased use of sophisticated defensive and offensive strategies and the computerized scouting of opponents.

For this reason the Super Bowl will never again be played in a situation that is likely to produce extreme weather conditions. A lot of regular season and playoff games in the East and Midwest are played in open air stadiums where winter temperatures often fall into the single digits; but Super Bowl games are being scheduled in cities that have warmer climates or domed stadiums. Fans enjoy the complicated alignments and sophisticated passing game that characterizes football today.

Baseball has never been good in cold or wet weather. For over a hundred years it's been recognized that baseball is not baseball when it rains. But unlike football, which has highly coordinated offensive and defensive strategies, baseball has a fielding strategy that is still a fairly loose affair. Fielders position themselves when a hitter comes to the plate, then hold those positions through all the pitches to him, even though there's no way a hitter is likely to hit a low-outside fastball the same way he's going to hit a low-inside fastball or a low-inside curve.

Anyone who has read *The Tenth Man* and the introductory chapters of this book knows how important it is for fielders to position themselves correctly for every pitch. When they use the BARS System fielding strategy to do this, they'll become as coordinatedt as the offensive and defensive units in professional football.

Two Main Objections

The two main objections to implementing the BARS System seem to be (1) pitchers can't throw the ball exactly where they want, so why bother, and (2) what managers really want is information based on how a hitter has performed against specific pitchers.

The first objection is easy to answer. It may be true that some pitchers will never be able to throw specifically to the medium-high outside location instead of to the low-outside or high-outside locations. But the fact is that the fielders have to be positioned *somewhere* on every pitch. They should be positioned so that their effectiveness can have the greatest potential. The pitcher may in fact not throw the ball to the medium-high outside location, but positioning the fielders accordingly will optimize the chance that they will be in the best positions to field balls hit in their directions.

The second objection is just as easy to answer. Sure, everyone would love to have batting and fielding strategy information that is 90 percent accurate for hitters against specific pitchers. Every manager would love to have it. I'd love to have it. But the fact is that it takes a lot of information to be able to get into the 90-plus percentage range of accuracy like the BARS System does. There's no way to get enough information for how hitters do against specific pitchers. Hitters don't face the same pitcher that often. Maybe they face a certain pitcher 20 or 30 at-bats in a season, but usually not even that often. BARS batting grids for how one hitter has done against a specific pitcher would be mostly zeros, especially in the curve and slider charts. Even in the fastball charts there wouldn't be much information, and that could be dangerous. A little information can sometimes be worse than no information at all

That's why the BARS System uses two main categories for the Super Summary charts: a hitter's performance against left-handed pitchers and against right-handed pitchers. As we get more information in the next few years, we may try to chart hitters and pitchers one-on-one. But for now, we'll stick to the two categories. We get over 90 percent accuracy using them, so we must be doing something right.

Home Runs

As I've mentioned before, because the BARS fielding strategy is accurate more than 90 percent of the time, it's often better to throw to a location in which a hitter has a high average, if there are a large number of instances recorded in that location. This is because there is a greater probability that the fielding strategy will be correct when the BARS System has recorded a large number of instances in a certain location. A batter may be hitting .400 in a location, but if you know how to position the fielders for pitches to that location, you'll get him out when he hits the ball.

One thing I am going to do very soon is show the number of home runs that a player has hit off pitches to specific locations. The number of home runs will be shown at the bottom left of every location in every BARS batting grid. Not only will this be valuable in a general sense, to show the areas of the strike zone in which a hitter tends to hit home runs, it will show specific locations to pitch away from in tight situations. The BARS fielding strategy shows where to position fielders, but there's no way to field a homer.

I'll work on this during the next year. It will be an added plus to the BARS System, and well worth the effort.

The Central Spark Of Baseball

The vital central spark of baseball involves the interaction between the pitcher and the hitter, and the overall coordinated effort of fielders positioning themselves correctly on a pitch-by-pitch basis. These factors determine how often pitches are hit and whether fielders are in position to field the hits, the number of runs scored, and ultimately whether games are won or lost.

Over the course of a season these factors, along with the capabilities of the players on a team and certain intangibles such as motivation and momentum, determine whether a team is a winner or an also-ran.

The interaction between the pitcher and the hitter includes three basic aspects:

(1) where the ball goes over the plate;
(2) what type of pitch is thrown;
(3) whether the batter is ahead, behind or even
in the count.

The location of pitches, the types of pitches, and even the count on the batter will affect how he hits the ball. The BARS System has found that, as a rule, hitters tend to pull fastballs more when they are ahead in the count than when they are behind. But when ahead and behind, the same batter will hit varying types and locations of pitches differently.

It is strange to say that almost all baseball fans, announcers and writers are entirely unaware of how important and fundamental these aspects are in determining the proper positioning of fielders. It seems that even baseball managers, coaches and players are unaware — because the fielders rarely shift once they assume positions for a hitter.

Part of the reason for this may be because it's difficult for fans at the ballpark to accurately see where the pitch comes in over the plate. A lot of seats are far away, and even fans sitting right behind the plate are often blocked by the catcher, the umpire or the netting of the screen.

It's also hard for fans to know what type of pitch is thrown every time. The difference between fastballs and curves can be obvious when watching closely, but sometimes the action is so fast that it's nearly impossible to tell what type of pitch was thrown, not to mention whether it was to the low-inside section of the strike zone as opposed to the medium-high inside section. Even radio and TV announcers from their vantage points have difficulty telling what the types and locations of pitches are. They're wrong a surprising amount of the time.

Aside from standing right behind the catcher or the pitcher, the best way to see where the ball comes in over the plate is the center field camera on T.V. A lot of the zest of baseball is missed on T.V., but there's nothing better for getting a close look at this vital element of the game.

Instant replays allow fans watching T.V. (or at the fortunate stadiums that have instant replays on the scoreboard) to study in slow motion where the ball came in over the plate, what type of pitch was thrown, and where the fielders were positioned at the time of the pitch. Only by studying these factors can a fan really see all the elements that relate to the BARS System.

It's instructive to follow along with the BARS batting charts and fielding strategy charts while watching an actual game, whether at the ball park or on TV. Time after time it will be seen that fielders were out of position for balls hit in their direction, considering the type and location of pitch and the count on the batter. Time and time again infielders dive and barely miss ground balls that could easily have been fielded if they had been shifted to the left or right according to the BARS System. Outfielders charge hard and barely miss catching line drives that could easily have been caught if they had been positioned according to the BARS fielding strategy.

Following along with the BARS batting charts and fielding strategy shows how often fielders are out of position, and how dramatic the difference will be when every fielder is part of an integrated strategy that adapts for different types and locations of pitches on different counts. The time is approaching when players, coaches and managers will have to put in a great deal of time studying statistics like those presented in this book.

BARS Batting Grids And Fielding Strategy On Television

Television is the best way for the BARS System to be followed in actual-game situations. T.V. announcers could superimpose the BARS batting grids over the strike zone right on screen as a player comes to the plate. That way fans could see at a glance where the batter's strengths and weaknesses are.

Then, after a ball is hit, announcers could replay the pitch and the hit, showing where the ball came in over the plate, the type of pitch thrown, and where the fielders were positioned at the time of the pitch. The announcers could then determine if the fielders were positioned correctly, according to the BARS fielding strategy for the particular type and location of pitch and the count on the batter. This would allow fans to become involved in the intricacies of the game as never before.

Even The Best Fielders Are Handicapped When Out Of Position

Fielders take their positions when a batter comes to the plate, playing him to pull the ball, to hit it straightaway, or to hit it toward the opposite field. But when the strategy between the pitcher and catcher is to throw a series of fastballs, curves and other types of pitches to various parts of the strike zone, the batter is being thrown pitches that he will tend to hit different distances and directions.

By taking their positions and holding them through all the varying pitches to a batter, fielders are fooling themselves. Without a coordinated effort by a team, using fielding strategy on a pitch-by-pitch basis, the defending against hitters is essentially random. Using traditional major league fielding strategy, fielders are positioned correctly only about 75 percent of the time.

This percentage is even lower for sharply-hit balls, because it's usually only when a ball is hit hard (or hit to a very unusual spot) that the positioning of fielders is put to a test. Easy grounders to the infielders or lazy pop flies to the outfielders are fairly routine, no matter where the fielders are positioned. But rockets through the hole between short and third or line shots into the gaps between outfielders are the acid tests of fielding strategy. At these times a fielder is either in the right position or not. If not, the ball is past him. Today's artificial surfaces increase the speed of hit balls, making fielding strategy even more important than it has been in the past.

The large amount of information collected by the BARS System and coordinated by the powerful BARS mainframe IBM 4331 computer allows each fielder to be positioned most effectively on every pitch. The BARS fielding strategy is accurate more than 90 percent of the time. This means that fielders will be in their right positions nine out of ten times for balls hit in their areas.

Since fielders are in the right position about 75 percent of the time following traditional major league fielding strategy and over 90 percent of the time when following BARS fielding strategy, by using the BARS strategy each team could prevent an average of two to three base hits that are now being allowed every game. Many of these hits go for extra bases, set up run-producing rallies and drive in game-winning RBIs. Over the course of a season, preventing an average of two to three hits per game would make a tremendous difference in a team's final standing.

How To Prevent One-Third Of All Base Hits

In *The Tenth Man*, the previously-published BARS book, over 100 base hits and extra-base hits that occurred in actual major league games are analyzed to show how fielders could have prevented the hits by following the BARS fielding strategy. Examples are taken from games involving the Yankees, Mets, Dodgers, Angels, Cubs, White Sox, Red Sox, Royals, Reds, Braves and other major league teams.

Understanding the importance of the BARS statistics for performance on the team level will make the BARS records for individual players more interesting and valuable. Understanding the fielding strategy and the BARS hitting charts for every player will make baseball more interesting for the fans. At this stage of major league strategy, it will allow fans to know more about the strengths and weaknesses of players than the players and managers themselves.

Controlling The Destiny Of a Game

Adopting the BARS System in regular play would allow a team to control the destiny of a game much more than before.

Baseball is unique in that the defense (the team on the field) initiates the action when the pitcher throws the ball. In football, basketball, hockey and other sports, teams take a defensive alignment without really knowing what their opponents are planning offensively.

In football, for example, the defensive team can adjust its strategy according to the setup of the offensive team at the line of scrimmage, but the defensive team never really knows if the play is going to be a pass or a run, or to what part of the field the pass or run will go.

In baseball the pitcher initiates the play, and by using the BARS System, the team on the field can coordinate fielders with the type and location of pitch. The BARS fielding strategy is right over 90 percent of the time. This high percentage of accuracy brings a new dimension to the game and opens speculation about how the style of play will change once teams begin using the BARS System regularly.

Larger Players May Become The Norm

When a fielder is in just the right position for each pitch, he won't have to move as far to field the ball. The effectiveness of fielders with greater mobility will be increased also — their range will enable them to cover an even greater area using the BARS System — but, overall, mediocre fielders will benefit most.

Fielders don't have to be as fast when they're perfectly positioned, and teams may go to larger fielders when they start using the BARS fielding strategy. Shortstops and second basemen are usually among the smaller players on a team because they need to be quick and agile. At present we're seeing players like Ozzie Smith or Alfredo Griffin who are like gymnasts on the field. The necessity for this may change as the BARS System is implemented. Both infielders and outfielders could become larger and even slower when a team uses a fielding strategy that positions players in the best possible position 90 percent of the time.

If the BARS System had been used in the past, it's possible that some of the power hitters that were considered too bulky and slow to play proper defense may have made it in the major leagues. If the BARS System had allowed them to use a fielding strategy that would have positioned them closer to where the ball would be hit, they wouldn't have been such a defensive liability.

The Ways To Beat The System

The best way to beat the BARS System is to hit the ball out of the park. You can't field a home run. This may also encourage teams to go with larger, stronger players, the power hitters who can hit the ball out of the park.

On the opposite side, implementing the BARS System may encourage hitters to emphasize increased bat control and placing the ball. Not every player can hit home runs, and when the high-average hitters suddenly find that there's always a fielder where they hit the ball, they're going to try to adjust.

Getting Every Edge Possible

Teams could make the most out of the BARS System fielding strategy in several ways. One would be to have fielders break toward their correct positions as the pitch is delivered. This would confuse the batter and make it more difficult for him to know beforehand where to place the ball. Shifting and stunting is common for defensive alignments in football. It confuses the offense and makes play changes more difficult.

Teams can also have their players use the BARS System to increase the percentages of making a play. For example, even though the BARS fielding strategy suggests that an outfielder play a hitter short for a particular type and location of pitch, the outfielder may not want to play short, thinking that the batter could possibly hit a deep drive. In this situation the outfielder could increase his chance of being in the right position by playing medium-deep to guard against deep drives while anticipating the likelihood that the ball may be hit short. In this way he could guard against both possibilities.

All in all, the BARS System will bring about many changes in the game once it is implemented by even a single team. Baseball will become much more coordinated and exacting, with the result that both offensive and defensive strategies will have to become more flexible than they are now.

The BARS System will make the game even more exciting and interesting for the fans. The most important overall consideration for excellence will be a team's level of coordination between players. This will be a major advancement in the evolution of baseball, and teams that do not adjust to the new strategies will fall to the bottom of the standings.

Index Of Players